CLAREND

General Editors

Brian Bosworth   Miriam Griffin
David Whitehead   Susan Treggiari
John Marincola

The aim of the CLARENDON ANCIENT HISTORY SERIES is to provide authoritative translations, introductions, and commentaries to a wide range of Greek and Latin texts studied by ancient historians. The books will be of interest to scholars, graduate students, and advanced undergraduates.

Frontispiece. Turin bust of Caesar. Permission granted by Ministero per i Beni e le Attività Culturali (© Sopraintendenza per i Beni Archeologici del Piemonte e del Museo Antichità Egizie)

Translated with an Introduction and Commentary

BY
CHRISTOPHER PELLING

OXFORD
UNIVERSITY PRESS

OXFORD

UNIVERSITY PRESS

Great Clarendon Street, Oxford OX2 6DP

Oxford University Press is a department of the University of Oxford.
It furthers the University's objective of excellence in research, scholarship,
and education by publishing worldwide in

Oxford New York

Auckland Cape Town Dar es Salaam Hong Kong Karachi
Kuala Lumpur Madrid Melbourne Mexico City Nairobi
New Delhi Shanghai Taipei Toronto

With offices in

Argentina Austria Brazil Chile Czech Republic France Greece
Guatemala Hungary Italy Japan Poland Portugal Singapore
South Korea Switzerland Thailand Turkey Ukraine Vietnam

Oxford is a registered trade mark of Oxford University Press
in the UK and in certain other countries

Published in the United States
by Oxford University Press Inc., New York

© Christopher Pelling 2011

The moral rights of the author have been asserted
Database right Oxford University Press (maker)

First published 2011

British Library Cataloguing in Publication Data

Data available

Library of Congress Cataloging in Publication Data

Data available

Typeset by SPI Publisher Services, Pondicherry, India
Printed in Great Britain

MPG Books Group, Bodmin and King's Lynn

ISBN 978-0-19-814904-0 (Hbk)
978-0-19-960835-5 (Pbk)

1 3 5 7 9 10 8 6 4 2

Preface

This book is a terrible warning for any young scholar. I began it in October 1970; I finished it in August 2010. It therefore took me one more year to write it than Caesar, 16 at the beginning of Plutarch's narrative and 55 at his death, to live it. Work on it has admittedly been rather less directed and sustained than was characteristic of Caesar himself. The years 1970–4 were spent on this as my doctoral thesis, a monstrosity that eventually contained over 200 pages of introduction and appendices, together with a commentary that reached only chapter 27. It was then laid aside, and my work on Plutarch took other forms, a series of articles that were then mostly collected in my *Plutarch and History* (2002), and a commentary on *Antony* that appeared in 1988 and a rather shorter Italian one on *Philopoemen–Flamininus* in 1997. Meanwhile the work on *Caesar* was bundled away in two box files firmly labelled 'Dead Caesar'. A window opened in 2000 to allow some revivification; but it closed after fifteen months, and my move to a new post in 2003, while opening many others, kept this one shut until a sabbatical year in 2008–9. The commentary was finished then, and the introduction in the following months.

Over those forty years the study both of Plutarch and of the Roman Republic has been transformed. The Plutarchan revolution has been largely peaceable and uncontested, and it is now widely accepted that Plutarch revised his material much more extensively and thoughtfully than scholars used to think. The debate on the texture of Roman political life has been more heated, and I say a little of that in Section 4 of the Introduction. I have been a participant in the first development but only an interested observer of the second, understandably as my institutional labelling is in Greek rather than Roman and in literature rather than history—though I would not be attempting this sort of commentary if I were not convinced that the study of history, literature, and indeed reception are mutually enriching if not indispensable. These changes in scholarly atmosphere may have left some impact on the commentary, though I have tried to smooth things out; certainly its early sections were drafted at a time when Symean views of the Roman oligarchy dominated the field, its middle parts when

Millar's emphasis on the democratic elements was widely accepted, and its final phase in a period when the debate seems to be moving on. Still, whatever view one takes, it remains important that most of the *Caesar* treats a time of great crisis, when political norms, whatever they may have been, were challenged and stretched to the limits; participants themselves must have been unsure about the rules of the game, about where power really lay. The book has certainly been written in the conviction that a commentator should not shy from the simple, unpostmodern, positivist question, 'Is what Plutarch says *true*?'—and that one can ask this question without assuming that there will be, or was at the time, a simple and uncontested answer. I do, however, assume that not all answers are as good as one another, and that even with such distant material one can occasionally get as close to certainty as one can in most human fields.

Inevitably the work, in particular the Introduction, overlaps with material that I have published elsewhere, and I apologize for that. Space could sometimes have been saved by simply referring to those other articles and papers, but I hope readers will feel that the convenience of not having to go elsewhere adequately compensates for the repetition. The text of *Caesar* that I have used is Ziegler's Teubner, except in cases where I have noted problems and variations in the commentary. The translation of the *Life* is my own, along with most of the other translations; the only exceptions are several cases where the unfailing elegance of Shackleton Bailey's Cicero translations has defied rivalry.

Many obligations have accrued over the years. The doctoral years were spent first as a Senior Scholar at Christ Church, Oxford, and then as a Research Fellow (in History, I proudly note) at Peterhouse, Cambridge: both were interesting and memorable experiences, offering a startling contrast to undergraduate years spent in the revolutionary Oxford air of 1960s Balliol. The middle phase came during my years as a tutorial fellow at University College, Oxford; the final one after my return to a very different Christ Church as Regius Professor of Greek. I am most grateful to all these colleges, and to Oxford's Classics faculty and the Craven Committee, not just for financial support (though there have been many conference and research trips, especially to battlefield sites) but for the extraordinarily stimulating intellectual environments they have provided: without discussion with colleagues and pupils, both graduate and undergraduate, there would have been no ideas in this book worth pursuing. Donald Russell and

A. N. Sherwin-White supervised the thesis, and Donald continues to this day to be an important source of inspiration, learning, and friendship. The international Plutarch community is an unusually close one; Frances Titchener takes most of the credit for that as Secretary of the International Plutarch Society, a body of which I currently have the honour to be President. Other Plutarchans with whom I have had many rich discussions are Simon Hornblower (who also very kindly checked my references to the forthcoming *OCD*[4] against the proofs), Philip Stadter, Judith Mossman, Ewen Bowie, Simon Swain, Luc van der Stockt, Tasos Nikolaidis, Alexei Zadorojnyi, Tim Duff, Lukas de Blois, Aurelio Pérez Jiménez, Frederick Brenk, and John Moles. Historiographic and historical discussions with John Marincola, Tony Woodman, Chris Kraus, Rhiannon Ash, Robert Morstein-Marx, Tim Rood, Maria Wyke, David Levene, Luke Pitcher, Mark Toher, Richard Rutherford, Katherine Clarke, Lisa Kallet, Anna Clark, Carolyn Dewald, Harriet Flower, Michael Flower, Emily Baragwanath, Jeff Tatum, Alan Bowman, David Stockton, and the late Christiane Sourvinou-Inwood have always been fruitful too. I have also learned a great deal from John Moles's unpublished Oxford dissertation on *Brutus*, as I have from pre-publication reading of Mark Toher's commentary on Nicolaus of Damascus and from some notes kindly sent me by David Yates and by John Ramsey, who read and commented on the crucial section on the outbreak of the civil war. I am particularly grateful to the series editors, Miriam Griffin and Susan Treggiari, not merely for their help and guidance on individual matters but also for their patience; the same goes for Hilary O'Shea and Oxford University Press, who have put up with an author whose bad example is the more culpable for his now being a Delegate himself.

The biggest debt is, of course, to my family. I began this book before meeting my future wife; we are now grandparents. Prefaces to my previous books have mentioned Margaret, Charlie, and Sally, but life moves on, and now I am proud and delighted to acknowledge Charlie, Claudia, and Sam; Sally and Adam; and, above all, Margaret.

Contents

List of Maps

Abbreviations

Plutarch *Lives* are cited according to the Teubner chapter divisions rather than those found in the older Loeb editions (more recent ones have been changed to fit the Teubner); the Teubner divides into the shorter subsections, so that e.g. *Ant.* 77.7 (Teubner and here) corresponds to the old Loeb *Ant.* 77.4. Scholars sometimes refer to the '*Comparisons*' or '*Synkriseis*' that follow a pair as continuations of the second *Life* (as e.g. *Brut.* 54), sometimes give them a separate numeration (as *Comparison of Dion and Brutus* 1), and sometimes use a combination of the two (as *Brut.* 54(1)): that final convention is the one that I have adopted here. References in the form '*Ant.* 12.6 n.' are to notes in my 1988 commentary on *Antony* (Cambridge). Those to 'Suet.' are to Suetonius, *Diuus Iulius*, except where stated; those to 'App.' are to Appian, *Bellum Ciuile*, except where stated; those to Nic. Dam. are to Nicolaus of Damascus' *Life of Augustus*; and 'Dio' is Cassius Dio, 'Dio Prus.' Dio of Prusa. References to Cicero's letters include in parentheses their alternative numberings in the various Cambridge editions of D. R. Shackleton Bailey (1965–80). Where essays of my own are included in the collected volume *Plutarch and History*, I give references only to the *Plutarch and History* version. The swung dash (~) between two references means that the passages are to be taken in combination or in contrast with one another.

AE	*L'Année Epigraphique* (1888–)
Alexander	M. C. Alexander, *Trials in the Late Republic, 149 B.C. to 50 B.C.* (Toronto, 1990)
André	J. André, *La Vie et l'œuvre d'Asinius Pollion.* (Paris, 1949)
ANRW	*Aufstieg und Niedergang der Römischen Welt* (Berlin and New York, 1972–)
Barrington Atlas	*Barrington Atlas of the Greek and Roman World*, ed. R. J. A. Talbert (Princeton, 2000)
Batstone and Damon	W. W. Batstone and C. Damon, *Caesar's Civil War* (Oxford, 2006)
BMC	*British Museum Catalogue*
Brenk	F. E. Brenk, *In Mist Apparelled: Religious Themes in Plutarch's Moralia and Lives* (Leiden, 1977)
Broughton	T. R. S. Broughton, *Magistrates of the Roman Republic* (Cleveland, OH, vols i–ii, 1951–2

	with Addenda, 1960; iii, 1986); except where stated, references are to volume ii
Bruhns	H. Bruhns, *Caesar und die römische Oberschicht in den Jahren 49–44 v.Chr.* (*Hypomnemata* 53; Göttingen, 1978)
Brunt, *FRR*	P. A. Brunt, *The Fall of the Roman Republic* (Oxford, 1988)
Brunt, *Manpower*	P. A. Brunt, *Italian Manpower* (first published 1971; reissued with postscript, Oxford, 1987).
CAH	*Cambridge Ancient History* (2nd edn, Cambridge 1961–)
Carsana	C. Carsana, *Commento storico al libro II delle Guerre Civili di Appiano* i (Pisa, 2007)
Carter i–ii	J. M. Carter, *Julius Caesar: The Civil War Books I & II* (Warminster, 1991)
Carter iii	J. M. Carter, *Julius Caesar: The Civil War Book III* (Warminster, 1993)
CJC	M. Griffin (ed.), *A Companion to Julius Caesar* (Malden, Oxford, and Chichester, 2009)
Clarke	K. Clarke, *Between Geography and History: Hellenistic Constructions of the Roman World* (Oxford, 1999)
Dettenhofer	M. Dettenhofer, *Perdita Iuuentus: zwischen den Generationen von Caesar und Augustus* (Munich, 1992)
Dobesch, *AS*	G. Dobesch, *Ausgewählte Schriften*, ed. H. Heftner and K. Tomaschitz, i–ii (Cologne, Weimar, and Vienna, 2001)
'Dreams'	'"With thousand such enchanting dreams . . .": The Dreams of the *Lives* Revisited', in L. van der Stockt, F. B. Titchener, H.-G. Ingenkamp, and A. Pérez Jiménez (eds), *Gods, Daimones, Rituals, Myths, and History of Religions in Plutarch's Works: Studies Devoted to Professor Frederick E. Brenk by the International Plutarch Society* (Málaga, 2010), 315–32
Duff	T. Duff, *Plutarch's Lives: Exploring Virtue and Vice* (Oxford, 1999)
ESAR	*Economic Survey of Ancient Rome*, ed. T. Frank et al., i–v (Baltimore, 1933–40)
Fehrle	R. Fehrle, *Cato Uticensis* (Darmstadt, 1983)
Flower	H. I. Flower, *Ancestor Masks and Aristocratic Power in Roman Culture* (Oxford, 1996)

Frei-Stolba	R. Frei-Stolba, *Untersuchungen zu den Wahlen in der röm. Kaiserzeit* (Zurich, 1967)
Fuller	J. F. C. Fuller, *Julius Caesar: Man, Soldier, and Tyrant* (London, 1965)
Garzetti	A. Garzetti, *Plutarchi Vita Caesaris* (Florence, 1954)
Gelzer	M. Gelzer, *Caesar* (tr. P. Needham, Oxford, 1968; 6th edn of the German original 1960)
Gelzer, *Cicero*	M. Gelzer, *Cicero* (Wiesbaden, 1969)
Gerlinger	S. Gerlinger, *Römische Schlachtenrhetorik: unglaubwürdige Elemente in Schlachtendarstellungen, speziell bei Caesar, Sallust und Tacitus* (Heidelberg, 2008)
Gesche	H. Gesche, *Caesar* (Darmstadt, 1976)
Goudineau	C. Goudineau, *César et la Gaule* (Paris, 1992)
Gruen	E. S. Gruen, *The Last Generation of the Roman Republic* (Berkeley and Los Angeles, 1974)
Hamilton	J. R. Hamilton, *Plutarch, Alexander: A Commentary* (Oxford, 1969)
Hardy	E. G. Hardy, *Some Problems in Roman History* (Oxford, 1924)
Heftner	H. Heftner, *Plutarch und der Aufstieg des Pompeius: Ein historischer Kommentar zu Plutarchs Pompeiusvita i* (Kap. 1–45) (Frankfurt, 1995)
Heinen, *Kleopatra-Studien*	H. Heinen, *Gesammelte Schriften für ausgehenden Ptolemäerzeit* (*Xenia* 49; Konstanz, 2009)
Heinen, *Rom und Ägypten*	H. Heinen, *Rom und Ägypten von 51 bis 46 v. Chr. Untersuchungen zur Regierungszeit des 13. Ptolemäers* (Tübingen, 1966), repr. in Heinen, *Kleopatra-Studien*, 13–153
Hellegouarc'h	J. Hellegouarc'h, *Le Vocabulaire latin des relations et des partis politiques sous la République* (Paris, 1963)
Holmes, *CCG*	T. Rice Holmes, *Caesar's Conquest of Gaul* (2nd edn, Oxford, 1911)
Holmes, *RR*	T. Rice Holmes, *The Roman Republic*, i–iii (Oxford, 1923)
HRR	H. Peter, *Historicorum Romanorum Reliquiae*, i–ii (1906, repr. and revised 1993)
IG	*Inscriptiones Graecae* (1873–)

IGR	*Inscriptiones ad res Romanas pertinentes* (1906–)
ILLRP	*Inscriptiones Latinae Liberae Rei Publicae*, ed. A. Degrassi (2nd edn, Florence, 1965)
JCAR	K. Welch and A. Powell (eds), *Julius Caesar as Artful Reporter: The War Commentaries as Political Instruments* (London, 1998)
Jehne	M. Jehne, *Die Staat des Dictators Caesars* (Cologne and Vienna, 1987)
Jones	C. P. Jones, *Plutarch and Rome* (Oxford, 1971)
Jullian	C. Jullian, *Histoire de la Gaule* (Paris, 1908–21)
Keppie	L. J. F. Keppie, *Colonisation and Veteran Settlement in Italy* (London, 1983)
Konrad	C. F. Konrad, *Plutarch, Sertorius: A Historical Commentary* (Chapel Hill, NY, and London, 1994)
Kremer	B. Kremer, *Das Bild der Kelten bis in augusteische Zeit* (Hist. Einz. 88; 1994)
Lambrecht	U. Lambrecht, *Herrscherbild und Principatsidee in Suetons Kaiserbiographien: Untersuchungen zur Caesar- and zur Augustus-Vita* (Bonn, 1984)
Leo	F. Leo, *Die griechisch-römische Biographie nach ihrer literarischen Form* (Leipzig, 1901)
LGPN	*Lexicon of Greek Personal Names* (Oxford, 1987–)
Linderski	J. Linderski, *Roman Questions* (Stuttgart, 1995)
Lintott, *Constitution*	A. W. Lintott, *The Constitution of the Roman Republic* (Oxford, 1999)
Lintott, *Evidence*	A. W. Lintott, *Cicero as Evidence: A Historian's Companion* (Oxford, 2008)
Lintott, *Violence*	A. W. Lintott, *Violence in Republican Rome* (Oxford, 1968)
LPPR	G. Rotondi, *Leges Publicae Populi Romani* (Milan 1922, repr. Hildesheim 1990)
LTUR	*Lexicon Topographicum Urbis Romae* (Rome, 1993–)
Maier	U. Maier, *Caesars Feldzüge in Gallien (58–51 v. Chr.) in ihrem Zusammenhang mit der stadtrömischen Politik* (Saarbrücker Beiträge zur Altertumskunde 29; Bonn 1978)
Meier	C. Meier, *Caesar* (tr. D. McLintock, London 1995: German original 1982)

Millar	F. Millar, *The Crowd in Rome in the Late Republic* (Michigan, 1998)
Moles, *Brutus*	J. L. Moles, 'A Commentary on Plutarch's Brutus' (Oxford D.Phil. thesis, 1979)
Moles, *Cicero*	J. L. Moles, *Plutarch: Cicero* (Warminster, 1988)
Mommsen, *Strafrecht*	T. Mommsen, *Römisches Strafrecht* (Berlin, 1899)
Mommsen, *Staatsrecht*	T. Mommsen, *Römisches Staatsrecht*, i–iii (3rd edn, Leipzig, 1887–8)
Moreau	P. Moreau, *Clodiana Religio: Un procès politique en 61 Av. J.-C.* (Paris, 1982)
Morgan, 'Autopsy'	Ll. Morgan, 'The Autopsy of Asinius Pollio', *JRS* 90 (2000), 51–69
Morstein-Marx	R. Morstein-Marx, *Mass Oratory and Political Power in the Late Roman Republic* (Cambridge, 2004)
MRR	T. R. S. Broughton, *Magistrates of the Roman Republic* (Cleveland, OH, vols i–ii, 1951–2 with Addenda, 1960; iii, 1986); except where stated, references are to volume ii
Münzer, *RAPF*	F. Münzer, *Roman Aristocratic Parties and Families* (tr. T. Ridley, Baltimore, 1999: German original as *Römische Adelparteien und Adelsfamilien (RAA)*, Stuttgart, 1920)
Napoléon I	Napoléon I, *Précis des Guerres de Jules César*, ed. M. Marchand (Paris 1836)
Nippel	W. Nippel, *Public Order in Ancient Rome* (Cambridge, 1995)
NP	*Der Neue Pauly*, ed. H. Cancik and H. Schneider (Stuttgart, 1996–), tr. as 'Brill's New Pauly' (Leiden, 2006–)
OCD[4]	S. Hornblower, A. Spawforth, and E. Eidinow (eds), *Oxford Classical Dictionary* (4th edn, Oxford, forthcoming)
OLD	P. G. W. Glare (ed.), *Oxford Latin Dictionary* (Oxford, 1968–82)
ORF	H. Malcovati, *Oratorum Romanorum Fragmenta* (4th edn, Turin, 1967)
Ottmer	H.-M. Ottmer, *Die Rubikon-Legende* (Boppard, 1979)
Otto	A. Otto, *Die Sprichwörter der Römer* (Leipzig, 1890)

Pelling	C. Pelling, *Antony: Plutarch: Life of Antony* (Cambridge, 1988)
Pelling, 'Augustus' Autobiography'	C. Pelling, 'Was there an Ancient Genre of "Autobiography"? Or, did Augustus Know what he was Doing?', in C. Smith and A. Powell (eds), *The Lost Memoirs of Augustus and the Development of Roman Autobiography* (London, 2009), 41–64
Pelling, 'Breaking the Bounds'	C. Pelling, 'Breaking the Bounds: Writing about Caesar', in B. McGing and J. Mossman (eds), *The Limits of Ancient Biography* (Swansea, 2006), 255–79
Pelling, 'Caesar's Fall'	C. Pelling, 'Plutarch on Caesar's Fall', in J. Mossman (ed.), *Plutarch and his Intellectual World* (Swansea and London, 1997), 215–32.
Pelling, 'Focalisation'	C. Pelling, 'Seeing through Caesar's Eyes: Focalisation and Interpretation', in J. Grethlein and A. Rengakos (eds), *Narratology and Interpretation* (2009), 507–26
Pelling, 'Judging Julius Caesar'	C. Pelling, 'Judging Julius Caesar', in M. Wyke (ed.), *Julius Caesar in Western Culture* (Oxford 2006), 3–26.
Pelling, 'Notes'	C. Pelling, 'Notes on Plutarch's *Caesar*', *RhM* 127 (1984), 33–45
Pelling, 'Roman Heroes'	C. Pelling, 'Plutarch: Roman Heroes and Greek Culture', in M. Griffin and J. Barnes (eds), *Philosophia Togata I* (2nd edn, Oxford, 1997), 199–232
Pelling, 'Roman Tragedy'	C. Pelling, 'Seeing a Roman Tragedy through Greek Eyes', in S. Goldhill and E. Hall (eds), *Sophocles and the Greek Tragic Tradition* (Cambridge, 2009), 264–88
Pelling, 'Thucydidean Intertextuality'	C. Pelling, 'Learning from that Violent Schoolmaster . . . : Thucydidean Intertextuality and some Greek Views of Roman Civil War', in C. Damon, A. Rossi, and B. Breed (eds), *Citizens of Discord: Rome and its Civil Wars* (Oxford, 2010), 105–17

PIR^2	*Prosopographia Imperii Romani* (2nd edn, Berlin and Leipzig, 1933–)
Plutarch and History	C. Pelling, *Plutarch and History: Eighteen Studies* (London and Swansea, 2002)
R-E	*Real-Encyclopädie d. klassischen Altertumswissenschaft*, ed. A. Pauly, G. Wissowa, and W. Kroll (Stuttgart, then Munich, 1893–)
Raaflaub	K. Raaflaub, *Dignitatis Contentio: Studien zur Motivation und politischen Taktik im Bürgerkrieg zwischen Caesar und Pompeius* (*Vestigia* 20; Munich, 1974)
Rambaud	M. Rambaud, *L'Art de la déformation historique dans les Commentaires de César* (2nd edn, Paris, 1966)
RDGE	R. A. Sherk, *Roman Documents from the Greek East* (Baltimore, 1969)
Riggsby	A. M. Riggsby, *Caesar in Gaul and Rome: War in Words* (Austin, TX, 2006)
Rives	J. B. Rives, *Tacitus: Germania* (Oxford, 1999)
Scardigli, *Essays*	B. Scardigli (ed.), *Essays on Plutarch's Lives* (Oxford, 1995)
Scardigli, *Römerbiographien*	B. Scardigli, *Die Römerbiographien Plutarchs* (Munich, 1979)
Schanz. and Hosius	M. Schanz and C. Hosius, *Geschichte der römischen Literatur* i–iv (Munich, 1914–35). Retitled in 1989 *Handbuch der lateinischen Literatur der Antike*
Schmidt	T. S. Schmidt, *Plutarque et les Barbares: La rhétorique d'une image* (Collection d'Études Classiques 14; Louvain-Namur, 1999)
Schmitzer	U. Schmitzer, *Velleius Paterculus und das Interesse an der Geschichte im Zeitalter des Tiberius* (Heidelberg, 2000)
Seager	R. Seager, *Pompey: A Political Biography* (Oxford, 1979)
SHA	*Scriptores Historiae Augustae*
Sherwin-White	A. N. Sherwin-White, *Roman Foreign Policy in the East 168 B.C. to A.D. 1* (London, 1984)
SIG^3	W. Dittenberger, *Sylloge Inscriptionum Graecarum* (Leipzig, 1915–23)
Spencer	D. Spencer, *The Roman Alexander: Reading a Cultural Myth* (Exeter, 2002)
Stadter	P. A. Stadter, *A Commentary on Plutarch's Pericles* (Chapel Hill and NY, 1989)

Steidle	W. Steidle, *Sueton und die antike Biographie* (Munich, 1951)
Stockton	D. L. Stockton, *Cicero* (Oxford, 1971)
StR	T. Mommsen, *Römisches Staatsrecht*, i–iii (3rd edn, Leipzig, 1887–8)
Strasburger	H. Strasburger, *Caesars Eintritt in die Geschichte* (Munich, 1938)
Strasburger, *CUZ*	H. Strasburger, *Caesar im Urteil seiner Zeitgenossen* (2nd edn, Darmstadt, 1968)
Sullivan	R. D. Sullivan, *Near Eastern Royalty and Rome, 100–30 BC* (Toronto, 1990)
Sumner	G. V. Sumner, *The Orators in Cicero's Brutus: Prosopography and Chronology* (Toronto, 1973)
Swain	S. Swain, *Hellenism and Empire: Language, Classicism, and Power in the Greek World,* AD *50–250* (Oxford, 1996)
Syme, *RP*	R. Syme, *Roman Papers*, i–vii (Oxford, 1979–91)
Syme, *RR*	R. Syme, *The Roman Revolution* (Oxford, 1939)
Szidat	J. Szidat, *Caesars diplomatische Tätigkeit im gallischen Krieg* (*Hist. Einz.* 14; 1970)
Tatum	W. J. Tatum, *Always I am Caesar* (Oxford, 2008)
Theander	C. Theander, *Plutarch und die Geschichte* (Bulletin de la Societé Royale des Lettres de Lund, Lund, 1951)
Thevenot	E. Thevenot, *Les Éduens n'ont pas trahi* (Coll. Latomus 50, 1960)
Thommen	L. Thommen, *Das Volkstribunat der späten röm. Republik* (*Hist. Einz.* 59, 1989)
TLL	*Thesaurus Linguae Latinae* (1900–)
Toher	M. Toher, *A Commentary on Nicolaus of Damascus' Life of Caesar* (forthcoming)
Townend, 'Oppius'	G. B. Townend, 'C. Oppius on Julius Caesar', *AJP* 108 (1987), 325–42
Veith, *Feldzug*	G. Veith, *Der Feldzug von Dyrrhachium zwischen Caesar und Pompeius* (Vienna, 1920)
Walser	G. Walser, *Caesar und die Germanen* (*Hist. Einz.* 1; 1956)

WdF	*Caesar (Wege der Forschung* 43, ed. D. Rasmussen, Darmstadt, 1967)
Weinstock	S. Weinstock, *Divus Julius* (Oxford, 1971)
Weippert	O. Weippert, *Alexander-Imitatio u. röm. Politik in republikanischer Zeit* (Augsburg, 1972)
Williams	J. H. C. Williams, *Beyond the Rubicon: Romans and Gauls in Republican Italy* (Oxford, 2001)
Wiseman	T. P. Wiseman, *Remembering the Roman People: Essays on Late-Republican Politics and Literature* (Oxford, 2009)
Woodman	A. J. Woodman, *Velleius Paterculus: The Caesarian and Augustan Narrative (2.41–93)* (Cambridge, 1983)
Woolf	G. Woolf, *Becoming Roman: The Origins of Provincial Civilization in Gaul* (Cambridge, 1998)
Woytek	B. Woytek, *Arma et Nummi: Forschungen zur röm. Finanzgeschichte und Münzprägung der Jahre 49 bis 42 v. Chr.* (Vienna, 2003)
Yakobson	A. Yakobson, *Elections and Electioneering in Rome: A Study in the Political System of the Late Republic (Historia* Einzelschr. 128, Stuttgart, 1999)
Zecchini	G. Zecchini, *Cesare e il mos maiorum* (Historia Einzelschr. 151, Stuttgart, 2001)

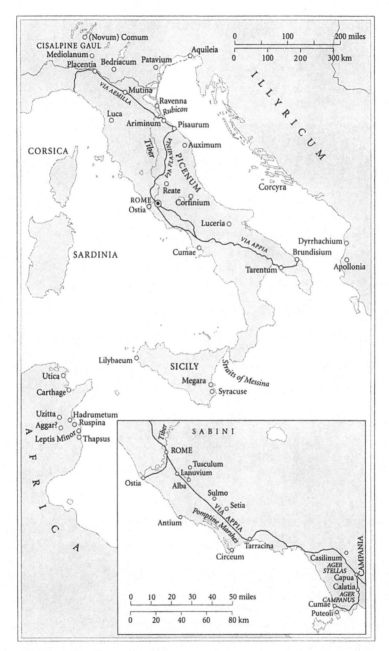

Map 1. Italy and Northern Africa

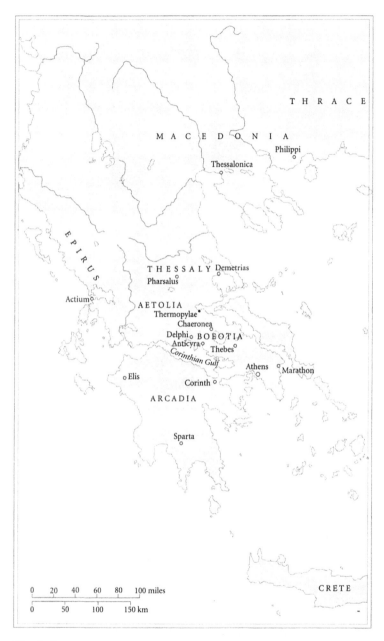

THRACE

MACEDONIA
Philippi

Thessalonica

EPIRUS

THESSALY Demetrias
Pharsalus

Actium

AETOLIA
Thermopylae
Chaeronea
Delphi BOEOTIA
Anticyra Thebes
Corinthian Gulf
Athens Marathon
Elis
Corinth

ARCADIA

Sparta

| 0 | 20 | 40 | 60 | 80 | 100 miles |

| 0 | 50 | 100 | 150 km |

CRETE

Map 2. Greece

Map 3. Asia Minor, the Near East, and Egypt

Map 4. Gaul

Map 5. Spain

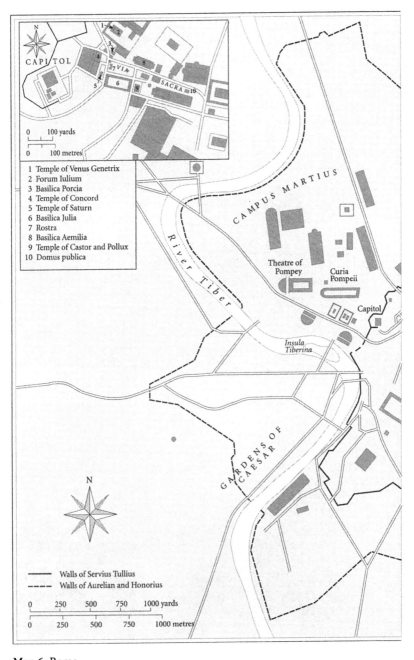

1 Temple of Venus Genetrix
2 Forum Iulium
3 Basilica Porcia
4 Temple of Concord
5 Temple of Saturn
6 Basilica Julia
7 Rostra
8 Basilica Aemilia
9 Temple of Castor and Pollux
10 Domus publica

Walls of Servius Tullius
Walls of Aurelian and Honorius

Map 6. Rome

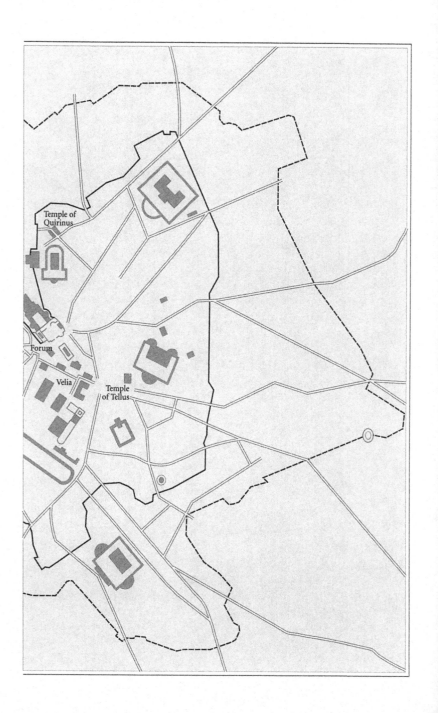

Temple of
Quirinus

Forum

Velia

Temple
of Tellus

Introduction

1. PLUTARCH AND THE CAESARS

> Brutus and Caesar. What should be in that 'Caesar'?
> Why should that name be sounded more than yours?
> Write them together, yours is as fair a name;
> Sound them, it doth become the mouth as well;
> Weigh them, it is as heavy; conjure with 'em,
> 'Brutus' will start a spirit soon as 'Caesar'.
>
> (Shakespeare, *Julius Caesar*, I. ii. 141–6)

Thus speaks Shakespeare's Cassius, working insidiously on the pride and self-respect of his friend. His words introduce themes of great importance to the play; Brutus' own spirit is stirred by appeals to that name of his, with all its resonance of the distant ancestor who freed Rome from the tyranny of the Tarquins (I. ii. 157–60, II. i. 53–4, cf. 61.9 n.); yet the spirit unleashed by Caesar after his death, both figuratively and more literally in the appearance of 'Caesar's ghost', will storm bloodily through the later scenes until vengeance is complete:

> And Caesar's spirit, ranging for revenge,
> With Ate by his side, come hot from hell,
> Shall in these confines with a monarch's voice
> Cry havoc and let slip the dogs of war...
>
> (*Julius Caesar*, III. i. 270–3)

'O Julius Caesar,' cries Brutus as he sees a senseless death on the battlefield of Philippi, 'thou art mighty yet!' (V. iii. 94). He is right.

Shakespeare's own audience would have been able to weigh the name of Caesar, and know how many 'spirits' it had indeed started over the centuries.[1] For Plutarch, writing once the rule of the Caesars—the Roman principate—had been established for nearly 150 years, the name of 'Caesar' would carry an even greater aura, and one of which he was of course fully aware; before starting the series of *Parallel Lives*, which includes the pair *Alexander and Caesar*, he had already written *Lives* of the emperors from Augustus to Vitellius, a series of which *Galba* and *Otho* survive. That series is normally referred to today as *Lives of the Caesars*, and that title is as likely as any. They were probably written under the reign of Domitian (81–96 CE) or, less likely, Nerva (96–8 CE);[2] Plutarch then seems to have begun the *Parallel Lives* some time around the accession of Trajan in 98 CE when he was something over 50 years old, and was still working on them at the time of his death in (probably) the early 120s.[3] *Alexander-Caesar* belongs somewhere just over halfway through the series (below, p. 36), and so, if we assume fairly even progress, he was probably at work on it some time around 110, perhaps a few years later. This is a time when Trajan was flushed with victories from his wars in the East against Dacia (101–7): he already carried the title *Dacicus*, and the gloriously celebratory Trajan's column was dedicated in 113. The further eastern war against Parthia then followed in 114. Trajan was indeed a man of the sword: 'the epoch of Trajan felt the attraction of a Caesar who was also a conqueror.'[4] Trajan himself was aware how Julius Caesar could be made a suggestive model to put in people's minds. In 107—so probably before Plutarch wrote *Alexander-Caesar*, but not many years before—he issued commemorative coins celebrating Caesar. In fact, Caesar figured in two coin series, one of Republican heroes and one of imperial figures:[5] that reflects not merely the continuing importance of Caesar as an image but also the way he could be made to point both ways, backward to the Republican past as well as forward to the

---

[1] On this, see now esp. *CJC*, pt V, together with M. Wyke, *Caesar: A Life in Western Culture* (2007) and the papers collected in M. Wyke (ed.), *Julius Caesar in Western Culture* (2006). Of earlier works, F. Gundolf, *The Mantle of Caesar* (Eng. tr. 1928; German original 1924), is especially rich in the material it collects, though its tendency to hero-worship and its lyrical style are not to modern tastes.

[2] A Domitianic date is favoured by Jones 72–3 and by G. W. Bowersock in W.W. Ehlers (ed.), *La Biographie antique* (Entr. Hardt, 44; 1998), 193–210; a date under Nerva by J. Geiger, *Hist.* 24 (1975), 444–53.

[3] On the date of his death, see S. Swain, *Hist.* 40 (1991), 320–2.

[4] R. Syme, *Tacitus* (1958), 434.

[5] *BMC Imp.* III[2] 141, nos 30–1, 142, nos 696–8; cf. Levick in *CJC* 217–18.

present. There is a more immediate relevance still, for Dacia and Parthia figured in the last plans of Caesar (58.4–10 n.), and he was planning to set out on that campaign three days after the Ides of March. It would have been easy for Plutarch to insinuate a point about this thematic parallel, doubtless subtly (rather as the last chapter of *Antony* glances forwards suggestively to Nero, *Ant.* 87); perhaps in a tragic register, with the assassins as the reckless ones but for whom Rome could have achieved those eastern conquests 150 years before they did; perhaps more adulatory, with the hint of Trajan as the one who was Alexander's truer successor. So Caesar, now, was a very hot topic indeed.

All the more striking, then, that Plutarch makes so little of this. There are indeed times when he seems to be going out of his way to avoid any contemporary resonance. Take that moment when he describes those eastern plans of Caesar:

He planned and prepared an expedition against the Parthians; once he had conquered them, he intended to march through Hyrcania along the Caspian and the Caucasus; then he would make his way around the Pontus and invade Scythia, then overrun Germany's neighbours and Germany itself, and finally return through Gaul to Italy, thus completing the circle of an empire that would have Ocean alone as its boundary.

(58.6–7)

Here Plutarch misses out Dacia, and does so twice. It looks as if Caesar's plan was to attack Dacia first and then go on to Parthia (58.6 n.), so Dacia is passed over right at the beginning. Then 'Germany's neighbours and Germany itself' is a remarkable way of describing Dacia, as if we were to talk of a traveller moving northwards through Guatemala, then Mexico, then Canada's neighbours, then Canada herself. Plutarch would seem to be taking considerable trouble to avoid the D-word.

Nor is that an isolated case. There is also the story of the young Caesar musing on the achievements of Alexander the Great, and weeping because at that age Alexander had conquered the earth and Caesar had so far achieved nothing (11.5–6). The usual version of that story (Suet. 7.1, Dio 37.52.2) places the scene in the temple of Hercules at Cádiz, where Caesar saw a statue of Alexander; and that setting has real point, for Cádiz was conventionally one end of the earth, that earth which Alexander had traversed to east and Hercules

to west. That theme is also Trajanic. Trajan himself favoured Hercu-
lean motifs,[6] for instance adopting Hercules as the emblem of the
newly raised *Legio II Traiana*, and it is usually thought that the
'Hercules' type that he included in his coinage was, precisely, Hercules Gaditanus, with all the point that this carries for this Spanish
emperor.[7] But in Plutarch the story is not like that at all. There is no
statue and no temple; Caesar is simply *reading* about Alexander, and
inspired by what he has read. The change will not be careless. It may
well carry a metatextual implication, pointing to the inspiration that
reading about the great can give, just as Plutarch's own readers of the
pair have now been reading his own *Alexander* (11.5–6 n.). That fits
his moral programme well enough (below, Section 2.2). But this is
another case where a Trajanic motif has loomed, and Plutarch has
deftly sidestepped, changing the story into something different.

Examples could be multiplied;[8] just one more here. At the beginning of his reign Trajan famously showed reluctance to take the title
'father of his country', *pater patriae* or *parens patriae*, but graciously
allowed himself to be persuaded. Pliny makes a great deal of this in his
speech of praise of the emperor, the *Panegyricus* (21). Caesar also,
again famously, was 'father of his country' (Weinstock 200–5), and
many authors stress the point.[9] Of our major sources only Plutarch
omits the detail, despite his awareness of the delicacy of the issues
raised by Caesar's honorific titles (57.2–3, 60.4–5 nn.). He certainly
realized the importance of this one, for in the earlier *Cicero* he had
talked about the honours Cicero received in 63 BCE:

Cato delivered a speech praising Cicero to the skies, so much so that they
voted Cicero honours on an unprecedented scale and gave him the title of
'father of his country'. It appears that he was the first to be given this title,
after Cato had addressed him in those terms before the people.

(*Cic.* 23.6)

[6] C. P. Jones, *The Roman World of Dio Chrysostom* (1978), 116–20, observing that
the prominence of Heracles in Dio's kingship orations is not coincidence; cf. also Plin.
Pan. 14.2.
[7] Thus, for instance, A. Fear in J. Elsner and I. Rutherford (eds), *Pilgrimage in
Graeco-Roman and Early Christian Antiquity* (2005), 324: this is argued in detail by P.
L. Strack, *Untersuchungen zur röm. Reichsprägung des 2 Jhdts*, i (1931), 95–104, and ii
(1933), 85–8, though H. Mattingly, *BMC Imp. III²* (1966), pp. lxvii–lxviii, is more
cautious. Cf. *Plutarch and History*, 264 n. 31.
[8] I give more at *Plutarch and History*, 255–9.
[9] App. 2.106.442, 144.602, Dio 44.4.4, Livy *per.* 116, Nic. Dam. 80, Suet. 76.1, 85,
Flor. 2.13.91.

'The first to be given this title': thus he 'unobtrusively links Cicero and the emperors'.[10] But which is the more obvious forerunner of the principate, Cicero or Caesar? And yet no point of that sort is made in *Caesar* itself; nor does Plutarch focus particularly on any other honours that could have been made to presage features of the principate (57–61 n.). When Suetonius came a few years later to write his own *Diuus Iulius*, he dwelt particularly on aspects of Caesar's life that looked forward to the principate. In many cases they were things that Caesar got wrong and Augustus got right—for instance, the question whether one should rise to show proper deference to consuls and senate (60.4 n.: Suet. *Iul.* 78.1, *Aug.* 53.3) or whether one should go looking for warfare gratuitously (Suet. *Iul.* 24.3, *Aug.* 21); in other instances it may be more a question of plotting the changing nature of leadership as the principate becomes established, for instance in the appropriate degree of camaraderie with one's troops (Suet. *Iul.* 67.1–2, *Aug.* 25.1).[11] That is largely a consequence of Suetonius placing Caesar at the beginning of his series of imperial biographies whereas Plutarch's Caesar is one of the latest of the figures included in the *Parallel Lives*; we shall later (pp. 33–5) see more specific ways in which Plutarch's *Caesar* looks backward just as Suetonius' looks forward. It remains true that Plutarch had opportunities to look forward to the principate a good deal more than he does.[12]

So: why does he not do so? Let us consider several possibilities; as we do so, this will give an opportunity to mention some further aspects of Plutarch and the way he relates to the world around him.

A first possibility, or rather two possibilities, can be dismissed quickly. Might Plutarch not have realized the topical relevance of Caesar? Or might he and/or his audience not have found it very relevant *to them*? The text itself suggests differently: if we were right to sense that Plutarch was deliberately avoiding mention of Dacia, that could only be because he was all too aware that it was a loaded theme—and, more than this, that he was writing for an audience that

[10] Moles, *Cicero*, ad loc.; in his n. on *Cic.* 2.1 Moles also brings out a more general theme of Cicero as imperial forerunner in that *Life*.
[11] More on this in *CJC* 252–66, esp. 261–2.
[12] Cf. e.g. the choice of material when he treats C.'s last plans (58.4–10 n.) and the quiet way in which he chooses to end the *Life* (69.14 n.).

would include people who might otherwise read him in that way, who
unless he avoided the word 'Dacia' might think he had something to
insinuate about Trajan's campaigns. True, Plutarch was writing at his
home in Chaeronea in Boeotia, some way from the centre of things,
deep in Roman Greece; there he kept something of a school, with
young acolytes coming to listen and to learn. True, too, he was
interested in many things beyond Roman politics; the *Lives*, volumi-
nous as they are, are less than half of his surviving output, and we also
know of many more works that have not survived. The other half,
usually collectively (and loosely) called *Moralia* or 'moral essays',
range over a vast array of topics, literary, religious (he was a priest
at Delphi and served the shrine 'for many Pythiads', *Should an Old
Man take part in Public Life?* 792f), homiletic (how to listen to
lectures, how to tell a flatterer from a friend, how to avoid offensive
self-praise, *Advice to Bride and Groom*), *Table Talk*, more or less
technically philosophical works, and more. But it would be wrong to
think of him as so isolated as all that, or so out of touch with politics.
Indeed, it is one of the most characteristic notes of his political advice
that public duty comes first; he is admittedly thinking more of local
public duties—he talks of the way that important visitors may be
surprised to find him deep in supervising building construction
when they come to seek him out at Chaeronea (*Advice on Public
Life* 811b–c)—but this is certainly not a man for an ivory tower. He
had himself travelled to Rome on several occasions, very likely on
public deputations,[13] and he had toured parts of Italy as well: as we
shall see in a moment, he was able to visit and examine one of the civil
war battlefields of 69 CE, an experience that clearly left a lasting
impression (*Otho* 14.2–3, 18.1). The *Parallel Lives*, like the *Table
Talk* and the *On Progress in Virtue*, are dedicated to Q. Sosius
Senecio. Sosius was a military man who was twice consul (99 and
107 CE), and also a man whose interest in Hellenic culture is
marked by his appearance in scholarly debates over the dinner table
(*Table Talk* 622c–623f, 635e–638a). Plutarch's choice of addressee is

---

[13] Cf. Jones 15–16, 20–4: notice the 'political business' that he mentions at *Dem.*
2.2, below, p. 000. Such embassies were a prominent feature of civic life; cf. e.g. *Advice
on Public Life* 805a, 819c, *Should an Old Man take part in Public Life?* 793d, 794a,
Roman Questions 275b–c, *On Exile* 602c; F. Millar, *The Emperor in the Roman World*
(1977), 228–40 and esp. 375–85.

itself expressive: action and culture can coexist, and the dedication of the work and the stories that it conveys are both testimony to that.[14]

So such themes mattered to his audience too; not perhaps equally to all of them, for some of his younger readers or listeners might not be so gripped by niceties (for instance) concerning *pater patriae*, but at least to some. For Sosius was not an isolated figure. The *Table Talk* pictures a world where Plutarch's dinner guests might be members of his family, might be local farmers or doctors, or might be visiting members of the Roman elite. These men of power can exchange intellectual conversation, even if their contributions are usually not the most learned and scholarly of all;[15] they know how to behave on such occasions, 'code-switching' to fit in with the Greek company they are keeping.[16] The conversation in fact dwells on Roman topics rather less than we might have expected, given Plutarch's own interest in Roman customs and antiquities.[17] Still, memory of the power of such guests is never far away, and there can occasionally even be light-hearted banter about their public lives. At one point, for instance, Plutarch presents a conversation of his own with Sosius when he recalls how one Roman, Aufidius Modestus, had twitted another, Avidius Quietus, about his governorship, presumably of Achaea.[18] Avidius' hands were chill with some disease, but Aufidius says 'but they're warm from your province'—warm with the heat of other people's money: that pleasantry can only work because Avidius was in fact beyond reproach (*Table Talk* 632a).

Of course there may be some idealization in such portrayal, and such conversations with the powerful may be presented as more frequent and more easygoing than they in fact were; and doubtless not every passing governor was quite so courteous or sympathetic to

[14] Cf. *Plutarch and History*, 270, where I also suggest that the placings of the particular dedicatory references to Sosius in the *Lives* are significant (*Thes.* 1.1, *Dem.* 1.1, *Dion* 1.1).

[15] Swain 145, and in *JHS* 110 (1990), 130–1 (= Scardigli, *Essays*, 237–8). I say more about the texture of such conversations in a paper to be published in a collection on the *Table Talk* edited by Frieda Klotz and Aikaterini Oikonomopoulou.

[16] On this see A. Wallace-Hadrill, *Rome's Cultural Revolution* (2008), esp. ch. 1.

[17] This too is discussed in my paper mentioned in n. 15.

[18] Avidius' proconsulship is epigraphically attested (*SIG*[3] 822) under Domitian, probably in 91–2 CE (Jones 23: cf. *PIR*[2], no. 1410, B. Puech in *ANRW* ii. 33.6 (1992), 4841–2). Jones assumes that the original conversation had taken place in Rome; that may be the case, but it is clear only that Sosius himself ('you remember!') and Plutarch had both been present, and that too may have been at Plutarch's own table.

his subjects. Indeed, the Avidius story works only because of the general expectation of personal enrichment, even if Avidius himself was spotless. In his *Advice on Public Life* Plutarch warns young politicians always to remember the 'weakness of Greek affairs' (824d) and the realities of Roman power: 'you are a subject as well as a ruler, the city is in the power of proconsuls, the men who do Caesar's bidding', and Roman 'shoes are above your head' (813d–e); you must be careful not to be carried away by memories of the glorious Greek past into untimely provocation (814a–c). That will draw Romans into more intervention than they would choose; much better to keep what control of one's affairs one can, and that requires a dignified and mature restraint (814e–815c). 'What sort of power is it', after all, 'that a little decree of a proconsul destroys or transfers to someone else, and does not extend to anything worthwhile in any case' (824e)? So, much as one may code-switch over a convivial dinner *à la grecque*, one must always remember that there are other, less comfortable codes too. Politically, one must watch one step.

All the more important, then, to make sure that 'one always has a friend among the powerful people above us' (814c), and it is clear that Plutarch's own familiarity with Roman grandees is not *simply* a fanciful literary construct.[19] He was himself a Roman citizen, and his Roman name 'Mestrius Plutarchus' figures on an inscription at Delphi (*SIG*[3] 829): his son was similarly 'Mestrius Autobulus' (*SIG*[3] 844a). The 'Mestrius' indicates that Plutarch owed the citizenship to L. Mestrius Florus, consul under Vespasian and another man who features in the *Table Talk*, three times as host (626e, 680c, 684e) and on several other occasions as guest (on one of these, below, p. 39). We hear more of Mestrius Florus in the *Otho*, where Plutarch tells how he toured the battlefield of Bedriacum in Mestrius' company; Bedriacum had been the site of some of the bloodiest fighting of the civil wars of 69 CE, and Mestrius had been there. He showed Plutarch an ancient temple, where after the battle he had 'seen a pile of corpses so high that they reached the temple's gables'. He told me that he had never been able to find out the explanation for their being heaped so high: 'no one had been able to tell him' (*Otho* 14.2–3).

---

[19] For more on Plutarch's 'Roman friends', see esp. Jones 22–3, 48–64; B. Puech in *ANRW* ii. 33.6 (1992), 4831–93.

Of course, not all of Plutarch's readers would be men like Sosius and Mestrius; many would be Greek rather than Roman, though that does not mean they would not be intrigued and flattered to think that the great and powerful might figure among their fellow-readers. Plutarch often takes the trouble to explain Roman customs or phrases in ways that Greek readers might find useful: the Bona Dea festival, for instance (9.4–8 n.), or the Attic equivalent of the Roman month of January (37.3 n.), or the punchy effect of the Latin *ueni uidi uici* (50.3 n.)—he does not in fact quote the Latin itself on that occasion, though he does do so in some cases elsewhere, as with *hoc age* ('do this!') at *Cor.* 25.4 or *deliciae* ('darling') at *Ant.* 59.8.[20] Sometimes, admittedly, such explanations may be an affectation, apologizing for a Latin intrusion into a Greek work; it is hard to think that many Greeks really needed *magnus* (*Pomp.* 13.7, *Crass.* 7.1) or *legio* (*Otho* 12.4) or *dicere* (*Marc.* 24.12) explained.[21] But many of the explanations may be real enough, and welcome to at least an appreciable number of his readers.

Still, these Greek readers too would be all too aware of the realities of power and conquest: legions bound for Parthia would be passing through Greece around the time he was writing. They would be aware too of the suffering that civil war could bring, even if they had not had such recent experience of it as those who had seen Bedriacum. There is a vivid moment in Plutarch's *Antony* which brings that home. We are in autumn 31 BCE, and the battle of Actium has just been fought.

Octavian then sailed to Athens, came to terms with the Greeks, and distributed among the cities the grain that he still had from the war. These cities were at the time in a dreadful state, stripped of their money, slaves, and cattle. There was one story that our own great-grandfather Nicarchus used to tell: all our citizens were forced to carry down a fixed measure of wheat to the sea at Anticyra [the nearest port on the Corinthian Gulf: this would be about a 30 km. march from Chaeronea, over steep and difficult country], and they were whipped as they went to make them go faster. They carried one load in this way, and the second had already been measured out ready for them to carry. Then the news arrived that Antony had lost: the city was saved!

---

[20] See index to Teubner *Lives* (3rd edn, Leipzig, 1998), 200–3; A. Wardman, *Plutarch's Lives* (1974), 37–48; A. Strobach, *Plutarch und die Sprachen* (*Palingenesia* 64; 1997), esp. 73–115, 145–57, 194–201.
[21] So P. A. Stadter in E. N. Ostenfeld (ed.), *Greek Romans and Roman Greeks* (2000), 123–4.

For Antony's stewards and soldiers immediately took to their heels, and the Greeks shared out the grain among themselves.

(*Ant.* 68.6–8)

Even 150 years later, memories of suffering like that would be hard to erase. Neither Plutarch nor his audience could have been unaware of all that would follow in Caesar's name. This is not a world populated by political innocents.

So the avoidance of a contemporary perspective is likely to be deliberate. But why should Plutarch turn his back on issues that must have concerned many of his readers, and in a different mindset would concern the writer himself? It is true that we can sometimes detect something of a detachment in the way he thinks about contemporary Rome.[22] The politics that most concern him in *Advice on Public Life* are clearly those of a Greek *polis*, with assemblies that need to be persuaded and an upper class that needs to develop leadership skills, some more devious and more manipulative than others. It is a good idea, for instance, for the elite to put on a few shows of internal disagreement about unimportant matters, so that their apparent consensus is more likely to prevail when it comes to the really important decisions (813a–c).[23] The Romans appear in that essay as the men of power, as we have already seen; but the nostalgia for the earlier days, when different and more inspirational lessons of freedom might be drawn from the past, may also be felt there. In another essay he is cool about those ambitions of young Greeks who aspire to a career as a Roman senator, international as the Roman political elite has now become:

Here's some Chian, here's some Galatian or Bithynian who is not content if he has acquired some reputation or power among a section of his own community, but bewails the fact that he is not yet wearing the patrician shoe; if he gets as far as wearing that, he's sad that he is not yet a Roman praetor; once praetor, that he is not consul; once consul, that he was proclaimed second rather than first.

(*On Peace of Mind* 470c–d)

---

[22] As I suggested more fully in the intr. to my comm. on *Antony*, 6–8.
[23] Swain 161–86 and M. Trapp in L. de Blois, J. Bons, T. Kessels, and D. M. Schenkeveld (eds), *The Statesman in Plutarch's Lives* (2004), i. 189–200, have good discussions of the way Plutarch's advice relates to the political circumstances of the time.

Admittedly, that is more a point about restlessness than about Rome, but it is still a telling example to come to mind, and we can sense Plutarch's ingrained sympathy with those content to stay at home. It is more telling still that the possibilities of a Roman career barely figure in *Advice on Public Life* at all, and when they do it is in a similarly dismissive vein: if you leave home dreaming of lucrative provincial posts, you will grow old on other people's doorsteps (814d).[24]

One should not overstate this distance: Plutarch is not a subversive, and this is not a text of resistance.[25] He is alert to all the advantages of the Roman peace, not an unbroken peace—69 and Bedriacum shows that—but still a time when Greece could prosper. He is certainly aware of the deficiencies as well as the glories of that Greek past, the ways that their own internal struggles and jealousies had so often been their undoing (*Flam.* 11.3–7, *Ages.* 15.3–8, *Tim.* 29.6, *On the Pythian Oracles* 401c–d).

Consider the greatest goods that cities can enjoy, peace, freedom, prosperity, a thriving population, and concord. As for peace, the peoples have no need of politicians at the present time; every war, Greek and barbarian, has disappeared. The people have as much freedom as the ruling power allows, and perhaps more than this would be no good thing . . .

(*Advice on Public Life* 824c)

There may again be some wistfulness in the tone of those final words, but there is also a stern awareness of what Rome had achieved. Elsewhere he puts it more exuberantly, talking of the way in which

Rome grew great and strong, and attached to herself nations and peoples and kingdoms of foreigners across the sea; that is when the world found stability and security, as the empire came round to one unwavering cycle and a world-order of peace.

(*On the Fortune of the Romans* 317c)

Why, the gods themselves had been involved, guiding Rome through those difficult days of the late Republic and steering towards the principate (*Brut.* 55(2).2, quoted below, at p. 20; also *Brut.* 47.7, *Ant.* 56.6, *Lucull.* 44(1).1)[26]—even if, for his own reasons, Plutarch

---

[24] Cf. Swain 169–71, 182–3.
[25] 'A statement of resistance' (Duff 309)—though Duff means that phrase in a nuanced and qualified way.
[26] Cf. Swain 157–61 and *AJP* 110 (1989), 272–302 at 288–92.

does not bring that point out so clearly in *Caesar* as in other *Lives* (below, Section 2.1). And even in *Caesar* itself the view is aired that the malaise of the Republic was such that a 'doctor' was needed, even if observers at the time identified the wrong man to apply the medicine, Pompey instead of Caesar (28.5–6 n., cf. 41.2, 57.1 nn.).

It must rather be that, at least in *Caesar*, Plutarch was more interested in other things. Where history was heading could be taken for granted; he had already covered that in the *Lives of the Caesars*. It was where history had been that mattered more—all the different factors that were now combining to promote Caesar's rise, and then to destroy the Republic. Many of those factors are clear enough within the *Life*'s narrative: they come together to form what he memorably calls Rome's *kakopoliteia*, the 'sorry state of politics' in Rome (28.4 n.) or, more literally, the 'bad-state' or 'bad-political-style' or 'bad-constitution'—the word combines all those dystopic suggestions. Greater depth is given by taking the *Life* with others in the series, so that we can see more clearly the roots of this *kakopoliteia*, with origins that go back at least to the Gracchi (below, p. 35). This is the sort of biography that requires a broader historical insight if it is to be understood.

But, if biography requires history for full comprehension, Plutarchan history also requires biography. It was the human beings who mattered: mattered because they made the history, and mattered because they allowed the most interesting morals to be drawn from that history. There is a sense—a qualified sense, perhaps, but still a real one[27]—in which the *Parallel Lives* fit together to build a composite picture of Greco-Roman history, rather as one of the classic histories of Rome, that of Drumann-Groebe, organized its material by chapters on families and individuals, with an entire volume on Cicero (vi, 2nd edn, 1929); and, if different *Lives* give different impressions of the same events—if *Cato*, say, or *Brutus* evinces more sympathy for the freedom-fighting ideal and less admiration for Caesar's charismatic leadership and energy and visionary plans for the future—then that too conveys an important historical insight, that good history is complicated and multivocal, admitting conflicting perspectives and requiring engagement with viewpoints that may eventually be incompatible. If Plutarch found

---

[27] I explore this perspective in a paper in Noreen Humble (ed.), *Plutarch's Lives: Parallelism and Purpose* (2010), 217–35.

room for different historical impressions, even apparently contra-
dictory ones, that is no sign of muddle, any more than it is in
Herodotus or Tacitus. It is a sign of the passionate engagement in
historical conflicts and in clashing viewpoints that, he felt, had timeless interest and appeal.

If individuals mattered, few mattered more than Caesar. But *how*
his story mattered to Plutarch is another question. As the founder or
precursor of the principate, of course—but, as we have seen, that is
not his interest here. As the culmination of the Republic, again of
course, and there is certainly material on that. But most of all, he
mattered for the moral questions he raised. Yet these too are not
altogether what one would expect. They are best seen against the
programme of the *Parallel Lives* as a whole, and it is time to see what
Plutarch himself says about that.

2. THE *LIFE OF CAESAR*

2.1. Biography and History

'Genre' is a slippery concept, and it is especially slippery when we talk
of ancient biography. By the time of Plutarch we can at least assume
that 'life-writing' was a familiar concept; 150 years earlier Cornelius
Nepos had begun his *Life* of Pelopidas by expressing a fear that 'if
I start to set out what happened, I might seem to be writing history
rather than narrating the man's life' (*Pelop.* 1), a snappy enough
phrase to suggest that the distinction was a familiar one;[28] but that
does not mean that there was anything like a firm expectation of
exactly what the genre might contain.

'Biography' is normally traced back to Xenophon's *Agesilaus* and
Isocrates' *Evagoras* in the fourth century, sometimes with a nod back
to Stesimbrotus and Ion of Chios in the fifth;[29] perhaps both *Agesilaus* and *Evagoras* might more properly be called encomia, but that

---

[28] Cf. J. Geiger, *Cornelius Nepos and Ancient Political Biography* (*Hist.* Einz. 47;
1985), 21-2, and, for a thoughtful recent treatment of Nepos' programmatic state-
ments and their relation to his practice, J. Beneker, *CJ* 105 (2009-10), 109-21.

[29] The standard treatment is A. Momigliano, *The Development of Greek Biography*
(2nd edn, 1993); a brilliant brief cross-period study is given by Hermione Lee,
Biography (2009). For brief surveys, see my own contributions on 'Biography,

distinction is itself a precarious one. Xenophon's *Cyropaedia* is also important, with a linear narrative structure that is close to that favoured by many later biographies, and adding a heavy admixture of fiction. There were other works, too, sharing many of the characteristics of biography, even if they are not normally counted as examples of the genre. Ptolemy's and Aristobulus' histories of Alexander, for instance, will evidently have focused their narratives on the leadership of the great man, whether or not they covered the whole life from birth; do they count as biographies? If they do, why not trace the genre all the way back to the *Odyssey*, which Aristotle took as his example when warning that centring a narrative on one person was not enough to give unity, and that writers needed to do more (*Poetics* 8.1451ᵃ16–19)? And would Theopompus' *Philippica* count, again taking one man as a central figure but ranging widely enough to include a whole book on 'The Demagogues'? And what of Dicaearchus' *Life of Greece*, not dealing with a single person at all, but rather with the lifestyle of a whole nation, its range of customs, its feasting, its dress, its origins, its debt to Chaldaean and Egyptian as well as indigenous influences? Or Xenophon's *Memorabilia*, built around the figure of Socrates and telling anecdotes without a linear chronological structure? Rather than any clear 'genre' with firm expectations, it is better to think of a loose family of works with overlapping features, allowing a range of different structures—Satyrus' *Life of Euripides* was in dialogue form—and a variation in other aspects as well, including a differing mix of fiction and truth and a differing degree of sympathy for the central figure. We should not be misled by the familiarity that we feel in reading these *Lives* of Plutarch, with their concentration on politicians and generals, their linear cradle-to-grave narrative, their interweaving of public and private life, their tendency to humane sympathy with the subjects, and their—qualified (below, Section 3.3), but genuine—commitment to truthfulness and their concern to get the person's character right. None of these features could be taken for granted when Plutarch

---

Greek' and 'Biography, Roman' in *OCD*⁴, and my articles on 'Biography' in G. Boys-Stones, B. Graziosi, and P. Vasunia (eds), *Oxford Companion of Hellenic Studies* (2009), 608–16, and on 'Plutarch and Biography', in F. B. Titchener and A. Zadorojnyi (eds), *Cambridge Companion to Plutarch* (forthcoming). I also make some comments on the fifth-century origins of the genre in V. Jennings and A. Katsaros (eds), *The World of Ion of Chios* (2007), 75–109.

wrote, and he had many choices to make. It is partly a mark of his success that we take so many of them for granted now.

Given those choices of Plutarch for public figures and linearity, his *Parallel Lives* might come particularly close to narrative historiography, and the earlier *Lives of the Caesars* will have come even closer.[30] Imperial historiography also often came close to biography, understandably in view of the immense power that a single individual now exercised, and indeed Tacitus' *Annals* and *Histories* are later once referred to as his *Lives of the Caesars* (Jerome, *Comm. in Zach.* 3.14.47); one of the epitomators of Cassius Dio could similarly say that an item on Vespasian 'will be recounted in his *Life* as well' (Xiphilinus at Dio 65.9.1). This generic proximity made it even more important for authors to stake out biography's distinctive territory. Andrew Wallace-Hadrill has brought out how Suetonius, writing only a few years after Plutarch, characterizes his *Lives* in terms of their being 'not-history';[31] we have just seen that Nepos also finds it natural to contrast 'narrating the man's life' and 'writing history', and when the same writer anticipates that some may think 'this kind of writing [*hoc genus scripturae*] trivial and unworthy of the roles played by great men', there is again an implied contrast with the obvious alternative, historiography (*Praef.* 1.1).

Plutarch too defines his biography against history, and it is no coincidence that he does so most elaborately in the proem to this very pair of *Alexander and Caesar*; these two great achievers, in their different ways, came as close as anyone could to turning the history of their countries into the history of themselves, into one-man stories.

For it is not histories we are writing, but Lives. Nor is it always the most famous actions that reveal a person's good or bad qualities; a clearer insight into character is often given by a small thing or a word or a jest than by engagements where thousands die, or the biggest of pitched battles, or the sieges of cities.

(*Alex.* 1.2)[32]

---

[30] Thus the first sentence of *Otho*—'The next day dawned, and the new emperor came out to the Capitol and sacrificed'—is a direct continuation of *Galba*, while 'as I have already mentioned' at *Galba* 2.1 refers back to a passage in *Nero*; Otho is introduced not at the beginning of his own *Life* but at *Galba* 19. See my introduction to *Galba* and *Otho* in the Penguin *Rome in Crisis* (2010).

[31] A. Wallace-Hadrill, *Suetonius* (1983), esp. 8–10.

[32] Duff 13–51 illuminatingly analyses this passage along with several more of the programmatic passages that are quoted below.

So character, *ēthos*, is the point:

I have spent time on this [a story of the quarrel and reconciliation of Cato and his friend Munatius Rufus] because I think it just as telling as Cato's great public actions in giving the reader illumination and insight into the man's character.

(*C.min.* 37.10)

That taste for 'small things' need not exclude the 'big things' as well; it is 'often', not always, that the small things give a clearer picture, and the personal story is 'just as telling as', not more telling than, the great public actions. The proem to *Nicias* seems[33] to make it explicit that his 'manner [*tropos*] and disposition were particularly revealed by his sufferings, many and great as they were'—in that case, the Sicilian disaster, a big thing *par excellence*. But even those sufferings (he goes on) will be treated lightly and with an eye to supplementing the well-known historical material.

Nor is this an accumulation of useless erudition: I am conveying material that is helpful for grasping the man's character [*ēthos*] and manner [*tropos*].

(*Nicias* 1.5)

He can leave extraneous detail to the writers of 'the histories that make their way through everything' (*Fab.* 16.6) or—echoing the language of Polybius[34]—'pragmatic histories' (*Galba* 2.5), though in those passages too he makes it clear that he includes momentous events when they suit his purpose ('I too should not omit anything of note in the doings and sufferings of the Caesars', the *Galba* passage goes on). But Plutarch's focus remains sharper than that of narrative history.[35]

[33] 'Seems', because there is a textual uncertainty here: most manuscripts have *kaluptomenēn* ('concealed' rather than 'revealed'), though a correcting hand in one (U) alters to *apokaluptomenēn* ('revealed'). Duff 25 gives good reasons for favouring the latter or for emending to *anakaluptomenēn* (also 'revealed': so Jones 104 n. 4).
[34] Polybius 1.2.8, 3.47.8, 6.5.2, etc. They are 'pragmatic' in the sense that they concentrate on political and military matters, perhaps with the additional implication that they aim to give practical guidance to readers for their own public activity.
[35] Though note that there is less interest in *character* in the programmatic formulation in the *Galba* than there is in those in the *Parallel Lives*. On this cf. A. Georgiadou, *ICS* 13.2 (1988), 349–56 at 350–1, and the introduction to *Galba and Otho* in my Penguin translation (*Rome in Crisis* (2010)).

In the proem to *Aemilius-Timoleon* Plutarch tells us more about this process of getting to know his characters, and expands on the way that this goes with an improving moral purpose. Writing the *Lives*, he says, has been like entertaining each of his characters as a house guest; as he and his readers (for at that point he drifts from 'I' into 'we')[36] deepen their understanding of each figure, it is like looking in a mirror; and Plutarch himself has become a better person for these encounters (*Aem.* 1). 'Like looking in a mirror . . .': the point seems to be that we explore the experiences and dilemmas of those figures from the past, and ask what we would have done ourselves in their circumstances, or what they would have done in ours.[37] The exercise will often prove inspirational; Plutarch is clear that narrative can be more uplifting and can produce virtue more constructively than any work of plastic art (*Pericles* 1–2). Sometimes the effect may be more one of deterrence, providing examples of how things can go wrong (*Demetrius* 1.4–7), especially when 'great natures' are in danger of being corrupted.[38] But overall the historical writer should dwell on the good things, not concealing a subject's faults but not overemphasizing them either, in the manner of a tactful portrait-painter (*Cimon* 2.4–5).

That is the theory, and it is not hard to find *Lives* that correspond. Take *Cato minor*, for instance. That is a *Life* that has a great deal of detail on 'small things'—a lot on the women of his family, for instance, or on his dealings with his friends such as Munatius;[39] we noted the passage above in which he justified such inclusions. That *Life* is also extremely moralistic, in the sense of delivering explicit or implicit praise and blame. Sometimes there is explicit criticism of Cato's political line: he spoke and behaved as if he were living in

[36] On this see *Plutarch and History*, 273.

[37] P. A. Stadter in L. van der Stockt (ed.), *Rhetorical Theory and Praxis in Plutarch* (*Collection d'Études Classiques*11; 2000), 493–510 at 505: cf. my *Plutarch and History*, 250–1 n. 27. The analogy with 'looking in a mirror' recurs at *Progress in Virtue* 85a–b, and is examined in detail by Duff 30–4 and by A. Zadorojnyi in N. Humble (ed.), *Plutarch's Lives: Parallelism and Purpose* (2010), 169–95. Zadorojnyi stresses that mirrors can (and were often acknowledged to) distort as well as reflect accurately: studying in a mirror requires the audience to be alert and thoughtful, with their power of moral reasoning fully involved.

[38] On 'great natures' and their corruptibility, cf. Duff, esp. 47–9, 60–5, 205–8, 224–8, and, with a detailed discussion of the *Demetrius* proem, *Hermes*, 132 (2004), 271–91.

[39] *C.min.* 24.4–25.13, 30.3–10, 52.5–9. Cf. *Plutarch and History*, 103.

Plato's *Republic* rather than the cesspool of the Roman state (*Phoc.* 3.2, quoting Cicero),[40] and consequently failed to make the compromises that might have avoided civil war (*C.min.* 30.9–10); his sloppy dress diminished the dignity of his rank as praetor (*C.min.* 44.1). Still, no one could fail to admire his attempt to apply principle to politics, even if he took this too far; and great emphasis falls on his thoughtful and principled behaviour in his final days at Utica, so concerned to protect the townspeople even though he had resigned himself to his own fate (*C.min.* 58–70)—though room is also found for his less admirable traits, in the angry blow he delivered to a slave (69.5).

What of *Caesar*? Julius Caesar would certainly seem to *invite* moralistic comment.[41] The rights and wrongs of the case for tyrannicide were hotly debated as early as Cicero's *de Officiis* later in 44,[42] and continued to be charged with ideological passion for a century afterwards.[43] A central concern of Suetonius' *Life* is to weigh up the case for and against Caesar, and eventually the verdict is negative: despite all Caesar's good qualities, especially his clemency and moderation,

the balance is tilted by his other actions and words, so that he is thought to have abused his power and to have been justly killed.

(Suetonius, *Diuus Iulius* 76.1)

Those are strong words: 'justly killed', *iure caesus*, is the legal term used for justifiable homicide, and this was the language in which the lynching of the Gracchi had been excused.[44] Two generations earlier

[40] Cf. below, p. 52 and n. 136.

[41] I have said more on the various verdicts in 'Judging Julius Caesar'; see in general the various studies in *CJC* 207–314 for Caesar's shifting reputation during the principate.

[42] Cic. *Off.* 2.23, 3.19, 3.82–5: see the outstanding discussion of H. Strasburger, *Studien zur alten Geschichte*, iii (1990), 407–502 at 495–7.

[43] E. Rawson in I. S. Moxon, J. D. Smart, and A. J. Woodman (eds), *Past Perspectives* (1986), 101–19 = *Roman Culture and Society* (1991), 488–507. Notice esp. the Cremutius Cordus case in 25 CE (Tac. *Ann.* 4.34–5) where praise of Brutus and Cassius proved fatal; presumably the praise centred on the killing, as did the attacks on them as 'brigands *and parricides*', which Tacitus' Cremutius says were current (4.34.3). Under Nero, Thrasea Paetus and Helvidius Priscus are said to have celebrated the birthdays of Brutus and Cassius (Juv. 5.36–7, cf. Tac. *Ann.* 16.22.5); and in 65 CE a statue of Cassius inscribed 'to our party leader' sealed the fate of one of his descendants (*Ann.* 6.7.2).

[44] Cf. *CJC* 262; I say more about Suetonius' weighing-up there and in Pelling 'Judging Julius Caesar', 9–10.

Seneca had disapproved of the assassination, but his judgements on Caesar himself were more nuanced, with earlier works tending to stress the good qualities and later works the bad; still, the moral register remains throughout, whether in approval of his self-restraint (*de Ira* 2.23.4) or in condemnation of his naked populism (*Letters* 94.65, 104.31, etc).[45] Nor were Caesar's conquests beyond criticism. When the elder Pliny considered the bloodshed in Gaul, he could wonder whether 'so great a wrong to the human race' could be justified (*NH* 7.92);[46] Suetonius too has reservations about some of Caesar's excuses for attack (*Iul.* 24.3, cf. 15.2–5 n.). Of course, judgement could be positive as well, with awe at the man's massive achievement in battle or in power, respect for his 'admirable moderation and clemency both in administration and as victor in the civil war' (Suet. 75.1), or simply admiration for the demonic energy and restlessness in everything that he did; fascination with such a character, even obsession, is clear enough in the complex interplay of different voices we can see in Lucan's poem. But there too one voice, and by no means the quietest, is a moral one, and it is not one of favour:

It may be their own fame that ensures that memory will survive amid distant races, the peoples of our grandchildren; it may be that our own labours can help the names of the Great. And when these wars are then read about, hope, fear, and doomed prayers will still move the readers, and all will be shaken as they hear of this destiny as if it is still to come, not a story of the past; and they will still, Great Pompey, take your side.

(Lucan 7.207–13)

Yet, in Plutarch's *Life* itself, the moral voice is strangely muted. The young Caesar plunged deeply into debt, and Plutarch would normally strongly disapprove (*Advice on Public Life* 822c–f and his whole essay *Avoid Debt!*); here he simply notes it (5.8–9 n.). Caesar's techniques were often those of the demagogue, and here too we would expect disapproval (4.4–7, 7.1–4 nn.; contrast *Advice on Public Life* 802d–e, 821f–822c). Sometimes we do indeed find a note of distaste:

---

[45] M. T. Griffin, *Seneca: A Philosopher in Politics* (1976), 183–8.
[46] Cf. L. Pitcher's acute remark: Caesar 'perverts the encyclopedist's love of large and precise numbers (cf. Plin. *Pref.* 17) into an arithmetic of carnage—the one million, one hundred and ninety-two thousand casualties that constituted the necessary evil of his conquests' (*CJC* 268).

Then as soon as he entered office he started introducing laws that would have been more fitting for the most reckless of tribunes than for a consul, some colonies to please the masses, and also some distributions of land...

(14.2)

But even there his sharper criticism is reserved for Pompey rather than Caesar:

Pompey even added that his opponents might have their swords, but he would face them with both sword and shield. That upset the aristocrats; and indeed Pompey's sense of personal dignity, as well as the respect owed to the senate, should have stopped him from making so lunatic and juvenile a remark. But the people loved it.

(14.4–5)

Similarly, Caesar's behaviour during the Catilinarian conspiracy was at least questionable, but it is not this *Life* that brings that out most clearly; there is a good deal more interest in that theme in *Cicero* and in *C.min.*[47] Nor is it simply the bad moral points that Plutarch passes over here, for some of his best qualities are equally unstressed: his clemency to the conquered, for instance, does come out and is clearly commended, but more could have been made of it (34.7, 42–6, 48.4, 57.4 nn.). Thus his generous treatment of the troops of Afranius and Petreius is stressed at *Pomp.* 65.2 but omitted at 36.2 (n.), and at the end of the civil wars the accent rests on his vindictiveness rather than his moderation (53.7, 54.3 nn.). Even the traditional moral question raised by his assassination—was it right for Brutus and Cassius to strike him down when they had received so many benefits at his hands?—is aired not here but in the *Comparison of Dion and Brutus* (*Brut.* 56(3).4–6, below, p. 73); and it is again in that *Comparison*, not here, that Plutarch makes his view clear on the even bigger question whether autocracy was justified.

Caesar's rule caused trouble for its opponents during its genesis, but once they had accepted it and been defeated it seemed no more than a name and an idea, and nothing cruel or tyrannical sprang from it. Indeed it seemed that the state needed monarchy, and Caesar was Heaven's gift to Rome as the gentlest possible doctor.

(*Brut.* 55(2).2)

---

[47] See 7.5–8.5 n., 7.7 n., and *Plutarch and History*, ch. 2.

Here as well Plutarch's principles of ethical generosity might seem to call for that big historical perspective to be emphasized; but *Caesar* is simply not that sort of *Life*.

It is, though, a very 'historical' *Life* in other ways. That initial programmatic statement in the proem to *Alexander* may define biography against history, but still many of the narrative themes are ones that would sit comfortably in historiography. Plutarch's explanation for Caesar's rise is clear: from the beginning, he was the champion and the favourite of the Roman people, the *dēmos*. He spends lavishly to secure their favour (4.4–7. 5.8–9, cf. 57.8 n.), and 'its impact on the people was so great that everyone sought new offices and new honours to repay him' (5.9). The demonstration of images of Marius is calculated to appeal to them too (6.1–5), and Caesar fends off the senatorial criticisms:

That encouraged his admirers even more, and they urged him not to bow to anybody. He had the people's support; with it he would conquer everyone, and win the highest place of all.

(6.7)

'New offices', 'new honours', 'the highest place of all': Caesar is not yet even praetor, but it is very clear where this is heading, and what the crucial element in Caesar's support is. Nor is it heading there peaceably or constitutionally: Cicero is wondering whether Caesar can really be plotting the 'overthrow of the Roman constitution' (4.9); Catulus accuses him of assailing the state with his siege engines (6.6). The themes recur as the narrative progresses (20.2, 21.2, 21.8–9, 23.7, 35.8 nn.), and other factors come into play too: the enthusiasm of his friends, for instance (17.9–11), and particularly the devoted, some-times even erotically tinged, loyalty of his troops (16–17, 29.4–7, 37.6–9, 38.7, 39.2, 42–6, 44.9–12 nn.). Then it is when these factors start to turn against him that his position becomes precarious. On his return to Italy from one of his most spectacular victories

he was met by popular disapproval. That was partly because his soldiers had mutinied and killed two former praetors, Cosconius and Galba, but Caesar had ventured no harsher punishment than to call the men 'citizens' instead of 'soldiers': he had then given each of them a thousand drachmas, as well as parcelling out to them a large part of the Italian countryside in land grants. Dolabella's madness also started tongues wagging against Caesar, and so did Matius' avarice; so too did Antony's drunken excesses and his ransacking and rebuilding of Pompey's private house, as if it was not big enough already.

The Romans did not like all this. Caesar himself knew what was going on, and it was against his will. But he had no choice. Political considerations forced him to make use of the men who were willing to be his agents.

(51.2–4)

People, soldiers, friends: the same factors that made Caesar great are now destroying him. The themes recur as the assassination looms (57–61, 64–5 nn.). Such patterning is a favourite of Greek thought: one can detect it in Herodotus' Persia, Thucydides' Athens, Sophocles' Oedipus or Antigone or Ajax, even the Achilles of the *Iliad*. And here those factors are fundamentally *historical* factors. Of course features of Caesar's personality—his brilliance, his phenomenal gifts, his intelligence, his ambition—matter too, but they are not the crucial elements now: indeed he 'knew what was going on', as Plutarch makes clear in the passage just quoted, but he had no choice. He was similarly aware of the dangers looming against him at the time of the conspiracy, and he feared Brutus and Cassius (62.9–10, 63.1 n.). But there was little he could do: he was trapped, trapped by his own past, trapped by the elements that had raised him to such might.

Even so, of course *Caesar* remains a biography, however close it may come generically to history (for more on this, below, in Section 2.2). There are many sections where Plutarch follows what has been called 'the law of biographical relevance',[48] telling events in this *Life* from Caesar's perspective or with particular emphasis on or exaggeration of his role, and moving the spotlight to one of the other figures when he tells of the same events in other *Lives*. That is particularly true of the accounts of the conspiracy in *Brutus* and here, which interlock with minimal repetition (62, 64–5, 67–8 nn.; cf. also 14, 39, 42–6 nn.). It remains true that there is rather less on those 'small things' or 'words' or 'jests' than that passage in the proem to *Alexander and Caesar* would have led us to expect. It is Suetonius who gives us a more rounded portrait of the man as a whole, with interest for instance in his sensitivity about his baldness or his restraint at the dinner table, much more on his broader culture and his literary achievements,[49] and a good deal on his notoriously active sex life (Suet. 45.2, 53, 49–52, 56); in Plutarch's *Life* there is not even much

---

[48] D. R. Stuart, *Epochs of Greek and Roman Biography* (1928), 78.
[49] On Plutarch's suppression of Caesar's philosophical interests, cf. B. Buszard, *TAPA* 138 (2008), 194.

on that love life, and it is once again other biographies, *Brutus* and
Cato minor, that tell a revealing story about his affair with Servilia (8.2
n.: contrast *C.min.* 24.1–3, *Brut.* 5.2–4, and cf. 62.1 n.). Even Cleopatra and the carpet (or rather kitbag, 49.2 n.) are given remarkably little
attention (49.3, 49.10 nn.), tempted though the author of the marvellous *Life of Antony* must have been to tell us more.

So this *Life* becomes a rather unusual one, not wholly isolated
among the *Parallel Lives—Themistocles,* for instance, is rather 'historical' as well, and Plutarch's moralistic voice ranges in register and
stridency elsewhere—but still well to one end of Plutarch's spectrum.
One reason for that is certainly the texture of the events themselves,
as we have already seen; under Caesar as under Alexander, history
comes close to being the story of this one man. But there is another
way of looking at it, seeing this not as a drift away from biography but
a moulding of biography in a way that this one man demanded. For it
was, after all, a choice of Caesar himself to direct his life so single-
mindedly towards power:

Caesar, they say, had a remarkable gift for political oratory, and he trained
and developed this talent with a great eagerness for glory. The second place
was unquestionably his, but he allowed the first to escape him: his attention
was devoted to becoming first in power and in armed strength. His campaigns and his politics won him dominion in the state, but robbed him of
that first prize in eloquence for which he was naturally fitted.

(3.2–3)

That passage is very early in the *Life,* and ensures that we know what
drives him. It is then no surprise that he would prefer to be first man
in an obscure Alpine village than second in Rome (11.4). Various
delicate touches make sure that the coming 'monarchy' and 'tyranny'
is kept before our eyes (29.5, 30.1, 35.6–11 nn.). Once it is achieved,
Platonic allusion marks the importance of this 'acknowledged tyranny: he already enjoyed a monarch's unaccountability, and now he
had a monarch's permanence as well' (57.1 n., echoing Plato *Republic*
8.569b: below, p. 63).

And was it worthwhile, all this ruthless dedication to power? That
question is highlighted at the end:

Caesar died after living fifty-six years in all, outliving Pompey by a little more
than four years. He had sought dominion and power all his days, and after
facing so many dangers he had finally achieved them. And the only fruit it

bore him was its name, and the perils of fame amid his envious fellow-citizens.

(69.1)

In a different mood Plutarch could address the topic in a different, more extended mode—in the dialogue of *Pyrrh.* 14, for instance, when the philosopher Cineas draws out Pyrrhus to say what the aim of all this warfare and conquest might be: to go on to conquer all Italy? Then Sicily? Then Carthage and Africa? Then Macedonia and Greece? And what then? Why, to relax in comfort and enjoy a lunchtime drink with our friends. But why, we can do that already, and spare ourselves all that toil and bloodshed ... Such expansiveness is alien to the taut style of *Alexander-Caesar*,[50] but the moral thought is similar, just as it is towards the end of *Alexander* when Taxiles asks the king whether they really need to fight (59) and Dandamis is said to have wondered 'why did Alexander make such a long journey to get here?' (65.4).[51] It all points to a more reflective type of moralism than the straightforward praise and blame that we have so far been discussing. Plutarch's readers might not be able to put themselves quite in Caesar's shoes, pondering whether to become the greatest orator in the Roman world or the most powerful man; but they—but we all—might still face analogous choices on a smaller, more everyday scale between a driven and a broader existence, and on gazing into that 'mirror' of Caesar's choices we might find material to reflect on our own.

So the manner of the *Life* reflects the manner of Caesar himself. There are few intimate personalia because this was a man with 'no time for love';[52] those 'small things' of the *Alexander-Caesar* proem are scarce because Caesar was such a big-thing person. That proem spoke also of 'comments and jokes'. Those of Caesar himself focus on achievement: 'Today, mother, you will see your son either

---

[50] Though, if Buszard is right to take *Alex.-Caes.* and *Pyrrh.-Mar.* closely together (below, n. 74), the Cineas passage in *Pyrrh.* may be taken as reflecting on Alexander and Caesar as well: B. Buszard, *TAPA* 138 (2008), 185–215, esp. 204–6, 210–11.

[51] To this extent Buszard's question concerning both men's 'ambition' (*philotimia*), 'Why disparage Caesar and not Alexander?' (*TAPA* 138 (2008), 194), may mislead: whether or not 'disparage' is too strong a word, the end of *Caesar* may anyway be seen as giving sharper formulation to, and encouraging retrospective reflection on, a moral issue that has run through both *Lives*.

[52] To use the phrase of J. Beneker, 'No time for love: Plutarch's chaste Caesar' (*GRBS* 43: 13–29).

a high-priest or an exile' (7.3); 'Let the die be cast' (32.8); 'Today the enemy might have won—all they needed was a winner' (39.8); 'It was their choice. They drove me to this pitch of necessity that I, Gaius Caesar, victor in the greatest of wars, would actually have been condemned in the courts if I had given up my armies' (46.1); 'I came, I saw, I conquered' (50.3); and more.[53] But they are not noted for humour: 'I thought my wife should be beyond suspicion' (10.9) is no joke at all. Just as striking are the 'comments and jests' of his enemies, initially suspicions or warnings (1.4, 4.8–9, 5.6, cf. 13.6), then towards the end some genuine jokes at his expense: those are especially launched by Cicero, evidently the man whose oratorical skill left Caesar in second place in that passage in 3.2–3. At the end Cicero is initially complimentary (57.6), but the barbs soon start: 'Let's hurry, or his consulship will be over' (58.3, on the elevation of Caninius Rebilus to be consul for the last day of the year); the constellation of Lyra will be rising 'on instructions' (59.6). The remarks plot, even partly orchestrate, the gathering resentment against Caesar. It is a favourite Plutarchan technique to 'characterize by reaction', to use the responses of contemporary observers to manipulate the reactions of his readers;[54] here those responses are also important in explaining Caesar's fall. The comments of his friends (Balbus at 60.8) are as damaging as those of his enemies; and by now Caesar's own remarks are themselves, one way or another, presaging his death (62.6, 62.9–10, 63.6–7).

So there may be more to that initial programmatic passage in *Alexander* than meets the eye, just as there is more to that choice between oratory and domination (3.2–3). Small things have a way of interacting with big things; jests and comments can play their part in bringing down the greatest of men; and eloquence may eventually have its own powerful weapons in the play for power.

2.2. *Alexander and Caesar*: Pair and Series

Long before Plutarch, Alexander had been a thought-provoking figure for the all-conquering Romans, a benchmark against which to measure themselves; it seems to have been Romans, not Greeks, who

[53] Examples: 11.4, 11.6, 14.13, 17.10, 18.3, 35.7–10, 38.5, 44.9, 52.9, 54.2, 56.4, 60.6.
[54] Cf. 6.3, 21.7, 28.5–6, 56.7, 66, 67.1 nn. and my comm. on *Antony*, index, s.v. 'characterisation by reaction'.

first called Alexander 'the Great'.[55] Livy had played with 'virtual history' in imagining what would have happened if Alexander had challenged the Rome of his day, and decided that Rome would have won (9.17-19): Plutarch too knew that this was a favourite topic for debate (*Pyrrh.* 19.2), whether or not he knew Livy's version of it. By the first century CE Alexander topics often preoccupied the declaimers, though interestingly their themes tend not to be those larded with the most obvious historical significance for Rome:[56] not 'should he adopt oriental customs and dress'—that would have had too much of the flavour of Antony and Cleopatra—nor even 'should he take on Rome', but 'should he sail the Ocean' once he had reached so far, or 'should he enter Babylon' when the prophets were saying that he would die there (Sen. *Suas.* 1, 4). Ocean, achievement, prophecies of death, and one's response: those are themes of interest in *Caesar* too, where the Alexander comparison may add an extra resonance, as we will see.

Much earlier, even before Caesar, Alexander had fascinated Roman generals themselves, and those who talked about them.[57] 'Alexander-*imitatio*', or at least a projection of a general as a latter-day Alexander conquering the world in the interest of Rome, can be traced in the legends that grew up around Scipio Africanus.[58] That fascination continued in Plutarch's day, and Alexander was another figure who featured heavily in the thought world of Trajan.[59] But it was above all Pompey and his supporters who made much of his claim, which was indeed more reasonable than that of others, to be the Roman

[55] That is first found at Plautus, *Most.* 775: for Greeks and Macedonians he had been just '(King) Alexander' or 'Alexander of Macedon' or 'Alexander son of Philip'. Cf. Weippert 17-22.

[56] But there is always a more tacit relevance of themes of kingship and excess for imperial Rome: 'being Alexander is the inescapable subtext for all subsequent autocrats'. This aspect is elaborately developed by Spencer, esp. ch. 2 (quotation from p. 79).

[57] On Alexander-*imitatio*, see esp. Spencer, Weippert, and P. Green, *AJAH* 3 (1978), 1-26; also D. Michel, *Alexander als Vorbild für Pompeius, Caesar, und Marcus Antonius* (1967), G. Wirth in *Alexandre le Grand* (Entr. Hardt 22; 1976), 181-221, S. Borszák, *Gymn.* 89 (1982), 37-56, and Woodman on Vell. 2.83.1, all with further bibliography.

[58] On Scipio note esp. Livy 26.19.1-7, Gell. 6.1.1-6, with the discussion of Weippert 37-55.

[59] Trajan and Alexander: G. Wirth in *Alexandre le Grand* (n. 57), 197-200, Spencer 177-8. Cf . above, pp. 2-6, on Trajan and Caesar.

Alexander, a Pompey the Great to match Alexander the Great.[60] That theme is visible in Plutarch's own *Pompey*. The nickname 'Alexander' attached to Pompey from his youth, as there was a physical resemblance (*Pomp.* 2.2–3), and his run of triumphant conquests echoed Alexander too—until his return from the East in 61 BCE:

> At this point he was, according to those who compare him to Alexander in everything and make much of the parallels, not yet 34 years old; in fact he was over forty. How fortunate he would have been if his life had finished at this point, for until now he had enjoyed Alexander's fortune! But the years that followed brought successes that provoked rancour and disasters that were beyond remedy.
>
> (*Pomp.* 46.1–2)

Plutarch must surely have thought about pairing Alexander with Pompey rather than Caesar, but one can see why he did not; there was eventually rather little that he could do with that comparison, other than developing that contrast of Pompey's Alexander-like beginnings and his catastrophic end. In particular, the finely drawn narrative in *Pompey* of the man's bemused leadership at Pharsalus, his forlorn flight, and his treacherous murder in Egypt would have little resonance with the last days of Alexander, whereas Egypt saw the final phase of Agesilaus' life as well, one that was inglorious rather than tragic (*Ages.* 36–40, esp. 37.9–11, with *Pomp.* 85(5)). There was more to be done with the comparison of Alexander and Caesar, the two great victors of Greek and Roman history. Still, if we take the two pairs *Alexander-Caesar* and *Agesilaus-Pompey* together, the acute reader of *Pompey* may catch the hint that it would be Caesar who more completely filled the Alexander role that was mapped out for Pompey, not unlike the way that in *Caesar* observers misidentify Pompey rather than Caesar as the 'gentlest possible doctor' for the sick state (28.6 n., above, p. 12), and just as it was Alexander who eventually carried through the eastern conquests that Agesilaus might have achieved (*Ages.* 15.4, cf. *Pomp.* 82(2).6, *Alex.* 37.7).[61]

Not that Caesar himself seems to have projected himself as a new Alexander: it would indeed have been unwise of him to do so at any

---

[60] Cf. esp. Weippert 56–104; Spencer, esp. ch. 5; Heftner, index, s.v. 'Alexander d. Gr.'; P. Greenhalgh, *Pompey: The Roman Alexander* (1980).

[61] On *Alexander-Caesar* as a benchmark for *Agesilaus-Pompey*, see also G. W. M. Harrison, *RBPh* 72 (1995), 91–104, esp. 100–2.

point before his final victory, for it would have been clear that
Pompey had a much stronger claim. Even after his victory, it seems
rather to have been others who drew that comparison, from Cicero
onwards.[62] It had certainly developed well before Plutarch came to it:
Velleius Paterculus, writing under Tiberius, says in his exuberant
introduction to Caesar's career that

> in the greatness of his thinking, his swiftness in war, and his willingness to
> face dangers he was most closely parallel to Alexander the Great—but to
> Alexander when he was sober and when his anger was under control.
>
> (Vell. 2.41.1)

We have already seen Plutarch at work on one aspect of this tradition,
adjusting that story of Caesar and Alexander's statue to make it a
matter of reading rather than viewing (above, p. 4; 11.5–6 n.).
A sentence or so later, and Plutarch is using language in such a way
as to keep Alexander in our mind: Caesar is marching 'on to the
Ocean at the end of the earth, conquering new peoples and subjecting
them to Rome' (12.1 n.). Later Caesar goes one better still, becoming
'the first man to sail the western Ocean with a fleet, and convey an
army into battle through the waters of the Atlantic' (23.2 n.)—better
even than Alexander in that case, who reached the eastern Ocean
but merely set foot on an island beyond (*Alex.* 62–63.1, 66.1–3,
cf. 44.1–2). And Caesar's last plans, like Alexander's, envisage a
great looping circle around the known world (58.4–10 (nn.) ~ *Alex.*
68.1–2), though neither lives to carry it through.

   Those are not the only ways that memories of Alexander are in play
as the *Life* reaches its end. Alexander and Caesar both felt they had to
rearticulate their position in the light of their conquests, and neither
did it without causing offence. In Alexander's case it was the adoption
of a new style of kingship, borrowing from the Persian court that he
had vanquished (*Alex.* 45.1–4, 46.5–7, 51.2–5, 54.4–6, 71.1–4); in
Caesar's it was kingship itself. When the Thebans tried to mobilize
Greece against Alexander in the name of freedom, they did not get
very far (*Alex.* 11.8, 12.5), and later Alexander can even turn Greek

[62] 11.5–6 n. and esp. P. Green, *AJAH* 3 (1978), 1–26; Spencer 170, 198–9 largely
agrees, but allows the possibility that Caesar himself took 'some tentative steps'
towards Alexander self-figuring after Pompey's death. Cicero: esp. *Att.* 12.40 (281).2
and 13.28 (299).2, with Spencer 53–64; also Weippert 123–53, though Weippert
emphasizes how unexpectedly little Cicero has to say about Alexander.

freedom-rhetoric opportunistically to his own advantage (*Alex.* 34.2). At Rome the cause and spirit of freedom had more vigour. Thus

the most visible and lethal hatred was provoked by his [Caesar's] passion to become king. That was the first grievance felt by the ordinary people, while those who had long nursed their resentments took it as the most plausible of their pretexts.

(*Caes.* 60.1)

And so the forces begin to gather against each man in turn, and the conspiratorial whispers begin. Here though they react in different ways. Alexander becomes extremely fearful and suspicious (*Alex.* 42.3–4); that is the key to several dramatic scenes, with his killing of Philotas and Parmenio, his unworthy suspicions of Cleitus and Callisthenes, and his strong response to the conspiracy of the pages (*Alex.* 48–9, 50.5–6, 55.2, 55.3–7). Omens presage the deaths of both Alexander and Caesar (*Alex.* 57.4, 73–5, *Caes.* 63); both men are shaken, but Alexander far more so than Caesar, and the tracing of his bizarre psychology is strong and explicit—'he was despondent, despairing already of the gods and suspicious of his friends', 'now that he had given in totally to superstition and was wholly disturbed and terrified in his thinking, there was nothing so unusual or absurd that he did not regard as a portent' (*Alex.* 74.1, 75.1)—while Caesar's thinking remains more enigmatic.[63] Alexander descends into irascibility and febrile drunkenness (*Alex.* 70.1–2, 75.3–6). We have come a long way by then from the brilliant Alexander of his youth, initially so keen and interested a pupil of Aristotle (*Alex.* 7–8); by now the name of Aristotle figures only in a gibe (*Alex.* 74.5). His encounter with the Gymnosophists in India exposes him to a different, stranger sort of wisdom (*Alex.* 64), almost as bewildering as Dandamis' remark that Socrates, Pythagoras, and Diogenes were philosophers of talent but were too respectful of convention and the laws (*Alex.* 65.3).[64] The disorienting perspectives are in keeping with the macabre atmosphere

---

[63] On Alexander, cf. also 48.6 n., Brenk 197–201. On Caesar as enigmatic, cf. 57.7, 63, 64–5 nn., Pelling, 'Focalisation', 514–15.

[64] On the Gymnosophists and their role in the *Life*, see T. Whitmarsh, *CQ* 52 (2002), 184–6; on Aristotle, B. Buszard, *TAPA* 138 (2008), 190–2. There is a marked difference of emphasis here between Plutarch's *Life* and his two essays *On the Fortune or Virtue of Alexander I* and *II*: the essays, particularly the first, develop the idea of Alexander as the 'philosopher in arms', civilizing the East with Greek wisdom, and have no hint of the darker elements of Alexander's decline. Cf. Hamilton, pp. xxiii–xxxiii.

of the closing chapters, and the atmosphere of terror is strong: one can understand why Cassander could not pass a statue of Alexander much later in life without tottering and nearly fainting (*Alex.* 74.6). With Caesar things are very different. Clemency is the order of the day (57.4 nn.). Statues once again become a charged theme,[65] and one that has some bearing on the mounting apprehensions of kingship (61.8 n.), yet one of Caesar's first acts in power is the restoration of the statues of his enemy Pompey (57.6 n.)—and it is ironically by one of those statues that he dies, emblematically marking the lack of vindictiveness that left him vulnerable to the men he had spared, Cassius and Brutus (62, 66.1 nn.). Despite the enigmatic way in which Plutarch treats Caesar's own thinking, it at least seems clear that he has caught wind of the conspiracy (62.10, 63.1 nn.); still, it is his calmness rather than an Alexander-like paranoia that dominates at the end. Kingliness turned lethal for both, but in different ways; there is indeed a sense in which external factors destroyed Caesar while Alexander destroyed himself.[66]

Kingliness, it should be stressed, rather than godliness: Plutarch makes relatively little of Caesar's divine honours (57.2, 63.9, 67.8 nn.). There he may well be historically right, and it probably was the regal rather than the divine honours that caused more offence.[67] But anyway the point draws attention to a noticeable rhythm through the pair concerning the divine. Alexander's godly presumptions are clear; they were evident from the beginning of the *Life*, with the possibility aired of divine birth (*Alex.* 2–3); they were there when Alexander visited Siwah (*Alex.* 26–7); they were probably there at the very end of *Alexander*, in a recently identified fragment.[68] But for Alexander they are pretensions, and it is not clear that they are anything more. Even the omens surrounding his birth are given an alternative secular explanation (*Alex.* 2.7–9), and that early sequence ends with an outburst of Olympias, 'I do wish Alexander would stop putting me at odds with Hera!' (*Alex.* 3.3); the discussion of Ammon includes the suggestion that the apparent address 'son of Zeus' was just a

---

[65] J. Mossman in M. A. Flower and M. Toher (eds), *Georgica: Greek Studies in Honour of George Cawkwell* (*BICS* Supp. 58; 1991), 98–119 at 115–19. On statues earlier in the *Lives*, cf. *Alex.* 4.1–2, 14.8–9, 16.16, 17.9, 21.11, 37.5, 40.5, *Caes.* 6.1.

[66] J. Mossman, *JHS* 108 (1988), 92, cf. 85 = Scardigli, *Essays*, 226, cf. 213; some qualifications are aired by T. Whitmarsh, *CQ* 52 (2002), 177 n. 18.

[67] E. Rawson *CAH* ix² (1994), 463–5; 60–1 n.

[68] See below, p. 131.

grammatical slip of the oracular priest (*paidion* ~ *pai Dios, Alex.*
27.9); the fragment from the end concludes with Alexander's resentment when his wife refuses to play along with his immortality
(p. 131).

Caesar by contrast has thought in resolutely secular terms, and
Caesar has for the most part been a resolutely secular *Life*. It is
Pompey (68.2), not *Caesar*, that mentions Pompey's dream of Aphrodite before Pharsalus, though what made that ominous was Caesar's claim of divine descent from Aphrodite/Venus (42.1 n.). True,
the gods have marked the importance of Pharsalus by suitable portents (43.3–6, 47 nn.),[69] but an omen can also be something that the
shrewd Caesar can exploit (52.4 n.). Caesar's position as pontifex
maximus matters for its political significance, particularly for its
humiliation of his distinguished opponents (7.1–4); any religious
implications remain unstressed, though they were arguably important
for, say, his reform of the calendar (59 n., cf. 7.1–4 n.). Nor is it just
Caesar himself; his wife Calpurnia too had never been given to superstition (63.11). But the very final days are different. A dreadful
portent and an eerie dream terrify Calpurnia, and discountenance
Caesar himself (63.8–11); the soothsayer knows that murder is afoot
(63.5–6). After his death, the divine involvement is unmistakable, and
extraordinary.

His great guardian spirit, which had accompanied him in life, continued to
avenge his murder, pursuing and tracking his killers over every land and sea,
until not one remained but everyone had been punished who had any
contact with the killing in thought or in execution.

(69.2)

This 'great guardian spirit' seems to merge with Brutus' own
'evil spirit', that appears to him twice (69.11, 13: cf. 69.2 n. and
below, p. 66).

It is uncertain how much we should make of this sudden intrusion
of the supernatural into the pair. It is unlikely to signify anything so
crude as 'Caesar was the greater hero, so the gods took more concern
for his passing'. It may be that the suggestion is more concerned with
the events than the persons: the end of the Republic was so momentous that *of course* divinities will take an interest in matters so

---

[69] Just as they had marked the critical phases of Alexander's career: *Alex.* 14.8–9,
18.7–8, 24.4–9, 26.9, and esp. 57 and 73–5 with above, p. 29.

significant and people so great, just as they would not leave Pharsalus unmarked by portents: Alexander's godly affectations reflect a wrong way of envisaging the gods' involvement in the world, but that does not mean an absence of any involvement at all. Probably we should simply leave it there, as thought-provoking, with Plutarch leaving it to the reader what particular thoughts he or she may choose.

So the pairing with *Alexander* matters a good deal to the way we read *Caesar*. In one way though it is irregular, as this is one of four pairs—the others are *Phocion–Cato Minor*, *Themistocles–Camillus*, and *Pyrrhus–Marius*—that lack the concluding few chapters that normally serve as a summing-up, comparing the two figures and constructing a balance sheet exploring the areas in which each outdid the other. (The answer is normally an honourable draw, or close to one.[70]) Scholarly opinion is divided on the explanation for this. It used to be assumed that an epilogue had been written and had been lost, in this case as in the other three. In 1956 Hartmut Erbse argued that, for particular reasons in each case, Plutarch may have decided to dispense with the usual summings-up when concluding these four pairs.[71] That is also my view, and in 1997 I supported it by an analysis of the manner of narrative termination in these four pairs; in three of the cases there is a stronger closure, with various standard terminal signals, than is usual in those second *Lives* that are followed by a formal epilogue.[72] Certainly the final chapter of *Caesar* is itself so powerful, and ends so perfectly with Brutus's own death, that Plutarch might understandably be reluctant to compromise it by adding anything more.

Possibly that is all we need to say; but in a further article[73] I added a more speculative suggestion, one that builds on that generic proximity of biography and historiography (above, pp. 13–15). It is relevant here that Appian ends the second book of his *Civil Wars* with exactly (or almost exactly—the manner is slightly different) the sort of synkritic epilogue comparing Caesar and Alexander that we might have expected to find in Plutarch (2.149.619–154.649). Might it be that history and biography in Caesar's case each come so near to

---

[70] Cf. Duff 257–62; S. Swain, *Eranos*, 90 (1992), 101–11.

[71] H. Erbse, *Hermes*, 84 (1956), 378–424.

[72] In D. H. Roberts, F. Dunn, and D. Fowler (eds), *Classical Closure: Endings in Ancient Literature* (1997), 228–50; repr. in *Plutarch and History*, 365–86. Duff 253–5 gives me a hearing, but is unconvinced.

[73] Pelling, 'Breaking the Bounds'.

the other that each genre momentarily takes over the other, so that by the end of Plutarch's *Life* a biographical conclusion no longer feels so apposite? And that, by the end of a historical book detailing Caesar's death, it becomes appropriate for Appian to include the sort of biographical conclusion he will have noticed to be missing from Plutarch?

Whether or not we find that suggestion appealing, we can anyway see ways in which the closing chapters of *Caesar* discreetly hint at the importance of those days to the whole of Roman history, rounding off not merely the one man's life but also the entire history of an age. This is where the whole series of the *Parallel Lives*, not just the pair, becomes an important perspective, just as it is with *Alexander*, which so often adds an extra perspective to other *Lives* of heroes before and (particularly) after Alexander's own day.[74]

It is a characteristic technique of Plutarch to find a hero's final days mirroring critical scenes from his earlier life, the moments of his greatest success or greatest joy or greatest menace; thus Pelopidas' death recalls the Liberation of the Cadmeia (*Pel.* 32, 35 ~ 8), Marcellus' fatal rashness in plunging into battle recalls his earlier single combats (*Marc.* 28 ~ 2.1, 7), and the hauling-up of the dying Antony brings back a carefree moment with Cleopatra when fishing in the harbour of Alexandria (*Ant.* 77 ~ 29.5-7). There is something of that here too, when Caesar's insulting behaviour to the senators reverses their own contemptuous treatment of his supporters (60.4-8 ~ 29.1-2), his humiliation of the tribunes recalls the way his own tribunes were driven out (61.1, 61.8-10 ~ 31.2-3), then the hesitation on the morning of the Ides recalls Caesar's uncharacteristic moment of doubt at the Rubicon (32, 64-5 n.). Brutus' end in its turn has elements of the Ides (66.10, 67.3, 69.3, 69.14 nn.).[75]

---

[74] Esp. *Pyrrhus*: cf. J. Mossman in P. Stadter (ed.), *Plutarch and the Historical Tradition* (1992), 90-108, esp. 103-4, and *CQ* 55 (2005), 498-517, esp. 512-15; B. Buszard, *TAPA* 138 (2008), 185-215, extends the comparative reading to all of the two pairs *Alex.-Caes.* and *Pyrrh.-Mar.* On *Agesilaus* and *Demetrius*, see G. W. M. Harrison, *RBPh* 73 (1995), 91-104.

[75] Cf. also 14.5 n., 64.6 n., 66.5-6 nn., and, for similar mirrorings towards the end of Caesar's campaigning, 52-4 n., 56 n. More on this technique at *Plutarch and History*, 375, and 'Roman Heroes', 207-8; for such repetition as a closural feature, see e.g. B. Herrnstein Smith, *Poetic Closure: A Study of How Poems End* (1968), esp. 31, 42-4, 48-9, 155-66.

Just as significant is the way in which the killing of Caesar recalls for a reader crucial scenes from other *Lives*.[76] One of those echoes is of *Romulus*. There too power led Romulus astray, and he adopted an uncomfortably autocratic style:

> This was Romulus' last war [cf. *Caes*. 56.7]. Next came the experience which falls to most, indeed virtually all who are raised to power and majesty by great and paradoxical successes; Romulus did not escape this either. His career had made him confident [or perhaps 'over-confident']; he became haughtier in spirit and abandoned his popular manner, shifting to a monarchy which gave offence and pain. This came about in the first place because of the way in which he presented himself . . .
>
> (*Romulus* 26.1)

Then we move into a description of his purple robes, his kingly throne, his bodyguard, and so on. The similarity to the end of *Caesar* is clear, with Caesar's semi-regal outfit and his golden throne, the humiliation of the senate, and the fears of his monarchy (60.1, 60.4, 61, 61.4 nn.). And Romulus too died; one version was that he was torn apart by hostile senators (*Rom*. 27.6). That death was followed by the uncanny dream that led the shaken Proculus Iulius to appear in public (*Rom*. 28.1–3); that turned out less murderous than the dream of the luckless Cinna (*Caes*. 68), but again the rhythm is similar. And in Romulus' case too a supernatural dimension is strongly suggested; certainly the naturalistic explanation mooted for his disappearance—the senators cutting up him up into little pieces— does not carry conviction, and Plutarch passes quickly to a purple passage on the immortality of the soul (*Rom*. 28.7–10). True, some of this patterning may already have been there in Plutarch's sources, and indeed some of it in the events themselves, when the conspirators may well have been modelling themselves on the Romulus pattern to make their point about kingship (61.1 n.).[77] But we should still accept

---

[76] I say 'recalls', even though in the case of the *Gracchi* the *Lives* covering the earlier events were probably not yet written (though *Romulus* is almost certainly earlier than *Caesar*). Plutarch can still be envisaging the series as a whole, as he certainly has already considered the material he has still to write in *Pompey* (notice the future tense at 35.2 (n.) with 45.9). Alternatively, we could put the point in terms of the *Gracchi* later being written in such a way as to mirror the version he had already written in *Caesar*: by then, at least, he could envisage readers taking all these *Lives* together.

[77] Cf. Weinstock 347, 358–9; Rawson, *CAH* ix² (1994), 445.

that Plutarch is making the theme his own: a clear pointer to that is the similarity here of *Romulus* to the paired *Theseus*, where again we can find foreshadowings of the events of the Peloponnesian War, with hints both of Pericles and of Alcibiades.[78] At Athens, as in Rome, the founders sowed the seeds not just of greatness but of destruction, as the magnitude of the city's achievements and of its massive individuals would eventually cause fatal tensions, and the wheel would turn full circle.

There are wheels and wheels; a further circle starts with the Gracchi. With Tiberius Gracchus too there is a question whether he should go forth on the morning of danger, but he is warned that he has to come to the senate to defuse the accusations of wanting tyranny (*Gracch.* 17.5–6 ~ *Caes.* 63–4 with 64.4–5 n.; cf. *Gracch.* 14.3); there too the pernicious advice of reckless friends plays an important part (*Gracch.* 34.1 ~ *Caes.* 60.8); there too a scene with a diadem proved inflammatory (*Gracch.* 14.3, 19.3 ~ *Caes.* 61.5 (n.)); there too graffiti in a public place play an important role, stimulating that all-important sense of honour (*Gracch.* 8.10 ~ *Caes.* 62.7; *Brut.* 9.5–7); there too public enthusiasm, the source of the brothers' success, wavers at the end, and plays an important part in their fall (*Gracch.* 32, 37.7 ~ *Caes.* 51, 56.7–9); there too the popular enthusiasm revives after their champions are dead, and they turn on the killers (*Gracch.* 21.4–5, 39.2–3 ~ *Caes.* 67–8). The point is not just a literary one of elegant intratextuality, important though such mirroring can be as a closural technique[79] (and important though that is in itself, pointing to the thematic coherence of the series as a whole and not just the individual *Life* or pair). The historical insight is impressive too. The Gracchi, for all their good intentions, have unleashed popular forces and revealed divisions that will in the end be destructive not just to them, but to the whole constitution; and Caesar, the man who exploits those forces and divisions most tellingly, will himself fall their victim at the end.

---

[78] Or so I argued in *Plutarch and History*, ch. 7.
[79] Cf. above, p. 33, with n. 75.

3. SOURCES AND METHODS

3.1. Gathering the Material

We can tell a little about the sequence in which Plutarch wrote the *Parallel Lives*, forty-six of which survive. It appears that the first in the series was the lost *Epaminondas and Scipio* (probably Scipio Aemilianus),[80] an opening pair that programmatically foregrounded men of action who combined public life with an appreciation of culture and wisdom. Plutarch himself tells us that *Demosthenes and Cicero* was the fifth pair, *Pericles and Fabius* the tenth pair, and *Dion and Brutus* the twelfth.[81] I argued in 1979 that we can detect that six of the *Lives* treating the late Roman Republic, including *Caesar*, were prepared together as part of a single project, then presumably published in reasonably swift sequence along with their pairs: these six are *Agesilaus–Pompey*, *Nicias–Crassus*, *Alexander–Caesar*, *Phocion–Cato minor*, *Dion–Brutus*, and *Demetrius–Antony*.[82] If this is right—and, with some reservations concerning *Nicias–Crassus*, subsequent scholarship has tended to accept the thesis[83]—then it is easier to find room for the other five pairs if they belong just after rather than before *Dion–Brutus* in its twelfth position; that would put *Alexander–Caesar* something after halfway through the sequence of the *Lives*, and this is the reason for assuming a date around 110 or a little later (above, p. 2).

Two other *Lives* treating the period belong earlier in the sequence along with their pairs, *Demosthenes–Cicero* in fifth place

---

[80] At least, that is what *Gracch.* 21.9 and 31.5 suggest, referring back to 'the *Life* of Scipio' for Scipio Aemilianus' damning verdict on Tiberius Gracchus and for the mysterious circumstances of his death. *Pyrrh.* 8.5, however, refers to 'my writing on Scipio' for Hannibal's praise of Scipio's generalship, and that is clearly Scipio Africanus. But Plutarch likes to sketch a person's ancestry in his proems (cf. pp. 129–30), and it is more likely that a *Scipio Aemilianus* would tell that anecdote in such a scene-setting introduction than that a *Scipio Africanus* would end with so elaborate a flash forward to the descendant.

[81] *Dem.* 3.1, *Per.* 2.5, *Dion* 2.7.

[82] *JHS* 99 (1979), 74–96, repr. with a Postscript in Scardigli, *Essays*, 265–318 and revised and repr. as *Plutarch and History*, ch. 1.

[83] See *Plutarch and History*, 26–9, for a response to some dissenting voices, esp. 29 on *Crassus*.

and *Cimon–Lucullus*, which seems to belong in one of positions II–IV.[84] There are some cases where we can trace Plutarch's knowledge expanding between those earlier *Lives* and the batch of six that were prepared together.[85]

If simultaneous preparation is accepted, there are further implications for the way we reconstruct Plutarch's practice as he set about writing. He will have had the opportunity to consider his distribution of material among different *Lives* (cf. 35.2 n.): of course there was bound to be extensive overlapping, and, for instance, the battle of Pharsalus was bound to be central to both *Pompey* and *Caesar*—but even there some material could be used in one *Life* rather than the other (42–6 n.), and a cross-reference in *Caesar* (45.9 (n.), cf. 35.2 (n.)) refers the reader to the other *Life* for a description of Pompey's death. He has clearly given similar thought to the distribution of material when it comes to the conspiracy, and another cross-reference (62.8, cf. 62 n.) directs the reader to *Brutus* for a treatment of Cassius' motives. In *Caesar* itself he can therefore concentrate on Caesar's fall as a consequence of Caesar's own actions, not as anything that depended on a particular mindset in those conspiring against him: as we saw in Section 2.2, that emphasis is important in directing the choice of interpretative themes that tie the *Life* together.

Simultaneous preparation also allowed Plutarch to draw on a wider range of material, including specialized works on, say, Brutus or Cato as well as on Caesar himself. I have discussed this 'cross-fertilization' elsewhere,[86] and return to it below (pp. 49–53). He can also draw in one *Life* on analyses that he developed for another; thus we see him in *Antony* emphasizing that 'Caesar's rule would have seemed anything rather than a tyranny as far as his own behaviour was concerned, but it was his friends that brought it into bad repute' (*Ant.* 6.7, cf. *Brut.* 35.4)—in one way a different emphasis from that in *Caesar*, which

[84] On the early date for *Cimon–Lucullus*, see C. P. Jones, *JRS* 56 (1966), 67–8 = Scardigli, *Essays*, 109. It rests on the cross-citation of *Cimon* in *Theseus* (36.2) and in *Pericles* (9.5); *Pericles–Fabius* was the tenth pair, *Theseus–Romulus* seems to belong in positions VII–IX, and positions V–VI are taken by other pairs. Such arguments are not conclusive (*Plutarch and History*, 9, following J. Geiger, *Athen.* 57 (1979), 61 n. 47), but do create a probability.

[85] I discuss the test cases of Caesar's first consulship (14 n.) and his assassination (62–6 nn.) at *Plutarch and History*, 2–7, and the Catilinarian conspiracy at *Plutarch and History*, 51; cf. my n. on *Ant.* 19.3.

[86] *Plutarch and History*, 10–11.

stressed that it *was* an 'acknowledged tyranny' (57.1 (n.)), but in a much fuller sense agreeing with and taking over *Caesar's* emphasis on the ruler's moderation in power (57.4–8) and, particularly, the disastrous effect of Antony and his other friends (51.2–3 with 51 n.; above, pp. 21–2). Within *Caesar* itself, we can similarly be confident that Plutarch knew more than he here says about, for instance, the politics of the fifties and Cato's high-principled opposition, or Pompey's weak leadership at Pharsalus, or Caesar's attacks in his *Anticato(s)*, or the Philippi campaign;[87] and, just as important, that he could assume that his readers could and would look elsewhere if they wanted to know more.

The days are long gone when scholars thought that Plutarch was simply a transcriber, 'slavishly'[88] reproducing what he found in his sources and adding little but mistakes and the odd moralistic gloss. He may not have first-hand knowledge of every writer he quotes, but we are now much readier to assume that he did read very widely and was capable of combining material from a number of sources; we can assume too that he regularly imposed on this material his own vision of what made a satisfactory literary and interpretative whole. Still, the circumstances in which he found himself were very different from those that face a modern scholar, surrounded as we typically are by books open on the desk or the floor, usually now with a website or so open too, with at least intermittent access to most published materials, and with a wealth of technology making it straightforward to write, rewrite, edit, and correct our text until we are content. In one way Plutarch might be in a better position than his modern counterparts, as he probably had educated slave and freedman assistants who could be sent to consult recherché texts as well as secretaries to whom he could dictate at every stage of composition;[89] but in far more ways he was much worse off. His own library was doubtless very big by the

[87] Cato's opposition in the fifties: *C.min.* 31–51, cf. 21.3–9, 22.4, 28–32, 28.5, 28.7 nn. Pompey's weak leadership in the Pharsalus campaign: *Pomp.* 66–73, cf. 40–1, 42–6 nn. here. *Anticato(s)*: see 54.6 n. and below, n. 117. Philippi campaign: *Brut.* 24–53, cf. 69.2–14 n.
[88] The word was used, for instance, by E. Kornemann, *Jb.f.cl.Phil.* Spb. 22 (1896), 577.
[89] Pelling, *Plutarch and History*, 24. Quint. 10.1.128 describes Seneca as 'a man of ready and fluent talent, great diligence, and wide-ranging knowledge, but in that respect he was sometimes misled by those to whom he had given questions to investigate'.

standards of his day—that is made clear by the extraordinarily wide reading that he displays in work after work—but equally doubtless it had gaps: a telling passage in the *Table Talk* depicts the excitement when a particular text of Aristotle reaches Thermopylae, and an educated Roman (Mestrius Florus, above, p. 8) wants to talk about it to his friends (8.10 734c–d). When Plutarch talks of the advantages of working in a big city rather than tiny Chaeronea (*Dem.* 2.1, below, p. 53), having access to 'an abundance of every sort of books' is the first point he mentions; when sending his *On the E at Delphi* to an Athenian friend and his circle, he says that he hopes for some compositions in exchange, 'given that you are all living in a big city and have plenty of leisure amongst a wealth of books and all sorts of ways of spending your time [*diatribai*]' (384e). True, there will have been possibilities for Plutarch to visit libraries on his own trips to Athens and to Rome, just as there will have been chances to grab city-conversations with the learned and voluble (those would figure among the other 'ways of spending your time' of *On the E*): more on this later (pp. 53–4). But very often Plutarch must have found himself knowing that relevant material existed while, frustratingly, he was unable to put his hand on it. The phrasing at *Cato minor* 23.3, '*they say that* this is the only speech of Cato to survive', is revealing.

Even when he had texts in front of him, weaving the material together was anything but straightforward. Texts came in rolls, perhaps as much as 20 feet long; reading them was a two-handed business, and it was not easy to have more than a single text open before one's eyes. Even if, say, a slave was asked to hold one open, systematic comparison of two works handling the same events was not easy, especially if they did not treat material in the same sequence (and that would be particularly frequent when it was a question of comparing a linear narrative account with material from a different genre, letters or speeches). Indexes, chapter headings, and line- and column-numbering were rudimentary or non-existent. That can help to explain a phenomenon that we often notice in Plutarch as in other ancient writers about the past, and one that renders less surprising that older prejudice that he followed a single source with little altera-tion; for we can see that Plutarch often *does* seem to be following a single source (though not exclusively) for a stretch of narrative. Sometimes we can see this particularly clearly as we still have that source: the clearest example is *Coriolanus*, closely based on the account of Dionysius of Halicarnassus.[90] More often, we see a continual series of close similarities between two accounts, perhaps an identical narrative structure and articulation, perhaps a regular tendency to reproduce the same items, perhaps even a series of verbal echoes: often these are explicable only if both authors are following a source that we now have lost. In the case of *Caesar* and the other *Lives* that appear to have been prepared simultaneously, this is clearest in a long sequence of parallels with the narrative of Appian in his fragmentary *Celtica* and especially his *Civil Wars*. These are best explained if we assume that Plutarch's wide reading came at a preliminary stage, and then this single source text was the only one before his eyes as he composed; it would be this that provided the skeleton and a fair amount of the flesh of his narrative.[91] More on this in a moment, when we shall see that that source text was probably the work of Asinius Pollio.

Still, the other reading that Plutarch had done was by no means wasted. It would initially have guided that choice of source: as his immersion in the period increased, his feel both for the accuracy of the accounts he found and for their suitability for his purposes would similarly deepen. If he decided that Pollio filled the bill particularly well, that was not a random or casual choice. Nor would that initial wide reading be forgotten. Plutarch's memory was doubtless very good; that is clear from the vast amount of erudition visible in so many of his works—all those literary quotations, for instance, which he simply would not have had time to look up and check in each case (and therefore he sometimes gets slightly wrong).[92] It would have been trained and strengthened by his education in rhetoric, where

[90] D. A. Russell, *JRS* 53 (1963) = 21–8 = Scardigli, *Essays*, 357–72. Russell estimates that the non-Dionysian material amounts to 'about 20%' of the *Life* (21 = 358). Similar is the debt to Thucydides in, for instance, his account of the Sicilian campaign at *Nicias* 12–29: at *Plutarch and History*, 119, I estimate that 'rather over half' of that comes from Thucydides, rising to 'over two-thirds' for the detail of the campaign itself.

[91] We might compare here what we can reconstruct of the procedures of Appian and Dio. For good arguments that, like Plutarch, both of those authors use a plurality of sources, see A. M. Gowing, *The Triumviral Narratives of Appian and Cassius Dio* (1992), 39–50, and (on Appian) *Phoenix* 44 (1990), 158–81. Gowing prefers to think that a single source would not be open before the eyes during compositions, but that 'the groundwork laid, he [Dio at least, and probably Appian too] worked primarily from notes, excerpts, and his own memory' (*Triumviral Narratives* 44). I think that more probable for Dio than for Appian.

[92] W. Helmbold and E. O'Neil, *Plutarch's Quotations* (1959), p. ix.

mnemonic skills were instilled and encouraged.[93] His recollections of
that wide reading would provide him with material that he could
integrate as deftly as he could into the framework provided by his
main source; of course, it would often confirm rather than comple-
ment it, and that would be valuable too, even if in such cases the
initial reading would usually leave no trace in Plutarch's own account.
Signs of the use of memory are duly found. For instance, at 22.5
Plutarch gives a figure of 400,000 dead for Caesar's massacre of the
Usipetes and Tencteri, and this seems to have been the figure he
found in his source (n.). Yet *Cato minor* 51.1 and *Crassus* 37(4).2 give
the figure as 300,000. That is presumably just a slip of memory: when
preparing *Caesar* he would be working through the roll carefully, but
in the briefer mentions elsewhere he would be confident—in this case
wrongly—that he could recall the detail. There is a very similar case
elsewhere with deviant figures for the number of dead in the proscriptions of 43–2, 300 in *Ant.* 20.2 and 200 in *Brut.* 27.6.[94]

Once Plutarch had decided which material to use, he still had his
own narrative to complete. It appears that the most regular form of
ancient composition was not to proceed immediately to a first attempt at a final version, but rather to complete a draft 'memorandum'
(*hypomnēma*), which would contain the material but would lack the
final literary polish that an accomplished stylist would give.[95] That
polish would then be given in a separate stage, where such artistry
would be the writer's dominant preoccupation; though doubtless, as
with all creative composition, the actual stages would never be distinct in so clear-cut a way, and a writer would find it as difficult at the
hypomnēma stage to refrain from all embellishment as he would at
the finished stage to resist some last-minute integration of material
that came to mind as he wrote. When he collects anecdotes of Aspasia
that 'came to mind at that moment' (*Per.* 24.12, below, p. 55), that
'coming to mind' is as likely to have been at the final stage as when he
was constructing a *hypomnēma*.

In 1979 I argued that traces of such a *hypomnēma* can be seen in
Plutarch's Roman *Lives*, and developed that thesis further in articles

[93] B. Vickers, *In Defence of Rhetoric* (1988), 65; Hamilton, p. xxii.
[94] See my n. on *Ant.* 20.2, and for further signs of the use of memory *Plutarch and History*, 21–2; Hamilton, p. xliv; Stadter, pp. xlvi, xlviii.
[95] Cf. *Plutarch and History*, esp. 23–4, 52–3, 65–8. The *locus classicus* describing this procedure is Lucian, *How to Write History* 47–8; other passages are collected by G. Avenarius, *Lukians Schrift zur Geschichtsschreibung* (1956), 85–104.

published in 1985 and 2002.[96] That thesis gains further support from work done in Leuven in the 1990s, which argued on quite different grounds for the detection of similar *hypomnēmata* in various texts of the *Moralia*.[97] Possibly Plutarch will have written separate *hypomnē-mata* for each new *Life*; possibly he combined into a single *hypom-nēma* material for all these *Lives* that he was preparing together, and in that case that draft would look very much like a continuous history of the period, lacking only its final artistic polish. If this is right, the frequent verbal similarities between (say) *Caesar* and *Pompey* may be explained by the way Plutarch had phrased the *hypomnēma* rather than by the wording that he found in a source, though there may well be cases of both. He might also still have the *hypomnēmata* that he had written some time ago for *Demosthenes–Cicero* and *Cimon–Lucullus* as well as the completed texts of those pairs, and we shall see that this research from years earlier could still be useful in providing information for this new raft of *Lives* (below, pp. 52–4).

So discussion of Plutarch's sources cannot limit itself to listing the works that might have provided him with information. It is important too to try, even though the attempt must often be only tentative, to identify *how* he used each source, as the single text before his eyes, as part of the initial general reading, as part of the recherché specialized material that he might have asked an assistant to check, as a text he might have read years before while composing an earlier pair and perhaps noted in a *hypomnēma*, or simply as part of the broad general culture that this utterly civilized bookworm had acquired over what was already a fairly long life.

3.2. The Sources

In *Caesar* Plutarch cites the following authorities by name:

- Caesar's *Anticato* (3.4, cf. 54.3–6)
- Cicero's *On his own consulship* (8.4)
- C. Oppius (17.7, cf. 17.11)

---

[96] *Plutarch and History*, chs 1–3.
[97] Cf. esp. L. van der Stockt, *AJP* 120 (1999), 575–99, and in P. A. Stadter and L. van der Stockt (eds), *Sage and Emperor* (2002), 115–40; B. van Meirvenne in J. G. Montes Cala, M. Sánchez Ortiz de Landaluce, and R. J. Gallé Cejudo (eds), *Plutarco, Dioniso y el Vino* (1999), 527–40; L. van der Stockt in A. Pérez Jiménez, J. García López, and R. Mª Aguilar, *Plutarco, Platón, y Aristoteles* (1999), 127–40.

- Caesar's *Commentarii* (22.2, citing *BG* 4.11.3 as Caesar's 'journal' (n.)); and 44.8, citing *BC* 3.92.4–5)
- Tanusius Geminus (22.4)
- Asinius Pollio (46.2, 52.8, cf. 32.7)
- Livy (47.3–6, 63.9)
- Strabo (63.3)

Some of those quotations may well be second-hand. Take, for instance, the citations of Caesar and Tanusius at 22.2–4. It cannot be coincidence that App. *Celt.* fr. 18 retails these in the same manner (Appian does not *name* Tanusius, but surely refers to him: cf. 22.1–5 n.); it looks even less like coincidence because we find the same with the other Caesar citation at 44.8, for Appian again quotes the same passage to the same effect (*BC* 2.79.329–30).[98] Possibly Appian may simply have read Plutarch and drawn the citations from him,[99] but the more likely explanation is that both writers have taken them over from the same intermediate source—presumably Pollio, as we shall see.

It will be noticed that Plutarch's possible sources include more works in Latin than in Greek. Plutarch mentions his Latin in the introduction to *Demosthenes–Cicero*:

When I was in Rome, and during the time I spent in Italy,[100] I did not have time to practise Latin because of my political business and because people came to talk to me about philosophy, and so it was only late and at an advanced age that I began to read Roman texts. The consequence was something surprising but true: I found that I was not so much understanding and recognizing what happened through the language, but it was more that the events, with which I already had some sort of familiarity, were helping me to follow the meaning of the words. But as for appreciation of the beauty and speed of Latin narrative, or of metaphor or smooth composition and all the other elements which are a cause of stylistic pride, that is another matter. I find such things attractive and they give me some pleasure, but practice and skill in them does not come easily, and must be left for those who have more time and whose age still allows such aspirations.

(*Demosthenes* 2.2–3)

---

[98] Appian admittedly quotes it from a 'letter': see 44.8 n.
[99] Cf. below, n. 104; *Plutarch and History*, 35 n. 69 and 36 n. 75. That explanation is the less likely, for the reasons given below.
[100] On these spells in Rome and Italy, see above, pp. 6 and 8.

There is some subtle self-projection there as a humble man, but one
who is also diligent, thoughtful, experienced, and respected, and
perhaps as one that rates content and substance higher than style
and showiness;[101] but that is no reason to doubt the essential truth of
what he says. That experience—understanding a foreign-language
narrative more easily because one is already familiar with the material
it treats—is one that will strike a chord with many modern scholars.
Plutarch's point is that his Latin was not adequate for the sort of
sophisticated *stylistic* comparison that a pairing of Demosthenes and
Cicero might lead a reader to expect (at least this early in the series,
before the other pairs had had a chance to guide such readerly
expectations). It certainly does not suggest that he avoided Latin
texts; indeed, the passage is explicit that he did read Latin, and *Caesar*
shows that too, including one remark on style as well as content (50.3
(n.)).[102] We have already seen him explaining Latin terms to his
audience elsewhere (above, p. 9). Still, it is probably true that he did
not have the same wide reading in Latin literature that he had in
Greek: below, pp. 54–5.[103]

1. **Asinius Pollio** (*HRR* ii. LXXXIII–LXXXXVII, 67–70, 224; 46.2 n.).
I have already mentioned the long sequence of parallels between
Plutarch's narratives and the accounts of Appian in *Celtica* and
Civil Wars (above, p. 40). The parallels are noted throughout the
commentary: cf. esp. 15–27 n., 28–32 n., 40–1 n., 42–6 n., 52–4 n.
That systematic contact is normally, and best, explained in terms of
their independent derivation from a common source. This is not the
only explanation that is theoretically possible, as we cannot exclude
the possibility that Appian is himself drawing on Plutarch;[104] still, it is
easy to show that Appian (and arguably Cassius Dio as well, for he too
shows some points of contact with this tradition) would have to know

[101] On this, see esp. J. Mossman in *Histos* (1999) (www.dur.ac.uk/Classics/histos/1999/mossman.html); A. Zadorojnyi, *PCPS* 52 (2006), 102–27.
[102] Cf. Zadorojnyi (n. 101), 105.
[103] On Plutarch's knowledge of Latin, the discussion of H. J. Rose, *The Roman Questions of Plutarch* (1924), 11–19, is still useful; see also more fully A. Strobach, *Plutarch und die Sprachen* (*Palingenesia* 64; 1997).
[104] So E. Gabba, *Appiano e la storia delle Guerre Civili* (1956), 255–8, and *Rend. Acc. Lincei*, 12 (1957), 340; R. Fehrle, *Cato Uticensis* (1983), 29–32. I discuss this possibility more fully at *Plutarch and History*, 36 n. 75. For cases in *Caesar* where Appian may be following Plutarch, see 7.8, 9.2–10.11, 14.8, 32 nn.

all six of the relevant *Lives* of Plutarch and combine material from each of them,[105] and that is much less plausible a hypothesis.

These points of parallel seem to start around the year 60, and it is an easy guess that they are owed to a common derivation from Asinius Pollio, who appears to have begun his narrative in that year (13.3 n.).[106] It is just possible that one or both of Plutarch and Appian read, not Pollio, but a later account closely based on his version;[107] still, there is no reason to prefer that explanation, and I have simplified throughout the commentary by speaking just of 'Pollio' rather than more cautiously of 'the Pollio-source'.[108] No such contact with Appian is visible in the earlier *Cicero* (or *Lucullus*, though that is less significant, as very little of *Lucullus* covers the years after 60), and in general the *Cicero* narrative of, particularly, the fifties is sketchier and scrappier than those in the later *Lives*. Presumably Plutarch gained access to a copy of Pollio in the period between *Demosthenes–Cicero* and the later, bigger project of the six interconnected *Lives*. He must have found it a godsend. The bulk of the narrative of *Caesar* from chapter 13 onward, probably three-quarters of the whole, seems to come from Pollio.

Pollio is often praised for what we assume to have been his political insight and shrewd, non-partisan interpretations: Syme took his own vision of Pollio as the model for his own incisive analysis in *The Roman Revolution* (1939).[109] Pollio's own career, as a follower first of Caesar, then of Antony, then possibly even of Octavian too before entering a sort of retirement from the fray,[110] certainly fits the picture

---

[105] *Plutarch and History*, 12.
[106] Horace, *Odes* 2.1.1. Strictly that passage shows only that Pollio traced the 'civil disruption' back to the consulship of 'Metellus', rather than starting his narrative in that year, but the interpretative point could easily carry that narrative strategy as a consequence. I follow the usual view in identifying Metellus as Q. Metellus Celer, the consul of 60, rather than Q. Metellus Numidicus, the consul of 109, as argued by A. J. Woodman in S. Braund and C. Gill (eds), *Myth, History, and Culture in Republican Rome* (2003), 191–216 (cf. also J. Henderson, *Fighting for Rome* (1998), 109–14): for my reasons, see Pelling, 'Breaking the Bounds', 271–2 n. 31.
[107] As suggested for instance by G. Delvaux, *LEC* 56 (1988), 27–48 at 37–48, who proposed Timagenes, supplemented by Fenestella. Delvaux makes a good deal of Fenestella (*HRR* ii. CVIII–CXIII, 79–87) in several other articles, esp. *LEC* 57 (1989), 127–46: cf. n. 125.
[108] As I did in 1979, in the article reprinted as *Plutarch and History*, ch. 1 (n. 82).
[109] R. Syme, *The Roman Revolution* (1939), 5–7, cf. vii.
[110] For discussion of Pollio's career, see André; Morgan, 'Autopsy'; B. Haller, *C. Asinius Pollio als Politiker und zeitkritischer Historiker* (1967); A. B. Bosworth, *Hist.*

of the man who has seen it all in his time, and has been disillusioned
with most of it; so do various anecdotes attesting his capacity to stand
up to Octavian/Augustus with striking independence.[111] The tren-
chant analyses found at various points in Plutarch often have close
counterparts in Appian (13.3, 20.1–3, 21.3–9, and esp. 28 nn., cf. 15–
27, 28–32 n.), and again support that reconstruction of Pollio's
qualities; not that he was as impartial as all that, so it seems—we
can trace, for instance, a considerable lack of sympathy in his portrayal of the urban *plebs* (67–8 n.), and he may well have been
ungenerous in his treatment of King Juba of Numidia (52.1 n.).
Other hallmarks of Pollio's account can also be detected in and
through the narratives that survive. One is the frequency with
which he parades his autopsy, a theme recently illuminated by Lle-
welyn Morgan.[112] Thus the first citation of Pollio in *Caesar* concerns
Caesar's famous utterance on the field of Pharsalus, 'It was their
choice' (46), and goes on to include a note of the casualties: Plutarch
does not quite say that Pollio was an eyewitness, but it is a clear
implication, and at *Pomp.* 72.4 he is explicit that 'Pollio was with
Caesar as he fought that battle', as he again cites him for the casualty
figures. Plutarch also notes that Pollio was present as Caesar crossed
the Rubicon (32.7) and at a perilous encounter in Africa (52.8). Both
should be taken as implicit quotations, indicating that Pollio was the
source, rather in the manner that a mention of 'Polybius' at the end of
Philopoemen (21.5, 21.11) or of 'the historian Dellius' in *Antony* (59.6,
cf. 25.3) is sufficient to indicate to the knowing reader where the
information comes from.

Emphasis on Pollio's interpretative insight should not obscure the
other merits that would have commended his account to Plutarch.
When Horace addresses Pollio and praises his history, he does it in

---

21 (1972), 441–73; Woodman on Vell. 2.78.2 and 86.3; F. Cairns, *CCJ* 54 (2008), 49–
79; and (briefly) my comm. on *Antony*, 27.

[111] For instance, his sharp line when explaining why he did not reply to some
jocular verses of Augustus at his expense: 'As for me, I keep silent. It is not easy to
inscribe anything against the man who can proscribe' (Macr. 2.4.21). Morgan, 'Autopsy', has acute remarks relating Pollio's 'retirement' to what we can reconstruct
about his history: 'Pollio's move into literature can be interpreted as a retreat from
public life, but it can also be seen as a turning of literature into an alternative form of
public activity' (66), one that expressively marks the absence of the traditional fora for
free and pointed self-expression.

[112] Morgan, 'Autopsy'.

terms of its vividness and suspense as well as its insight and boldness (*Odes* 2.1); we can see those features too, not least in that graphic account of the Rubicon (32 n.) or the narrative of the Pharsalus campaign (42–6 n.). Not all the details of Caesar's assassination scene will come from him (below, pp. 51–2), but much of that drama too will be owed to Pollio's descriptive skills (64.6 n., 66 n.), as will the marvellous depiction of Caesar's spirit at the end (69.6–11 n.); and Plutarch was wise enough to take all this over, just as Shakespeare in his turn was wise enough to follow Plutarch. At times we can also detect systems of imagery that recur in different parts of the narratives of Plutarch and Appian, recurrent pictures for instance of flower-throwing (30.2 n., cf. 28.3 n.) or figures of wild beasts (39.3, 66.10 nn.).[113] Neither author has the full system, nor indeed does Plutarch himself concentrate all his own examples in a single *Life*. Here, too, we should probably infer that the systems originally come from Pollio, just as we can combine elements from Plutarch and Appian to detect echoings of the Rubicon at later critical moments (32.7 n., 38 n. and n. 21). Once again we should reconstruct an author who was less austere and more concerned with vivid effect than some of his modern idealizations would suggest.[114]

2. **Caesar** himself. We have seen (p. 43) that the two citations at 22.2 and 44.8 correspond to passages in Appian where exactly the same Caesar citations are deployed, and we should presume that it was Pollio who cited Caesar and that Plutarch and Appian both took over the citations from his account. In that case, it is likely that the contact that is often visible between Plutarch's campaign descriptions and Caesar's *Commentarii* is also to be explained in terms of Pollio using Caesar, then Plutarch using Pollio (15–27, 39, 41, 42–6 nn.).

Pollio did not take over Caesar's account uncritically: Suetonius reports some pointed criticism.

Asinius Pollio thinks that the *Commentarii* were composed with insufficient care and insufficient respect for truth, given that in many cases Caesar was too rash in accepting things that had been done by others, and in many cases

---

[113] Cf. also p. 344 n. 21, 28.3 n., 28.6 n., 60.6 n., and 66.12 n. for further possible cases.

[114] On Pollio's narrative flair, cf. W. Syndikus, *Lucans Gedicht vom Bürgerkrieg* (1958), 1–12; J. L. Moles, *CW* 76 (1983), 287–8; Nisbet–Hubbard on Hor. *Odes* 2.1; Morgan, 'Autopsy', 57.

48 *Introduction*

too gave false versions of things done by himself, perhaps deliberately or perhaps through slips of memory; and Pollio thinks that he would have rewritten the work and corrected the mistakes.

(Suet. 56.4)

The barbed nature of the comment is clear, even if the precise degree and nature of the barb is hard to analyse,[115] and the comment may come from a preface or second preface in the *Histories*, building up Pollio's authority as one who knows—and will tell—better than even the most authoritative of sources. That goes with the stress on autopsy that we have already noticed: Pollio knows, because he was there. When we find some additions to or subtractions from Caesar's material in Plutarch and Appian, that too should be no surprise, and the later authors will again be indebted to Pollio for these (18.2, 20.1, 22.6 nn. with pp. 203–4; 42–6, 43.1–2, 44.3–4, 45.2–4, 46.2–3 nn.). It need not follow that Pollio was always right: the claim at 18.2 that it was Labienus rather than Caesar who 'crushed the Tigurini' in 58 BCE is likely to be captious and wrong-headed (n.).

Other literary works of Caesar were extant in Plutarch's day, including some speeches, poems, and letters (Suet. 55–6): Plutarch is aware of Caesar's speeches (3.2–4 n.) and of his poetry (2.4 n.) and mentions his letter-writing (17.7–8, 50.3, cf. 63.7 (nn.)), but there is no sign that he had read any of these.[116] Nor is it likely that he knew the *Anticato*(s) (3.4, 54.3–6 (nn.)), even though it is likely that several items in the *Cato minor* come ultimately from that work.[117] He does not make any claim to have read it himself, and it is more probable that he knew it indirectly through the mediation of Munatius Rufus and/or Thrasea Paetus (54.6 n.).[118]

3. **Other historical narratives.** The other two narrative sources that he quotes, **Livy** (47.3–6, 63.9) and **Strabo** (63.3, *FGrH* 91), both offered full narratives of these events. There is no reason, however, to suppose that they provide more material than the specific items for

[115] I attempt some of that analysis in Pelling, 'Judging Julius Caesar', 19–20; see also Morgan, 'Autopsy', 58–9, and C. S. Kraus in T. Reinhardt, M. Lapidge, and J. Adams (eds), *Aspects of the Language of Latin Prose* (PBA 129; 2005), 97–115 at 99–100.
[116] J. Geiger in L. van der Stockt (ed.), *Rhetorical Theory and Praxis in Plutarch* (2000), 211–23 at 219–20.
[117] *C.min.* 11.7–8, 36.5, 44.1–2, 52.6–8, 54.2, 57.4: cf. 54.6 n. here.
[118] Cf. H. J. Tschiedel, *Caesars 'Anticato'* (1981), 29–30; J. Geiger in the Rizzoli *Focione e Catone Uticense*, ed. C. Bearzot, J. Geiger, and L. Ghilli (1993), 297–8.

which Plutarch quotes them. It may be that he had read them at an earlier stage, and stray items happened to lodge in his memory or his notes; it is certainly possible that he used other parts of Livy's history elsewhere, for instance, for *Flamininus, Fabius,* and *Marcellus.*[119] The same may be true of Strabo, whom he cites at *Sulla* 26.4 and *Lucull.* 28.8 (see 63.3 n.). Alternatively, these may well be passages that were reported to Plutarch by an assistant. It is notable that the Livy passages both concern omens (so in fact does the Strabo). Elsewhere too we can detect him supplementing his main source with additional omens and portents: in *Nicias* he supplements Thucydides with such items from, probably, Timaeus,[120] and at *Brut.* 48 he adds to his Pollio material an omen from Volumnius. If Pollio did not exhaust Plutarch's taste for omens here, he would have known from his reading for other *Lives* that Livy was a rich source for such material, and for all we know the same may have been true of Strabo too; he might well have asked an assistant to check and report.

4. **Biographical material** of various types (it is important to recall that the genre was a fluid one, above, pp. 13–15). Any work on Caesar himself would be particularly useful, but if Plutarch was preparing several *Lives* together he could also draw on biographical treatments of the other main players in these events, just as he could draw on Caesar-works when writing the *Lives* of those other players ('cross-fertilization', above, p. 37).

Caesar's own companion C. **Oppius** (17.7 n., *HRR* ii. LXIII–LXIIII, 46–9) wrote an account of Caesar that presumably appeared fairly soon after the events: Plutarch seems to have known it, and known also that it needed to be treated with caution. He also quotes it in *Pompey*, in a particularly clear case of cross-fertilization. Oppius there provides a story about an atrocity committed by the young Pompey, but Plutarch adds a caveat:

but one must be very cautious about believing Oppius when he is talking about Caesar's friends or enemies.

(*Pomp.* 10.8–9)

---

[119] *Flamininus*: see my Rizzoli comm. on *Phil.–Flam.* (1997), 263–83. *Fabius*: *Plutarch and History*, 234–5 n. 113. *Marcellus*: Pelling, 'Roman Heroes', 203 n. 7. Plutarch's use of Livy is discussed further by C. Theander, *Plutarch und die Geschichte* (1951), 72–8.

[120] *Plutarch and History*, 118.

Within *Caesar* itself Plutarch quotes Oppius for an item on Caesar's gift for dictation on horseback (17.7), then Oppius himself appears in an anecdote at 17.11 about Caesar's considerate behaviour towards his friends: this may again (cf. above, p. 46) be a concealed indication that Oppius is the source. Other items in chapter 17 may also come from him (15–17 n.);[121] so may a fair amount of the material in the early chapters, where it is clear that Plutarch has more material than he does in some other *Lives* for his subjects' youthful experiences.[122] In particular, there seems to be some non-coincidental overlap not merely with Suetonius but also with material that Velleius includes in his own striking introduction to Caesar (2.41–3); Velleius' chapters too have something of the flavour of biography, and Oppius may well be the source.[123] Pliny (*NH* 11.252) also quotes Oppius for an item on Marius' varicose veins; if that comes from the work on Caesar[124] (a big 'if'), then it would follow that Oppius went into Caesar's family connection with Marius in some detail, and in that case Plutarch's own stress on Caesar's 'Marianism' (1.2, 5.2–5, 6, 18.1, 19.4, 26.2 nn.) may owe something to him.[125]

'Biographical' works on other figures included **Theophanes** (*FGrH* 188; *Pomp.* 37.4 etc., cf. 48.1 n. here) on Pompey[126] and various works, largely encomiastic, on Cato (54.5 n.);[127] the most important

---

[121] On Oppius' work, see also Strasburger 30–3 (noting that Oppius' work on Caesar is never described as a 'biography', but his works on Scipio Africanus and Cassius (n. 124) are attested as 'Lives', and biographical form was anyway fluid); Townend, 'Oppius'; J. Geiger, *Cornelius Nepos and Ancient Political Biography* (*Hist.* Einz. 47; 1985), 83–4.

[122] Cf. *Plutarch and History*, 13.

[123] See esp.1–3 n., 4–14 n.; also 1.1–8, 1.8–2.7, 2.6, 2.7, 5.6, 5.9, 7.1–4 nn. Cf. Strasburger 72–89, though the detail of his attempt to disentangle the tradition is not convincing. I discuss this 'biographical' flavour of Velleius further in E. R. Cowan (ed.), *Velleius Paterculus: Making History* (2011).

[124] As Peter thought, *HRR* ii. LXIIII, followed by G. Delvaux, *Lat.* 50 (1991), 88–91. But 'Lives' of Scipio Africanus and on 'Cassius' are attested for Oppius (*HRR* ii. 46–8), and it is not unlikely that there was a separate volume on Marius as well.

[125] Plutarch himself has a similar story of varicose veins at *Mar.* 6.5–7 and that too may come from Oppius. G. Delvaux, *Lat.* 50 (1991), 88–91, also suggests that 'C. Oppius' should be read for the manuscripts 'a certain C. Piso' as the authority for an item at *Mar.* 45.8: that is not impossible, whether or not Delvaux is right to think that all came from the work on Caesar (previous n.). Delvaux, however, thinks that Plutarch did not know Oppius directly but via Fenestella: cf. n. 107.

[126] For traces of Theophanes in *Pompey* itself, see esp. Heftner 53–7.

[127] R. Macmullen, *Enemies of the Roman Order* (1967), 1–45; A. Afzelius, *C&M* 4 (1941), 198–203; J. Geiger in the Rizzoli *Focione e Catone Uticense*, ed. C. Bearzot, J.

of those, and one that has clearly left its mark on *Cato minor*, was that of Cato's companion **Munatius Rufus** (*HRR* ii. LVIII, 42–4). In *Cato minor* itself Plutarch comments that **Thrasea Paetus** (*HRR* ii. CXXX–XXXI, 99), well-known for the ostentatious opposition to the emperor Nero which eventually led to Thrasea's own death, 'particularly followed' Munatius in his own work on Cato (*C.min.* 37.1, cf. 25.2), and it may well be that Plutarch knew Munatius' material only at second-hand through Thrasea.[128] *Cato minor* itself is especially rich in personalia on Cato's own family, especially his wife and daughters, and the sometimes spiky relationship of Cato with his friends, including Munatius himself (notice esp. 7, 9.1–3, 25, 27.6, 30, 36–7, 52.4). *Caesar* understandably finds no use for such items, but the personality of Cato is still strongly felt (e.g. 21.8, 22.4, 28.7, 41.1); and Plutarch will certainly have known more than he here says about the fraught politics of the fifties thanks to Munatius, and he includes much more detail in his narrative in *Cato minor* (31–51).

One characteristic of these narratives is the unusually high proportion of apparently non-Pollio material at times of high descriptive intensity,[129] and once again Plutarch has presumably gone elsewhere at times when he wants to spread himself. Caesar's killing is one of those moments; he seems here to be supplementing Pollio's material not merely with the omens from Strabo and Livy (63.3, 63.9) but also with other items. These include the 'Brutus will wait for this flesh' story (62.6, *Brut.* 8.3), Caesar's special fear of 'the thin and pale' (62.10, *Brut.* 8.2, *Ant.* 11.6), his baring his neck to a hostile crowd (60.6, *Ant.* 12.6), and, less spectacularly, the details of the provinces Brutus and Cassius were to receive (67.9, *Brut.* 19.5).[130] Appian has none of that material. 'Biographical' material is here an obvious candidate. In *Brutus* Plutarch quotes several specialist works, including 'a short but valuable book on Caesar's assassination entitled *Brutus*' by **Empylus** (*FGrH* 191, *HRR* ii.LXVIII; *Brut.* 2.4) and a 'small book of stories about Brutus' by his stepson **Calpurnius Bibulus** (*HRR* ii. LXVII, 51–2; *Brut.* 13.3, cf. 23.7); it is very likely that

---

Geiger, and L. Ghilli (1993), 288–310; R. J. Goar, *The Legend of Cato Uticensis from the First Century BC to the Fifth Century AD* (1987).

[128] On Munatius and Thrasea, see esp. J. Geiger, *Athen.* 57 (1979), 48–72, and the introduction to *Cato minor* in my Penguin *Rome in Crisis* (2010).

[129] *Plutarch and History*, 15–16.

[130] See also *Plutarch and History*, 14, where I list some further non-Appianic items found in *Brutus* but not in *Caesar*.

they provide material for *Caesar* too, and that those non-Appianic items come from one or both of these.

The final chapter of *Caesar* also summarizes events of the Philippi campaign that are much more extensively treated in *Brutus*. In *Brutus* he several times cites the works of **P. Volumnius** (*HRR* ii. LXVII–LXVIII, 52–3; 69.13 n.) and **Messala Corvinus** (*HRR* ii. LXXVIII-LXXXIII, 65–7), and both those men are tellingly prominent in the narrative of those chapters.[131] It is hard to identify particular items in *Caes.* 69 that come from them, but it is reasonable to regard the whole chapter as an abbreviated amalgam of all the material that Plutarch is weaving together in *Brutus*.

5. Other **first-hand material** from Caesar's own lifetime has left a mark on some of Plutarch's other *Lives*: in particular, he seems to have read some works of **Cicero** at the earlier stage of the *Lives'* production when he was collecting material for *Cicero*, especially the work *On his own Consulship* for the events of 63.[132] He may also have read at that stage Antony's reply to the *Second Philippic* and some of Brutus' letters to Atticus.[133] Once read, such works might continue to provide material for the later series of *Lives*, and the reference to the *On his own Consulship* at 8.4 (n.) is probably drawn from his memory or from the *hypomnēma* that he took at that time (below, p. 54). Close analysis of *Caes.* 7.5–8.7 reveals several further items that will have been known to him at the time of *Cicero*, even though he omitted them from the *Cicero* narrative.[134] We can also detect some use of Cicero's correspondence in *Pompey* and *Brutus*,[135] and Plutarch also recalls a famous Cicero gibe in his introduction to *Phocion–Cato minor* (Cato behaving as if he were living in Plato's *Republic* rather than Romulus' cesspool, *Phoc.* 3.2: above, pp. 17–18).[136]

---

[131] Messala: *Brut.* 40.1, 42.5, 45.1. Volumnius: 48.1–4, 51.1. See the introduction to *Brutus* in my Penguin *Rome in Crisis* (2010).

[132] *Plutarch and History*, 45–9; cf. 8.4 n. and Moles, *Cicero*, 28.

[133] Moles, *Cicero*, 28–9; cf. *Plutarch and History*, 16.

[134] Namely, the youths' attack, 8.2; the senatorial session where Caesar delivered his apologia, 8.5; Cato's corn dole, 8.6–7 (nn.). For the detailed argument, see *Plutarch and History*, 51–2.

[135] *Pomp.* 42.13, 63.12; *Brut.* 21.6, 22.4–6, 24.3. cf. 29.8–11, with J. L. Moles in J. Mossman (ed.), *Plutarch and his Intellectual World* (1997), 141–68.

[136] Plutarch there adds that Cicero 'says that this was why he failed to win the consulship'. The gibe about 'Romulus' cesspool' in fact comes in Cic. *Att.* 2.1 (21).8, a letter of 60 BCE, well before that failure to win the consulship of 51 (*C.min.* 49–50): cf.

Elsewhere we can trace an extensive debt to Cicero's *Second Philippic* in *Antony*, so extensive and detailed that in this case he had probably reread the work;[137] in *Caesar* the fleeting reference to 'Antony's drunken excesses and his ransacking and rebuilding of Pompey's private house' (51.3) probably owes something to that rereading (51 n.). Still, there is no indication that Plutarch undertook any further reading of Cicero for this later series,[138] any more than he read Caesar's own speeches and letters; as we saw (above, p. 43), the reference to **Tanusius Geminus** (*HRR* ii. LXV–LXVI, 49–51) at 22.4 is likely to be drawn second-hand from Pollio. Probably Plutarch felt that the discovery of his Pollio narrative gave him such a rich extra source of material that he did not need to dig any further.

6. **Oral tradition** mattered too.[139] In the same passage in *Demosthenes–Cicero* where Plutarch mentions his Latin (above, p. 43), he also discusses how his work has been affected by living in small-town Chaeronea. One can be virtuous anywhere, he says, but a writer of history finds it so much easier when living in a big city. One advantage is the 'abundance of books' in libraries (above, p. 39); another is that one can 'pick up and ask questions about' oral traditions, 'all those things' (as he puts it) 'that have escaped the written sources, but are still remembered and have gained a more remarkable credibility' (*Dem.* 2.1). The passage is echoed at the end of *Demosthenes*: the *Life* has been based on 'what we have read or heard' (31.7, cf. 31.1). The clearest cases of such oral traditions come in *Antony*, stories of the dining in Alexandria and the hardships of Greece during the Actium campaign that had been transmitted within Plutarch's own family (*Ant.* 28.3–12, 68.6–8). Nothing in *Caesar* would have come quite so close to home (though we should remember that the battlefield of Pharsalus was only some two days' ride away to the north), but some items do look to be a survival of oral

54.5 n. Plutarch is probably just misremembering that distant reading: cf. above, pp. 40–1, for similar cases.

[137] See my comm. on *Ant.* 26–7; *Plutarch and History*, 17–18.

[138] Cf. J. Geiger in L. van der Stockt (ed.), *Rhetorical Theory and Praxis in Plutarch* (2000), 211–23, arguing at 221–2 that the *Second Philippic* may have been the only speech of Cicero that Plutarch knew.

[139] On the importance of this, cf. *Plutarch and History*, 18–19; Stadter, pp. lxxxiv–v; Theander 2–32 and *Eranos*, 57 (1959), 99–131; A. Georgiadou, *Plutarch's Pelopidas* (1997), 27–8.

tradition even 150 years after the events—not perhaps so surprising as all that, as these were after all among the most epoch-making events of history. At 26.8 Plutarch notes that the Arverni 'still display a small sword hung in one of their shrines as a spoil from Caesar', and adds a tale of how Caesar smiled on seeing it and allowed it to remain in place. Notice the present tense, this is still 'on display', and the accompanying story is exactly the sort of embellishment that such items tend to attract (below, p. 57). At 6.6–7 (n.) he mentions a 'celebrated remark' of Q. Lutatius Catulus: 'celebrated' is literally 'recalled' (*mnēmoneuomenon* in the present tense), still remembered and talked about in Plutarch's own day. There may be more examples: perhaps the story of Domitius' attempt at suicide (34.6–8); perhaps an anecdote or so of Caesar on campaign (15–17 n.); perhaps some of the *bons mots* of Cicero (4.8–9, 57.6. 58.3, 59.6 nn.: above, p. 25).[140]

7. There is also a sense in which Plutarch would sometimes be using **his own earlier work and reading** as a 'source'. We have already mentioned the work that he had done when composing *Cicero* (above, p. 52, cf. p. 42); perhaps some of that was lodged in his memory, perhaps he reread his own earlier text when describing, say, the Catilinarian conspiracy or the Bona Dea (7.5–8.5, 9.2–10.11 nn.), perhaps he consulted whatever *hypomnēma* he had written at that stage.[141] His remarks on Caesar's calendar reforms will similarly owe something to the reading he had undertaken for *Numa* (59 nn.), just as the antiquarian material on the Bona Dea and the Lupercalia will draw on the work he had done for the *Roman Questions* and for *Romulus* (9.4, 61.1 nn.).

There is also a broader category of material, including the sort of literary culture that sometimes surfaces in his stylistic allusions to classical authors,[142] which covers items and texts that he had known for years, very likely for so long that he would no longer be able to recall when he had first come across them. One case might be the story of the soothsayer at 43.3–4 (n.). Still, this is one area in which

---

[140] Though some or all of these may come from the work of Cicero's freedman Tiro, his biography of Cicero or his *On Jokes*: Plutarch may well have read both works for *Cicero*.

[141] As I suggested at *Plutarch and History*, 49–53. Cf. esp. 8.4 n.: might an inconsequential argument in *Caes.* arise from a note made in that original *hypomnēma*, when his train of thought was different?

[142] e.g. at 6.1, 15.3, 27.7, 37.9, 64.6, 66.12 (nn.).

the Roman *Lives* are very different from the classical Greek ones. Those are replete with citations of the literature of the day. Thus *Pericles* could quote several comic poets, Aristophanes, Eupolis, Cratinus, Telecleides, Hermippus, Plato, and more;[143] it could quote odd passages of the philosopher Plato;[144] a few more philosophers could be exploited along the way, Timon of Phlius, Critolaus, Heraclides Ponticus; so could Theophrastus.[145] Plutarch probably did not read any of those for 'research' purposes; he had read them for themselves. Recollections of them could now be very useful, and there is no need to doubt it when he says that a chapterful of anecdotes of Aspasia just 'came to mind' as he wrote (24.12).[146] The Roman *Lives* are not like that. Suetonius' *Diuus Iulius* is rich in the same sort of material that Plutarch used for *Pericles*: quotations from contemporary pamphlets and lampoons, from Calvus, Catullus, Curio, and so on. Plutarch has nothing like that. He never quotes Catullus, though Catullus 93—'I am not too keen, Caesar, to give the impression of wanting to please you; nor to know whether you are a white man or a black'—might have added something when he was discussing Caesar's attempts to conciliate public opinion. He never mentions Virgil, though the ninth *Eclogue* would have been apposite at 69.4 (n.). The Roman poets might have added useful material for the triumviral period in *Antony*, not least in what they said about Cleopatra; Ennius' famous 'by delaying he rescued our cause' (*cunctando restituit rem*) would have been a useful adornment for *Fabius*. The one reference to Horace at *Lucull.* 39.5 shows that there was no generic rule to exclude such references, but Plutarch just did not have the same immersion in Latin literature for its own sake as he had in Greek.[147]

---

[143] *Per.* 8.4, 26.4, 30.4; 3.7, 24.10; 3.5, 13.8, 13.10, 24.9; 3.6, 16.2; 33.8; 4.4; *fragmenta adespota* at 7.8, 8.4, 13.15, 16.1, 24.9.

[144] *Per.* 7.8, 8.2, 13.7, 15.2, 24.7.

[145] Cf., respectively, *Per.* 4.5, 7.7, 27.4 and 35.5, 38.2. On these and other 'sources' for *Pericles*, see Stadter, pp. lviii–lxxxv. Another telling *Life* here is *Themistocles*: A. Zadorojnyi, *AJP* 127 (2006), 261–92, argues that Plutarch's characterization here exploits thoroughly his own and his readers' acquaintance with two poets, Simonides and Timocreon. One Roman *Life* that does exploit such material is *Flamininus* (9.2, 9.4, 16.7), and there it is Greek epigrams that are in point: cf. my Rizzoli comm. on *Phil.–Flam.* (1997), 319–24.

[146] Which is not to exclude an element of artificial self-projection there: *Plutarch and History*, 30 n. 9.

[147] Cf. also A. Zadorojnyi (as 'Zadorojniy') in C. Schrader, V. Ramón, and J. Vela (eds), *Plutarco y la historia* (1999), 497–506, esp. 503–5 on the Horace quotation.

So that is one way in which his late acquisition of Latin (above, pp. 43–4) genuinely does seem to make a difference to the texture of the Roman *Lives*. All the more credit, then, to him for all the Latin reading that he did, very clearly, undertake. The *Parallel Lives* were a very big project indeed.

3.3. Remoulding the Material

Once the material was gathered, Plutarch then had to shape it so that it told the story and conveyed the interpretations he wanted to tell and convey. On the larger scale, the themes he chose to emphasize have already been discussed in Section 2.2. On the smaller scale, too, he often found that his material was not quite as he would want it, and some adjustment was necessary. Where we can trace what he has done, the commentary will bring this out; it may be useful here to summarize some particularly typical techniques. Here I list only examples from *Caesar* itself.[148]

1. *Alteration of sequence.* A clear case comes in the organization of Caesar's early foreign adventures, grouping together the trip to Nicomedes (1.7), the pirate adventure (1.8–2.7), and the study in Rhodes (3): the return to Rome restores the reader to domestic politics at 4.1, and the ordering may insinuate the idea that Caesar's rhetorical successes of 4.1–4 are the consequence of his Rhodian teaching (3.1 n.). But those rhetorical successes came in 77/6; the piracy story belongs later, in 74–3 (1.8–2.7 n.), and the journey to Rhodes was also later (3.1 n.).

2. *Conflation of similar items*—for instance the merging-together of two agrarian bills in Caesar's legislation in 59 (14.2 with ch. 14 n.); he separates them in the fuller account in *C.min.* (32–3). He similarly gives the impression that the Catilinarians were exposed and their punishment was decided at the same debate at 7.7: the fuller account in *Cicero* makes it clear that he knew better (n.).

---

[148] For similar cases elsewhere, see *Plutarch and History*, 91–7, and collections of material in various introductions to and discussions of other *Lives*: in *Marius*, T. F. Carney, *JHS* 80 (1980), 26–7; in *Cicero*, Moles, *Cicero*, 37; in *Pericles*, Stadter, p. xlviii; in *Sertorius*, Konrad, p. xl; in *Alcibiades*, F. Frazier (1997), 25–7; in *Phil.–Flam.*, my Rizzoli comm. (1997), 119–20, 283, 406 n. 196; in *Lysander* and *Alcibiades*, Duff, 313–14.

3. *Chronological compression.* At 21.8 Plutarch explains Cato's absence from a crucial debate 'for they had deliberately spirited him away to Cyprus'. That suggests a measure to safeguard this particular piece of legislation; in fact he knew that Cato had been sent two years earlier (n.).

4. *Transfer of actions from one character to another.* A complex, but disputed, example of this comes in his treatment of tribunicial activities in the final few weeks before the outbreak of war in January 49, where it is arguable that he has transferred items from one year's tribune (Curio) to the next (Antony): cf. 30.5 n.

5. *Creation of a context.* The item of 26.7–8—the sword that the Arverni still display—probably comes from oral tradition, as we have seen (p. 54). Plutarch notes that this was captured at an early stage of the battle when 'it looked as if he was having the worse of it'. There is no hint in the fuller narrative in Caesar's *Commentarii* of such an initial reverse, though he often notes such passing crises elsewhere, and it is likely that Plutarch has simply inferred such a phase to give a plausible context for the sword's capture (26.8 n.).

6. *Imaginative elaboration.* 9.2–10.11 tells of Clodius and the Bona Dea, a tale that he had already recounted in detail in *Cic.* 28–9. There are further picturesque touches here: the doors of the house are open; the maid runs off to fetch Pompeia; Clodius is too nervous to stay where he was left; Aurelia's maid is playful — 'Come on, join in the fun'—then pulls him out from the shadows; Aurelia is formidable and decisive; the wives return and gossip to their husbands. Some of this may come from notes taken at the time of *Cicero* or from his memory, but some—probably most— is likely to be 'creative reconstruction'.[149]

We naturally find such manipulation of detail uncomfortable and cavalier; or at least we would in a contemporary historian or biographer, though we cope with it without too much trouble in, say, a film, just as Shakespeare's contemporaries coped with similar techniques

---

[149] As, perhaps slightly euphemistically, I described it at *Plutarch and History*, 153–4; I also there insisted that such imaginative expansion was fairly limited in Plutarch, and did not extend to the 'big invention' that could have allowed him to fill, for instance, the considerable gaps in the narrative of *Lives* like *Phocion*, *Aristides*, *Philopoemen*, *Poplicola*, *Artaxerxes*, and even *Crassus*.

well enough in his plays (below, p. 67). T. P. Wiseman, discussing
Roman historiography, wondered if possibly a writer might have
thought that it 'must have happened like that' in such cases, with
a priori likelihood overriding the authority of whatever the
sources happened to tell him.[150] That approach may sometimes be
appropriate, but Plutarch provides good evidence for its limitations,
for in several of those cases we have seen that he provides different
and incompatible versions in other *Lives*, probably composed at the
same time and as part of the same exercise. If he noticed—and
sometimes he may not have noticed, for such smoothing of material
may on occasion have been unconscious—he could not have thought
them all equally true.

It is better to realign our expectations. Such tweaking techniques
are quite regular in ancient historiography; indeed, Plutarch could
reasonably have assumed that his own sources had felt similar free-
doms, and it would have been as inappropriate for him to take his
own sources' arrangement as completely reliable as it would be for us
to rely on his. But his energy was spent on other things, exploiting
such smoothing techniques as a way of conveying as sharply, lucidly,
and engagingly whatever it was that he wanted to make of this period
and these people. It is time to examine how successful he was in those
historical interpretations.

4. PLUTARCH AND ROMAN POLITICS

Caesar, we have already seen, is a very 'historical' *Life*, plotting
Caesar's rise and fall against the background of the historical forces
that made them possible (pp. 21–5). We have also seen that this
reflects, not merely the life choice made by Caesar himself in devoting
his energy so exclusively to power, but also themes developed in other
Roman *Lives*: threats and tensions now come to a head that have been
gathering for several generations, perhaps even since the city's birth
(above, pp. 34–5). It is a characteristic feature of Greek narrative
not to set out every relevant feature at the beginning, but to hold

---

[150] T. P. Wiseman, *History*, 66 (1981), 389, followed by A. J. Woodman, *Rhetoric in
Classical Historiography* (1988), 93. I discuss the issues much more fully in *Plutarch
and History*, ch. 6, esp. 152–6, and in the introduction to my *Antony* comm., 35–6.

themes back until they are most telling.[151] This is no exception, and thus Caesar's relations with Pompey and Crassus rarely emerge in the early years (1.8–2.7, 5.8–9, 9.1, 28.2 nn.); there are passing references only at 5.7 and 11.1–2. That makes them all the more prominent when the 'first triumvirate' is formed in 60 BCE (13.3 nn.), and by then Caesar's own rise has been presented more in terms of his relation with the Roman people (*dēmos*), a matter between him and them. The description of the city's political malaise (*kakopoliteia*, above, p. 12) comes with the height of the crisis at the end of the fifties (28–32 n.), not at any of the earlier points when it might have been relevant—the Catilinarian conspiracy (7.5–8.5), for instance, or Caesar's consulship of 59 (14). Plutarch's timing here is not always in line with the emphases that we might choose ourselves; a modern writer, for instance, might introduce political bribery as a factor in explaining Caesar's own rise (4.4–7, 5.8–9, 7.1–4, 7.5, 11.1–2, 13 nn.), whereas Plutarch prefers to hold it back and present it as part of the *kakopoliteia* (28–32 n.), explaining the problems that by now required a radical 'doctor' to cure. Still, he had his reasons, probably not so much a matter of simple generosity to his subject (cf. *Cimon* 2.4–5, above, p. 17) as of tracing the Romans' shifting perspectives, as the prospect of one-man rule, like the identity of the man most likely to exercise it, comes closer and clearer (28–32, 28.5–6, 41.2, 57.1 nn., and above, p. 12).

In other cases, too, we can see a biographical *inflection* of Plutarch's favoured historical themes, so that, for instance, Roman political divisions are even more sharply bipolar, the people (*dēmos*) against the few (*oligoi*), than in other *Lives* (8.6, 15–27, 21.8–9, 60.1, 61.10–62.1, 67–8 nn.): that fits the strong emphasis on the *dēmos* as the force that carried Caesar to power and then destroyed him, and the *oligoi* as the ruthless enemies who are at first humiliated and then adroitly successful (above, pp. 21–2). Still, these are indeed inflections, matters of emphasis rather than complete differences of interpretation (though some of those can be found too, for instance, in the presentation of Clodius or the alertness of Pompey to the threat that Caesar posed[152]). Elsewhere, too, Plutarch favours a two-party

---

[151] See above all E. Fraenkel, *Aeschylus: Agamemnon* (1950), Appendix A; Fraenkel's insight is applied illuminatingly to Thucydides by T. Rood, *Thucydides: Narrative and Explanation* (1998), index, s.v. 'delay, narrative'. See also my *Literary Texts and the Greek Historian* (2000), 69, 89–94.
[152] *Plutarch and History*, 96–100; cf. 9.2, 28.2 nn.

emphasis on the model of Greek stereotypes,[153] with the *dēmos* on one side and another grouping on the other, variously called the 'respectable group' or 'gentlemen' (14.3 n.), or the 'aristocrats' (13.5, 14.6) or 'the most powerful' (10.6) or the 'best people' (7.4) or the 'notables' (e.g. *Brut.* 24.4) or the 'gentlemen' (e.g. *C.min.* 27.8) or 'the oligarchically minded' (e.g. *Gracch.* 32.4) or the 'most well-known' (*Marc.* 27.4);[154] fine distinctions among such categories—for instance, the distinction between 'nobles' and 'patricians' (9.2, 61.2 nn.) or the differences among the various popular assemblies[155]— are of less interest. This, for him, was how Roman politics worked: and not just Roman, as we shall see.

Plutarch's general assumptions may also be influencing what he does *not* discuss. Suetonius discusses whether Caesar had aimed at tyranny all his life (*Diu. Iul.* 30, cf. 32 n.), and we can see that this was an interpretation aired soon after his death (Cic. *Off.* 3.83, cf. above, p. 18). Plutarch does not discuss the question. He takes it for granted that he had sought one-man rule from his early career (69.1 n., cf. 3.3, 28.1, 32 nn. and e.g. *Cic.* 20.6, *Ant.* 6.2–3), and scatters various hints that this is where his ambition is heading (1–3, 5.6, 5.9, 6.7, 29.5, 30.1, 33.6, 35.5–11 nn., cf. above, pp. 21 and 23–4); but this is not problematized, either morally (above, pp. 19–21) or historically. Perhaps we should not be surprised: in Plutarch's mind, such ambitions—or at least the allegation of such ambitions—were not so remarkable. Similar things are said in the *Lives* about Cicero, about Pompey, even about Cassius (*Cic.* 23.4, *Pomp.* 25.3, 30.3–4, 43.1, 54.5, *Brut.* 29.5); just as it is regularly assumed that 'revolution' was the aim of statesmen at the time, not just of the likes of Catiline but—at least it could be claimed—of Saturninus, of Antony and Dolabella, and of the supporters of Pompey (*Mar.* 30.1, *Ant.* 9.1, *Pomp.* 43.5). And, fully in line with the stereotypes of Greek political theorizing, demagogic

---

[153] *Plutarch and History*, 211–17: typical passages from other *Lives* that I quote there are *Mar.* 4.7 (referring to 'both groups' in a way that makes it clear that there are only two), *Marc.* 6.2, *Gracch.* 7.3–4, 8.10, 10.1, 15.1, 21, and 26, *Mar.* 4.6 and 28–30, *Pomp.* 21.7 and 22.3, *Lucull.* 35.9, *C.min.* 51.7, and *Brut.* 21.2–3. The list could easily be extended. On this and on the other themes treated in this section, see also L. de Blois in *ANRW* ii. 33.6 (1992), 4568–615: de Blois accepts my emphasis on Plutarch's bipolar categorization, but at 4578–83 gathers a few cases ('[a]lthough the harvest is small') where Plutarch qualifies or renuances this 'simplified portrayal'.

[154] *Plutarch and History*, 218, 231–2, collecting other examples.

[155] *Plutarch and History*, 222; de Blois (n. 153), 4577–8.

methods are thought of as the natural path to tyranny (28.5 n.), and indeed the natural way to protect tyranny when it is threatened (57.8 n.). The programmatic banners of demagogic agitation are again thoroughly Greek in flavour, land redistribution, and a remission of debts (14.2, 37.2, 57.8 nn.; cf. my n. on *Ant.* 9.1). The word Plutarch uses for the latter is the distinctive Solonian *seisachtheia* ('unburdening', 37.2 n.), as Greek as can be.

The Greekness of all these categories repays further thought.[156] Aspects that do not fit the Greek patterning tend to be discarded: *clientela*, for instance, or *equites*;[157] or the value of gladiators for urban street-violence (5.9, 67.7 nn.); or Caesar's family connections with the old aristocratic houses of the Aemilii Lepidi and the Aurelii Cottae (1.4, 60.2 nn.). Plutarch prefers to emphasize the family connection with Marius and Caesar's self-presentation as his successor in that popular tradition (5.2–5, 6, cf. 1.2, 18.1, 19.4, 26.2 nn.).

It is easy to see this as simply a limitation of Plutarch's historical vision, blinkered against Roman realities because of presuppositions deeply embedded in his Greek mentality; perhaps there is something in that. But we should also acknowledge two further factors, both of them themes which feature elsewhere in this introduction: first, the desire to create a framework where the comparison between Greek and Roman (Section 2.2) can obtain maximum purchase, as his figures confront similar issues in a similar political climate; secondly, the taste for timeless themes rather than those which are more specific to a particular period and culture (below, p. 76, 67–8 n.). If Plutarch felt that *clientela* and patricians were likely to be of less permanent significance than class conflict and demagogy and tyranny and revolution, he was absolutely right.

Nor is it clear that his historical emphases are as off-beam as all that; here today's historians are more likely to give him a generous hearing than those of fifty years ago. Gelzer's and Münzer's work on 'nobility' and Syme's emphasis on the Roman oligarchy dominated the field in their time; more recently Brunt has emphasized social conflict and Millar has highlighted the 'democratic' elements in

[156] For a fuller discussion, see *Plutarch and History*, 207–36, esp. the postscript paragraph on pp. 225–6, where I reconsider the emphasis I had given in the original 1986 paper; this emphasis on the Greekness of the categories is accepted by de Blois (n. 153).
[157] *Plutarch and History*, 220.

Roman political debate, and that has been no less influential.[158] These are continuing debates, as much about which acknowledged truths deserve more emphasis as about what counts as truth; it is clear both that the political elite continued to exercise immense political power and that many issues were genuinely open when they came to debate in senate and people, both that the 'oligarchy' could usually dominate elections and that not every member of the elite was successful, both that elections were often corrupt and that votes needed and mattered enough to be bought. And we should not write as if the rules of the political game were cut-and-dried at the time. A major theme of the last generation of the Republic, as it was to be of the triumvirate, is the degree to which politicians were themselves unsure how far, say, the Roman crowd could influence high politics, how far Roman legions could be relied upon to follow general rather than state, how far a maverick could simply be slapped down, how far senatorial authority could be overridden or ignored. One-man rule was a genuine danger; if one looks back to the last generation and Sulla or forward to the

---

[158] M. Gelzer, *The Roman Nobility* (tr. R. Seager, 1969: German originals 1912 and 1915), though Gelzer's definition of 'nobility' is challenged by P. A. Brunt, *JRS* 72 (1982), 1–17; Münzer, *RAPF*; Syme, *RR*. 'Oligarchy is imposed as the guiding theme, the link from age to age whatever be the form and name of government' (R. Syme, *The Augustan Aristocracy* (1986), 13). For more emphasis on social conflict, see esp. Brunt, *Social Conflicts in the Roman Republic* (1971) and *FRR*, esp. 1–92; 'democratic aspects' are stressed by Millar in *Crowd* and in several of his earlier studies that are reprinted in H. M. Cotton and G. M. Rogers (eds), *Rome, the Greek World, and the East I: The Roman Republic and the Augustan Revolution* (2002). Wiseman, *Remembering*, is a further attempt to repair the 'ideological vacuum' (ch. 1) that he sees in older analyses, and in particular to recover the voice of the Roman people: 'we do, I think, have to accept . . . that the republic was divided into two ideological camps—two *partes*, as [Cicero] put it in a speech to the Senate [*post red. in sen.* 33]—and that this rivalry had been fundamental in Roman politics since the time of the Gracchi' (14). Millar's approach is taken further e.g. by Yakobson (1999); it is criticized by H. Mouritsen, *Plebs and Politics in the Late Roman Republic* (2001). Morstein-Marx (*Mass Oratory*) agrees with Millar in emphasizing the role of public speech in mass–elite relations but has deep reservations about 'democratic' features and the possibility of any genuine 'debate': on the contrary, skilful use of the *contio* 'strongly reinforced its [the governing élite's] hegemony and buttressed the traditional order' (32). Useful recent compendia are the two *Companions to the Roman Republic* published by Cambridge (ed. H. I. Flower, 2004) and Blackwell (ed. N. Rosenstein and R. Morstein-Marx, 2008); the Blackwell *Companion* begins with a good summary by M. Jehne of the historiographic debate during the last few generations (3–28), and this is also the subject of K.-J. Hölkeskamp, *Reconstructing the Roman Republic: An Ancient Political Culture and Modern Research* (2010, German original 2004), who is highly critical of Millar: notice esp. his ch. 6 (76–97), pointedly entitled 'Between "Aristocracy" and "Democracy": Beyond a Dated Dichotomy'.

next generation and Augustus, it is clear enough that the scaremongering was not dealing in the unthinkable.

It is clear, too, that similar categories featured in political debate and analysis at the time, even if Plutarch pushes them more relentlessly and with fewer variations. His bipolarity is not very different from Sallust's picture of the 'two factions' or 'parts' (*partes*) of the Roman state, the 'few' and the 'people' (esp. *BJ* 41, *Cat.* 37–8, *Hist.* 1.6–13 M). Us-and-them language is always a temptation in partisan rhetoric, and in *pro Sestio* (96–147) Cicero tendentiously theorizes a contrast of good-people-like-us and bad-people-like-them that frequently features in a cruder way in his other speeches.[159] Charges of aiming at tyranny or the overthrow of the constitution were commonplace;[160] land distribution genuinely figured in agrarian proposals, and was fiercely contested on both sides; there was a real crisis of debt (37.2, 51.3 nn. and M. Frederiksen, *JRS* 56 (1966), 128–41), and fears of *tabulae nouae*—new tablets, the tearing up of current obligations—were articulated often enough. The analytical terms did not have to wait for Greeks to construct in their own image (for Polybius, Dionysius, Dio, and Appian at least sometimes write in similar terms[161]), familiar and welcome as those authors would have found them.

Nor does Plutarch apply the categories uncritically. He knows, for instance, that the polarities could blur, and Cato too could strike a populist line (14.8 n., though cf. also 8.6 n.). But particularly important here is the Platonic vocabulary with which he describes Caesar's eventual rule: this was 'acknowledged tyranny', he says (57.1 n.), echoing a prominent passage in Plato's *Republic* (8.569b). That summons up Plato's picture of a cycle of constitutions (cf. also 28.5–7, 29.5 nn.), and in particular his model of the ambitious demagogue whose popular support offers him the path to power. Yet, strikingly, Caesar does *not* now behave like Plato's tyrant, turning to ever more brutal and repressive measures as his power wanes and he strives to eliminate his enemies (57–61 n., cf. also 57.1, 57.4 nn.). Caesar does have his 'passion to become king' (60.1, cf. above, p. 29), one that is no longer so erotically reciprocated as before (above, p. 21, cf. 58.1, 58.4 nn.), and he does make mistakes in power (57–61 n.): still, he

---

[159] Cf. R. Kaster's Clarendon Ancient History Series edn of *Pro Sestio* (2006), 31–7; Wiseman 5–6; and my *Plutarch and History*, 222.

[160] Cf. Hellegouarc'h 560–5.

[161] *Plutarch and History*, 212–14.

also shows himself 'unimpeachable' (57.4 n.), championing clemency
and mildness, generous to Pompey's memory, refusing a bodyguard,
alert to the importance of popular goodwill (above, p. 30). As we have
seen, it is more his past than his present that brings him down (above,
pp. 21–2). And eventually it is his good qualities that leave him
so vulnerable, his sparing of Brutus and Cassius, then his accessibility
as the crowds and the assassins cluster round on the Ides (57.7,
64–5 nn.).

Such is the stuff of tragedy. Shakespeare knew it. But what Shakespeare did with it is another story, one that invites analysis in its
own right.

5. *CAESAR* AND *JULIUS CAESAR*: PLUTARCH AND SHAKESPEARE

Amyot, North, and Shakespeare

For *Julius Caesar* (1599), as for the later Roman plays *Coriolanus* and
Antony and Cleopatra, Shakespeare drew on Plutarch as his main,
indeed almost his only, source. He did not know Plutarch's text in the
original, but in the 1579 translation by Sir Thomas North; in fact
North himself did not know Plutarch, but translated the 1559 French
version of Amyot. There are times, as we shall see, when this double
distance from Plutarch's original has interesting consequences.

There is much to say about Shakespeare's adaptation, and I have
recently treated this in more detail in 'Roman Tragedy', a paper from
which much of the following discussion is drawn. (See now also Julia
Griffin in *CJC* 371–98, with illuminating comparisons with other
early modern Caesar plays: see both papers for a fuller guide to the
extensive bibliography.) Here I concentrate on points where the
comparison is particularly illuminating for Plutarch's technique, not
just Shakespeare's. It will be no surprise that Shakespeare was a
particularly sensitive reader of Plutarch, and was particularly alert
to the various dramatic possibilities that Plutarch's material offered.
Where he chose to develop these in a different way, it is always
worthwhile to examine why, and to see if Plutarch has simply missed
a trick or if the different choices illuminate broader narrative strategies in the two writers. Scarcely less illuminating are those cases

where Shakespeare decided that Plutarch's artistic ideas, once transposed into dramatic form, would suit his own purposes very well.

Often Shakespeare is content to take over Plutarch's dramatic ideas fairly closely. Plutarch's narrative of the killing itself is particularly vivid and visual (66 n.), and transposed very well for the theatre; some of the more reflective passages of *Brutus* are also taken over—for instance, the weighing of the arguments for suicide at *Brut.* 40, where Shakespeare's language is particularly close to North's version, even in minor details of rhythm and phrasing (*JC* v. i. 93–121).[162] In *Coriolanus* we can see that the shaping of the story is in many ways a continuous process, with Plutarch remoulding his source Dionysius of Halicarnassus in precisely the same directions as Shakespeare goes on to remould Plutarch: Plutarch takes the dramatic refiguring halfway, and Shakespeare goes on to finish the job.[163] *Julius Caesar* does not offer such clear-cut examples, but there is something of the same here.

Even more interesting are a few cases where Amyot and North might have been expected to give Shakespeare the wrong impression, but do not. It is as if Shakespeare can sense the real Plutarch even when his translators stray.[164] Take the picturing of the murder as sacrifice, something important to the righteous self-image of the conspirators—'Let us be sacrificers but not butchers, Caius...' (II. i. 165). The idea of sacrifice is there in the original Plutarch too, for *Caesar* describes the violence with imagery both of the hunt and of sacrifice:

He was run through like some wild beast, rolling to and fro in everyone's hands, for each person there needed to begin the sacrifice and taste of the slaughter.

(66.10–11)

(The word in Greek is *katarkhesthai*, often used of sacrifice.) But the image was not there in Amyot ('car il était dit entre eux que chacun lui donnerait un coup et participerait au meurtre') and so it is not there in North either, who has:

---

[162] There are some interesting minor divergences: see Pelling, 'Roman Tragedy', 268–70.

[163] *Plutarch and History*, 387–411.

[164] For some similar cases in *Brutus*, see Pelling, 'Roman Tragedy', 266–70; for one in *Coriolanus*, see *Plutarch and History*, 410 n. 35.

For it was agreed among them, that every man should give him a wound, because all their parts should be in this murder.

North's language of 'parts'—his rather than Plutarch's—may even have suggested to Shakespeare the language of metatheatre that follows at precisely the point where all are bloodied from the strike (III. i. 111–16), but it could not have been North that suggested the figure of sacrifice. That was Shakespeare's own, and it re-created what Plutarch's translators had suppressed.[165]

The most interesting example concerns the apparition that twice visits Brutus. What is it, exactly? In Shakespeare it seems to be at the same time 'Caesar's ghost'—the stage direction, confirmed by Brutus' own words at v. v. 16—and Brutus' own 'evil spirit' (IV. iii. 279). As we have seen (p. 31), that is not untrue to Plutarch, for the last chapter of *Caesar* talks of 'the great *daimōn* of Caesar' that now ranges so widely to secure revenge, and then has the apparition introduce itself as 'your evil *daimōn*, Brutus' (69.2 n., 69.4). But it is again untrue to the translators, who obscure the spiritual depth that the word *daimōn* carries for Plutarch.[166] North's version of that 'great *daimōn* of Caesar' has 'his great prosperity and good fortune that favoured him all his lifetime'; Amyot's had a little more of the supernatural, but is still weaker than the original—'cette grande fortune et faveur du ciel qui l'avait accompagné tout le long du cours de sa vie'. No reader could have interpreted the translations as suggesting the demonological equivalence of the two spirits: yet that is what Shakespeare has, and once again it is important to him. The two men's fates are becoming one, as history replays itself; Caesar's spirit is indeed ranging for revenge (III. i. 270). And Brutus knows it: 'O Julius Caesar, thou art mighty yet!' (v. iii. 94, above, p. 1). True, Shakespeare need not have drawn the idea of 'Caesar's ghost' directly from Plutarch, for it may well be that the anonymous play *Caesar's*

---

[165] Thus N. C. Liebler, *Shakespeare's Festive Strategy* (1995), 100, is only half-right to say that all the sacrificial imagery is 'Shakespeare's embroidery over the plain presentation in Plutarch': Shakespeare's embroidery, yes, but the 'plain presentation' is not Plutarch's own. This is recognized by R. A. Brower, *Hero and Saint: Shakespeare and the Graeco-Roman Tradition* (1971), 227, noting a further case where North and Amyot suppress Plutarch's sacrificial imagery at *Brut.* 10.1 but missing the instance at *Caes.* 66.10.

[166] Cf. J. A. K. Thomson, *Shakespeare and the Classics* (1952), 195–205, an insightful discussion, though it underplays the complexities to say that 'Shakespeare *confused* [emphasis added] Caesar's daemon with that of Brutus' (204).

Revenge, featuring just such an apparition of Caesar's ghost, pre-dates Shakespeare's play by a few years.[167] It is still remarkable that Shakespeare and Plutarch should have merged the two spirits together in so similar a way. Perhaps one might think of a friend carefully conning the Greek and alerting Shakespeare to nuances that North had missed, or of Shakespeare consulting a Latin translation of Plutarch as well as North,[168] but such scholarliness hardly fits the hurly-burly of rushed theatrical practicality. More likely, once again we should simply accept that the sensibilities of the two writers, and their sense of the dramatic possibilities of the tale they told, took them along uncannily similar paths.

The Shaping of the Story

Many of the more routine techniques of storytelling are similar too. That could be illustrated through matters, for instance, of the sort we saw in Section 3.3: compression of time, say, or transfers of actions to different characters (such as the transfer of the squabble over which wing each general should command: between Brutus and Cassius in Plutarch, *Brut.* 40.10, between Antony and Octavian in Shakespeare, v. i. 16–20).[169] That is familiar ground, but there are times when one can trace the similarities particularly closely. In Act I, Scene ii, for example, Shakespeare fuses several Plutarchan episodes together, most notably the Lupercalia incident with the triumph over Pompey's sons (61.1–7 n.). Plutarch knew that those two events were separate and keeps them apart in *Caesar* (56.7–9, 61–2), understandably as he wishes to trace the mounting discontent; but he can do his own fusion too, and thus in the rapid version in *Antony* (12.6) Plutarch displaces to the Lupercalia the instance where Caesar, annoyed by a popular demonstration, drew the toga down from his neck and invited his enemies to strike. Shakespeare also puts it there (i. ii. 261–4), presumably finding this economical *Antony* version dramatically attractive and preferring it to the more detailed account in *Caesar*, which makes it clear that the toga display was a separate, earlier incident

---

[167] G. Bullough, *Narrative and Dramatic Sources of Shakespeare*, v (1964), 33–5, 50, 209–11. (But the date of *Caesar's Revenge* is not quite certain.)

[168] D. Daniell, *Julius Caesar* (The Arden Shakespeare; 3rd edn, 1998), 91–2.

[169] For similar techniques in Plutarch, see above, pp. 56–7, and *Plutarch and History*, 91–115.

(60.6 (n.)). The displacement is surely a matter of deliberate choice both in Plutarch's *Antony* and in Shakespeare.

Of course Shakespeare had to deal with bigger problems of 'shaping' as well, and ones that were different from those that would face him when he returned to Plutarch for *Antony and Cleopatra* and *Coriolanus*. For each of the other plays he is handling a single Plutarch *Life*, and, despite all the subtle renuancings and adaptations, the basic themes retain their Plutarchan stamp. With *Julius Caesar* things are much less close. Shakespeare here draws from several different *Lives*, combining the last few chapters of *Caesar* with the whole of his *Brutus* and a smaller amount of *Antony*, and welding the material together was a very unstraightforward matter.

One important technique of Shakespeare here is particularly reminiscent of Plutarch himself. We have already noticed the way in which Plutarch often makes a terminal scene mirror an earlier critical episode of a hero's career; one example of that was the way in which Caesar's death has elements that look backwards to the Rubicon and others that look forward to Philippi (above, p. 33). Shakespeare takes the technique much further. We can even see it in the way that Caesar's spirit is 'mighty yet': just as Pompey's spirit was sensed in many parts of the first half of the play, so now Caesar's spirit destroys Brutus. There is indeed 'a tide in the affairs of men' (IV. iii. 216, cf. III. i. 256), and the same 'affairs' come back in different form.

Nor is it hard to see the same type of crisis recurring with Brutus as with Caesar. Shakespeare's Caesar is so frail: the man who could not swim across the Tiber (I. ii. 100–18), who has to call Antony to come to his other side 'for this ear is deaf' (I. ii. 212), who 'had a fever when he was in Spain' (I. ii. 119) and now collapses at the Lupercalia (I. ii. 247), who looks so vulnerable in his nightgown (Act II, scene ii). But there is also the Caesar who speaks of himself in the third person, all that 'illeism'[170]—'Caesar shall go forth': and when he speaks as Caesar,

---

[170] It may well have been suggested by Caesar's use of the third person in his *Commentaries*, a familiar grammar-school text (thus Griffin, *CJC* 382 and e.g. J. W. Velz, *Shakespeare Survey*, 31 (1978), 9–10), and if so Shakespeare was not the first to pick up the hint: 'Caesar' also uses the third person in Kyd's *Cornelia* of 1594 and in *Caesar's Revenge* (pp. 66–7 and n. 168); so he had also in Muret's *Julius Caesar* as early as 1544. 'Shakespeare's Caesar engages in conscious self-dramatization as the great man' (C. and M. Martindale, *Shakespeare and the Uses of Antiquity* (1990), 151). Nor, significantly, is it just Caesar who uses the third person of himself, but also Brutus, Cassius, Portia, and even Titinius. Role-playing is everywhere.

whether in the first person or in the third, he sounds quite different. 'Danger knows full well | that Caesar is more dangerous than he' (II. ii. 44–5, cf. 57.7 n.); 'I am as constant as the northern star . . .' (III. i. 60): there is a grandeur about that, so different from the frail and vulnerable inner person, and when he is struck down not merely the inner person but also the outer 'Caesar' is destroyed, leaving that Caesar-shaped gap at the top of the state that is impossible to fill. So there is the man; there is also the role he has to play, and it is no coincidence that there is so much *theatricality* in the play, most strikingly in the metatheatre of III. i. 111–16 but also in all the literally cloak-and-dagger material, as the conspirators come together and unmuffle to reveal the true figures beneath their outer disguise (reversed so expressively when Caesar muffles his face as he falls (III. ii. 188)). They have their roles to play too.

When we come to Brutus, things are not so different. There too we see a difference between the inner Brutus, a very private person, and the outer role that the pressure of circumstances puts upon him. That is the best way of explaining the familiar problem about the second half of the play, when Brutus seems to hear the news of his wife's death twice, and react very differently on the two occasions. The private, inner Brutus is distraught and devastated; the outer shell, though, must be put on, and when the news comes publicly the response has to be different:

> Why, farewell, Porcia. We must die, Messala,
> With meditating that she must die once,
> I have the patience to endure it now.

> (IV. iii. 188–90)

—itself an echo of similar words that Brutus spoke himself over Caesar's corpse, 'That we shall die, we know . . .' (III. i. 99). Theme and moment are alike coming back in Brutus' own crisis. And here again this can be seen as a development—but a vast one—of a theme already in Plutarch, for in *Caesar* too we have some mirrorings of Caesar in Brutus, but here they are of a very different nature. Caesar's 'eagerness for glory' (*philotimia*) is still as active in his final days as it has been all his life (58.4–5 nn.); now it is the same quality in Brutus that drives him to action (62.4). And it is not just Caesar who is trapped by forces beyond his control, in particular the popular pressure that raised Caesar to power and is now turning against him (above, p. 22). In *Caesar*, more clearly than in *Brutus* itself, the genuine reluctance of

Brutus to be involved is emphasized (62.2 n.), and it is popular opinion that forces him on when 'the ordinary people' turn to him (62.1); they appeal, precisely, to that 'eagerness for glory', *philotimia* (62.8), the quality that is so firmly embedded in Roman political culture (above, p. 60) as well as in the temperaments of both Brutus and Caesar. The pressures of public life are seen differently in the *Life* and the play, but the mirroring effect is not so very different.

Shakespeare's audience does not have to wait for the Philippi campaign for such scenic echoes to be sensed. Brutus has stolen from Portia's bed, and she pleads with him on her knees (ii. i. 234–309, esp. 278: 'Kneel not, gentle Portia'); Caesar, in his night-gown, faces the pleas of the kneeling Calpurnia (ii. ii. 8–56, esp. 54: 'upon my knee'). In each case, the domestic scene shows a wife who can penetrate to an inner uncertainty; in each case, though, the public figure must go forth, and put those uncertainties aside. Slight adaptations of Plutarch again help the point. In Shakespeare it is Caesar who 'is superstitious grown of late' (ii. i. 194), pointing that inner apprehension; in Plutarch it was Calpurnia (63.11 n.). That baring of the neck at the Lupercalia is another significant gesture, preparing in Shakespeare (as it does in Plutarch, 60.6, 66.6–7 nn., and as in Shakespeare the kneeling does too, 66.7 n.) for the real strike upwards at the throat on the Ides; it also, though, recurs in Shakespeare's quarrel scene, when Cassius too, very theatrically, bares his breast and offers a dagger (iv. iii. 99–106), bidding Brutus 'strike, as thou didst at Caesar'. At that point it is a *false* re-enactment of the Ides, just as the gesture at the Lupercalia was a false anticipation, but one which like that will soon give way to the bloodier equivalent, with Cassius dying by the same sword as killed Caesar (v. iii. 45–6 ~ *Caes.* 69.3). The rhythm is reasserting itself, just as it does when Cassius too grows superstitious as the time for battle approaches (v. i. 75–91) or muffles himself as he dies (v. iii. 44), and just as it does when Brutus too calls for his nightgown (iv. iii. 229, 237, 251). And, if the appeal to the gowned Brutus comes not from a loving wife (for she is no more) but from Caesar's ghost, that too reflects that unsettling intimacy and interlinking of Caesar's spirit and his own.

Once again, though, even these adaptations of Plutarch are highly Plutarchan in manner. Plutarch too has a feeling for gesture: he has Decimus Brutus lead Caesar by the hand as he goes to his doom, just as Cinna a few pages later will dream of Caesar leading him, once again by the hand and once again lethally (*Caes.* 64.6, 68.3 nn.). As it happens, Shakespeare did not find room for this, for the action is moving too fast in another direction;[171] but in the technique he would have recognized something of his own.

Caesar

The real-life Caesar was anything but frail. This vigorous man in his mid-fifties was planning to leave for Parthia three days after the Ides, something that Shakespeare knew from Plutarch (58.6) but suppressed; and this, so Plutarch says, was to be only the start of his ambitious plans for world conquest (58.6–7). So where does that bodily frailty of Shakespeare's Caesar come from? It is indeed from Plutarch, but from an unexpected direction. It comes from the time when Caesar failed to rise to his feet when the whole senate was coming to meet him. Later all manners of excuse were found, including the suggestion that he had had an attack of dizziness, perhaps connected with his epilepsy (60.6–7 n.). That last reason is mentioned by Plutarch:

Later he blamed it on his disease, and explained that people in his condition find that their senses do not stay steady when they stand and speak to a large crowd; they quickly blur and become dizzy, and this brings on faintness and loss of consciousness. But on this occasion it was not like that. Indeed, people say that Caesar was very willing to stand up to receive the senators, but was restrained by one of his friends, or rather his flatterers, Cornelius Balbus. 'Remember you are Caesar,' said Balbus. 'You are their superior; you should expect them to show you the proper respect.'

(60.6–8)

So for Plutarch, Caesar *did* want to get to his feet, and was dissuaded by his officious friends who advised him to make a spectacle of his power. So it is the false excuses, especially the dizziness and the epilepsy, that leave an impression of frailty: that is what Shakespeare seizes on—he borrows this incident too to add to that mix of Lupercalia and triumph (I. ii. 244–52)—but he turns it from falsity to truth.[172] Notice too that Shakespeare does not accept the explanation

---

[171] Had Decimus led Caesar off it would have left no room for the 'last supper' with his supposed friends (II. ii. 126–7). But anyway this Caesar, once his public mask is on, is not one to be led: 64.6 n.

[172] Once the frailty has been accepted as a theme, Shakespeare adapted other Plutarchan details: the Tiber swim may well have been inspired by the very different

that Plutarch himself preferred, in terms of the bad advice of Caesar's friends. That ties into what we have seen to be a major theme of the *Caesar* (above, p. 21), and it is an analysis that in a different mood Shakespeare might have welcomed: think of those history plays, where it is the manœuvrings of the great men at the court that eventually explain as much as the best efforts, often extremely well-intentioned efforts, of (say) a Henry VI. Nor, for all the talk in the play of 'flattery', is there much on the difficulties for Caesar that the flatterers caused, generating such envy by their excessive veneration (*Caes.* 57.2–3). Balbus' bad advice is part of that picture, and it is suppressed.

As we saw in Section 2.1, Plutarch is himself analysing the pressures upon Caesar of his rule, his position, and his past, a version of the theme that Shakespeare's own patterning, with those outer shells and inner persons, is exploring too. But Plutarch is exploring it in a very different way, dwelling on the *particular* political factors that were causing Caesar such problems. In the play it is not these pressures themselves that form the interest, it is Caesar's own perception of his position: it is he, not any friend, who proclaims that 'always I am Caesar' (I. ii. 211). He himself defines what being Caesar amounts to: 'Caesar shall go forth' (II. ii. 48: cf. 64.6 n.). It is symptomatic that, when Artemidorus urges him to read the schedule first because it touches Caesar nearer, he replies so grandly that 'What touches us ourself shall be last served' (III. i. 8, 65.3 n.). Plutarch's Caesar had responded very differently, trying as hard as he could to read it, but prevented by the crowd of people 'coming to meet him' (65.3), the physical emblematization of those pressures he faced. Once again, the reality of those pressures absorbs Plutarch; Caesar's perception of his role dominates the play.

And Plutarch, as we have seen, is very interested in where the pressures come from, some from as far back as the Gracchi or even Romulus (Section 2.2), some from Caesar's own past. There is little of that in Shakespeare; even the great soldier of the past is sensed only when the military man Antony speaks, in particular when he recalls the summer evening when Caesar overcame the Nervii (III. ii. 171–3). Shakespeare is more interested in where the events will lead: perhaps,

item at 49.7–8, where Caesar's strong swimming enables him to escape at a dangerous moment in the harbour of Alexandria. But the adaptation has the effect of reversing Plutarch's point.

on a broader view, even to Christianity;[173] certainly to the principate. Hints of the succession come early in the play, with Caesar telling Calpurnia to 'stand . . . directly in Antony's way' and hold out her hand for the leather lash at the fertility ceremony of the Lupercalia (i. ii. 1–9, 61.3 n.);[174] the true heir will be clear by the end of the play. 'Here was a Caesar! When comes such another?' proclaims Antony at the end of the forum scene (iii. ii. 253, cf. the plebeian at iii. ii. 112), and a moment later news arrives that Octavius has arrived in Rome: the stony determination with which Octavius enforces his will to command the right wing (v. i. 16–20: above, p. 67) is a harbinger of the future, and the noble humanity of Antony at the play's end also does something to mark him out as the next victim. There is something of that in *Brutus*, where several hints towards the end of the *Life* suggest what looms for the future;[175] but *Caesar* avoids ending on that note (69.14 n.). Once again, as we saw in Section 1, he shies away from a theme that might still have a contemporary resonance in Trajan's day.

Brutus and Cassius

Different spectators of Shakespeare's play doubtless took different views of the moral issue. What, though, *is* that moral issue? In antiquity it was above all a question of *ingratitude*:[176] can it ever, no matter what the circumstances, be justified to strike down one to whom one owes so much? That was the moral problem Shakespeare found emphasized by Plutarch himself, in *Dion and Brutus* if not in *Caesar* itself:

The biggest charge they lay against Brutus is that he had been saved by Caesar's generosity, had also been allowed to save as many of his fellow-prisoners as he wanted, was thought to be his friend and favoured above many others, and then became the murderer of his saviour.

(*Brut.* 56(3).4)

---

[173] Cf. Pelling, 'Roman Tragedy', 280–1 and esp. D. Kaula, *Shakespeare Studies*, 14 (1981), 197–214, who finds suggestions of anti-papal rhetoric in the play's treatment of Caesar's regality.

[174] Griffin in *CJC* 385–6.

[175] Esp. at *Brut.* 47.7 and 53.2–3, but there may be hints at 50.9 and 51.1 as well: see the notes in my Penguin translation (*Rome in Crisis* (2010)). At *Brut.* 41.7 Heaven seems to be protecting Octavian just as surely as it is opposing Brutus: cf. Pelling, 'Augustus' Autobiography'.

[176] E. Rawson in I. S. Moxon, J. D. Smart, and A. J. Woodman, *Past Perspectives* (1986), 101–19 = *Roman Culture and Society* (1991), 488–507.

Yet there is little of this in Shakespeare. 'Ingratitude' is raised, certainly—but by Antony, in the forum scene (III. ii. 186), and it is part of his skilful and tendentious rhetoric. The play has little on the honours Caesar had paid Brutus (62.3-4 n.), no mention, for instance, of the past bad feeling when Caesar preferred Brutus to Cassius for the urban praetorship, something of which Plutarch had made a great deal (62.4 n., *Brut.* 7.1). Any quarrelling between the two is delayed to the scene at Sardis, and the past relations of the pair are marked only by love (I. ii. 31-5). This, presumably, is also a reason why the possibility is suppressed that Brutus might be Caesar's biological son (*Brut.* 5.2), an idea that Shakespeare himself played with some years earlier ('Brutus' bastard hand | stabbed Julius Caesar' (*2 Henry VI* IV. i. 137-8)). The play is simply not about that sort of clash between personal ties and public good, and it similarly plays down Cassius' past grudges, a theme developed in *Brutus* (8.5-7). Shakespeare does give more of a personal tinge to Cassius' feeling of outrage than to Brutus, but this is in his indignation that Caesar should be so great *when Cassius is not*, that the frail man is the Colossus when he is as nothing. The sense of affront is self-directed, but it is not connected with past honouring or dishonouring. Not, of course, that Cassius and Brutus see things altogether the same way. Shakespeare makes them more different than they were in Plutarch: Plutarch makes Caesar's 'lean and hungry' remark a comment on both Brutus and Cassius (62.10, *Brut.* 8.2, *Ant.* 11.6): Shakespeare makes it refer to Cassius alone (I. ii. 193, cf. 62.10 n.), picking up the one point where Plutarch's Caesar eyes Cassius in particular and comments 'I do not like him; he is too pale' (62.9). But, whatever their differences of temperament in Shakespeare, past honours and favours are not what these differences concern. For both, the issue is the one posed by the monarch and the monarchy itself,[177] for Brutus more a question of what Caesar may become (II. i. 10-34),[178] for

---

[177] That, indeed, is probably what the audience expected of a Roman play: in his outstanding essay on 'Shakespeare and the Elizabethan Romans', T. J. B. Spencer emphasized that 'the moral purpose of history in general, and of Roman history in particular, was directed towards *monarchs*' (*Shakespeare Survey*, 10 (1957), 27-38 at 30; emphasis in original). Spencer goes on to demonstrate that there was no single, dominant view on the rights and wrongs of the assassination (33-4). Cf. Griffin in *CJC*, esp. 380-1, 391.

[178] More on this in Pelling, 'Judging Julius Caesar', 3-5.

Cassius one of what Caesar is already. The issue is one of regicide, not of ingratitude.

Other displacements of Plutarchan material are here telling. One idea that clearly had to go was any suggestion that Cassius might have been aiming for tyranny himself (*Brut.* 29.5). Brutus is allowed a striking image to express his horror at the notion of living under a king:

> Brutus had rather be a villager
> Than to repute himself a son of Rome
> Under these hard conditions as this time
> Is like to lay upon us.

(I. ii. 171–4)

That too is Plutarchan in origin, but drawn paradoxically from the thinking of Caesar himself: that remark of his as a young man that he 'should prefer to be first man here' in an obscure Alpine village 'than second in Rome' (11.4 n.). And it is this villager determination that Shakespeare finds in Brutus that will ultimately thwart those first-man ambitions that Plutarch saw in Caesar.

So for Shakespeare the issue is the general one of the justifiability of rebellion: the affront to free persons, whatever their past experience, of having a fellow-human—any fellow-human—who is so powerful; that is where the contrast comes in between the weak, frail old man and the 'Caesar', the position and the idea as much as the person. The more frail the ruler, the sharper the contrast. It is the dramatist's way of presenting the moral question with the clarity of extremes.[179]

Nor is it hard to relate this to 1599, the date of the play, and a government already nervous of the Earl of Essex two years before his open rebellion against the ageing Elizabeth; nor to see this as part of the lively contemporary debate on Republicanism.[180] If we were in

---

[179] Just as the lawyer Edmund Plowden phrased it in extremes when writing in 1578: 'The king has in him two bodies, viz. a body natural, and a body politic. His body natural (if it be considered in itself) is a body mortal, subject to all infirmities that come by nature or accident, to the imbecility of infancy or old age, and to the like defects that happen to the natural bodies of other people. But his body politic . . . is utterly void of infancy, and old age, and other natural defects and imbecilities which the body natural is subject to, and for this cause, what the king does in his body politic cannot be invalidated or frustrated by any disability in his natural body' (quoted by R. H. Wells, *Shakespeare, Politics, and the State* (1996), 104–5).

[180] On the contemporary relevance, cf. J. Shapiro, *1599: A Year in the Life of William Shakespeare* (2005), esp. chs. 7–8, who stresses other themes as well: demagogic methods ('popularity', in the language of the day), the political manipulation of

danger of missing the point, there are other hints of Elizabeth too: for instance, the words of Porcia: 'I have a man's mind, but a woman's might' (II. iv. 8). We inevitably think of Tilbury and Elizabeth's speech just eleven years earlier—'I know I have the body of a weak, feeble woman; but I have the heart and stomach of a king . . .'. Would not the original audience think of Elizabeth too? And that contrast—bodily weakness, but the heart and stomach of a king—is very much the one that Shakespeare articulates in *Julius Caesar*.

Shakespeare does this sort of thing all the time. In *Coriolanus* he gives the differences over grain even more prominence than Plutarch had done, at a time when the Midlands suffered from a series of bad harvests and famines.[181] In *Antony and Cleopatra* the extraordinariness of the power of a woman, dominating so much of the world, would have its contemporary ring as well, even now that Elizabeth herself was dead: that legendary Victorian response to Lillie Langtry's Cleopatra—'how very different from the home life of our own dear Queen'—is not perhaps so off-key after all, even if the original 'dear Queen' with which an audience might draw comparisons was Elizabeth rather than Victoria.

That, however, suggests the final point about Plutarch, and takes us back to the first section of this Introduction: for it is striking how little Plutarch does himself along such lines. When a contemporary theme beckons, Plutarch turns his head away. This too is something to do with his moralism, and the way he preferred the bigger, more timeless themes rather than those narrowed down in place and time; he aligns with Greek tragedy, concerned as it is to make points about the nature of democracy or of war, rather than comedy, with its sharper points about the deficiencies of Cleon or the rights and wrongs of the Peloponnesian War. For Plutarch, Caesar mattered because of the thoughts he might provoke about tyranny, about the pressures of ruling, about the life choice that the man made; and those are points for all time, not just for Trajan's Rome. That was indeed why Shakespeare could give them particular twists that made them particularly relevant for the world of late Elizabeth I; and, if we so choose, we can find them thought-provoking still.

---

the calendar and its holidays, and—less plausibly—the rights and wrongs of censorship in the Cinna-scene of Act III, scene iii, and the untimely intrusion of the poet at IV. iii. 123-36.

[181] See esp. D. George, *Shakespeare Survey*, 53 (2000), 6-72; more on this in *Plutarch and History*, 254 and 389-90.

Translation

[**Fragment.**] Some think he was called Caesar because his mother died as he was being born, and he was 'cut out' of her womb into the light of day. But that is not true: his mother was alive even after Caesar had grown to manhood, as the accounts of his life make clear. It was not this Caesar who was 'cut out' at birth, but one of his ancestors, and that was the origin of the family name.

1.... Caesar had married Cornelia, daughter of the Cinna who had once been monarch. Then Sulla won control, but he could not entice or intimidate Caesar into divorcing her, so finally he confiscated her dowry. (2) This bad feeling between Caesar and Sulla went back to his connection with Marius, for the elder Marius was married to Caesar's aunt Julia, and the younger Marius was their son and Caesar's cousin.

(3) At first Caesar was overlooked by Sulla amid all the killings and the pressure of affairs. But that was not enough for Caesar, who came before the public as a candidate for a priesthood, though still a very young man. Sulla discreetly opposed this, and made sure that he failed. (4) Then he thought about killing him. Some argued that it was senseless to kill a boy of his age: Sulla replied that they were the senseless ones, if they could not see there was many a Marius inside this 'boy'. (5) The remark was relayed to Caesar, and he spent a long time moving from place to place in Sabine country and staying out of sight. (6) Then one night he was travelling from one house to another, carried in a litter because he was sick. He fell into the hands of some of Sulla's soldiers who were searching the district and capturing those in hiding. (7) Their leader was a man called Cornelius, and Caesar managed to bribe him with two talents to let him go; then he immediately fled to the sea, and sailed off to Bithynia and the court of King Nicomedes. (8) He did not stay there long, but on the return voyage he was captured near the island of Pharmacusa by pirates,

who were at that time already masters of the sea with their large fleets
and their countless smaller ships.

2. First they asked him for a ransom of twenty talents. He laughed:
'you don't know who it is you've captured,' he said, and promised
them fifty instead. (2) Then he sent his companions around to the
various cities to collect the money. While they were away he was left
on his own among these Cilicians, the most bloodthirsty people in the
world, with just one friend and two attendants; yet he was so contemptuous of them that, whenever he went to bed, he would send
someone to tell them to keep quiet. (3) Thirty-eight days passed, and
it was as if they were his bodyguards rather than his captors. He
played games with them and shared their exercises, without a hint of
fear; (4) he wrote poems and speeches and tried them out on this
audience, and if any of them were unappreciative he called them total
illiterates and barbarians. 'I'll see you hanged,' he would often say
with a laugh. They were most amused by what they took to be his
rather simple sense of humour. (5) Then the ransom arrived from
Miletus, and he handed it over and was released. He immediately
manned some ships and set sail from the harbour of Miletus against
the pirates, and found them still waiting in ambush near the island.
(6) He captured most of them, took the money as a prize for himself,
then left the men in gaol at Pergamum while he went to Iuncus,
who was governor of Asia and as governor should have had the
responsibility of punishing the prisoners. (7) Iuncus eyed the
money greedily—it was a sizable sum—and said that he would consider the prisoners' case at his leisure. Caesar decided to ignore him.
He returned to Pergamum, where he took out all the prisoners and
crucified them. He had often promised them that on the island, and
they had thought he was joking.

3. Soon Sulla's power began to decline, and Caesar's friends at
home encouraged him to return. He sailed to Rhodes to study with
Apollonius son of Molon, a distinguished rhetorician, who also had
the reputation of being an admirable person. Cicero too attended his
lectures.

(2) Caesar, they say, had a remarkable gift for political oratory, and
he trained and developed this talent with a great eagerness for glory.
The second place was unquestionably his, (3) but he allowed the first
to escape him: his attention was devoted to becoming first in power
and in armed strength. His campaigns and his politics won him
dominion in the state, but robbed him of that first prize in eloquence

for which he was naturally fitted. (4) Later, in his reply to Cicero's essay on Cato, he himself begged his readers not to compare his style with Cicero's: he was the military man, Cicero the accomplished orator, with natural talent and the time to cultivate it.

4. On his return to Rome he prosecuted Dolabella for maladministration, and many of the Greek cities provided him with evidence. (2) Dolabella was acquitted, but Caesar repaid Greece for its enthusiasm by supporting the nation when it prosecuted Publius Antonius for corruption. The case was heard by Marcus Lucullus, governor of Macedonia. (3) Caesar was so effective that Antonius appealed to the tribunes, claiming that he could not have a fair trial when contending against Greeks in Greece.

(4) In Rome Caesar's support grew. That was partly due to his rhetorical gifts and the goodwill he won by his advocacy; but the ordinary people were very enthusiastic too, won over by the charm with which he greeted people and talked to them, for his talent for winning popularity belied his years. (5) Other factors too ensured that his political power slowly grew, the dinners he gave, the generosity of his table, the general glamour of his style. (6) Some were envious, but at first they thought that his funds would run out and that would be the end of his power, and so they let that power increase among the people. (7) Then it became too great to overthrow and marched on inexorably to revolution, and they realized the moral too late: that no beginnings should ever be thought so small that persistence cannot raise them to greatness, if they remain neglected and therefore unchecked. (8) The first suspicions of Caesar were felt by Cicero, who feared the smiling surface of his political style like that of the sea, and who sensed the formidable personality beneath the generous and amiable exterior. He remarked that he could see the tyrannical ambition in all Caesar's other plans and political ploys; (9) 'but when', he added, 'I see that exaggerated hairstyle, and the way he parts it with a single finger, I cannot bring myself to believe that this man would ever conceive anything so dreadful as the overthrow of the Roman constitution'. But that was later.

5. The first indication of the people's enthusiasm came when he and Gaius Popillius were rivals for a military tribunate, and Caesar was elected first. (2) The next was even clearer, and it followed the death of Marius' widow Julia. Caesar was her nephew, and he delivered a brilliant eulogy in the forum, then had the audacity to display images of the Marii at her funeral. This was the first time these had

been seen since the time of Sulla, when the men had been voted public
enemies. (3) Some criticized Caesar fiercely, but the people shouted
them down, greeting the sight with brilliant enthusiasm and applause.
They were delighted and surprised at the man who had brought back
Marius' honours as if from the dead, when they had been absent from
the city for so long.

(4) This practice of funeral speeches for elderly women was a
Roman tradition, but Caesar was the first to extend this to younger
women, giving a speech for his own wife when she died. (5) This too
brought him goodwill. Together with his grief, it was most effective in
winning the favour of the ordinary people, who admired him as
a man of tender and sensitive feeling. (6) After his wife's funeral he
went out to Spain, serving as quaestor to one of the praetors called
Vetus. Caesar always showed respect for Vetus himself, and, when he
was ruler himself, he made Vetus' son quaestor in his turn. (7) When
he had completed this office, he took Pompeia as his third wife;
Cornelia had left him with a daughter, the later bride of Pompey
the Great.

(8) And the spending went on, with no restraint. People thought he
was paying a fortune for some brief and fleeting acclaim; in fact he
was buying the greatest thing of all, and it was cheap. Before he held
any office it is said that his indebtedness amounted to 1,300 talents.
(9) Then he was put in charge of the Appian Way, and he contributed
immense sums from his own pocket; as aedile he gave a display of 320
pairs of gladiators. There was also his lavish spending on public
displays—the theatrical performances, the processions, the banquets.
It was enough to wash away anything the ambitions of his predecessors
sors had achieved. And its impact on the people was so great that
everyone sought new offices and new honours to repay him.

6. There were two factions in Rome, the one dominant since
Sulla, the other the 'Marians'. This one was now in a very lowly
state, cowering in humiliation and totally fragmented. Caesar decided
to revive it and win it for his own. Those aedileship displays were
reaching their climax, and he had portraits of Marius made in secret,
along with statues of Victory carrying trophies. He took these to the
Capitol by night and set them up. (2) At dawn they could be seen
glittering with gold and beautifully crafted, with inscriptions recording the Cimbrian successes, and bystanders were amazed at the
audacity of the man who had set them up. Nor was it hard to guess
who had done it. Word spread quickly, and everyone gathered to see

the sight. (3) There were some who cried out that Caesar was aiming for tyranny: here he was, restoring honours that had been buried by law and official decree; this was an experiment on the people, and he was eager to see whether his ambitious enterprises had softened them to such submissiveness that they would allow him to play the revolutionary in this tomfool way. (4) But the Marians turned to one another in mutual encouragement. It was extraordinary how many they suddenly showed themselves to be; they noisily took over the Capitol, (5) and the sight of Marius' face even made tears of joy come to many of them. They praised Caesar to the skies, the one man (they said) worthy to be Marius' kinsman.

(6) The senate gathered to discuss it. Lutatius Catulus, the most respected Roman of the day, stood up and denounced Caesar, and this was when he made that celebrated remark, 'you are no longer undermining the state, Caesar; you are assailing it with your siege engines'. (7) But Caesar spoke in his own defence, and it was he who carried the senate. That encouraged his admirers even more, and they urged him not to bow to anybody. He had the people's support; with it he would conquer everyone, and win the highest place of all.

7. Now Metellus died, the pontifex maximus. This priesthood was a tempting prize, and Isauricus and Catulus stood for it, both highly distinguished men, and both with great influence in the senate. But Caesar would not be put off. He went down to the people, and announced that he would stand too. (2) The contest turned out to be fierce, and it was very close indeed. Catulus was the more distinguished man, and this made him the more nervous about the uncertainty: he sent to offer Caesar a vast sum of money to abandon his ambitious campaign. Caesar replied that he would borrow even more, and fight it to the end. (3) The day of the election came, and Caesar's mother was tearfully seeing him off from the house. He embraced her, and said: 'today, mother, you will see your son either a high-priest or an exile'. (4) Then the votes were cast. It was a close struggle, but Caesar won. The senate and the best people were terrified. He would encourage the ordinary people to be reckless and aggressive: where would it end?

(5) That was why Piso and Catulus and their followers criticized Cicero for letting Caesar off the hook during the Catiline affair. (6) Catiline had planned not merely constitutional reform, but the total devastation of the empire: utter chaos was his aim. Catiline himself had left Rome, trapped by lesser charges before his final

plans were revealed, but he had left Lentulus and Cethegus in the city to take over the conspiracy. (7) Perhaps Caesar gave them some secret encouragement and help—that is unclear. But he certainly played a role when they had been decisively exposed in the senate. Cicero as consul was asking each senator for his opinion on the question of punishment. Everyone before Caesar had proposed the death penalty, (8) but then Caesar rose and delivered a most thoughtful speech. His argument was that it was untraditional and unjust to execute without trial men of such birth and such distinction, if there was any alternative at all. (9) It would be better to take them to Italian cities of Cicero's own choice, and keep them under guard for the duration of the war; once Catiline had been crushed, the senate could take its time and deliberate peacefully about each of the accused.

8. The proposal struck the senate as humane, and it was a very powerful speech. Those who rose after Caesar supported him, and also many of the previous speakers said they were changing their votes and taking Caesar's view. Then it came around to the turn of Cato and Catulus. (2) They opposed him vehemently; Cato even insinuated that Caesar was himself involved, and confronted him most vigorously. The men were handed over for execution. Then Caesar himself was attacked as he was leaving the senate, for at the time a group of young men were serving as Cicero's bodyguard, and many of these set upon Caesar with drawn swords. (3) They say that Curio threw his toga around him and bundled him away, and Cicero too shook his head when the young men looked towards him: perhaps he was afraid of the people; perhaps he simply thought that such a murder was wholly illegal and unjust. (4) But, if this story is true, I cannot understand why Cicero did not mention it in his account of his consulship. He was certainly accused later of missing an ideal opportunity of foiling Caesar because of his terror of the ordinary people. And they were indeed most enthusiastic for Caesar: (5) they showed that a few days later, when Caesar had gone into the senate and was defending himself against the insinuations of complicity. His opponents heckled him loudly, and the senate-sitting was lasting longer than normal: so the people marched noisily on the senate house and surrounded it, shouting for Caesar and insisting that he should be allowed to leave.

(6) That impressed Cato. He was particularly afraid that the poor might start a revolution: they were the spark that could set the populace alight, and all their hopes rested with Caesar. So Cato

persuaded the senate to give the poor a monthly allowance of corn. (7) This added 7,500,000 drachmas a year to the state's expenditure, but it was clearly most effective in damping down the immense immediate danger. It also broke up and dispersed most of Caesar's power, and that was most timely, for he was about to be praetor, and the office made him even more formidable.

9. Still, nothing violent came of it. Caesar was involved in some domestic unpleasantness instead. (2) Publius Clodius was a noble, wealthy and articulate, and a man who outdid the most notorious of scoundrels in his arrogance and reckless aggression. (3) He was in love with Caesar's wife Pompeia, and she was herself not unreceptive. But the women's quarters were closely guarded, and Caesar's mother Aurelia was in constant attendance on his young wife. Aurelia was a most virtuous and respectable woman, and the meetings of Pompeia and Clodius were always most difficult and hazardous.

(4) The Romans have a goddess whom they call 'the Good Goddess'. She is like the Greek 'Women's Goddess', and the Phrygians claim her for their own as the mother of King Midas; the Romans think she was a Dryad nymph and the wife of Faunus; the Greeks regard her as one of the mothers of Dionysus, the one it is forbidden to name. (5) That is the origin of the custom of covering the tents with vine branches during the festival, and a sacred snake sits by the goddess, just as the myth says. (6) No man is allowed to come to the festival, nor even to be in the same house when the rites are celebrated. Instead the women are left by themselves, and it is said that many of their rites are similar to Orphic ritual. (7) So, when the day arrives, the festival is celebrated in the house of a consul or a praetor, but the master himself leaves along with all the other males, while his wife takes over the house and arranges everything. The most important rites take place after dark, and this night-time festival also has an element of revelry and fun, with a good deal of musical accompaniment.

10. Pompeia was now presiding over this festival. Clodius was still beardless, and this encouraged him to think that he might remain unnoticed: so he dressed himself as a lute-girl and took up the tools of her trade. (2) He was indeed quite like a young woman in appearance. When he arrived, he found the doors open. A servant girl let him in, and so far he had nothing to fear: the girl was in on the scheme, and she ran on ahead to tell Pompeia. But time passed, and Clodius was too nervous to stay where he had been left; instead he wandered

around the large house, trying to stay in the shadows. Then a maid of Aurelia came up. 'Come on,' she said, 'join in the fun'—it was very much one woman talking to another. Clodius demurred, and she pulled him out from the shadows: 'who are you?' she asked; 'where do you come from?' (3) 'I'm waiting for Habra, Pompeia's servant girl', Clodius replied—and Habra was indeed the servant's name. But his voice gave him away, and Aurelia's maid immediately gave a shriek and ran off to the lights and the crowd. 'I've found a man here,' she cried. The women were most agitated, and Aurelia immediately put a stop to the ceremony and concealed the sacred objects; she also gave instructions for the doors to be shut, while she searched the house with torches, looking for Clodius. (4) He was found hiding in the bedroom of the servant girl who had let him in; the women saw who it was, and drove him out through the doors. (5) The affair soon became known, for that very night the women went away and told their husbands, and the next morning it was the talk of the town. Clodius had committed sacrilege, they said, and he owed retribution not merely to the victims of his outrage, but to the gods and the city as well.

(6) So one of the tribunes indicted Clodius for impiety, and this soon gained the backing of the most powerful men in the senate. There were plenty of extraordinary outrages of Clodius to point to, including incest with his sister, the wife of Lucullus. (7) But the people equally took sides in Clodius' support, and that was very useful to him with the jurors, who were quite terrified of the mob. (8) As for Caesar, he immediately divorced Pompeia, but when he was called as witness he said that he had no knowledge that any of the charges were true. (9) That seemed paradoxical. 'In that case, why did you divorce your wife?' the prosecutor asked. 'Because I thought my wife should be beyond suspicion,' Caesar replied. (10) Some say that Caesar was being sincere, while others think that he was playing to the people, eager as they were to save Clodius. (11) So Clodius was acquitted, with most of the jurors spoiling the letters on their votes. They did not want to convict, for that would mean taking risks with the people; but they did not want an acquittal either, for that would lose them the respect of the nobility.

11. Straight after his praetorship Caesar took Spain as his province. But his creditors were most intractable: they came clamouring around and obstructed his departure. So he took refuge with Crassus, the richest man in Rome, who himself needed Caesar's vitality and fire for

his political activity against Pompey. (2) Crassus took over those creditors who were fiercest and most uncompromising, and went surety for 830 talents. That allowed Caesar to leave for his province.

(3) There is a story told of his journey across the Alps. He came to a tiny barbarian village, with just a handful of wretched people living there. Caesar's companions started to laugh and joke: 'do you think that here too there are rivalries for office, and struggles for top place, and jealousies of one mighty man against another?' (4) Caesar replied in all seriousness: 'I should prefer to be first man here than second in Rome.' (5) And there is another story too, relating to his time in Spain. He had some time to himself, and was reading a book about Alexander. He fell quiet for a long time, then he began to weep. (6) His friends did not know what to make of this, and asked him why. 'Don't you agree that it is a matter for tears?' he said. 'When Alexander was my age, he was already master of so many nations— and I have not yet done anything distinguished at all.'

12. But he was certainly active as soon as he set foot in Spain. Within a few days he had raised ten cohorts to add to the twenty that were waiting for him, then he marched on the Callaici and the Lusitani, beat them, and went on to the Ocean at the end of the earth, conquering new peoples and subjecting them to Rome. (2) And he was as masterful in his peacetime administration as on campaign, bringing harmony to the cities, and in particular healing the differences between creditors and debtors. (3) He decreed that two-thirds of a debtor's income should pass to the creditor each year, but the owner of the property should retain the rest, until the debt was paid off. (4) This brought him acclaim as he left his province. He had become rich himself, and he had also made sure that his men benefited from the campaigns; and they had responded by saluting him as 'Imperator'.

13. On his return to Rome he was faced with a legal dilemma. Those requesting a triumph had to remain outside the walls, but those who sought the consulship had to do this within the city itself; and the time of the election was very near. Caesar sent to the senate to ask for permission to stand for the consulship in absence, with his friends canvassing on his behalf. (2) At first Cato relied on the letter of the law in opposing Caesar's petition; then, when he saw that many senators had been won over by Caesar's attentions, he turned to filibustering, and talked out the proposal by speaking until sunset. Caesar decided to abandon the triumph and try for the consulship.

(3) And as soon as he arrived in the city he adopted a stratagem that fooled everyone except Cato. This was the reconciliation of Pompey and Crassus, the two most powerful men in Rome. (4) Caesar persuaded them to put their differences aside and become friends, and thus he concentrated both of their strengths in his own support. It seemed an altruistic policy, when in fact it was concealed revolution. (5) For it was not, as most people think, the rift of Caesar and Pompey that brought about the civil wars, it was rather their friendship: first they linked to destroy the aristocracy, and it was only after this had been achieved that they quarrelled. (6) Cato often gave dark prophecies of what would come, and at the time all he won was a reputation as an ungenerous troublemaker; it was only later that people applauded him for his sagacious and ill-starred advice.

14. Anyway, the friendship of Crassus and Pompey made them virtually Caesar's bodyguards, and they escorted him to the consulship. (2) He won a brilliant success, and was elected along with Calpurnius Bibulus. Then as soon as he entered office he started introducing laws that would have been more fitting for the most reckless of tribunes than for a consul, some colonies to please the masses, and also some distributions of land. (3) In the senate he met with opposition from the respectable group. That was the excuse he had long been looking for, and he responded with a solemn cry. It was not by his own choice, he swore, that he was driven to the people; now he would court them, but it was the arrogance and inflexibility of the senate that were to blame. With those words he leapt out to the people. (4) He stood before them with Crassus on one side and Pompey on the other, and asked them if they approved of the laws. They said they did. Caesar then called on them to help against those who threatened to oppose him with their swords, (5) and they promised they would; Pompey even added that his opponents might have their swords, but he would face them with both sword and shield. (6) That upset the aristocrats; and indeed Pompey's sense of personal dignity, as well as the respect owed to the senate, should have stopped him from making so lunatic and juvenile a remark. But the people loved it.

(7) Caesar now clutched even more at Pompey's power. He had a daughter, Julia, who was betrothed to Servilius Caepio. Caesar now promised her to Pompey, and told Servilius he could have Pompey's daughter instead. (She too had a commitment, for she had been promised to Faustus, Sulla's son.) (8) A little later Caesar married

Calpurnia, daughter of Piso, and designated Piso himself consul for the coming year. That was when Cato spoke with particular earnestness: it was intolerable, he shouted out; the men were the pimps and marriage-brokers of empire, they were giving one another provinces, armies, and massive forces—and using females to do it.

(9) Caesar's colleague Bibulus tried to prevent the laws, but achieved nothing. Indeed, he was often in danger of being killed in the forum, and so was Cato. Finally Bibulus shut himself up at his home, and spent the rest of his term of office there. (10) Pompey celebrated his marriage by immediately filling the forum with arms to help the people pass the laws; these gave Caesar both Cisalpine and Transalpine Gaul, along with Illyricum and four legions, and he was to hold the province for five years. (11) Cato tried to speak against the bill, but Caesar hauled him off to prison, thinking that he would call on the tribunes to intercede; but Cato simply walked in silence. (12) Caesar saw that this had offended not merely the men of power and influence: even the ordinary people were following silent and downcast, for they respected Cato's virtue. So Caesar himself quietly asked one of the tribunes to release him.

(13) As for the other members of the senate, very few came to its meetings; the rest marked their displeasure by staying away. (14) But there was one very old senator called Considius, who told Caesar that it was the senators' fear of arms and soldiers that was keeping them away. 'Then why aren't you afraid as well?' asked Caesar; 'why don't you too stay at home?' (15) 'My years take away my fear,' Considius replied. 'I have little life to come, and it is not worth much concern.'

(16) The most shameful measure of all during Caesar's consulship was the election of Clodius as tribune, the man who had treated him so outrageously in the affair of his wife and the secret ceremonies. (17) He was elected to destroy Cicero, and Caesar did not leave for his campaign until he had helped Clodius to crush Cicero and force him out of Italy.

15. That is the end of Caesar's story before the Gallic Wars. (2) The period that followed—that of the wars he fought, and the campaigns by which he tamed the land of the Celts—marks a new start, and it is as if he had begun a new way of life, a new path of achievement. He showed himself as good a warrior and commander as any of history's greatest and most respected generals. (3) One can compare Fabii and Scipios and Metelli; or Caesar's own contemporaries and immediate predecessors, Sulla, Marius, and both Luculli; or even Pompey

himself, whose glory at the time blossomed through the whole firmament for every sort of military virtue. (4) Caesar's achievements outdo them all. Some he excelled in the difficulty of the terrain over which he fought; others in the extent of territory he acquired; others in the numbers and formidable qualities of the antagonists he defeated; others in the bizarre and faithless characters of the peoples he brought over to Rome; others in his mildness and clemency to prisoners; others in the gifts and favours he bestowed on the soldiers who shared his campaigns; (5) and every one of them in the vast number of battles he fought and enemy he killed. The campaigns in Gaul lasted for less than ten years, and in that time he took over eight hundred cities by force of arms; he conquered three hundred nations, he faced a total of three million enemy in successive battles, and he killed one million of these in action and took the same number again as prisoners.

16. He inspired his soldiers with a quite remarkable enthusiasm and devotion. In their other campaigns they were no better than anyone else, but they were invincible and irresistible and ready to face any peril, now they were fighting for Caesar's glory. (2) One example was Acilius. In the sea battle off Massilia he boarded an enemy ship, then had his right hand chopped off by a sword; but with his other hand he held tight to his shield, and kept thrusting it into the faces of the enemy until he forced them all back and took the ship. (3) Another was Cassius Scaeva. At the battle of Dyrrhachium he had one eye shot out by an arrow, his shoulder was transfixed by one javelin and his thigh by another, and 130 missiles had landed on his shield. He called the enemy to come to him, as if he was going to surrender. (4) Two men came up: he cut one man's arm off with his sword, and struck the other in the face and forced him away. He himself got away safely, as his comrades gathered round to protect him. (5) Again, in Britain the leading centurions once fell by mistake into a watery swamp, and the enemy launched an attack. One soldier, under full view of Caesar himself, forced his way into the middle of the enemy and performed many brilliant exploits of gallantry and valour, and saved the centurions as the enemy fled. (6) The man himself was the last of all to struggle across, and hurled himself into the muddy streams; finally, by a mix of swimming and wading, he just managed to get back across without his shield. (7) Caesar and his companions were full of admiration, and they greeted him with cries of delight. But the man himself came before Caesar with downcast

eyes and in floods of tears, begging for forgiveness for losing his shield. (8) In Libya Scipio's men once took a ship of Caesar, with the quaestor-elect Granius Petro on board. They regarded all the others as spoils of war, but said they granted the quaestor his life. (9) His reply was that Caesar's men were accustomed to grant mercy, not to receive it, and he thrust his sword into his body and killed himself.

17. That was what his men were like, full of spirit and eagerness for glory, and Caesar himself cultivated those qualities and made them even more effective. First, he was unsparing in the favours he granted his men and the respect he showed for them; he made it clear that he was not collecting riches from the enemy for his own comfort or pleasure, but storing up prizes for valour that were open to anyone, and taking no more of the wealth than he was willing to give to any deserving soldier. Secondly, he was ready to face any sort of personal danger, and never shirked any sort of work. (2) They were less impressed by his readiness to take risks because they knew of his eagerness for glory. But they were highly impressed by his resilience, which they found remarkable in one of his physique. For he was a thin man, and his skin looked white and soft; he suffered from headaches, and was prone to epileptic fits. They say that he suffered the first of these while he was at Cordoba. (3) But he never made his physical weakness an excuse for slacking, preferring to use campaigning as a way to strengthen his physique: his way of fighting against his illness and keeping his body fit was a prescription of long marches, strict personal regime, nights in the open air, and constant hard work. (4) For example, he took most of his sleep while travelling in his litters or carriages; even his hours of rest had to be used in the service of action. Then at daybreak he would drive to the garrisons and cities and camps; at his side would sit one slave boy, trained to take dictation while Caesar was driving, and behind him would stand a single soldier with a drawn sword. (5) In this way he made such good speed that when he first left Rome he reached the Rhône in only seven days.

(6) He had found riding easy since he was a boy: he had trained himself, for instance, to pull back his arms and link them behind his back, then spur his horse to the gallop. (7) On this campaign he also developed the ability to dictate letters while riding, and he could keep two secretaries busy at once—perhaps even more, as Oppius claims. (8) It is also said that Caesar was the first to introduce the habit of

conducting conversations with his friends by letters, for he did not have time to see them personally on matters that required an urgent decision: the pressure of business was simply too great, and the city too large.

(9) As for his personal lifestyle, there is another example quoted of his lack of pretension. Once his host Valerius Leo was entertaining him in Mediolanum, and served perfumed oil instead of olive oil with the asparagus. Caesar ate contentedly, and when his friends protested he gave them a rebuke: (10) 'you could always leave what you did not like, and the person who complains at this sort of bad manners is just as bad-mannered himself.' (11) Again, he was once on a journey, and forced by a sudden storm to take shelter in the cottage of a poor man. There was only one room, barely large enough for a single person. When Caesar saw this, he said to his friends that honours should go to the strongest but necessities to the weakest, and told Oppius to take the bed, while he himself slept with the others in the porch.

18. The first of his Gallic Wars was against the Helvetii and Tigurini. These tribes had burnt their twelve cities and four hundred villages, and now they were moving forward through the part of Gaul that was subject to Rome. It was just like the Cimbri and Teutones of old: these peoples now appeared to be just as daring, and the numbers were about the same—300,000 in all, including 190,000 combatants. (2) The Tigurini were crushed at the River Saône, not by Caesar himself but by Labienus, whom Caesar had sent against them. Then the Helvetii fell upon Caesar unexpectedly while he was on the road, leading his army to some friendly city. Caesar moved quickly, and managed to make his way to a strong position, where he collected his forces and drew them up for battle. (3) When a horse was brought to him, 'I shall use that later,' he said, 'for the pursuit, when I have won. For the moment, let us attack the enemy.' With those words he plunged into them on foot. (4) It was a hard fight, but he eventually forced the enemy army back; but then he found even more trouble at their wagons and fortifications, for there it was not merely the men themselves who rallied and fought, it was the women and children too. They did their best to defend themselves and fought to the death, till finally they were cut down along with the men. The battle was barely finished by midnight.

(5) It was a fine victory, but even better was what followed. He resettled those barbarians who had fled from the battle, forcing them to return to the land they had left and the cities they had destroyed.

Their numbers were more than 100,000. (6) Caesar did this because he was afraid that the Germans might cross to the land if it were left deserted, and take it over themselves.

19. The second war was fought directly against the Germans themselves, and Caesar was here acting in the Gauls' interest. It was true that previously, in Rome, he had made the German king Ariovistus an ally; (2) but the Germans were intolerable neighbours to the peoples under Caesar's control, and there was little doubt that they would grasp the first opportunity to move into action, sweeping over Gaul and occupying it. (3) Caesar could see that his captains were afraid, especially those young nobles who were accompanying him. Their idea had been to use Caesar's campaign as an excuse for a money-making pleasure trip. Now he called an assembly and told them to go away rather than face unwanted dangers, if they were so feeble and cowardly. (4) He would take the tenth legion alone and march on the barbarians: after all, he was not going to fight any enemy more formidable than the Cimbri, and he himself was no less a general than Marius. (5) The tenth legion responded by sending a deputation to thank Caesar, while everyone else poured abuse on their captains—but they were certainly filled with eagerness for the fight, marching for many days until they pitched camp within 200 stades of the enemy.

(6) Their very arrival did something to break Ariovistus' nerve. (7) Here were Romans attacking Germans—and he had thought that it would be the other way round, indeed that the Romans would not even stand their ground. He was taken aback by Caesar's boldness, and he saw that his army was shaken too. (8) Their resolve was further weakened by the prophecies of the holy women, who examined the eddies of rivers and streams and whirlpools and listened to the noises they made, and were telling Ariovistus not to fight before the new moon. (9) Word of this reached Caesar, and he saw that the Germans were making no move. This persuaded him that it was better to attack now, when the Germans were reluctant to fight, than to sit waiting for the moment that suited them. (10) So he launched several attacks on the fortifications and the hills where they were encamped, and he provoked them into coming down to the plain and fighting it out in a rage. (11) The Romans routed them brilliantly, and Caesar pursued them all the way to the Rhine, a full 400 stades. The whole plain was full of spoils and corpses. (12) Ariovistus got away with just a few companions and crossed the Rhine. The dead, they say, numbered 80,000.

20. After this success he left his army to winter among the Sequani, while he himself came back to Cisalpine Gaul, which had been included in his province: the Cisalpina is divided from the rest of Italy by the river they call the Rubicon. From here he could keep an eye on developments in Rome, (2) and he used it as a base for his demagogy. He had many visitors, and he gave all of them what they wanted. None went away unsatisfied; some things they were given now, others they were promised for the future. (3) And the same was true of the other years of the campaign. Caesar was playing Gauls and citizens against one another, though Pompey did not realize it. Part of the time he was using citizen arms to conquer Gauls, and the rest he was using Gallic wealth to capture and subdue the citizens.

(4) Then he heard that the Belgae had revolted. These were the most powerful Celtic tribe, occupying a third of the whole country, and they had gathered a vast force of armed men. (5) So he turned back and moved on them with great speed, and fell on the enemy as they were plundering his Gallic allies. The strongest and most concentrated Belgic force put up a poor show, and Caesar routed them completely. Lakes and deep rivers became fordable to the Romans, choked as they were with corpses. (6) Among the other rebels, the coastal tribes all submitted without a fight; then Caesar marched on the Nervii, who were the fiercest and most warlike tribe of the region. (7) These were a people who lived in thick woods, and they now hid their families and possessions deep in the forest, far away from the Romans. Then a force of 60,000 men fell on Caesar as he was building a rampart around his camp. He was not expecting an immediate attack, and was taken by surprise. They routed the Roman cavalry, then surrounded the twelfth and seventh legions, killing all their centurions. (8) Only one thing saved the Romans from complete massacre, and that was Caesar himself, who grabbed his shield, forced his way through the men fighting in front of him, and hurled himself into the enemy: the tenth legion saw that he was in danger, charged down from the surrounding hills, and cut its way through the enemy ranks. (9) So Caesar's daring brought them what people call an impossible victory. Even so they could not turn the Nervii to flight. They had to cut them down as they continued the battle. (10) Only 500 are said to have survived of 60,000 Nervii, and only 3 of their senators out of 400.

21. When the Roman senate heard the news, it voted a thanksgiving festival of fifteen days, more than had been decreed for any previous victory. (2) That was a mark of the immense danger, with so many tribes bursting into revolt at once. But the victory also seemed more brilliant because it was Caesar who had won it. The affection of the ordinary people made sure of that.

(3) For Caesar himself, too, was again spending the winter in the Cisalpina cultivating the city, now that he had settled Gallic affairs so successfully. (4) Candidates for office relied on him as their paymaster, spending his money on bribing the voters: they were duly elected, and they did everything they could to increase his power. But that was not all. (5) A large number of the most distinguished and powerful Romans also gathered for a meeting with Caesar in Luca—Pompey and Crassus, and Appius the governor of Sardinia, and Nepos the proconsul of Spain. A total of 120 lictors were there, and more than 200 senators.

(6) They held a council, and agreed terms. Pompey and Crassus were to be elected consuls, while Caesar was to be voted money and an extension of his command for five years. (7) That was what seemed most paradoxical to intelligent observers. The men who had got such vast sums from Caesar were now urging the senate to vote him money as if he did not have any: indeed, it was a matter of compelling rather than urging, for the senate groaned at the decrees it passed. (8) Cato was not there, for they had deliberately spirited him away to Cyprus; but Favonius, a fervent admirer of Cato, achieved nothing by speaking against the proposals, so he rushed out through the doors of the chamber and cried to the people for support. (9) But no one paid any attention to him. In some cases this was because of people's respect for Pompey and Crassus, but most were living in hopes of Caesar, and it was to please him that they stayed so quiet.

22. On his return to the forces gathered in Gaul, Caesar found a great war waiting for him. Two large German tribes had just crossed the Rhine to occupy new territory, one called the Usipi, the other the Tencteri. (2) Caesar's own version of the battle with these tribes is given in his journal. He claims that the barbarians were negotiating with him, but then attacked him on the road during a truce: this allowed them to surprise and rout the 5,000 Roman cavalry with their own force of 800. (3) Then he says that they sent a second deputation to him on a further mission of deceit; he took the envoys prisoner, then led his army towards the enemy, for he thought it simple-minded to keep faith with this sort of faithless treaty-breakers. (4) Tanusius reports that, when the senate was voting a thanksgiving

for the victory, Cato proposed that Caesar should be handed over to the enemy: that would be the way to clear the city of blame for such treachery and fix the curse on the guilty man. (5) 400,000 of those who had crossed the Rhine were killed, and only a very few crossed back. These found refuge with the Sugambri, another German tribe.

(6) Caesar took this as his excuse for attacking them—and he was anyway eager for glory, and wanted the honour of being the first man ever to cross the Rhine with an army. So he began to bridge the river. It was very wide and rough and turbulent, for at that point of its course the current is at its strongest: the supports of the bridge were exposed to a terrible battering from the trunks and logs that were sweeping down the river. (7) But Caesar fixed large timber breakwaters in the current to keep them off, and thus managed to bridle the force of the stream against the bridge. It was an incredible spectacle, a bridge like this finished in just ten days.

23. Once the army was across, all the enemy disappeared. Even the Suebi, the most dominant of the German tribes, departed into their deep and wooded dells. So Caesar burnt the enemy territory and encouraged the peoples who always remained loyal to Rome, then returned again to Gaul. His stay in Germany had lasted eighteen days.

(2) Then came the invasion of Britain, an exploit of celebrated audacity. For he was the first man to sail the western Ocean with a fleet, and convey an army into battle through the waters of the Atlantic; (3) and the island itself had been said to be so large that no one could believe it existed at all. Writer after writer had entered the bitter controversy. Britain was just a name and a legend, they said; the island did not exist and never had existed. Now Caesar attempted to conquer it, and advanced the Roman Empire beyond the bounds of the human world. (4) He sailed twice to the island from the opposite shore in Gaul, and in a long sequence of battles he did more damage to the enemy than good to his own men, for there was nothing worth taking from a people of such wretched poverty. The war did not end as Caesar had hoped, but he did take hostages from the king and impose a tribute before he left.

(5) As he was about to cross back to Gaul, a letter reached him from his friends at Rome. It told him of his daughter's death: she had died when bearing Pompey's child. (6) Pompey himself was as distressed as Caesar, and their friends were altogether shaken. This had been the family bond that had kept the ailing state in peace and harmony, and now it was broken: for the baby died too, outliving its

mother by only a few days. (7) Julia's body was seized by the people, who defied the tribunes and carried it to the Campus Martius. There the funeral rites were held, and there she still lies.

24. Caesar's forces were now so large that he had to divide them among many different winter camps. He himself returned as usual to Italy, but while he was away all Gaul burst out in revolt once again: vast armies were roaming around, trying to destroy these winter camps and attacking the Roman fortifications. (2) The largest and strongest of these rebel forces was led by Ambiorix, and these destroyed Cotta and Titurius and all their camp, (3) then surrounded and besieged the single legion of Cicero with a force of 60,000 men. They all but took the camp by storm. Every one of Cicero's men was wounded, but such was their gallantry that they put up a superhuman resistance.

(4) Caesar was a long way away, but when the news reached him he moved with great speed, collecting a force of 7,000 men and hurrying to relieve Cicero's camp. (5) The besieging Gauls heard that he was on his way, and they marched to meet him, thinking they would have no trouble in destroying so small a force. (6) But Caesar outsmarted them. He kept moving back stealthily, then he occupied a position that would favour a small and outnumbered force, and there he fortified his camp. He kept all his men back from fighting, instructing them to give the impression of terror as they built their rampart and barricaded the gates. His strategy was to win contempt. (7) Then finally the enemy were so overconfident that they attacked in a random and uncoordinated way: Caesar swept out against them, turned them to flight, and killed many of their number.

25. This victory brought calm to the area, and the many rebellions ceased; Caesar himself made sure of that, making his way everywhere during the winter and attending quickly to any disturbances. (2) He was helped by the arrival from Italy of three legions to replace those he had lost. Two of these were lent by Pompey from his own forces, while the third was made up of new recruits from the Cisalpina.

(3) But far away there was danger. The seeds had been there long before, sown secretly and scattered among the most formidable tribes by the most powerful individuals; now they were coming to the surface, and they brought on the greatest and most hazardous of all the Gallic Wars. The movement drew its vigour from the immense numbers of young men under arms, gathered from all over the country; and vast sums of money had been collected, the cities

involved were powerful, and the terrain made movement very difficult. (4) The season of the year was winter: rivers were frozen, woods
cloaked with snow, plains turned into lakes by torrential rains; in
some parts the paths were hidden under the depth of snow, in others
they had been submerged by marshes and overflowing torrents, and it
was a bewildering matter to find a route. All these things seemed to
make the rebels' position invulnerable to Caesar. (5) Many peoples
had joined the revolt, but the Arverni and Carnutes were the leading
tribes, and total control of the war lay with the elected leader Vercingetorix, whose father had been put to death by the Gauls when
they thought he was aiming for tyranny.

26. Vercingetorix began by splitting his force into many different
divisions, and appointing many commanders. Then he set about
bringing over all the nearby country as far as the watershed of the
Saône. His aim was to bring every part of Gaul into the war, now that
Caesar was faced by more concerted opposition at Rome. (2) Had he
done this just a little later, when Caesar had become embroiled in the
civil war, Italy would have been beset by dangers just as serious as in
the days of the Cimbri. (3) As it was, Caesar was able to respond. He
was a master of every aspect of warfare, but he had a special gift for
sensing and grasping a critical opportunity, and now he set off
immediately he heard of the insurrection. The very routes he took,
the vigour and speed of his march, the severity of the winter weather
he overcame all showed the enemy that this was a general whom it
was inconceivable to fight or defeat. (4) For this was a region where it
was hard enough to believe that a single Roman herald or messenger
could slip through in a long time; now here was the man himself,
appearing with his whole army, ravaging their land as he went, reducing their forts, conquering their cities, and welcoming those who
came over to him. (5) Then finally the Aedui went to war against
him, a tribe that had so far paraded themselves as brothers of the
Roman people and enjoyed a special position of honour; but now
they joined the rebels, and this threw Caesar's army into great despon-
dency. (6) So he moved his force from the area and began to cross the
land of the Lingones, hoping to establish contact with the Sequani, a
friendly people who formed a buffer between Italy and the rest of Gaul.

(7) There the enemy fell on him, surrounding his force with many
tens of thousands of men. He moved quickly to bring on a decisive
battle, and won an overall victory, driving the enemy back after
a protracted and bloody exchange: (8) but in the early stages it looked

as if he was having the worse of it, and the Arverni still display a small sword hung in one of their shrines as a spoil from Caesar. He himself saw it later, and he smiled; his friends told him to take it down, but he refused, saying that this would be sacrilege.

27. There was still fighting to do, for most of those who escaped were able to regroup with their king at the city of Alesia. (2) Caesar laid it under siege. The city seemed impregnable, so great were its walls and so numerous the defenders; and then a further danger came from outside, one that beggars description. (3) For the most powerful forces of Gaul gathered from every nation and came in arms to Alesia, a total of 300,000 men, (4) while the defending force inside the city numbered at least 170,000. That was the dimension of the war that enveloped Caesar, trapped and besieged as he was. He had to build two walls in defence, one facing the city and one to ward off the relieving force, for it was clear that if the two armies could link his position was utterly hopeless.

(5) There were many reasons why the dangers of Alesia became justly celebrated: it indeed afforded more instances of heroism and brilliance than any other campaign. But the most striking feature of all was the way in which Caesar managed to take on and defeat that vast force outside, without the Gauls in the city even knowing what was happening. Indeed, even the Romans who were guarding the inner wall were unaware of the battle, (6) and the first they knew of the victory was when they heard noises from the city, the men wailing, the women beating their breasts: for the Gauls had seen what the Romans were carrying into the camp—many shields decorated with silver and gold, many bloodstained breastplates, even goblets and Gallic tents. (7) That was how swiftly this massive force had vanished and dispersed, like a phantom or a dream, with most of them falling in battle.

(8) The defenders in Alesia caused considerable trouble to Caesar as well as to themselves, but they too finally surrendered. (9) Vercingetorix, the supreme commander, took up his finest armour, decorated his horse, and rode out through the gates. (10) Caesar was sitting there, and Vercingetorix circled him three times on horseback, then leapt down, threw off his armour, and sat quietly at Caesar's feet. There he stayed till he was handed over to the guards, a prisoner to be kept for the triumph.

28. Caesar had long ago taken the decision to destroy Pompey, just as Pompey had decided to destroy Caesar. For a time Crassus had

acted as a curb on both, waiting like a reserve competitor ready to challenge the victor; but now Crassus was dead, fallen among the Parthians. Only one thing now remained for Caesar to become greatest, and that was to destroy the man who was greatest already; only one thing was necessary for Pompey to defend that position, to strike first and eliminate the man he feared. (2) In Pompey's case these fears were recent ones, for he had previously felt dismissive of Caesar. He had been the one who had built Caesar up, and he thought it a straightforward task to bring him down once more. (3) But Caesar had from the beginning made this his programme, and like an athlete had put himself far away from his rivals; the Gallic Wars had been his own training ground, and he had also used them to prepare his army and enhance his glory. (4) His achievements there had now raised him to rival even Pompey's past successes. There were pretexts at hand. Pompey himself afforded some, and others were furnished by the crisis and the sorry state of politics at Rome. It had reached the stage that candidates for office would set out their banking tables in public and offer bribes shamelessly to the common people; the people were already purchased as they came down to the elections, and they gave their support not with their votes, but with their arrows and swords and slings. (5) When the two sides separated, they often left the rostra defiled with blood and corpses; they left the city in anarchy, like a ship drifting without a helmsman. Where would all this crazy turbulence end? Sensible people would be content if the outcome were monarchy, and nothing worse. (6) Indeed, by now there were many who were ready to say in public that the state could be cured only by a monarchy, and the right thing to do was to take the remedy from the gentlest of the doctors who were offering it—meaning Pompey. (7) Meanwhile Pompey himself was putting on a respectable show of reluctance, but in fact plotting more than anyone or anything to get himself appointed dictator. Cato and his followers realized what was afoot, and they persuaded the senate to make Pompey sole consul. The purpose was to satisfy him with a more constitutional form of sole rule, so that he would not grab the dictatorship by force. (8) They also voted to continue his tenure of his provinces. He held two of these, Spain and all Africa, and he governed them by sending out legates and maintaining armies, for which he drew 1,000 talents each year from the public treasury.

29. Then Caesar sent to ask for a consulship and a similar extension of his own provincial commands. Pompey at first kept his

silence, but Marcellus, Lentulus, and their followers opposed the request. They hated Caesar anyway, and now were so eager to snub and humiliate him that some of their actions were quite unnecessary. (2) For instance, they took away the citizenship from the inhabitants of Novum Comum, a colony that Caesar had recently established in Gaul. Marcellus, who was consul, even used his rods to flog a councillor from Novum Comum who had come to Rome. 'I give you these marks to show you are not a Roman,' he added. 'Now go away and show them to Caesar.'

(3) Marcellus' lead was soon followed. Caesar was already opening the streams of Gallic wealth, and inviting any politician who wished to take a deep draught; he had freed the tribune Curio of his many debts, and given 1,500 talents to the consul Paullus, a sum that enabled him to adorn the forum with his famous basilica (it replaced the Fulvian basilica). (4) That finally brought Pompey to feel alarm at the coalition that was gathering against him. He now took action, both openly and through his friends, to have a successor appointed to take over Caesar's command; he also sent to demand the return of the soldiers he had lent Caesar for the Gallic Wars. Caesar duly returned them—after giving each man 250 drachmas. (5) The officers who conducted these troops to Pompey began a shameful and disgraceful whispering campaign among the ordinary people on Caesar's behalf. At the same time they deceived Pompey with empty hopes. 'Caesar's army is yearning for you,' they told him. 'In Rome you are finding things difficult: there is too much envy here in this festering state. But his army there is waiting to support you, and will come over to you as soon as they invade Italy. That's how unpopular he has become with them because of all those campaigns, and that's how frightened and suspicious they are of his monarchical ideas.' (6) That tickled Pompey's vanity, and he let his military preparations slip, giving the impression he had nothing to fear. Instead he tried to conduct the campaign in the political sphere, with various speeches and proposals, thinking Caesar *** Then there was a vote against Caesar: (7) Caesar was unimpressed. Indeed, there is a story told of one of the centurions who had come from his army. He was standing in front of the senate house, and heard that the senate was refusing to give Caesar any extra time in his command. 'They may not give it; this will,' he said, slapping the hilt of his sword.

30. Yet Caesar's claim had the appearance of being strikingly just. His proposal was that he should lay down his arms and Pompey

should do the same. Both should become private individuals, and find what advantage they could from their fellow-citizens. He complained that they were stripping him of his forces at the same time as confirming Pompey in his: they were accusing one man of seeking tyranny, only to set up the other as tyrant. (2) Curio made this case in the popular assembly on Caesar's behalf, and the people responded with loud applause. Some even showered him with garlands of flowers, just like a victorious athlete. (3) Then a letter of Caesar on the subject arrived: Antony as tribune brought it before the people and read it aloud, even though the consuls tried to suppress it.

(4) In the senate, however, Pompey's father-in-law Scipio proposed that Caesar should be declared a public enemy if he failed to lay down his arms before a specified day. (5) The consuls asked the senate whether they thought Pompey should dismiss his soldiers, and then put the same question about Caesar: only a few supported the first, nearly everyone voted for the second. But then Antony and his followers proposed that both of them should give up their command, and everyone unanimously agreed. (6) Still, Scipio forced the matter through, and Lentulus the consul cried out that arms were what were needed against this brigand, not votes. That was the end of the meeting, and the senators put on mourning clothes to mark the civil discord.

31. Then came letters from Caesar that gave the impression of being most accommodating: he offered to give up everything else on condition that he was granted Cisalpine Gaul and Illyricum, together with two legions, until he stood for his second consulship. The orator Cicero, too, who was freshly arrived from Cilicia, was working for a reconciliation and trying to soften Pompey's line. Pompey responded by agreeing to the rest of Caesar's suggestion but insisting that he give up the soldiers. (2) Cicero then urged Caesar's friends to reach an agreement on the basis of the provinces already mentioned, together with just 6,000 troops. Pompey was inclined to change his mind and allow this, but Lentulus, who was consul, refused; indeed, he and his associates humiliated Antony and Curio and drove them out of the senate, (3) an act of disrespect that gave Caesar the best of his justifications and the one that was most effective in stirring up his soldiers. For he could now display to them these distinguished men, in positions of authority, who had arrived in hired carriages and wearing slaves' clothing: for that was how they had dressed

themselves when they stole out of Rome, frightened as they were for their safety.

32. Caesar had with him no more than 300 cavalry and 5,000 infantry. The rest of his forces had been left beyond the Alps, and he had sent men to bring them to him. (2) But he knew that it was not numbers of men that were now needed to launch the attack and begin this great enterprise that lay before him; what was wanted was an audacity that would amaze his enemy and a speed in seizing all opportunities, for he would find it easier to stun the enemy by surprise than to crush them with a fully prepared assault. (3) So he instructed his lieutenants and captains to take their swords and no other weapons, and to advance and seize the large Gallic city of Ariminum. They were told to do everything they could to avoid bloodshed and disturbance. Hortensius was put in command of this force.

(4) Caesar himself spent the day where people could see him, visiting some gladiators and watching them as they trained. Shortly before evening he bathed and prepared himself, then entered the dining room. He spent a little time with the dinner guests, then rose from his seat as darkness was beginning to fall. He spoke politely to the others, asking them to wait for him, for he would soon return; but he had already told some of his friends to follow him, not all together, but each by a different way. (5) He himself took one of the hired carriages, and first drove off in a different direction, then turned and took the road for Ariminum. On his way he reached the river that marks the boundary between Cisalpine Gaul and the rest of Italy. They call it the Rubicon. Thoughts came upon him on this very brink of danger, and he was turned this way and that by the greatness of his enterprise. (6) He reined in the horses, and ordered a halt. Silently, within his own mind, his thoughts veered first one way and then the other, and this was when his resolve was most shaken; (7) and for some time he also spoke of the dilemma with his friends that were present, including Asinius Pollio—if he crossed, how great the ills that it would bring upon the world; how great the story of it they would leave among later generations. (8) Then, finally, as if with a burst of passion, he abandoned his counsels and hurled himself forward into the path that lay before him. As he went he uttered those words that so often serve as the prelude for some incalculable risk or audacious enterprise: 'let the die be cast.' Then he moved

swiftly to cross the river. He galloped the rest of the journey, and burst into Ariminum before dawn and took the city.

(9) It is said that, the night before he crossed, he dreamed a monstrous dream. It seemed to him that he was lying with his own mother—the unspeakable union.

33. With the fall of Ariminum, it was as if the broad gates of war had been opened to every land and sea. No respect was paid to the laws of the city, just as none had been given to the boundary of Caesar's province. It no longer felt as if men and women were dashing terrified across Italy—that had happened before—but now it was more as if whole cities were rising up to flee and rushing across one another. (2) Rome itself was filled by a torrent of flights and migrations from the nearby towns, and it was no easy matter for any leader to control the city by persuasion or to restrain it by words. It was a swirling maelstrom; Rome all but destroyed herself. (3) Contending passions and violent impulses dominated everywhere. Some were pleased, but even their jubilation had no quiet: in a great city it clashed time and again with fear and pain, and its brash confidence about the future gave rise to violence and quarrels. (4) Pompey himself was bewildered, hounded on every side by conflicting criticisms. Some accused him of being the one who had built Caesar's power, and claimed he should now be held responsible for the man's dominance; others protested that Pompey had allowed Lentulus and his group to insult Caesar just when he was giving way and offering a reasonable solution. (5) Favonius told him to stamp on the ground, for Pompey had once boasted to the senate that they need not trouble themselves about any war preparations: he had only to strike his foot on the earth to fill all Italy with armies.

(6) Even so, Pompey's force still outnumbered Caesar's. But no one would allow him to be his own man. One report arrived after another, many of them false, and there was panic after panic. The war was at the gates, they said, sweeping all before it. Pompey was borne along by the universal tide. He carried a vote to establish a state of emergency, then left the city, giving orders to the senate to follow, and forbidding anyone to remain whose allegiance lay with country and freedom rather than slavery.

34. The consuls fled, without even conducting the normal sacrifices before leaving. Most of the senators fled too, grabbing what they could from their own property as if they were plundering other people's. (2) Even some of Caesar's most enthusiastic former

supporters were so amazed at this time that they lost their nerve, and were carried along with the torrent of this rush out of the city, even though there was no real need. (3) The sight of the city was most pitiful. The storm was sweeping down upon her, yet she lay abandoned, like some ship left by its despairing helmsmen to drift randomly to land. (4) So dreadful a thing was it to abandon the city. Yet, for Pompey's sake, people even felt exile to be their home, and left the city feeling it was Caesar's camp. (5) There was, for instance, Labienus, one of Caesar's closest friends, who had served as his legate and fought most valiantly in all the Gallic campaigns. Now he abandoned Caesar and came to Pompey. Caesar sent all Labienus' possessions and equipment after him.

(6) Then he moved on Domitius, who held Corfinium with thirty cohorts, and pitched camp against him. Domitius gave up hope, and asked his doctor, one of his slaves, for a drug: he took it and drained it down, thinking it would kill him. (7) Soon afterwards he heard that Caesar was treating prisoners with a remarkable generosity, and he began to lament his own death and chide himself for his hasty decision. (8) His doctor told him to take heart, for he had taken only a sleeping drug, and it was not lethal. The delighted Domitius rose, went off to Caesar, and took him by the hand; then he stole away again to Pompey. (9) When this news reached Rome it raised people's spirits, and some who had fled turned back to the city.

35. Caesar enlisted Domitius' troops among his own army, and did the same with the levies of Pompey that he had overrun in the various cities. He had now grown to be a great and menacing force, and he moved on Pompey himself. (2) Pompey withdrew before his advance. He fled to Brundisium, then sent the consuls with a force over to Dyrrhachium, and he himself sailed after them a little later as Caesar came up. (The details will be given more fully in my projected *Life* of Pompey.)

(3) Caesar was eager to pursue at once, but did not have the ships, and so he returned to Rome. In sixty days he had become master of Italy, and not a drop of blood had been spent. (4) He found the city in a more stable condition than he expected, with many senators still there; he addressed them in moderate and popular tones, encouraging them to send envoys to Pompey to propose a reasonable settlement. (5) But no one did. Perhaps they were nervous of Pompey, whom they had abandoned; perhaps they felt Caesar's fine words were insincere.

(6) But when the tribune Metellus tried to prevent him from taking money from the treasury and cited certain laws in his support, Caesar replied by saying that there was a time for laws and a time for weapons. (7) 'If you do not like what I am doing, the right thing now is to go away. War is not the time for free speech. When peace is made and I lay down my arms, come back and play the demagogue then. (8) What is more,' he added, 'I am giving up my own rights in saying this. For you are my slave, you and all the others I have captured who took sides against me.' (9) With those words to Metellus he moved towards the doors of the treasury. The keys were nowhere to be seen, and so he sent for blacksmiths and ordered them to break down the doors. (10) Metellus intervened again, and some of the onlookers showed their approval; at that Caesar's voice hardened, and he threatened to kill him if he did not stop his obstruction. 'And, young man,' he added, 'you know very well that that is harder for me to say than to do.' (11) That was enough to intimidate Metellus into going away, and it also ensured that everything else Caesar needed for the war was carried out readily and quickly.

36. Then he launched an expedition into Spain. His plan was to drive out Afranius and Varro, Pompey's legates there, as a preliminary for the campaign against Pompey himself: once he had brought the forces there and the provinces under his own command, that would ensure that he was leaving no enemy in his rear. (2) In Spain he was often exposed to personal danger in ambushes, and his army was also at risk: lack of food was the main difficulty for them. But Caesar continued his pursuits and challenges and circumvallations until he seized control of the enemy camps and forces. The commanders took to flight, and made their escape to Pompey.

37. Once Caesar had returned to Rome, his father-in-law Piso encouraged him to send a deputation to Pompey to discuss terms for a peace; but Isauricus, eager to please Caesar, spoke against. (2) Then the senate appointed Caesar dictator. He allowed some exiles to return, restored their political rights to the children of those who had suffered under Sulla, and introduced some unburdening of interest to lighten the load on debtors; and there were other similar measures, but not very many, for within eleven days he resigned his position as sole ruler, declared himself and Servilius Isauricus consuls, and set out on the campaign.

(3) As he pressed on with his march he swept past the rest of his troops, then embarked with just 600 elite cavalry and 5 legions, even

though it was close to the winter solstice: it was in fact the beginning of January, the equivalent of the Athenian month Posideon. (4) Crossing the Ionian Sea he took Oricum and Apollonia, then sent the ships back to Brundisium for the soldiers who had been left behind on the march. (5) As long as those men were on the road, they were critical of Caesar: these were men who were past their physical peak, and were finding this amount of hard work too much for them. (6) 'Where is this man taking us now? What's the purpose of it all? Where is he going to put us down, after hauling us around everywhere and treating us as if we weren't human at all, and as if nothing could wear us out? Even swords get worn out with striking; even shields and breastplates are finally allowed some rest after so much time. (7) Aren't our wounds enough to tell Caesar that he has mere human beings under his command, who suffer human pain and agony? Even a god cannot impose his will on the winter season and the winds of the sea. But this man takes risk after risk, as if he were fleeing from the enemy, not pursuing them.' (8) That was what they were saying as they trailed slowly into Brundisium. But when they arrived and found that Caesar had already put to sea, they soon changed again, and berated themselves as traitors to their general: they berated their captains too for not making them march more quickly. (9) They sat on the cliffs and gazed out towards the sea and the land of Epirus opposite, watching for the ships that would carry them over to Caesar.

38. Meanwhile Caesar sat in Apollonia, without sufficient forces to fight. Time went on, still the troops from Italy did not arrive, and Caesar was at his wit's end. Finally he conceived a remarkable plan. He told no one what he was about to do, then secretly climbed aboard a twelve-oared boat to put out to Brundisium, despite all the vast enemy fleets that controlled the sea. (2) It was night-time, and he had disguised himself in slave's clothing, then he climbed into the ship, threw himself down like some passenger of no importance at all, and stayed there quietly. (3) The river Aous carried the ship down towards the sea. Normally in those parts a morning breeze calms the waters at the point where the river flows into the sea, driving the waves back; but on that occasion a strong sea wind had been blowing during the night, and that stopped the morning breeze. (4) The river grew rough as it hit the sea tide and the oncoming swell; the waters chopped and swirled and reared; the roar was deafening. The master of the boat could not see how he could make any headway, and gave orders to his

crew to turn back. (5) When Caesar saw this he showed himself and grasped the hand of the astonished master. 'Go on, my good man,' he said, 'be bold, and fear nothing. It is Caesar you are carrying, and Caesar's Fortune sails with us.' (6) The sailors immediately forgot about the storm. They threw themselves at their oars and forced their way down the river, straining their utmost. It was still impossible; but it was only after he had taken in large quantities of sea water in the river mouth, and exposed himself to great risks, that he very reluctantly allowed the master to put about. (7) When he returned, his men turned out in force to meet him, shouting their anger and indignation. Did he not think that they could bring victory on their own? Why was he so worried and why was he taking these risks, just for the men who were away in Italy? Could he not trust the men on the spot?

39. Then Antony arrived with the forces from Brundisium, and Caesar's spirits rose. He even challenged Pompey to battle. Pompey's position was a strong one, adequately supplied by both land and sea, whereas even at the outset Caesar was badly off for provisions, and as time went on he was in severe difficulties because of the shortage of necessities. (2) His men even found a certain kind of root that they would mash, mix with milk, and eat. On one occasion they moulded this into cakes, rushed up to the enemy outposts and threw the cakes over so that they scattered inside the camp, shouting that, as long as the earth provided roots like this, they would never give up besieging Pompey. (3) But Pompey himself gave instructions that his troops should not be shown the cakes nor told of the shouts. They were already dispirited and frightened enough by the toughness and endurance of Caesar's men, who seemed just like wild beasts.

(4) There was a succession of skirmishes around Pompey's fortifications, and Caesar won them all except one. On that single occasion his men were completely put to flight, and the camp itself came close to being captured. (5) The troops all fled as Pompey attacked and the trenches were full of the dead and dying, while others, driven back in headlong rout, were cut down in front of their own palisade and rampart. (6) Caesar himself came forward to meet his men and try to make them turn back, but he could achieve nothing. When he grasped the standards, their bearers just threw them away, so that the enemy eventually captured thirty-two of them. Indeed, Caesar himself was very nearly killed. (7) He had laid hands on a soldier who was fleeing past him, a powerful giant of a man, and

ordered him to face the enemy and stand his ground: the soldier, full of panic at the fearful situation, raised his sword and was about to strike, but Caesar's shield-bearer landed his blow first and cut off his arm at the shoulder. (8) Caesar was now in despair. Yet Pompey somehow failed to put the finishing touch to this great exploit, whether because of his caution or because fortune took a hand; instead he retreated after forcing the routed enemy back into their camp. 'Today,' said Caesar to his friends as he left the field, 'the enemy might have won—all they needed was a winner.' (9) He then withdrew into his tent and lay down, and this was his worst night of all. He was totally at a loss, thinking how incompetent his generalship had been. Here he was, with broad plains at hand, and all the flourishing cities of Macedonia and Thessaly: yet he had lost the chance of drawing the fighting into that direction, and instead was hemmed in here by the coast, with the enemy in complete control of the sea. It was not so much that he was besieging them with arms; they were besieging him, through lack of provisions.

(10) Such was his dismay and his agitation, tossed this way and that by the hopeless difficulties he faced. He finally ordered his men to break camp, intending to march against Scipio in Macedonia: (11) either he would draw Pompey where he would fight without such a strong line of supply from the sea, or at least he would be able to beat the isolated Scipio.

40. That stirred up Pompey's army and lieutenants to think that Caesar was already defeated and in flight, and they wanted to keep at his heels. (2) Pompey himself was cautious and reluctant to let so much turn on the throw of a single battle. He was supremely well provided for a lengthy campaign, and he wanted to follow a strategy of slow attrition: his enemy's strength, he thought, could not last long. (3) The most formidable part of Caesar's army was certainly experienced, and showed invincible valour in battle; but their age left them ill-suited to long marches and encampments and siege fighting and night watches. Their bodies could not cope with the exertions; their enthusiasm was undaunted, but their physical weakness let them down. (4) At that time too there was talk of an epidemic going around in Caesar's camp, brought on by their outlandish diet. And, most important of all, Caesar had no money and no supplies. It looked as if his army would destroy itself, and it would not take long.

41. That was why Pompey was reluctant to fight. But Cato was the only one to praise him for it, and Cato's motive was to save the lives of his fellow-citizens: indeed, when he saw the enemy dead lying on the field of battle, some thousand in number, he covered his face and went away in tears. (2) Everyone else berated Pompey for shirking battle, and tried to stir him into action. They kept calling him 'Agamemnon' or 'king of kings', implying that he was concerned to hold on to his one-man rule and that it pleased his vanity to have so many commanders dependent on him and coming constantly to his tent. (3) Then there was Favonius, who went around affecting the outspoken style of Cato like a madman: it would be a dreadful thing, he said, if Pompey's lust for rule was going to stop them enjoying the figs of Tusculum for yet another season. (4) Afranius, newly arrived from his poor generalship in Spain, was accused of betraying his army for a bribe, and retaliated by asking Pompey why they were not fighting against this merchant to whom he had sold the provinces. (5) All these men hounded Pompey into fighting against his will, and he set out in pursuit of Caesar.

(6) Caesar's march was not an easy one. No one allowed him to buy food, for everyone had heard of his recent defeat, and they were writing off his chances. (7) But then he captured Gomphi, a city of Thessaly, and this allowed him not merely to feed his army but also, paradoxically enough, to rid them of their sickness. (8) For they captured large quantities of wine and drank their fill, then continued the march reeling about in drunken revelry. That drove the illness away and restored them to health, for the drunkenness had changed the whole constitution of their bodies.

42. Both armies came to the district of Pharsalus and pitched camp. Pompey now reverted to his earlier strategy: he was influenced too by certain unfavourable omens, and also by a dream in which he had seen himself back in his theatre, applauded by the Romans. (2) But his company were full of themselves and confident of victory, so much so that Domitius and Spinther and Scipio were already wrangling among themselves as to who should succeed Caesar as pontifex maximus, and there were many who sent representatives to Rome to rent and put in early bids for houses that would be suitable for consuls and praetors: so sure were they that they would take office immediately after the war. (3) The cavalry were especially keen to fight. They were particularly impressive with their splendid arms and their well-fed horses and their handsome physical appearance, and they were also confident because of their numbers, 7,000 of them to Caesar's

1,000. (4) The infantry also outnumbered Caesar, with 45,000 men against 22,000.

43. Caesar called his men together, and began by telling them that Cornificius was close at hand with two legions, while Calenus was stationed at Megara and Athens with a further fifteen cohorts. Then he asked them whether they wanted to wait for those extra forces, or preferred to risk the decisive battle on their own. (2) They shouted out and told him not to wait, but to try everything he could to get to grips with the enemy as soon as possible.

(3) He went on to purify his force, and when he had sacrificed the first victim the soothsayer immediately told him that the decisive battle would come in three days' time. (4) Caesar asked him if he could see any good indications in the auspices about the outcome. 'You yourself', said the soothsayer, 'are the man to answer that: for the gods are showing that there will be a mighty change and revolution from the present state of affairs. So if you regard yourself as doing well, expect failure; if badly, success.' (5) Then, on the night before the battle, Caesar was making his way around the guard posts at about midnight when a flaming light was seen in the sky: it passed over their own camp, then Caesar thought he saw it fall into Pompey's, blazing brilliantly. (6) During the morning watch Caesar's men could also see an attack of panic among the enemy. (7) Still, Caesar did not expect to fight on that day. He was already beginning to break camp, intending to march towards Scotussa.

44. The tents had already been taken down when his scouts came riding up, telling him that the enemy was marching to the field to fight. Caesar was delighted. He prayed to the gods, then drew up his men in a triple formation. (2) He put Domitius Calvinus in command of the centre, while Antony took the left wing and Caesar himself the right, where he would fight along with the tenth legion. (3) He saw that the enemy cavalry was taking up position opposite this part of the line. Their splendid appearance and their numbers made him nervous, and he gave orders that six cohorts should secretly move across to him from the rear. He stationed them behind the right wing, and told them what they should do when the enemy cavalry attacked. (4) Pompey commanded his own right wing and Domitius his left, while his father-in-law Scipio commanded the centre. (5) All the cavalry were stationed to throw their weight towards the left: the plan was that they should outflank the enemy right, and create a splendid rout of the part of the line where Caesar himself was

stationed. (6) They were confident that no depth of ranks would be able to resist, but would be crushed and shattered when so great a force of cavalry swept down on them in a single movement.

(7) When both sides were about to sound the attack, Pompey gave instructions that his legionaries should take up their stance with spears levelled and stand their ground firmly as the enemy charged, until the two armies were within javelin range. (8) Caesar claims that this was another error: he says that Pompey failed to realize the advantages of speed and momentum at the first clash of arms: that is what adds vigour to the initial blows, and helps to inflame the men's spirit as it is fanned up by the encounter.

(9) Caesar himself was on the point of ordering the legions to charge and was already moving forward into action, when he saw one of the centurions encouraging his men and challenging them to a competition in valour. (10) The man was a loyal follower of Caesar, and he had fought many campaigns. Caesar called out to him by name. 'How are our prospects, Gaius Crassinius?' he asked. 'Are we confident?' Crassinius stretched out his right hand and gave a great shout: 'we will win a splendid victory,' he cried; 'and today, living or dead, I shall win your praise!' (11) With those words he led the charge at the double, taking his 120 men with him. (12) He cut his way through the front line and plunged on, cutting down man after man, and he was still pressing onwards when he was killed by a thrust of a sword through the mouth. The blow was so powerful that the point pierced through the head and came out by the occipital bone.

45. That marked the beginning of the infantry clash in the centre, and while they were fighting the cavalry of Pompey launched their magnificent charge, sweeping forward in squadrons to encircle Caesar's right. (2) But before they made contact the cohorts came running out from Caesar's force. These men did not throw their javelins in their usual way, nor did they thrust at the enemy's thighs or legs at close quarters; instead they aimed for the enemy's eyes and tried to wound their faces. Those had been Caesar's instructions, (3) for he had thought that Pompey's men were so inexperienced in battle and unused to wounds, so young and vain and proud of their good looks, that they would be particularly apprehensive of that sort of blow and would not face up to them, fearful both of the immediate danger and of disfigurement for the future. (4) And that was exactly what happened. They did not stay as the spears lunged up towards them, and did not have the courage to face the steel before their eyes;

instead they turned their heads away and covered them up, protecting their faces, (5) till finally they threw themselves into utter confusion and turned to flight. The damage they did to their cause was disgraceful, (6) for the cohorts that had defeated them went on to turn the flank of Pompey's infantry, then fell on their rear and set about cutting them to pieces.

(7) From the opposite wing Pompey saw his cavalry routed. He was no longer the same man, he had no memory that he was Pompey the Great; he was more like a man whom Heaven had robbed of his wits. Silently, he moved away to his tent, sat down, and waited for what was to come. Finally his entire force had been routed, and the enemy reached the fortification of the camp and began to fight its defenders. (8) Then he seemed to come to his senses. He said only this (so the story goes): 'surely, not as far as the camp?' Then he took off his cloak of action and command, put on clothes more fitting to a fugitive, and stole away. (9) As for his later fortunes, and his death after entrusting himself to the Egyptians, we tell that story in his own *Life*.

46. Soon Caesar himself was in Pompey's camp. As he gazed on the piles of enemy corpses and the men who were still being cut down, he gave a groan. 'It was their choice,' he said. 'They drove me to this pitch of necessity that I, Gaius Caesar, victor in the greatest of wars, would actually have been condemned in the courts if I had given up my armies.' (2) These were his words: according to Asinius Pollio he uttered them in Greek at the time, then they were written down by Pollio himself in Latin.

(3) Most of the dead (Pollio goes on) were servants, cut down as the camp fell; not more than 6,000 soldiers were killed. (4) Most of those who were taken alive Caesar incorporated into his own legions. He spared many of the more prominent figures as well. These included Brutus, the man who went on to kill him. It is said that Caesar was most distressed when Brutus initially appeared to be lost, and was extraordinarily relieved when he was safely brought before him.

47. There were many portents to indicate the victory: the most remarkable one was that recorded at Tralles. (2) Here, in the Temple of Victory, stood a statue of Caesar. The area around was naturally hard and paved with solid stones: yet they say that a palm tree sprang up from this at the foot of the statue. (3) Again, at Patavium Gaius Cornelius, a well-known prophet and an acquaintance and fellow-citizen of Livy the historian, happened to be sitting on that day studying the auguries. (4) And first, according to Livy, he recognized

the precise moment of the battle, and told those present that the event was indeed in progress and the armies had begun to fight. (5) He resumed his watch and inspected the signs again, then jumped up in a frenzy and cried, 'Caesar! You are victorious!' (6) Everyone there was astonished, but he took the wreath from his head and swore not to replace it before his skill was vindicated by events. Livy firmly attests the truth of this.

48. Caesar gave the people of Thessaly their freedom to celebrate his victory, then set off in pursuit of Pompey. Once he had reached Asia, he liberated the Cnidians—that was a favour to Theopompus, the collector of myths—and granted all the peoples of Asia remission of a third of their tribute.

(2) He sailed into Alexandria just after Pompey's death. When Theodotus came to him with Pompey's head, he turned away; he took up the man's signet ring instead, and wept for him. (3) Some of Pompey's friends and companions had been captured by the king as they roamed around the country, and Caesar treated them all well, welcoming them to his side. (4) Indeed, he wrote back to his friends at Rome that this was his greatest and most delicious reward of victory, the chance to save one man after another who had fought against him.

(5) As for the war in Egypt itself, some claim that it was unnecessary. On their view it was a shameful and hazardous escapade, inspired by his passion for Cleopatra. Others blame the king's courtiers, especially the eunuch Pothinus. He was the most powerful of them, and it was he who had killed Pompey a little earlier and had driven out Cleopatra. (6) Now he was secretly plotting against Caesar (and this is why they say Caesar now began his practice of all-night drinking parties as a ploy to protect his person), while openly he was quite intolerable, with act after act and remark after remark that were spitefully and aggressively directed at Caesar. (7) He gave the soldiers rations of the worst and stalest grain, and told them they should be content with whatever they got: it was after all other people's food they were eating. At table he used wooden and earthenware dishes, claiming that Caesar had taken all the gold and silver to settle a debt. (8) Caesar was in fact owed 17,500,000 drachmas in payment of a debt contracted by the father of the present king. He had previously granted the old king's children remission of everything beyond ten million drachmas, but now he demanded the ten million immediately for the support of the army. (9) Pothinus told him to go away for the

present and attend to his great affairs, promising him that he would be welcome to the money later. Caesar retorted that he had no need for Egyptian advisers, and secretly sent for Cleopatra to come from the country.

49. She set out with just a single companion, Apollodorus of Sicily, and embarked on a tiny boat. It was dusk as she came to the palace. (2) There was only one way to come in unobserved, and so she got into one of those sacks that are used for bedclothes and stretched herself out full length. Apollodorus rolled up the sack, fastened it with a strap, and brought it in through the doors to Caesar. (3) And that, they say, was the beginning of Caesar's captivation: the trick showed such style, and he was also overcome by all the charm and grace with which she behaved towards him. He reconciled her with her brother, and arranged that the two would rule jointly. (4) A banquet was held to celebrate the reconciliation. During this a servant of Caesar—his barber, in fact—gathered that a plot was being hatched against Caesar by Achillas the general and Pothinus the eunuch. The barber had found this out by eavesdropping and snooping: he was the most cowardly man alive, and this led him to keep his eye on everything. (5) Once Caesar had discovered the plot, he ordered troops to surround the banqueting hall, then had Pothinus killed. Achillas escaped to the army camp, and the war that followed was a particularly difficult and awkward one for Caesar, who had to protect himself against so great a city and so large an army with so few men of his own.

(6) First he ran into difficulties with his water supply, for the conduits were dammed by the enemy. Then he was nearly cut off from the fleet, and had to use fire to avoid the danger: the fire spread from the shipyards and destroyed the great library. (7) Thirdly, there was a battle around the island of Pharos, and Caesar leapt down from the bank into a small boat to come to the help of the men who were fighting. The Egyptians bore down on him from all sides, and Caesar hurled himself into the sea: he only just managed to escape by swimming. (8) According to the story, he was carrying a bundle of papers and managed not to let them go, even when the missiles were flying at him and he was sinking beneath the waves. He held them above the surface and swam with his other hand, for the small boat had been sunk straight away. (9) But finally the king left to join the enemy, and Caesar marched on their forces and defeated them in battle. Many were killed, and the king disappeared. (10) Caesar left

Cleopatra in control of Egypt, and a little later she bore him a son, whom the Alexandrians called Caesarion. Caesar himself set out for Syria.

50. Then he travelled on through Asia. There he received news that Domitius had been defeated by Pharnaces son of Mithridates, and had fled from Pontus with a few followers; that Pharnaces was making every use he could of the victory, and was already master of Bithynia and Cappadocia, with aspirations to take over the land called Lesser Armenia; and that he was already encouraging all the kings and tetrarchs of the area to revolt. (2) Caesar immediately marched against the man with three legions. A great battle ensued at the city of Zela, and Caesar drove Pharnaces out of Pontus and destroyed his entire army. (3) When he was reporting back to Rome on the sharpness and speed of the battle, he wrote to Matius, one of his friends, using just three expressions: 'I came, I saw, I conquered.' In Latin the three words all end with the same inflection, and the compression of the phrase is very powerful.

51. Caesar then crossed to Italy and travelled to Rome. It was just at the end of the year for which he had been elected dictator for the second time, though this office had never before been an annual one. He was now declared consul for the following year.

(2) He was met by popular disapproval. That was partly because his soldiers had mutinied and killed two former praetors, Cosconius and Galba, but Caesar had ventured no harsher punishment than to call the men 'citizens' instead of 'soldiers': he had then given each of them a thousand drachmas, as well as parcelling out to them a large part of the Italian countryside in land grants. (3) Dolabella's madness also started tongues wagging against Caesar, and so did Matius' avarice; so too did Antony's drunken excesses and his ransacking and rebuilding of Pompey's private house, as if it was not big enough already. The Romans did not like all this. (4) Caesar himself knew what was going on, and it was against his will. But he had no choice. Political considerations forced him to make use of the men who were willing to be his agents.

52. After the battle of Pharsalus the followers of Cato and Scipio had taken refuge in Africa, and with the help of King Juba they had by now gathered a considerable force. Caesar now decided to launch his campaign against them. (2) It was around the time of the winter solstice when he crossed to Sicily. Then some of his own captains were hoping that the fighting might be held back and delayed: Caesar

wanted to put an end to any such thoughts, so he pitched his tent on the seashore itself, and as soon as he had a favourable wind he set sail with 3,000 infantry and a small force of cavalry. (3) He managed to land these unobserved, and immediately put to sea again, anxious for the main force: he found them already at sea, and he brought them all safely into camp.

(4) He now discovered that the enemy were drawing confidence from an ancient oracle, which said that it was the prerogative of the Scipios always to win mastery in Africa. Perhaps Caesar wanted to make fun of the enemy general Scipio, perhaps he really wanted to claim the oracle for his own; (5) anyway, he took one of his own men called Scipio Salvito, a descendant of the Africani but otherwise unimpressive and undistinguished, and continually placed him in the front line of the battle as if he was the real commander.

Caesar was indeed forced to engage the enemy frequently and look for every chance of fighting, (6) for he was short of food for the men and fodder for the animals. They were indeed forced to give the horses a diet of seaweed, washing off the salt and adding a little of the local grass to disguise the flavour. (7) The problem was that the Numidians controlled the countryside, and they kept appearing with rapid movements in considerable numbers. There was one particular occasion when Caesar's own cavalry were off duty: in fact they were being entertained by an African, who was a gifted dancer and flute-player. They were sitting there enjoying themselves, and had handed over the horses to the slaves. Meanwhile the enemy had surrounded the camp, and now they suddenly attacked. Many of Caesar's men were killed and the rest fled headlong to the camp, but the Numidians forced their way in with them. (8) If Caesar himself, together with Asinius Pollio, had not managed to check the rout by coming promptly from the fortifications, that would have decided the war. (9) There was another battle, too, when the enemy were getting the better of the engagement. Caesar, so they say, grabbed the standard-bearer by the neck as he fled, jerked him around, and said 'the enemy are over there!'

53. These successes encouraged Scipio to risk a decisive battle. He left Afranius and Juba in separate camps nearby, while he himself began to build a fortification for his army above a lake near the city of Thapsus. This was to serve the entire force as a base for the battle and a place to which they could retreat. (2) While he was working on this Caesar made his way with extraordinary speed through a terrain that

was wooded and had some concealed approaches. He surrounded some of the enemy and attacked others in a frontal charge: (3) after turning these to flight, he exploited the momentum of his victory and took the camp of Afranius without resistance. Nor was there any resistance from Juba: he fled, and the Numidian camp was ransacked. (4) In a small part of a single day Caesar had taken three camps and killed 50,000 of his enemy, losing fewer than 50 of his own men.

(5) That, at least, is one version of that battle. Others say that Caesar was not on the field himself, following an attack of his usual illness while he was drawing up and organizing his battleline: (6) he recognized its early symptoms, and left before his already blurred senses were totally confused and overcome by the disease. Instead he went to a nearby fortification and passed the battle there undisturbed. (7) A good many men of consular and praetorian rank survived the battle: some took their own lives as they were captured, and Caesar put many to death himself.

54. But Cato was one man he had ambitions of taking alive, and he hurried to Utica. The city was under Cato's guard, and that was why he was not present at the battle. (2) When news came that Cato had killed himself, Caesar was clearly very annoyed, though it is uncertain why: at any rate, he exclaimed, 'Cato, I grudge you your death, just as you grudged me the chance of saving your life'. (3) Yet the work he later wrote against the dead Cato does not suggest a mood of generosity or reconciliation: would he really have spared him alive, when he poured out so much anger on the man when he was a senseless corpse? (4) Still, he was generous towards Cicero and Brutus and countless others who fought against him, and that leads people to infer that the work was not born of enmity, but rather served some political ambition. This was how it came about. (5) Cicero had written a eulogy of Cato ('Cato' was in fact its title), and it won considerable acclaim: that was not unnatural, given that it was composed by the most accomplished of orators on the most excellent of themes. (6) That irritated Caesar, who took the view that praise of the man whose death he had caused was equivalent to an accusation of himself. So he collected many charges against Cato and published them under the title 'Anticato'. Both works have many admirers, for Caesar's and for Cato's sake.

55. Anyway, Caesar now returned from Africa to Rome. First he gave a grand speech about his victory to the people: he had conquered land large enough (he claimed) to produce for the treasury a yearly

income of 200,000 Attic bushels of grain and 3 million cups of olive oil. (2) Then he celebrated his triumphs, from Egypt, from Pontus, and from Africa: the last masqueraded as a victory over King Juba rather than Scipio. (3) This was the time when Juba, the small son of the king, was also paraded in the triumph. His was the most fortunate of captures, for he was born a barbarian and a Numidian and was eventually counted among the most learned of Greek authors.

(4) After the triumphs he gave great rewards to the soldiers, and cultivated the people with banquets and spectacles: he gave one banquet for the entire people, with 22,000 separate triple-couches, and put on gladiatorial shows and mock naval battles in honour of his daughter Julia, who had died years earlier.

(5) Once the spectacles were over, he conducted a census. The citizen population was found to be 150,000; before it had been 320,000. (6) That was the dimension of the destruction caused by the civil war and of the depletion of the Roman people, to say nothing of the disasters that befell the rest of Italy and the provinces.

56. When that was completed, he was declared consul for the fourth time, then set out to Spain to fight the sons of Pompey. They were still young, but they had collected a force of astonishing size, and their daring was such as to justify their claim to leadership: in fact they went on to bring Caesar into perils that were nearly the end of him. (2) The great battle took place near the city of Munda. Caesar could see his troops being pressed back, and in great trouble: so he himself dashed amid the weapons and the ranks. They should take him, he cried, and hand him over to those boys, if they had no more self-respect than this. (3) It was a hard fight and it required much strenuous effort, but finally he pushed the enemy back, killing over 30,000 of the Pompeians but losing 1,000 high-quality men of his own. (4) 'I have often fought to win', he remarked to his friends as he left the battlefield; 'never before to survive'. (5) He won his victory on the feast of the Dionysia, the very day, they say, that Pompey had left for the war. Since then four years had passed. (6) The younger of Pompey's sons escaped: a few days later Didius brought in the head of the elder.

(7) This was Caesar's final war. The triumph that he celebrated for it was the most distressing thing of all to the Romans. (8) These were not foreign or barbarian generals he had defeated; Caesar had destroyed the sons and the entire family of the man who had been the greatest of the Romans, and who had fallen on misfortune. It could

not be right to celebrate the nation's disasters like this, (9) nor to preen oneself on a victory whose only possible defence before gods and men was one of necessity: especially as before this Caesar had sent no official messengers or despatches about victory in the civil wars, but had had the decency to shun that sort of glory.

57. Still, the Romans bowed before the man's fortune and accepted his bridle. Thinking that monarchy could afford a respite from civil war and national calamities, they proclaimed him dictator for life. This was acknowledged tyranny: he already enjoyed a monarch's unaccountability, and now he had a monarch's permanence as well.

(2) The first honours were proposed to the senate by Cicero, and these at least kept to some level of magnitude appropriate to a human being. But then others suggested more and more, and it became a sort of competition. The result was that they rendered the man offensive and loathsome even to the most mild-mannered of observers, so extravagant and bizarre were the decrees. (3) They say that those who hated Caesar were no less active here than his flatterers; their aim was to collect as many pretexts for their hostility as they could, so that they would have the best possible case for their attack. (4) For Caesar himself behaved in a way that was unimpeachable, now that the civil wars were over. It seems utterly appropriate that in gratitude for his mildness they decreed a temple to Clemency. (5) He pardoned many of those who had fought against him and even gave offices and honours to some, such as Brutus and Cassius. (Both men became praetors.) (6) Nor did Caesar allow the statues of Pompey to remain lying on the ground; when he restored them, Cicero remarked that by raising up Pompey's statues he had firmly fixed his own. (7) His friends urged him to use a bodyguard and many offered their own services, but he would not allow it. Better to meet death once, he said, than always to be anticipating it. (8) He regarded people's goodwill as at once the fairest and the firmest protection, and he put this on as his magic charm—so once again he cultivated the people with banquets and doles and the military with colonies. The most celebrated of these were Carthage and Corinth, two cities whose destinies were linked for a second time, now in their restoration as once in their fall.

58. As for the men of power, he promised some of them consulships and praetorships for the future, and gave others various positions of authority and honours as a consolation; he afforded hope to all, for he was courting rule over willing subjects. (2) One instance came when the consul Maximus died, and he declared Caninius

Rebilus consul for the one remaining day of the term of office. (3) Naturally enough, many people were making their way to greet and escort him; 'let's hurry', said Cicero, 'or his consulship will be over'.

(4) He had a natural magnificence in his energy and an eagerness for glory, and his many successes did not now divert this into the quiet enjoyment of his achievements. They were rather the spark that inflamed his thoughts for the future and lent them confidence: they generated greater plans and a passion for new glory, as if he had used up all the old. (5) What he felt was nothing else than envy of himself, as if he were his own rival; he was eager to contend with his past achievements and outdo them with those to come. (6) He planned and prepared an expedition against the Parthians; once he had conquered them, he intended to march through Hyrcania along the Caspian and the Caucasus; then he would make his way around the Pontus and invade Scythia, (7) then overrun Germany's neighbours and Germany itself, and finally return through Gaul to Italy, thus completing the circle of an empire that would have Ocean alone as its boundary. (8) During this expedition he also planned to dig a canal through the Isthmus of Corinth, and he appointed †Anienus as his engineer; another plan was to take the Tiber as soon as it left the city and capture its waters in a deep canal, then divert it to Circeum and let it flow into the sea near Tarracina; that would add to the safety as well as the comfort of traders travelling to Rome. (9) He also planned to drain the Pomptine marshes near Setia, producing a plain that could be farmed by many tens of thousands of men; (10) to build moles and breakwaters at the point where the sea is nearest to Rome; and to clear the treacherous waters near the shore at Ostia, and build instead harbours and docks that could safely accommodate so much maritime traffic. All these projects were in preparation.

59. Then, however, there was his calendar reform, and his correction of the misalignments that had crept into the reckoning of time: this was extremely useful as well as subtle. He had worked it out with learning and elegance, and he took it through to its conclusion and brought it into effect. (2) It was not just that in remote antiquity the Romans had used a confused method of combining the lunar and solar cycles, so that the timetable for sacrifices and festivals had gradually become distorted and everything now fell in the opposite season of the year; (3) even in Caesar's day the only people who understood the system were the priests, and they would suddenly and without notice slip in the intercalary month known as 'Mercedonius'.

(4) It was traditionally King Numa who introduced this month: as I explained in his *Life*, the deviations in the heavenly orbits were causing some errors, and he invented this as a minor and makeshift corrective. (5) Caesar now put the problem before the best philosophers and mathematicians of the day; his solution drew on the various approaches that already existed, but combined them in an individual way to produce a more accurate correction. The Romans still use his system, and it seems that they cope better than anyone else with the irregularity between the cycles.

(6) Still, this too fuelled the grumbles of those who criticized Caesar and resented his power. That seems to be the point of the orator Cicero's remark. Someone said that tomorrow the constellation Lyra would rise; 'yes', he said, 'on instructions'—as if this too was an imposition that mortals had to accept.

60. But the most visible and lethal hatred was provoked by his passion to be king. That was the first grievance felt by the ordinary people, while those who had long nursed their resentments took it as the most plausible of their pretexts. (2) Yet it was those who were trying to procure this honour for Caesar who actually spread a rumour among the people: an oracle had been found in the Sibylline books, they claimed, which said that Parthia would only fall if the Romans marched on them with a king. (3) Then there was an occasion when Caesar was returning to the city from Alba, and they hailed him as king. The people were bewildered and shocked; Caesar, annoyed, said that his name was 'Caesar', not 'King'. Everyone fell silent, and Caesar went on his way, looking sullen and displeased.

(4) There was another scene too. They had been voting him some extravagant honours in the senate, and Caesar was sitting above the rostra. The consuls and praetors approached, with the whole senate following behind. Instead of standing up to receive them, Caesar treated them as if they were merely some private petitioners, and said that the honours needed to be cut down, not increased. (5) That distressed the people as much as the senate: they thought that an insult to the senate meant an insult to the whole state. Immediately those who could do so left the meeting, their eyes downcast in intense disapproval. (6) Caesar himself realized what he had done, and returned home immediately. As he went he drew his toga away from his throat and cried to his friends, 'does anyone want to kill me? Here, come and strike.' Later he blamed it on his disease, (7) and

explained that people in his condition find that their senses do not stay steady when they stand and speak to a large crowd; they quickly blur and become dizzy, and this brings on faintness and loss of consciousness. (8) But on this occasion it was not like that. Indeed, people say that Caesar was very willing to stand up to receive the senators, but was restrained by one of his friends, or rather his flatterers, Cornelius Balbus. 'Remember you are Caesar,' said Balbus. 'You are their superior; you should expect them to show you the proper respect.'

61. On top of these reverses came his insults to the tribunes. It was the festival of the Lupercalia: many authors give descriptions of this as an ancient pastoral festival, with some similarities to the Arcadian Lycaia. (2) Many of the younger nobles and magistrates run naked through the city, using leather thongs to flick people they meet, and it is all done with good humour and laughter. (3) Indeed, many of the magistrates' wives deliberately get in the way of the thongs, putting out their hands to be hit like children at school: they think that this helps women to have an easy labour if they are pregnant, and to conceive if they are barren. (4) Caesar was watching the spectacle, seated above the rostra on a golden throne, wearing rich triumphal dress. (5) Antony was one of those running the sacred race, for he was consul. When he entered the forum and the crowd stood back to make way for him, he brought up a diadem with a laurel crown wound around it, and offered it to Caesar. There was some applause—not too much, but small, as had been prearranged. (6) Caesar pushed it away; the people cried loudly in approval. Antony offered it a second time, and again a few applauded; Caesar rejected it, and again everyone cheered. (7) The attempt had evidently failed, and Caesar stood to his feet, ordering the crown to be taken and dedicated on the Capitol.

(8) His statues were also seen decorated with royal diadems, and two tribunes, Flavius and Marullus, came and tore them down; they also sought out the people who had been the first to hail Caesar as king, and hauled them off to prison. (9) The people followed them, applauding loudly, and called the men true Brutuses. (Brutus was the one who overthrew the regal dynasty and transferred authority from the kings to the senate and people.) (10) Caesar was furious, and dismissed Marullus and his colleague from office; and in his invective against them he was insulting to the people as well, for again and again he called the men 'Brutuses' and 'Cumaeans'.

62. These were the circumstances in which the ordinary people turned to Marcus Brutus. He was thought to descend from that ancient Brutus on his father's side, while on his mother's he belonged to the Servilii, another distinguished family. He was also the nephew and son-in-law of Cato. (2) He had received honours and favours at Caesar's hands, and these had blunted his own zeal to overthrow the monarchy: (3) he had been rescued at Pharsalus from sharing Pompey's flight, and he had even been allowed to extend this rescue to many of his friends by a simple request to Caesar. That was not all, for Caesar also placed great confidence in him, (4) and he already held the most distinguished of the praetorships. He was also going to be consul in three years' time. Cassius had been his rival, but Brutus was preferred, (5) with Caesar remarking (so they say) that Cassius' claim was the fairer, but that he himself would not pass over Brutus. (6) There was also an occasion when some people came to Caesar and accused Brutus—the conspiracy had already begun—but Caesar paid no attention; instead he touched his own body and replied to the accusers, 'Brutus will wait for this flesh'. The implication was that Brutus' virtue was such as to make him worthy to rule, but also such as to prevent any act of ingratitude or dishonour.

(7) As for those who were eager for revolution and looked to Brutus above anyone else, they did not dare to approach him openly; instead they worked by night, covering with writings his tribunal and the chair where he sat for official business as praetor. Most of them said things like 'Brutus! You are asleep!' or 'You are no Brutus'. (8) These began to stir his eagerness for glory: Cassius noticed, and began to press him harder than before and try to stir him into action. Cassius himself had certain personal reasons to hate Caesar, as we have explained in the *Brutus*. (9) Caesar was in fact suspicious of Cassius, and once said to his friends: 'what do you think Cassius wants? I do not like him: he is too pale.' (10) Again, there is a story of a time when Caesar was told that Antony and Dolabella were plotting; 'it is not those fat long-haired fellows I fear,' he said; 'it is rather those who are thin and pale'—meaning Cassius and Brutus.

63. Yet fate, it would seem, is not so much unexpected as unavoidable, for they say that there were some remarkable portents and apparitions to show what was to come. (2) In the case of so great an event it is perhaps not worth mentioning the blazing lights in the sky, or the strange sounds moving around in many directions at night, or the birds that swooped down into the forum by day. (3) But the philosopher Strabo narrates that many men saw human beings coming towards them in flames; that there was a particular soldier's slave who appeared to bystanders to be on fire, with a great flame bursting from his arm, yet was perfectly unharmed once the blaze died down; (4) that Caesar himself found that the heart was missing from an animal he was sacrificing, a dreadful prodigy, for no natural animal could exist without a heart. (5) One often hears another story too, that a certain soothsayer told Caesar to beware of a great danger on the day of March that the Romans call the Ides. (6) The day came, and Caesar greeted the man as he left for the senate. 'The Ides of March have come,' he light-heartedly said to him. 'Yes, they have come,' calmly answered the soothsayer; 'but they have not gone'. (7) The day before, Marcus Lepidus had been entertaining him to dinner, and Caesar was reclining on the couch adding his personal notes to letters as usual. The conversation turned to the most desirable way to die. 'Unexpectedly,' Caesar cried out, before anyone else said a word. (8) Later that evening he was in bed besides his wife as usual, and suddenly all the doors and windows of the room flew open. The room was bathed in moonlight, and Caesar himself was startled by the noise and the light; then he noticed Calpurnia still deeply asleep, but murmuring confused words and groaning disjointedly as she slept. (9) She was dreaming that she was holding Caesar's murdered body in her arms and weeping for him. (There is another version that her dream was a different one: according to Livy's account there was a gable built on to Caesar's house, voted by the senate as a mark of honour and distinction, and Calpurnia dreamed that this had broken off and she was weeping in frenzy for it.)

(10) At daybreak Calpurnia begged Caesar, if it was at all possible, not to leave the house but to postpone the meeting of the senate; or if he planned to treat her dreams as worthless, he should at least consult some other form of augury or sacrifice about the future. (11) And it would appear that Caesar himself felt some misgivings and unease, for he knew that Calpurnia had never before succumbed to such womanly superstition, and now he saw her in great distress.

(12) The soothsayers duly sacrificed, and after repeating the procedure many times they reported that the omens were unfavourable. Caesar decided to send Antony and dismiss the senate.

64. Then Decimus Brutus Albinus intervened. This was a man who was in Caesar's trust (so much so that he was included in his will among the second class of heirs), but who had joined the conspiracy of the other Brutus and Cassius and their followers. (2) He was nervous that Caesar might put matters off for that day and news of the conspiracy might leak out; so he made fun of what the soothsayers had said and warned Caesar that he was stirring up resentment and bad feeling among the senators, for he was giving the impression of treating them like playthings. (3) There they all were, gathered at his command, and everyone eager to vote for him to become king of the overseas provinces and to wear a diadem wherever he travelled outside Italy, by land or by sea. (4) They had already taken their seats: if anyone told them now to leave and reconvene on some day when Calpurnia's dreams had improved, what would be said by those who were jealous of him? (5) And who would listen to his friends if they denied that this was tyranny and slavery? But, Brutus added, if Caesar thought it absolutely essential to rule out the day for religious reasons, then it would be far better for him to come himself and make the announcement of a postponement in person. (6) As Brutus spoke he took Caesar by the hand and began to lead him out.

When he had taken a few steps from the door, a slave belonging to someone else tried to get to him, but could not force his way through the jostling crowd. Instead he forced his way into the house and gave himself up to Calpurnia, asking her to keep him there until Caesar returned, for he had great matters to reveal to him.

65. There was a man of Cnidus called Artemidorus, a Greek sophist, and for that reason close to some of Brutus' followers. He therefore knew most of what was going on, and he came carrying a document with details of what he was planning to reveal. (2) When he saw Caesar taking each document he was given and handing them unread to his attendants, Artemidorus came very close and said: 'Read this, Caesar, by yourself, and read it quickly: it is about great matters, and they concern your own person.' (3) Caesar took the document, but there were so many people coming to him that he could not read it, though he tried time after time. That document was the only thing he was still holding in his hand when he went into the senate. (4) Some claim that it was some other person who gave Caesar this letter, and that Artemidorus could not get near him at all, but was forced away by the crowd all along the route.

66. All that might simply be the result of coincidence, but it is harder to explain the place where the senate had gathered on that day, the scene of the murder and the violence. For it had a statue of Pompey standing there, and the whole building had been dedicated

by Pompey as one of the additional decorations to his theatre. That made it plain that there was some heavenly power directing events and guiding the plot into action at this spot. (2) Indeed, there is a story that Cassius looked at the statue of Pompey before they attacked, and called him silently to his aid, even though Cassius was sympathetic to Epicurean doctrine; (3) but it would seem that, in this critical and terrifying moment, a type of frenzied emotional transport drove out those earlier rational calculations.

(4) Antony was loyal to Caesar and physically powerful, and so Brutus Albinus kept him outside the senate, deliberately striking up a lengthy conversation. (5) As Caesar came in, the senate rose as a mark of respect. Some of Brutus' followers gathered behind Caesar's official chair, while others came to meet him: they pretended that they were coming to support a petition of Tillius Cimber to restore his exiled brother. (6) They came with Caesar right up to the chair, joining in with Tillius' entreaties. Caesar took his seat and waved the petitioners away. They responded by pleading with even greater force, and Caesar began to speak angrily to one man after another. Then Tillius grabbed Caesar's toga with both hands and ripped it down from the neck, the signal for the attack to begin. (7) Casca struck first, with a blow by the side of the neck that was not fatal nor even very deep: it was natural enough for him to be apprehensive at the beginning of so great and bold a venture. The wound was slight enough for Caesar to be able to spin round, grasp the dagger, and hold it firm. (8) The two men cried out at the same time, the victim in Latin, 'Casca, you scoundrel, what are you doing?' and the assailant in Greek to his brother, 'brother, help!'

(9) That was how it began. Those who knew nothing of the plot were bewildered and terrified: they dared not flee, nor go to Caesar's help, nor even utter a word. (10) As for the conspirators, they gathered round, each brandishing a naked blade. Caesar was surrounded; wherever he looked he met blow after blow, with the rush of steel towards face and eyes. He was run through like some wild beast, rolling to and fro in everyone's hands, (11) for each person there needed to begin the sacrifice and taste of the slaughter. That was why Brutus too struck a single blow to the groin. (12) Some say that Caesar fought gamely against the others, shouting and throwing his body in every direction, but when he saw Brutus with drawn blade he pulled his toga over his head and gave in before the attack.

He fell by the pedestal on which Pompey's statue stood, perhaps by chance, perhaps dragged there by the assassins. (13) It was drenched in streams of blood, so that it gave the impression that Pompey himself had presided over the vengeance inflicted on his enemy, lying there beneath his feet, still writhing convulsively from his many wounds. (14) There were twenty-three of these, they say, and many of his assailants were wounded by one another, as they aimed all those blows at the one single body.

67. Once Caesar was dead, Brutus came forward before the senators to say something about what they had done. The senators would not let him: instead they rushed out of the doors, and their flight filled the ordinary people with confusion and blind terror. Some shut up their houses, others left their counters and their places of business, some were rushing to the place to see what had happened, others were rushing back once they had seen the sight. (2) Antony and Lepidus, Caesar's closest friends, stole away into other houses. (3) Brutus' followers, just as they were, still hot from the killing, brandished their naked blades, and all of them left the senate house together and began to make their way to the Capitol. They did not seem like fugitives, but their faces were radiant with pride and confidence, as they called the ordinary people to freedom and welcomed the men of quality among those they met. (4) There were some who joined them and went up with them to the Capitol, just as if they had played a part in the killing themselves, and claimed a share of the glory. These included Gaius Octavius and Lentulus Spinther. (5) These men later paid the penalty for their shallow ostentation, for they were put to death by Antony and the younger Caesar; they did not even win the glory for which they died, for no one believed their claims. (6) Not even their killers were taking vengeance for what they did, only for what they wished they had done.

(7) Next day Brutus and his followers came down from the Capitol, and Brutus made a speech. The people listened to what was said without any hostility, but without showing any approval of what had been done: their utter silence hinted at pity for Caesar, but respect for Brutus. (8) The senate tried to bring about some sort of amnesty and general reconciliation, and so they voted that Caesar should be honoured as a god and that there should be no alteration in even the smallest particular of anything he had planned while in power, (9) while provinces and appropriate honours were given to Brutus

and his friends. So everyone thought that the situation had stabilized, and the best possible compromise had been reached.

68. But then Caesar's will was opened, and it was found that he had given a sizable sum to every single Roman citizen; and they saw the body as it was borne through the forum, all disfigured by its wounds. Now the popular passion no longer brooked any discipline or restraint: they brought benches and railings and tables from the forum, piled them round the corpse, and set it alight just where it was: (2) then they lit blazing torches and ran to the houses of the assassins to burn them down. Different groups roamed everywhere in the city, searching for the men to tear them to pieces.

None of them met the gangs, for they were all well barricaded away. (3) But there was a certain Cinna, a friend of Caesar, who (so they say) had had a strange dream on the previous night. He dreamed that Caesar was inviting him to dinner, and he was trying to decline; but Caesar led him along by the hand, even though he was unwilling and trying to resist. (4) When Cinna heard that Caesar's body was burning in the forum, he rose from his bed and went to pay respect, even though his dream caused him some misgiving and he was suffering from a fever. (5) When he was seen, one of the mob asked another what this man's name was, and he was told that it was Cinna. This was passed along, and there was an angry shouting everywhere, as they cried that this was one of Caesar's killers; (6) for there was a man of the same name among the conspirators. They assumed that this was the same man, rushed on him straight away, and tore him apart there and then.

(7) It was this incident more than anything that unnerved Brutus and Cassius, and a few days later they left the city. In the *Brutus* I have described what they did and suffered before they met their ends.

69. Caesar died after living fifty-six years in all, outliving Pompey by a little more than four years. He had sought dominion and power all his days, and after facing so many dangers he had finally achieved them. And the only fruit it bore him was its name, and the perils of fame amid his envious fellow-citizens.

(2) His great guardian spirit, which had accompanied him in life, continued to avenge his murder, pursuing and tracking his killers over every land and sea, until not one remained but everyone had been punished who had any contact with the killing in thought or in execution. (3) The most remarkable human event was what happened to Cassius, who after his defeat at Philippi killed himself with the very

dagger he had used against Caesar. (4) As for the supernatural, there
was the great comet that shone brightly for seven nights after Caesar's
death, then disappeared; and also the dimming of the sun's rays.
(5) For that entire year the sun rose pale, with no radiation, and its
heat came to earth only faintly and ineffectually, so that the air hung
dark and thick on the earth because of the lack of radiance to
penetrate it. The fruits of the earth consequently never matured, but
shrivelled and withered away when they were only half-ripe because
of the coldness of the air.

(6) More than anything else, it was the phantom that appeared to
Brutus that gave a particularly clear sign that Caesar's killing had been
unwelcome to the gods. It happened like this. (7) Brutus was about to
transport the army from Abydus to the other continent: it was night-
time, and he was resting as usual in his tent. He was not asleep, but
deep in thought about the future. (8) They say that this man needed
less sleep than any other general in history, and spent many hours
awake and alone. (9) He thought he heard a noise by the door, and
looked towards the lamp, which was already burning low. He saw a
terrifying apparition of a man, a giant in size and menacing to look at.
(10) At first he was shaken, but then he saw that the apparition was
doing nothing and saying nothing, but just standing silently by the
bed. Brutus asked him who he was. (11) The phantom replied: 'Your
evil spirit, Brutus. You will see me at Philippi.' For the moment
Brutus calmly replied 'I will meet you there', and the phantom
immediately went away.

(12) Then, later, Brutus faced Antony and the young Caesar in
battle at Philippi. In the first battle he defeated and forced back the
detachment stationed opposite himself, and drove on to destroy
Caesar's camp. (13) When he was about to fight the second battle
the phantom visited him again at night. It said nothing, but Brutus
recognized his fate, and plunged into danger in the battle.

(14) Yet he did not die fighting. After the rout he took refuge on a
rocky prominence, and forced his breast against his naked blade, with
a friend, so they say, adding weight to the blow. So he met his death.

Commentary

The Initial Lacuna

B. G. Niebuhr (*Vorträge über röm. Geschichte*, iii (1848), 28–9), and others before him, saw that several paragraphs had been lost; K. Ziegler, *RhM* 84 (1935), 387–90, suggested that the lacuna extended to the end of *Alexander*. Both hypotheses are confirmed if the identification of two fragments is admitted (below), but the *Caesar* lacuna at least was always indisputable. P. deals with his subject's ancestry even where there is little to say (e.g. *Sert.* 2.1, *Eum.* 1.1, *Cam.* 2.1: *Flam.* is the only exception among the Roman *Lives*), and there was much to say about the *gens Iulia*. He can hardly have omitted the entire story of C.'s youth, and the abruptness of 1.1 (n.) is itself suggestive. The mutilation seems to have taken place very early: a third-century papyrus (*PKöln* 47) begins with the same words as our manuscripts, but has them at the right-hand edge rather than the start of its first line. The first part of that line is missing, and so are any that preceded (G. Indelli, *Atene e Roma* 40 (1995), 49–50). Perhaps it was that papyrus itself that suffered the crucial damage, or perhaps its scribe may be indicating knowledge of a gap. Still, a parallel, unmutilated tradition seems also to have survived: see on Zonaras and the fragment, below.

What would the lacuna have contained? The fifth/sixth-century CE rhetorician Emporius takes C. as his example to illustrate ways of finding and treating material: 'he will be praised for his family... then his name will be treated... next education...' (*Rhet. Lat. Min.*, pp. 567–8 Halm). Dio 44.37 and Vell. 2.41.1 give some idea of the material available on the *gens Iulia*. P. knew of the paraded descent from Venus/Aphrodite (*Pomp.* 68.3), and may have mentioned it (cf. e.g. *Alc.* 21.1, *Ant.* 4.1–2; though cf. 42.1 n.); for such genealogies, cf. T. P. Wiseman, *G&R* 21 (1974), 153–64. Perhaps he also included C.'s grandmother's descent from the king Ancus Marcius (Suet. 6.1), and there was a treatment of the origin of the name 'Caesar' (below). C.'s father, who in the nineties reached the praetorship and became proconsul of Asia (T. R. S. Broughton, *AJA* 52 (1948), 323–30, *MRR* iii. 104–5), might rate a brief mention, and his mother Aurelia (9.3 n.) a more extensive one: she was of similar stature to Cornelia, the mother of the Gracchi (Tac. *Dial.* 28.6), whom P. treats enthusiastically at *Gracch.* 1.6–7 and 25.4–6. There will not have been much more on C.'s ancestors. They were respectable but not remarkably impressive (cf. Meier 52–4; E. Badian, *CJC* 11–16), and 'the fact that, for the time being, mattered most, was that Marius had married the sister of C.'s father' (Gelzer 19). That link is introduced, clearly for the first time, at 1.2.

C.'s youthful engagement and (in P.'s view) marriage to Cossutia was clearly mentioned (1.1, 5.7 nn.). But the lacuna will not have contained much more. Leo 180–2 enumerated the categories often found in a *Life*'s opening chapters: family, appearance, character, way of life, education, and style of speech. Education may have figured here, but the rest are held back till later, style of speech to 3 and most of the rest to 15–17, where they introduce C.'s 'second beginning in life' (15.2). This technique of postponing the 'categories' and weaving them into the narrative is seen elsewhere (e.g. *Ant.* 2.2–8 and 4, *Them.* 22.3, *Cic.* 3.6–7 and 8.3–6, *Dem.* 6.3–4), but never elaborated to such a degree. That is significant. P. is in this *Life* more interested in C.'s public life than in personalia: the tableau portrait comes naturally as a preparation for the Gallic campaigns, the period that brought the first spectacular achievements.

Suet.'s *Life* is also acephalous, and begins the narrative at precisely the same point. That may be coincidence: beginnings and ends of rolls were especially vulnerable to physical damage. Still, that explanation works better with Suet. than with P., where we would have to infer that the pair *Alexander–Caesar* was contained in two rolls rather than the usual one, presumably because of its length: so Stadter, *ICS* 13.2 (1988), 279. That is not impossible, but the continuous damage to the end of *Alexander* and beginning of *Caesar* would more naturally imply that the passages were together in the middle of a single roll. Alternatively, some element may have been particularly offensive to monkish sensibilities (something on Venus/Aphrodite, perhaps), and the destruction was deliberate. We cannot tell.

The Fragment
This is preserved by the twelfth-century Byzantine historian Zonaras (10.11, p. 368), who includes it not in its chronological place but as a note

attached to the story of *Caes.* 60.3 (he 'said that his name was "Caesar", not "King"'). In *CQ* 23 (1973), 343-4, I suggested that Zonaras had found the note in the proem of an unmutilated text of *Caesar*, and transplanted it to its new context: he does the same in epitomizing *Alexander*, working the story of 3.4 into the context of ch. 28 (4.10, p. 291). Alternative explanations—an addition from Zonaras' own general knowledge, perhaps, or a fleeting use of a secondary source—fit less well with Zonaras' technique elsewhere. I also suggested that 4.14, p. 304, was drawn from the lost conclusion to *Alexander*:

It is said that, as Alexander realized his life was departing, he wanted to drown himself secretly in the Euphrates: his object was to disappear and leave behind the story that he had now returned to the gods, just as he had come from them. But Roxane realized what was in his mind, so they say, and stopped the plan. Alexander said to her with a groan, 'So you envied me, wife, the fame of apotheosis and immortality'.

If these suggestions are right,[1] we do not have P.'s exact words, but Zonaras usually paraphrases closely, and most of his alterations are minor changes of order and the substitution of familiar words for recherché ones. He can be taken as a reliable indicator of P.'s content.

The mistake P. corrects—that C. owed his name to his own 'Caesarian' birth—is found at Serv. *ad Aen.* 1.286 and Isid. *Orig.* 9.3.12; Lydus *de Mens.* 4.102 attributes it to 'the ancients'. The argument of the correction itself—that Aurelia survived, and that it must have been one of his ancestors who was born in this way—is not found elsewhere: we would expect the more obvious 'but his ancestors were already called "Caesar"'. More usual is the simple attribution of the Caesarian birth to an ancestor: Plin. *NH* 7.47 ('first of the Caesars'[2]), Serv. *ad Aen.* 10.316, and esp. *SHA Ael. Ver.* 2.3-4, who also lists alternative etymologies: that an ancestor killed an elephant ('caesai' in Moorish), or had a thick head of hair (*caesaries*), or had eyes that were bright grey (*caesiis*). At *Met.* 15.840 Ovid seems to play on a 'Caesarian birth' etymology when his Jupiter talks of the 'body cut open and the spirit torn out', then sent heavenwards, on the Ides of March. Cf. *TLL*, s.v. 'Caesar', col. 34; R. Maltby, *A Lexicon of Ancient*

---

[1] They are countered by M. Manfredini, *Prometheus*, 19 (1993), 18-23, to my mind unconvincingly: in particular, he gives too little weight to the other indications that the end of *Alexander* and the beginning of *Caesar* are lacunose. But Manfredini may be right in suggesting that Zonaras is using an earlier epitome rather than P. directly; in that case, it will be that epitomist, not Zonaras, who had access to a non-lacunose Plutarch text.

[2] Scholars usually take this to mean 'first of the *imperial* Caesars', i.e. C. himself, but that would be an extraordinary mistake for Pliny to make, especially if, as seems likely, he is here using Varro (cf. Varro *gramm.* frs 145, 323, 327, 337, 347).

Latin Etymologies (1991), 93. In fact all these etymologies seem wrong, and 'Caesar' is Etruscan in origin: A. Ernout and L. Meillet, *Dictionnaire étymologique de la langue latine*[4] (1959), 84.

1–3: First Steps

Here as in *Alexander* the narrative presages future greatness, but in a different way. In *Alexander* there is the hint of a divine register, with extraordinary occurrences—thunderflashes, significant dreams, unnatural snakes, Philip robbed of his eyesight, the coincidence of three pieces of good news on the same day (2–3)—all indicating the possibility of a heavenly father. Most of the possible omens are given an alternative secular interpretation (see Intr., pp. 30–1), but the question is already opened whether the gods are taking an interest. In *Caesar* the register is purely secular: the interest falls on the qualities that the perceptive Sulla sees (1) and the doltish pirates miss (2), and on the rhetorical skills that will fit C. for greatness—but also on the future preoccupations that will rob him of first place (3). As yet, though, there is nothing on C.'s own hopes or ambitions: the future is seen through others' hopes and fears, and through P.'s own authorial prolepsis (3.3–4). A subtler prefiguring is the emphasis on Roman 'monarchy'. C. is first seen as son-in-law of the 'monarch' Cinna, then as understood and feared by Sulla. His relation to absolute rule is already foregrounded.

P.'s material is so similar to that of Suet. 1–4 that it probably comes from the same source; but there are various differences in emphasis and sequence. In most of these it seems likely that P. rather than Suet. is adapting (nn.). Vell. 2.41–3 also seems to rest on similar material.

1.1–8: CAESAR AND SULLA   Cf. Vell. 2.41.2 and esp. Suet. 1. Suet. has a different sequence:

Plutarch	Suetonius
1. C. refuses to divorce Cornelia; Sulla deprives him of the dowry.	1. C. refuses to divorce Cornelia; Sulla deprives him of the dowry, the priesthood, and the patrimony.
2. C. seeks a priesthood.	2. C. flees.
3. Sulla deprives him of the priesthood.	3. C. bribes the searchers.
4. Intercession: Sulla utters his *dictum*, and refuses to concede.	4. Intercession; Sulla concedes, but utters his *dictum*.
5. C. flees.	
6. C. bribes his searchers.	
7. C. flees to Bithynia.	

For P., the result is historically inaccurate (nn.) but biographically superior. Sulla is the centre of the Suet. account, and the sequence must finally return to him; P. makes it an event in C.'s story, not in Sulla's. In P. the priesthood represents an additional provocation, and Sulla's move seems less extreme; then Caesar secures his own safety, with no concession from Sulla himself. His flight to Bithynia gives a smooth transition to the next item. P. cuts away material which might distract: Julia's birth, postponed to a later context (5.7 n., contrast Suet. 1.1); the names of those who interceded (§4 n.).

P. is fond of such adventure stories: cf. *Crass.* 4–5, *Mar.* 36–40, both with a wealth of (doubtless imaginative) detail and coloured style. This version is austere in comparison. P. hurries on towards 'the vast number of actions which form my subject-matter' (*Alex.* 1.2).

The episode is discussed by R. T. Ridley, *Hist.* 49 (2000), 211–29.

1.1. The style of the Greek is abrupt, and it may be that our text begins in mid-sentence (Pelling, 'Notes', 33). **Caesar had married Cornelia:** at the age of 16, i.e. according to Suet. (88.1, cf. 69.1 n.) in 84 or 83, 'when designated as *flamen Dialis*, after discarding Cossutia, a fairly rich girl of equestrian family, who had been betrothed to C. while he was still an adolescent' (Suet. 1.1). 5.7 (n.) shows that, according to P., Caesar and Cossutia had been married, not just betrothed. But a *flamen Dialis* could not be divorced (1.3 n.), and it is anyway hard to find room for a marriage and divorce before C. was 16, especially as the marriage should presumably precede 87–6, the probable date of C.'s designation as priest (below). Suet.'s 'discarding' must simply mean that an engagement was broken off, and P. must have misunderstood a source.

As Suet.'s language suggests, Cossutia's rejection was linked to C.'s nomination to the flaminate (§3): a *flamen Dialis* was required to be married by the ritual of *confarreatio* (see *OCD*[4], s.v. 'manus', S. Treggiari, *Roman Marriage* (1991), 21–4) to a patrician wife, herself the daughter of parents married by *confarreatio*. P.'s misdating of the flaminate 'candidature' (below) has obscured the connection. Cf. G. de Sanctis, *Riv. fil.* 12 (1934), 550–1.

The Cinna who had once been monarch: a strong phrase for the domination of Cinna as consul from 87 to 84. The language may owe something to the prophecy related at *Cic.* 17.5, that the Cornelii would provide Rome with 'three monarchs' (i.e. Cinna, Sulla, and P. Cornelius Lentulus Sura, 7.6 n.). It also suits the themes of the *Life* (above). **Then Sulla won control:** in 82. **He could not entice or intimidate Caesar into divorcing her.** Sulla's motives are unclear, and initially may not have been vindictive: when he forced Pompey to divorce, it was to set up a new union linking the young man more closely to Sulla himself (*Pomp.* 9, *Sulla* 33.4). Cf. Strasburger 80, Meier 93, and esp. Ridley, art. cit. (1.1–8 n.).

1.2. Sulla...Marius...   Here as in §1 P. assumes that his readers are familiar with the outline: hence he does not have to explain that Sulla and Marius were bitter enemies, nor sketch the history of the civil wars of the eighties. Julia (*Mar.* 6.4, *OCD*[4], no. 1) married Marius at some time between 115 and 110. She died before or during 69: 5.2. The **younger Marius** (*OCD*[4], no. 2) became consul in 82 and died at Praeneste in the same year. P. disapproved of him: *Mar.* 46.7–9.

1.3. came before the public as a candidate for a priesthood.   This was the position of *flamen Dialis.* It was a considerable honour, but was also hedged around by various ritual restrictions, listed by Gell. 10.15: the priest, for instance, was forbidden to mount a horse, or to see armed troops outside the *pomerium,* or to touch a corpse, or to spend more than two nights away from Rome. It is uncertain how many of these provisions still applied in practice; they had not prevented the previous *flamen,* L. Cornelius Merula, from becoming consul in 87 (Ridley, art. cit., 214). But we know of no provincial command for Merula, and it remains possible that, had C. become and remained *flamen,* his political enemies could have put serious difficulties in his later path. Cf. Tatum 29–31, with good remarks on the reasons why the flaminate might still have seemed attractive to the young C. and his family: if his epilepsy was already a problem (but 17.2 indicates that the first onset was later), a more active career may at that stage have seemed unrealistic.

Suet. 1.1 and Vell. 2.43.1 agree that Sulla took the priesthood away from C., but differ from P. on other details. Appointment to the priesthood apparently involved two stages that might normally follow closely on one another, nomination and then inauguration. Vell. has 'when, as not much more than a boy, he had been made [*creatus*] *flamen Dialis* by Marius and Cinna...': that language suggests a date in late 87 or very early 86, before Marius' death on 13 January. 'Creatus' is normally taken to suggest that C. actually became priest, but Woodman, ad loc., argues that it may refer only to the nomination, not the full inauguration. Suet., we saw (§1 n.), has C. marry Cornelia in 84 or 83 when 'designated *flamen Dialis*'. His 'designated' seems accurate, for it seems likely that C. was never installed: at *Ann.* 3.58.2 Tacitus makes his Servius Maluginensis say that there was no *flamen Dialis* appointed for seventy-two (or seventy-five: the MS number may be corrupt) years after Merula (died 87); Dio 54.36.1 similarly speaks of the 'first appointment of a *flamen Dialis* since Merula' in 11 BCE. Suet. is usually read as implying that the 'designation' also took place in 84 or 83, but that need not follow: Suet. may be suggesting a causal rather than chronological link (C. discarded Cossutia and married Cornelia '*as* f. D. designate'), and the designation could still go back to 87–86, presumably to replace Merula. Hence Suet. and Vell. can be reconciled.

The alternative is to assume that C. *was* installed to replace Merula, but his name was removed from the list of priests when Sulla annulled Cinna's *acta*: so E. Badian, *CJC* 16, *Gnom.* 33 (1961), 598 and 62 (1990), 33; Sumner 139–40. This is less likely: all memory of it would seem to have vanished by the time of Tacitus' Maluginensis, whose language—no priest was 'appointed to fill the vacancy' during that period (*suffectus*: cf. Dio's 'first appointment')—is not appropriate if one was appointed but annulled; nor would Maluginensis have weakened his argument if he had said 'for seventy years since C.' rather than 'since Merula'—indeed, he could have made capital from having such a man of action as a predecessor, for he is arguing for permission to govern a province ('what would have happened if C. had remained *flamen* and been prevented from governing Gaul? Think what Rome would have lost...'). Nor does it save us from positing a long delay after nomination, if C. was genuinely nominated 'by Marius and Cinna' in 87–86 and his marriage to Cornelia was not till 84–83.

P. must refer to the same priesthood, but C. will not now have been 'a candidate' for it for the first time. Perhaps C. did now seek full inauguration: a *flamen Dialis* could not be divorced (Gell. 10.15.23), and C. would therefore acquire an excuse to place in the way of Sulla's request. But P.'s version is anyway confused. (1) The flaminate was not in the gift of 'the public': the priest was chosen from a short list of

three by the pontifex maximus (Tac. *Ann.* 4.16), and the short list
was presumably drawn up by the college of *pontifices* (*StR* ii³. 25–6).
(2) P. himself clearly is not presenting this as a double stage of
'designation' and full inauguration, for if he had mentioned 'designation' in the initial lacuna he would not have written in these terms
here. It is better to regard the candidature as a narrative displacement
to this point, underlining C.'s provocative boldness. In this presentation C.'s first resource, when threatened by his enemies, is to turn
to the people of Rome. That is P.'s own favoured theme, and it makes
it likely that the whole embellishment is his own, not a source's.

On all this see esp. L. R. Taylor, *CPh* 36 (1941), 115–16, and *TAPA*
73 (1942), 4–5; Strasburger 79–82; Syme, *RP* i. 153–4; Weinstock 30;
M. Leone, *Studi … E. Manni* (1976), 193–212; Linderski 554–6; Rid-
ley, *Hist.* 49 (2000), 213–15; and in general on the flaminate
J. Vanggaard, *The flamen: A Study in the History and Sociology of
Roman Religion* (1988).

though still a very young man: assuming that C. was born in 100
(69.1 n.), he would be about 18 (the age given by Vell. 2.41.2): 'at first'
should date this to 82 or soon afterwards.

1.4. Some argued that it was senseless to kill a boy of his age.   Suet.
1.2 names C.'s supporters as 'the Vestal Virgins and his relatives and
kinsmen Mam. Aemilius and Aurelius Cotta', i.e. probably Mam.
Aemilius Lepidus, cos. 77, and C. Aurelius Cotta, cos. 75. C.'s mother
was an Aurelia (9.3 n., cf. 60.2 n.); his relationship to the Aemilii was
more distant (Münzer, *RAPF* 287–8, 298 = *RAA* 312–13, 324). The
Vestals were closely connected in cult with the *flamen Dialis*, and the
two men were apparently *pontifices* and may have interceded in that
role: Münzer, *Philol.* 92 (1937–8), 221. These were highly influential
gentes at the period, with the Aemilii Lepidi providing a consul in 78
as well as 77 and the Aurelii Cottae in 74 as well as 75. The connections doubtless helped the young C. in less conspicuous ways as well,
perhaps, for instance, in connection with C.'s own remarkable election as *pontifex* in 73: see 4.1 n. **there was many a Marius inside this
'boy'.** Sulla's dictum comes at the end of Suet.'s account (1.3), where it
is associated with the pardon. P.'s Sulla does not relent. It seems that
the pardon at least is historical, and P. is wrong: C.'s military service
(omitted by P., §7 n.) shows that he was back in favour by 81. Either
P. has displaced Sulla's remark, or, just as likely, both he and Suet.

have exploited a floating apophthegm and attached it to the stage of their story where it fitted best. Cf. Dio 43.43.4: like Suet., he thinks that Sulla pardoned C., and, like Suet., he thinks a parting shot is needed; but he prefers the other Sullan *dictum*, that 'they should beware the badly belted boy' (cf. Suet. 45.3, Macr. *Sat.* 2.3.9).

1.7. a man called Cornelius: Cornelius Phagita, whom C. later 'could never bring himself to harm' (Suet. 74.1). **two talents:** the drachma was generally equated with the denarius. One talent = 6,000 dr./den. = 24,000 sesterces. 'Two' is probably a rounding of 50,000 sesterces. This was the usual reward offered by Sulla to murderers of the proscribed (*Sull.* 31.7, *C.min.* 17.5), and search parties doubtless did a good trade in bribes of this order; but C. himself was probably never placed on a proscription list (B. R. Motzo, *Ann. Fac. Filos. Lett. Cagliari* 4 (1933), 62–4). **Nicomedes** IV Philopator, king of Bithynia from *c.*94 to 74: see *OCD*[4], R. Sullivan, *Near Eastern Royalty and Rome* (1990), 33–5.

1.8. He did not stay there long: defensive phrasing. C.'s stay with Nicomedes became notorious for sexual reasons: Suet. 49 lists examples of his enemies' obscene verses on the subject, and tells how at his Gallic triumph the soldiers sang of 'Caesar grinding the Gauls and Nicomedes grinding Caesar'. Suet. mentions the scandal in the present context (2.1): here as elsewhere (8.2, 10.7, 49.10 nn., and Intr., pp. 22–3) P. passes discreetly over C.'s sexual diversions. Perhaps he was right to do so: J. Osgood, *CQ* 58 (2008), 687–91, suggests that the charge, typical of Roman invective, may well have originated in the exchanges of the Dolabella trial in 77–76 (4.1 n.), and that C. was probably spending his time in Bithynia building up connections and *clientelae*.

P. also omits the circumstances of the visit. In 80–79 C. was serving his first campaign under M. Minucius Thermus, governor of Asia (*MRR* 76, 78, 81), and Minucius 'sent him to Bithynia to collect a fleet' (Suet. 2.1). P. also omits C.'s brief service in Cilicia under P. Servilius Vatia Isauricus (7.1 n.), probably in 78 (if the chronology of Suet. 3.1 can be trusted) in a year given mainly to preparations (*MRR* 88). Normally P. likes such first campaigns: cf. e.g. *C.mai.* 1.8, *Mar.* 3.2, *Sert.* 3.1, and especially *Cor.* 3.1, with D. A. Russell, *JRS* 53 (1963) 23–4 = Scardigli, *Essays*, 362–3; and these were not without incident or importance, for C. was decorated by Thermus for valour (Suet. 2), and this will have boosted his early political prestige (E. Badian, *Gnom.* 62 (1990), 28–9). But P.'s recasting of the Sullan adventure (1.3 n.) left no room for that here. C. secures his own escape, is never pardoned, and hence cannot serve the Sullan regime.

On C.'s early activity in the East, see also 2.7 n.

1.8–2.7: CAESAR AND THE PIRATES   The story is also told by Vell. 2.41–2 (well discussed by Schmitzer 164–76), Suet. 4, Polyaenus 8.23.1, and Val. Max. 6.9.15. It probably has a core of truth. 'Piracy', the opportunistic reassignment of ownership of cargoes and other goods, was a familiar aspect of maritime enterprise culture in the eastern Mediterranean, based especially on Cilicia ('these Cilicians, the most bloodthirsty people in the world' (2.2)) and Crete. At this period the Romans periodically sought to act as spoilsports, most notably with Pompey's vast command of 67 BCE (5.8–9 n.): that is itself testimony to the scale of the problem. C. was not the only Roman noble to be taken and held to ransom, for the same thing happened to Clodius a few years later (*MRR* 148; W. J. Tatum, *The Patrician Tribune* (1999), 50). Here the precise detail of 'Iuncus' (2.6 n.) also suggests some factual basis, as does Polyaenus' mention of the historical figure Epicrates (2.5 n.).

That core lent itself to embellishment: 'pirate-captures' were a favourite theme of rhetorical declamation (e.g. Sen. *Contr.* 1.2, 6–7, 3.3, 7.4; [Quint.] *Decl. min.* 257, 342–3, 373), and became a favourite of the novelists too (e.g. Chariton 1.7–14, Heliod. *Aethiop.* 5.20–7, Xen. Ephes. 1.13–14, Ach. Tat. *Leuc. and Cleit.* 2.17–18, 3.9–14); and it was doubtless embellished even before P. came to it. Our different versions elaborate further, variously stressing the humiliation of it all (Suet., Vell.), the unnerving terror C. inspired in his captors (Vell.), the vicissitudes of a divine figure (Val. Max.), the hackneyed but dramatic stratagem of the pirates' undoing (C. drugged their wine at a farewell banquet and killed them: thus Polyaenus, who therefore leaves no room for Iuncus). P. too doubtless adds his own touches: the poetry recitals (§4 n.) and the demands for silence do not occur in the other versions. Still, his point remains uncomplicated, C.'s confident disdain and ruthless speed of vengeance. Notice especially the additional detail of *Crass.* 7.5, surely acquired from the same source during P.'s reading for *Caesar* but suppressed here as distracting: at one point C. exclaimed, 'Crassus, how delighted you'll be to hear of my capture!'

Polyaenus, like P., connects the story with C.'s trip to Nicomedes, Polyaenus preferring the outward journey, P. the return. But a later date is almost certain. Suet. connects it with the journey to Rhodes that P. mentions at 3.1, and puts it after the Dolabella trial (4.1 n.): that puts it between 77 and 73, and is confirmed by the very precise detail of Vell. 2.42.3. C. there refers the matter to 'Iunius Iuncus', proconsul of Bithynia and Asia. This must be our 'Iuncus' of 2.6, who apparently held this unique province for a short period of 74–3 (n.). C. was detained for thirty-eight days: his capture should therefore be dated to late 74 or very early 73. So *MRR* 98, 100 n. 6 and A. M. Ward, *AJAH* 2 (1977), 26–36, with a necessary chronological correction by D. G. Glew, *Chiron*, 11 (1981) 128–9; for a different view, see L.-M. Günther, *Chiron*, 29 (1999), 321–37, who to my mind underrates P.'s capacity to revise chronology in the interest of narrative smoothness (3.1 n.).

P.'s transposition hangs together with the similar antedating of the visit to Rhodes (3.1 n.). It will have been aided by the two trips to Bithynia.

For the spread of Mediterranean piracy and Roman countermeasures, see esp. *Pomp.* 24, App. *Mith.* 63, 92–3, Dio 36.20–3, Cic. *de Imp. Cn. Pomp.* 31–3, 55; *OCD*[4], s.v. 'piracy'; H. A. Ormerod, *Piracy in the Ancient World* (1924), ch. 6; P. de Souza, *Piracy in the Greco-Roman World* (1999), chs 4–5, discussing this incident at 140–1.

1.8. Pharmacusa: south of Miletus, some 10 km. south-west of Cape Monodendri. For piracy in the area, cf. *Greek Questions* 303d, Strabo 14.1.7, *SIG*[3] 567–70. **large fleets:** noted as a recent development: so also *Pomp.* 24.4, App. *Mith.* 63.262, Vell. 2.31.2, Dio 36.21.1. This was one aspect of the pirates' growing unity and improved organization.

2.1. twenty talents. Suet. and Val. Max. mention the fifty talents C. paid, Polyaenus has C.'s bravado in 'doubling' the sum. Such numbers in literary sources are very stylized, often dealing in powers of ten (W. Scheidel, *CQ* 46 (1996), 222–38), but pirates may have liked powers of ten as well. Less valuable citizens were treated more mockingly: cf. the colourful plank-walking at *Pomp.* 24.11–13.

2.4. poems and speeches. The touch seems to be P.'s own (1.8–2.7 n.): it coheres with the themes of 3.2–4 (n.), where C. *could*, if he had chosen, been the master wordsmith rather than the master politician.

For C.'s youthful poetry, cf. esp. Suet. 56.7. 'Caesar and Brutus wrote poems . . . no better than Cicero, but with better luck, for fewer people know it' (Tac. *Dial.* 21.6).

2.5. Then the ransom arrived from Miletus. Polyaenus 8.23.1 names a Milesian intermediary 'Epicrates', who is known epigraphically and was worshipped as a hero after his death: cf. L.-M. Günther, *Chiron*, 29 (1999), 329-33, emphasizing the role of Miletus in the story, and suggesting that the hunting-down of the pirates owed less to C. himself than to a Milesian public initiative. It may well have been a mixture of both.

2.6. Iuncus, who was governor of Asia: cf. Vell. 2.42.3, 'he came to Bithynia to the proconsul Iunius Iuncus [on the reading, cf. Woodman, ad loc.], who was governing that province along with Asia'. Praetor in 76, Iuncus became proconsul of Asia in 75. Nicomedes' death is now dated to late 74: coins show he was still alive in October. He bequeathed his kingdom to Rome, and Vell. implies that Iuncus administered it along with Asia for the rest of his term (so *MRR* 98 and iii. 113). The new governors (the two consuls of 74, Lucullus coming to Cilicia and Asia and M. Aurelius Cotta to Bithynia) may have arrived before the end of 74 or in early 73. On the chronology, see *MRR* 106-9; W. Bennett, *Hist.* 10 (1961), 460-3; D. G. Glew, *Chiron*, 11 (1981), 128; Sherwin-White 162-5.

At some point C. also pleaded a case 'for (certain) Bithynians', and addressed 'M. Iuncus' in the proem (Gell. 5.13.6, as emended = fr. 44 M.). That was probably during this same short period in Bithynia, with C. addressing Iuncus as judge. H. Dahlmann, *Hermes*, 73 (1938), 341-6, less plausibly assigns it to a later trial for extortion, with C. addressing Iuncus as the accused. **governor.** The Greek is the non-technical *strategos* ('commander'), used of Roman 'governors' of various title and rank (Mason 86-7, 155-62). Here Iuncus was apparently 'proconsul' (Vell.).

2.7. Iuncus eyed the money greedily. P. is muddled. 'The' money seems to identify it with 'the money' that C. had extracted from the pirates at §5, which will have included the fifty talents ransom, but it is obscure why this should recommend delay in allowing the prisoners' execution: Iuncus' ability to extract this money for himself seems unaffected by that. Vell. 2.42.3 suggests the truth of the matter: 'Iuncus said he would not execute them, but would sell them instead',

presumably as slaves. P. has either streamlined or misunderstood.
crucified them: after first cutting their throats (Suet. 74.1, citing it as
an instance of C.'s mercifulness). Fenestella fr. 30 P. has their heads
cut off instead.

P. ignores various other eastern experiences of C., several of which
would have involved further brushes with pirates. He served under
P. Servilius Vatia Isauricus, probably in 78 (so Suet. 3: above, 1.8 n.),
and he may well have been the C. Iulius who held a legateship
under M. Antonius in 73–2 (SIG^3 748, *MRR* iii. 105). He was also
involved in fighting against Mithridates in Asia Minor (Suet. 4,
cf. Meier 109–10), probably in 73, and at some point, perhaps in 78
or 75–3, became a guest-friend of King Deiotarus of Galatia. Vell.
2.43.1–2 also tells of C.'s return to Italy, and his attempts to evade the
pirates' revenge.

On C.'s eastern service, see also E. Badian, *CJC* 17–19; T. R. S.
Broughton, *TAPA* 79 (1948), 63–7 (the legateship under Antonius,
doubted by Sumner 138 and Badian); H. W. Ritter, *Hist.* 18 (1969),
255–6 (Deiotarus); B. C. McGing, *The Foreign Policy of Mithridates
VI Eupator* (1986), 147.

3.1. Sulla's power began to decline. P. thus dates the Rhodes
journey to 79–8. A later date is again likely: Suet. 4 dates it after the
failure of C.'s prosecution of Dolabella (4.1 n.), when C. 'decided to
leave Rome and go to Rhodes, both to escape his unpopularity and to
use the opportunity of his leisure to study with Apollonius Molon, the
most distinguished teacher of rhetoric of the day'. The journey will
presumably be later than the Antonius case as well as the Dolabella
trial (4.1–3): that implies a date of 76 or later. If Suet. is right to
connect this with the pirate story, that should give a date during 74–3
(1.8–2.7 n.): C. probably arrived at Rhodes in the first months of 73.

P.'s antedating of the pirate episode (1.8–2.7 n.) and the Rhodian
journey enables P. to group C.'s early foreign adventures together
(1.7–3.1); the return to Rome (4.1) concentrates attention exclusively
on domestic events. There is also advantage in placing the visit to
Rhodes before the Dolabella and Antonius lawsuits (4.1–3), as C.'s
rhetorical triumphs now follow as a natural consequence of this study
under Apollonius. Suet.'s sequence, with C. *failing* in the Dolabella
case and *then* betaking himself to Apollonius, is probably the one that
P. knew (1–3 n.), but that would compromise P.'s picture of

consistent success. For similar tendentious transplants, cf. Intr., p. 56, and *Plutarch and History*, 92–3.

Caesar's friends at home encouraged him to return. P. may here have conflated the Rhodes episode with the item of Suet. 3, 'when news of Sulla's death [March 78] arrived, Caesar hastened home; he was also influenced by his expectation of the new unrest which M. Lepidus was stirring up...' (though Suet. may here himself be incorporating some of his own imaginative interpretation). The involvement with Lepidus did not come to anything, and P. naturally omitted it. **He sailed to Rhodes.** P. does not make the logic clear, but the point is similar to *Cic.* 4.4–5: when Cicero heard of Sulla's death, 'his friends in Rome sent him many messages and requests, and Antiochus himself [Cicero's philosophical teacher] also strongly encouraged him to launch himself on public life: Cicero once again developed his political rhetoric as a tool...'. Caesar like Cicero responded to his friends' encouragement towards political life, *and so* went to Rhodes to study rhetoric. This notion of rhetoric as an instrument for politics, not an end in itself, is a favourite of P.: cf. e.g. *Advice on Public Life* 801c–802e, *Per.* 8.1 with Stadter's n., *Fab.* 1.7, *C.min.* 4.3, *C.mai.* 1.5.

On Rhodes as a cultural centre, cf. F. Portalupi, *Sulla corrente rodiese* (1957); on such cultural visits of young men to the Greek world, L. W. Daly, *AJP* 71 (1950), 40–58.

Apollonius son of Molon: more usually called 'Apollonius Molon' or just 'Molon': see *OCD*[4], no. 9, and A. E. Douglas on Cic. *Brut.* 307. He taught not only C. and Cicero, but also T. Torquatus (Cic. *Brut.* 245) and perhaps M. Favonius (Cic. *Att.* 2.1 (21).9). **who also had the reputation of being an admirable person.** Note the emphasis on character as well as skill. There may be some hint of the Roman ideal of 'a good man and a skilled speaker' (*uir bonus dicendi peritus*), but P. is probably applying his own evaluative criteria here (cf. *Advice on Public Life* 800a–801d) and assuming that the young C. would have shared them. Elsewhere P. makes Demosthenes admire Callistratus, Brutus admire Antiochus, and the Romans admire Philo for similar reasons (*Dem.* 5.4, *Brut.* 2.3, *Cic.* 3.1), and at *Ant.* 80.3 he makes Octavian show disapproval for an eloquent rhetorician with a despicable character.

F. Gerber, however, prefers (*RhM* 134 (1991), 157–61) to assign this 'high moral reputation' to a source that P. has encountered since

writing *Cicero*, and thinks that P. welcomed it as a reply to Josephus'
denunciation of Apollonius (*Against Apion* 2.145, 148, 236, 255, 295).
But there is no sign elsewhere that P. knew Josephus' work. He may,
however, have been aware that Apollonius was a controversial figure,
and P. may be quietly indicating that C. learnt nothing more sinister
from him than rhetorical skill.

Cicero too attended his lectures: *Cic.* 4.5; Cic. *Brut.* 307, 312, 316,
with Douglas's nn.

3.2–4: CAESAR'S ELOQUENCE   P. does not seem to know C.'s
speeches at first hand, though several survived to his day: the references at 4.1–3, 5.2–5, 6.7, and 7.9–8.1 do not suggest direct acquaintance. See Intr., p. 48, and *Plutarch and History*, 17; J. Geiger in
Rhetorical Theory and Praxis in Plutarch, ed. L. van der Stockt
(2000), 219–21. C.'s rhetorical fragments are collected in Malcovati,
ORF, pp. 383–97, and discussed by K. Deichgräber, *Gymn.* 57 (1950),
112–23 = *WdF* 208–23. For praise of his eloquence, cf. esp. Cic. *Brut.*
252, 261; Tac. *Dial.* 25.3–4, *Ann.* 13.3; Suet. 55.1.

P. makes no comment on C.'s rhetorical *style*, though often elsewhere he uses this as a way of illuminating a man's character, whether
or not he knew their writings directly: cf. *Ant.* 2.8 with my n., *Gracch.*
2.2–3, *Fab.* 1.8, etc. Here he stresses only the *quality* of its rhetoric,
stressing the admiration it aroused. That directed the political result,
the adhesion of the masses: cf. 4.1–3, 5.2–5, and 6.7; and the prolepsis
of C.'s final success ('his attention was devoted to becoming first in
power...') indicates how successful he would be. It will also be
important that he attains only 'second place' in rhetoric. If we had
not already sensed the identity of the first-place winner, §4 makes it
clear: Cicero, of course. In the closing chapters a series of Ciceronian
barbs will play an important part in undermining Caesar's supre-
macy: the worlds of rhetoric and of power will not eventually prove so
easy to keep separate. Cf. Intr., p. 25.

he trained and developed this talent: P.'s advice for any aspiring
politician (*Advice on Public Life* 801c ff.). **The second place was
unquestionably his:** while Cicero 'advanced to first place: it was not
a slow progress, but he immediately won a glorious reputation and far
outmatched his contenders in the forum' (*Cic.* 5.3).

3.3...he allowed the first to escape him...   The Greek is here
difficult and corrupt (cf. Pelling, 'Notes', 34), but the sense is reasonably clear. Similarly Quint. 10.1.114, 'if Caesar had had time to

concentrate only on the forum, no other Roman would be named as Cicero's rival'; Tacitus' 'Aper' puts the same point more negatively (*Dial.* 21.5). Notice also Cicero's similar judgement on Pompey, *Brut.* 239.

Alexander too was culturally as well as politically gifted, but he initially told Aristotle 'I should wish to excel in my skills in the highest pursuits rather than in power' (*Alex.* 7.7). C.'s choice seems different. But it is a question whether P.'s Alexander lived up to those initial protestations: Intr., p. 29.

3.4. his reply to Cicero's essay on Cato: i.e. the *Anticato*, 54.5–6 nn. **he himself begged his readers not to compare his style with Cicero's...** There was surely irony here, especially in 'and the time to cultivate it': the apparent self-deprecation insinuates that C.'s own time has been better spent. So H. J. Tschiedel, *Caesars 'Anticato'* (1981), 76–9. It would be a mistake to take this too literally as an acknowledgement of Cicero's stylistic superiority. P.—or his source, for he is unlikely to have known the *Anticato* at first hand (Intr., p. 48)—may have missed the sardonic tone, here as at *Cic.* 39.5 (see 54.5 n.); but P. may have chosen to use the item anyway, welcoming the chance to prepare for the later Ciceronian exchanges (above). **Cicero the accomplished orator:** echoed at 54.5 (n.).

4–14: Rome: The First Phase

We have so far had hints of C.'s coming power (1–3 n.), but only fleeting suggestions of the methods and qualities that will gain that power: his turning to the people at a moment of crisis (1.3), his eerie determination and ruthlessness (2), his rhetorical training (3.1 n.), but also the second place this takes to 'becoming first in power and in armed strength' (3.3). The next chapters will transpose these qualities into Roman politics, where the rhetorical skills (esp. 4, 5.4–5, 7.8–9), the popularity they brought him (esp. 4–6), his successes on campaign (11–12), and his uncompromising ruthlessness before his opponents (6, 7.1–4, 13–14) render him formidable. So far only Sulla, attuned to autocracy as he is, has sensed the danger C. posed (1.4); the following chapters trace the gradual wakening of C.'s senatorial enemies to the threat. A series of *apophthegmata* (short pithy utterances) point this development, functioning almost as a refrain: Antonius at 4.3, Cicero at 4.8–9, Catulus at 6.6–7, Cato's reported 'dark prophecies' at 13.3–6, Considius at 14.14–15. Meanwhile C.'s own *apophthegmata* correspondingly convey his own determination (7.4,

10.9, 11.3–4). In the *Life*'s closing chapters a similar series of *apophthegmata* will track C.'s gathering vulnerability, as the factors that initially build his power finally turn against him: Intr., pp. 24–5.

As at 1–3 (n.), Suet. continues to present similar items, and can often convey an idea of the material open to P.; but, as C. begins to play a part in general history, the material open to both authors grew greater, and the source picture becomes more complex. From ch. 13 it seems that P. begins to draw on his Pollio source. See Intr., pp. 44–7.

4.1. On his return to Rome. The displacements of 1.8–2.7 and 3.1 (nn.) have obscured the chronology. C.'s *first* return from the East is dated to 78 BCE (3.1 n.), and it was after this that he prosecuted Dolabella and appeared against Antonius (below). Then came his second eastern phase, and the pirate and Rhodian episodes (75–3). In 73 C. heard that he had been co-opted as *pontifex*, and hurried home: Vell. 2.43.1–2, with L. R. Taylor, *CPh* 36 (1941), 117–20; cf. Weinstock 30–1 and esp. F. Hinard, *BMCR* 2008.07.26, observing how unusual it is for a man to be appointed to priesthoods by several different priestly colleges (cf. 1.3–4 nn.). **he prosecuted Dolabella for maladministration:** so also Suet. 4.1. This is Cn. Cornelius Dolabella, the Sullan commander and admiral: *OCD*[4], no. 1, *Sull.* 28.9, 29.8, 40 (2).7. Consul in 81, he governed Macedonia in 80–77 (*MRR* iii. 65). His trial was probably in 77 or early 76: on its circumstances, E. S. Gruen, *AJP* 87 (1966), 385–9, and cf. 1.8 n. C.'s speech was published (unusually for a prosecution that failed), and became well known (*ORF*, pp. 386–7).

4.2. Caesar repaid Greece for its enthusiasm. C. Damon and C. S. Mackay, *Hist.* 44 (1995), 54, suggest that this motive statement goes back to some remark of C. himself; it is more likely to be P.'s own construction linking the two episodes. C. already knows how to respond to popular enthusiasm, here the Greeks' as later the Roman people's. **Publius Antonius:** a mistake. This is *Gaius* Antonius 'Hybrida', the consul of 63 (see *OCD*[4]). His exactions in Greece date from the civil war: Asc. 84 C., 'he had plundered many people in Achaea after getting some cavalry squadrons from Sulla's army. Then the Greeks who had been despoiled brought Antonius to trial before M. Lucullus, the praetor who delivered judgement in cases between foreigners. The young <C. Caesar> ... spoke for the Greeks; and when Lucullus had granted the Greeks' request, Antonius appealed to the tribunes and swore that he rejected the procedure [*iudicium*] on oath [*eiurare*], on the grounds that he could not have a fair trial.' The case is dated to 76, the date of Lucullus' praetorship. It is discussed by C. Damon and C. S. Mackay, *Hist.* 44 (1995), 37–55. Antonius' escape was short-lived: in 70 he was ejected from the senate, and the charges included 'plundering the allies' (Asc. 84 C.). **for corruption.** The Greek word *dōrodokia* can mean either 'giving' or 'taking' bribes. This does not seem to have been a maladministration trial like Dolabella's. P.'s language seems to distinguish the two charges ('extortion . . . corruption . . .'); Antonius was a private citizen or subordinate officer at the time of his exactions—Damon and Mackay suggest that he obtained a 'sham prefecture' to command these cavalry in the same way as Scaptius twenty-five years later, Cic. *Att.* 5.21 (114).10–12 and 6.1 (115).5–7—and the *quaestio repetundarum* did not apparently deal with such cases (Damon and Mackay 40–6, D. Daube, *JRS* 27 (1937), 43); in the passage quoted above, Asc. shows that the case came before the 'praetor for foreigners' or 'who administers justice among foreigners' (*praetor peregrinus*, 62.4 n.) rather than the 'praetor for maladministration trials' (*praetor repetundarum*: see *OCD*[4], s.v. 'praetor [*Republic*]'); and anyway it appears that under the Sullan dispensation *peregrini* could not prosecute in maladministration trials (P. A. Brunt, *Roman Imperial Themes* (1990), 497–8). In fact it was probably a civil case: so Damon and Mackay, and e.g. Marshall on Asc., 84C, Alexander 71–2. Regular procedure would then be for the praetor to specify a 'judge' (*iudex*) or 'recoverers of goods' (*recuperatores*). It may be that Antonius objected to Lucullus' choice, for 'reject on oath' (*eiurare*), the word Asc. uses, is the appropriate word for such an objection (Brunt, *FRR* 230); but Damon and Mackay prefer to think that Antonius rejected the praetor's formulation of the charge on which the trial would be based, i.e. rejected 'not the *iudex* but the *iudicium* itself'.

Marcus Lucullus: M. Terentius Varro Lucullus (*OCD*[4], s.v. Terentius, 15.3 n.), the brother of the famous L. Licinius Lucullus. His praetorship is dated to 76 (*MRR* 93). Consul in 73, he then governed Macedonia for two years; but **governor of Macedonia** here is a mistake. Asc. 84 C. makes it clear that Lucullus tried the case as *praetor peregrinus* (above), and, despite P.'s 'in Greece', the case was naturally heard in Rome. Perhaps P. misunderstood 'praetor peregrinus'; perhaps his source spoke of 'the Lucullus who governed Macedonia' (i.e. in 72–1).

4.3. Antonius appealed to the tribunes. Millar 56–7 points out that the tribunal of the *praetor peregrinus* was only some hundred metres from the regular seat of the tribunes in the forum. For tribunicial intercession in court cases, both criminal and civil, see also A. H. J. Greenidge, *The Legal Procedure of Cicero's Time* (1901), 290–2, 516; Thommen 225–6, 233–4, 257. **when contending against Greeks in Greece.** The lemma from Cicero's *In Toga Candida* at Asc. 84 C. has 'who in his own country said that he could not contend on fair terms with a foreigner': so also *Comm. Pet.* 8, probably building on the same Cicero passage. That is doubtless Cicero's tendentious summary of what Antonius' protest amounted to, and we should not assume that Antonius said precisely those words. Both Cicero and *Comm. Pet.* are pointing the absurdity of Antonius' plea. P., thinking that the hearing took place in Macedonia, transforms the apophthegm, places it in Antonius' mouth, and makes it state his justification. **against Greeks.** Cicero's own 'with a foreigner' (previous note) makes it clear that only a single 'foreigner' formally brought the case. It may be that a legal fiction was necessary to represent the prosecutor as a citizen to allow the proceedings, and Damon and Mackay suggest that this was the basis for Antonius' appeal.

4.4–7: C.'S POLITICAL METHODS P. likes to use such surveys to break up the narrative and introduce central themes: they often, as here and at 15–17 (n.), mark off an important new phase. Cf. my n. on *Ant.* 4.

This treatment reflects P.'s own stereotype of the way to win popular favour: he gives tellingly similar analyses elsewhere, e.g. *Per.* 11.4, *Nic.* 3.2, *Alc.* 16.4, *Ag.-Cl.* 1–2, 34.8–9. The most instructive comparison is with *Advice on Public Life*, for there P.'s own strong views emerge. Timely generosity is acceptable (818c–e), and the rich man should not be mean (821e ff.). But there is only one good way to win popularity, the use of eloquence. P. despises those who court popularity by extravagant spending, or luxurious entertainment, or spectacular shows: 'such techniques for taming the masses are no better than the hunting or tending of mindless animals' (802d). Elsewhere he shows his distaste for the 'greetings and handshakes and liberal gifts' used by young Roman nobles to court the people (*Aem.* 2.6, cf. *C.min.* 49.6, *Brut.* 10.6). Here P. is interested in the political result, and passes no such moral judgement: cf. Intr., p. 19. It is the historians who are more moralistic: P. is as removed from the enthusiasm of Velleius (2.41.1, 'most unrestrained in liberality', cf. Sall.

Cat. 49.3) as from the harshness of Dio (37.37.3, 'he did not shrink from immediate grovelling if it would gain ultimate power...').

4.4. the charm with which he greeted people and talked to them: again P.'s stereotype (cf. *Cic.* 7.1–2, *Gracch.* 25.6, *Crass.* 3.5), but stereotypes can be accurate, and Roman politics were indeed like this: cf. e.g. *Comm. Pet.* 41–2.

4.5. his political power slowly grew.   At *Advice on Public Life* 804e P. comments that such slow growth arouses envy (cf. 'some were envious' at §6 here), and contrasts those like Pompey who rise suddenly. **the dinners he gave, the generosity of his table, the general glamour of his style.** Cf. *Per.* 11.4, *Cic.* 10.5, etc, but again this is not far from political realities: cf.*Comm. Pet.* 44 on 'kindness' (*benignitas*): 'it can be a matter of private wealth: even though that cannot reach the masses, it is praised by friends and is welcome to the people. It can be a matter of banquets: ensure that you and your friends hold these everywhere and in all the tribes.' It seems likely that vigorous electioneering, including generous handouts and entertainment, was a particular feature of the sixties and fifties: A. W. Lintott, *JRS* 80 (1990), 8, 15–16; Yakobson 26–43 and *JRS* 82 (1992), 35–43; Millar 69. On C.'s rise in particular, note Cic. *Phil.* 2.116: 'he had softened the inexperienced people by his gifts and shows, his buildings, his doles, his banquets...'.

4.7. that no beginnings should ever be thought so small...   'Small things lead to great' (*Advice on Public Life* 825a) was proverbial: cf. e.g. Arist. *Pol.* $1303^{b}17$, Tac. *Ann.* 4.32.2 with Martin and Woodman's n., Livy 27.9.1. But P.'s elaboration, especially **if they remain neglected and therefore unchecked**, ties it closely to his theme of the initial negligence and gradual wakening of C.'s enemies (4–14 n.). The Greek is heavy, with an accumulation of verbal abstracts, rather in the manner of Thucydides (33–5 n.): this analysis of human nature and power is thereby pointed as incisive and telling.

4.8. Cicero: for his foresight cf. *Cic.* 20.6; for its historicity, Strasburger 45–72. Cicero himself dates this foresight no earlier than 63 (*Att.* 10.4 (195). 5).

4.9. '...he parts it with a single finger':   a sign of effeminacy (Juv. 9.133, Sen. *ep.* 52.12; A. Corbeill, *Nature Embodied* (2004), 134–5), along with certain other hand gestures (M. Gleason, *Making Men* (1995), 62–4). The insult was also thrown at Pompey (*Pomp.* 48.12,

Sen. *Contr.* 7.4.7, 10.1.8). For C.'s dandified appearance, cf. Suet. 45.3, Dio 43.43.4, Macrob. *Sat.* 2.3.9; Morstein-Marx 272–3. **But that was later**: probably in 63 BCE (§8 n.: so Strasburger 66–8) or a little later: the remark presumably came in a speech, with Cicero striking a balance between scaremongering (not plausible before 63) and dismissiveness (not plausible after 59).

5.1. he and Gaius Popillius were rivals for a military tribunate, and Caesar was elected first: i.e. came out above Popillius on the list. On *tribuni militum*, see *OCD*⁴, s.v.; J. P. Suolahti, *The Junior Officers of the Roman Army in the Republican Period* (1955), 35–187; Konrad on *Sert.* 3.5. C., like Servilius Caepio and Cato (*C.min.* 8.1, 8.4–9.1), was one of the superior class of military tribunes elected directly by the people; others were appointed directly by the general. This tribunate is dated to 72 or 71: *MRR* 115–16, 125–6, iii. 105, 168; Sumner 136; F. X. Ryan, *Maia*, 47 (1995), 295–7.

Popillius (or Popilius) is very obscure; he may be the same man as a tribune of 68 (*MRR* 138, iii. 168, cf. Syme, *RP* i. 155–6 and ii. 564; Ryan, art. cit.). The item evidently fits P.'s theme of popular enthusiasm, but his language is still inconsequential: it should be no great achievement for C., the newly appointed pontifex (4.1 n.), to come out above Popillius, who was perhaps not even a member of the main branch of his *gens* (Suolahti 92), though Ryan prefers to think that the item would only have been remembered if Popillius came from the noble Popillii Laenates and carried some further weight as well, perhaps as an ex-quaestor. In Pelling, 'Notes', 34–5, I suggested that, as the strong phrasing 'were rivals for' suggests (cf. 62.4 n.), there was some specific wrangle of the two during the campaign, and it became a point of honour which won the more support. If so, P. has abbreviated to the point of obscurity.

While military tribune, C. 'most vigorously supported' agitation for the restoration of the powers of the *tribuni plebis* (Suet. 5), a burning topic of the day. Pompey and Crassus restored those powers the following year (*Pomp.* 22.4). The agitation would have suited P.'s picture of C. as a popular politician; but it did not lead to any success that could be seen as C.'s own, and P. omits it, just as he omits other mentions of Crassus' and Pompey's political prominence (5.8–9 n.).

5.2–5. C.'S FUNERAL SPEECHES Suet. 6.1, 'as quaestor C. delivered laudations of his aunt Julia and his wife Cornelia from the front of the *rostra*, as was traditional', and he goes on to quote a fragment

from the eulogy on Julia. For the striking Roman custom of the
funeral laudation, see *OCD*⁴, s.v. *laudatio funebris*, and esp. Plb.
6.52–4, D.H. *Ant. Rom.* 5.17.3–6; Flower, chs. 4–5; W. Kierdorf,
Laudatio funebris (1980).

   C.'s quaestorship was in 69 (*MRR* iii. 105–6). P. has therefore
hurried over the portentous events of 70, the first consulship of
Crassus and Pompey: that is not the sort of background he considers
necessary to give. It may be that C.'s own speech supporting 'Plotius'
bill concerning the return of Lepidus' supporters is to be dated to 70:
cf. Suet. 5, *MRR* 128, 130 n. 4, iii. 158, and F. Hinard, *Sullana Varia*
(2008), 117–18; but P. could not have tied that item, even if he knew
it, into his narrative without a good deal of distracting explanation.

5.2. Marius' widow Julia: 1.2 n. nephew. The funeral laudation
regularly fell to the nearest male relative (Plb. 6.53.2, *Fab.* 24.6, etc.).
to display images of the Marii at her funeral: i.e. funeral masks, worn
by actors in the procession: cf. *OCD*⁴, s.v. *imagines*, and Flower, ch. 4.
These displays offered a chance to show off long lineages of office-
bearing ancestors, and masks of the Marii would be far outnumbered
by those of the *gens Iulia*: the quotation at Suet. 6.1 shows that
C. dwelt on those too. But there is no need to doubt that the Marii
had most impact. It suggests that 'a family's use of their *imagines* was
not aimed simply at an enumeration of previous offices held, but
could identify a specific political programme' (Flower 124, cf. Kierdorf, *Laudatio funebris*, 135).

   'Of the Marii' is Reiske's emendation for the manuscripts' 'of
Marius': in fact only one *imago* of each ancestor would be displayed,
and 'when the men...' also suggests that likenesses of more than one
man are in point. Probably only two 'Marii' were paraded, father and
son (1.2 n.).

   The elder Marius was, famously, a 'new man'. At *Jug.* 85.25, 29–30
Sallust's 'Marius' makes much of his lack of *imagines*, contrasting his
own merits with the degenerate failings of his noble antagonists, and
at *Mar.* 9.2 P. too makes him attack his opponents for 'priding
themselves on other men's *imagines*'. Marius' own funeral in 86
would then have been memorably unusual, parading a single mask,
his own, along with other triumphal mementos of his career and
possibly with Julia's patrician *imagines* too. That effect—all the
greater if Sallust's emphasis goes back to words of Marius himself
(so Flower 16–23)—would now be recalled.

when the men had been voted public enemies: originally in 88 (both father and son: Liv. *Per.* 77, App. 1.60.271, etc.). Flower 103 and n. 68 infers that Sulla as dictator explicitly banned any future display of the Marian *imagines*: if so, this is the first case of such a banning, a precursor (as Flower brings out) of imperial *damnatio memoriae*. But it may be that there was no such formal ban, only a fear that such a display of sympathy for public enemies could be regarded as treacherous. In 98 BCE even possession of an *imago* at home (one of Saturninus, perhaps a portrait rather than a funeral mask) had become a critical issue in, probably, a *maiestas* trial: Cic. *Rab. Perd.* 24–6.

5.3. brilliant enthusiasm and applause: picking up the 'brilliant eulogy' of 5.2: C. gives the lead, the people respond in kind. Cf. 6.3 n.

5.4. a Roman tradition. It was one of which P. strongly approved, *Virtues of Women* 242e–f. P. probably here reflects the antiquarian tradition of *Cam.* 8.4: such eulogies were first granted to women in 390, as a reward for the matrons' contribution for a dedication to Delphi. Cf. the related tradition of Livy 5.50.7, with Ogilvie's n.; but at *de Or.* 2.44 Cicero's Antonius says 'I think'—this suggests that it was controversial—that the first such eulogy was that of Popilia, which was in (probably) 102 BCE. Cf. Flower 122, 130–2; Kierdorf, *Laudatio funebris*, 111; Badian, *CJC* 21–2. Popilia's son was Q. Lutatius Catulus (6.6 n.), and it had been he who delivered that famous laudation. C.'s performance now may have been sensed as a gesture of emulation, doubtless one unwelcome to Catulus himself: cf. the brushes with the old man that P. goes on to highlight, 6.6 n.

There is no reason to doubt that C. was the first to praise a young woman. The speech will surely have continued some 'Marian' agitation: family was a natural theme, one that could be developed as readily for women as for men (cf. J. A. North, *JRS* 73 (1983), 170), and Cornelia was Cinna's daughter (1.1). Such Marianism would have special point if that rivalry with the Sullan Catulus was sensed. C. also seems to have vaunted the Cinnan connection in 70, supporting moves for the restoration from exile of his brother-in-law L. Cinna (Suet. 5).

C.'s Marianism continued to be important: in 47 it won him some support in Africa from men whose ancestors Marius had favoured sixty years before (*B.Af.* 32.3, 35.4, 56.3, Dio 43.4.2). Cf. also 18.1, 19.4, 26.2, 57.6 nn.; on its popular appeal, cf. Syme, *RR* 65, Morstein-Marx 110–11.

5.6. C.'S QUAESTORSHIP. He will have reached Spain in spring-summer 69; his return is probably to be dated to the first months of 68 (L. R. Taylor, *CPh* 36 (1941), 122–4). Suet. 7–8 makes much of the episode. For the moment P.'s narrative is thoroughly Rome based (3.1 n.), and he omits or displaces several stories that Suet. includes:

1. C.'s wistful envy for Alexander's triumphs, aroused (for Suet.) when he sees a statue in Cádiz. P. leaves his version of this episode for 11.5–6 (n.), where it helps to elucidate the background of the Pompey–Crassus–Caesar alliance.

2. C.'s dream of intercourse with his mother: see 32.9 n.

3. C.'s early departure from Spain, eager for great deeds in Italy. P. makes a lot of a similar theme at *Gracch.* 21.6–10.

4. C.'s agitation in the 'Latin colonies', i.e. those of Cisalpine Gaul. Any modern analysis of C.'s rise, and for that matter of his later policies, would include a treatment of the Cisalpina: cf. 29.2, 37.2 nn., Williams 120–6; but for P. the relevant background is simply the popular fervour at Rome.

Spain: more precisely Further Spain (Suet. 7), confirmed by the recurrent mentions of Cádiz (Suet. 7, *B.Hisp.* 42.1, Dio 37.5.2, 41.24.2). **Vetus:** C. Antistius Vetus, the praetor of 70, now propraetor of Further Spain. **Vetus' son:** probably C. Antistius Vetus, the cos. suff. of 30 BCE (see *OCD*[4]), despite the unusually large gap in the generations: so *MRR* iii. 17–18: D. R. Shackleton Bailey, *Two Studies in Roman Nomenclature* (2nd edn, 1991), 8–9. **when he was ruler himself:** i.e. dictator, perhaps in 45 (*MRR* iii. 17): another hint of the power that will eventually come to C. But this still seems a trivial item, especially given all the juicy material that P. suppresses (above). Possibly P., like Vell. 2.43.4 (who makes the point explicit), is influenced by the later fortunes of this distinguished family. Six consuls are attested between 6 BCE and 96 CE; the last of them was doubtless known to many of P.'s friends, if not to P. himself.

5.7. he took Pompeia as his third wife: 'third' rather than 'second', so P. clearly thinks that C. married Cossutia, 1.1 n. Suet. 6.2 has: 'to replace Cornelia he married Pompeia, daughter of Q. Pompeius [son of the consul of 88] and grand-daughter of L. Sulla.' Unlike Suet., P. gives no hint of Pompeia's parentage: the detail would be embarrassing, for the bride of the 'Marian' Caesar should hardly be Sulla's grand-daughter. For the Clodius scandal and the divorce, see 9–10. **a daughter:** Julia. We do not when she was born; more likely 76 or 75 (Syme, *RP* iii. 1237) than 81–79 (B. Marshall, *AncSoc* 18 (1987), 91–2). For her marriage to Pompey, 14.7; for their romantic love, *Pomp.* 48.8, 53.1–5; for her death, *Caes.* 23.5–7.

5.8–9: CAESAR'S EXTRAVAGANT SPENDING   P. abruptly reverts to the themes of 4.4–7 (n.), again in strong language and again without moralizing. The extravagance gives the transition to the aedileship and the *curatio* of the Via Appia (§9 n.), both dated to 65. P. again suppresses important items:

1. C.'s support for the *lex Gabinia*, which in 67 gave Pompey his vast command against the pirates (1.8–2.7 n.). P. highlights this support at *Pomp.* 25.8, making C. do so 'not caring at all about Pompey, but insinuating his way into the favour of the people and gaining them for his own'. On the *Pompey* passage, see O. Watkins, *Hist.* 36 (1987), 120–1, Morstein-Marx 179–80 n. 83.

2. C.'s support for the *lex Manilia* in 66, described in very similar terms by Dio 36.43.2–4.

The two reports are so similar that they may well be doublets (Strasburger 63, 100–1). We might anyway have expected P. to include his *lex Gabinia* story here: the alleged motivation suits his general thesis. But it would have introduced Pompey, and that is not the background P. gives. Except for the fleeting reference in §7, Pompey, like Crassus, is excluded from the narrative until ch. 11, and C.'s rise remains his own self-contained story, a matter between him and the people of Rome: cf. Intr., p. 59.

3. P. also gives no treatment of the so-called first Catilinarian conspiracy, and C.'s alleged complicity. Contrast the lavish treatment of Suet. 9.

4. C.'s attempt to secure a command in Egypt (Suet. 11), possibly in some sort of cooperation with Crassus (cf. *Crass.* 13.2; A. M. Ward, *Hist.* 21 (1972), 244–50; M. Siani-Davies, *Hist.* 46 (1997), 312–13 and her edn of Cic. *Rab. Post.* (2001), 8–10; *contra*, A. Drummond, *Athen.* 87 (1999), 154–6). The aim may have been annexation, but '[p]ossibly no more was intended than a profitable sequestration of the treasuries of the Ptolemies under specious pretexts' (Sherwin-White 265).

People thought he was paying a fortune for some brief and fleeting acclaim: cf. the excited language of *Advice on Public Life* 821f, arguing that popularity bought by over-extravagance is inevitably short-lived: 'the falsely named and falsely witnessing "honours" coming from theatrical performances or doles or gladiators are like a prostitute's tricks, flattering the crowds, who smilingly grant some brief and unstable acclaim to whoever gives them a favour.' That again shows how strongly P. would normally disapprove.

Before he held any office it is said that his indebtedness amounted to 1,300 talents. This must mean that C. owed 1,300 talents before his first public magistracy, i.e. the quaestorship of 69. The word for office, *archē*, could in itself equally mean 'provincial governorship', i.e. Spain in 61, and that would make better historical sense (below); but no reader could take the sentence as meaning that. The same word *archē* means simply 'magistracy' in both §7 and §9, and the logical sequence of §§8–9 is that C. already owed a large sum in 69 and spent much more in 65. But this is difficult. 1,300 talents should = 31,200,000 HS (1.7 n.), probably a rounding of 30,000,000 HS = 1,250 talents. A very similar item is preserved by App. 2.8.26: C. owed 25,000,000 HS in 61, before departing for his Spanish proconsulship. It is not credible that C.'s debts decreased during the decade: P. notes his expenditure in 65, App. 2.1.3 notes that C. incurred vast debts 'as aedile and praetor' in 65 and 62, and it was common for candidates to run up debts in an election campaign against expectations of a future province. Spain in 61 was C.'s first opportunity to recoup his outlays. At 11.1–2 P. notes his creditors' importunity at that date: Crassus' sureties for 830 T = 19,920,000 HS, presumably 20,000,000, are there to placate only the 'fiercest and most uncompromising' creditors.

It is likely that P. and App. reflect a single original item, which one of them has displaced. If so, App.'s date is surely the correct one: 61 is the natural time for C.'s debts to reach their height. Has P. misunderstood a Greek source that referred similarly to *archē*, but meant Spain? As for the figure, it is likely that '30,000,000 HS' was the original: this is a particular favourite stylized round number (W. Scheidel, *CQ* 46 (1996), 222–38, cf. 2.1 n.). It is difficult to have much faith in its accuracy.

For C.'s debts, cf. *ESAR* i. 325, 351; I. Shatzman, *Senatorial Wealth and Roman Politics* (1975), 346–8 (agreeing at 347 n. 444 that P. has misdated); M. W. Frederiksen, *JRS* 56 (1966), 130; Woytek 10–13;

and note Syme, *RP* v. 704, 'the brief paradox about Roman political life is that it's a good thing... to become indebted. For the obvious reason that your backers have to support you later on.'

5.9. he was put in charge of the Appian Way: i.e. *curator uiae Appiae.* Such posts were an expensive but good way of gaining popularity: cf. esp. Cic. *Att.* 1.1 (1). 2, *Gracch.* 26.1, App. 1.23.98; T. P. Wiseman, *PBSR* 38 (1970), 122–52 = *Roman Studies Literary and Historical* (1987), 16–56. For a similar *curatio* of a specific road, cf. Cic., loc. cit., Minucius Thermus, *curator uiae Flaminiae* in 65 BCE. Such appointments seem to have been ad hoc measures of the censors, who let out contracts for construction and repair. A high proportion of the attested *curationes* fall within the sixties: apparently a tribune *curator uiarum* in ?68 (*ILLRP* 465a); Minucius and Caesar; L. Fabricius *curator uiarum* in 62, possibly as tribune (*ILLRP* 379 with Dio 37.45.3, *MRR* 141 n. 8, 174). Perhaps a fad of the moment, perhaps a reflection of the newly increased importance of Italian support in Roman politics?

It seems that these *curationes* were regularly entrusted to men already holding another office; if necessary, they were presumably prorogued into later years. It is, therefore, likely that C. received his *curatio* either in 69 as quaestor (*MRR* iii. 106, putting too much weight on P.'s ordering here) or, more likely, in 65 as aedile.

as aedile: in 65 (*MRR* 158). **he gave a display of 320 pairs of gladiators:** for C.'s lavish games, cf. Suet. 10, Pliny *NH* 33.53, and esp. Dio 37.8; F. Bernstein, *Ludi publici* (*Hist.* Einz. 119; 1998), 300–1, 327–8. They were formally in memory of his father, who had died twenty years before. C. was in fact forced to reduce the number of gladiators after his enemies had taken fright (Suet. 10.2), a point that P. would hardly include: it would show his enemies clearly taking note of C., and the episode represents a setback. It also hints at another reason for C.'s use of gladiators, their value for everyday street thuggery (Lintott, *Violence*, 83–5). P. has no hint of this (Intr., p. 61). **the ambitions of his predecessors had achieved.** The word for 'ambitions' is *philotimia* (58.4 n.), literally 'love of honour', and is picked up by these 'new honours' with which the public now try to reciprocate. **everyone sought new offices and new honours to repay him:** elegantly vague language: this could mean 'new for Caesar', i.e. the next step on the ladder; it also presages the 'new', i.e. unprecedented, offices and honours that this popularity will eventually secure for him. Still, those honours are a long way ahead (57.3 n.), and such language at this stage of his career is highly anachronistic. See also 6.3 n.

6: THE DISPLAY OF MARIAN PORTRAITS   Suet. 11 and Vell. 2.43.4 both treat the same incident, but give much less charged versions: P.'s emphasis on the Marian theme is all his own, and the style is allusive and heightened. He concentrates less on the display itself than on the varied emotions it aroused, as C.'s audacity polarizes friends and enemies. The end of the chapter reverts, with another enemy's apophthegm, to the theme of C.'s coming success, with language that is again (cf. 5.9 n.) ominously vague.

6.1. cowering in humiliation: a single bold word in the Greek (*kateptēchei*), probably echoing its use at Dem. *Phil.* 1.8: those recently conquered by Philip are there 'cowering', waiting only for Athens to give them a lead—in that case against the tyrant. Now Caesar plays Demosthenes, and the Marians respond to *his* lead; but the relation to 'tyranny' is more complex. **portraits of Marius:** not here funeral *imagines* as at 5.2 (though the Greek word is the same), but simply statues. They remained in place on the Capitol: Val. Max. 6.9.14, Prop. 3.11 46 with Dio 50.5.4. On the importance of statues in *Alex.-Caes.*, see Intr., p. 30. **statues of Victory carrying trophies.** Both Marius and Sulla had made play with the cult of *Victoria* (Weinstock 92 and *HTR* 50 (1957), 224–7), and Marius had once been infuriated by a similar Sullan display of 'Victories carrying trophies' (*Mar.* 32.4, *Sulla* 6.1–2). He seems to have replied in kind: Suet. 11 says that the trophies he placed were destroyed by Sulla, and that it was these that C. now 'restored'.

6.2. the Cimbrian successes: in 102 (strictly over the Teutones) and 101. Marius had naturally made much of these in connection with the cult of *Victoria* (Weinstock, *HTR* 50 (1957), 224), but Suet. 11 says that C.'s trophies commemorated the Jugurthine victories as well. The Cimbrian emphasis prepares for C.'s own northern successes in Gaul, when he will emerge as Marius' military as well as political successor: 18.1, 19.4 (nn.)—an aspect that gives added point to Catulus' military imagery in §6.

6.3. that Caesar was aiming for tyranny. P. is 'characterizing by reaction' (Intr., p. 25), and reconstructing how onlookers would think: he naturally stresses his own tyranny theme. It is wrong to assume that he had source authority: thus e.g. Gelzer 39 n. 4, using this to explain Cicero's alleged remark that 'C. confirmed in his consulship the tyranny he had thought of as aedile' (Suet. 9.2) as a reference to the Marian display. If that remark is historical, Cicero doubtless intended a wider application, thinking especially of C.'s extravagant spending and perhaps also to the failed Egyptian project of Suet. 11 (5.8–9 n.). **honours that had been buried by law and official decree:** referring both to Sulla's suppression of Marius' own similar trophies (§1 n.) and to the designation of the Marians as public enemies, initially in 88 (5.2 n.) and implicitly or explicitly confirmed by the later proscriptions. **on the people . . . to such submissiveness** (lit. 'taming'). As at 5.3, P. immediately ties in the 'Marian' display to his theme of C. as a popular politician, and any higher-status supporters of Marius are ignored. At 5.3, as here, the people's enthusiasm is the main point. But the more perceptive of the enemies wonder if C. is not merely playing for their support, but softening them up for 'taming' like a domestic pet. Again, the hints of the future are strong. **play the revolutionary.** The Greek word (*kainotomein*) is basically 'innovate': the 'new' element is the same as in 'everyone sought new offices and new honours to repay him' at 5.9, as both C. and the people reciprocally seek something new for one another. In a political context, such 'newness', like Latin *res nouae*, is usually pejorative, easily suggesting 'revolution' (*Ag.–Cl.* 24.4, *Sulla* 34.6, Plato *Laws* 4.709a, Arist. *Pol.* 5.1305^{b}41, Plb. 3.70.4, etc.). It therefore hangs closely together with the charge of 'aiming for tyranny', and presages the constitutional change that C. will bring.

6.5. made tears of joy come to many: a reminiscence of the climax of Plato *Phaedo* 117c, 'my tears came [the same verb is used] in floods . . .' as Socrates drains the hemlock: the same passage is recalled at *Socrates' Sign* 595d. The last chapters of the *Phaedo* are often recalled by P., e.g. at 119f (~ *Phd.* 115a), 379d and 707f (~ *Phd.* 115e), 499b (~ *Phd.* 117b), 554e (~ *Phd.* 117e), 920c (~ *Phd.* 114d), 924b (~ *Phd.* 111e ff.). In Plato's original, immortality is central; in this context, where 'return from Hades' (5.3) is relevant, those suggestions are not casual.

6.6. (Quintus) **Lutatius Catulus:** the consul of 78 and censor of 65, *OCD*^{4}, no. 2. This is the first of several such brushes with C.: cf. 7.1–5, 8.1–2, and Vell. 2.43.4, 'his very well-known clashes with Q. Catulus'. Here his role had special point. His father, the consul of 102, had initially shared with Marius the glory for the 'Cimbrian triumphs',

and they shared a triumph in 101; but there was dispute over who had
really deserved the glory (cf. esp. *Mar.* 25.8, 27.6–10), and the feud of
the two men finally led to Catulus' death in 87 (*Mar.* 44.8). Moreover,
the present Catulus had been responsible for restoring the Capitol
after its destruction in the civil wars, and his name was engraved
prominently on the face of the temple of Jupiter Optimus Maximus
(*ILLRP* 367–8, cf. *Popl.* 15.1, Val. Max. 6.9.5, etc.). It must have gazed
down on this very display. The Capitol again became a symbolic
battleground between the two in early 62: 9.1 n. **that celebrated
remark:** lit. 'often recalled', in conversation and anecdote (cf. e.g.
Alex. 31.12, *Per.* 18.2, *Marc.* 21.5, *C.mai.* 15.4)—a valuable reminder
of how much of P.'s information may rest on oral tradition: Intr.,
p. 54. However famous in P.'s day, the apophthegm is not mentioned
elsewhere, but it may be historical (Strasburger 68–9).

In the context of the Marian display, Suet. 11 adds that C. announced in court that 'he held those men too to be assassins, who had
taken money in the proscriptions for bringing in the heads of Roman
citizens...'; cf. F. Hinard, *Les Proscriptions de la Rome républicaine*
(1985), 204–7. It was well known that C. had prosecuted the agents of
the proscriptions (Dio 37.10.2–4, Cic. *Lig.* 12, etc.), and P. is well
informed about these events (cf. esp. *C.min.* 17.4–7): he probably
knew the tale, and it would have fitted his Marian thesis. But he
characteristically leaves the point simple.

There may also have been some agitation from C. in support of the
children of the proscribed (cf. 37.2 n.). Vell. 2.43.4 says that in 65 C.
'recalled' the sons of the proscribed to their rights to stand for office,
which would naturally be taken as indicating that he was successful.
That cannot be right, for it was still a sensitive topic in 63 when some
tribunes proposed restoring their rights and perhaps secured some
transient success (Dio 37.25.4, cf. Cic. 12.2). Cf. Woodman's n. on the
Velleius passage: possibly Vell. has simply misplaced C.'s measure as
dictator in 49 (37.2 n.), but it is more likely that he reflects either some
support from C. for the tribunicial move in 63 (so Woodman) or
some earlier agitation of C. himself in 65.

7.1–4: CAESAR BECOMES PONTIFEX MAXIMUS At 6.7 the people have given their unequivocal encouragement: C. now responds,
'going down to the people' (§1), and it is again Catulus who is humiliated. This is the point when the senate and the optimates all sense the
danger (7.4): contrast the ease with which C. persuaded them at 6.7.

Suet. 13 and Dio 37.37.1–3 may well come from the same source as P.: cf. also Sall. *Cat.* 49.2, Vell. 2.43.3. Suet. hints at the large-scale bribery that was probably involved ('not without most extravagant largess'); Dio moralizes angrily on C.'s tactics. P. as usual does not present this so starkly (Intr., pp. 19, 60–1). Big money is clearly necessary ('C. replied that he would borrow even more'(§2)), but at 4.5–6 and 5.8–9 C.'s spending was more open and straightforward, and we are left to assume that the same sort of electioneering is in point here. The only 'bribe' is that offered by Catulus to C., a point on which the other sources are silent.

For the weight C. attached to the post, cf. Jehne 163–5, 172–3: pontifical symbols are frequent on his coinage during the Civil War and up to his final months, and inscriptions record the pontificate more regularly than his magistracies.

7.1. Now Metellus died…:   Q. Caecilius Metellus Pius, pontifex maximus since ?81, best known for his fighting against Sertorius in Spain: see *OCD*[4]. He is last heard of in 65 (Asc. 60 C., etc.). C.'s election was apparently in 63, before the Catilinarian debates of early December (Sall. *Cat.* 49.2, etc.) and probably later than the Rabirius trial(s) in mid-summer (Suet.): cf. A. Drummond, *Athen.* 87 (1999), 150–1. Metellus will have died in late 64 or early 63. P. Servilius Vatia **Isauricus**, cos. 79 and cens. 55 (see *OCD*[4]), had commanded with distinction in the East in the seventies (cf. 1.8 n.); the deceased Metellus was a kinsman. **Catulus** (6.6 n.) may well have been the senior member of the college of *pontifices*: Macr. *Sat.* 3.13.11 with L. R. Taylor, *AJP* 63 (1942), 400–1. **both highly distinguished men.** Cic. *Verr.* 2.3.210 had already linked Catulus and Isauricus as 'leaders of the state, with such authority and achievements that they should be counted along with the most distinguished men of the highest antiquity'.

7.4. Then the votes were cast.   C. was elected by the traditional procedure for the pontifex maximus, where only seventeen of the thirty-five tribes voted: see e.g. Linderski 241–2. According to Dio 37.37.1–2 this procedure had only just been restored by a law of the tribune Labienus, backed by C., after Sulla had changed the system to one of co-optation. That may be right; but the traditional mode of election was apparently in place in early 63, as Rullus' agrarian proposal specified that the commissioners should be selected 'in the same way as in the elections for pontifex maximus' (Cic. *Leg. Agr.*

2.16–18). The pontifex maximus procedure had been extended to all *pontifices* only in 104 BCE by the tribune Cn. Domitius, and possibly Sulla and Labienus were concerned with the appointment of *pontifices* alone, reversing and then reinstating the procedures of the *lex Domitia* (notice that C. had himself been 'co-opted' in 73, 4.1 n.); in that case the pontifex maximus procedure will have remained unaffected throughout. Thus L. R. Taylor, *CPh* 37 (1942), 421–4, followed by e.g. J. Scheid, *Religion et piété à Rome* (1985), 69 n. 21. Dio, typically eager to reconstruct political motives, might naturally infer that C. was behind Labienus' bill and wrongly assume that it was connected with C.'s own candidature. The alternative is to assume that Dio is right, as Millar 105–6 thinks. In that case, we should have to date Labienus' bill before Rullus'; that is not impossible, but Rullus' bill was introduced very early in the year (Cic. *Leg. Agr.* 2.13, etc.) and there hardly seems time. **reckless and aggressive:** a single word in the Greek (*thrasutēs*), which had long formed part of the demagogue stereotype: Ar. *Knights* 304, 331, 637, 693, Dem. 8.68–9, and my note on *Ant.* 2.6. Cf. 9.2, 14.2 (nn.).

7.5–8.5: THE CATILINARIAN CONSPIRACY   This is one of P.'s four accounts of the conspiracy. His earliest was his fullest, at *Cic.* 10–24; the others are *C.min.* 22–4 and *Crass.* 13.3–5. At *Plutarch and History*, 45–63, I gave a detailed comparison of the four accounts and tried to infer something of P.'s working method, drawing on my earlier argument (= *Plutarch and History*, 1–44) that *Caesar, C. min.,* and *Crass.* all rest on the same source material and were prepared as a single project. The present account is close in language and articulation to the version in *Cicero*. It is likely that P. (naturally enough) looked again at his earlier narrative, but he may also have looked again at the notes or first draft (*hypomnēma*) that he will have made for *Cicero*. Some material is added from his more recent reading (7.5 n.) and from his imagination (7.8–9 nn.). See Intr., pp. 52, 54.

   A modern biographer of C. might use the Catiline affair in various ways. Catiline, or perhaps the other main 'conspirator' Manlius, could illuminate the economic troubles and social disintegration, the interplay of country and city, the domestic shadow cast by a great general abroad, the skilful scaremongering of the elite to outmanoeuvre a radical politician: Catiline could be made a more depraved and less gifted precursor of C. himself, and there is much of that in Sallust's *Catiline* and in Appian. Such effects were not beyond P. In *Cor.*, for instance, he uses the tangential Menenius Agrippa to illuminate background and provide a foil to Coriolanus himself. But in *Caesar* he is more economical, limiting himself to C.'s own part in these events. The stress falls on the failure of C.'s enemies to grasp their opportunity, the moral authority of his rhetoric in the senate, and the enthusiasm of the people: all these build on the themes of the earlier narrative (4–14 n.). Other material is suppressed. *Cicero* had discussed C.'s own possible complicity, including a digression on C.'s long-term plans (20.6–7): *C.min.* 22.5 develops a similar emphasis. Here that theme is dismissed perfunctorily at 7.7, and P. is more interested in C.'s defence against those charges, revealing his popular support (8.5). An important detail of C.'s proposal (7.9 n.) is obscured. The background is sketched incisively but briefly (7.6–7), and some aspects are again misleading (nn.). P.'s language is lucid, but less heightened than in 6.1–7.4 or 8.6–7: the stylistic contrast with *C.min.* is particularly marked (*Plutarch and History*, 55–7).

The modern bibliography on Catiline is vast. N. Criniti, *Bibliografia Catilinaria* (1971) and Gesche 24–9 collect material up to the early 1970s; see also the commentaries on Sall. *Cat.* by K. Vretska (1976), P. McGushin (1977), and J. T. Ramsey (2nd edn, 2007), and on Cic. *Cat.* by A. R. Dyck (2008). Among earlier work, E. G. Hardy's *The Catilinarian Conspiracy in its Context* (Oxford, 1924 = *JRS* 7 (1917), 153–228), Gelzer 47–55 and *Cicero* 81–104, and Syme, *Sallust* (1964), are particularly useful; so is the vigorous revisionism of R. Seager, *Hist.* 23 (1973), 240–8. More recently, see esp. A. Drummond, *Law, Politics, and Power: Sallust and the Execution of the Catilinarian Conspirators* (*Hist.* Einz. 93; 1995), and T. P. Wiseman in *CAH* ix^2 (1994), 346–60.

7.5. That was why… P. begins with these criticisms of Cicero as they bring out the episode's main significance for C.'s career, his enemies' failure to capitalize on their chance. He returns, rather awkwardly, to the same point at 8.4. **Piso and Catulus and their followers.** The Greek is an idiomatic phrase (cf. 29.1, 30.5, 31.2, 61.10, 68.7 nn.) that may mean no more than 'Piso and Catulus'. This is C. Calpurnius Piso, consul in 67 and then proconsul of both Gauls: *OCD*^{4}, s.v. Calpurnius (no. 1). Earlier in 63 C. had attacked him in his maladministration trial for the unjust execution of a Cisalpine Gaul (Sall. *Cat.* 49.2, Cic. *Flacc.* 98). Piso was prominent in the final scenes of the conspiracy, giving evidence against Cethegus (*Cic.* 19.1), participating in the debate of 5 December (Cic. *Att.* 12.21 (260). 1), and commending Cicero's conduct (Cic. *Phil.* 2.12). He was doubtless familiar to P. from his notes; but he was not really a famous character, and few of P.'s readers would know much of him. His introduction is abrupt here. For similar cases, cf. 8.3, 21.5, 32.3, 37.1, 56.6, 58.8 nn. and e.g. Culleo at *Pomp.* 49.4, 'Appius' at *Pomp.* 57.7. **criticized Cicero for letting Caesar off the hook.** Sall. *Cat.* 49.1 has a more loaded version: 'around the same time [the context is 4 December, but Sall.'s language is vague] Q. Catulus and C. Piso were not able to bribe or influence Cicero into getting Caesar falsely accused by the Allobroges or some other witness'. Sall. explains it in terms of the two men's personal grudges. P.'s notice may derive directly or indirectly from Sall.: if so, he or an intermediate source has made it blander, suppressing the unscrupulousness ('bribe... falsely accused') of the optimates, and leaving the impression that the motives were more political (the optimates' fears for the future) than personal.

7.6. Catiline had planned not merely constitutional reform, but the total devastation of the empire. Cicero has similar outbursts, stressing the danger to 'city and empire': e.g. *Cat.* 1.9, 3.9, 3.20, 3.25, 4.7 ('destroy the empire'), *Mur.* 80. In his other accounts P. similarly characterizes Catiline's ambitions (*Cic.* 10, *C.min.* 22.2–3, *Crass.* 13.3), but even in *Cicero* he has little on Catiline's *programme*: we could there have done with material similar to that of Sall. *Cat.* 21.2. **Catiline himself had left Rome:** after the debate on 7 or (more likely) 8 November, when Cicero delivered *Cat.* 1: on the dating issue, see Dyck's comm. on Cic. *Cat.* (2008), 243–4. **trapped by lesser charges...:** a misleading summary of the events of *Cic.* 16, which makes it clear that by these 'lesser charges' P. means the allegations of an assassination plot against Cicero himself (apparently 7 November: Sall. *Cat.* 28, Cic. *Cat.* 1.9–10, etc.): *Cic.* 16.2–4 presents this as the theme of the debate of 7 or 8 November and the reason for Catiline's departure. But P. knew that there had been strong suspicion of Catiline's alleged 'final plans' (*Cic.* 15.3–5) and that Catiline decided voluntarily to leave Rome (*Cic.* 16.1); and Sall. *Cat.* 31.4–9 and Cic. *Cat.* 1–2 make it clear that the debate of 7 or 8 November was more widely based, in fact dealing more with the 'final plans' than with the 'lesser charges'. P. Cornelius **Lentulus** Sura (*OCD*[4] 1.1 n.) and C. Cornelius **Cethegus** (Berry on Cic. *Sull.* 53) are often linked together as prominent Catilinarians and the leaders of the conspiracy at Rome (e.g. *Cic.* 17–19, 22.3 and 8, 30.5, Sall. *Cat.* 48.4, Vell. 2.34.4, Juv. 10.287). Cethegus was allegedly deputed to murder Cicero himself. It has been doubted how closely any 'plot' of Lentulus was associated with Catiline himself: Seager, *Hist.* 22 (1973), 241–5.

7.7. Perhaps Caesar gave them some secret encouragement and help. Here P. is non-committal ('that is unclear'). But he had earlier given a broad hint that C. was guilty (*Cic.* 20.6), and he thought that complicity would suit C.'s policy (*Cic.* 20.6., *C.min.* 22.5). He could certainly have said more here: in *Crass.* 13 he mentions that Cicero implicated both Crassus and C. in 'a certain work published after both men [Crassus and Caesar, it seems, rather than Crassus and Cicero] were dead'—probably the vitriolic 'Account of his own Policies' on which Cicero was still at work in 44 (E. Rawson, *LCM* 7/8 (1982), 121–4 = *Roman Culture and Society* (1991), 408–15, as corrected by J. L. Moles, *LCM* 7/8 (1982), 136–7). But in *Caesar* he is more interested in other things (above, 7.5–8.5 n.).

According to Asc. 83 C., Caesar, like Crassus, had backed Catiline in mid-64 for the consulship of 63. That evidence is suspect, as some of Asc.'s material comes from that Ciceronian 'Account of his own Policies' (Asc. 83 C.: Marshall on Asc., loc. cit., and P. A. Brunt, *CR* 7 (1957), 193–5), though that does not make it necessarily wrong (see E. Rawson, *Roman Culture and Society* (1991), 408–15). In itself such support would be no surprise. For Catiline to have been so serious a consular candidate, then and a year later, he must have had strong backing, and from many sectors of society: Cic. *Cael.* 12–14 talks of the respectable people initially 'taken in by' Catiline. Many will have backed off as Catiline's hopes and tactics later became more extreme.

C. himself does not seem to have been initially suspected of complicity in the 'plot', for on 3 December he, like Crassus, was selected to keep one of the accused under house arrest (Sall. *Cat.* 47.4: admittedly, this may have been some complicated double game of Cicero). Sall. himself is clear that the accusations against C. were 'false' (*Cat.* 49.1, quoted at 7.5 n.). But during the final debates many names were in the air. To judge from Sall. *Cat.* 40.5–6 and 47.1–2 (cf. also 49.4 and Cic. *Sull.* 36), several allegations originated in the lists of supporters that Gabinius and Umbrenus had produced for the Allobrogian ambassadors and T. Volturcius. These would naturally seek to impress by including as many figures as possible, especially grand ones, even if the commitment and sympathy of some of them had waned: Sall. *Cat.* 40.6 is explicit that many 'innocent' people were added in order to hearten the Allobroges. Crassus was then named in the senate on 4 December: the accusations were not found plausible (Sall. *Cat.* 48). Doubtless, some of the lesser men suspected were no more reliably implicated, but there was probably firmer evidence against the five men executed on 5 December (D. A. March, *CW* 82 (1988–9), 225–34).

in the senate. P. gives the impression that the debate on punishment followed in the same session as their exposure, but the conspirators were denounced in the senate on 3 December, Crassus was attacked on the 4th, and the final debate on punishment took place on the 5th. (See 8.1 n. for the possibility that there was already some preliminary debate on this on the 4th.) P. knew that the sittings of 3 and 5 December were distinct (*Cic.* 19.1–4, 20.4–21.5), and he already knew of the sitting of the 4th as well (*Crass.* 13.3). For the conflation, and similar cases elsewhere, cf. Intr., p. 56, *Plutarch and History*, 91–2.

Everyone before Caesar had proposed the death-penalty: all the consulars: Cicero lists them at *Att.* 12.21 (260).1. P. elsewhere names D. Iunius Silanus, who as consul designate was the first to deliver his view, and some dramatic capital is gained in *Cic.* (20.1, 21.3) and *C. min.* (22.4 and 6) by Silanus' subsequent volte-face under the influence of C.'s speech (Sall. *Cat.* 50.4). P. here prefers to concentrate on his leading figures C., Cato, and Catulus. On the voting sequence, see 7.8, 8.1 nn.

7.8. Caesar rose and delivered a most thoughtful speech. He spoke 'in the praetor's position' (Cic. *Att.* 12.21 (260).1) after the consulars: as praetor designate he presumably preceded the ex-praetors (*StR* iii. 966–7, 973).

For this speech, cf. esp. Sallust's version at *Cat.* 51. We might hope for accurate reports of this speech, as the proceedings were taken down by stenographers (*C.min.* 23.3–4, cf. Cic. *Sull.* 41–4). Yet P.'s brief version is inconsistent with Sall.'s. P.'s Caesar stresses the social status of the conspirators (cf. *Cic.* 14.4, 19.6), but Sall.'s does not. P.'s version makes the proposed execution 'unjust' as well as untraditional; Sall.'s has 'they will deserve whatever their fate turns out to be' (51.26, cf. 15, 17, 23, 25, 27). Sall.'s Caesar takes the prudential line: this would be a bad precedent. Even the terms of C.'s proposal are different, with P. making imprisonment temporary, Sall. permanent (§9 n.).

We may or may not believe Sall.'s version of the speech: the *content* may well be historical, substantiated as it largely is by Cic. *Cat.* 4.7–10, though it may also be that Sall. is himself using Cicero's speech to aid his own reconstruction (Drummond, *Law, Politics and Power*, 38–47); in any case, the style is doubtless Sall.'s own (M. Paladini, *Lat.* 20 (1961), 3–32, esp. 12–20). But P.'s cursory treatment deserves no credence. It seems that he is wrong over the terms of the proposal (§9 n.), and has misunderstood a source. But his final argument is directly dependent on that misinterpretation: 'the senate could take its time and deliberate peacefully…'. P., composing imaginatively, picked the argument of social standing, which would come naturally to a Greek of the Roman empire (P. Garnsey, *Social Status and Legal Privilege* (1970), esp. 105–11). So does App. 2.6.20, but here he may well be following P.

7.9: C.'S PROPOSAL   The language is taken over closely from *Cic.* 21.1, but that passage along with 21.5 makes it clear that the conspirators' property was also to be confiscated: so also Cic. *Cat.* 4.8, 10; Suet. 14; C. 'alone proposed that the men should be shared out around the municipalities and kept in custody, with their property confiscated'. **keep them under guard for the duration of the war…:** i.e. the imprisonment was to be temporary: so also *Cic.* 21.1. App. 2.6.20 agrees, but is probably dependent on P. or (less likely) on his source. The other versions clearly imply that C. proposed permanent imprisonment: Cic. *Cat.* 4.8 and 10, Sall. *Cat.* 51.43, and Dio 37.36.2 mention a *sanctio*, fixing a punishment for anyone who should bring up the question again. The same impression is given by Cic. *Cat.* 4.10, 'consigning them to eternal darkness and chains', and 7, 'everlasting chains'. Nor is it easy to think, with Hardy, *The Catilinarian Conspiracy*, 93, and McGushin and Ramsey on Sall. *Cat.* 51.43, that C.'s proposal was really for temporary imprisonment but Cicero misrepresented it in the *Fourth Catilinarian* and misled later authors: the confiscation of property (above) would be odd if imprisonment were not to be permanent, and life imprisonment was 'not totally unprecedented', even though it was 'distinctly unusual' (Lintott, *Violence*, 169, cf. Vretska on Sall. *Cat.* 51.43). It is probably P. himself who has misinterpreted a source (as Drummond, *Law, Politics and Power*,

37 n. 74 agrees): Suet. 14 seems to rest on similar material, and does not mention the possibility of the case being reopened.

P.'s version is inaccurate, but it does coincide closely with the proposal of Ti. Claudius Nero, 'who had proposed that the issue should be discussed with guards removed from (or "added to") the prisoners' (Sall. *Cat.* 50.4 with McGushin's n.)—at least as that proposal was later interpreted, I think rightly (App. 2.5.19: Drummond, *Law, Politics, and Power*, 24–6, believes that App. was mistaken and that Nero proposed only a brief adjournment, but that leaves more inconsequential Silanus' later support for Nero and the sharp criticism he incurred). P. omits Nero's proposal. Perhaps he simply confused the two (Holmes, *RR* i. 469); perhaps he first misinterpreted his source's version of C.'s proposal, then discovered he had no logical room for Nero's.

8.1. The proposal struck the senate as humane, and it was a very powerful speech. Closely based on *Cic.* 21.2, 'the proposal was reasonable and the speaker most eloquent'. Cf. *C.min.* 22.5 and Sallust's Cato, who ridicules C.'s 'gentleness and pity' (*Cat.* 52.11, 27, cf. 54.2) but allows that he had spoken 'in a good and well-ordered way' (52.13). **Those who rose after Caesar:** i.e. the *praetorii* and below. These included Q. Cicero (Suet. 14.2). **many of the previous speakers...:** in particular, D. Iunius Silanus, whose role is stressed in the other *Lives*: 7.7 n. **Cato and Catulus.** Despite this ordering, *Cic.* 21.4 makes it clear that Catulus was the first to check the tide, followed by Cato.

P.'s picture is clear. *All* whose turn to speak came after C. supported him, *many* of those who had spoken before changed their minds. So also Dio 37.36.2; Suet. 14.2, 'C. would have won, for the majority had already come over...', does not contradict it. But it cannot be quite accurate. Ti. Claudius Nero will not have spoken until after C.'s speech (Holmes, *RR* i. 468–9, McGushin and Ramsey on Sall. *Cat.* 50.4–5), and Nero had a proposal of his own. Sall. *Cat.* 52.1, 'the others indicated in a word which side they took, some supporting one and some the other', also gives a rather different impression.

Not all who spoke after C. supported him, but some clearly did, and others (Silanus, Nero) at least refused to support the death penalty. Yet Cicero later seems to claim that all the senators before Cato, save C. himself, supported the death penalty (*Att.* 12.21 (260).1). That is hard to believe (*pace* Shackleton Bailey, ad loc.); even if the rest is discarded,

Sall.'s evidence seems decisive. In that letter Cicero's indignation centres on Brutus' claim, made in his *Cato* in 46 or 45 (54.6 n.), that Cato was the first to propose death: Cicero fairly claims that many others had done the same, and adequately explains why it was Cato's proposal, not any of the others, that he had put to the vote. That point is unaffected by this detail, and his 'all' is a pardonable exaggeration.

As a senior consular Catulus will first have spoken early in the debate, well before C., and Cic. *Att.* 12.21 (260).1 gives the impression that he spoke immediately after the consuls designate, Silanus and Murena. He must have spoken twice; so did Silanus; so, to judge from *Cic.* 21.5, did C., intervening a second time to drop confiscation from his initial proposal. All this is very unusual. It was *possible* for a senator to speak a second time—for instance, to question a later speaker (Sch. Bob., p. 170 St.)—but the privilege was rarely exploited: apart from the present instances, Mommsen, *StR* iii. 985 cites only Cic. *Att.* 1.16 (16).10 and Tac. *Hist.* 4.7.1 and M. Bonnefond-Coudry, *Le Sénat de la republique romaine* (1989), 504, adds Cic. *Q.fr.* 2.3 (7).3, all altercations of a very different type from this. A closer parallel is C. *BC* 1.2.6, M. Marcellus 'abandoning his proposal' for delay, i.e. presumably verbally withdrawing it, in the debate of 1 January 49 (30.4–6 nn.): Bonnefond-Coudry, *Le Sénat de la république romaine*, 512–13. (*Magistrates* could speak at any time when no other senator held the floor—hence such altercations as Livy 28.45.3, 33.22 and Cic. *Fam.* 1.2 (13).1—but most of the senators in point here were not magistrates.) True, senate-meetings may have been less strictly formal than scholars have often imagined, as Bonnefond-Coudry in particular stresses; but a cluster of so many exceptional instances remains striking. It is certainly hard to believe that 'many of the previous speakers', as P. here has it, would avail themselves of this rare option.

One possibility is that there were two debates on punishment, that Cicero's *Fourth Catilinarian* introduced the second, and that therefore all senators had a chance of speaking twice. In that case, P. has conflated the two, here and in *Cicero* and *C.min.*: in itself that is perfectly possible, 7.7 n. So S. J. Heyworth and A. J. Woodman, *LCM* 11 (1986), 11–12, who find traces of this in Sallust's tenses at *Cat.* 50.3–5 ('the senate *had* a little before judged ... Silanus *had* proposed the death penalty ... and later, moved by a speech of C., *had* said that he would vote for Ti. Nero ...'); they suggest that Nero's proposal (7.9 n.) was procedural, to adjourn while security was improved. They leave it open whether this first debate was earlier on the 5th, or took place in the later stages of the meeting on the 4th (Moles on *Cic.* 21.4 tentatively favours the latter). There are, however, difficulties in this interpretation of Nero and Silanus (7.9 n.), and it is not the only way of taking Sall's Latin (Ramsey on Sall. 50.4; J. Briscoe, *LCM* 12 (1987), 50–1; Drummond, *Law, Politics, and Power*, 23 and n. 2).

It is better, with e.g. Gelzer 52 and *Cicero* 99 and Vretska on Sall. *Cat.* 50.3, to assume that the *Fourth Catilinarian* is the written version of Cicero's intervention in the middle of a (single) debate, and that after his intervention he began anew the process of asking the senators for views: this gives particular force to Cic. *Cat.* 4.6, 'I have set in motion the procedure of consulting you as if the matter was untouched' (*institui referre ad uos ... tamquam integrum*). That would give all the consulars in order a chance to express their change of view, and P.'s 'many' may be right; it also gives force to the emphasis on Catulus, who was probably the first consular to speak after Silanus had changed his mind. It fits P.'s ordering in *Cic.* 20–21, Silanus–Caesar–Cicero (but P. misunderstands the tone of the *Fourth Catilinarian*)–Silanus again–Catulus–Cato; he may then be right there in putting C.'s second intervention after rather than before the final vote, if Cicero 'divided' C.'s proposal and intended to take the confiscation item separately.

The main difficulty is presented by the speech of Ti. Claudius Nero, who spoke before Silanus' second intervention (Sall. *Cat.* 50.4). If Silanus spoke immediately after Cicero, then Nero must have spoken before Cicero too, yet the *Fourth Catilinarian* shows no awareness of Nero's intervention (unless, as Miriam Griffin suggests to me, the insistence in §6 that delay is unthinkable should be taken as an oblique attempt to brush aside Nero's proposal). The normal inference is, therefore, that Nero spoke after Cicero, not before (so e.g. Dyck on Cic. *Cat.* 4.7–8 and, tentatively, Ramsey on Sall. *Cat.* 52.1). Still, this difficulty may not be decisive, for this is a speech where Cicero may well have made particularly extensive revisions in the published version (Lintott, *Evidence*, 17–18, 147–8; cf. Dyck's comm., 208). If the speech was in some sense 'published' only in 60 (*Att.* 2.1 (21).3), tradition may already have been obscuring the light-weight Nero, especially as it seems his proposal was not voted upon. It was not in Cicero's interest to correct that tendency, for Nero's proposal, unlike both Cato's and C.'s, allowed the conspirators to be tried constitutionally: life imprisonment and confiscation, like execution, constituted a 'capital' judgement on Roman citizens, and the *lex*

Sempronia outlawed this without the endorsement of the people, i.e. the possibility of appeal (cf. *Cat.* 4.10, where Cicero's unease on the issue is clear). Cicero would have no wish to remind his critics of his failure to put that proposal to the vote.

8.2: THE SPEECH OF CATO   Cato was called on as tribune designate, 'almost the last to be asked his opinion' (Vell. 2.35.3), after consulars, *praetorii*, and *aedilicii* (*StR* iii. 967, 973). Sall. *Cat.* 52 gives him a version stressing the magnitude of the peril, the dangers of a false softness, the debt of Rome to her ancestors. This is confirmed and perhaps supplemented by Vell. 2.35.3–4, which may be based on Brutus' *Cato* (8.1 n.): Vell. also has Cato (1) praising Cicero's conduct and (2) casting suspicion on those who urge a milder course. The first of those two points is historical (Cic. *Att.* 12.21 (260).1); the second is surely hinted by Sall. *Cat.* 52.16 ('if C. alone is fearless when everyone else is so fearful, that gives me all the greater reason to fear for you and for me') and may be confirmed by P., here and at *Cic.* 21.4 and *C. min.* 23.1–2. The original may well have made more of this than Sall. allows: M. Paladini, *Lat.* 20 (1961), 20–5, and Drummond, *Law, Politics and Power*, 74.

P. here omits an item he certainly knew, as he includes it in *Brutus* (5.2–4) and *C.min.* (24.1–3). While Cato was speaking, a message was brought to C.: Cato bade C. read it aloud. C. silently passed it to Cato. It was a love letter, written by Cato's own sister Servilia. Cato hurled it back at C.: 'take it, you drunken oaf!' Once again (1.8 n.) *Caesar* shows no interest in sexual personalia: cf. 62.1 n. and Intr., pp. 22–3.

a group of young men were serving as Cicero's bodyguard: 'a band of armed Roman *equites*, attending Cicero as a bodyguard' (Suet. 14); 'some Roman *equites*, who were serving as an armed protection around the temple of Concord' (Sall. *Cat.* 49.4). This is presumably the bodyguard continually attested as Cicero's escort through 63 (Cic. *Mur.* 52, Sall. *Cat.* 26.4, *Comm. Pet.* 33, 50, etc.), and may well be identical with the 'number of young men picked from the district of Reate', if they were *equites*, who had played a large part in the arrest a few days earlier (Cic. *Cat.* 3.5). For these, cf. Lintott, *Violence*, 59 and 90; Nippel 52. **set upon Caesar with drawn swords.** The same incident is related by Sall. *Cat.* 49.4, representing the *equites* as inspired by Piso and Catulus (7.5 n.), and by Suet. 14.2. Sall. appears to put this incident earlier, after the revelations of Volturcius and the Allobroges but before the critical senate debate, but it is not clear that he is ordering events there in strict chronological sequence. P. probably came across this item at the time when he was preparing *Cicero* (*Plutarch and History*, 51; Intr., p. 52 and n. 134).

8.3. Curio: another unfamiliar individual abruptly introduced: cf. 7.5 n. His introduction at *Sulla* 14.11–12 is no less awkward. This is the elder C. Scribonius Curio (*OCD*[4], no. 1), cos. 76, sometimes known as 'Curio the father' to distinguish him from his homonymous son, C.'s tribune and lieutenant (*OCD*[4], no. 2, 29.3 n.). He now supported the execution (Cic. *Att.* 12.21 (260).1), and praised Cicero (Cic. *Phil.* 2.12). Later he became a bitter and vocal enemy of C., issuing his attacks in a dialogue (*c.*55 BCE). That makes the present story surprising: P. is himself doubtful ('they say that'), though his reasons for doubting are incoherent (§4 n.). The whole story may be fabrication, or at least an exaggeration, of the fifties (Strasburger 124–5), when it could have been used against either Curio or C. If so, the toga item may have been borrowed from an incident a few weeks later (*C.min.* 28.3, Murena and Cato). **perhaps he was afraid of the people:** P.'s favoured theme: it recurs at *C.min.* 22.6. His analysis of Cicero's motivation at *Cic.* 20.7 is rather different. **perhaps he simply thought that such a murder was wholly illegal and unjust.** As at 9.10 (n.) and e.g. *Cic.* 19.6, the double motivation is interesting. It is not unlike Thucydides' manner of introducing a more 'realistic' alternative to a morally specious motive in cases like 3.86.3 (where see Hornblower's n., speaking of 'conservative' and 'radical' motive-alternatives) and 6.6.1, and as in the Thucydidean cases the possibility that both alternatives coexist is not excluded. The first, more realistic motive serves P.'s political analysis better, but, as at 9.10, he includes the more creditable motive as well.

8.4. I cannot understand why Cicero did not mention it in his account of his consulship: i.e. the 'memoir of my consulship written in Greek' (Cic. *Att.* 1.19 (19).10) rather than Cicero's later Latin prose version or his poem (Cic., ibid., cf. *Att.* 2.1 (21).1): Intr., p. 52. P. quotes it again at *Crass.* 13.4, and it is likely that much of the narrative in *Cicero* is drawn from this work and that P. knew it at first hand: O. Lendle, *Hermes*, 95 (1967), 90–109, and *Plutarch and History*, 45–9.

Yet the argument here is inconsequential. 'It is exactly the sort of incident which Cicero might be expected to omit' (Hardy, *The Catilinarian Conspiracy*, 104 n. 1), for the very reasons P. goes on to discuss: Cicero, criticized for letting C. escape, would have no wish to remind contemporaries of this incident. P.'s mind does not seem to have been concentrated on this 'later criticism' when he formulated this argument; perhaps he added this comment to the *hypomnēma* he drafted when preparing *Cicero*, and has not here worked it properly into the context (*Plutarch and History*, 47–8, 53). Cf. Intr., p. 54 and n. 141.

8.5. a few days later. Ziegler thinks that this contradicts Suet. 14.2, C. 'not merely withdrew, but did not attend the senate for the rest of the year'. But Suet.'s account is otherwise closely similar; it was not long till the end of the year, and P. probably refers to a session of early 62, that of Suet. 17. If so, P. has omitted details included by Suet. This denunciation of C. came from Q. Curius, who had been the initial informer on the conspiracy; there was also a further denunciation in court by L. Vettius. C. defended himself by showing that he had given Cicero details of the conspiracy, and Cicero confirmed this on oath. C. now retaliated by ensuring that Curius did not get his reward and Vettius was thrown into prison. P. had mentioned Vettius in the earlier *Lucull.* (42.7–8), but here the details would complicate and confuse.

P. has also disturbed the chronology, for Cato's corn dole followed shortly after the debate, between 5 and 29 December (§§6–7 n.), and therefore before this senate-meeting.

8.6–7: CATO'S CORN DOLE The people are aflame for C.: Cato's timely measure now calms them. P. tells the story again at *C.min.* 26.1 and at *Advice on Public Life* 818d, in both cases most enthusiastically. Here too the language is richer in imagery ('spark...damping... broke up and dispersed', all stronger in Greek than in English) and warmer than is usual in this *Life*.

P. is our only evidence for this bill. He seems to know that there was already some sort of dole before: *C.min.* has this measure 'include in the distributions those who were destitute and had hitherto been ineligible' (below, §7 n.). Distributions began with the law of C. Gracchus, mentioned at *Gracch.* 26.2, but the bill now in force was the *lex Terentia Cassia* of 73 BCE. This apparently fixed distributions of 5 *modii* a month for a precise number of recipients, perhaps 40,000 (cf. Sall. *Hist.* 3.48.19 M. = 3.34.19 McG., Cic. *Verr.* 2.3.72; G. Rickman, *The Corn Supply of Ancient Rome* (1980), 168). Then came Cato's measure, and in 58 P. Clodius made distributions free.

The price of the distributions before 58 was still the Gracchan figure, $6\frac{1}{3}$ asses a *modius*: Cic. *Sest.* 55, cf. Asc. 8 C. (as emended). If P.'s language in *C.min.* can be trusted, Cato's measure simply extended a previous measure, on the same terms, to greater numbers (above). It is thus assumed that the Gracchan price was already provided by the *lex Terentia Cassia*, and that Cato's law also continued the allowance of 5 *modii* a month. Both are dangerous hypotheses to rest on the unsupported implication of *C.min.*, but may be right.

The number of recipients under Cato's law can be calculated only within wide margins. This is not the place for a full discussion: I criticize more precise calculations in *LCM* 14.8 (1989), 117–19. The calculations of Rickman, *Corn Supply*, 171 are more cautious, and suggest a figure of 150,000. Even if P.'s figures are reliable (and they may well not be (§7 n.)), I doubt if we can do better than limits of 130,000 and 190,000. Cf. also 55.4 n. On all this, see *LCM*, loc. cit.; Rickman, *Corn Supply*, 166–72; Brunt, *Manpower*, 378–9; P. Garnsey, *Famine and Food Supply in the Graeco-Roman World* (1988), 208–13.

8.6. persuaded the senate. P.'s language, here and in *C.min.* and *Advice on Public Life*, suggests that this was a matter only of a senatorial decree. That is accepted by e.g. Fehrle 98–9 and C. Virlouvet, *Famine et émeutes à Rome* (1985), 111, and may be right, especially if this measure was essentially an extension of the *lex Terentia Cassia*: in other operational details, that law does seem somehow to have operated in conjunction with senatorial decrees (Cic. *Verr.* 2.3.163, 2.5.52). But this extension was substantial (above), and such distributions were normally ordered by law. It is likely that Cato too, perhaps with senatorial backing, introduced this as a bill before the people: thus, tentatively, Rotondi marks this as a *lex* (*LPPR* 384), though noting that the evidence is uncertain. P., who tends to operate with a polarized view of Roman politics (Intr., p. 63), will have obscured this popular tactic of an optimate figure.

This has implications for the measure's dating: §7 n.

8.7. This added 7,500,000 drachmas a year to the state's expenditure: *C.min.* 26.1 characteristically revamps the passage: Cato 'persuaded the senate to include in the distributions the poor and destitute, men who had hitherto been excluded. The annual cost was 1,250 talents...': that figure is the equivalent of these 7,500,000 drachmas/denarii (1.7 n.). R. J. Rowland, *Acta Antiqua Acad. Scient. Hung.* 13 (1965), 81–3, and A. J. Cullens, *LCM* 13.7 (1988), 98–9, take *C.min.* to refer to the total 'cost' to the state, whereas *Caesar* clearly refers only to the additional expenditure that Cato's measure involved: they therefore prefer an alternative reading here of '5,500,000 drachmas'. In *LCM* 14.8 (1989), 117–18 I gave reasons for taking *C.min.* too to mean additional rather than total cost, and for retaining the better attested '7,500,000' here. As usual (2.1 n.), these figures are suspect, especially as they may represent yet another stylized '30,000,000 sesterces' (5.8 n.) and may anyway originate in political polemic.

he was about to be praetor: smoothly leading into the next item. C.'s praetorship began on 1 January, and so this implies that Cato's measure was passed before the end of December but after the 5 December debate.

It may be that we can be more precise. Did it come after or before 10 December, the date on which the new tribunes assumed office?

1. If, as I believe, it was a law proposed by Cato as tribune (§6 n.), it will have been *after* 10 December when he took up the tribunate.

2. After treating the corn dole *C.min.* 26.2 continues: 'next, after bursting into office as tribune, Metellus began to hold turbulent assemblies...'. In their comm. (1993) on the passage, J. Geiger and L. Ghilli conclude that Cato's measure should be dated *before* Metellus entered office on 10 December (though they think it was a law rather than a decree). But P.'s language cannot be so pressed: he is frequently unreliable on such matters in the interest of narrative smoothness (Intr., p. 56; *Plutarch and History*, 92–3), and anyway the Greek may simply mean 'then Metellus, now tribune, began to hold...'.

9.1: CAESAR'S PRAETORSHIP, 62 BCE   **nothing violent came of it:** a brazen mis-statement, for P. knew that C.'s praetorship was anything but peaceful; but the troubles would not fit his themes. In particular:

1. C. played a part on the attacks on Cicero: together with Bestia and Metellus Nepos, he tried to prevent Cicero from making a public speech on the last day of his consulship (i.e. strictly the day before C. entered office, but at *Cic.* 23.1 P. makes him already 'praetor'): cf. Lintott, *Evidence*, 149–50. P. had told the story at *Cic.* 23.1–3, and had probably looked again at *Cicero* and/or his notes when writing this part of *Caesar* (Intr., p. 54 and 7.5–8.5 n., 9.2–10.11 n.). But Cicero had won the day, swearing his individual oath 'to have saved his country and

preserved the empire', and P. here suppresses C.'s failures; *Cicero* had also stressed that the people warmly supported Cicero, and that would not fit here at all.

2. Again with Nepos, C. supported the proposal to recall Pompey 'as the man to break Cicero's one-man domination' (*Cic.* 23.4), or less extravagantly to assume command against Catiline in the field (*C.min.* 26.2): cf. *MRR* 173–4. Once more this was a proposal that failed; and P. is so far avoiding the suggestion of any link between C. and Pompey (Intr., p. 59).

3. On the first day of his praetorship C. attempted to have Catulus' name erased from the Capitol (cf. 6.6 n.), claiming that Catulus had embezzled funds, that the restoration was incomplete, and that the task should be transferred to Pompey (Suet. 15, Dio 37.44.1–2, cf. *Cic. Att.* 2.24 (44).3). If P. knew this item, the same considerations would come into play as with (2), and P.'s Caesar is anyway more dignified than to indulge such petty vindictiveness.

4. Suet. 16 has a tale that C., together with Nepos, was removed by office by senatorial decree; a few days later he restrained some popular demonstrations on his behalf, and the senate restored him to office (the truth of the story is doubtful: Strasburger 103–5). P. probably knew a different version, which had Cato dissuading the senate from passing the original motion (*C.min.* 29.3, not naming C. but only Nepos). The whole story, if it involved C. at all, would now be too trivial to mention.

9.2–10.11: CLODIUS AND THE BONA DEA This episode is related in a more leisurely style than the tense preceding chapters. In telling of Clodius' intrusion and capture, P. is more expansive than in his earlier version in *Cic.* 28–9, adding picturesque new detail (Intr., p. 57). With the trial and its outcome, it is the other way round: *Cicero* was fuller on Cicero's own testimony (he was bullied into giving it by his wife Terentia), on Clodius' incestuous affairs, and on the strong rumours of bribery. In *Cicero* the sequence forms a suggestive contrast with the earlier Bona Dea scene at 19–20, as he in turn confronts the two demagogues, Catiline and Clodius (cf. Moles, ad loc.). The first scene there marks the height of Cicero's success, the second the beginning of his reverses, and P. therefore stresses the unscrupulous forces and the domestic unpleasantness that will face him. *Caesar* prefers its usual, less morally charged political polarity, with the 'most powerful men in the senate' attacking Clodius, the people enthusiastic in his defence, and the jurors influenced by their nervousness rather than any bribes.

P. is never at his most acute with those he sees as demagogues, and his Clodius is simply motivated by lust for the willing Pompeia. That must be too simple: there would be easier ways to consummate the affair. But C.'s swift divorce of his wife does suggest that some sexual explanation was in the air at an early stage, and tells against the more straightforward attempts to reduce Clodius' motive to a political one, provoking a confrontation with the optimates (thus e.g. H. Benner, *Die Politik des P. Clodius Pulcher* (*Hist.* Einz. 50; 1987), 38–40). Such a view anyway underplays the element of serious religion involved in the sacrilege, and it makes Clodius too stereotyped a demagogue; nor should we assume he *wanted* to be discovered. We do better to concentrate on Clodius' association with other gilded young aristocrats (on which see esp. Dettenhofer 36–8), and see this as an act of self-admiring social audacity, rather in the style of the eighteenth-century Hell-Fire club. Cf. the parallels O. Murray collects in discussing the mysteries outrage of 415 BCE (*Sympotica*, ed. Murray (1990), 158–60): '[t]he Eighteenth century understood better the purpose of sacrilege: there too it was an intrinsic part of the life-style of certain groups of aristocrats.' Clodius was about to enter office as quaestor, probably the next morning (9.7 n.). It carried a certain *frisson* to begin a senatorial career fresh from the bed of the pontifex maximus' wife, and from an unthinkable impiety: a new Alcibiades.

App. (2.14.52 and *Sic.* 7) and Sch. Bob. (pp. 85–91 St.) show contact with P.'s version; App. may perhaps derive from P., Sch. Bob. from his source. The complicated sequence of events leading up to the trial (shortly before 15 May 61) is elucidated by Cic. *Att.* 1.12–16 (12–16 Shackleton Bailey). Fragments of Cicero's *Against Clodius and Curio*, reflecting the altercation in the senate on 15 May, are preserved by Sch. Bob., loc. cit., along with his comments (cf. W. J. Tatum, *The Patrician Tribune* (1999), 87–8, 281). The fullest modern treatment is Moreau, but Tatum is better on religious aspects; Lintott, *Evidence*, 6–8, 154–9 discusses the Ciceronian material, and has particularly good comments on the dynamics of senatorial debate.

9.2. Publius Clodius. Cicero's notorious adversary (see *OCD*[4] and esp. Tatum, *The Patrician Tribune*) was at the time of the scandal quaestor designate; later tribune in 58, aedile 56, murdered 52. For P.'s treatment of him, which varies according to the themes of

different *Lives*, see *Plutarch and History*, 98–100. **noble:** possibly
here = *patricius* (*Sulla* 1.1, cf. 61.2 n.), possibly *nobilis*: Clodius was
in fact both, and P. may not have understood the difference (*Plutarch
and History*, 219–20 and 231–2 n. 88). **reckless aggression:** the same
word *thrasutēs* as at 7.4. Here as there (n.) the demagogue stereotype
is in point, and the phrasing ('outdid the most notorious of scoundrels') suggests that P. had Cleon, the demagogue's perpetual para-
digm, in mind. Cf. *Dtr.* 11, where the introduction of Stratocles
evokes an explicit comparison with Cleon.

9.3. Caesar's wife Pompeia: 5.7 n. **women's quarters.** Susan Treggiari points out to me that these were a feature of Greek houses rather
than Roman: P. is elaborating the story according to his own concep-
tions. **Aurelia** probably figured in the introductory lacuna (above,
p. 130), which fits her prominence here and at 10.3: *Cicero* has no
such emphasis. Cf. *Gracch.* 25.4–6, stressing the similarly (Tac. *Dial.*
28.6) formidable Cornelia and picking up *Gracch.* 1.6–7.

9.4–8: THE FESTIVAL OF THE BONA DEA   Such antiquarian di-
gressions are characteristic of P. (Leo 152–3), especially where he inter-
prets Roman customs for his largely Greek audience: cf. 61.1–3 and e.g.
Pomp. 4.7–10, 13.10–11, 22.5; *Mar.* 1, 5.1–2; *Marc.* 22; Intr., 9; C.
Theander, *Eranos* 57 (1959), 102–3. *Cic.* 19.4–5 had already shown P.'s
interest in the Bona Dea, and at some time before *Caes.* he had written a
detailed chapter of the *Roman Questions* (268d–e) discussing why
myrtle branches were excluded from the festival. The tentative authorial
voice here ('the Phrygians claim... the Romans think... the Greeks
regard... the one it is forbidden to name... it is said') conveys the
respectful uncertainty appropriate for a male dealing with female religious secrets; it contrasts with the crassness of a Clodius, bursting in and
(as P. presents it) thinking of the festival only as a sexual opportunity.

The cult was secret, and exercised men's imaginations even in
antiquity : cf. esp. Macr. *Sat.* 1.12.20–9, Prop. 4.9.23–30, Juv. 2.86–7
and 6.314–51, Arnob. *adu. nat.* 1.36 and 5.18. On the cult, cf. esp.
H. H. J. Brouwer, *Bona Dea: The Sources and a Description of the Cult*
(1989), esp. 359–70; T. P. Wiseman, *Cinna the Poet* (1974), 130–7;
and briefly *OCD*[4], s.v.

At *Alex.* 2.5–9 Alexander's mother Olympias is connected with
snake-handling and with Dionysiac and 'Orphic' (cf. §§5–6 here)
cults. That forms part of that *Life*'s uncertain religious atmosphere,
into which Alexander himself was to enter so willingly: Intr., p. 30.

The world of C. and his family is different. The dignified Aurelia is no Olympias, pursuing the rites 'more energetically than the others and in a rather barbarian way' (*Alex.* 2.9); and we here swiftly return to the hard realities of Roman politics.

like the Greek 'Women's Goddess'. *Cic.* 19.4 more bluntly identifies the two, 'the goddess whom the Roman call "Good" and the Greeks "Women's"': so also Prop. 4.9.25, Macr. *Sat.* 1.12.27. Little is known of this Greek 'Women's Goddess'. **mother of King Midas:** i.e. Cybele, the 'Great Mother', especially associated with Phrygia (hence 'claim her for their own'): on her frequent identification with Bona Dea, see esp. Macr. 1.12.20–1 with Brouwer, *Bona Dea*, 251, 353, 388–9, 412, 415–17, and in *Hommages...J. Vermaseren* (1978), i. 142–59. **a Dryad nymph and the wife of Faunus.** In *Roman Questions* 268d–e Fauna is again Faunus' 'wife'; she is more usually Faunus' daughter, in one version a daughter whom he incestuously tried to ravish. For these and other versions, see Wiseman, *Cinna the Poet*, 134–7; Brouwer, *Bona Dea*, index, s.vv. Fauna, Faunus. **one of the mothers of Dionysus, the one it is forbidden to name:** presumably Persephone (so Brouwer, *Bona Dea*, 341–3), who was euphemistically worshipped as 'Kore' ('the Girl'): cf. e.g. Eur. *Hel.* 1306–7, 'the girl who is gone, the one we may not name', and, for Dionysus as son of Persephone and Zeus, Diod 3.64.1, 4.4.1, and *Orph. hymn.* 29.5–7, 30.6–7 (with M. L. West, *The Orphic Poems* (1983), 74, 95–7, for the notion in earlier Orphic literature); for Bona Dea as Persephone, Macr. 1.12.23. The Bona Dea was also equated with Semele, Dionysus' more usual mother (Macr., ibid.).

9.5. sacred snake...just as the myth says: probably the myth of Eur. *Bacch.* 101–4: Zeus bore Dionysus from his thigh 'and crowned him with crowns of snakes...'. That provided an aetiology for the prominent role of snake-handling in the Dionysiac cult: Dodds on *Bacchae* 101–4. For snakes as a feature of the cult cf. Brouwer, *Bona Dea*, 340–8.

9.6. No man is allowed... Indeed, 'anything male' was excluded from the house (*Roman Questions* 268e), i.e. male animals and images of males: Brouwer, *Bona Dea*, 255. **the women:** including the Vestal Virgins (*Cic.* 19.5, etc.). **similar to Orphic ritual.** It is unclear what 'similarities' P. had in mind (if he knew himself: notice 'it is said...'): perhaps the mime of the Orphic 'holy story' or other features of initiation (Wiseman, *Cinna the Poet*, 134): this prepares for Aurelia concealing the 'sacred objects' at 10.3. Or it may be just that 'Orphic' should be 'taken as a label that could be (but was not necessarily) applied to religious material that seemed extra-ordinary, unusual in either a positive or negative sense' (R. G. Edmonds III, *BMCR* 2004.12.29). The sexual licence alleged of both Orphic and Bona Dea rituals (Brouwer, *Bona Dea*, 369–70, cf. A. Dieterich, *Philol.* 52 (1894), 8) may also be relevant—but for Clodius' lubricious way of viewing the proceedings, not too far from that of Juv. 6.314 ff., rather than P.'s own (above, 9.4–8 n.).

9.7. when the day arrives.   In 63 the rites took place on the night of 3–4 or more likely 4–5 December (*Cic.* 19–20, Dio 37.35.4), and this was probably the regular fixed date (Wiseman, *Cinna the Poet*,130 and n. 1, Moreau 15–20). Cicero first refers to the 62 scandal in a letter of 1 January (*Att.* 1.12 (12).3). If the 4th–5th is right, Clodius was due to enter office as quaestor the next day. **in the house of a consul or a praetor:** in 63 of Cicero as consul, in 62 of C. as urban praetor. This was probably the *domus publica* on the Sacred Way (*LTUR*, s.v., 63.9 n.), where C. had presumably by now taken up residence as pontifex maximus (Suet. 46.1): Moreau 20–2. 'C.'s status as *pontifex maximus* made his house a natural choice' (Shackleton Bailey on Cic. *Att.* 1.12 (12).3), but it is not clear who was responsible for choosing it: probably the Vestals, perhaps consulting with the pontifices. **musical accompaniment.** So Clodius disguised himself as a lute-girl.

10.1. Pompeia was now presiding…:   not Aurelia (*pace* Balsdon, *Hist.* 15 (1966), 66 and Moreau 12). At §3 Aurelia takes matters into her own hands. **Clodius was still beardless.** But he was at least 29 years old. His beardlessness was from choice, and may have been adopted for the occasion: the small trimmed beard was more the style of his coterie (Cic. *Cael.* 25 with R. G. Austin's n., *Att.* 1.14 (14).5, etc.).

10.3. Habra   was also a word for a favourite waiting-maid, so Habra **was indeed the servant's name** as well as her description. This was the usual Greek form of 'Aura', a common name for slaves; but Sch. Bob., p. 91, St., suggests that here it = 'Hibera'. **put a stop to the ceremony:** the Vestals later repeated the disturbed sacrifice (Cic. *Att.* 1.13 (13).3, Dio 37.46.1, Sch. Bob., p. 89): we do not know when or where. Cf. Moreau 80.

10.4 He was found hiding in the bedroom of the servant girl…: so also Cic. 28.4 and Sch. Bob., pp. 89, 91, but Cic. *Att.* 1.12 (12).3 has Clodius first 'discovered' (cf. Cic. *Mil.* 72), then helped by a slave girl or girls to escape surreptitiously (rather than P.'s picture of Aurelia and the others 'driving him out'). So also Cic. *Har. Resp.* 44. It is unclear which version is right: Moreau 15 n.11 is tempted to favour P. The slave girl was later demanded for torture (Sch. Bob., p. 91).

10.6. one of the tribunes: almost certainly a mistake. Clodius' formal prosecutor was L. Cornelius Lentulus Crus, the future pr. 58 and cos. 49 (29.1 n.), with three *subscriptores*, Cn. and L. Lentulus and C. Fannius. Moreau 133 n. 385 and Tatum, *The Patrician Tribune*, 278 n.137, think that P.'s 'tribune' is a garbled reference to Q. Fufius Calenus (39.9 n.), who was not prosecutor but played a part in the political dispute concerning the jury composition (Cic. *Att.* 1.14 (14).1, 1.16 (16).2). If so, the confusion is considerable: Fufius was on Clodius' side (cf. also Cic. *Phil.* 8.16). It is more likely that P. has imaginatively expanded (9.2–10.11 n.) his *Cicero* account, where 'someone' prosecuted Clodius (28.4: cf. Moles, ad loc., Pelling, *Plutarch and History*, 40 n. 119, followed by Moreau 43). It may be a simple error, but it may also relate to a wider theme: this is not the only time where P. introduces 'tribunes' who turn out to be helpless against C. (23.7, 35.6–11, 60.1, 61.8–10 nn.).

indicted Clodius for impiety. The charge was *incestum*, assimilating (so it seems) the religious outrage to the defilement of the Vestals' chastity: so Moreau 83–9, followed by Tatum, *Patrician Tribune*, 74–5. Here and in *Cic.* P. refers loosely to 'an indictment for impiety', the normal *Athenian* method of trial for behaviour prejudicial to the sanctity of festivals (A. R. W. Harrison, *The Law of Athens*, ii (1971), 62–3). The trial took place before, probably not long before, 15 May 61 (Cic. *Att.* 1.16 (16).9: Moreau 152–7).

the most powerful men in the senate. P. could have named names—Cicero, Lucullus, Catulus (*Cic.* 29); for other optimates whose sympathies were clear, cf. Cic. *Att.* 1.13 (13).3, 14 (14).5. Evidence was also given by Aurelia and C.'s sister Julia (Suet. 74.2, Sch. Bob. p. 89), and perhaps by Cato (Sen. *Ep.* 97.3, doubted by Moreau 200). **plenty of extraordinary outrages:** 'acts of perjury, fraud, bribery of the masses, and seduction of women' (*Cic.* 29.4). **incest with his sister, the wife of Lucullus.** As *Cic.* notes more fully, this is not the famous sister Clodia Metelli (the star of Cicero's *Pro Caelio* and possibly Catullus' Lesbia). Lucullus' wife was the youngest of the three sisters: Clodius was alleged to have slept with all three. Lucullus now provided maids to substantiate the allegations. P. could evidently have said more here about Clodius' brotherly loves, but as usual *Caesar* eschews gratuitous smut.

10.7. the people equally took sides in Clodius' support: so *Cic.* 29.6, adding that the jurors asked for a bodyguard: cf. *Cic. Att.* 1.16 (16).5. There was a demonstration against Cicero when he came to give evidence (*Cic. Att.* 1.16 (16).4). P. gives the impression of a spontaneous demonstration; he has no inkling of the efficient organization of Clodius' bands (on which see esp. Lintott, *Violence*, 74–88, Nippel 70–9).

10.8. he immediately divorced Pompeia: before 25 January 61 (*Cic. Att.* 1.13 (13).3). **when he was called as witness:** so also *Cic.* 29.9, Suet. 74.2. But he was probably not even in Rome at the time of the trial. The allocation of provinces had taken place before 15 March (*Cic. Att.* 1.15 (15).1), and C. left quickly (11.1 n.). Strasburger 111 n. 55 concludes that C.'s famous apophthegm is fictional, but that need not follow: writers would naturally have assigned an anecdote to what seemed a plausible context.

10.9. 'Because I thought my wife should be beyond suspicion': a crisper version than at *Cic.* 29.9, Suet. 74.2, or Dio 37.45.2. C.'s statement would sound less pompous in a world where 'reputation' could in itself count among virtues, especially female ones: e.g. Prop. 4.11.12, 72, *laud. Turiae* 1.33, 2.58, 65, *OLD*, s.v. 'fama' 6 a. 'Without reproach' is a common theme on epitaphs. Lintott, *Evidence*, 155, may also be right in pointing to C.'s position as pontifex maximus: he 'could not retain his authority in a matter like this, if his own wife was compromised'.

10.10. Some say that Caesar was being sincere, while others think that he was playing to the people: cf. 8.3 n. for the double motivation. Here too the second, more cynical alternative suits P.'s themes better, but he includes the more creditable version as well.

10.11. So Clodius was acquitted, with most of the jurors spoiling the letters on their votes: expanding *Cic.* 29.6, 'and most of the jurors submitted their votes with the letters spoiled'. P. surely has no authority for his guess at the jurors' motivation. He also knew that the voting was close (*Cic.* 29.8), but does not weaken his point by saying so here. Thirty-one voted for acquittal, twenty-five for conviction (*Cic. Att.* 1.16 (16).5, Sch. Bob., p. 85, St.), and P. may be right that others spoiled their votes, though he doubtless exaggerates their number. The total number of jurors is unknown: the *lex Aurelia* prescribed a minimum of fifty-one jurors, but that could be and here clearly was exceeded: cf. Shackleton Bailey on *Att.* 1.16 (16).5.

Wax-tablets could easily be erased. J. L. Strachan-Davidson, *Problems of the Roman Criminal Law* (1912), ii. 129–34, thinks that the procedure of the (? Gracchan) *lex Acilia* still applied: if so, the tablets had A written on one side, C on the other (*absoluo, condemno*), and the juror was expected to erase one before dropping his ballot into the urn. If a juror wished to abstain, he should erase both. P.'s vague 'spoiled the letters' probably reflects this last procedure, but P. perhaps did not understand what happened: no reader would think of a simple abstention here.

11–12: CAESAR PROCONSUL IN SPAIN, 61–60 BCE   These inconspicuous chapters are important to the structure of the *Life*. So far we have heard a lot of the popular enthusiasm for C. and the danger this posed for the optimates; we have heard less of his own ambitions, and nothing of C.'s relations to Crassus and Pompey. Now 'Crassus needed C . . . . for his political activity against Pompey': apart from the incidental 5.7, this is the first mention of either. Anecdotes are rarer in *Caesar* than in other *Lives*, but now we have two to illustrate C.'s ambition, one of them displaced for the purpose (11.5 n.). A neat ring composition ties the Spanish episode together: C. begins crippled with *debts*, but riding on his popularity at Rome; in Spain he wins new popularity by managing *debtors* sensitively (so P. has it, most implausibly: 12.3 n.); he returns a rich man. The next chapters illustrate the sequel, and by 13.4–6, in league with the other two great men, he is exercising his full influence on Roman politics. And the wise Cato shudders.

The account of the governorship at App. 2.8.27 and *Hisp.* 102.442 shows little contact with P., and App. takes a different view of C.'s administration (12.2 n.). The emphasis of Dio 37.52–3 is also different, but may well go back to the same source, as P. Dio has more detail on the warfare, and does not even mention the peacetime administration: that bias of interest is true to the traditions of Roman historiography. P. is less steeped in the Roman tradition, and here and elsewhere he shows considerable interest in administration: cf. 23.2–4 n. and e.g. *Lucull.* 20, 29, *Cic.* 6.1–2, 36, 52(3), *Pomp.* 10.2, 28, 39, *C.min.* 34–40; *Plutarch and History* 233 n. 91.

The evidence for C.'s Spanish governorship is examined by R. Schulz in *Res publica reperta: Festschrift . . . J. Bleicken* (2002),

263–78. F. Fischer, *Klio*, 91 (2009), 435–42, argues that C.'s interest in
Spain may suggest an ambition, perhaps as early as his quaestorship
in 69 (5.6 n.), to build a power base of his own in the West on the
model of Pompey's in the East, and that 'C.'s move against Gaul
therefore would have many roots, some of them stretching a long way
back' (p. 440): that is not very plausible, and it is not clear that C.'s
proconsular ambitions focused initially on Gaul rather than on Illyricum (18–27 n.).

11.1. Straight after his praetorship. Lots were normally cast for
provinces during the magistrates' term of office (*StR* ii³. 214–15), but
this year that was delayed and took place between 13 February and 15
March 61 (Cic. *Att.* 1.14 (14).5 and 15 (15).1). C. left hurriedly soon
afterwards (Suet. 18.1, though this is doubted by Moreau 199–200).
Caesar took Spain as his province: Further Spain, where he had been
quaestor eight years earlier (5.6 n.). **his creditors were most intractable:** for C.'s debts, see 5.8 n.; for his creditors' importunity, Suet.
18.1, App. 2.8.26. *Crass.* 7.6 adds graphic and perhaps imaginative
detail—the creditors grabbed hold of C.'s baggage train.

11.2. Crassus...went surety for 830 talents: i.e. 20,000,000 HS
(2.1 n.). See 5.8 n.: here too there should be the usual reservations
about the reliability of stylized round numbers. A. Drummond,
Athen. 87 (1999), 154, notes the important implication that Crassus
had not hitherto been C.'s major creditor.

11.3–4: THE ALPINE VILLAGE Whereas Sertorius would 'prefer
to be the most nameless citizen in Rome than to rule the whole of the
rest of the world' (*Sert.* 22.8): *Sert.* is probably later than *Caesar*, and
the reader of *Sert.* may well catch the contrast. S. Grazzini, *Maia*, 50
(1998), 77–80, suggests an allusion to Eur. *Hipp.* 1016–18, where
Hippolytus protests his preference for a quiet life as 'second in the
city'; not impossible, but there seems little point in characterizing C.
as 'no Hippolytus'. More thought-provoking would be a hint of
Achilles in the underworld, *Od.* 11.488–91 (so Schmitzer 221 n.
178), where Achilles would prefer to be a poor serf amid the living
than king among the dead; for it is the Achillean life of achievement
to which C. is in fact drawn, and eventually 69.1 may suggest the
question whether it was all worthwhile (Intr., p. 23–4).
    At *JC* i. ii. 171–4 Shakespeare's Brutus gives his first response to
Cassius' approach: 'Brutus had rather be a villager | than to repute
himself a son of Rome | under these hard conditions as this time | is
like to lay upon us.' Cf. Intr., p. 75. Shakespeare's transfer of the motif

to Brutus is suggestive. P.'s story points the ambition that, once C. has realized it, will make others think of a 'village' existence with a different wistfulness and a different sense of honour. That is why, and how, C. will be destroyed by the greatness for which he yearns.

11.5–6: C MUSES ON ALEXANDER   Cf. 5.6 n, and, on the significance for the pair, Intr., pp. 3–4, 28. The story of Suet. 7.1 and Dio 37.52.2 is basically the same, except that:

1. Suet. and Dio have C.'s musings inspired by the sight of a 'representation', presumably a statue, of Alexander in the temple of Hercules at Cádiz—an appropriate place, for Cádiz is at one end of the earth (Juv. 10.1, etc.), this earth that Hercules had traversed to west and Alexander to east: cf. F. della Corte, *Maia*, 41 (1989), 95–9, and A. Fear in J. Elsner and I. Rutherford (eds), *Pilgrimage in Graeco-Roman and Early Christian Antiquity* (2005), 319–31. The 'statue' story could have tied into a recurrent motif of the pair (Intr., p. 30), and at first sight P.'s 'reading' version has less colour. Perhaps the difference derives from an ambiguous reference in a Greek source to *graphē*, which could mean either 'writing' or (painted) 'representation'. Or perhaps there is something subtly metatextual, with P. suggesting, just as C. is about to reach Ocean for the first time (12.1 n.), the inspiring power of reading about Alexander, just as his own readers have read about Alexander in the paired *Life*, and just as P.'s Alexander looked forwards to writings about himself (*Alex.* 14.9). *Per.* 1–2 is explicit on the way in which written narrative is a more powerful incentive to virtue and achievement than any statue. Cf. *Plutarch and History*, 257, and, on P.'s avoidance here of a possible Trajanic perspective, Intr., pp. 3–4.

2. Suet. dates the episode to the Spanish quaestorship in 69–8 (cf. 5.6 n.); so, apparently, does Dio, although he relates it among the proconsulship items. P. clearly (*pace* Green, *AJAH* 3 (1978), 18–19 n. 20) implies that it belongs to the proconsulship. It seems that the original version dated the item to the quaestorship (so Steidle 18–19; *contra*, Strasburger 94–7), when C. was genuinely 'at the age when Alexander had already conquered the world' (Suet.). Dio's odd arrangement may reflect the genesis of the displacement, but it anyway suits P.'s narrative strategy to have the item here: this is the time when C.'s ambitions become central (11–12 n.).

P. liked comparisons with Alexander (Jones 96). They also appealed to the Romans, and at the time Pompey was the great Alexander figure (*Pomp.* 2.2–4 with Heftner's nn., *Pomp.* 46, etc.): see Intr., pp. 25–7. For C. in particular, cf. Weippert 105–92 and esp. P. Green, *AJAH* 3 (1978), 1–26, drawing the important distinction between C. *imitating* Alexander and others *comparing* the two; the second is frequent in later literature and is hinted even in Cicero (Intr., p. 28 and n. 62), but Green is rightly sceptical of the first. The present anecdote, like the preceding one of the Alpine village, may well be the product of later imaginative hindsight: so Weippert 108–12, cf. Green 3. It could naturally fit into the debate about C.'s ideas of world domination (Suet. 30, Cic. *De Off.* 3.82–3, etc.: see 69.1 n. and Intr., p. 18), and could have been put about by supporters, by detractors, or simply by romanticizers.

12.1. raised ten cohorts . . . : this may simply = 'enrolled one extra legion to add to the two he had already', as P. can give army strength in terms of cohorts even where exact numbers of legions are involved: *Lucull.* 11.4, 17.1, *Pomp.* 20.4, 62.3, etc. C. presumably enrolled most of these from Roman citizens in Spain (R. E. Smith, *Service in the Post-Marian Roman Army* (1958), 48: cf. *Sert.* 6.9, with Konrad's nn.; J. M. Roldán Hervas, *Zephyrus*, 25 (1974), 458–71, unnecessarily doubting at 470 whether these cohorts constituted a regular legion); if so, C. may have been capitalizing on contacts with Roman settlers established eight years earlier as quaestor (5.6 n., Schulz, *Res publica reperta . . .* (11–12 n.), 269–70). But he may have included natives too (Brunt, *Manpower*, 471–2). **marched on the Callaici and the Lusitani:** see Map 5, and on these campaigns cf. M. Ferreiro López, *Actas 1er Congreso Peninsular de Historia Antigua* (1988), ii. 363–72; Schulz, *Res publica reperta . . .*, 270–3, speculating that C. had his eye on the rich mineral deposits of the region. Dio 37.52–3 stresses that C. might easily have limited himself to clearing up brigandage, but instead deliberately provoked the Spanish; Suet. 54.1 is also unsympathetic—'he plundered some towns of the Lusitani as if they were enemies, even though they were not disobedient to his orders and opened their gates to him as he arrived'. P. is interested in the achievement, not its dubious moral circumstances. **went on to the Ocean at the end of the earth.** Pointed language: C. is indeed a new Alexander. Cf. *Alex.* 66.1. At *Pomp.* 38.4 similar language suggests a similar point about Pompey (so Weippert 87–9): 'a certain passion and emulation [in Alexander's case the word was often *pothos*, "yearning"] came over him to recover Syria, drive through Arabia to the Red Sea, and equate his conquests with the Ocean that marks the circumference of the human world...'. See also Intr., p. 28; 23.2 and 58.7 nn.

12.2. masterful in his peacetime administration. *B.Hisp.* 42 gives C. a speech extolling his own administration; similar praises at Cic. *Balb.* 43 (prudential) and Vell. 2.43.4 (conventional). A different picture emerges from Suet. 54.1, 'he displayed restraint neither in his commands nor in his magistracies...', and esp. App. 2.8.27, 'after arriving in Spain he gave no attention to conducting public business or giving judgements or anything of that sort...'. In the Civil War, Spain (with some exceptions) was fairly solid for Pompey and his sons.

12.3. two-thirds of a debtor's income should pass to the creditor each year. C.'s debt legislation was probably inspired by Lucullus' example in the East: cf. *Lucull.* 20, with Gelzer, *R–E* 13 (1927), 394; Sherwin-White 252–3. Lucullus imposed an interest limit of 12 per cent a year, and ordered a complete remission on any back interest due above the sum of the capital; he forbade compound interest, and allowed the creditor to claim no more than 25 per cent of the debtor's income against the total. If P.'s figures are accurate here, C.'s legislation was much more severe: no order on interest, no remission, and the creditor allowed $\frac{2}{3}$ of the debtor's income. P.'s optimistic phrases have no hint of the harshness of this measure.

12.4. as he left his province. C. left the province early, before a successor arrived: Dio 37.54.1, cf. Suet. 18.1. (Strasburger 96 unnecessarily supposes this a doublet with his haste in early 61 to leave Rome, Suet. 11.1, but Suet. may well be building an expressive sequence here of C. doing everything ahead of schedule: Pelling in *CJC* 259.) Elsewhere too P. passes over such haste in silence (5.6, 11.1 nn.): it is too undignified for his C., and here the compassionate administrator would hardly leave Spain without a government. **He had become rich himself.** For the wealth C. acquired there, cf. Catull. 29.19 and esp. Suet. 54.1, 'when proconsul in Spain he took money from the allies which he had begged for the relief of his debts...'. P. is again not interested in making moral points about such financial exploitation: contrast the tone of *C.mai.* 10.4–6. **made sure that his men benefited:** cf. 17.1. C.'s troops would certainly expect a share of the booty, and so would his staff (cf. Catull. 29); there was also some responsibility for C. to deliver something to the state treasury, as App. 2.8.27 claims he did. But there was no moral or legal sanction against a general using a lavish amount of the proceeds for his own purposes:

the elder Cato (*C.mai.* 10.4–6) was quite unusual. Cf. I. Shatzman, *Senatorial Wealth and Roman Politics* (1975), 63–7, 105–6, 123–4 and in *Hist.* 21 (1972), 177–205; K.-H. Vogel, *Zschr. d. Sav.-Stift. f. Rechtsgesch.* 66.2 (1948), 394–422; Brunt, *FRR* 263–5; Y. le Bohec in *NP* 6 (1999), 837–8. **saluting him as 'Imperator'.** No other source mentions this acclamation.

13: CAESAR'S RETURN; THE PACT WITH POMPEY AND CRASSUS
P. accepts the view of Asinius Pollio (§3 n., cf. Intr., p. 45): it was the pact of the three great men which set Rome on the path to war. The point is a purely historical one, but it is important to the biography, the first of C.'s 'friendships' to have catastrophic effects, and it is the more marked for the small role that Pompey and Crassus have so far played in the *Life* (Intr., p. 59). The emphases here are characteristic. No moralizing on the death of freedom; but the reappearance of Cato once more introduces some warmth into an austere account (§6 n., cf. 8.6–7 n.). No speculation on C.'s motivation: P. does not debate whether C. *intended* all these far-reaching consequences (though the anecdotes of 11.3–4 give a strong hint); cf. Intr., p. 23. The emphasis is historical, but there is no larger-scale historical judgement, no ascription of the Republic's decline to less personal causes: contrast e.g. Lucan 1.70–2, 158–82, Flor. 1.47 and 2.13.8, and Sall. *Cat.* 6–13, 36.4–39.5; M. Pohlenz, Ἐπιτύμβιον *H.* Swoboda (1927), 201–10; Syme, *RP* i. 205–17; A. W. Lintott, *CQ* 21 (1971), 493–8; B. M. Levick, *G&R* 29 (1982), 53–62. P. could doubtless have found something to say: cf. e.g. *Cic.* 10–11, *Sulla* 12.11–12 and 39(1).2–5, *Pomp.* 3.3 and 70. But, at least in *Caesar*, that is not his style of historical biography. He observes how historical factors affected his subject's career and how his career affected history; but wider 'background', with less relevance to the personal subject, is eschewed. Cf. 28 n. and Intr., pp. 15–25.

P. omits complicating detail, some at least of which he probably knew:

1. Suet. 19.1 mentions C.'s electoral pact with L. Lucceius, and the rival bribery campaigns. So far *Caesar* has played down bribery (Intr., p. 59), and for P., as for Dio (below), C.'s election is adequately explained by the support of Pompey and Crassus.

2. Suet. 19.2 has the senate's decision to decree 'the woods and drove-paths of Italy' as the consular provinces, and represents this as the last straw that drove C. into the coalition. For P., once again, results matter more than motives or antecedents. On these provinces, cf. J. W. Rich, *Lat.* 45 (1986), 505–21.

They were not necessarily 'sinecures', as Meier 183 thinks, as the
aftermath of 63 clearly left some genuine rustic troubles: cf.
Oros. 6.6.5–7 (presumably from Livy), Dio 37.41.1, Suet. *Aug.*
3.1, 7.1. But the possibilities for consular self-enrichment were
doubtless disappointing. As Miriam Griffin suggests to me, the
task of clearing out Catilinarian supporters (cf. esp. Suet. *Aug.*
3.1) may have been intended as a deliberate embarrassment for
C., given the suspicions of his involvement (7.7 with 7.5–8.5 n.).

3. Dio distinguishes two phases: C. first secured the support of
   Crassus and Pompey independently, then later reconciled the
   two (37.54–56; see 13.4 n.). Suet. 19.2 and App. 2.9.33 also seem
   to distinguish two steps; App. makes first Pompey approach C.,
   then C. set up the 'reconciliation' with Crassus. P. prefers the
   simpler and clearer picture, with the initiative unequivocally C.'s.

P. also treats the coalition at *Lucull.* 42.5–6, *Pomp.* 47.1–4, *Crass.*
14.1–4, and *C.min.* 31.2–5.

13.1. Those requesting a triumph.   P.'s language implies only that
C. sought a triumph, not necessarily that one was granted: App. 2.8.28
and Dio 37.54.1–2, 44.41.3–4 say or imply that the senate did award
the triumph. We might have expected the triumph to be contentious
and discussion to be protracted, yet we heard nothing of any dispute;
C. T. H. R. Ehrhardt, *Prudentia*, 19 (1987), 50–8, suggests, with some
reason, that C. abandoned his request before it came to a vote. **outside
the walls:** i.e. outside the *pomerium*, StR i^3. 63–4, 127 and n. 2. **those
who sought the consulship had to do this within the city itself.** The
point at issue is the announcement of candidature (*professio*), which
had to be delivered in person: StR i^3. 503–4, Lintott, *Constitution*, 44–
5, Linderski 87–8, 91–4, 635–6, R. Morstein-Marx, *Historia*, 56
(2007), 168–9 and n. 44. **the time of the election was very near.** C.
arrived over a month before the elections (Cic. *Att.* 2.1 (21).9), but he
needed to deliver his *professio* in time to leave a period of 'three
market-days' before the elections (*trinum nundinum*, cf. *OCD*^{4}, s.v.,
and A. W. Lintott, *CQ* 15 (1965), 281–5). Even if a triumph had been
granted, this did not give him time to prepare it (App. 2.8.29, 'his
procession was not yet ready'). **to ask for permission to stand for the
consulship in absence:** 'he knew that it was against the law, but also
that it had been done by others' (App. 2.8.29), and there were indeed
precedents: J. P. V. D. Balsdon, *JRS* 52 (1962), 140–1. Linderski 93–4

infers from Cic. *Leg. Agr.* 2.24 that a law requiring personal *professio* dated only from 63 or later; in my view that makes too little allowance for rhetorical disingenuousness in the Cicero passage.

13.2. talked out the proposal by speaking until sunset. Cato's favourite tactic (*C.min.* 5.4, 31.5, C. *BC* 1.32.3, cf. *C.min.* 33.1–4 (with 14.11–12 n., below), 43.2–6), effective because senatorial decrees passed after sunset were not valid (Gell. 14.7.8, citing Varro): P. Groebe, *Klio*, 5 (1905), 229–35, L. de Libero, *Obstruktion: Politische Praktiken im Senat und in der Volksversammlung der ausgehenden römischen Republik (70–49 v.Chr.)* (*Hermes* Einz. 59; 1992), 15–22, as corrected by A. Drummond, *CR* 44 (1994), 124. Cato may already have used it a few months earlier to frustrate the *publicani* (Cic. *Att.* 1.18 (18).7 with Shackleton Bailey's n.; de Libero 16–17). At *Advice on Public Life* 804c P. generalizes: 'When Cato did not expect to persuade the people or the senate because they had been won over in advance by his opponents' favours or attentions, he would get up and speak all day, and thus avert the crisis by procrastination.' **to abandon the triumph.** The troops C. had brought home from Spain may well have been sent northwards to Aquileia (F. Fischer, *Klio*, 91 (2009), 435–52, cf. C. *BG* 1.10.3). If C. was already thinking of reclaiming them for a proconsular command (so Fischer), that would fit an expectation of a campaign in Illyricum (18–27 n., cf. 12 n. above).

13.3. the reconciliation of Pompey and Crassus, which produced the famous coalition of the three that was long mis-called 'the first triumvirate': cf. esp. Holmes, *RR* i. 474–6; H. A. Sanders, *MAAR* 10 (1932), 55–68; R. Hanslik, *RhM* 98 (1955), 324–34; G. R. Stanton and B. A. Marshall, *Hist.* 24 (1975), 205–19; Seager 80–4. Contemporary sources make no certain reference to a triple coalition in 60–59,[3]

---

[3] Cic. *Att.* 2.4 (24).2 and 2.9 (29).2 look like allusions, but Sanders, art. cit., shows that different interpretations are possible. App. 2.9.33 says that Varro 'described this agreement [of 60] in a book which he entitled "The Three-Headed One"' (*Trikaranos*); but we know no more of the work, and despite App.'s dating we cannot be sure that it dealt with an alliance of 60 (as e.g. R. Astbury, *CQ* 17 (1967), 403–7, and B. Zucchelli, *Atti del Congresso Internazionale di Studi Varroniani* (1976), ii. 609–25, assume) rather than, say, 56. Other points too are problematic, especially the hostile tone that is usually assumed (the phrase is often translated 'Three-Headed Monster'); but it is surprising to find Varro attacking Pompey, with whom he was often closely associated (36.2 n.). Perhaps the title mocked a phrase of his opponents, perhaps we need a more nuanced view of Varro's politics (so Zucchelli, in a most careful discussion), but most likely his point was simply that three heads were better than one—or alternatively, in

indicating only that in late 60 C. *hoped* to 'join Crassus with Pompey' (Cic. *Att.* 2.3 (23).3, see below). It is the secondary sources who are fulsome about the pact and its consequences.

Not that they are helpful in determining the coalition's date. Here as elsewhere, P. puts the alliance before the consular elections of mid-60 (cf. esp. 14.1), and so does Livy *per.* 103; but both P. and Livy may represent an abbreviation of Dio's more complex sequence, with Crassus and Pompey first separately supporting C.'s campaign and then, later ('after this', 37.56.1), C. reconciling the two (above, ch. 13 n.). Dio leaves it vague whether that further reconciliation came before or after the elections, for 37.54.3–55.1 cannot be exploited chronologically. Suet. and App. also seem to distinguish two steps (ch. 13 n.), but App. 2.9.33 says that the reconciliation followed 'immediately' and perhaps implies that it came before the elections. Vell. 2.44.1 dates the coalition to 59 ('with Caesar as consul'), but it is rash to put weight on that: 41–3 have introduced a retrospect of C.'s early career as Vell. reaches 59 BCE, 'now followed the consulship of C. Caesar, which arrests the writer...' (41.1): his quaestorship and praetorship had been 'conducted with wondrous excellence and diligence' (43.4); now Vell. hurries back to that consulship, which forms the climax. Had the coalition in fact been formed in the preceding months, Vell. would hardly have wrecked his narrative sweep to tell us so. It is equally dangerous to build on the vague phrases of Flor. 2.13.10.

Suet. 19.2 treats the formation of the pact immediately after his notice of the consular elections, and this at least has seemed to scholars to offer a precise dating, though many have rejected it. That, however, misunderstands Suet.'s technique. He narrates the electoral alliance of C. and Lucceius (19.1), and the worries this caused the optimates. Hence (1) they launched a rival bribery campaign in suppport of Bibulus, and Suet. traces this through to its logical consequence, 'therefore Caesar was elected consul with Bibulus'. (This, rather than the preceding sentence, should be marked in texts as the end of Suet.'s paragraph.) 'For the same reason', (2) the optimates took care that 'trivial provinces, the woods and drove-paths, should be decreed', and this drove C. into coalition with Crassus and Pompey. As Holmes, *RR* i. 475, saw, Suet. is carrying

hindsight, that one head (Pompey's) was better than three. Cf. also Wiseman 117 and 139 n. 43.

through two different chains of consequences of the optimates' fears, leaving their chronological relation imprecise: the consular provinces, for instance, must have been decreed before the elections, despite Suet.'s order. There is nothing here to exclude a date before the elections for the coalition too.

The secondary sources are therefore unhelpful. The combination of Dio, Suet., and App. suggests that there were two stages, with C. gaining the two men's separate support before the 60 elections; the date of any 'reconciliation' remains uncertain. Cicero's correspondence gives no hint of a reconciliation in the letters up to early summer 60, shortly before the elections; then *Att.* 2.3 (23).3–4 (December 60) has C.'s friend Balbus assuring Cicero that C. would 'consult both Pompey and Cicero in everything'—Cicero took this as an offer of alliance that he found tempting but resistible—'and would try to join Crassus with Pompey'. It need not follow that no Pompey–Crassus pact yet existed: it was better-judged rhetoric for Balbus to suggest that all was still in the air, with a hint that Cicero might himself be a key player, than to present him with a *fait accompli* that he could take or leave. But it does show that nothing was yet firmly known of such a pact, even by someone as well informed as Cicero. Dio 37.58.1 says that the pact was initially kept secret for some time (cf. 38.5.5): that may be Dio's own inference or guess (he has a good nose for conspiracies), but as usual it is intelligent.

The continuing silence of the primary sources remains telling. It seems that little was *ever* known about the coalition, and that contemporaries did not regard any such triple coalition as being of central importance. The unity of the secondary sources, speaking of a firm and important triple pact, is therefore striking. The picture must derive from a single original source, and it is an easy guess that this was Pollio, who found the origins of the civil war in the year 60 and apparently began his history at that point (Hor. *Odes* 2.1.1, Intr., p. 45 and n. 106). He would naturally herald his leading themes in an arresting opening.

We should not, however, push scepticism too far. At *some* time between mid-60 and early 59 there was probably *some* understanding between Crassus and Pompey: Crassus supported one item of Pompeian legislation in early 59 (14.4 n.), and there was a time when Pompey and Crassus were anticipated as the two consuls for 58 (*Att.* 2.5 (25).2). Nor is there any reason to doubt (with Stanton and Marshall, art. cit.) that C. played a crucial part in initiating this, despite being the least established figure of the three: Cicero did not find such a role preposterous for C. (*Att.* 2.3 (23).3), and neither should we. As consul, C. was indispensable for any legislation to pass, and he knew it. Still, it is not likely that the 'reconciliation' went deep. It did not last long, and by mid-59 Crassus and Pompey were estranged (*Att.* 2.21 (41).4, cf. the story of Suet. 21; Seager 93–4, 96, Meier 216–17). The three presumably always envisaged this alliance as a temporary union for temporary political ends, however vaguely specified (Suet. 19.2 has 'to prevent anything from being done in the state which any of the three disliked'): cf. Ch. Meier, *Res Publica Amissa* (1966), 280–1, Seager 84. The agreement at Luca in 56 was probably more far-reaching: 21.3–9 n.

the two most powerful men in Rome: P. knows that C. was not yet their equal.

13.5. it was not...the rift of Caesar and Pompey...it was rather their friendship. According to *Pomp.* 47.4, P.'s view here reflects the view of Cato (and this may be what underlies §6, see n.). It was doubtless quoted by Pollio. The view was also expressed by Caelius Rufus (Cic. *Fam.* 8.14 (97).2), and was probably a commonplace before Pollio. **to destroy the aristocracy.** For the view of Roman politics this implies, cf. Intr., p. 60, and *Plutarch and History*, 218.

13.6. Cato often gave dark prophecies of what would come. *Pomp.* 47.4 also puts the more general statement of §5 in Cato's mouth. *C.min.* 31.7 finds it useful to transfer the motif of Cato's foresight to the events of 59, with Cato expressing misgivings at C.'s agrarian legislation: the theme is then elaborated to make Cato's foresight deepen gradually, *C.min.* 42.6, 43.3, 43.9. Such 'warners' are familiar from earlier historiography, especially but not only Herodotus (cf. H. Bischoff, *Der Warner bei Herodot* (1932), R. Lattimore, *CP* 34 (1939), 24–35): Thucydides' Nicias (6.9–14, 20–23) and Archidamus (1.80–5), Polybius' Lyciscus (9.32–9), and Livy's Hanno (21.10) are other elaborate examples of wise advisers, some of them distinctly wiser than others: on Archidamus, for instance, cf. Pelling in *Georgica*, ed. M. A. Flower and M. Toher (*BICS* Supp. 58; 1991), 120–42. P.'s warners tend to be given smaller roles, and in his most elaborate cases the wisdom is again often disputable or ill-timed or otherwise problematic: cf. e.g. *Cor.* 16, *Phil.* 16–17, *C.mai.* 26–7. There are more straightforward cases too, e.g. *Crass.* 16, *Sol.* 27–8 and 30.

In other *Lives* Cato's political wisdom too is problematized, even though the eventual verdict remains overwhelmingly positive. *C.min.* emphasizes his high-minded and counterproductive style (cf. esp. the proemial *Phoc.* 3.1, quoting Cicero's remark that Cato speaks as if he were in Plato's *Republic* rather than the cesspool of the Roman people); it also, like other *Lives*, highlights the way that Cato's intransigence drove his opponents into dangerous corners (*C.min.* 31.2 and *Lucull.* 42.6 make this point in this same context of 61–60 BCE); and P. is more sensitive than C.'s enemies to Rome's needs and C.'s merits (cf. esp. *Brut.* 55(2).2 on Brutus: 28.5 n., below). In *Caesar* the moral problematic is less prominent: Intr., pp. 20–1. Cato's sagacity rather gives point to the establishment's failure to grasp or meet the threat, and the contrast with C.'s own alertness and energy.

14: CAESAR'S FIRST CONSULSHIP, 59 BCE   Ch. 13 had ended weightily, and this chapter continues the tone: in particular, it is unusually explicit in its moral judgement (Intr., p. 20). C's laws are appropriate for a demagogic tribune, not a consul (§2); Pompey's threat is 'senseless and juvenile' (§6); the climax is reached with Clodius' election, 'the most shameful measure of all' (§16). P.'s treatment is highly selective (below), concentrating on items that underline the moralistic point. They are sharpened by *apophthegmata* (§§4–5, 8, 14–15), and bold figures and phrases enhance the solemn register of disgraceful deeds. Several of the scenes are very visual—for instance, C. 'leaping out' (a very strong word) to the people in §3, the public appearance of the trio in §§4–6, and especially the crowd escorting Cato in downcast silence at §12 (n.). The historical thesis is also developed. C. at last brings his anti-senatorial policy into the open (§3); the reactions of the people are traced (§§6, 12); C.'s opponents—Bibulus, Cato, Cicero—are helpless; the aristocrats have missed their chance, and can only grieve (§6).

P. treats the consulship also in *Lucull.* 42.6–8, *Cic.* 30.1–4, *Pomp.* 47–8, *C.min.* 31–3, and *Crass.* 14.1–5: for a comparison of these versions, see *Plutarch and History*, 3–5, where I argue that in the four later *Lives* P. has access to fuller information than for *Lucull.* and *Cicero*: cf. Intr., p. 45. That new information shows contact with the accounts of Dio 38.1–12 and also with some parts of Suet. 20–22 and App. 2.10.34–14.53, and probably derives (at least ultimately) from

Pollio.[4] This helps to indicate information known to P. but here suppressed:

1. Many details of the agrarian laws (cf. esp. Dio 38.1), including the distinction of two separate measures (Dio 38.7.3), though P. does hint at that here with the plural 'laws' (§2). At *C.min.* 33.1 he distinguishes the measures, presumably because each is linked with separate acts of heroism from Cato that he wishes to include. *Caesar* has little on agrarian matters, and has even avoided mentioning Pompey's veterans. The material would also have been politically awkward, for Dio stresses the moderation of the first measure and C.'s eagerness to conciliate senatorial opinion: cf. §10 n. for a similar suppression of moderate behaviour.

2. The details of the opposition. P. knew that Lucullus had played a role (*Lucull.* 42.6, *Pomp.* 48.6–8, *C.min.* 31.7), but he does not say so here. Several clashes of C. and Bibulus are also suppressed: *Pomp.* 48.2, 5, *C.min.* 32.3–4, Dio 38.4.1–3, 6.1–6, 8.2, Suet. 20.1–2, App. 2.11.37–9. Here the opposition centres around Cato (§§8, 9, 11–12), and others fade away.

3. Unsurprisingly, matters most personally affecting C. are stressed: thus the election of Piso, C.'s new father-in-law, as consul for 58 is mentioned (§8), but not that of his colleague Gabinius (*Pomp.* 48.4, *Cic.* 30.2, *C.min.* 33.7). This 'law of biographical relevance' (Intr., p. 22) is however observed even more than we should expect: thus not merely the rebate to the *publicani* and the proposal of Q. Calenus (Dio 38.7.4, 8.1, Suet. 20.3, App. 2.13.47–8) are omitted, but also the crucial ratification of Pompey's eastern *acta* (*Pomp.* 48.4, Dio 38.7.5, Suet. 19.2, App. 2.13.46).

4. L. Vettius claimed that their opponents had tried to procure him to kill Pompey; when the charges seemed implausible, Vettius himself was thrown into prison, where he died mysteriously

---

[4] G. Zecchini, *CISA* 17 (1978), 99–110, followed by Carsana on App. 2.10–14, finds a strong anti-Caesarian, pro-senatorial register in the senatorial material shared by P. and App., and Zecchini thinks that this excludes Pollio: he prefers to think of the obscure Scribonius Libo (Cic. *Att.* 13.30 (303).3, 32 (305).3, 44 (336).3). He seems to me to underestimate the degree to which features of the account (e.g. the fusion of the two laws, §2 n., or the omission of the senate's role in giving C. his command, §10 n.) are owed to P. rather than the source. Rather than seeking partisan bias, we should attribute more to the strands of historical interpretation that P. and App. independently favour.

(Cic. *Att.* 2.24 (44), etc.; Lintott, *Evidence*, 173–5). P. knew of the affair (*Lucull.* 42.7–8, cf. Dio 38.9, Suet. 20.5, App. 2.12.43–4). But it was less telling than the other acts of violence; and P. has already suppressed another mention of Vettius (8.5 n.).

5. The marital bliss of Pompey and Julia, which suits a theme of *Pompey* and is stressed there (*Pomp.* 48.7–8), finds no place in this, much less personal *Life*.

6. Many details of the antecedents of Cicero's exile, especially Clodius' 'transfer to the *plebs*' (§16 n.), the trial of C. Antonius (Dio 38.10–11, Suet. 20.4, E. S. Gruen, *Lat.* 32 (1973), 301–10), and C.'s offer of a legateship to Cicero (§17 n., Cic. *Att.* 2.18 (38).3 and 19 (39).5, *Cic.* 30.3 with Moles's n.).

A balanced view of C.'s measures is given by E. S. Gruen at *CJC* 31–5: they were not extreme or unreasonable, but C. was uncompromising in forcing them through. Their chronological sequence has been greatly disputed, with few firm conclusions. Cf. esp. F. B. Marsh, *CJ* 22 (1927), 504–24; M. Gelzer, *Hermes*, 63 (1928), 113–37 = *Kl. Schr.* ii. 206–28; L. R. Taylor, *Hist.* 1 (1950), 45–51, *AJP* 72 (1951), 254–68, *CQ* 4 (1954), 181–2, *Hist.* 17 (1968), 173–93, and with T. R. S. Broughton, *Hist.* 17 (1968), 166–72; Ch. Meier, *Hist.* 10 (1961), 68–98 (the best discussion); Linderski 71–90; Shackleton Bailey, *Cicero's Letters to Atticus*, i (1965), 406–8; G. Gottlieb, *Chiron*, 4 (1974), 243–50; Lintott, *Evidence*, 167–75. In what follows these works are referred to by author and (where necessary) publication year alone.

As Marsh and Meier stress, none of the secondary sources follows any chronological sequence. That is no surprise with App. and Suet., who generally prefer thematic to sequential organization of such material. Dio and P. often prefer more sequential strategies, and here it seems that they share material with Suet.: but the three here show a remarkable series of discrepancies, including discrepancies among P.'s own accounts. Dio postpones the Antonius trial to the end of his account (38.10–11); in fact it can be no later than April (Cic. *Att.* 2.7 (27).2, *Dom.* 41 etc., cf. Gruen, *Lat.* 32 (1973), 305 n. 20). At *C.min.* 31.6 P. advances Julia's marriage to the beginning: cf. §8 n. for the true date. Suet 22.1 and P. (§10 n., *Pomp.* 48.4, *C.min.* 33.5) put the *lex Vatinia* after the marriages; Dio 38.9.1 puts it before. Dio 38.9.1 and Suet. 21 put the consular elections before the marriages; P. is explicit that they were later at §8 and *Pomp.* 48.4, but *C.min.* reverses the sequence. P. puts the abortive imprisonment of Cato late in the year (§§11–12); elsewhere he connects it with the second agrarian bill (in April, §2 n.; *C.min.* 33.2–4); Dio 38.3.2–3 puts it early, and links it with the first bill; and a further version connects it with a filibuster against the *publicani* (Val. Max. 2.10.7, see §11 n.).

Such chronological vagueness must surely be inherited: the material on which our sources draw was itself arranged thematically, at least in Pollio and very likely in further strands of the tradition as well, and individual authors imposed their own orders and patterns. Cicero's letters allow us to do something to sort out the chronological mess (nn.), but the arrangements adopted in the secondary texts carry no weight at all.

14.1. virtually Caesar's bodyguards...they escorted him to the consulship: vigorous language, and only semi-metaphorical: P. builds on the practice of escorting candidates to the *comitia* on the morning of the elections; the two most prominent supporters would doubtless flank him on each side. Cf. two versions of Ap. Claudius Pulcher's rebuke to Aemilius Paulus: 'Philonicus the tax-collector is your son's *bodyguard* as he comes down for the censorship' (*Advice on Public Life* 810b) and 'Aemilius the herald and Licinius Philonicus are *leading your son down* for the censorship' (*Aem.* 38.5).

14.2. M. Calpurnius Bibulus (*OCD*[4], s.v., Syme, *RP* vi. 193–204) was C.'s colleague in aedileship (65) and praetorship (62) as well as consulship. On his obstruction to C. (going 'far beyond anything normally held acceptable' (Syme)), see Linderski 72–5, 512–14, 634, Tatum 71–4 and *The Patrician Tribune* (1999), 129–33, F. X. Ryan, *Lat.* 55 (1996), 384–8.

laws (cf. §4, *Pomp.* 47.6). P. knows that there were two distinct bills (*C.min.* 33.1; above, ch. 14 n.). App. 2.10.35 also has a plural (cf. Carsana, ad loc.), but both authors find it useful to speak as if both bills were debated simultaneously. Vell. 2.44.4 ignores the first bill and speaks only of the second. It is credible that the first bill was introduced 'as soon as he entered office': it was expected at the very beginning of the year (Cic. *Att.* 2.3 (23).3), and its commissioners were elected by mid-April (*Att.* 2.6 (26).2, 2.7 (27).3–4). Taylor (1968), 179–81, thinks that the bill was presented to the senate on 1 and 2 January, and was eventually passed by the people on 29 January; Meier (1961), 69 n. 2, makes a date after 18 February more likely for the final enactment, but Linderski 81–4 seems wrong to impugn the early presentation (Taylor and Broughton (1968), 166–72). The second bill was introduced in late April (Cic. *Att.* 2.16 (36).1). For the two bills' provisions, see below on 'some colonies...'.

more fitting for the most reckless of tribunes than for a consul: 'reckless' is the same demagogic word *thrasutēs* as at 7.4 and 9.2 (nn.). The language has the ring of contemporary propaganda: cf. Cic. *Rab. Perd.* 22, 'did he follow a tribune's madness or a consul's authority?', *Sest.* 20, 'a tribune of the *plebs* who is mad and reckless... a consul who is brave and weighty' (*Planc.* 86, *Mur.* 82; Strasburger, *CUZ* 21).

some colonies to please the masses: including Novum Comum, 29.2 n. and also some distributions of land. Land distribution was a traditional populist measure, and would for P. have a tang of 'revolution': cf. *Ag.-Cl.* 8.1, 12.1, 28.5, etc.; Plato, *Laws* 3.684d–e, Arist. *Pol.* 5.1305^{a}3–7, How and Wells on Hdt. 4.159.2; Intr., p. 61, and *Plutarch and History*, 215, 217–18. 'To please the masses' again suggests P.'s favourite theme of C. as the champion of the urban 'people'. We are left to assume that they were to gain, and in *C.min.* 31.5 and 33.1 and *Pomp.* 47.5 the land is distributed to 'the poor and needy'. In fact, the crucial (though not the only) beneficiaries were Pompey's veterans, not yet settled after his return to Italy two years before; but here and in the other *Lives* P. does not bring out the connection, even though he knows that Pompey 'filled the city with soldiers' to get the measure passed (*Pomp.* 48.1, cf. §6 here). Cf. *Plutarch and History*, 221 and n. 96.

Under the first law, all the *ager publicus* in Italy except the *ager Campanus* was to be divided among the veterans and perhaps some of the *plebs*; additional land was to be purchased with the revenues of Pompey's eastern conquests. The second law added the *ager Campanus* and the neighbouring *ager Stellas*, with distributions limited to soldiers and members of the *plebs* with three or more children. It was apparently only in this area that colonies were established, at Capua and perhaps also at Casilinum and Calatia. If so, it is even clearer that P. and App. 2.10.35 have conflated the details of the two bills.

On this, see Holmes, *RR* i. 312–7, 476–9; Gelzer 72–4 and 80–3; L. R. Taylor, *Studies... in honor of A. C. Johnson* (1951), 68–78; Brunt, *Manpower*, 312–19; Seager 86–8; Gruen 397–401; L. Richardson in G. Schmeling and J. D. Mikalson (eds), *Qui miscuit utile dulci* (1998), 299–312; Morstein-Marx 166–7, 175–7.

14.3. the respectable group: i.e. the *kaloi kagathoi* or 'gentlemen', apparently identical with the 'aristocrats' of §6: for the vocabulary, cf. Intr., p. 60, and *Plutarch and History*, 218. These included Bibulus, Lucullus, Cicero, and especially Cato (*Pomp.* 47.6, *C.min.* 31.7). Dio

38.3.2–3 attaches the imprisonment story (§§11–12 below) to the present senatorial sitting.

14.4. This is **Crassus'** one securely attested act of support for Pompey and Caesar in the first months of 59. Crassus' link with C. goes back earlier (11.1), but it is striking that he should support such a Pompeian measure, enabling the veterans to be settled: see 13.3 n.

14.5. with both sword and shield: reversed at 29.7, where a later, equally ill-judged policy of Pompey is countered by C.'s centurion's threat of the sword. Politics and swordplay should not mix: the climax of their interaction will come on the Ides of March.

14.6. Pompey's sense of personal dignity, as well as the respect owed to the senate: perhaps from a Latin original which talked of *dignitas* and *uerecundia*. **so lunatic and juvenile a remark:** harsh words, perhaps hinting at the 'insane and juvenile' ideas that Plato thought might corrupt a guardian into trying to take over absolute power (*Rpb.* 5.466b). There may also be a hint of Cleon's 'lunatic' promise to win in Pylos within twenty days (Thuc. 4.39.3), suggesting again (cf. §2 n.) that this is how demagogues behave: Catiline too gave a 'lunatic answer' before the elections of 63 (*Cic.* 14.3). But political 'lunacy' is not infrequent in the Roman *Lives*, answering to the Latin catchword *furor* (itself part of the demagogic stereotype): e.g. 51.3 below, *Fab.* 5.5, 14.4, *C.min.* 26.5, 35.7, 51.2, *Ant.* 2.7, *Cic.* 31.5.

At *Alex.* 31.12 Parmenio has suggested a night attack at Gaugamela, and Alexander retorts 'I am not a thief of victory': that reply seemed 'juvenile and empty' to some, but in fact (P. suggests) was not, as it robbed Darius of any excuse for his failure. For the moment, C. and Pompey seem the more immature.

14.7. Julia: 5.7 n. She was the fourth of Pompey's five wives; he had divorced his third, Mucia, in 61 BCE. **who was betrothed to Servilius Caepio.** A less austere *Life* might have expressed pity for the victims of an inhumane barter: cf. *Pomp.* 9.3, when Sulla is equally ruthless, 'the marriage affair had the brand of a tyrant about it…'. Here the only moral is the inadvisability of appointing generals on the basis of a marriage settlement (§8). This Servilius Caepio supported C. against Bibulus (Suet. 21), but further identification is difficult. J. Geiger, *AncSoc* 4 (1973), 143–56, identifies him with the legate of Pompey in 67 (Flor. 1.41.10), the creditor of Q. Cicero (Cic. *Q.fr.* 1.3 (3). 7), and the adoptive father of the tyrannicide Brutus: the first two identifications are plausible, the last more difficult. Münzer *RAPF* 310–1 = *RAA* 338–9 thought that this Caepio was Brutus himself under his adoptive name, but this is unlikely: see Geiger, art. cit., 153.

Caesar... told Servilius he could have Pompey's daughter instead. In fact this projected marriage did not take place, and Pompeia married the original choice Sulla (*B.Afr.* 95). Unless Suet. 27.1 is confused, that marriage did not take place till 54 or later: presumably Pompeia was too young to marry immediately (B. Marshall, *AncSoc* 18 (1987), 92–101). Caepio probably rejected his off-hand treatment and refused to play along, but he may simply have died young (Gelzer 80 n. 1). Pompeia bore Sulla two children: cf. 53.7 n. C. himself later thought of divorcing Calpurnia and marrying her (Suet. 27.1). **Faustus, Sulla's son.** Quaestor in 54 and then a Pompeian in the Civil War, he died in Africa (53.7 n.): *OCD*[4], s.v. 'Cornelius Sulla'.

14.8. A little later. Cicero heard of the marriage of Pompey and Julia in late April or early May ('that sudden marriage connection' (*Att.* 2.17 (37).1)). We cannot tell how soon afterwards the wedding of C. and Calpurnia took place, nor whether it preceded or followed the consular elections. **Calpurnia** becomes important in the ominous days before the Ides of March: 63.8–11, 64.6. **Piso** is L. Calpurnius Piso Caesoninus, the target of Cicero's *In Pisonem*: see Nisbet's comm., pp. v–xvii, and *OCD*[4], s.v. He was **consul** in 58, along with A. Gabinius. The elections probably took place on 18 October: cf. Cic. *Att.* 2.20 (40).6. On these elections, cf. Linderski 71–90; Taylor and Broughton (1968), 166–72; Taylor (1968), 188–9.

Cato's opposition to C. in 59 is presented much more fully, and fulsomely, in *C.min.* 31–3. It is discussed by J. Bellemore in *Roman Crossings*, ed. K. Welch and T. W. Hillard (2005), 225–57, who doubts whether he ran any serious risks: she argues that Cato was in fact more active in 58 than 59 (cf. Cic. *Sest.* 60–3), and that features of his 58 activity have been transferred to 59. That may be the case, though we should not discount the possibility that several confrontations took similar forms; and Cicero has good reasons in *Sest.* for concentrating on 58, the year of Cato's most prominent brushes with Clodius (20.1 n.), rather than anything that occurred in 59. If so, it should be seen as a further feature of the non-chronological character of the whole tradition (above, pp. 194–5). Bellemore herself prefers to think that P. has used *Sest.* directly—not impossible, but not very likely (Intr., pp. 52–3); that it is he who has transferred the material to 59;

and that App. and Dio follow P. (more plausible for App. than for Dio).

Here P. makes him use very strong language: **pimps** uses an image that is rare in the morally proper Plutarch, but that he discusses at *Table Talk* 632c (cf. also 693c); the Greek word used here (*diamastropeuesthai*) is very rare, found only here and in the counterpart passage in App. (2.14.51: this is one reason for suspecting that App. may here be using P.'s text, Intr., p. 44 and n. 104). Then **females** is a word with a dismissive tone, 'mere' or 'little' women (*gunaion*, cf. *Ant.* 2.4, 10.5 with my notes, *Arat.* 6.4, etc.); and he **shouted out**, just as he often does (21.9, *C.min.* 43.4 and 7, 51.7, 68.5, *Pomp.* 59.4, *Brut.* 5.3). Elsewhere demagogues 'shout' to an appreciative crowd (e.g. *Fab.* 14.2, 26.1, *Cor.* 13.1, 17.3, 39.8, *Mar.* 9.2; *Plutarch and History*, 224 on *Fabius* and 391–2 on *Cor.*): here, as at 8.6–7, Cato strikes an unexpectedly populist style as he attacks the irresponsible possessors of power, and at §12 he too gets a popular response. The strong political polarities, with C. as the people's champion confronting the unbending and powerful establishment, are beginning to blur. Nor was P.'s insight here amiss: there *was* a populist strand in the style and tactics of Cato and others, even if Cic. *Att.* 2.20 (40).4, 'nothing is now so popular as hatred of the popular politicians', shows some wishful thinking.

14.9. P. abbreviates the description of **Bibulus**' opposition, and **often in danger of being killed** omits the degrading details of physical violence: contrast *Pomp.* 48.2, *C.min.* 32.3–4, Dio 38.6.3; Millar 128–31, Tatum 72. **shut himself up at his home.** Bibulus' self-incarceration has generally been associated with the failure of his opposition to the first agrarian bill: so Suet. 20.1 and Dio 38.6.5–6, accepted by e.g. Taylor (1951), 256–7, and Meier (1961), 73 n. 19. But the indications of Suet. and Dio are worth little (ch. 14 n., above), and *Pomp.* 48.5 is explicit that Bibulus remained in his house for eight months. If he came out at the end of his term of office (Suet. 20.1, Dio 38.6.5, 12.3), we should associate his retirement rather with the *second* agrarian bill: so Shackleton Bailey, *Cicero's Letters to Atticus*, i. 406–8, not all of whose arguments are met by Taylor (1968), 174 n. 3 and 185 n. 34.

14.10. immediately. P. finds piquant the sequence of 'marriage, then arms': he need not be drawing the implied chronological sequence from a source, despite the apparent agreement with Suet. 22.1. Dio 38.9.1 puts the sequence the other way round, but anyway none of these orderings carries weight: see above, ch. 14 n., and, for similar cases where P. imposes his own chronological schemes, *Plutarch and History*, 92–3. **these [laws] gave Caesar both Cisalpine and Transalpine Gaul, along with Illyricum.** In fact the people, by the *lex Vatinia*, gave C. only Cisalpine Gaul and Illyricum; it was the senate that later added Transalpine Gaul after the death of its designated governor Q. Metellus Celer (cos. 60) in April. P. will have known this (cf. Dio 38.8.5, Suet. 22.1), but prefers to avoid any suggestion of senatorial cooperation. For the details of the *lex Vatinia*, see esp. Gelzer 86–7 and *Hermes*, 63 (1928), 113–37; the question is also treated in much of the bibliography on the terminal date of his Gallic command (29.1 n.).

The dating of the law is the most debated of all the chronological issues. Taylor (1951), 264–6 and (1968), 182–8, follows Gelzer in favouring a date in May or early June; Meier (1961), 69–88, seems to make a date in March or early April more likely. One crucial point is the interpretation of Cic. *Att.* 2.16 (36).2, where on 29 April or 1 May Cicero imagines Pompey saying to him 'I shall hold you in check with Caesar's army'. Meier and Shackleton Bailey, i. 408, insist that this must mean a real army, accompanying a province; Taylor (1968), 183–8, accepts this, but thinks that the Gallic province was by that point firmly anticipated; Gottlieb (1974) retorts that in context it should refer to people present in the forthcoming assemblies on the second agrarian bill, and hence Gelzer and Taylor (1951), 264–5, were right in taking it as 'C.'s gang of supporters'; at *Violence*, 75, Lintott thinks of C.'s army recently returned from Spain, but at *Evidence*, 170–1, prefers C.'s supporters in the city, who would include many of Pompey's veterans. On balance I follow Meier: at that point of the letter Cicero's train of thought is already broadening from the immediate to the wider context, how Pompey will be able to defend his position and what constraints will limit Cicero's behaviour. There is no need to limit this vision to the debates of the immediate future.

and four legions. The *lex Vatinia* gave him three legions, the *senatus consultum* added a fourth (Dio 38.8.5). **for five years.** The *lex Vatinia* seems to have forbidden any proposal or decree to provide a successor 'before the Kalends of March of the fifth year', i.e. 54 BCE. The grant of Transalpine Gaul, granted by *senatus consultum*, rested on a different footing; it did not quite have to be 'renewed annually' (Gelzer 87), but would last until the senate included Transalpina again in the annual assignment of provinces, something that it might choose to do at any time.

Cf. 21.6 n. for the terms of the renewal in 55, when the *lex Licinia Pompeia* included Transalpine as well as Cisalpine Gaul. That removed the danger of its premature subtraction from C.'s command.

14.11–12. Caesar hauled him off to prison. *C.min.* 33.1–4 associates the story with Cato's opposition to the second agrarian bill. Dio 38.2–3 seems to derive from the same source (ch. 14 n.), but places the scene in the senate house and attaches it to the first bill. Suet. 20.4 gives no occasion, but agrees in placing it in the senate house. Val. Max. 2.10.7 connects it with a senatorial filibuster of Cato against the *publicani* bill. Gell. 4.10.8, quoting Ateius Capito, again puts it in the senate, and he too associates it with an (unspecified) filibuster. Cf. Bellemore, art. cit. (§8 n.), 235–7.

Dio has more circumstantial detail than P., though he omits the 'tribune' item of §12 (~ *C.min.* 33.4); and it looks as if he is right to place it in the senate. If so, he is probably also right to put it early in the year, given Cato's subsequent boycott of the senate (§13 n.). But we cannot be sure of the precise occasion; the anecdote may well have been timeless in the source that Dio, Suet., and P. share (cf. §8 n.), and Val. Max. may be confusing this *publicani* legislation with that of early 60 (Cic. *Att.* 1.18 (18).7), where there may well have been a Cato filibuster (13.2 n.). P.'s placing of it here contributes deftly to the picture of mounting senatorial disgust, and also introduces the important notion of *popular* disquiet (§8 n.). Dio preferred a context where it would illustrate the senate's unreasonable opposition to C.'s conciliatory overtures.

in silence: whereas in the version at *C.min.* 33.2 he continues orating as he walks. Here there is a contrast with his shouting at §8. P. knows how to exploit the dramatic silence, especially after turbulence: cf. 60.3 and 67.7 nn., *Cic.* 22.2, *Gracch.* 12.2–3, *Alex.* 51.11, etc. It was an old historiographic trick: cf. Ogilvie on Livy 3.47.6. Here the ordinary people respond in kind to Cato, **following silent and downcast,** a paradoxical travesty of the usual picture of a great man escorted noisily by a retinue of supporters: here it is silence rather than noise, and with disapproval and embarrassment rather than enthusiasm. Cf. A. J. E. Bell, *JRS* 87 (1997), 9 and n. 54. **downcast** (*katēphēs*): an epic and tragic word that could be used in parodies of the grand style (Cic. *Att.* 13.42 (354).1). P. felt its visual connotations

(*On Bashfulness* 528e, 'they define *katēpheia* as a feeling of grief which makes one look downwards'), and favours it in vivid and emotional narrative (e.g. *Mar.* 29.7, *Pomp.* 73.5, and predictably often in *C.min.*, 27.2, 33.3, 50.1, 53.1 67.4).

14.13. the rest marked their displeasure by staying away.   Thus Cicero retired to his estates and relied on Atticus for information (Cic. *Att.* 2.4–17 (24–37), esp. 2.4 (24).2); even after his return to Rome he took little part in public life (*Att.* 2.23 (43).3). Cato too boycotted the senate (Cic. *Sest.* 63), in contrast to his usual behaviour (*C.min.* 18.2, 19.1–2).

14.14.   Q. Considius was renowned for his riches (Cic. *Att.* 1.12 (12).1, Val. Max. 4.8.3) and his incorruptibility (Cic. *Verr.* 2.1.18). This present demonstration was much respected, it seems: cf. Cic. *Att.* 2.24 (44).4, 'we were recently fearing a massacre, but the words of that brave old man Q. Considius put paid to that'.

14.15. 'My years take away my fear . . .'.   If this is historical, Considius had his precedents: Solon to Pisistratus (*Sol.* 31.1, *Should an Old Man take part in Public Life?* 794f, Cic. *de Sen.* 72) and M. Castricius to Cn. Carbo (Val. Max. 6.2.10).

14.16. the election of Clodius as tribune: yet another chronological puzzle. Taylor (1950), 45–51 and (1968), 189–93, argued that the tribunicial elections must have been held in July: this involved the assumption that the ordering of Cic. *Att.* 2.22–5 (42–5) is out of chronological sequence. P. A. Brunt, *CQ* 3 (1953), 62–4, showed this assumption to be improbable, and Meier (1961), 88–98, more plausibly prefers a later date for the elections. See also Linderski 85–8, Seager 99 n. 99. First Clodius needed to 'transfer to the *plebs*', a complicated procedure that, at least in his case, involved adoption into a plebeian family: Cic. 34.2, *C.min.* 33.6, *MRR* 195, and on the technicalities Tatum, *The Patrician Tribune* (1999), 87–113. This 'transfer' had happened by March or early April: Cic. *Att.* 2.7 (27).2, etc. According to Cic. *Dom.* 41, Dio 38.10.4–12.1, and Suet. 20.4, it followed within hours of Cicero's defence speech for C. Antonius, which included a vicious attack on the state of the times. **the affair of his wife and the secret ceremonies:** the Bona Dea affair, 9–10.

14.17. He was elected to destroy Cicero: a simplification, but one that derives from a source: cf. Dio 38.12.1–2, App. 2.14.53. The great men's initial support of Clodius' 'transfer to the *plebs*' was doubtless aimed at Cicero (§16 n.), but by the time of his election their relations with Clodius may have been more complicated: cf. Gelzer 77–8, 89 and the partly divergent analyses of Gruen 98–9, Seager 91–102 and *Lat.* 24 (1965), 519–31, Meier 213–15, Tatum, *The Patrician Tribune*, 97–8, 104, 107–13.

In this *Life*, but not in *Pompey* or *C.min.*, P. gives the impression that C. as well as Clodius wanted Cicero exiled. Here we are not given any clear reason why; it simply forms the disgraceful climax of the year's misdeeds. In *Cic.* 30.3–5 the alienation springs from Cicero's rejection of a legateship. On the differences among the *Lives* here, cf. *Plutarch and History*, 98–100, and, on the circumstances of Cicero's exile, see *Cic.* 30–2 with Moles's nn. **Caesar did not leave for his campaign:** see Shackleton Bailey, *Cicero's Letters to Atticus*, ii. 227: it seems likely that C. left for Gaul around 15–20 March 58 BCE, and that Cicero departed into exile just a little earlier.

15–27: The Gallic Campaigns

Gaul marks C.'s 'new beginning' (15.2), and C.'s force of personality now emerges in all clarity: the opening survey is thus a sort of 'second preface' (15–17 n.), exploiting many of the characterizing themes that might have been expected earlier (above, p. 130). The narrative first pits C. against formidable adversaries—Helvetii, Ariovistus, and the Germans, Belgae, Nervii; then it moves on to show C. confronting not human adversaries but nature itself, with the Rhine crossing and the British expedition. Verbal echoes emphasize the point (23.2–4 n.). The closing chapters turn to the critical perils presented by Gallic insurgents, Ambiorix and then Vercingetorix; the sequence finishes with Vercingetorix acknowledging his master (27.9–10). This warmth is not wholly inherited: P.'s source, it seems, was sometimes less sympathetic to C. (18.2, 22.1–5 nn.). The admiration is P.'s own, and there are no moral reservations to qualify it (15.2–5, 17.1, 22.1–5 nn.)—no reflections, for instance, on 'so great a wrong to the human race' in the manner of the elder Pliny (*NH* 7.92, Intr., p. 19); nothing along the lines that *Pomp.* 24–6 might have suggested, allowing a contrast between C.'s uncompromising treatment of barbarians and the more 'modern and promising' (H. Strasburger, *JRS* 55 (1965), 52) style adopted by Pompey.

More can be said about that source. It is at this point that the long sequence of parallels with Appian begin (Intr., pp. 40, 43–7), and they point to a common origin, the 'Pollio-source' (I simplify by just calling this 'Pollio', Intr., p. 45). That source described the campaigns in some detail (e.g. 18 n., 23.3–4 n., 25.3–27 n.), deriving much of it from C.'s own *Gallic Wars*, traces of which often survive into P.'s account. Into C.'s framework the source incorporated some additions, most clearly well informed (17.5, 19.12, 22.6–23.1, 23.2–4, 27.5–7, 27.9–10 nn.): it questioned C.'s veracity (18.2, 20.1, 22.6 nn.); it could even add an item on the strength of the Rhine's current (22.6 n.)— another pointer to Pollio, whose interest in the Rhine flow is attested elsewhere (Strabo 4.3.3). It may also have included an introduction, cataloguing the numbers of enemy slain, tribes conquered, and battles fought (15.5 n., cf. 15–17 n.); a penchant for statistics can also be seen later in the account (18.1, 18.5, 19.12, 20.10, 21.5, 22.5, 24.3–4, 27.3–4). There may also have been some errors (18.1, 20.5, 20.7 nn.). P. largely relied on this source, but added some items from elsewhere: some from Oppius' 'biographical' work on C., it seems (15–17 n., 16 n., Intr., p. 49–50); and at least one from oral tradition (26.7–8 n., cf. 15–17 n., Intr., p. 54).

The combination of App., Suet., and P.'s other *Lives* suggests that Pollio punctuated his narrative with a series of general political analyses: one before Luca (cf. *Pomp.* 51.1–3, App. 2.17.61–2, Suet. 23.2), at least, and one after Julia's death (*Pomp.* 53.7–54.2, App. 2.19.68–20.73, and cf. the brief hint at *Caes.* 23.6–7). P. took over many of the source's interpretations closely: Pompey as C.'s dupe (20.3 n., cf. 28.2 (n.), 29.5–7), Cato as the opposition figurehead (22.1–5 n., cf. 21.8), the importance of C.'s Gallic wealth (20.3 n.) to his machinations in Rome (20.1–3, 21.3). But P. here delays many themes to the skilful pastiche of 28 (n.): Crassus' death, the electoral anarchy, Pompey's sole consulate. Other material is simply omitted, not merely general points such as Cicero's recall from exile or the violence of 55 BCE (*Pomp.* 51–2, *Crass.* 15, *C.min.* 41–3: cf. *Caes.* 20.1, 21.3–9 nn.), but also more specifically Caesarian points: the epistolary attack on Cato (*C.min.* 51.3, cf. *Caes.* 22.2–4 n.), or C.'s encouraging letter to Crassus (*Crass.* 16.3, cf. *Caes.* 21.6 n.). The focus remains on the war.

Even in so brief a political treatment, P. remains true to his themes. C. is still the favourite of the people; his machinations in Rome are 'demagogy' (20.2 n.); the fifteen-day thanksgiving was partly driven by 'the affection of the ordinary people' (21.2); the reaction of 'the people' to Favonius' outburst is traced and explained (21.8–9); the popular reaction to Julia's death is emphasized (23.7, cf. *Pomp.* 53.6). Other *Lives* do not develop the same emphasis: *Pomp.* 53.6 indeed plays down the enthusiasm of the people for C. The campaigns too echo the previous themes. C. commands the devotion of his men (16, 19.3 n.) just as he won the enthusiasm of the people; he becomes Marius' military (18.1 n., 19.4, 26.2) as well as political (5.3, 6) successor.

15–17: INTRODUCTION TO THE GALLIC CAMPAIGNS The powerful treatment of 1–14 has left little room for personalia. 15–17 redress the balance, as personal details suppressed in the early chapters are now exploited (esp. in ch. 17: cf. above, p. 130). Such characterizing sketches frequently introduce and mark off a crucial stage in the biography, e.g. *Alc.* 16 and 23, *Ant.* 4 (with my note), 24.9–12, 27.3–5, and 70, *Cor.* 9, 11, 14, 32, and 38, *Pomp.* 45, etc.: the artistic device appears in Greek biography as early as Isoc. *Evag.* 33–46. This instance also has much in common with the 'second prefaces' often used by historians and other writers (on these, see esp. G. B. Conte, *YCS* 30 (1992), 147–59), which frequently stress that the coming theme is bigger, bloodier, and more breathtaking than what has preceded in the narrative (e.g. Virg. *Aen.* 7.36–44), or indeed than all previous counterparts (e.g. Thuc. 1.23, Hdt. 7.20–1, Livy 21.1: cf. 15.2–5 here). Particularly similar is Arrian's second preface at *Anab.* 1.12, introducing the glorious period of Alexander's achievements in Asia: there, as here, the delay of proemial elements marks the preceding events as *merely* preliminary, with the period of great achievement about to begin (J. L. Moles, *JHS* 105 (1985), 162–8, esp. 167); there, as here, it heralds an admiration for the coming achievements that overlays the response to previous, more morally equivocal actions (J. Marincola, *JHS* 109 (1989), 186–9, esp. 187), in this case the strong disapproval for the consulship (ch. 14).

This 'preface' accordingly introduces themes that are important not merely for the Gallic narrative (15.4–5 n.) but also for the rest of the *Life*, in particular C.'s closeness to his troops (16, drawing from the later wars as well as from Gaul: cf. then 29.4–7, 37.6–9, 38.7, 39.2, 44.9–12), his mercy to enemies (15.2–5, 34.7, 57.4 nn.), and his readiness to face dangers himself (17.2–4, cf. 18.3, 20.8, 38.1–6, 49.7–8, 52.8–9, 56.2): all these elements will play their part in his fall (51.2, 56.7, 57.4, 57.7) as well as building his greatness.

Some of the present material is probably drawn directly from Pollio, which may have prefaced its account with some general introduction (as at App. *Celt.* fr. 1.2.4–7, though we should not exclude the possibility that that is App.'s own compilation from the later narrative). That could provide the statistics of 15.5 (n.), which are similar to those of App. *Celt.* fr. 1.2.6, *BC* 2.73 and 150. The general remarks of 15.2–5 need not come directly from anywhere (n.), but the four anecdotes of 16 are probably taken over *en bloc* from a source: Val. Max. 3.2.22–3 groups the first three together in the same, non-chronological order and Suet. 68.4 similarly juxtaposes the tales of Acilius and Scaeva. That source may be Oppius (Intr., p. 50), as suggested by Townend, 'Oppius' (cf. A. Wallace-Hadrill, *Suetonius* (1983), 12 n.1 9);[5] or it may be Pollio's introduction, for one of the stories is told very similarly by Appian (16.2–4 ~ App. 2.60.248), and the omission of the others is consistent with App.'s own manner (he has less of a taste for good stories than e.g. Plutarch or Dio). The material of ch. 17 may be more heterogeneous: there is no longer contact with App. Several items here do seem to point to Oppius, who is quoted at §7 and seems to lie behind the two stories of §§9–11 (nn.). But 17.5 (n.) may have been culled from Pollio, who clearly handled the Helvetii campaign in detail (18). Not all the items need have a literary source at all. Oral tradition will still have preserved anecdotes about C.'s life (Intr., pp. 53–4), and surviving statues, as often (*Mar.* 2, *Arat.* 2, *Sulla* 2, *Flam.* 1; A. E. Wardman, *CQ* 17 (1967), 414–20), may have influenced P.'s description of his subject's personal appearance (17.2).

15.1–2. Gallic Wars . . . land of the Celts.   P. assumes an unproblematic equivalence of 'the land of the Celts' with 'Gaul': so do other writers (e.g. App. 2.16, 3.4–5, Dio 44.43.1, Strabo 1.4.3, etc.), though 'Celts' can also be used more generally of those who dwell in northern and western Europe (cf. e.g. *Mar.* 11.6). Scholars now increasingly see 'the Celts' as (at least in part) a cultural construct of the Greco-Roman

---

[5] Wallace-Hadrill and Townend infer that Oppius organized his material 'thematically', as P. does here, and suggest that in that case he may have been a precursor of Suet. and his 'category' mode of organization. That need not follow from the instances here in ch. 17: P. himself could easily have collected material from Oppius' narrative, perhaps from memory, and exploited it here. If the material and ordering of ch. 16 come from Oppius, that is better evidence for a 'category' organization, but such organization need have been in no more than an introductory section, just as it is here.

mentality, eliding differences among many smaller groupings who would not themselves have recognized mutual ethnic linkage. Strabo 1.2.27 was already clear about this tendency. It is hotly disputed how far any cultural unity corresponds to this overall category. Recent stages of the debate are valuably synthesized in B. Cunliffe, *The Celts: A Very Short Introduction* (2003), and can be traced in C. Renfrew, *Archaeology and Language: The Puzzle of Indo-European Origins* (London, 1987), 211–49; Williams, esp. 5–13 and in T. Cornell and K. Lomas (eds), *Gender and Ethnicity in Ancient Italy* (1997), 69–81; J. V. S. and M. R. Magaw, *Antiquity*, 70 (1996), 175–81 and 72 (1998), 432–5; B. Arnold, intr. to *The Oxford Handbook to the Archaeology of the Continental Celts* (forthcoming); and, focusing on British Celts, S. James, *The Atlantic Celts: Ancient People or Modern Invention?* (1999). Cf. also Rives 1–11 for the similar problem with 'the Germans'.

C. deftly exploited the vagueness for his own purposes in *BG*, representing 'all Gaul' as a unity (even if 'divided into three parts' (1.1)), bounded by the physical limits of the Rhine and the English Channel, and distinct from the Germans (19.1, 22.1 nn.): on his narrative subtlety here, see Riggsby 28–32, 59–71, C. Krebs, *AJP* 127 (2006), 111–36, and H. Schadee, *CQ* 58 (2008), 158–80. He is thus able to present his conquest of 'Gaul' as logically coherent and complete: he can claim credit for overcoming even those natural boundaries of Rhine and Channel (22.6, 23.2–3 nn.), while deflecting criticism for failing to establish a Roman presence beyond 'Gaul' itself.

15.2–5: THE MAGNITUDE OF CAESAR'S ACHIEVEMENTS
These historical reflections, like that of 26.2 (n.), will be P.'s own, inspired by his narrative and especially by the figures of §5. He often incorporates such brief comparisons with predecessors or, more rarely, successors: e.g. *Gracch.* 2, *Cim.* 19.3–4, *Flam.* 11.3–7, 21.2–6, *Brut.* 1.1–4, *Pel.* 4.3, *Dem.* 13.6–14.1, and see Leo 151–2; Duff 251–2. The technique comes naturally to biography, especially at its most encomiastic: cf. Xen. *Ages.* 8.6–9.7, Isoc. *Evag.* 37–8. As is usual (but not universal: cf. *Sert.* 1.8–10, *Sulla* 6.5–7), P. limits such 'internal' comparisons to compatriots, here C.'s Roman predecessors. He does not bring to the surface the underlying comparison with the Greek pair. In this case comparison with Alexander would anyway have been less flattering to C.

P.'s admiration for the achievement is uncompromised: cf. above, 15–27 n. This is one of those passages (for others, see Schmidt 176–201) where vast enemy numbers and casualties simply enhance the glory of their Greek or Roman victor. There is no room here for moral reservations: contrast Suet. 24.3, 'after that [i.e. in the final stages of his command] he overlooked no opportunity for war, not even if it was unjust or dangerous, with unprovoked aggression against allied as well as hostile and uncivilized peoples' (cf. also 54.1); or Plin. *NH* 7.92, quoted above at p. 203 and at Intr., p. 19. P. even makes something of C.'s 'mercy and generosity' to those he defeated (§4, cf. 18.5–6), not an obvious theme for the *Gallic* wars (though it is for the civil: 34.7, 57.4 nn.). Little touches reinforce the positive impression: see nn. on 'tamed', below, and on 'bizarre and faithless characters', §4; also 17.1 n., 18.5–6 n.

tamed: i.e. 'conquered and pacified', continuing the imagery from C.'s political strategy at 6.3 (n.). The word P. uses here is strong (cf. e.g. Hdt. 4.118.5, 5.2.2, 7.5.2) and rare in later Greek (cf. Ael. Arist. 38.238, Dio Prus. 3.127), and yet also bland, for it intimates a justi-fication for such aggression in the enemy's feral qualities. Such beast-liness is characteristic of barbarians in P. (Schmidt 27–67) as in others (Oakley on Livy 7.10.3, Woodman on Vell. 2.106.2, 118.1, Woolf 60). **a new start . . . a new way of life, a new path of achievement:** more strong language (cf. *Sert.* 9.3 and, for instance, Cicero's 'second birth' on returning from exile, *Att.* 4.1 (73). 8, 6.6 (121). 4), even though the 'path' of life metaphor is a traditional one (e.g. Plato *Rpb.* 10.600b1, Isoc. 1.5, NT Acts e.g. 22:4).

15.3. Fabii and Scipios and Metelli. P.'s language could mean simply 'men like Fabius, Scipio, and Metellus'; but there are also hints of a genuine plural, embracing the various members of each family who had won military glory. The list is fairly predictable: cf. e.g. *On the Fortune of the Romans* 317d–e. We might have expected Marcelli, as at 317d, rather than Metelli, but there is unlikely to be any significant point in the selection. The most distinguished **Fabius** was Q. Fabius Maximus Cunctator, Hannibal's adversary and the subject of P.'s *Life*. **Scipios:** primarily Scipio Africanus, the eventual victor of Hannibal. There is also a hint of Scipio Aemilianus, distinguished for both fighting and diplomacy in the Third Punic War. The *Life* of one or other Scipio, probably Aemilianus, figured in P.'s (lost) opening pair along with *Epaminondas*: see Intro., p. 36 and n. 80. **Metelli:**

principally Q. Caecilius Metellus Numidicus, consul 109 and the adversary of Jugurtha; also L. Caecilius Metellus, the consul of 251 and victor at Panormus in the First Punic War; perhaps Q. Caecilius Metellus Pius as well, adversary of Sertorius in the seventies (7.1 n.). **both Luculli:** L. Licinius Lucullus (*OCD*[4], no. 2) was the victor of Mithridates and the subject of P.'s *Life*. M. Lucullus (4.2 n.) is rather a surprise in this illustrious company. P.'s respect for his generalship may have been inspired by the incident of *Crass.* 11.3, Crassus' suggestion that M. Lucullus, along with Pompey, should be recalled to oppose Spartacus: cf. *Crass.* 36(3).7, Crassus getting his own command in that war 'when Pompey and Metellus and both Luculli were away'. The man caught his imagination: cf. also *Lucull.* 1.8–9, 43.4, *Sulla* 27.14–16. **whose glory ... blossomed:** a complex amalgam of classical and especially epic allusions, implying a comparison of Pompey too to the greatest figures of legend: this is to be a worthy adversary for C. For 'glory ... through the whole firmament', cf. e.g. Hom., *Od.* 9.20, 264, *Il.* 8.192, 10.212 (familiar enough for Aristophanes too to exploit, *Clouds* 461). For 'glory blossomed', cf. Pind. *P.* 1.66, *N.* 9.39 and P.'s similar language at e.g. *Arat.* 13.1, *Dtr.* 27.3, *Lucull.* 6.3. For 'every sort of ... virtue', cf. e.g. *Il.* 22.268, *Od.* 4.725, Simon. fr. 10 W.[2] (cited at *On Herodotus' Malice* 872d), Plato *Critias* 112e. Notice too the less elaborate *Sert.* 18.3, 'Pompey's glory was not slight, but was then blossoming to its height of fame ...': if *Sert.* is later than *Caes.* (thus Konrad xxix; *Plutarch and History*, 35 n. 68), that passage will be borrowing from, perhaps alluding to, this earlier conceit.

15.4–5 introduce themes that will be important in the narrative: **difficulty of the terrain:** 22.6, 25.3–4, 26.4. **extent of territory he acquired:** 23.2. **numbers and formidable qualities of the antagonists:** 18.1, 20.4, 20.7, 24.1–3, 25.3, 26.7, 27.3–4. **bizarre and faithless characters:** 22.2–3 (and see below). **mildness and clemency:** possibly 18.5–6 (though cf. n. ad loc.; also 20.6 n., 20.6–10 n.); and cf. 57.4 n. **vast number ...:** 9.12, 20.9, 22.5, 24.7, 27.7.

 bizarre and faithless characters. The word for 'faithless' is *apistiai*, which can also mean 'incredible', thus expanding the point already made by 'bizarre' (lit. 'out of the way', *atopiai*): thus Isoc. 17.48 can use the same two words for 'the bizarre and incredible things which Pasion always tried to say'. But more usually in P. *apistia* does mean 'faithless', 'perfidious': e.g. *Tim.* 11.6, *Ant.* 63.4, *Pyrrh.* 23.4, etc.; that is the way Schmidt 209 takes the way here, relating it to other cases where P. represents barbarians as perfidious, e.g. *Ages.* 9.3–4, *Crass.* 30.5, 33.7, *On the Fortune of Alexander* 341e–f (for the stereotype elsewhere, cf. e.g. Kremer 39–43, Riggsby 56, Woodman on Vell. 2.118.1). The ambiguity prepares the way for the incident of 22.2–3, where the same word represents C.'s view of the 'faithless' Usipi and Tencteri, and once again downplays any moral problematization of C.'s conduct. Notice in any case the interest in 'bizarre', extraordinary customs. The point is not expanded in the narrative, but it corresponds to the interests of earlier ethnographers and of ethnographic passages in historians, seeking out distinctive and paradoxical customs. Cf. esp. C. *BG* 4.1–3, 6.11–28, and, briefly and conveniently, Rives 11–21.

15.5. vast number of battles...   P.'s source (below) seems to have given the figures: thirty battles in Gaul alone (App. 2.150.627) and fifty in all (Plin. *NH* 7.92; Solin. 1.106 is corrupt); the only man to surpass M. Claudius Marcellus, who fought thirty-nine (Plin., Solin., cf. *Marc.* 32(2).1). **lasted for less than ten years...** P. gives similar but less precise statistics at *Pomp.* 67.10, evidently based on the same reading: cf. also *Crass.* 37(4).2 with 22.5 n. below. The parallel figures at App. *Celt.* fr. 1.2.6, echoed at *BC* 2.73.305 and 2.150.627, are likely to derive from the same source (15–27 n.). Plin. *NH* 7.92 reflects the same statistics; Vell. 2.47.1 is more problematic (see n. on 'four million' below). Solin. 1.107 is based on Pliny, Julian *Caes.* 21 p. 321a on P.

App.'s figures mostly agree with P.'s, but twice differ: he has C. conquering 400 rather than 300 'nations' (*Celt.*, *BC*) and C. facing over four million, not three million, enemy troops (*Celt.* alone). Simple textual corruption does not seem to explain the divergences: P.'s figures are safeguarded by the concordance of *Caesar* and *Pompey*, App.'s '400 nations' by the agreement of *Celt.* and *BC*. P. may have been using a text that was already corrupt, but it is more likely that he has rounded down, while App. has rounded up, more precise figures. Alternatively the source perhaps included figures both for Gaul and for C.'s campaigns as a whole, including Spain in 61–60 (cf. App. 2.73.305, 'after we had acquired for Rome four hundred nations of *Spanish*, Celts, and Britons', and above on 'vast number of battles'), and P. scrupulously limited himself to the lower figures.

The figures are likely to be based on C.'s own estimates. Roman generals, competitive for glory in the present and for eternity, had a taste for such bloody statistics: they figured especially on triumphal inscriptions (T. P. Wiseman in Wiseman (ed.), *Roman Political Life 90 B.C.–A.D. 49* (1985), 3–10), Williams 38–9), and may well have figured on the placards carried at the triumphs themselves (Ovid. *Tr.* 4.2.19–20, *ex P.* 2.1.37–8, cf. e.g. *Pomp.* 45.2–4, *Lucull.* 37.6, App. *Mith.* 117), in this case at C.'s Gallic triumph in 46 (55.2 n.). P. too liked figures: notice the similar triumphal statistics at *Pomp.* 45.3–4 (cf. Plin. *NH* 7.97), *Lucull.* 37.4–6 (cf. Plin. *NH* 3.18), *Mar.* 12.6; non-triumphal instances are *Sulla* 28.15 and *Sert.* 12.2.

Even if they do derive from C. himself, few of the items will be accurate. C. had no mechanism to enable an exact estimate of enemy he faced; he is unlikely to have counted corpses or prisoners. The statistics will represent the total of a series of generous estimates, stylized into the usual round numbers (cf. 2.1, 5.8 nn.), and are 'totally unreliable' (Brunt, *Manpower*, 703). It is very bad method to seek from them any pointer to the total population of Gaul (so e.g. E. Kirsten, *Raum und Bevölkerung in der Weltgeschichte*, i (1956), 227). The figures anyway include Germans and British as well as Gauls, and any man who faced C. twice was doubtless counted twice (cf. P.'s 'in successive battles' and App.'s 'if one were to total the individual figures' (*Celt.* fr. 1.2.6)).

'Vast number' typifies P.'s portrayal of barbarian armies: see Schmidt 141–201. And Romans tended to regard Celts as especially multitudinous: Kremer 28–30, Gerlinger 125–33.

over eight hundred cities: rounded up at *Pomp.* 67.10 to 'a thousand'. **three hundred nations.** *Pompey* has '*over* three hundred'— perhaps exaggeration again, but App.'s figure of 400 (above) suggests that P. has indeed rounded down. 'Nations' represents the Greek *ethnē*, a word used with great freedom for anything conceptualized as a racial or cultural unit (see e.g. J. Hall, *Ethnic Identity in Greek Antiquity* (1997), 34–6): 'tribe' or 'people' might be better, but there are advantages in the vagueness and emotive power of 'nation', and its consequent suitability for sloganizing. **one million:** more precisely 1,192,000 (Plin. *NH* 7.92 = Solin. 1.106). Vell. 2.47.1 seems to say 'over 400,000' (though the numeral has sometimes been emended)— odd, as we would not expect him to understate: perhaps there is some confusion with C.'s number for the enemy he *faced* (four million at

App. *Celt.* fr. 1.2.6: see above). Goudineau 308–11 regards one million as historically plausible.

16.1. fighting for Caesar's glory (or 'reputation' (*doxa*, 69.1 n.)): perhaps an echo of a Latin original, talking of C.'s *dignitas*: for that favourite watchword, cf. 30.1, 61.10 nn. and esp. Cic. *Att.* 7.11 (134).1, C. *BC* 1.8.3, 9.2, 3.91.2, etc., Hirt. *BG* 8.52.4, Suet. 33 and 72.

16.2. Acilius. Val. Max. 3.2.22 and Suet. 68.4 tell the story similarly, though both have the hand lopped off as it grabs the stern rather than Acilius 'boarding' the ship: both explicitly compare the tale of Cynegirus at Marathon (Hdt. 6.114), who similarly lost his hand while grasping the stern, and that comparison may be directing this choice of detail. The man's praenomen was Gaius (Suet.); he was a soldier of the tenth legion (Val. Max.). **In the sea battle off Massilia.** P. does not seem to be aware that there were two naval battles at Massilia (36.1 n.), both in summer 49: C. *BC* 1.56–8 and 2.4–7. **took the ship.** Val. Max. says he sank it.

16.3. Cassius Scaeva. The spelling of his name is disputed: probably M. Cassius Scaeva, though the MSS of Val. Max. 3.2.23a have 'Caesius' (see Shackleton Bailey's n. in the Loeb edn). **Dyrrhachium:** in 48, in one of the 'skirmishes' of 39.4 (n.): C. *BC* 3.52–3. Suet. 68.4 and Val. Max. 3.2.23a both tell the story, probably from the same source (above, 15–17 n.); App. 2.60.247–9 also tells the story in a way very similar to P. Lucan 6.118–262 elaborates extensively: for discussion, see M. Leigh, *Lucan: Spectacle and Engagement* (1997), 158–90. Flor. 2.13.40 also mentions the incident. Scaeva had been entrusted with the guard of a 'fort' (C., Suet., Val. Max., Lucan), and defended it against the Pompeian prefect Iustuleius (Val. Max.); C. promoted him to *primus pilus* as a reward for his feat (C.). P. leaves the story simple. **130:** in the other sources the figure is generally 120.

16.4. forced him away. App. 2.60 says that Scaeva killed him; Lucan 6.238–40 seems to agree.

16.5. In Britain. Val. Max. 3.2.23b tells the same tale, including many additional details of the terrain and the fighting. Dio 37.53.3 apparently reflects the same story, but refers it to the Spanish campaigns of 61–60. The divergence may arise from the Spanish town of Brigantium, named in the next section of Dio (53.4) and easily confused with the British tribe Brigantes: so Townend, 'Oppius', 337. But, *pace* Townend, the mistake is probably Dio's rather than

P.'s, for Val. Max. agrees in setting the item in Britain. Dio is probably taking an item that his source included in a general survey, and trying to incorporate it into his chronological structure: there is a similar instance in his next chapter (C.'s horse, 37.54.2: see 17.6 n.), and the previous ch. also displaced an item from an earlier context (52.2, C.'s incest dream: see 11.5–6 n.). **the leading centurions:** 'a most improbable group for a joint action', Townend, 'Oppius', 334. **One soldier.** He was consequently promoted to centurion (Val. Max.). Dio calls him 'P. Scaevius' (or 'Scaefius'); the MSS of Val. Max. have 'Scaeva'. Most, including Leigh, *Lucan: Spectacle and Engagement*, 175 n.24, have assumed that the story refers to the same 'Scaeva' as §§3–4, but P. clearly regards this 'soldier' as a different figure, and Shackleton Bailey observes that Val. Max. too seems to regard his 23b story as referring to a different figure from 23a. He therefore follows Kempf in restoring 'Scaevi' in Val. Max.

16.8–9. This story of **Granius Petro** is not told elsewhere, and may be the same episode as underlies *B.Af.* 44–6 (an unnamed centurion in 47–46 BCE) and Val. Max. 3.8.7 (a 'Titius' in an unspecified campaign against Scipio). If so, the episode's absence from *B.Af.* perhaps suggests that it should be dated before that work's narrative begins in 47, but this is all very uncertain (cf. R. P. Bruère, *CPh* 50 (1955), 201): Suet. 68.1 suggests that there were several such incidents: 'several of his men refused, when taken captive and offered their lives if they were willing to fight against him.' If the 47–46 date is right, Granius was presumably quaestor designate for 46: so *MRR* 296. He came of a prominent family of Puteoli (Syme, *RR* 90–1; C. Nicolet, *L'Ordre équestre*, ii (1974), 905–7).

17: C.'S TREATMENT OF HIS MEN On P.'s source(s) here, cf. 15–17 n. Notice the skill of the arrangement, which is likely to be P.'s own: sharing wealth (§1) leads into 'sharing toils and dangers' (§2), especially remarkable because of his bodily weakness: that links with physical description (§2) and the way he fought against that weakness (§§3–4), where 'journeys' offer a series of connections into further themes, including horsemanship (§6); 'dictation on horseback' leads into other letter-writing (§7), and that then into the wider treatment of friends (§§7–11), picking up various themes from the austerity mentioned earlier in the chapter; 'Oppius', perhaps the source of some of this material, is also useful here as a connecting motif (§§7, 11).

17.1. eagerness for glory: the same word (*philotimia*) as in §2, where
it is used of C. himself: he and his men deserve one another. Cf. 58.4 n.
unsparing in the favours... C.'s generosity to his lieutenants and troops
(cf. *BG* 7.11.9, 89.5, 8.4.1, *BC* 3.6.1, etc.; Brunt, *FRR* 261–2, Woolf 42) was
notorious in his own day, naturally arousing suspicions among his
peers and rivals: e.g. Cic. *Att.* 7.11 (130).9, 8.14 (164).1, *Fam.* 7.13
(36).1, *Phil.* 2.50 and 116, Catullus 29.3. P. treats the theme with uncomplicated warmth: cf. 12.4, 15.4 above. The tone of other authors is
more complex: contrast Suet. 26.2 (in the late fifties he promoted his
ambition by 'neglecting no kind of largesse (*largitionis*) or favours, public
or private, to anyone') with the more positive 68.1; Dio 42.49.3. In a
different mood P. himself would have disapproved: cf. *Sulla* 12.11–14.

  any sort of personal danger...any sort of work...: so also Suet.
57, Dio 44.38.2, 5. Both traits form part of the stereotype of the good
general: cf. esp. *Mar.* 7.3–6 and e.g. *Ant.* 4.4 (with my note), *C.min.*
9.9, *Sert.* 4.7, 12.7–13.5; Xen. *Cyr.* 1.6.25, Cic. *Mur.* 38, Tac. *Ann.*
13.35, *Hist.* 3.17.

17.2. he was a thin man...:   Suet. 45.1: 'he is said to have been tall,
pale-skinned, with smooth round limbs, a rather fuller face [or
"mouth"] than one would expect, and dark and lively eyes; his health
was good, except that towards the end of his life he was prone to
fainting and even night-terrors. He was twice attacked by epilepsy
while conducting business...'. Suet. goes on to talk of C.'s baldness,
and his delight in being able to conceal it with an honorific laurel
crown. So Suet.'s emphasis is rather less on physical frailty; P.'s
slanting helps the linkage of themes, 17 n. above.

The surviving sculptures, many of uncertain attribution, and coins
are of several different styles: cf. J. M. C. Toynbee, *Roman Historical
Portraits* (1978), 30–9. The overall impression is of a high brow,
thinning hair, deep-set eyes, a large curved nose, hollow cheeks, a
pointed chin, and a long, thin, often creased neck with a prominent
Adam's apple. The 'best large-scale piece of evidence for what C.
really looked like' (Toynbee 37) is the Turin head depicted above as
the frontispiece. The 'Arles bust' discovered in 2007 (www.telegraph.
co.uk/news/worldnews/1954876/Divers-find-bust-of-Julius-Caesar-
in-Rhone-River.html) is not in fact particularly likely to represent C.

  P.'s age was alert to physiognomic indications of character (cf. esp.
E. C. Evans, *TAPA* 72 (1941), 96–108; T. S. Barton, *Power and*

Knowledge: Astrology, Physiognomics, and Medicine under the Roman Empire (1994), 95–131; M. Gleason, *Making Men* (1995), esp. 55–81; S. Swain and G. Boys-Stones in *Seeing the Face, Seeing the Soul: Polemon's Physiognomy...* (2007), 11 and 123 n. 239 respectively): *Alex.* 1.3, 'just as painters pick up similarities from the face and the appearance around the eyes, where the personality becomes visible...'. P. himself uses physiognomic indications with some reserve (A. Georgiadou, *ANRW* ii. 33.6 (1992), 4616–23, W. J. Tatum, *JHS* 116 (1996), 135–51): appearance can match character (Marius' acerbic manner, *Mar.* 2; Aratus' athleticism, *Arat.* 3) but can also mislead (*Ages.* 2, *Phoc.* 5, etc.). Here as elsewhere P. uses appearance not as a direct reflex of personality, but more dynamically to illustrate character or career. Thus Pompey's appearance aids his popularity (*Pomp.* 2), while Antony's promotes his imitation of Heracles (*Ant.* 4 with my note). Here C.'s character is shown not by his physique directly, but by the way he fought to overcome its frailties.

C. shares 'white skin' with his pair Alexander (4.3), but Alexander's appearance was more straightforwardly (and paradigmatically, 4.2, *Pomp.* 2.2–3) 'regal': for P.'s interest in such regal appearance cf. Tatum, art. cit. For P., that makes C.'s achievement all the more striking.

epileptic fits: cf. 1.3, 53.5–6, 60.7 nn.; Suet. 45.1, App. 2.110.459. Some doubts have been expressed whether C.'s attacks were really epileptic (A. Donnadieu, *Mém. Soc. Antiq. de France*, 80 (1937), 27–36), but D. T. Benediktson has shown that the narratives of C.'s seizures are convincing, and indeed suit the pathology of epilepsy better than ancient medical descriptions of the symptoms (*AncW* 25 (1994), 159–64). **at Cordoba:** possibly during his Spanish quaestorship (69, 5.6) or proconsulship (61–60, chs 11–12); possibly as late as 49 (37.1–2 n., cf. *BC* 2.19–21), as Benediktson thinks. An 'illness' is attested for C. at Cordoba in 46 (Dio 43.32.6), but it is hard to think that this was the 'first' onset of epilepsy; certainly the case of 53.5–6, if historical (n.), was before that.

17.5. when he first left Rome: in mid-March 58 (14.17 n.). **reached the Rhône in only seven days:** C. *BG* 1.7.1, he 'hurried to Further Gaul by the biggest marches he could...'. 'Only seven days' does not come from C., but may well come from the source for ch. 18 (n.). For C.'s renowned 'incredible speed', cf. esp. Suet. 57, Cic. *Att.* 7.22 (146).1, 16.10 (422).1, and Gerlinger 159–76; for speculation on his route in 58, G. Walser, *Bellum Helveticum* (*Hist.* Einz. 118; 1998), 51 (probably *not* the Grand St Bernard, still snow-covered in March, but the coast road through the south of France).

17.6. He had found riding easy since he was a boy.   Suet. 57 also comments on C's equestrian skills. P. omits an item that he probably knew: C. rode a splendid horse whose forefeet had human-style toes; he was the first to mount it, and it would carry no other rider (Suet. 61, Dio 37.54.2 (treated under the Spanish campaign of 62, 16.5 n.), Plin. *NH* 8.155). In *Alex.* 6 he had made much of a similar item, but P. prefers his synkritic points to be more substantial and thought-provoking: Intr., pp. 25–32.

17.7. keep two secretaries busy.   When not riding C. could dictate even more letters simultaneously—four, or sometimes seven, according to Plin. *NH* 7.91. C.'s secretaries would have taken dictation in longhand, as tachygraphy was in its infancy (*OCD*[4], s.v. 'tachygraphy'). Simultaneous dictation was a good way of speeding up the process. On dictation in general, see N. I. Herescu, *REL* 34 (1956), 132–46. **Oppius:** C.'s famous and powerful aide. He is credited with biographies of Scipio Africanus and C. Cassius; his most important work was his book on C., probably another biography. See Intr., pp. 49–50, and (with caution) Townend, 'Oppius'.

17.8. conducting conversations with his friends by letters.   Suet. 56.6 seems a better-informed version of the same item: 'there are surviving letters to Cicero, and also to his friends on domestic matters, in which he conveyed in code [*per notas*] anything that needed to be treated with some secrecy'. Dio 40.9.3 also mentions this code, which simply substituted for each letter of the alphabet the fourth letter beyond. P. may have misunderstood the phrase *per notas* in a Latin source (Oppius?), taking it as 'by notes' or 'letters' (*OLD*, s. v. *nota* 6a–b). Some commentators have assumed that P. too meant 'in code': but the Greek cannot mean that, and 'the pressure of business was simply too great, and the city too large' provides no reason for using code, but does for using messages. Some of Cicero's correspondence, especially with Atticus, illustrates the rapid exchange of notes within the city: there was no need there to wait for a convenient traveller, for one could always send a slave.

17.9–10. Valerius Leo.   Nothing more is known of him. Valerii are frequent in Cisalpine Gaul: G. E. F. Chilver, *Cisalpine Gaul* (1941), 75.

Mediolanum: the modern Milan in what was then Cisalpine Gaul, mentioned here to bring out that this was a countryman rather than a person of Roman city manners. **perfumed oil** (Greek *muron*). Suet. 53 cites the same story (for C. Lucarini, *RhM* 146 (2003), 426–9 shows that this is what Suet.'s *oleum conditum* must mean) as coming from Oppius. Suet.'s C. makes his show of compliance 'so as not to give the impression of criticizing his host for either carelessness or boorishness'. P.'s C. is less tactful ('at this sort of bad manners...'). The dish was clearly unappetizing, and Lucarini shows that such perfumed oil was never used in cooking; so part of Valerius' 'bad manners' (lit. 'country manners' or 'boorishness', as in Suet.) was in not knowing proper cuisine. Another part, though, was in trying to over-impress, for such an oil was too valuable to waste in the kitchen. Cf. the proverb 'perfume [*muron*] on lentils' for something costly wasted on something cheap: Athen. 160b–c and Cic. *Att.* 1.19 (19).2 with Shackleton Bailey's n.

Townend, 'Oppius', 339, thinks that P. is confused, and Oppius referred not to *muron* but to *muria*, i.e. 'brine': the point is then that Valerius was being cheapskate (cf. Pers. 6.19–21 for a mean man dressing vegetables with brine). That seems unlikely in view of the 'perfume on lentils' proverb.

17.11. told Oppius to take the bed. It is an easy conjecture that this too derives from Oppius (above, 15–17 n.). Suet. 72 tells the same story, making it clear that Oppius had been taken ill on the journey, and using it to illustrate C.'s 'easy-going and generous treatment of his friends'; P. may suggest that theme as well, but leaves the explicit point as still the 'lack of pretension'.

18–27: FIGHTING IN GAUL In 59 C. was originally given only Illyricum and Cisalpine Gaul (14.10 n.), and at that time a campaign in Illyricum might have been expected (cf. 13.2 n.); Roman interests might indeed have been advanced by the development of a better land route from the west to the new conquests in the east (M. Griffin, *CJC* 8; N. Rosenstein, *CJC* 88–9). But Transalpine Gaul offered richer possibilities in wealth and glory, and C. would have welcomed, and doubtless machinated for, the senate's additional grant of the Transalpine 'province' (14.10 n.)—i.e. 'Gallia Bracata' or 'Trousered Gaul' (modern scholars often use its sober post-Augustan name of 'Narbonensis'), the part of Gaul regarded as Roman since the conquests of the late second century. (For thoughtful discussion of how 'Roman' it really was, see E. Hermon, *Rome et la Gaule Transalpine avant César* (1993) and G. Soricelli, *La Gallia Transalpina tra la conquista a l'età cesariana* (1995).) For several generations Roman influence had also been seeping north through the free tribes of Gallia Comata or 'Long-haired Gaul': C. revealingly comments that the Belgae 'are furthest removed from the civilization of the province, and therefore merchants reach them least often' (*BG* 1.1.3 (cf. 2.15.4)).

In recent years there had been hints of trouble in the northern parts of the province. There had been fighting with rebellious Allobroges in 62–61, and in 60 the threat from the Helvetii created a stir in Rome (Cic. *Att.* 1.19 (19).2). Thoughts of action outside the province, too, were clearly in the air: in 61 the senate authorized governors of Transalpine Gaul to do what they could to protect the Aedui and the friends of the Roman people, presumably against the Helvetii, or the recently victorious (19.2 n.) Ariovistus, or both; there was a diplomatic initiative too among the Gallic tribes (Cic., loc. cit.). C. now had the chance of representing the time as ripe for vigorous defence against threats, and defence could lead on to expansion; 'fear of the Gauls' was a particularly easy scare to monger (e.g. Cic. *Cat.* 3.4, 9, *Prov. Cons.* 32–5, Sall. *Cat.* 52.24; H. Bellen, *Metus Gallicus-Metus Punicus*, Abh. Akad. Wiss. Litt. Mainz 1985.3, esp. 36–46; Williams, esp. 170–82). True, the decree of 61 could mean 'anything or nothing' (Meier 238); and isolated actions outside the province were one thing, while it would be quite another to launch a major war of conquest on a governor's personal initiative. That was highly questionable both legally and politically (Meier 236–8; D. Timpe, *Hist.* 14 (1965), 189–214). But this was to be no ordinary governor.

Not that an immediate war was necessarily expected, even by C.: the threat from the Helvetii in 60 BCE had seemed to pass (Cic. *Att.* 1.20 (20).5, 2.1 (21).11); in early 58 there was only a single legion in Transalpine Gaul (*BG* 1.7.2), whereas three were at Aquileia (*BG* 1.10.3), better placed for an Illyricum campaign. But the hint of further Helvetian movement was excuse enough, and C. quickly adapted his plans—unless he had been playing a double game with the Helvetii all along, encouraging them to think that he would not oppose their journey through Roman Gaul and thereby stimulating the move that would justify his attack (so, ingeniously but not at all implausibly, W. Wimmel, *RhM* 123 (1980), 127–37 and 125 (1982), 59–66). Two recent studies independently conclude that C. had decided in 59 or early 58 to concentrate on Gaul, and issued orders

for troop movements before he left Rome in March 58: F. Fischer in
H. Heftner and K. Tomaschitz (eds), *Ad Fontes! Festschrift...Do-
besch* (2004), 305–15, and J. Thorne, *Hist.* 56 (2007), 27–36.

Now as later, the pattern of C.'s campaigning was a series of sharp
thrusts into and beyond Gallic territory, aimed against real or imagined threats to himself or to his Gallic allies. Then larger tracts of
land to the rear of these campaigns could be regarded as 'pacified';
C. expected, and often received, delegations from those tribes offering
'surrender' (cf. esp. D. Timpe, *Chiron*, 2 (1972), 277–95). Any Gauls
who found this less than attractive became 'rebels', most notably at
20.4, 25.1, and 25.2–27 (nn.)—even if their 'revolt' represented their
first contact with Rome.

18: C. AGAINST THE HELVETII, 58 BCE   Our principal account
is C. *BG* 1.2–29, from which most of P.'s material seems ultimately to
derive. The clear contact with App. *Celt.* frr. 1.3.8, 15 suggests that it
was transmitted by Pollio. Dio 38.31–3 is, I think, wholly based on C.,
with Dio's own inferences and elaborations.[6] P.'s source was clearly
detailed, including material on the preliminary negotiations (App. fr.
15, conflating C. *BG* 1.7–8, 13–14: such conflation is typical of App.,
and is probably his own rather than the source's); on the dimensions
of the Rhône fortifications (App. fr. 15 ~ C. *BG* 1.8.1); on some Gallic
reinforcements for C.; and on some details of the Tigurini battle (both
App. fr. 15). P.'s precise 'in only seven days' at 17.5 (n.) may also
come from here. And the source was certainly polemical: §2 n.

P. cuts most of the detail away, concentrating instead on the
picturesque. The campaign raised moral and juristic questions:
should C. have involved himself in an external war without senatorial
approval? Dio was worried by such matters (cf. 38.41.1, of the
Ariovistus campaign), but not P. Instead he continues the themes of
15–17, vast numbers, great dangers, and then at the end peaceful
settlement.

[6] The origin of Dio's account of the Gallic Wars is disputed: see I. McDougall, *Lat.*
50 (1991), 616–38, with full bibliography, who argues that Dio combines C.'s *Commentarii* with at least one further source. G. Zecchini, *Cassio Dione e la guerra gallica
di Cesare* (1979), argued that Dio is independent of C.'s account, and derives his
material from a well-informed and anti-Caesarian source: he suggests Q. Aelius
Tubero. For the alternative view, that almost all of Dio rests on Caesar's material
together with his own imaginative embellishments, see my review of Zecchini, *CR* 32
(1982), 146–8. See also 19 n. with n. 8.

For the migration, campaign, and settlement, see Holmes, *CCG* 46–57, 616–34; Jullian iii. 193–220; Walser 1–7 and his *Bellum Helveticum* (*Hist.* Einz. 118; 1998); E. Taübler, *Bellum Helveticum* (1924); A. Furger-Gunti, *Die Helvetier* (1984), 95–119; Kremer 133–42, 219–28; D. Lohmann, *Altspr. Unt.* 33.5 (1990), 56–73, 36.1 (1993), 37–52, and 39.1 (1996), 19–31 (a brilliant series of articles primarily concerned with *BG* 1 as a school text, and as rich interpretatively as pedagogically); F. Fischer in H. Heftner and K. Tomaschitz (eds), *Ad Fontes! Festschrift...Dobesch* (2004), 305–15; J. Thorne, *Hist.* 56 (2007), 27–36; and the speculations of C. E. Stevens, *Lat.* 11 (1952), 167–76, are still stimulating.

18.1. Helvetii and Tigurini.   P. clearly regards them as two distinct peoples. App. *Celt.* fr. 15 agrees, so this was presumably the version of Pollio. C. himself, however, has the 'canton [*pagus*] of Tigurini' as one of the four Helvetian 'cantons' (*BG* 1.12.4), and the statistics of *BG* 1.29 clearly include the Tigurini among the total of Helvetii. Posidonius fr. 272 EK = Strabo 7.2.2, apparently followed by Strabo himself, similarly counts the Tigurini as a subdivision of the Helvetii. At 4.3.3, however, Strabo—probably again following Posidonius (thus Kidd on fr. 272 EK)—speaks of three rather than four Helvetian 'tribes' at the time of the Cimbrian invasion. Cf. E. Meyer in W. Drack (ed.), *Ur- u. Frühgeschichtliche Archäologie der Schweiz*, iv (1974), 199, and R. Frei-Stolba, *ANRW* ii.5.1 (1976), 298, 327, both inclined to think that the Tigurini enjoyed some measure of independence. The position may not have been clear-cut, as the relationship of a subservient tribe to a stronger neighbour can readily be ambiguous: cf. the Mandubii and the Aedui (Holmes, *CCG* 446–7), and perhaps the Rauraci and the Helvetii themselves (G. Walser, *Klio*, 77 (1995), 217–23).

C. had reasons for exploiting any ambiguity in the way he did: including the Tigurini among the Helvetii enabled him to treat the whole campaign (*BG* 1.7.4, 13–14), not only the crushing of the Tigurini themselves (1.12.5–7, §2 n.), as appropriate vengeance for a defeat in 107 BCE, when the Tigurini had beaten and humiliated the army of L. Cassius.

twelve cities and four hundred villages: so also C. *BG* 1.5.2, presumably the ultimate source. Some traces of this burning have been tentatively identified at Mont Vully on the Murtensee: G. Kaenel and P. Curdy, *Archäologie der Schweiz*, 6 (1983), 102–9. **the part of**

Gaul that was subject to Rome: probably an error, for this phrase would more naturally mean the Roman 'province' (above, pp. 217–18) than territory belonging to Roman allies. If the imperfect 'they were moving forward' implies that they were already in the province, this is incorrect: the Helvetii originally planned to travel through the province, and asked C.'s permission to do so (*BG* 1.6.2–3, 7.3). But C. refused, and the Helvetian attempt to use force failed (*BG* 1.8.3–4). They then took their alternative route, through the independent Sequani (*BG* 1.9.1–4). The error seems inherited: cf. App. *Celt.* fr. 15.1, 'they invaded Roman Gaul'. That version left it obscure how the Helvetii came to the Saône (§2), whose course lay entirely outside the province. Neither P. nor App. knew enough Gallic geography to correct that version (cf. 20.6, 26.1, 26.6 nn.), and indeed at 19.2 and 20.4 P. speaks as if most of Gaul was already 'subject' to Rome. The alternative would be to take the imperfect as conative, 'they were trying to make their way': so Amyot. But Appian's clear 'they invaded' makes this less likely.

like the Cimbri and Teutones of old. They entered the Rhône valley around 110, won the great victory of Arausio (Orange) in 105, and were defeated by Marius in 102–1: 6.2 n. Some at least of the Helvetii and Tigurini had attached themselves to them (Posidonius fr. 272 EK), winning a victory over the Romans in 107 (see on 'Helvetii and Tigurini' above). The names continued to exercise Roman imagination and fears (Williams 172–6, H. Callies, *Chiron*, 1 (1971), 341–50, D. Timpe in B. and P. Scardigli (eds), *Germani in Itali* (1994), 21–60), remembered as a threat to Italy (26.2 and e.g. Cic. *prov. cons.* 32, *de off.* 1.38) and—at least once they had been redesignated as 'Germans', which may well have been C.'s own doing (Walser 37–8 n. 8, Rives 271–3)—to Gaul as well (Tac. *Hist.* 4.73): both themes were exploited by C. in *BG* (1.33.4, 2.4.2, 7.77.12; G. Pascucci, *SIFC* 27–8 (1956), 361–73, Riggsby 116–17, 177–8). The tribes caught P.'s interest: he describes them lavishly at *Mar.* 11, and goes on to give a generous and impressive narrative of Marius' campaigns (*Mar.* 12–27). In *Caes.* the theme recurs at 19.4 and 26.2, as C. emerges as Marius' military as well as political successor (above, p. 205; 19.2 n.; Gerlinger 79–80). **the numbers were about the same:** a pardonable exaggeration. According to *Mar.* 11.3, the Cimbri and Teutones numbered 300,000 fighting men, 'and they were said to have with them a much bigger following of children and women'.

300,000 in all, including 190,000 combatants. These figures must be taken with §5, 'more than 100,000' returning home. C. *BG* 1.29 claims that 'tablets written in Greek' (a plausible detail: Rives 126–7, Woolf 92) were discovered in the Helvetian camp, with a complete register of the barbarian host. These gave 263,000 Helvetii and 105,000 other peoples, of whom 92,000 were combatants. C. adds that a census of those who returned home gave a total of 110,000. That figure should exclude 32,000 Boii who were settled by the Aedui (*BG* 1.28.5). These figures, along with those given by P, and other sources, have been much debated: cf. esp. K. J. Beloch, *Die Bevölkerung der gr.-röm. Welt* (1886), 451–3; A. Grenier, *ESAR* iii. 449–51; F. Stähelin, *Die Schweiz in röm. Zeit* (3rd edn, 1948), 73 n. 2; Kremer, 298–9; E. Meyer, *Zeitschr. f. Schweiz. Gesch.* 29 (1949), 65–70; J. Harmand, *Les Celtes* (1970), 62–4; R. Kasser, *Yverdon*, ed. Kasser (1975), 222 n. 10; Gerlinger 126–8.

Table 1. Comparison of numbers of combatants

Source	Totals	Combatants	Killed	Returned
(C. *BG* 1.29)	(368,000 in all)	(92,000)		(110,000)
Plutarch	300,000 H + T	190,000		over 100,000
App. *Celt.* fr. 1.3.8		*c.*200,000	80,000	
Polyaenus 8.23.3	300,000 H	200,000		
Strabo 4.3.3			400,000	8,000
Orosius 6.7.5	157,000		47,000	110,000

Note: H = Helvetii; T = Tigurini.

The figures given by sources other than C. are shown in Table 1. Do they carry any authority? Most treatments have taken these figures, especially those of Orosius, very seriously. Yet all may well arise from misunderstandings or roundings of C.'s own figures, or early corruptions in the texts they were using.

P. and App. will derive from their usual shared source, Pollio; it looks as if Polyaenus draws on the same tradition. That source apparently gave 300,000 migrants, 190,000 combatants, and 110,000 returning; App. presumably estimated the '80,000 killed' on that basis. The '110,000' agrees with C., and other figures in the P./App. tradition similarly reflect C.'s numbers (e.g. the 'twelve cities and four hundred villages' above, cf. 20.7, 20.10, 22.5, 24.3, 27.3–4 nn.; also 19.11 n.). In that case the 300,000 total, obscured in App.'s epitome, should also come ultimately from C.: probably a rounding of the '263,000 Helvetii' rather than the grand total of 368,000. The '190,000 combatants' remains: in view of the closeness of the other figures, this is most likely to derive from an early corruption in C.'s text or in the P./App. source (192,000 ~ 92,000).

Strabo's figures are oddities, especially as he goes on to give a reason for the 'settlement' ('fearing to leave their land empty and vulnerable to their German neighbours'), which seems to derive from C. *BG* 1.28.4 (see §6 n.). That makes it more likely that the '400,000' is a rounding of C.'s 368,000, perhaps derived via Pollio (whom Strabo has just quoted for the Rhine flow, above, p. 204), and a misunderstanding, presumably Strabo's own, of its significance. The '8,000' may be a false inference from C. *BG* 7.75.3, where the Helvetii send a force of 8,000 to Alesia. Orosius too reflects C.'s figures elsewhere in his Gallic account,[7] and here his 110,000 should derive from C. His other two figures of 157,000 and 47,000 clearly cohere with the 110,000 and are mutually dependent: it seems unlikely that they, and they alone, have independent authority. More probably one was copied from a corrupt or erroneous text, and the other calculated from it. Perhaps someone ineptly subtracted C.'s 105,000 from his 263,000 instead of adding.

Are C.'s figures credible in themselves? The population density implied for Helvetian territory is credible: depending on the area allowed for Helvetian territory (cf. C. *BG* 1.2), between 8 and 10 per square km. (E. Kirsten, *Raum und Bevölkerung in der Weltgeschichte*, i (1956), i. 229) and 16 per square km. (J. Harmand, *Les Celtes* (1970), 62). The 92,000 combatants are exactly 25 per cent of the 368,000 total, and one may well be an estimate based on the other; but if so the larger figure is likely to be primary (C.'s figures specify grand totals, not combatants, for the other tribes), and the estimate may anyway be a good one. Modern parallels would suggest a ratio of *c*.1:3 rather than 1:4 for combatants : total, but few modern states indulge in 'daily battles' (*BG* 1.1.4, cf. 1.40.7), and the combatant sector had surely suffered disproportionate losses. H. Graßl discusses the logistic problems of moving such a host in *'Troianer sind wir gewesen'—Migrationen in der antiken Welt*, ed. E. Olshausen and H. Sonnabend

[7] Oros. 6.7.12–16 (confused) ~ *BG* 2.4.8–10; 6.8.22 ~ *BG* 3.26.6; 6.9.2 ~ *BG* 4.22.3; 6.9.3–4 ~ *BG* 5.2.2, 11.2; 6.10.3 ~ *BG* 5.42, 44; 6.10.9 ~ *BG* 5.49.1; 6.11.4 ~ *BG* 7.28.5; 6.11.8 ~ *BG* 7.76.3; and note 6.7.10 ~ *BG* 1.53.1, with 19.11 n.; 6.8.23 ~ *BG* 4.15.3, with 22.5 n. Cf. F. Fischer, *BJb* 199 (1999), 60–4, arguing that Orosius was using a fourth-century MS of *BG* itself rather than deriving these figures via Livy.

(2006), 14–19, but does not consider them as insuperable, even though the numbers given are considerably greater than those he reconstructs for other migrations (e.g. 150,000 for the Cimbri and Teutones). True, the length of column would be such that the front would have to pitch camp for the night well before the rear could even begin its daily march; but wherever possible the host may have split into two groups following different but neighbouring routes.

One question remains: when was so detailed a register taken (C. specifies 'by name'), and how accurate could it be? Hardly on the march; presumably it would be some sort of census taken before the migration. If so, the figures are surely inflated. It was planned that all should migrate (*BG* 1.5), but some, especially the old, infirm, and disaffected, might prefer to take their chance at home. Others will not have survived much of the journey. But the total should still not be far below C.'s figures, and we have nothing better to put in their place. They deserve more credence than those of 15.5 (n.).

18.2. The Tigurini were crushed...: C. *BG* 1.12; perhaps near Trévoux, some 20 km. north of Lyon: Holmes, *CCG* 616–19; C. Jullian, *REA* 30 (1928), 120; A Fridh, *Eranos*, 94 (1996), 13–14, 19. P.'s source went into detail: App. *Celt.* fr. 15. **not by Caesar himself but by Labienus:** so App. *Celt.* fr. 1.3.3, 15.2–3, and so this was the version of the shared source. C.'s account does not mention Labienus, and gives the impression that he conducted the action himself. On variant versions of this stamp, cf. 53.5–6 n. P.'s language is oddly insistent, and seems to reflect a polemic against C.'s version. P. himself hardly intended such hostility in this enthusiastic chapter; this will be the emphasis of the source (Intr., p. 48). In fact C. was probably present at the action, as he implies: otherwise the distortion would be easily exposed, and he does give credit to lieutenants, especially Labienus, elsewhere (see K. Welch in *JCAR*, esp. 98–101)—though it is also true that he has particular reasons for emphasizing his own role here, in extracting private as well as public vengeance for events forty-nine years earlier (*BG* 1.12.5–7, cf. G. Lieberg, *Caesars Politik in Gallien* (1998), 55–8). If Labienus did play a large part in this action, the earliest form of the dispute may have centred on whether Labienus or C. deserved more credit. By the early forties Labienus had gone over to the Pompeians (34.5 n.), and the polemic could naturally intensify.

For T. **Labienus**, tribune in 63, praetor before 59, legate of C. from 58 to 49 and of the Pompeians from 49 to 45, cf. Syme, *RP* i. 62–75 (making much of Labienus' origin in Pompey's heartland of Picenum); W. B. Tyrrell, *Hist.* 21 (1972), 424–40.

to some friendly city: Bibracte (C. *BG* 1.23.2), the principal town of the Aedui: i.e. Mont Beuvray, 22 km. west of Autun. Intensive excavations were resumed there in 1984: D. Bertin and J.-P. Guillaumet, *Bibracte* (Guides archéologiques de la France 13; 1987), C. Goudineau and C. Peyre, *Bibracte et les Éduens* (1993).

For this march, cf. *BG* 1.16 and 23: C. says that he was running short of grain; with the enemy at hand and with the Aedui evidently divided about supporting C., it is understandable that he chose not to split his forces. One ingenious reconstruction turns this into a feint, luring the Helvetii into an attack (Lohmann, *Altspr. Unt.* 36.1 (1993), 46–50); but the terrain was not especially difficult for C., and he should have had more reliable ways of enforcing battle on the slow-moving Helvetian column.

For the fighting, *BG* 1.23–6, an enigmatic account of one of the bloodiest afternoons in European history. The battle's location is uncertain. It is normally put near Toulon-sur-Arroux, where Col. E. C. Stoffel found what he took to be traces of C.'s earthworks (*BG* 1.24.3: *Guerre Civile*, ii (1887), 439–52). Recent excavations have confirmed at least this part of Stoffel's findings (L. Flutsch, *Zeitschr. Schweiz. Arch. u. Kunstgesch.* 48 (1991), 38–48), but carbon-dating shows that the finds are considerably later than Stoffel thought (Flutsch, loc. cit., 44), and there are severe problems in Stoffel's reconstruction of the fighting. R. Rau, *Klio*, 21 (1927), 374–84, is not wholly satisfactory, but there is more to be said for his suggestion, a site east of Luzy, on the course of the pre-Roman road (E. Thevenot, *Les Voies Romaines de la Cité des Éduens* (Coll. Lat. 98, 1969), 291–2), perhaps near Thil or La Guette. Cf. also A. Fridh, *Eranos* 94 (1996), 15–18, who similarly rejects Stoffel's location.

18.3. When a horse was brought to him ... The story comes from *BG* 1.25.1; cf. Suet. 60. Lohmann, art. cit. (§2 n.) 43, observes that P. shifts the tenor of the story: in C.'s account and Suet.'s, it is an index of the desperate situation (C. removes *everyone*'s horses 'to take away all hope of flight', though Lohmann has good reason for doubting whether the situation was really so desperate); in P., of his inspirational confidence. Such stories were commonplace: cf. e.g. *Crass.*

11.8–9 (where the general's cry is 'if I win, I shall have many fine horses – the enemy's!'), *Phil.* 6.8, Sall. *Cat.* 59.1, Livy 3.62.8; Gerlinger 63–5. **'I shall use that later ...'**: not in C.'s own account, and P. has presumably made up this apophthegm himself, like that at *Crass.* 11.9: cf. Intr., p. 57.

18.4. women and children too: no mention of this in *BG* 1.26.1–5, though that passage confirms that there was fierce fighting around the wagons till late at night. P. will have known that women and children would be waiting there: he may simply have inferred their picturesque and conventional (cf. e.g. Dio 56.15.4–5) heroism. Such themes appealed to him: cf. *Mar.* 27.2–5.

18.5–6. He resettled those barbarians: ultimately based on *BG* 1.28–9: even C.'s motivation (§6) is inherited (*BG* 1.28.4; cf. Strabo 4.3.3, above, p. 223). We should not, however, regard this resettlement as simply an act of humanity, despite 15.4 and the possible implication of P.'s **better** here; there were good reasons of expedience for **forcing them to return**, as P. brings out in §6. The archaeological evidence for Helvetian resettlement is surveyed by G. Kaenel and D. Paunier, *Archäologie der Schweiz*, 14 (1991), 153–68. It tends to support the picture of severe depopulation. In 56 BCE Cicero refers to a 'treaty' between Rome and the Helvetii (*Balb.* 32): that may have been agreed now (F. Fischer, *BJb* 185 (1985), 1–26), but is just as likely to date back to the end of the second century, during or after the Cimbrian invasions (R. Frei-Stolba, *ANRW* ii.5.1 (1976), 328–38). **more than 100,000:** §1 n. **the Germans might cross:** for the German threat to Helvetian territory, probably a factor in the original Helvetian migration, see 19.2 n.

19: CAESAR AGAINST ARIOVISTUS, 58 BCE   Most of P.'s material derives from C. *BG* 1.30–54, again presumably via the usual source, for App. *Celt.* frr. 1.3.9, 16–17, shows contact at §12 (n.). Dio 38.34–50 differs substantially from C.'s, and has often been exploited as if it carried independent authority (thus H. Hagendahl, *CetM* 6 (1944), 29–40; D. Timpe, *Hist.* 14 (1965), 205–8; Walser 27–31). That is dangerous, for it is likely to be Dio's own imaginative and intelligent response to C.'s material;[8] but that response, concentrating

---

[8] It is typical of Dio himself both to reconstruct psychology and to pose problems concerning morality and legality (*CR* 32 (1982), 146–7: cf. above, p. 219): here he makes the soldiers protest that they were 'taking on a war that was not right and had

as it does on the campaign's moral and legal questionability and on C.'s ruthless motivation, is a pointer to other ways in which the material *could* have been handled, had P. chosen to pursue rather than abandon the moral reservations of ch. 14 (above, p. 203).

P.'s account suppresses military details and concentrates on a simplified version of the Vesontio mutiny and on the battle itself. Both themes are governed by an emphasis on psychology, as first the Roman and then the German nerve breaks, and C. deals brilliantly with both. Finally stereotyped barbarian terror and superstition gives way to stereotyped barbarian fury, and the result is a stereotypically massive slaughter (nn.).

For this campaign and C.'s narrative, cf. esp. Holmes, *CCG* 57–68 and 636–57; Jullian iii. 221–41; Gerlinger 78–81, 160–3, and 186–93; H. Hagendahl, *CetM* 6 (1944), 1–40; Walser 1–36; K. Christ, *Chiron*, 4 (1974), 251–92; and F. Fischer, *BJb* 199 (1999), 31–68.

19.1. directly (as opposed to the indirect measures of 18.6) **against the Germans themselves... in the Gauls' interest.** C. operates in *BG* with a tendentious and over-sharp distinction between Gauls and Germans, in particular elaborating the notion of the Rhine as the natural frontier between two different peoples: see 15.1, 22.1 nn., and Walser, esp. 37–51, A. Lund, *Altspr. Unt.* 38.2 (1995) 12–15 and 39.2 (1996), 12–14, A. C. King, *Roman Gaul and Germany* (1993), 31–2 (in fact 'the Rhine... seems not to have been a cultural barrier at all'), J. Loicq, *REL* 85 (2007), 66–80 ('une fiction géo-politique'), Rives 24–7, Riggsby 63–70, and, for discussion of how this fits into C.'s broader 'imaginary geography', C. Krebs, *AJP* 127 (2006), 111–36, and H. Schadee, *CQ* 58 (2008), 158–80. It is doubtful how many Gallic tribes in fact requested C. to intervene. According to C. *BG* 1.30–3, 'envoys from almost all of Gaul, the first citizens of each state' had gathered at a 'meeting' (*concilium*) 'of all Gaul' to ask for Roman action against Ariovistus. But this 'meeting' may well have represented no more than the Aedui and their client-tribes (Walser 11–12),

not been decreed, all for C.'s own ambition (*philotimia*)', and his C. delivers a long, Thucydidean speech, arguing for the war's necessity and paying especial note to the juristic point (38.41.1). It is in Dio's manner to state his own conjectures, especially psychological conjectures, as fact, and here he naturally applies (and makes his characters apply) his own view of the issues. W. Steidle, *WJb* 14 (1988), 211–24 and K. Christ, *Chiron*, 4 (1974), 272–80 have good remarks on the relation of these themes to those that Dio develops elsewhere. See also p. 219 with n. 6.

Ariovistus' previous relations with the Gallic tribes are controversial: see esp. E. Taübler, *Bellum Helveticum* (1924), 3–32; Holmes, *CCG* 37–40, 553–5; Jullian iii. 150–74; Hagendahl, *CetM* 6 (1944), 16–18; Barwick, *RhM* 98 (1955), 52–68; Walser 8–20; Maier 41–4. Around 62 BCE Ariovistus had won a decisive victory at Magetobriga (C. *BG* 1.31.12). Taübler's careful analysis demonstrated that this is likely to be identical with the battle of *BG* 1.31.6, where Ariovistus defeated the Aedui and their clients. It follows that at 1.44.3 C. makes 'Ariovistus' exaggerate when he claims that 'all the states of Gaul came to attack him...', and 'Diviciacus' exaggerate similarly at 1.31.12 (quoted in next n.): that is no surprise (cf. §1 n.).

intolerable neighbours: cf. 'Diviciacus' at C. *BG* 1.31.12, 'after Ariovistus had conquered all the forces of Gaul at Magetobriga, he had been ruling arrogantly and ruthlessly, demanding as hostages the children of the highest nobles, and subjecting them to all manner of torture if anything was not done according to his whim or his wish...'. Cruelty is part of the stereotype of barbarians in general, and the Germans in particular (Schmidt 36–45). P. does not fragment the reader's attention by giving details. **they would grasp the first opportunity to move into action:** ultimately from C. *BG* 1.31.11, where 'Diviciacus' claims that 'within a few years everyone would be driven beyond the boundaries of Gaul and all the Germans would cross the Rhine' (again notice C.'s tendentiously clear definition of 'Gallic' territory).

19.3–5: THE MUTINY AT VESONTIO   Cf. esp. C. *BG* 1.39–41 (well analysed by B. James, *Hermes*, 128 (2000), 54–64) and the elaborate version of Dio 38.35–47, probably based on Dio's own critical reading of C. (19 n.). Most of P.'s material comes from C., presumably transmitted by the usual source (cf. App. *Celt.* fr. 17 fin.). P. has a few non-Caesarian items: the inexperienced young men's lust for luxury and riches, and C.'s invitation to them to leave the campaign altogether. These are easy guesses, probably P.'s own, because both themes recur later: for the young nobles' distaste for danger, cf. 45.2–3, where C. turns such Roman dandiness to his advantage a second time, this time among his enemies; for the invitation to leave C.'s service, cf. 51.2.

19.3. captains ... young nobles ...:   more precisely 'the tribunes of the soldiers, prefects [*praefectis*], and those who had followed C. from the city out of friendship but had little military experience...' (C. *BG*

1.39.1, who goes on to give a vivid description of their panic). **Now he called an assembly**: at Vesontio, the modern Besançon. C. had already made some move towards the enemy; P. reserves C.'s first movement for §§4–5, his vigorous reaction to the soldiers' change of heart. **assembly.** P. gives the impression of a mass meeting of all the soldiers. In fact it was a 'meeting' (*concilium*) of centurions (*BG* 1.40.1): for the workings of that gathering, cf. J. Vogt, *Orbis* (1960), 97–8. P. has turned C. into the campaign equivalent of a popular politician, attacking the well-born before a mass audience. Dio adapts C.'s account in the opposite direction: he makes the 'soldiers' rather than the captains nervous (38.35.1), and C. rallies the officers to re-establish control (35.3)—again (cf. 19 n. with n. 8, Christ, *Chiron*, 4 (1974), 277–9), a theme that coheres with Dio's treatment of mutinies elsewhere.

19.4. He would take the tenth legion alone: so C. *BG* 1.40.14–15. The legion's position of favour and trust is often clear: *BG* 1.42.5–6, 2.21–6, 4.25.3, 7.47.1, 7.51.1, *B.Afr.* 16, *B.Hisp.* 30.7. **Cimbri...he himself was no less a general than Marius**: 18.1 n. Here the comparison is drawn from *BG* 1.40.5, where C. reports his own speech: 'Rome had faced the danger of confronting that enemy in their fathers' day, when the Cimbri and Teutones had been repulsed by C. Marius, and at that time the army had won as much glory as the general himself.' P. sharpens the point, especially the personal implication for C. himself.

19.5. summarizes *BG* 1.41, excising much detail. **within 200 stades**: 'twenty-four miles' (*BG* 1.41.5). 'A [Roman] mile is a little less than eight stades' (*Gracch.* 28.3), and 1:8 is the equivalence with which P. works elsewhere, e.g. *Cam.* 18.7, 29.5 ~ Livy 5.37.7, 49.6. 'Stade' can be an inexact term in Greek (cf. R. Bauslaugh, *JHS* 99 (1979), 5–6, Hornblower on Thuc. 1.63.2), and other equations were possible: thus Dio works with a 1:7.5 equivalent, e.g. 38.17.7, 46.44.4, 51.9.6 with A. Lintott, *CR* 21 (1971), 5–6, 52.21.2.

19.6–7. P. here omits the second sequence of talks (*BG* 1.42–7), though he probably knew of them (App. *Celt.* fr. 17). He prefers this elaborate if stereotyped (cf. *BG* 6.8.6, Tac. *Ann.* 2.14.3; Schmidt 212–9, Oakley on Livy 7.12.11) picture of failing German nerve: this has no explicit parallel in *BG*, though it was natural for later writers to have been a little delayed (*Lat.* 40 (1981), 756–7), and most of this slaughter probably took place on the river bank.

19.12. Ariovistus got away... He found a small boat tied to the bank, *BG* 1.53.2–3. He was probably wounded and died soon afterwards: cf. *BG* 5.29.3, 'the Germans were very grieved by Ariovistus' death and our earlier victories...'. **and crossed the Rhine:** forming a ring with §§1–2: far from 'sweeping over Gaul' with a horde, Ariovistus is forced back where he belongs, with just a handful of men. **The dead...numbered 80,000:** not in C., but evidently from the shared source, as App. *Celt.* fr. 1.3.9 has the same figure. C.'s despatch to the senate probably gave an estimate of enemy dead, and that may be the original source. At *BG* 1.31.5 C. has 'Diviciacus' speak of 120,000 Germans who had originally crossed the Rhine: it is not clear whether he includes women and children. Numbers of barbarians, dead or alive, are typically massive: 15.5 n. These may well be too high.

20.1–3: CAESAR IN THE CISALPINA The similar analysis of *Pomp.* 51.1–3 is more indignant and wider-ranging, adding for instance that C. plied the men's wives too with money: 'wives' are an important theme in that *Life*. *C.min.* 49.1 briefly echoes the same ideas. The picture of regular and extensive suborning may well be taken closely from the source (cf. App. 2.17.62 and esp. Suet. 23.2, quoted on §§2–3 below): if so, that source probably placed the analysis just before Luca (above, p. 204). Despite his tendency to political abbreviation in this part of the *Life*, P. thought it worthwhile to incorporate this separate section at the close of the first year's campaigns. This involved some duplication with ch. 21, but paints a man who from the outset does not allow warfare, however glorious or engrossing, to distract him from his political schemes. One of P.'s favourite stereotypes is that of the military man who is lost in the devious world of politics (Coriolanus, Philopoemen, Marius, Pompey): C. is very different.

20.1. he left his army to winter among the Sequani, while he himself came back to Cisalpine Gaul: ultimately from C. *BG* 1.54.2–3, where C. 'led his army to winter-quarters among the Sequani, and put them under Labienus' command; he himself went back to Nearer Gaul to conduct assizes'. Either Pollio or Plutarch has substituted political activity for C.'s bland 'assizes'. **the Cisalpina is divided from the rest of Italy by the river they call the Rubicon.** We do not need to know this here, and such 'they call it...' formulations are anyway usually given to less familiar names. Here it is more like the stereotyped 'there was a man called...' introduction to stories (e.g. Xen. Ephes. 1.1), a pointer to the river's fame and significance, relying on audience knowledge that it will play a later part in the story. Thus C.'s early political activity is already under the shadow of what it will lead to eight-and-a-half years later (32.5, where 'they call it the Rubicon' echoes the language here). The point involves geographical simplification, conscious or not. P. writes as if the river forms at least a large part of the province's boundary; in fact— whatever its precise identification, 32.5 n.—it is little more than a stream at the eastern end. **the rest of Italy.** It had long been possible (though also contestable: see Williams 129–39, E. Bispham, *From Asculum to Actium* (2007), 59–60) to see Cisalpine Gaul as *geographically* part of Italy: cf. 32.5 and esp. Plb. 2.14, Cato *Orig.* fr. 85 P = 4.10 Ch., Livy 21.35.4 ~ Plb. 3.54.2. This becomes relevant at 29.2 (n.).

developments in Rome: where a lot had been happening during Clodius' tumultuous tribunate of 58 (on which, see esp. Tatum, *The Patrician Tribune* (1999), chs. 5–6; Millar 136–46). Some of it concerned Cicero's exile (14.7 n.) and the mounting pressure for his return. P. knew a good deal about this (*Cic.* 30–33). C. was in contact with Pompey on the topic by late summer: Cicero found his attitude difficult to read (*Cic. Att.* 3.15 (60).3, 3.18 (63).1, *Fam.* 14.1 (8).2).

Other events mattered just as much. Cato had been deftly removed to Cyprus (*C.min.* 34): C. had written to congratulate Clodius on his ploy, or so Clodius claimed (Cic. *Dom.* 21–2). Relations were strained between Pompey and Crassus (Cic. *Att.* 3.10 (55).1), as they had been already in 59 (13.3 n., above, p. 191). The tribune Q. Terentius Culleo had been urging Pompey to break with C. too (*Pomp.* 49.4). And Clodius himself, developing a style of confrontational and charismatic populism that in some ways rivalled C.'s own, was a most uncertain quantity. Clodius was already at odds with Pompey, and was harrying and humiliating him (*Pomp.* 48–9, Tatum, *Patrician Tribune* 167–75); and by the end of the year he was also taking the position that C.'s legislation of 59 was illegal (Cic. *Dom.* 40, *Har. Resp.* 48)—although there may also have been some proposal that the legislation might be re-enacted legitimately (Cic. *Prov. Cons.* 46, though that is vague and undated). Much of this was doubtless just teeth-baring, but the style of Roman politics was changing, and no one could predict how effective or powerful Clodius might become.

C.'s response required careful calculation. A waiting game would seem attractive. Most of the major players, individual and collective, looked weaker at the end of 58 than they had at the beginning: Cicero, the senatorial conservatives, the bruised Pompey, the reticent Crassus. The exceptions were the urban *plebs*, who were being taught new methods of assertiveness; and Clodius—though only time would tell how effectively he could maintain his authority after demitting his office, and there were beginning to be signs of over-reaching, perhaps even of desperation. C. had little interest in stemming the disorder. A more effective *plebs* might be turned to his own benefit in the future; and, if anarchy spread beyond the city walls, there might even be the prospect of recalling a successful general to put things right. But Clodius himself was going too far too soon; it may even be, as Miriam Griffin suggests to me, that he was contemplating a deal with the *optimates* to rescind C.'s legislation while protecting his own transfer to the *plebs*. Just as Clodius had been useful for curbing Cicero (14.7 n.), so Cicero could now be useful for clipping Clodius' wings. Besides, events were moving in Cicero's favour, and (as Dio 39.10.1 shrewdly infers) C. was not a man to be associated with a losing cause. By early 57 he was coming out in favour of Cicero's recall (*Pis.* 80, *Prov. Cons.* 43, *Fam.* 1.9 (20).9).

20.2–3. his demagogy: cf. esp. Suet. 23.2, 'to protect his future he would take great care always to place the annual magistrates under obligations; he would help or allow to succeed only those candidates who had promised to protect his interests while he was away, and he went so far as to exact oaths and even contracts from some of them'. P. rejected the concluding detail (if he knew it), which would overload his narrative, and left the 'magistrates and candidates' item (cf. *Pomp.* 51.3) for 21.4–5. Individual cases of 'purchased' supporters cannot be identified till later (29.3 (n.)), but our evidence for the early fifties is not extensive (Gelzer 112). C. certainly took an active interest in Roman events (§1 n.), and he doubtless had fingers in several pies.

'Demagogy' continues the theme of C. as the popular politician; but P. surely, like Suet., envisages C.'s visitors as politicians and candidates for office (21.4), not members of the people. But such a use of 'demagogy' does sometimes recur, normally in passages of heightened language: to 'captivate by popular arts', 'court people's favour' (Clough). Thus 'playing the demagogue with the young men, pandering to their hopes' (*Fab.* 26.1), and e.g. *Lucull.* 23.1.

He had many visitors. Only one is identified, with a mission of a different kind: P. Sestius, seeking support for Cicero's recall (*Sest.* 71).

20.3. though Pompey did not realize it: for Pompey as C.'s dupe, cf. 28.2 (n.), 29.5–7, *C.min.* 43.8–10, 49.1. It seems to come from the source: cf. App. 2.30.116–8; above, p. 204). The picture in *Pompey* (esp. 51.1, 57.6–9) is rather different: 28.2 n. **Gallic wealth:** so also *Pomp.* 51.3: another theme, it seems, emphasized by the source (cf. App. 2.17.61–2). Gallic wealth was already famous, perhaps exaggerated in greedy Roman minds: cf. Catull. 29.1–4, 'who can bear to see this, who can put up with it, unless he is a shameless greedy gamester—Mamurra having whatever Long-haired Gaul and far-flung Britain used to own?' Suet. 54 says that C. brought back so much gold that he had to exchange it for silver at two-thirds of its normal price. The impact on Gaul of the war was immense: it can be traced in the collapse of the metal content of Belgic coinages during the decade, which suggests a massive drain of precious metals. Some may have been used to finance the fighting, some would be taken away by refugees to e.g. Britain, but most was surely plundered. Cf. C. C. Haselgrove, *Oxf. Journ. Arch.* 3 (1984), 81–105 and more generally Woolf 40–7, esp. 42. **capture and subdue:** military language, emphasizing the parallel. C.'s ruthless and effective policy was itself conducted as a sort of military operation.

20.4–5: THE BATTLE OF THE AISNE P.'s version derives ultimately from C. *BG* 1.15, presumably via the usual source (cf. App. *Celt.* fr. 1.4.10 with §5 n.). See also Dio 39.1–2, discussed not wholly cogently by I. McDougall, *Lat.* 50 (1991), 628–38. For the campaign, cf. esp. Holmes, *CCG* 69–74 and 658–70; Jullian iii. 246–56; C. Peyre, *REL* 56 (1978), 175–215; Goudineau 249–52. I discuss the location of the battle in *Lat.* 40 (1981), 742–7: somewhere a little north of Reims, perhaps Chaudardes, perhaps Berry-au-Bac.

The contrast between Roman politics (§§1–3) and Gallic warfare is left at its strongest, and so P. has no interest in C.'s *diplomacy* in Gaul: 'his Gallic allies' (§5) glides over the important accession of the Remi (C. *BG* 2.3, Szidat 52–4: contrast the stress given this by Dio 39.1.2–3). The battle is described briefly though powerfully, with stress yet again (cf. 15.5 n.) on the numbers of slain, this time put more melodramatically, §5; but the narrative climax is left for C.'s personal heroism in the Nervii battle, §8.

20.4. the Belgae had revolted. Yet they had in no sense been Rome's subjects: see above, p. 219. Some may have been under the control of the Aedui, Rome's allies (cf. *BG* 2.14), but that is clearly a different matter. Dio 39.1.2 may rest on good evidence (Jullian iii. 247, McDougall, art. cit., 636–7): 'previously some had had alliances with the Romans, some had taken no thought for them at all.' **the most powerful Celtic tribe, occupying a third of the whole country.** This derives presumably from C. *BG* 1.1–3, 2.1.1. **a vast force of armed men:** C. *BG* 2.4.4–10 tells of a report C. received from the Remi, with the numbers each Belgic tribe had promised (not all of them will have materialized, and the Remi had no interest in playing down the danger): they total either 296,000 or 306,000. Strabo 4.4.3 gives the number of Belgae who can bear arms as 'about 300,000', presumably deriving from C. The numbers in the field were doubtless lower, but still considerable, as the size of the Belgic camp shows ('more than eight miles wide' (*BG* 2.7.3)).

20.5. Lakes and deep rivers ... choked ... with corpses: ultimately from C. *BG* 2.10.2–3, 'our troops attacked the enemy while they were hampered in mid-river. They killed a great number; when others most courageously tried to cross by trampling over the dead bodies, the Romans forced them back with a hail of missiles.' It seems to have been the source that made the Romans, not the Belgae, use the corpses as stepping-stones: cf. App. *Celt.* 1.4.10. The exaggeration of the single river Aisne to 'lakes and deep rivers' seems to be P.'s own. There is also some recasting of sequence: the 'rout' seems to refer to the massacre of the withdrawing Belgae (*BG* 2.11.4–6), after the river carnage.

20.6. the coastal tribes all submitted. P. is probably guessing at the geography, and getting it wrong (cf. 18.1, 26.1, 26.6 nn.). The Suessiones, Bellovaci, and Ambiani submitted (C. *BG* 2.12–15), but of these only the Ambiani were 'coastal'. Also important was the decision of the dangerous Treveri to support C. with cavalry (*BG* 2.24.4; cf. E. Mensching, *Lat.* 38 (1979), 902–31); they were not coastal either. The other maritime tribes mentioned at *BG* 2.4.5–10—Caletes, Morini, and Menapii—did not support the Nervii (2.16.2), but the Morini and Menapii clearly did not come to terms with C. either (*BG* 3.28.1, 6.5.4), and probably all three tribes stayed outside the conflict.

P. makes nothing of C.'s mercifulness in accepting these submissions: contrast C.'s own version, *BG* 2.14.4, 28.3, 31.3. Cf. above, p. 208 and 15.4 n.

20.6–10: THE CAMPAIGN AGAINST THE NERVII   Ultimately from C. *BG* 2.15–28, via the usual source (cf. App. *Celt.* fr. 1.4.11, very close to P.: cf. §7 n.). Dio 39.3 also seems to be erratically dependent on C. For the campaign, cf. Holmes, *CCG* 75–80; Jullian iii. 260–8; P. Turquin, *LEC* 23 (1955), 113–56; H. P. Kohns, *Gymn.* 76 (1969), 1–17; Goudineau 280–2; and my brief discussion in *Lat.* 40 (1981), 747–9. On C.'s narrative, see R. D. Brown, *CJ* 94 (1999), 332–42, J. E. Lendon, *ClassAnt* 18 (1999), 317–20, and Gerlinger 37–43, 81–2. This is often known as 'the battle of the Sambre', but that rests on a false fourteenth-century identification of C.'s river *Sabis* (M. Arnould, *RBPh* 20 (1941), 29–106, esp. 84–5, 91–5). That river is more likely to be the Selle, as Turquin thought (the Escaut is also a possibility). Turquin's elaborate discussion points to a site near Saulzoir for the battle.

P. concentrates on C.'s personal heroism: §8: the good general does not shy from danger (17.1 n.). To heighten the effect, the Roman plight needs to be critical. P. therefore obscures the successes won by the Roman left and centre (C. *BG* 2.23.4–5, 25.1, 26.1), and concentrates on the struggling right wing (§7). There is no interest in the final settlement, no praise of C.'s mercifulness: cf. §6 n., and contrast *BG* 2.28.3, 15.4 n.

Nervii: cf. Rives 236. **the fiercest and most warlike tribe of the region:** from C. *BG* 2.4.8, 15.4–5.

20.7. **in thick woods.**   There is a textual difficulty here, and I translate Madvig's conjecture *sunecheis*, suggesting woods that joined together to form a 'continuous' forest. But the corruption may go deeper. C.'s own account has nothing like this, but does mention that the Nervii now concealed themselves on wooded slopes, 2.18.2–3: it may be that P. too is here referring to their temporary military disposition rather than where they 'lived', and that we should read *katakeimenoi*, 'lying concealed', rather than *katōikēmenoi*, 'dwelling in'. See Pelling, 'Notes', 39–40. **hid their families and possessions deep in the forest:** C. *BG* 2.16.4, 'they had taken their women and those they thought too old to fight, and consigned them to a location where the marshes prevented our army from access …'; 2.28.1. These 'marshes' may have been those at Ostrevant, between the Escaut and the Selle close to Valenciennes and St Amand (Turquin, art. cit., 138–9); but that position is surprisingly to the flank rather than the rear of the Nervian position, and a location further north-east is also possible (Holmes, *CCG* 674–5).

Then a force of 60,000 men fell on Caesar . . . : App. *Celt.* fr. 1.4.11 is here very close to P.; both derive ultimately from C. *BG* 2.19–23, 28.2. For the cavalry rout, cf. *BG* 2.19.7; for the Nervian encircling, 2.23.5; for the plight of C.'s right wing, 2.23.4, 25.1; and for the stereotypically large numbers, 15.5 n. **killing all their centurions:** so also App. *Celt.* fr. 1.4.11, so this was the source's version; but it is based on a misreading or over-abbreviation of *BG* 2.25.1, 'all the centurions of the fourth cohort were cut down, their standard-bearer killed, and the standard lost, and almost all the centurions of the other cohorts were wounded or killed . . .'.

20.8. Caesar himself . . . grabbed his shield . . . and hurled himself into the enemy: *BG* 2.25, a spectacular sentence cataloguing all the things necessary in the crisis: 'so C. grabbed a shield from one of the rear rank (for he himself had gone there without a shield), went forward to the front line, called on the centurions by name and encouraged the rest of the soldiers, and ordered them to advance and break up their maniple formation, so that they could use their swords more easily. This brought hope to the soldiers and heartened them . . .'. P. avoids the complicating detail that it was another man's shield; he has to suppress the rallying of the centurions (he has already killed them all off, §7); and he makes C.'s example the important point, not his order to break formation.

P. revels in such stories: cf. 39.6–7, 56.2, *C.min.* 63.11, *Sulla* 21.3, etc. This one caught the imagination of others too: cf. Flor. 1.45.4, Val. Max. 3.2.19. They fit a conventional pattern of the general who leads from the front: Gerlinger 37–43.

the tenth legion . . . : cf. C. *BG* 2.26.3, App. *Celt.* fr. 1.4.11. The legion had been sent to C.'s aid by Labienus; P. prefers to give the impression of the legionaries' own response to the sight of their general in danger, and so makes C.'s tactic of 19.4–5 bear further fruit. The legion had earlier, along with the ninth, occupied the enemy's camp, which was on higher ground than the Roman position (*BG* 2.26.3); that is the basis for **from the surrounding hills.** P. does not mention another important factor, the intervention of two further legions, probably XIII and XIV, which only now arrived on the field (*BG* 2.19.3).

20.9. They had to cut them down as they continued the battle: *BG* 2.27.3–5. P. omits the striking detail of 2.27.3, the Nervii climbing on their comrades' corpses to continue the flight. It was too similar to §5.

20.10. Only 500 are said to have survived of 60,000 Nervii, and only 3 of their senators out of 400. C. *BG* 2.28.2 makes the Nervian envoys say that 'they had been reduced from 600 senators to 3, and from 60,000 to barely 500 who could bear arms'. P.'s '400' should not, however, be emended to bring it into line: cf. the similar divergences at 18.1, 19.11, and 27.4 (nn.). Whether or not P.'s **are said** suggests scepticism, the Nervian strength three years later (24.3 (n.)) suggests that either the envoys shrewdly exaggerated their losses or C. the hugeness of his victory: Holmes, *CCG* 205–6, Gerlinger 134–7.

P. omits the remaining fighting of 57, the suppression of the Aduatuci (*BG* 2.29–33) and the adventures of Ser. Galba (*BG* 3.1–6): contrast the less sensitive anticlimax of Dio 39.4–5.

21.1. voted: on the proposal of Cicero (*Prov. Cons.* 26, *Balb.* 61). For varying estimates of the vote's significance, see Gelzer 116; J. Lazenby, *Lat.* 18 (1959), 68–9. **a thanksgiving festival of fifteen days, more than had been decreed for any previous victory:** from C. *BG* 2.35.4 (almost identical phrasing). Since the Punic Wars, the normal length had been three days, sometimes five. Ten days had been granted to Pompey in 63; C. was later granted twenty days in 55 (22.4 n.) and 52; forty days were voted after Thapsus in 46 and fifty after Munda in 45. Cf. Weinstock 62–4.

Crass. 37(4).3 seems to refer to this thanksgiving, but it suits his rhetoric there to put it after the defeat of the Usipi and Tencteri (22.1–5 n.): far from giving C. up to the Germans as Cato urged, they voted him a thanksgiving instead.

21.2. This interpretative expansion is likely to be P.'s own, with its typical emphasis on the **affection of the ordinary people:** that prepares for the account of Luca, where the popular enthusiasm for C. is again an important factor in guiding the city's response (§9). The transition at §3—'*For* Caesar himself, too…'—suggests that there was more than spontaneous affection at play in making the victory so 'brilliant'.

21.3–9: THE CONFERENCE OF LUCA, APRIL 56 BCE   P. does not try to paint the shifting political relations that made it pressing for C. to patch up an arrangement with Crassus and Pompey. It all looked less good for C. than it had done in late 58 (20.1 n.). The street violence had intensified during 57, but in ways that C. might find less easy to turn to his own advantage: Milo's and Sestius' bands had emerged to challenge Clodius (cf. *Cic.* 33.4), but these were hired thugs rather than enthusiastic amateurs, and the agitatory possibilities of the urban plebs themselves might seem to be diminishing. Clodius himself remained a loose cannon, and had not lost all his strength of 58. He was elected on 20 January 56 as aedile for the year. More agitation followed, with a prosecution of Milo (interestingly, C.'s follower P. Vatinius appeared as a witness against Milo), and much accompanying violence; Clodius' attacks on Pompey were continuing too.

And Cicero was back. He had returned to Italy in August 57 and reached Rome on 4 September (*Cic.* 33, *Pomp.* 49.4–6, *C.min.* 40.1, cf. 20.1 n.); his silver tongue could do as much damage as Clodius' and Milo's clubs and fists. Cicero might protest in public that any talk of a rift between him and C. was exaggerated (*Sest.* 39, 41), and he may indeed have given undertakings not to undermine the big three (Cic. *Fam.* 1.9 (20).9, 12, cf. J. T. Ramsey, *CJC* 38), but the Sestius trial in March 56 offered him the chance for a viciously humiliating attack on C.'s friend Vatinius. More worrying still, by early April—too late to have inspired the meeting at Luca, but soon enough to have been discussed there—he was involving himself in attacks on C.'s agrarian legislation of 59, 'invading', as he later put it, 'the very citadel of that cause' (Cic. *Fam.* 1.9 (20).8). It may have been around now that the tribune L. Antistius attacked C., also presumably over his acts of 59 (Suet. 23.1, with E. Badian in *Polis and Imperium: Studies . . . E. T. Salmon* (1974), 145–66; *MRR* iii. 17). There was more than a hint that Pompey too was involved: the land issue had been raised at the end of 57 by the new tribune P. Rutilius Lupus (Cic. *Q.fr.* 2.1 (5).1), a man who at that time was apparently acting for Pompey or at least playing for his favour (*Fam.* 1.1 (12).2, 1.2 (13).2).

Pompey himself was certainly in difficulties. 'He is not the man he was', thought Cicero (*Q.fr.* 2.5 (9).3). True, in September 57 he had been voted his five-year *cura annonae*, with massive powers (*Pomp.* 49.6–7, 50). But he was still being bruised by Clodius; there were also signs of increasing hostility within the senate (cf. esp. Gruen, *Hist.* 18 (1969), 71–108); and Crassus too was thought, at least by Pompey himself, to be plotting against him (*Q.fr.* 2.3 (7).3–4). The burning issue of the moment was the jockeying for the lucrative commission to restore Ptolemy XII to Egypt. There was much speculation that it would fall to Pompey, as the King himself was said to want (*Pomp.* 49.9–13). Pompey prevaricated (Cic. *Fam.* 1.5b (16).2, *Q.fr.* 2.2 (6).3); if he did want the job, he had clearly not found it straightforward to get it. If there was one prospect less attractive to C. than a massively strong Pompey, it was that of an opposition to Pompey, senatorial or thuggish or both, who felt strong enough to face him down. If they could outmatch Pompey, they could outmatch C. too.

Finally there was the threat of a hostile consulship in 55 of L. Domitius Ahenobarbus, who was threatening to remove C. from his command. It was time to act. An arrangement with Pompey was the best option (though not necessarily the only one, §5 n.), especially as Pompey himself was feeling particularly insecure (cf. Cic. *Q.fr.* 2.3 (7).4) and might find a deal attractive. Crassus would not want to be left out (on one speculative view he even played a part in engineering the crisis: A. M. Ward, *LCM* 3 (1978), 156–7); nor would it be safe to exclude him. He would be a stabilizing force. Events after his death would confirm his value all too clearly.

Suet. 24.1 represents the prospect of Domitius' consulship as the crucial factor driving C. to negotiate. But, here and in *Pomp.* 51, P. is content to describe the dealing as a natural consequence of the court paid to C., a sign of his strength and success rather than of any political problems.

P. gives further versions at *Pomp.* 51.4–5, *Crass.* 14.6–15.1, and *C.min.* 41.1; he is again (cf. 20.1 n.) more indignant elsewhere, especially in *C.min.* ('this amounted to a conspiracy to share out the empire and destroy the constitution'). He draws his material from the usual source: cf. App. 2.17.61–3, Suet. 24.1. Dio omits the conference, though he must have known of it (cf. A. W. Lintott, *ANRW* ii. 34.3 (1997), 2512–13): that is probably for his own interpretative reasons (Pelling, 'Focalisation', 517).

Comparison with the other accounts reveals how much material P. has omitted or displaced. He does not here mention the full terms of the agreement, the soldiers C. sent to the Roman polls (§6 n.), or the secrecy of the talks: this last is an important point, for Cic. *Prov. Cons.* makes it clear that the plans for the 55 consulship could not have been known in June. The source seems to have had a political disquisition at this point (above, p. 204): some of this P. has already used at 20.2–3, most he delayed to ch. 28 (nn.). P. stresses the decisions that favoured C., and does not dwell on the provinces and armies that Pompey and Crassus will receive in return (§6 n.). Only the immediate political sequel is traced, the ineffectiveness of opposition and Favonius' fruitless protest, for that again—at the cost of some exaggeration (§7 n.)—illustrates P.'s popular theme: 'most were living in hopes of C., and it was to please him that they stayed so quiet.'

The stress on the relations of the three great men recalls the treatment of 60–59 (13.3 n.), and is again presumably owed to Pollio. This time his stress on their pact is less questionable, for the importance and exceptional nature of the Luca agreement should not be impugned. J. F. Lazenby, *Lat.* 18 (1959), 67–76, is here less convincing than Gruen 146–7 and in *Hist.* 18 (1969), 71–108, C. Luibheid, *CPh* 65 (1970), 88–94, and A. M. Ward, *AJAH* 5 (1980), 48–63. See also Seager 114–25; T. P. Wiseman in *CAH* ix² (1994), 391–5; Gelzer 120–8 and *Cicero* 167–72; Meier 265–73; Maier 51–5; and, for an alternative view of Cicero's politics in the months before Luca, T. N. Mitchell, *TAPA* 100 (1969), 295–320, and *Cicero: The Senior Statesman* (1991), 168–81.

21.4. Candidates for office...: apparently reflecting the same source as Suet. 23.2, quoted at 20.2–3 n. **paymaster:** the Greek is *chorēgos*, i.e. the wealthy individual who paid for a tragic or comic chorus: so also of C. at *Pomp.* 51.2 and *Ant.* 5.2. Perhaps we ought to translate as 'impresario', and find a hint not just of the financial backing but also of the way his creatures sang the tunes he wished, and of the showy spectacle of their public displays (cf. 5.9, where it is used for the 'theatrical performances' put on by C. himself). But the word is often used weakly for 'supply' or 'support', e.g. at 39.1 and 39.11, and the metaphor is probably deader than so strong a translation would suggest.

21.5. Luca: conveniently on the southern boundary of C.'s province, only 239 miles from Rome. At *Pomp.* 51.3, P. has C. spending the winter there: in fact he spent part of the time in Illyricum (C. *BG* 3.7.1), was in Aquileia on 3 March (*RDGE* 24A, p. 140), and had been in Ravenna a week or so before the Luca meeting. He came to Luca to meet Pompey, who was travelling to Sardinia and detoured to sail from a northern port.

C. had already had discussions at Ravenna with Crassus and with Appius (Cic. *Fam.* 1.9 (20).9, *Q.fr.* 2.5 (9).4), in Pompey's absence. It may be that C. was simply preparing the ground, as both men had recently been at odds with Pompey; or it may be that other constellations were being explored—Appius' senatorial connections, his brother Clodius, and Crassus could themselves add up to a formidable alliance. But a deal with Pompey was always the most likely option.

Pompey and Crassus...   The Greek phrasing, like the punctuation in this translation, ties the pair closely together as a separate and significant subgroup within the list. Pompey reached Luca a few days after 8 April: Gelzer 121. C. and Crassus had already met at Ravenna (see previous note), but, *pace* J. Jackson, *LCM* 3 (1978), 175-7, and Seager 123, there is no reason to doubt that he was at Luca as well: so also Suet. 24.1. It would be most odd if Crassus, however bad his previous relations with Pompey, had relied on C. to protect his interests in such sensitive and unpredictable negotiations.

Appius Claudius Pulcher, brother and usually supporter of Clodius, had been praetor in 57; he governed **Sardinia** from 56 to 55, was consul in 54, then was Cicero's predecessor as governor of Cilicia in 53-51. He took Pompey's side in the civil war, and died before Pharsalus. For speculation on his role, now see J. Ramsey, *CJC* 42 and 53 n. 4. Q. Caecilius Metellus **Nepos**, another kinsman of Clodius, was the tribune of 62 whose Pompeian demagogy is strongly stigmatized in *C.min.* 20.8, 26.2-29.4. He was consul in 57, governed Further **Spain** in 56-55, and died soon afterwards. P. seems to introduce him, like Appius, as a familiar figure, but it need not follow that he is assuming his reader's knowledge of other *Lives*: cf. 7.5 n.

The sonorous names underline C.'s current stature; they might also have led P. to doubt the adequacy of his simple 'popular' analysis of C.'s support. Men of this stature and blood were not going to be anyone's tools. Even their support of their kinsman Clodius during 57 had been qualified, and Metellus in particular had abandoned him over Cicero's recall. Now bargains may well have been struck: Clodius dramatically changed his tune, and began supporting Pompey warmly (Cic. *Har. Resp.* 50-52, Dio 39.29); and this may have been the context when Appius' daughter was betrothed to Pompey's son (thus W. J. Tatum, *Klio*, 73 (1991), 122-9). But any deals would not bind either Appius or Metellus to unquestioned adherence. When Appius was consul in 54, his support of the big three was decidedly qualified: see Gruen, art. cit., 102-3 (unnecessarily assuming an opportunist drift away from the 'dynasts' at that point).

Appius had seen C. at Ravenna (above); like Crassus, he may have been at Luca too—but, if P. is conflating events at Luca with those elsewhere (see next note), it may be that he and/or Metellus had merely seen C. there, and not followed on to Luca.

120 lictors...and more than 200 senators: clearly from the source, who liked numbers (above, p. 204): cf. *Pomp.* 51.4, App. 2.17.62. The figure is not incredible. Pompey, Caesar, and Metellus between them would be entitled to thirty-six fasces; Appius perhaps a further twelve, if he governed Sardinia as proconsul; and any *legati pro praetore*, such as Labienus, would have added more. For speculation on who the other visitors might have been, see L. Hayne, *CPh* 69 (1974), 217–20, and Ward, art. cit., 52–5. Still, it is not likely that all these were present *at Luca*. App. 2.17.62 says that this great number of lictors and senators were present 'at some time' during the winter, but does not specify when or where. That 'at some time' is probably intended to mean 'at one (specific) time', but the figure may still represent the *total* of C.'s winter visitors, in Ravenna, Luca, or anywhere else, rather than the number with him at any one point: so also Ward, art. cit., 51. Presumably most had left C. before the three great men conferred, though P. chooses to obscure this in §6 (see next n.).

21.6. council: the word is the same as for the 'senate' at Rome, and is used in the second sense only a few lines later in §7. After a mention of so many 'senators', the effect is to suggest that 'they'—notice the skilful vagueness—were having their own unofficial senate-meeting at Luca, so powerful has C. become. But *Crass.* 14.6 shows that P. envisaged this as a private meeting of C., Pompey, and Crassus; *Pomp.* 51.5 also suggests that the senators left before this meeting. The decisions remained secret for some time (*Crass.* 15.2–3, *Pomp.* 51.6–8), and Cicero at least, despite the pressure put on him (see next n.), seems to have been unclear about their precise plans.

and agreed terms: P. simplifies, omitting details that he knew. C. was to aid the canvass of Pompey and Crassus by sending troops to the polls (*Pomp.* 51.5, *Crass.* 14.7): that would not fit here, where the people's support does not need to rest on intimidation. Once consuls, Pompey and Crassus were to secure large provinces with armies (*Pomp.* 51.5, *C.min.* 41.1, *Crass.* 14.6): those can be left till later (28.1 and 28.8 nn.), and so can the two legions that Pompey was to lend C. for Gaul (25.2, 29.4, cf. *Pomp.* 52.4).

Nor, naturally enough in so selective a treatment, does P. trace through the events in Rome that followed. Cicero was cowed (Pompey's words were blunt, *Fam.* 1.9 (20).9): that generated the eloquent praise of C. given, even if through clenched teeth, in his *Prov. Cons.* of (probably) June 56. The issue of the 59 land law (above, p. 242) was quietly dropped. The consular election campaign was violent, and the vote could not be held until January 55 (*Pomp.* 51.6–52.3, *Crass.* 15.1–7, *C.min.* 41.3–42.1, App. 2.17.64). The consulship itself was violent too. C.'s province was finally conferred by the *lex Licinia Pompeia* (see below), while the *lex Trebonia* gave Syria to Crassus and the two Spanish provinces to Pompey (*Pomp.* 52.4, fusing the *lex Trebonia* with the *lex Licinia Pompeia*, *Crass.* 15.7, and, erratically, *C.min.* 43.1–7),

Once the Syrian command had been agreed, C. wrote to congratulate Crassus and to urge him on to conquest. P. mentions that at *Crass.* 16.2, but it would involve too much sidetracking to include it here. It would also raise questions about C.'s motivation: was he *playing* for a Crassus disaster, in which case the moral issue would be problematic? Or was he just being comradely, which would not fit the shrewd politician?

money: §7 n. **an extension of his command:** eventually granted by the *lex Licinia Pompeia* (*MRR* 215), passed probably in the second half of 55 (Stevens, *Lat.* 12 (1953), 16). This *lex* included Transalpine Gaul, whereas the *lex Vatinia* had not: thus there was no need this time to rely on senatorial goodwill, and both Transalpine and Cisalpine Gaul were secure in C.'s hands for the five-year period (14.10 n.). **five years:** so App. 2.17.63,18.65 as well as P.'s other versions, but Dio 39.33.3 says that this law prolonged C.'s tenure for '*three* more years, on a precise count'. He presumably noted that C. still had two years to run of his original five (14.10 n.), so that a five-year grant at this stage gave him an *extra* three years.

The law's other terms become important in 50, and are discussed at 29.1 n.

21.7. That was what seemed most paradoxical to intelligent observers: for P.'s habit of conveying comment by reconstructing observers' response, see Intr., p. 25. **were now urging the senate to vote him money.** This apparently refers to the senate's grant of pay for the additional four legions, over and above the four authorized by the *lex Vatinia*, which C. had levied since 58. It seems that C. sought this grant before March 56, if these are the 'monstrous proposals concerning C.' to which Cicero refers at *Q.fr.* 2.5 (9).3. Despite the monstrosity, Cicero was instrumental in persuading the senate to agree to this later in the spring (*Prov. Cons.* 28, *Balb.* 61)—presumably after Luca, but before the debate on the consular provinces in (?) June. At the same time they voted 'ten *legati*', as C. had asked. These were presumably ten lieutenants of his choice, rather than the 'commission of ten' to organize a new province, as Dio 39.25.1 thought, for C. had no interest in representing the war as over. See Gelzer 123–4; J. P. V. D. Balsdon, *JRS* 52 (1962), 137–9.

A really 'intelligent observer' might not have found this so 'paradoxical'. The vote of pay was valuable not so much for the money, more for the retrospective recognition of C.'s levies.

it was a matter of compelling. The other *Lives* portray the senate as less helpless, with a real chance that the senatorial conservatives might foil the plans of the big three: *Pomp.* 52.2, *C.min.* 41.4–6, *Crass.* 15.5–6. That reading is the better one: cf. §§8–9 nn., Gruen 147 and *Hist.* 18 (1969), 96–108.

21.8. Cato was not there. Cato returned from Cyprus in 56 (*C.min.* 39.5), probably in spring or early summer (S. I. Oost, *CPh* 50 (1955), 107–8), but P. may well be right that he was not there in time for the debate on the legions' pay. He probably arrived soon afterwards: the 'man of the utmost authority and eloquence' of Cic. *Prov. Cons.* 45 is best taken to be Cato (*pace* Gelzer, *Cicero* 172: cf. *Cic.* 34.2–3, *C.min.* 40.2–4), and in that case he was presumably back in time for the debate on the consular provinces in (?) June. **they had deliberately spirited him away to Cyprus:** in 58 (20.1 n.), though P.'s language here would more naturally suggest a tactic to safeguard this particular legislation (Intr., p. 57). For Cato's mission, cf. *C.min.* 34–40; S. I. Oost, *CPh* 50 (1955), 98–112; E. Badian, *JRS* 55 (1965), 110–21.

M. Favonius was quaestor before 59, aedile 53, praetor 49; active for the Pompeians in the Civil War; executed after Philippi. His **fervent** admiration for Cato was consistent, fanatical, and may not have been limited to Cato's mind: at *Brut.* 12.3 and 34.4 P. calls him 'Cato's lover' (*erastēs*). Despite P.'s sympathy for Cato and Republican causes, he disapproved of Favonius' tactlessness and outspokenness: cf. the criticisms at 41.3, 'affecting the outspoken style of Cato like a madman', *C.min.* 46.1, *Brut.* 34.4–5, *Pomp.* 60.7, 67.5; more sympathy at *Pomp.* 73.9–11. For a rare hint of moderation, see *Brut.* 12.2–3: 'worse than a lawless monarchy is civil war.'

Here Favonius emerges as naive, not realizing the degree to which the people were in C.'s hand. P. overplays this analysis here: there was an interesting streak of populism in Cato too (14.8 n.), something to which Dio, for instance, is sensitive (cf. esp. 37.22.3, 39.39.1, 43.11.6), and Favonius' attempt to stir popular support was not hopeless. Something of that emerges at *Pomp.* 52.2–3, where Pompey's supporters fear that Cato may mobilize the people against him in the consular elections, and the people are then on the point of electing Cato praetor; and especially in *C.min.* 42–4, stressing popular enthusiasm and demonstrations for Cato. In *Caes.* P. leaves the political picture much simpler. Cf. Intr., pp. 59–60, 63.

21.9. people's respect for Pompey and Crassus... in hopes of Caesar: neatly completing the ring with 20.2–3, though now there is an implied contrast between C. and the other two. Pompey and Crassus are here almost elder statesmen, the objects of 'respect'; other *Lives* bring out that they were playing the people as carefully, if not as skilfully, as C. himself. This requires some adjustment of the earlier emphases of *Caes.* (the Pompey of 14.5 was not a man to win respect) and some oversimplification of the political realities. *Pomp.* 52, *Crass.* 15, and *C.min.* 41–3 dwell on the disreputable violence and bribery used by Crassus and particularly Pompey in 56–55, first to get themselves elected and then to drive through their programme once in office.

22.1–5: THE USIPI AND TENCTERI CAMPAIGN, 55 BCE P. passes over the campaigns of 56 (C. *BG* 3.7–29)—D. Brutus' naval victory over the Veneti, Titurius Sabinus' conquest of the Venelli, P. Crassus' successes in Aquitania, C.'s own abortive campaign in the north. His source probably treated at least one of these themes (App. *Celt.* fr. 17a, a garbled version of an episode from the Veneti campaign: the garbling may be App.'s own or his epitomator's). But most of the action was conducted by C.'s lieutenants rather than C. himself, who is notably inconspicuous in *BG* 3. P. hurries instead to the Usipi and Tencteri campaign a year later, allowing the story of Cato's partisan proposal, §4, to echo 21.8–9, the bitter but ineffectual opposition of the optimates.

For this campaign, cf. esp. C. *BG* 4.1–15. Dio 39.47–8 is largely, probably wholly, dependent on C.'s account. App. *Celt.* fr. 18 is very close to P., even including the same quotations (though App. leaves Tanusius unnamed: 'one writer says . . .'). Both are presumably deriving closely from the shared source, and the quotations too will be drawn second-hand from there. The Tanusius citation is at first sight unnecessary: at *C.min.* 51 and *Crass.* 37(4).2 the item is mentioned without supporting evidence, and it is indeed unquestioned that Cato made the proposal. But the mirroring quotations still intimate that there was *some* partisan dispute here, with different authors leaving different impressions; they also convey an authorial persona of learning and judiciousness, especially as P. here leaves open the rights and wrongs of the issue. Contrast *Alex.* 59.6–7, where he leaves no doubt of Alexander's faithlessness in a similar instance.

For compositional reasons, *C.min.* 51 shifts the whole debate to a later context: cf. *Plutarch and History*, 92. There P. adds the political sequel: C.'s next letter to the senate included a vicious attack on Cato, who replied with a denunciation of C.'s ambitions; these charges were 'true'; C.'s friends stood dismayed. That would disturb the picture of humbled and frustrated optimates, and could not be included here. Nor would so unambiguous a stress on C.'s ambitions suit the texture of *Caes.*

For the campaign, cf. esp. Holmes, *CCG* 95–9 and 691–706; Jullian iii. 323–30; A. Grisart, *LEC* 28 (1960), 169–71; in *Lat.* 40 (1981), 749–51, I briefly discuss the topography, and C.'s simplification of it in *BG*. For Cato's proposal, cf. M. Gelzer, *Festgabe . . . P. Kirn* (Berlin 1961), 46–53.

22.1. Two large German tribes had just crossed the Rhine to occupy new territory: some time before the end of winter 56–55, according to C., after wandering for three years (*BG* 4.1.1–2, 4.1, 6.1). P., like C. in *BG*, continues the themes developed during the campaigns of 58: C. is taking action against an invasion of a migrant horde (cf. 18.1, 19.1), presumably again *on behalf of* the Gauls (cf. 19.1), with the Rhine envisaged as a firm boundary dividing Gauls from Germans (15.1, 19.1 nn.). **crossed the Rhine:** 'not far from the sea' (*BG* 4.1.1), in the territory of the Menapii (*BG* 4.4): perhaps near Kleve (Holmes, *CCG* 689–90). **Usipi** (C. calls them 'Usipetes', but most imperial writers prefer 'Usipi') . . . **Tencteri:** on these two neighbouring tribes, often linked together in the sources, cf. Rives 252–4, doubting whether they were 'German' in any real sense.

22.2. Caesar's own version of the battle with these tribes is given in his journal: i.e. at *BG* 4.11–13. App. too here (*Celt.* fr. 18.3, see above) refers to the *BG* as a 'journal', literally a 'day-by-day account' or 'diary' (A. Samuel, *Hist.* 14 (1965), 1–3), which like *commentarii* can be contrasted with a polished history (Gell. 5.18.7 = Sempronius Asellio fr. 1 P.). The same title is used of the calendar of Alexander's final days, *Alex.* 76.1, 77.1. Some Latin authors too use this title for C.'s commentaries, and it is also found in several MSS of C.'s text: cf. Symm. *Ep.* 4.18.5 and the muddled Serv. *Aen.* 11.743; J. Rüpke, *Gymn.* 99 (1992), 202. It is not inappropriate for a type of writing that affected an impression of collecting material in 'a simple paratactic structure... with items arranged like beads on a string' (Riggsby 137–8), perhaps creating 'the illusion [of] a write-as-you-go basis without redaction' (Riggsby 155). For a similar shared, and therefore probably second-hand, quotation from C., cf. 44.8 (n.). **He claims that the barbarians were negotiating with him:** *BG* 4.11, claiming that the German envoys had requested a three-day truce to enable them to send negotiators to the Ubii; C. refused, thinking that they were buying time to allow their cavalry to return (§5 n.). He did, however, promise to delay his advance, and invited them to come again the next day in 'the largest possible numbers'. Then the German attack came 'when the Romans were off their guard, given that the envoys had only just left and that this day had been requested by them as a truce' (4.12.1—not quite saying that this 'day' had been designated by C. himself as a 'truce'). C. refused all further dealings with people 'who had deceitfully asked for peace and then made war' (*BG* 4.13.1: that phrasing again glosses over the fact that C. had *refused* the German request). **during a truce** here simplifies, but is doubtless the impression that C.'s evasive language was designed to create. (On C.'s narrative technique in this passage, see also Rambaud 118–22; Gerlinger 278–82; A. Powell in *JCAR*, 124–8.) **5,000 ... 800:** thus *BG* 4.12.1.

22.3. a second deputation to him on a further mission of deceit: or so C. claimed, *BG* 4.13.1, 'early the next morning the Germans, employing the same faithlessness and deceit, came to him in large numbers together with all their leading and senior figures...'. This is the further visit that C. himself had requested, §2 n. **he thought it simple-minded...:** cf. *BG* 4.13.2, C. 'judged it sheer madness to wait for the enemy forces to build up and their cavalry to return': P. prefers the more general and less tactical formulation **to keep faith with this sort of faithless treaty-breakers**, echoing the emphasis on **bizarre and faithless characters** at 15.4 (n.).

22.4.   For the historian **Tanusius** Geminus, see Peter, *HRR* ii. 49–51 and pp. lxv–vi. An anti-Caesarian stance is normally inferred from this passage and from Suet. 9.2, where we discover that he implicated C. in the 'first Catilinarian conspiracy' (5.9 n.); but very little is really known about him or his work. **a thanksgiving:** this time, twenty days (21.1 n.). The vote came at the end of the year, after the crossing of the Rhine and the first British expedition (*BG* 4.38.5); but this was the better place to put it, where Cato's alternative proposal could be brought in most conveniently. **for the victory:** skilful narrative speed, as §3 did not get as far as the fighting itself. For the battle, cf. *BG* 4.14–15. C.'s account simplifies the topography, but it was probably fought close to Goch or Kleve (*Lat.* 40 (1981), 749–51).

Cato proposed that Caesar should be handed over to the enemy: the traditional vindication of Roman good faith when a breach of international justice (*ius gentium*) was admitted. There had been famous instances in 321–20 and 136–5 (*Gracch.* 7 and the other texts cited at *MRR* i. 150–1, 484), in each case conveniently allowing Rome to repudiate a peace agreement made in the field; and *Cam.* 17–18 and Livy 5.36.8–9 have a version (doubtless based on the retrojection of later events) that the Gauls made similar demands after a breach of ambassadorial propriety in 391. For the present instance, cf. Suet. 24.3 (above, 15.2–5 n.): such was C.'s unprovoked aggression 'that the senate at one point resolved to send a commission to investigate the situation in Gaul' (we know nothing else about that, and *pace* Maier 63 it need not have been at the same time as Cato's proposal) 'and some proposed surrendering him to the enemy'. Evidently unfavourable reports were reaching Rome, and C. did not have total control of the flow of information (E. Mensching, *Hermes*, 112 (1984), 53–5). The same impression is left by C.'s evasive language (§2 n.): he could not pretend that the 'truce' issue had not arisen at all. But it is not likely that such a prosecution could have succeeded: R. Morstein-Marx, *Hist.* 56 (2007), 161.

The incident took place some time at the end of 55 (above, on 'thanksgiving'). It may (so Gelzer, *Festgabe Kirn*, 52–3 and *Cicero*, 185) or may not be identical with some 'altercations in the senate' that Cicero was glad to miss, as he would have had 'either to back a

proposal he did not like or let down someone he ought to support'
(*Att.* 4.13 (87). 1). *C.min.* 51.3 expands Cato's argument into a brief
speech.

22.5. 400,000 . . . were killed. C. *BG* 4.15.3 has the enemy numbering 430,000, and gives the impression that very few escaped. (Oros.
6.8.23 has 440,000, probably deriving from a corrupt text of C.: see
18.1 n. with n. 7.) App. *Celt.* twice gives 400,000 dead (1.4.12 and
18.1), and this was doubtless the version in the shared source; but at
C.min. 51.1 and *Crass.* 37(4).2 P. says '300,000'. This will be no more
than a slip, probably a misremembering when P. was composing
without his source open in front of him (Intr., p. 41; *Plutarch and
History*, 21–2). Gelzer is wrong to give the 300,000 figure any authority (*Festgabe Kirn*, 49 n. 19). Both 300,000 and 400,000 are favourite
round numbers, and as usual may be wild exaggerations (cf. 15.5 n.,
Gerlinger 108–11), but we have nothing to put in their place. **only a
very few crossed back:** the cavalry band that had been despatched a
few days before the battle (*BG* 4.9.3, 16.3). **Sugambri:** an important
Rhineland tribe who dwelt near the modern Cologne. They were still
acting together with the Usipi and Tencteri in 17 BCE, when a
combined force defeated the Roman governor M. Lollius (Dio
54.20.4–6); that suggests that the Usipi and Tencteri were less
wiped out than C. and P. here imply.

22.6–23.1: C. CROSSES THE RHINE, 55 BCE P.'s material
comes ultimately from *BG* 4.16–19, transmitted by the usual source
(cf. App. *Celt.* fr. 1.5.13, Suet. 25.2). C. himself had given a strategic
and political justification, especially the desire to deter the Germans
from further aggression and convince them that 'a Roman army
could and would dare to cross the Rhine' (4.16.2). It was apparently
Pollio who introduced the stress on C.'s ambition to be 'the first man
ever to cross the Rhine with an army' (§6; App., Suet., and Dio 39.48.4
and 50.1 have similar emphases): that reading is true enough to the
realities of Roman political ambitions, where such 'firsts' could be a
claim to overwhelming glory (cf. *ILLRP* 319, C. Duillius as 'the first
consul to conduct a naval action and the first to construct a fleet' in
260 BCE). Pollio also added a relevant item on the Rhine's current (§6
n.). In some moods P. might have reservations about such hazardous
glory-hunting (cf. esp. *Ag.–Cl.* 1–2), but not here: this is the point
where C. moves on to begin his conquest, not merely of human
enemies, but of nature itself. Cf. 23.2; Clarke 32. This river-crossing

24: THE REVOLT OF AMBIORIX, AUTUMN 54   P. has dismissed
the British campaigns briefly, and will shortly pass over the summer
of 53 in silence (25.2 n.); the greater scale here might seem surprising.
But the British disappointments (23.4 n.) mark a turning point. The
tale is no longer of spectacular advance, breaking the bounds of the
world; the theme is now the sequence of critical perils that will
culminate with Vercingetorix, but it would be too harsh a contrast
to move to that climax immediately. Ambiorix usefully prepares
the way.

The material comes ultimately from C. *BG* 5.24–8, derived through
the usual source (cf. App. *Celt.* fr. 20, *BC* 2.150.630, Suet. 25.2). Dio
40.4–11 depends on C.'s account. P. simplifies (nn.), concentrating on
C.'s own part in it all: thus the relieving operation is given the space,
and P. sacrifices the more dramatic earlier events—the argument of
Cotta and Sabinus, the troops' suicide, the brave resilience of Q.
Cicero, the epic competition in valour of the centurions Pullo and
Vorenus, the difficulty of getting messages through (*BG* 5.28–31, 37.6,
40.7, etc., 44, 45.1–4, 48). The interest lies in C. as general, not in
anything more personal: C. had reacted to the disaster by swearing
that he would not cut his hair or shave his beard until he had taken
vengeance (Suet. 67.2, Polyaenus 8.23.3). P. probably knew that, but
as at 23.5–7 (n.) an emphasis on C.'s personal response to grief would
be discordant. Cf. Intr., p. 20.

For the campaigns, cf. Holmes, *CCG* 103–20, 371–84, and 726–31;
Jullian iii. 365–95; A. Grisart, *LEC* 28 (1960), 171–5 and 188–93.

24.1. Caesar's forces were now so large.   C. had commanded eight
legions since early 57 (*BG* 1.7.2, 1.10.3, 2.2.1, 2.8.5), and he had
recently levied a further one (5.24.4): see Brunt, *Manpower*, 466–7.
But C.'s own list of the present dispositions seems to give a total of
only eight legions and five cohorts at this point (5.24), and that also
coheres with the implications of 6.1.4, 32.6–33.3, and 44.3. Presumably five cohorts of one veteran legion had been redistributed among
the others. Auxiliaries are to be added to the total. For his numbers
later, cf. 25.2, 32.1 nn. **that he had to divide them.** The year's bad
harvest was crucial (*BG* 5.24.1): the burden of supporting so large a
force had therefore to be spread over a larger area than in previous
years.

He himself returned as usual to Italy. Wrong: he did not, though
Titurius Sabinus thought that he had (*BG* 5.29.2). C. in fact kept to his

decision to winter in Gaul (5.24.8), probably at Samarobriva (Amiens). Dio 40.9.1 shares the mistake, which may derive from an over-swift reading of 5.29.2.

24.2–3. Ambiorix: king of one half of the Eburones' territory (C. *BG* 5.24.4, 6.31.5). L. Aurunculeius **Cotta** and Q. **Titurius** Sabinus were C.'s legates probably from 58 and certainly from 57. For their disaster, cf. *BG* 5.26–37. Their camp had been at Aduatuca, which may be Limbourg: so Grisart, *LEC* 28 (1960), 188–91. **these destroyed Cotta and Titurius ... then surrounded and besieged the single legion of Cicero:** a simplification. It was the Eburones alone who massacred the force of Cotta and Sabinus; they were then only a part of the 60,000 who attacked Cicero (*BG* 5.38–9, 49.1). Nor is there any suggestion that the second force was under Ambiorix's command.

24.3. Cicero. P. might have made himself clearer, for this is not the orator but his brother Quintus, who had joined C. as legate in 54 (*MRR* 226). To avoid repeating the confusion he reintroduces Marcus as 'the orator Cicero' at 31.1.

Quintus was clearly allowed to choose which winter quarters to command (Cic. *Att.* 4.19 (93).2). The site of his camp is quite uncertain: perhaps Brussels (Grisart, *LEC* 28 (1960), 173–4). For the siege, cf. *BG* 5.39–52. **60,000 men:** so *BG* 5.49.1. **Every one of Cicero's men was wounded:** mild exaggeration: when C. arrived 'he discovered that not one man in ten was left without a wound' (*BG* 5.52.2).

24.4. 7,000 men: from *BG* 5.49.7; and for C.'s swift relieving march (from Samarobriva, §1 n.?), cf. 5.46–8.

24.6–7. For the engagement, cf. *BG* 5.49–52. **there he fortified his camp.** P. again simplifies. C. *first* pitched his camp; *then*, next day, a cavalry battle was fought, and C. 'deliberately ordered his cavalry to retreat into the camp' (5.50.4); in order to reinforce the impression of terror, he told his men to strengthen the fortifications. But it was the same camp as the day before, and P.'s sequence is misleading. **His strategy was to win contempt:** from *BG* 5.49.7, where C. makes his camp as small as possible 'in order to produce the utmost contempt amongst the enemy'; then at 5.51.3 the Gauls are so 'contemptuous' that they try to tear down the earthworks by hand.

24.7. they attacked in a random and uncoordinated way: a rather over-simple summary of *BG* 5.51.1–3.

25.1–2: THE WINTER OF 54–53, AND POMPEY'S LOAN OF
TROOPS   P. is hurrying on and will shortly omit all the events of
summer 53 (§2n.), but he still finds room for Pompey's loan. This is
its chronological place (cf. C. *BG* 6.1), but it still sits uncomfortably
here: it interrupts the sequence of revolts, and nothing is made of it in
the subsequent Gallic account. But at 29.4 these troops will become
crucial in the political crisis of 50–49 BCE, and it would be disruptive
to that tight narrative to introduce a flashback explanation there.

A few words may have dropped out of the Greek here (Pelling,
'Notes', 42–3), but the general sense is clear.

**25.1. Caesar himself made sure of that, making his way everywhere
during the winter (of 54/3):**   at *BG* 5.53–4 C. writes of the atmosphere of persistent unrest and at 6.3.1 he mentions his swift march to
quell the Nervii 'before the end of winter'; but the most important
winter victory was not one of 'Caesar himself', but Labienus' defeat of
Indutiomarus and the Treveri (5.55–8). **making his way everywhere**
may anticipate some of C.'s own campaigns of *summer* 53: see §2 n.

25.2. the arrival from Italy of three legions.   Cf. *BG* 6.1, but P.
probably knew of this through his usual source (cf. App. 2.29.115).
These three legions were XIV (*BG* 6.32.5), replacing the legion of the
same numeration lost with Cotta and Sabinus; XV (*BG* 8.24.3, 54.3);
and I, lent by Pompey (*BG* 8.54.2, *BC* 3.88.2). Here and at *Pomp.* 52.4
(but not *C.min.* 45.5, where his Cato speaks of a loan of only one
legion), P. is wrong to say that **two** rather than one **were lent by
Pompey.** The error presumably springs from the manœuvrings of 50
BCE (29.4 n.), when the senate decreed that Pompey and C. should
each give one legion for a Parthian War, and C. was asked to return
Pompey's legion along with one of his own (*BG* 8.54). He sent I and
XV, and Pompey retained both in Italy. The error is probably P.'s
own, as App. 2.29.115 gets it right.

P. here omits the events of summer 53 (C. *BG* 6), unless that
'everywhere' (§1 n.) vaguely fuses them with the preceding winter:
the swift campaigns against Senones, Carnutes, and Menapii (6.3–6,
but too uneventful); Labienus' victory over the Treveri (6.7–8, but not
C.'s own); the second Rhine crossing (6.9–19, spectacular but too
similar to the first); the second attack on Aduatuca (6.35–41, again
too similar to the events of ch. 24); the pursuit of Ambiorix (6.29–35,

42-4, exciting but hard to abbreviate and eventually fruitless). He hurries to the climax: Vercingetorix.

25.3-27: THE GREAT GALLIC UPRISING, 52 BCE   P. like C. calls this a 'revolt' (25.5); for the inappropriateness of the word, cf. above, p. 219.

Most of the material comes from C. *BG* 7, probably transmitted as usual by Pollio, who clearly treated the story in some detail (App. *Celt.* fr. 21 with M. Gelzer, *R-E* VIIIa (1955), 991). Dio 40.33-41 is largely (but not wholly, 27.8-10 n.) an intelligent rewriting of C.'s own account. Flor. 1.45.20-6 muddles Gergovia and Alesia (the Budé editor P. Jal generously assumes the fault is his copyist's rather than his own, i (1967), 166-7), but he seems to be using the same material as App. and P.; it may have reached him via Livy. P.'s account of Alesia itself has several non-Caesarian items (27.5-6, 9-10 nn.), which also seem to come from Pollio (cf. Flor. 1.45.26). But the 'small sword' item of 26.8 seems different: 'the Arverni still display' it, and P. probably incorporated this from his general knowledge rather than from a written source. It may well be based on oral tradition: see n.

Everything builds to the climax of Alesia, and earlier detail is cut down: there is no mention of Avaricum or Gergovia or Labienus' campaigns in the north (*BG* 7.13-28, 34-53, 57-62). Misleading conflation adds force and speed (26.3-4 n.). The battle of 26.7-8 is included (indeed exaggerated, n.), as that explains the siege. Otherwise P. prefers the powerfully phrased generalizations of 25.3-4, developed imaginatively from a bare hint at *BG* 7.8.2 (n.). The range and organization of Vercingetorix's operations are exaggerated (26.1 n.); the siege narrative is also streamlined by chronological distortion (27.5-7, 8 nn.). The result is historically wild but artistically powerful, with some hints of epic (26.2, 27.5-10 nn.): and Vercingetorix's proud final display brings the Gallic narrative to a fitting conclusion.

There is a large modern bibliography: see the catalogues in J. Harmand, *Une campagne césarienne: Alesia* (Paris, 1967), pp. xiii-xxii, and Gesche 268-73 for works up to that point, and J. Le Gall, *La Bataille d'Alésia* (1999), for an update. For a sophisticated treatment of the archaeological perspective, see A. Duval in J. Collis, A. Duval, and R. Périchon (eds), *Le Deuxième Age du Fer en Auvergne et en Forez* (1982), 298-335, esp. 323-7, and more popularly in *Archéologia*, 163 (Feb. 1992), 6-23. The archaeological evidence for the Alesia siege is particularly extensive: see esp. Le Gall, *Alésia*; also Harmand, *Alesia* (though he is sometimes over-sceptical), for the position as it was in 1967, and his *Vercingétorix* (Paris, 1984). Much has been established by recent excavations and especially by aerial photography: see esp. M. Reddé et al., *Ber. d. röm.-germ. Komm. des Deutschen Arch. Instituts*, 76 (1995), 73–158, and more recent developments can be traced in Reddé's contributions to M. Reddé and S. von Schnurbein (eds), *Alésia: Fouilles et recherches franco-allemandes sur les travaux militaires romains autour de Mont Auxois (1991–1997)* (2001), 489–506, and to M. Reddé (ed.), *Alésia et la bataille du Teutoburg: Un parallèle critique des sources* (2008), 277–89. Another contribution of Reddé to the second collection (153–63) gives a fascinating account of the fierce controversies the various identifications have aroused. Further convenient archaeological surveys are given by J. Bénard and S. Sievers in M. Reddé (ed.), *L'Armée romaine en Gaule* (1996), 40–80: in particular, these authors and Reddé in his contribution to the 2008 collection bring out the implications of the archaeological finds for our interpretation of *BG* (pp. 51, 56, 59–60, 63), and it emerges that, as usual (cf. *Lat.* 40 (1981), 741–66), C. has simplified drastically. Cf. Gerlinger 94–104, arguing that C.'s detailed presentation is 'unbelievably systematic' when compared with the archaeological data: C. 'proceeds very cleverly, without needing any direct lies' (100). Goudineau 202–12 and esp. 287–305 has some good remarks on the campaign; still useful too are Jullian iii. 418–535 and *Vercingétorix* (1901), Holmes, *CCG* 129–83 and 736–824, and M. Gelzer, *R-E* VIIIa (1955), 981–1008 and 2418–19. Thevenot has some helpful topographical material. For the important numismatic evidence, see J.-B. Colbert de Beaulieu, *Ogam* 8 (1956), 11–36, *Mélanges . . . A. Piganiol*, i (1966), 321–42, and *Hommages . . . J. Carcopino* (1977), 39–46, with Duval, art. cit., 323–4 and 331 n. 42.

25.3. far away: i.e. from Northern Gaul, 'the area' of 25.1. **the most powerful individuals:** 'the first men of Gaul', C. *BG* 7.1.4. **vast sums of money had been collected:** not mentioned in *BG*, and this is probably P.'s guess (presumably a good one).

25.4.   P. here generalizes some much more specific material, ultimately derived from *BG* 7.8.2 on crossing the Cevennes (cf. 26.3–4 n.): 'the Cevennes mountains . . . hampered his route, for it was the most difficult time of year and the snows were at their deepest; but thanks to his men's immense exertions the snows were cleared to a depth of six feet and the path was opened, and he reached the land of the Arverni.' P.'s source doubtless made much of these difficulties (cf. Flor. 1.45.22), but much of this detail—the **rivers which were frozen, the plains turned into lakes, the paths . . . submerged by marshes and overflowing torrents**—is imaginative expansion, probably P.'s own.

25.5. Many peoples had joined the revolt. At *BG* 7.4.6, C. lists the Senones, Parisii, Pictones, Cadurci, Turoni, Aulerci, Lemovices, Andi, and 'all the others who border on Ocean'. They were soon joined by the Bituriges, the Ruteni, the Nitiobriges, and the Gabali (7.5.7, 7.7.1–2). **the Arverni and Carnutes were the leading tribes.** The Carnutes began the revolt by killing the Roman citizens at Cenabum (Orléans), *BG* 7.2–3; but leadership soon passed to the Arverni and **Vercingetorix**, 'son of Celtillus, an Arvernus, a young man of the highest power' (*BG* 7.4.1). He was acclaimed as king of the Arverni at the beginning of the uprising, and shortly afterwards as commander-in-chief of the Gallic forces (7.4.5–6). **whose father** (Celtillus, above) **had been put to death by the Gauls when they thought he was aiming for tyranny:** simplifying *BG* 7.4.1, 'his father *had held a position of primacy of all Gaul* and had been killed *by his countrymen* because he was aiming for kingship (*regnum*)'. It is not clear what a 'primacy of all Gaul' might mean, and 'tyranny' or 'kingship' also sounds Roman or Greek as much as Gaulish. Perhaps (as Susan Treggiari suggests to me) P. hints at the universality of such ambitions and the dangers from those who resent them, with a glance forward to the Ides of March?

26.1 seems to be a summary of the campaigns of *BG* 7.5–7, but has several exaggerations and errors. C. mentions only a twofold division of the Gallic forces, some marching with the Cadurcan Lucterius against the Ruteni, Nitiobriges, and Gabali, others moving with Vercingetorix against the Bituriges: contrast **into many different divisions.** C. mentions no subordinates except Lucterius: contrast **appointing many commanders.** And **as far as the watershed of the Saône** (if the text is correct: 'Saône' is only a plausible emendation) is another oddity, for P. knew that the Aedui, west of the Saône, had not yet joined the rebels (26.5). P.'s narrative canvas is too small to admit the tribes' names, and he seems to have guessed at their position and got it wrong: cf. 18.1 n., another geographical mistake concerning the Saône, 20.6, and 26.6 nn. **to bring every part of Gaul into the war:** cf. the fine words that C. gives Vercingetorix at *BG* 7.29.6, 'he would create a single council for all Gaul; and if Gaul acted together, the whole world could not resist'—words now inscribed on the statue of Vercingetorix (impressive, fanciful, and looking suspiciously like Napoleon III) erected at Alesia in 1865.

now that Caesar was faced by more concerted opposition at Rome: perhaps inspired ultimately by *BG* 7.1.1–3, where C. mentions the mayhem at Rome in early 52 BCE ('Clodius' death, and the senatorial decree demanding an oath from all the young men of Italy') and the presumption in Gaul that 'C. would be detained by the disruption in the city and would be unable to join his army'. P. leaves the political background vague. More detail will come at 28–9 (nn.). But, along with §2, **when Caesar had become embroiled in the civil war**, this hint usefully prepares for the next act, which will begin as this final Gallic episode closes.

26.2. Had he done this just a little later . . . P. is fond of such 'virtual history': cf. e.g. *Ant.* 50.4 with my note, *Pomp.* 70.5, *Crass.* 37(4).3, *Lucull.* 36.5, *On the Fortune of the Romans* 321f–322a (with Jones 69). Elsewhere too he speculates on how near history came to a concurrence of factors that could have been shattering: *Flam.* 9.9–11, *Marc.* 3.2, *Gracch.* 3. The technique recalls a favourite epic way of marking a moment when something cataclysmic—the Greeks' unsuccessful return (*Il.* 2.155–6), or Troy's fall (*Il.* 6.73–6, 16.698–701), or Odysseus' death (*Od.* 5.436–8), or 'the last day of the war and of the people' (Virg. *Aen.* 9.756–9)—almost happened but was just averted. (On that technique, see H.-G. Nesselrath, *Ungeschehenes Geschehen: 'Beinahe-Episoden' im gr. u. röm. Epik* (1992).) In epic it is often because a god intervenes; here it is simply fortune, so it seems.

dangers just as serious as in the days of the Cimbri: 18.1 n.

26.3. he had a special gift for sensing and grasping a critical opportunity: as the good general always should: cf. e.g. *Pyrrh.* 31.4, *Arat.* 36.2, *Cor.* 31.3, *Pomp.* 17.2, *Sert.* 6.6, 16, Vell. 2.106.3.

26.3–4. These sections are again (cf. 25.4 n.) largely developed from C.'s crossing of the Cevennes, described at *BG* 7.8.2–3: in particular, **it was hard enough to believe that a single Roman herald or messenger could slip through** will derive from 7.8.3, 'the paths had never been passable even to a single individual at that time of year'. But in that case it is very misleading. **appearing with his whole army** is one oddity: C. crossed the Cevennes with only 'a part of his forces from the province and the reinforcements he had brought from Italy' (7.7.5), and was separated from his main army in the north (6.44, 7.6.2–4). Nor was there anything in the Cevennes crossing that could be described as **ravaging their land as he went, reducing their forts**, etc. P. is presumably conflating this with several later events: the Roman forces united soon after the crossing (7.9.5–10.4), and the fort reduction and city conquests are inspired by the subsequent sieges of Vellaunodunum, Cenabum, Noviodunum, Avaricum, and Gergovia (though not even those were conducted 'with his whole army': cf. 7.10.4, 34). Flor. 1.45.22–3, clearly based on the same material, suggests that Pollio kept the phases more firmly distinct.

26.5. finally the Aedui went to war against him. The behaviour of the Aedui has produced passionate attacks and defences: cf. esp. Thevenot, *Les Éduens n'ont pas trahi.* C. gives considerable space to their dissensions in *BG* 7, insinuating some parallels (esp. at 7.32–3) between their senseless self-destructive strife and the equivalent at Rome. Unease appeared as early as 7.5, when Aeduan troops refuse to aid the Bituriges against Vercingetorix; by 7.17 they are reluctant to provide C. with corn; internal divisions are clear by the time of the conference of Decetia (7.32–4). C. there supported Convictolitavis, who was soon himself involved in the plotting (7.37–40). Trouble within Aeduan territory bursts out at 7.42–3; soon afterwards the Roman station at Noviodunum was attacked, and secession was clear (7.54–5). **brothers of the Roman people... special position of honour.** This probably comes ultimately from C. *BG* 1.33.2, 'the Aeduans, who had often been called brothers and kinsmen by the Roman senate': the point recurs several times in *BG* 1 (36.5, 43.6, 44.9), where C. has reason to stress that his fighting against Ariovistus, accepted as 'friend of the Roman people' by the senate in 60 (19.1 n.), was at least in support of another people with whom the senate had similarly acknowledged a bond. P. shifts the focalization: what matters here is not only, as in C., that Rome had accepted them **(enjoyed a special position of honour)**, but also the Aeduans' own pride in the link (**had... paraded themselves as...**), which makes their defection all the more telling.

Others too accepted that the Aedui had a special position as Romans' 'brothers' (Cic. *Att.* 1.19 (19).2, *Fam.* 7.10 (33).4, Strabo 4.3.2, Tac. *Ann.* 11.25.1–2), and this kinship was taken literally: cf. D. C. Braund, *CQ* 30 (1980), 420–5, arguing plausibly that it was viewed as a shared descent from Troy.

26.6. he moved his force from the area. P. does not bring out that some time, perhaps a month, elapsed between C.'s departure from the Aedui and his march towards the Sequani. He first linked with the troops of Labienus, then clearly rested for some time (cf. the events of 7.63–6), perhaps among the Senones. **began to cross.** Most editors read the aorist 'crossed', but the imperfect 'began to cross' or 'was crossing' has equal manuscript authority, and corresponds to the original 'was marching' in C.'s text (see next n.). **to establish contact with the Sequani:** ultimately from *BG* 7.66.2, 'C. was marching to the Sequani through the borders of the Lingones: this was to make it easier to bring help to the province'. P. might naturally infer that the Sequani were **friendly**, but his notice has no independent authority, despite the ingenious argument of J. Carcopino, *Alésia et les ruses de César²* (1958), 116–18, 152–3. The attitude of the Sequani was in fact more equivocal (cf. esp. Thevenot 119–21), and they were soon to be openly hostile (7.75.3). **who formed a buffer between Italy and the rest of Gaul.** P. elaborates on the assumed friendliness. His geography is again vague (cf. 18.1, 20.6, 26.1 nn.), as the Allobroges separated 'Italy' (20.1–3 n.) from the Sequani: but his language need not imply literal contiguity, only that the Sequani lay protectively somewhere in the way.

26.7–8: C. ROUTS VERCINGETORIX Cf. C. *BG* 7.66–7, strikingly brief for so critical an encounter. P. does not bring out that only the cavalry of the two forces were engaged. On the strategic background of the battle, cf. esp. the acute remarks of C. E. Stevens, *Lat.* 11 (1952), 17–18. **There:** or less plausibly 'then', as E. St-Denis thought, *LEC* 18 (1950), 428–30: the Greek word *entautha* could just mean that, but the strong local indications of §6 suggest that it would more naturally be taken in its usual spatial sense. But 'there' need not mean 'chez les Séquanes' (J. Le Gall, *Bull. Soc. Ant. France* (1984), 210, and others): rather, just as in *BG* 7.66.2 (previous note), 'as he was passing through the Lingones'. Dio 40.39.1 unambiguously places the battle 'among the Sequani', presumably misunderstanding *BG* 7.66.2.

The location of this engagement is unresolved: possibly north or north-west of Alesia (e.g. Thevenot 133–4, Harmand, *Vercingétorix*, 260–2); less likely a site some 7 km. north of Dijon (Holmes, *CCG* 791–801, St-Denis, art. cit.), but that is a long way from Alesia;

possibly one near Baigneux-les-Juifs or Aignay-le-Duc (Carcopino, *Alésia*², 200–25); more likely one on the Tille near Beire-le-Châtel (E. Renardet, cit. St-Denis, *RPh* 36 (1962), 82–3). **many tens of thousands:** 27.4 n.

26.8. the Arverni still display a small sword: for a similar instance, cf. *Nic.* 28.6, 'I gather that till this day a shield is on display in a temple in Syracuse, said to be that of Nicias'. This item in *Caes.* does not come from *BG*; nor does C.'s account make it clear that the Romans initially had the worst of it. Hence Gelzer, *R-E* VIIIa (1955), 998, and Thevenot 132 and 151 inferred that P.'s notice goes back to an early independent source. That misunderstands P.'s technique. The story must come from a source much nearer to P.'s time (note the present tense 'display'), and as in the *Nicias* example we should probably think of an oral source: cf. p. 204 and Intr., p. 54. It may be a Gallic local tradition. Once P. had learnt of this anecdote, the rest was easy guesswork. C.'s own account shows that the battle was hard, and the very existence of the spoil would show that C. had **the worse of it** at some point, presumably **in the early stages.** The inference is intelligent, but carries no authority.

    G. Zecchini, *BJb* 191 (1991), 126–33, plausibly identifies this 'small sword' with the 'Sword of the Deified Julius' offered to Vitellius in Gaul in 69 CE (Suet. *Vit.* 8.2). That sword had been 'removed from a shrine of Mars': this may be the same as the **one of their shrines** mentioned here, or it may have been rededicated. Zecchini also thought this the origin of an anecdote in a romanticized passage of Geoffrey of Monmouth (*History of the Kings of Britain* 4.3–4), telling of a Sword of Julius that brought inevitable death to all it wounded, and was buried in Britain (not Gaul) with one 'Nennius' in 54 (not 52). (I am grateful to Professor Zecchini for sending me a pre-publication copy of his article and for correspondence.)

27.1. were able to regroup with their king at the city of Alesia: *BG* 7.68.1. The site of **Alesia** has long been (and is still) disputed, but its identification as Mont Auxois (Alise-Ste-Reine) is beyond all reasonable doubt.

27.2. The city seemed impregnable: a rather hyperbolic summary of material deriving from *BG* 7.69: cf. esp. 7.69.1, the town was on 'a hilltop, on quite an elevated location, so that it did not seem possible to take it by any means other than siege'. In that case **so great were its**

walls is odd. C. mentions but does not describe the town wall proper
('under the wall' (7.69.5)); the Gauls now built an additional 'wall'
(*maceria*, often used of garden walls), but that was only 6 feet high
(ibid.). It is possible that as at 5–10 (nn.) P. is here deriving non-
Caesarian material from his source: cf. Flor. 1.45.24, 'eighty thousand
men were defending a great city with a wall and citadel and steep
banks'. But it is more likely to be imaginative expansion, assuming the
obstacles that long sieges always confront (*Cam.* 2.7, *Sert.* 21.4–5,
etc.). P.'s imagination may still have been on the right lines, for the
man-made defences of Alesia were indeed substantial: M. Mangin in
Les Celtes en Belgique et dans le nord de la France (*Revue du Nord*
special edn, 1984), 241–54. **one that beggars description.** The phrase
has classical models in famous passages (Hdt. 2.35.1, 148.1, Thuc.
2.50.1), appropriately to the moment's importance (cf. §7 n.).

27.3. the most powerful forces of Gaul gathered.   This abbreviates
the material of *BG* 7.71, 75–6, 79. **a total of 300,000 men.** C. gives
figures of 8,000 cavalry and, depending on the choice of reading,
240,000 or 250,000 infantry (*BG* 7.76.3). The detailed list of contin-
gents *summoned* by the Gallic 'council' (7.75) is likewise bedevilled by
textual uncertainties, but seems to give a total between 267,000 and
288,000 (K. J. Beloch, *RhM* 54 (1899), 414–45 at 419). P.'s source
seems to have given 250,000 (Flor. 1.45.23, cf. Polyaenus 8.23.11;
Oros. 6.11.8 will derive from *BG*, cf. p. 223 and n. 7). P. rounds up;
Strabo 4.2.3 exaggerates still more, with the Arverni 'fighting with'
(the formulation could include their allies) 400,000 men. On these
figures, see Harmand, *Alesia*, 265–78, with references to earlier discussions: Beloch, art. cit., is especially valuable.

27.4. at least 170,000:   another mistake, if the text is right. **defending force** should mean combatants, and so should C.'s own formulations at *BG* 7.71.3 ('picked men') and 77.8: C. gives the figure as
80,000. That also seems to have been the version of P.'s source
(cf. Flor. 1.45.24). P.'s error is similar to that of his '190,000' at
18.1 (n.), but here there is no obvious mechanical explanation. It
may go back to some confusion between combatants and total numbers, or may just be a slip. C.'s figure of 80,000 seems credible: Holmes,
CCG 243–4; Harmand, *Alesia*, 97–105, 257–65; Goudineau 262.

 two walls in defence... P. abbreviates what may have been a fairly
detailed treatment in his source (cf. Flor. 1.45.25), deriving ultimately

from *BG* 7.69.6–7, 72–4. For these fortifications, see esp. Reddé et al. 1995 (cit. 25.2–27 n.), 81–125.

27.5–7: THE DECISIVE BATTLE   Cf. esp. *BG* 7.83–8, but not all P.'s information comes from C., who has nothing like the **without the Gauls in the city even knowing what was happening** item (unless this is a wild inference from 7.88.5, where at the end the Gauls 'catch sight from the town of the destruction and flight of their countrymen'; but that does not imply that this was the first they knew of the fighting— in C. the besieged clearly do know what is going on, 7.79.3–4, 80.4–5, 84.1—nor does it imply anything for **the Romans who were guarding the inner wall**). It is hard to believe that P. fabricated so elaborate a tale, and he probably took it over from his source along with the other non-Caesarian item at §§9–10. Apart from that detail, P. is very brief: his source may have been fuller (cf. Flor. 1.45.25). He does not explain that the besieged Gauls attacked the Roman camp at the same time as the external onslaught (7.84.1): that would sit uneasily with the notion that they did not know that the external army was attacking. The brave resistance of the besieged is delayed till §8, where at the expense of chronology (n.) it gives an easy transition to Vercingetorix' surrender.

27.6. many shields decorated with silver and gold, many bloodstained breastplates, even goblets and Gallic tents: the sorts of prizes that would eventually be displayed at the triumph, and so P. already prepares for his keynote final word of §10.

27.7. like a phantom or a dream.   P. evokes the famous similes when Odysseus meets his mother in the underworld, *Od.* 11.207, 'three times she flew from my arms like a shadow or a dream' (echoed again at *Epicurus Makes a Pleasant Life Impossible* 1089b), and 222, 'her soul flew away like a dream' (quoted at *On the Face in the Moon* 944f). After Homer, other memorable passages had used the image to explore the unreality of all human existence: cf. esp. Pi. *P.* 8.95–7, Soph. *Ajax* 126; the theme had become clichéd (e.g. *Anth. Gr. Epig. Sepulc.* 749.1, 'everything is a dream, a shadow, nothing more'). Whether or not the original underworld connections are felt here amid so much death, the intertext may (*a*) evoke generally the epic register for this climax of the war, and (*b*) suggest a wider sense that formidable dangers and achievements can swiftly collapse into un- reality. The narrative will shortly revert to different types of crisis at

Rome, where the whole of the Gallic challenge might similarly seem
to have belonged in a different world.

most of them falling in battle: *BG* 7.88, esp. §4, 'from so great
a host only a small number returned safely to the camp'.

**27.8, caused considerable trouble to Caesar... they too finally
surrendered.** P. misleadingly leaves the impression that this resistance was mounted after the final battle. The besieged fought bravely,
but *before* (7.70, 79–82) and *during* (7.84.1, 86.4–87.1) the decisive
battle; they then surrendered on the next day (7.89.1).

27.9–10. Vercingetorix surrenders The surrender is magnificent:
there is a greatness and dignity about C.'s Gallic enemy very different
from the style of politics in Rome, the world to which we will shortly
return.

BG 7.89.5 has only 'C. himself sat down within the fortifications in
front of the camp. The leaders were brought before him. Vercingetorix was surrendered. The arms thrown down.' (On that staccato
war-communiqué style, much more evocative to a Roman than to a
modern audience, see E. Fraenkel, *Eranos*, 54 (1956), 189–94 = *Kl.
Beitr.* ii (1964), 69–73.) P.'s elaboration again seems to come from the
usual source (cf. Flor. 1.45.26) and shows contact also with Dio 40.41.
A religious significance might well have been sensed in the detail of
Vercingetorix' display, as Jullian suggested (*Vercingétorix* 308–11 and
REA 3 (1901), 131–9): see J.-Y. Guillaumin, *Lat.* 44 (1985), 743–50,
who defends the episode's historicity against the scepticism of Harmand, *Vercingétorix* 323–6. That may be right, but some details are
dubious (by now any horse in Alesia would have made someone
a good lunch); and Greek or Roman writers too—perhaps originally
Pollio—may have been attracted by the notion of a ceremonial self-
sacrifice and elaborated the surrender accordingly.

27.10. triumph: a powerful final word for the Gallic narrative,
indicating without describing the natural sequel at Rome to such a
victory: but the next chapter suggests that a very different Roman
story is unfolding. The triumph was eventually celebrated in September 46 (55.2 n.). Vercingetorix was afterwards executed (Dio 40.41.3,
43.19.4), a note that could have been used to add pathos here had P.
preferred a different terminal effect.

P. does not compromise that effect by mentioning the subsequent
campaigns in Gaul (nor, for similar reasons, does C. himself in *BG*

1–7: it was Hirtius who later filled the gap by writing *BG* 8). Those campaigns were substantial: the siege of Uxellodunum in 51 was specially hazardous. Nor, despite his interest in provincial administration (11–12 n.), does P. mention the organization of Gaul (but probably not now Britain: cf. 15.1–2 n., 23.4 n.) into a province, with the vast tribute it would pay to Rome (Suet. 25.1, cf. C. E. Stevens, *Antiquity*, 21 (1947). 8–9, D. Timpe, *Chiron*, 2 (1972), 295; Goudineau 335–40). P.'s interest is more on what Gaul and its wealth had done for C. himself, not for Rome: and that will now be tested politically in the following chapters.

28–32: The Outbreak of War

Except for the brief, ominous notices of Cato's proposal (22.6) and Julia's death (23.5–7), this is the first we have heard of Roman politics since Luca (21.3–9). P. melds important particular facts—Crassus' death, Pompey's sole consulship—into a broader survey of the crisis. The abrupt beginning—'Caesar had long ago taken the decision to destroy Pompey'—moves the narrative from one sort of 'destruction', that in Gaul, to another; it also ensures that the focus is immediately on the coming war, and the following survey is seen as prospective as much as flashback. The technique has something in common with that of 15–17 (n.), where a characterizing sketch of C. himself marks off an important new phase; but by now we know enough of C.'s own traits, and the new information we need concerns historical background.

The main points are familiar; some have already been assumed in the side glances at Rome in 15–27 (see p. 204). They also re-emerge in other authors. Lucan 1.98–182 puts it all most memorably: 'this unharmonious harmony lasted for a brief time, and there was peace, though this was not the leaders' will. The only thing to delay the coming war was Crassus, standing between them... The pledge of joined blood, the death-bearing ill-omened marriage torches, were borne off to the underworld when Julia was snatched away by the ruthless hand of the Fates... The men were forced on by their rivalry in prowess.... Caesar can bear no superior, Pompey no equal... These were the reasons of the leaders; but there were underlying public seeds of conflict too, those which always bring down great peoples. Once the world had been conquered, fortune brought in an excess of wealth; morals gave way to prosperity, booty and the enemy's spoils urged luxury.... Anger now came easily ... violence was the measure of right; thence came laws and decrees extorted by

28.2. In Pompey's case these fears were recent ones, for he had previously felt dismissive of Caesar. The analysis here and at 20.3 (n.) reflects the picture of *C.min.*, where Cato's foresight during the fifties is contrasted with Pompey's blindness: Cato 'often warned' him of the danger, but Pompey 'paid no attention and let things slide: this was because he believed in his own good luck and power, and therefore could not believe that C. would change' (*C.min.* 43.10). It is only after the sole consulship of 52 BCE that Pompey realizes the danger, though even then he does little about it (*C.min.* 49.1–2). The picture in *Pompey* is different. There too Pompey is outsmarted (51.1), but he is alert to the danger earlier, apparently as early as 54 BCE (53.9, 54.2: so also Dio 39.25–6), and his neglect is put down to conscious policy, 'not wanting to give an impression of distrust but rather of turning a blind eye to what was going on...' (54.2). For P.'s reasons, cf. *Plutarch and History*, 96–8; for the change in Pompey in mid-50, below, 29.4 n. **He had been the one who had built Caesar up...:** focalized through Pompey: this is his view, not necessarily P.'s. At least in this *Life*, P. has not been so clear that C. owed his success to Pompey (Intr., p. 59), though he has stressed that the alliance was useful to both (esp. 13.3–6, 21.3–9). At *Pomp.* 46.4 P. is more unambiguous that 'C. rose through Pompey's strength to challenge the city, then used that strength to bring down and destroy Pompey himself'. The thought was current at the time of the events: Cic. *Att.* 7.3 (126).4, 'I should have preferred Pompey not to have given C. so much power, rather than now stand up to him when he is so strong'; 8.3 (153).3, 8.8 (158).1, etc.

28.3. like an athlete had put himself far away from his rivals; the Gallic Wars had been his own training-ground... *Pomp.* 51.2 also uses athletic imagery: 'C. himself put on his army's power as if it were a human body; it was not a question of using it against the barbarians, but rather of using the fighting against them as a training ground as if for the hunt, and he exercised it to the point that he had made it formidable and invincible.' *Caesar* takes the idea further, suggesting an athlete who goes to a distant training ground where his rivals cannot see him. The Greek might also be taken as 'far ahead of' his rivals, suggesting that this training opened a gap of achievement between him and his less skilled rivals. *Pompey* later develops the image into a real contest with further athletic touches (53.9); in *Caesar* too it will soon be time for Caesar's man to be crowned and acclaimed 'like an athlete' as victor (30.2). Pollio too developed a system of athletic imagery (30.2 n., Intr., p. 47), and the ideas may come from there.

28.4. Pompey himself afforded some. P. goes on to explain in §§7-8. **the people were already purchased as they came down to the elections.** App.'s language is very similar (2.19.69): 'the magistrates were elected by faction and by bribes, with dishonest tricks and stones and swords; bribery and corruption was particularly rife at that time, and *the people were already purchased as they came down to the vote.*' Unless App. is echoing P. here, both are presumably following Pollio closely. Cf. 4.5 n. for lavish and corrupt electioneering as a feature of the fifties: Cicero commented that the 54 campaign marked a new low (*Q.fr.* 2.15 (19).4, 2, 3.2 (22).3, *Att.* 4.15 (90).7, etc.), and 53 was apparently just as intense (Yakobson 32-3). In 52 Pompey introduced new laws against bribery and violence and streamlined the court procedure for hearing cases (*MRR* 234), and this led to a flood of trials and convictions.

28.5. they often left the rostra defiled with blood and corpses. Pollio probably generalized in a similar way (cf. App. 2.19.69, quoted on §4). P. knew of several particular instances, including the violence of 59 BCE (14.10-12 nn., *C.min.* 32.3-4, *Pomp.* 48.1-2): the alleged assassination attempt on Pompey in 58 (*Pomp.* 49.2); further violence in the debate about Cicero's return in 57, with tribunes wounded and Q. Cicero left for dead (*Cic.* 33.4, *Pomp.* 49.5); the violent canvassing after Luca in late 56 (21.6 n.), when Domitius Ahenobarbus' torchbearer was killed and on a later occasion Pompey's clothing was carried home stained with blood (*Crass.* 15.6, *Pomp.* 52.2, 53.3-4, *C.min.* 41.6-8); more bloodshed in 55 when Cato opposed the *lex Trebonia* (21.6 n., *C.min.* 43.7) and in 54 when he proposed a measure on *ambitus* (*C.min.* 44.3-4); then the disorder after Clodius' death in 52 (§7 n.), which was the first peacetime occasion when an army was called in to the city (Lintott, *Violence*, 91). **anarchy...monarchy.** The jingle is in the Greek, as at *C.min.* 45.7, where in 54 Cato attacks Pompey for deliberately 'courting monarchy through the use of anarchy'. It is more than wordplay. The idea rests on a traditional insight of political theory, that one-man power often springs from civic disorder (note esp. the fifth- or early fourth-century *Anonymus Iamblichi* 7.12-14, 'if anyone thinks that a king or a tyrant comes about from any other cause but lawlessness and greed, that person is a fool' and e.g. Theognis 51–2, Arist. *Pol.* 1304b19–5a10, 1319b27–32). Usually that disorder is associated with democracy and its excesses, and the tyrant is himself a demagogue (Plato *Rpb.* 8.560d–1a, 562a–6d, Hdt. 3.82.4, Arist. *Pol.* 1305a7–10, 1310b14–6, *Ath. pol.* 22.3, cf. e.g. *Alc.* 34.7, *Pyrrh.* 23.3). Rome's story too is to fit into that pattern, but in a more regular way than Pompey and his supporters envisage; for the monarch here, as so often in those classical models, is to be the man who himself is 'champion of the demos'—Caesar.

like a ship drifting without a helmsman. The familiar 'ship of state' image is continued in **turbulence**, and picked up at 33.2 and 34.2–3 (nn.). At 38 C. will memorably take charge of a real storm-tossed ship, with the helmsman in despair, and bring it home to safety; but steering the state itself will not be so straightforward. **Sensible people would be content . . .** P. often makes points by reconstructing onlookers' reactions (Intr., p. 25, and *Antony*, Index 2, s.v. 'characterisation by reaction'). **monarchy, and nothing worse:** i.e., presumably, civil war.

28.6. many who were ready to say in public . . . : not necessarily identical with 'the sensible people' of §5; P. himself might agree **that the state could be cured only by a monarchy**, but not that Pompey was the answer: see below. **to take the remedy from the gentlest of the doctors who were offering it—meaning Pompey** (so also App. 2.20.72): or, as Cato puts it at *Pomp.* 54.7, 'any government [*archē*] is preferable to anarchy, and no one would govern better than Pompey in turbulence like this'. *Pomp.* 55.4 goes on to speak of the city 'choosing Pompey as doctor', and *C.min.* 47.2 has 'using the mildest of illegalities as a medicine to avert the most severe'. App. uses the same medical image in this context ('the crisis seemed to require such a course of treatment' (2.23.84), cf. 25.95, 28.107), and it probably goes back to Pollio. The idea of statesman-as-doctor is an old one: cf. Hornblower on Thuc. 6.14. It figures in Plato *Rpb.* 8.564b–c, but there the statesman's medicine is preventative, to *avoid* tyranny: cf. 57–61 n. and Intr., pp. 63–4, for further expressive Platonic tweaks. By the late Republic talk of a 'cure' for the state's ills had unsurprisingly become a cliché, and one that, as Woodman (*Rhetoric in Classical Historiography* (1988), 133–4) says, was particularly associated with dictatorship or one-man rule: cf. e.g. Cic. *Att.* 1.18 (18).2, 4.3 (75).3, 9.5 (171).2, *Fam.* 16.11(143).2, *Q.fr.* 2.16 (20).5. It was a cliché still for

P., though he sometimes turns it in interesting ways: cf. *Advice on Public Life* 818d–e, or the development of the image through the double pair *Agis–Cleomenes–Gracchi* (*Ag.-Cl.* 31.7, *Gracch.* 11.6, 42(2).2, 44(4).3).

meaning Pompey. But were they wise? P.'s own view seems different: 'Caesar's rule caused trouble for its opponents during its genesis, but once they had accepted it and been defeated it seemed no more than a name and idea, and nothing cruel or tyrannical sprang from it. Indeed it seemed that the state needed monarchy, and Caesar was God's gift to Rome as the gentlest possible doctor' (*Brut.* 55(2).2). Still 'it seemed', with the characteristic use of reaction (§5 n.), but this time a view informed by hindsight, 'after they had accepted it'. *Ant.* 6.7 similarly talks of C.'s rule as 'something that in itself seemed anything other than tyrannical'—'seemed' again—but was tainted by his friends (cf. 51 n.). Cf. also *Pomp.* 75.5, an exchange between the defeated Pompey and the philosopher Cratippus: Pompey claimed that 'the state needed monarchy because of its *kakopoliteia*', and Cratippus retorts, 'how, Pompey, can we be sure that you would have used your good fortune better than Caesar if you had won?'

It is noticeable that all these passages are in other *Lives*. We might have expected this to be the great moral issue raised by C.'s life; it seemed so to contemporaries. But P. chooses to do things differently. See Intr., pp. 20–1.

28.7. but in fact plotting more than anyone or anything to get himself appointed dictator: in particular (Pollio seems to have stressed, *Pomp.* 54.3 ~ App. 2.19.71–20.74) by conniving at the disorder in 53, when the consuls for the year could not be elected until July, a full twelve months after the elections were due. (That is not the only way to read Pompey's role in those months: for Gruen 149 n. 120 'the affair [of the delayed elections] underlines not Pompey's shrewdness but his ineptitude'.) More turmoil followed in the canvassing for 52, and once again no consuls had been appointed by the beginning of the year. The central theme of that campaign was the candidature of T. Annius Milo, opposed by Pompey but supported by Cicero's rhetorical ingenuities, by Cato, and by his own thugs. On 18 January 52 Clodius and Milo clashed in a fight on the Appian Way and Clodius was killed. The ensuing disorder was so severe that Pompey was appointed sole consul two months later. In April Milo was found guilty and went into exile. Here and in *Pomp.* 54,

P. simplifies by omitting any mention of Clodius and Milo; *C.min.* 47 is fuller, but still does not mention Clodius' murder. But P. knew its relevance: cf. *Cic.* 35.1 and App. 2.21.75–23.84.

Cato and his followers. The proposer was the senior figure Bibulus (14.2 n.), but Appian too makes Cato the force behind it (2.23.84). That is probably right: true, the tradition tends to attach any optimate initiative to Cato, but at the time too he was seen as a moral figurehead, and his authority would have been important. **to make Pompey sole consul**: early 52, in the intercalary month, four days before the beginning of March (the dating is complicated: Marshall on Asc. 36.4 C.). 'Dictator' (cf. *OCD*[4], s.v.) was the obvious position and the one that had been mooted for several years (*Pomp.* 54.3–5, Cic. *Att.* 4.18 (92).3, *Q.fr.* 2.14 (18).5, 3.4 (24).1, etc.: Gelzer 137 n.1, 146). Already in November 54 Pompey was saying he did not want it, but had earlier given Cicero a different impression (*Q.fr.* 3.6 (26).4). How much difference there was between the two positions is uncertain, and would have been uncertain at the time: some of a dictator's constitutional powers were unclear (Lintott, *Constitution*, 111–12), and that might itself be a reason for preferring 'sole consul', where the powers of the office were less open to creative manipulation and there was a clear terminal date. P.'s reading of the significance is probably right, and this seemed **a more constitutional form of sole rule** (a phrase that D. Sedley, *JRS* 87 (1997), 48–9, suggests is influenced by Plato, *Politicus* 302e, perhaps mediated via the influence of the Academic Brutus)—even though in an important sense it was less rather than more 'constitutional', destroying the principle of checks and balances intrinsic to the double consulship. A dictatorship was amply, if distantly, precedented; this was not. It was also only three years since Pompey's last consulship, not the ten-year gap that Sulla's legislation had imposed. Still, the alternatives would have seemed worse to C.'s enemies: there was even talk of recalling C. himself as consul, perhaps in combination with Pompey (Dio 40.50.3–4, Suet. 26.1). Pompey alone was better than that, and 'consul' sounded better than 'dictator'. The one recent dictator was Sulla, and that was not a comfortable memory. Cf. also 37.2, 57.1 nn.; Seager 144–5.

In any case, the optimates' parade of (their own brand of) constitutionalism may have been intended as a signal to Pompey that the hard-line optimates might welcome him, provided some appeasing constitutional gestures could be made. If so, they judged their man well. A position of authority within a grateful and appreciative state had always been acceptable to him, and often been his aim; too many times he had been disappointed by curmudgeonly opposition from uncompromising optimates or ambitious demagogues. In late 61 he had made a sort of constitutional gesture of his own in demobilizing his armies, expecting the senate and state to reciprocate by recognizing his *acta* and settling his veterans. They had not, and this had done much to bring on the crisis of 59 (13.3 n., 14 n., 14.2 n.). Now it was becoming clear that the optimates needed and wanted a general; they were fortunate that their general wanted them.

28.8. voted to continue his tenure of his provinces. In 55 both provinces of **Spain** had been given Pompey for five years (21.6n.). That was now prorogued for another 'four' (*Pomp.* 55.12) or 'five' (Dio 40.44.2, 56.2) years: P. is probably right in saying that this was done by senatorial decree rather than by law (Millar 185–6). Pompey's *imperium* would now outlast C.'s. The new terminal date was probably 45 (so Gruen 459 n. 36); the previous date is unclear, and perhaps was specified in the same way as for C.'s command in Gaul, outlawing decision on a successor before March 50 (29.1 n.). In that case Pompey, like C., would have expected to retain his province for a good deal longer, and the difference between Dio and Plutarch is understandable. Cf. the variation between 'five' (P., App.) and 'three' (Dio) years at 21.6 (n.). **all Africa** may be a mistake, as most scholars tacitly assume, but if so it is an odd one. It recurs not merely at *C.min.* 43.1 and *Pomp.* 52.4 but also at App. 2.18.65, and so it seems to go back to Pollio. It is just possible that Pompey really did have Africa as well as Spain. *MRR* gives two other governors of Africa during these years, but both are uncertain (*MRR* 237, 242, 250, but C. Considius may have governed as Pompey's legate rather than as proconsul, Cic. *Lig.* 2, and the dates and status of P. Attius Varus are unclear, Caes. *BC* 1.31). But at *BC* 1.85.8 C. gives himself a speech protesting that Pompey stayed at Rome with his army while governing by proxy 'two most warlike provinces', presumably Nearer and Farther Spain (Africa was not 'warlike'); if Pompey was governing Africa as well, it is odd that C. should not have said so there.

I include verbatim a suggestion of David Yates: 'a possible solution to the Africa problem might lie in Pompey's *cura annonae*, which was granted in 57 for 5 years. This would mean that he retained that command at least until 52 if it was not extended (*pace* R. T. Ridley *RhM* 126 (1983), 136–48, especially 143 ff.; cf. Dio 39.39.4 for the

continued existence of this commission in 55 and *ad Fam* 13.75 [60]
for perhaps later—though the date of the letter is uncertain [Shackle-
ton Bailey puts it in 52 or early 51, CP]). This command gave Pompey
some authority at least in Africa and Sardinia (Cic. *Q.fr.* 2.6(5)(10).3
and *ad Fam.* 1.9.(20).9). Perhaps Pollio/a Pollio-source took some
literary license to paint Pompey in a particularly unconstitutional
light by lumping all his commands together.' **legates.** Rather as
Augustus would later send out legates to govern the imperial provinces on his behalf. Pompey's legates in Spain were Afranius, Petreius, and Varro (36.1 n.). **maintaining armies.** The size of his army is
uncertain. At *Pomp.* 52.4 P. says that Pompey had been voted four
legions in 55, but that passage is confused; according to Dio 39.33.2,
he was authorized in 55 to raise as many troops as he wanted (cf. 29.4
n.); App. 2.24.92 says that he was now given an extra two legions. By
49 he had raised a local legion in Spain, and had seven there in all.
Even if he did have Africa as well (above), there were probably no
legions there. Cf. Brunt, *Manpower*, 451–2, 472, and esp. Addenda
714. **1,000 talents each year:** so also *Pomp.* 55.7. Cf. Brunt, *Manpower*, Addenda 714–15: this sum (= 24,000,000 HS, 1.7 n.) is 'aston-
ishingly large', almost double what was required to pay the wages of
(say) six legions. An army costs more than its pay, but still Pompey
could expect to be comfortably in pocket. Woytek 43–5 rightly doubts
whether this sum represents the true expense, but does not take into
account the possibility of unscrupulous over-estimation by Pompey's
friends or C.'s enemies.

Through most of 52 Vercingetorix was ensuring that C. had other
things to worry about; but the rapprochement of Pompey and senate
could not be welcome to him. Some of Pompey's particular measures
could look particularly threatening—for instance, one allowing citizens to call to account anyone who had held office since 70 BCE: C.'s
consulship of 59 was particularly vulnerable (29.2 n.). Another very
important measure provided for a five-year gap before a consul could
move on to a provincial command, something C. later claimed was
aimed against him (*BC* 1.85.9), though that is anything but clear
(below, pp. 287–8). Other developments of 52 were hard to gauge.
The elimination of both Clodius and Milo would stabilize the city,
and urban stability might reduce C.'s options—but equally the violent
elements of the mob had not disappeared, and he might find ways of
exploiting them later. And he soon had charismatic demagogues of
his own (29.3, 30.2–3 nn.).

It would have been unwise for C. to enmesh himself in further Gallic entanglements, and it is no surprise that British and German adventures were at an end: 51 and 50 were to be years of consolidation in Gaul (27.10 n.: cf. esp. Hirt. *BG* 8.49 on the year 50). C.'s eyes were turning to Rome. And there was no reason to regard the political prospects there as hopeless. He had plenty of support, and able politicians to exploit it, not merely the men he was fostering with funds (29.3 n.) but also weighty figures like Cicero, whom he had continued to flatter and cultivate (Cic. *Q.fr.* 2.14 (18).1–2, *Att.* 4.16 (89).7–8, 4.19 (93).2, *Fam.* 1.9(20).21, etc.: Gelzer 136–40). And the glory C. had won in Gaul would weigh with all but the most intransigent. Nor would relations between Pompey and the harder-line optimates be easy. Neither side there would trust the other, if they had sense. There was every prospect of a rift that C. would exploit, and once again as at Luca the great men might be able to come to an understanding. C. would be unwise to alienate Pompey despite his unwelcome new friends, and he suggested a renewed marriage link, with Pompey marrying C.'s grand-niece Octavia while C. himself was to divorce Calpurnia and marry Pompey's daughter (Suet. 27.1). Pompey declined—but he too knew it would be unwise to destroy all his bridges to C. Some careful footwork may be sensed in 52 when Pompey did not oppose the law of the ten tribunes allowing C. to stand for a second consulship in absence (*MRR* 236, 29.1 n.; Cicero too backed this, *Att.* 7.1 (124).4, though possibly under duress); and again a year later when Pompey refused to back M. Marcellus' proposal to appoint a successor to C. in Gaul (29.1 n.). There was coolness too on the optimate side towards Pompey (*C.min.* 48, *Pomp.* 54.8–9). Options were being kept open on all sides, and the future was deeply unpredictable.

29.1. Caesar sent to ask for a consulship and a similar extension of his own provincial commands. *Pomp.* 56.1 has C.'s friends saying that he deserved *either* a second consulship *or* an extension of his command: the version here makes C. seek something that is more closely equivalent to what Pompey has already been given, just as he and his friends will be seeking only equal treatment in ch. 30 (30.1 nn.).

According to Suet. 26.1, the tribunes of 52 had talked of giving C. a consulship as Pompey's colleague (28.7 n.), and C. had asked them instead to propose to the people that he be allowed to stand for a second consulship in absence (cf. 13.1 nn.). This was agreed by the 'law of the ten tribunes', with Pompey's support (see previous note)—though a subsequent law by which Pompey excluded such candidatures *in absentia* muddied the water (Suet. 28.2–3, quoted below, at p. 292: cf. esp. Seager 148–51, Raaflaub 129–32, and Gruen 456–7). It is this concession, rather than the **consulship** itself, to which P. is here referring. He must have known that he was simplifying (cf. *Pomp.* 56.2, quoted in next paragraph), but it reinforces the impression that C. is merely asking for what Pompey already had. C. was presumably still thinking primarily of standing for 48, the first year in which he could be consul after the legally required ten-year gap (28.7 n.); but the two-year gap between Pompey's consulships of 55 and 52 might already have suggested that C. too might stand for an earlier consulship, perhaps in 49, and this possibility was in the air a year later (for 'this year' at Cael. *Fam.* 8.8 (84).9 must surely refer to a candidature during 50).[9]

There is no mention in Suet. of a request in 52 for a further prorogation of C.'s command, even though Pompey's extra five years would mean that his *imperium* would outlast C.'s (28.8 n.). P.'s language here and at *Pomp.* 56.1 might suggest that C. did react to Pompey's prorogation with an immediate request for a similar extension, but P. is here collapsing together the events of several years, and if there was any such proposal it was probably made during the diplomacy of 51 rather than 52, presumably as a response to the intensified optimate opposition during that year: cf. below on 'Marcellus' and §7 n. If it had been made in 52, it would have provoked fierce debate, and we would hear of it in Cicero's correspondence. That suggests that at this point C. was more concerned with the permission to stand in absence rather than any extension of

---

[9] This possibility is aired thoroughly by K. Girardet, *Chiron*, 30 (2000), 679–710. It may be that this is what underlies Hirt. *BG* 8.39.3, where in mid-to-late summer 51 C. knows that 'all the Gauls realized that he had one summer of his command remaining'; or, less likely, the 'one summer' may be that of 51 itself, assuming 1 March 50 to be some sort of end point (so O. Hirschfeld, *Kl. Schr.* 317–18, but Holmes, *RR* ii. 303–4 has strong arguments against this); or it may be simply disingenuousness on Hirtius' part, reading back from what did happen to indicate what was expected to happen. That maximizes both the danger (this anticipation makes the Gauls more likely to 'rebel') and the need for C. to act quickly; that could be seen as 'tendentious', but it also fits a traditional literary pattern whereby a peril reaches its height just as the prospect of deliverance looms (cf. my note on *Ant.* 48). Stevens too thinks that Hirtius has here imported hindsight, *AJP* 59 (1938), 187 n. 76.

command, even though this command was not due to run all the way through to a consulship in 48. Perhaps he regarded the legal issue as secondary and manageable (see below); perhaps he was nervous of putting in people's minds the possibility that he could be kept safely away in Gaul for a further five years. This was not the future that he was planning, certainly not with Pompey dominating the city as he was. According to *Pomp.* 56.2, Pompey at some point claimed in public that he 'had a letter from C. in which he himself expressed the wish for a successor and for an end of his campaign': that need not be a total lie. Pompey added that it was right to allow him to seek the consulship in *absentia*, which was consistent with the line he had taken in 52 (see previous note).

So far it looks as if this permission to stand in absence mattered more than any 'terminal date' of C.'s command: that may be an important clue as we approach the so-called *Rechtsfrage*, the legal issue of C.'s command and his enemies' threat to end it. This is famously and endlessly controversial. Syme, *RR* 48 n.1, borrowed a phrase of Gelzer (*Hermes*, 63 (1928), 131) and declared that it all came down to a *Machtfrage* rather than a *Rechtsfrage*. In one sense that is clearly right, but the legal and constitutional questions were debated hotly and tendentiously at the time, and mattered at least in terms of rhetoric and public image. The most important discussions include Th. Mommsen, *Die Rechtsfrage zwischen Caesar und dem Senat* (1857) = *Gesammelte Schriften*, iv. 92–145; O. Hirschfeld, *Kl. Schr.* 310–29; Holmes, *RR* ii. 299–310; Hardy 150–206; C. G. Stone, *CQ* 22 (1928), 193–201; J. P. V. D. Balsdon, *JRS* 29 (1939), 57–74, 167–83; G. R. Elton, *JRS* 36 (1946), 18–42; R. Sealey, *C&M* 18 (1957), 75–101; P. J. Cuff, *Hist.* 7 (1958), 455–71; S. Jameson, *Lat.* 29 (1970), 638–60; K. M. Girardet, *Chiron*, 30 (2000), 679–710; G. R. Stanton, *Hist.* 52 (2003), 67–94; R. Morstein-Marx, *Hist.* 56 (2007), 159–78; Gruen 475–6, 492–4; Seager 193–5. For fuller bibliography, see Gesche 113–20, and for a general narrative of 52–50 Wiseman, *CAH* ix². 408–23. These works are referred to in what follows by author's name alone.

In 55 the *lex Licinia Pompeia* had given C. 'another five years' (21.6 (n.)) in Gaul, but what did this mean? In 59 the *lex Vatinia* (14.9 n.) had fixed 1 March 54 as the first possible date for a successor to take over Cisalpine Gaul (Cic. *Prov. Cons.* 37: cf. Cuff 454–62, and see K. Bringmann, *Chiron*, 8 (1978), 348–52, for discussion of why this unexpected date might have been chosen). Dio 39.33.3 (see 21.6 n.)

seems to have taken the new grant to extend not from that previous terminal date but from that on which the law was passed in 55; this would give a term that would be expected to run until 50 (cf. 40.59.3). That 50 was a crucial year seems confirmed by a further provision, either part of the *lex Licinia Pompeia* or a separate measure, that no one should decide on the supersession of C.—decide, it seems, rather than 'discuss' (below, pp. 290–2)—until 1 March 50; and probably this was the only form in which any 'terminal date' was specified.[10] It was indeed anything but clear what a terminal date for the command would mean, or what would happen when it passed. (A similar lack of clarity recurred during the second triumvirate when such law-granted commands expired: Pelling, *CAH* x^2. 26–7, 48, 67–8.) Most provincial commands were granted not by law but by senatorial decree, and lasted not for a fixed time but until a successor was appointed and arrived. Analogy would suggest that a command granted by law would be similar, and C. would continue in Gaul until a successor (or successors, if the Gauls were to be separated) took over. In that case the crucial issue would indeed be that appointment rather than the terminal date of the command, and the 'no one should decide on the supersession . . .' provision was the central one.

Under the *lex Sempronia* provinces for the next year's consuls had to be fixed before they were elected, i.e. some eighteen months before they would expect to take those provinces over. C.'s friends would assume, at least at first, that (*a*) after C.'s command Gaul, or at least Transalpine Gaul, would be taken over by a consul; (*b*) the provinces for the consuls of 50 would be fixed before their election in 51, and the embargo on proposing supersession would exclude Gaul from that discussion; so (*c*) the first time that Gaul could be assigned would therefore be for a consul of 49, who would presumably not take over until 48, and this would take C. through to a second consulship.

---

[10] This, then, would be the 'law's date' (*legis dies*) of Cic. *Att.* 7.7 (130).6, cf. 7.9 (132).4. The centrality of 1 March 50 to so much of the political manœuvring creates a presumption in that direction: the case for 1 March 49, the alternative most frequently aired in the scholarly debate, relies on the assumption that a firm terminal date *for the command* must have been specified. If the terminal date had indeed been 1 March 49, it is hard to think that C. would not have made more capital in *BC* of the extreme moves against him before the date that the Roman people had decreed: so, fairly, Stevens 194–6.

That—or so it is normally assumed—was all changed by Pompey's law of 52, which confirmed a senatorial decree of 53 demanding a five-year gap after a consulship (above, p. 282) and specified that, for an interim period, governorships should be filled by ex-consuls and ex-praetors who had not yet ruled provinces: for it would now be possible to appoint a successor to take over immediately after 1 March 50, someone who had held a consulship in an earlier year. (On this *lex Pompeia*, see Wiseman 413 and esp. A. J. Marshall, *ANRW* i.1 (1972), 887–921; for this view of its significance, cf. e.g. Mommsen 45–7, Hirschfeld 320, Hardy 188–9, Gelzer 122, 152–3, 170, Cuff 464–6, 470, Carter i–ii.10–11, Stanton 76–9, Lintott, *Evidence*, 435–6; *contra*, Balsdon 173–4, Gruen 457–9, Sealey 97–8, H. Gesche, *Chiron*, 3 (1973), 205, C. T. H. R. Ehrhardt, *Antichthon*, 29 (1995), 30–41.) That, again it is assumed, is why C. claimed that legislation was aimed against him (*BC* 1.85.9, though what C. emphasizes there, in *popularis* vein, is the control that a small faction was given over provincial appointments). But we should be cautious about this. In all their epistolary chewing-over of events and possibilities, neither Caelius nor Cicero brings out, or even seems to hint or assume, that the *lex Pompeia* had changed things in this way. One can see why. (*a*) It had never been a wholly safe assumption that C. could not be superseded before January 48: it was not unusual for consuls to leave for their provinces before the end of the consular year—most recently Crassus in November 55, *MRR* 215—and, if Gaul were allocated to a consul of 49, it would be wholly proper for him to take it up before December (cf. Balsdon 58–65). Anyway, a private citizen could always be given a special command; it had happened to Pompey several times before, and it could happen again now. (It very nearly did happen, though for Syria rather than Gaul: Cic. *Fam.* 8.10 (87).2.) (*b*) More significantly, we can doubt whether the *lex Pompeia* really opened Gaul up to a pool of possible successors, for very few ex-consuls—and, *pace* Girardet 691 and 700, it would surely have to be an ex-consul who took over at least Transalpine Gaul—were eligible. Most had governed provinces already. Of those who had not, perhaps only Bibulus, cos. 59, and Cicero (if he could be got to do it) would be reliable optimates: yet by mid-51 these two had been despatched to other provinces, Syria and Cilicia, so they too were taken out of the equation at precisely the time when their availability ought to have been crucial. C. *BC* 1.6.5 may suggest (it is certainly hard to find other names[11]) that the only two other consulars available were L. Aurelius Cotta, cos. 65 (60.2 n.), and L. Marcius Philippus, cos. 56, both relatives of C. who might be reluctant to be used as pawns against him. If the measure had really been designed to hit at C., that provision 'who had not governed provinces already' would not have been included; without it figures like P. Cornelius Lentulus Spinther, cos. 57 (34.7, 42.2 nn.), or L. Afranius, cos. 60 (36.1 n.),[12] would have been eligible. The surface reason for this law of Pompey's can after all be the real one, namely, the need to combat electoral bribery by making it more difficult for a successful consular candidate swiftly to recoup his losses.

Even if the measure was not aimed against C., people must of course have calculated its implications for him. But those were hard to read. The most predictable consequence would be that it would be harder to find *any* plausible successor to C., at least before he could take up a second consulship in 48.[13] It might make it more likely that

---

[11] Stone 195 n. 1 and Marshall 898 suggest that Cicero and Bibulus were the first to be assigned provinces as the senior eligible consulars; that cannot be quite right, as it ignores at least Cotta and probably others (below), but it may well be that those other senior figures were willing to be passed over. Besides Cotta and Philippus there were others who had held consulships in the sixties and, as far as we know (but our evidence for the sixties is much sketchier than for the fifties), had not gone on to govern provinces: M'. Aemilius Lepidus, cos. 66, was still alive at the outbreak of war, and so was his consular colleague L. Volcacius Tullus. But both seem to have been conciliatory (Cic. *Att.* 7.3 (126). 3 with Shackleton Bailey's n., 7.12 (135).4, 8.9a (160).1, 9.10 (177).7), and it is anyway hard to think that such unbellicose or shadowy figures were major factors in calculations. L. Iulius Caesar, cos. 64, was currently a legate of C. in Gaul, so again was unlikely to be deployable against him. Q. Hortensius, cos. 69, may have been another technically eligible for a governorship when the law was passed, but he died in 51 and could surely not have been seen as a possible proconsul even in 52. M. Valerius Messalla Niger, cos. 61, may also have been alive in 52 but was probably dead before the outbreak of war (F. Münzer, *R-E* viiia. 165). Cn. Cornelius Lentulus Marcellinus, cos. 56, was probably dead by 52; so, again probably, was M. Pupius Piso, cos. 61 (cf. *MRR* iii. 177, right I think against *MRR* 269).

[12] Assuming that Afranius governed Cisalpine Gaul in 59: cf. *MRR* 183.

[13] It may be significant that it was planned in October 51 to convert Cilicia to be a praetorian province in 50, despite the feared Parthian danger (Cael. *Fam.* 8.8 (84).8). Stevens 28 and others have thought this a ploy to leave C.'s as the only consular provinces available for allocation in 50; one reason may also have been the simple shortage of available consulars. That same passage, Cael. *Fam.* 8.8 (84). 8, shows a parallel shortage in men eligible for the praetorian provinces: the procedure there proposed—but vetoed—envisages sending ex-praetors who had not ruled provinces even if the gap was not as large as five years; but it anyway seems clear that the more sensitive consular issue was not handled in the same way (see *StR* ii. 248–9), and any attempt to introduce a similar scheme would equally have been vetoed.

C.'s enemy L. Domitius Ahenobarbus would be the eventual successor to a province where he had ancestral links (Syme, *RR* 44), but that
could not legally be till 1 January 48, five years after the end of his own
consulship in December 54.[14] Pompey's measure also seems to have
removed a ban under the *lex Sempronia* on vetoing provincial appointments for consuls, and in 50 that was to prove crucial in C.'s
interest (31.2 n.): it is understandable that C. should have spent so
much effort in the next few years in securing reliable tribunes (29.3,
30.2–3, 31.2–3 nn.). The more serious threat to C. might seem the
difficulty that he could now anticipate in moving on to a further
province—Syria, perhaps, for a new Parthian War—immediately
after a second consulship; but if Paullus, the consul of 50, could
hope for some exemption for himself (29.3 n.), most certainly C.
could do the same.

True, the *lex Pompeia* may have introduced a further degree of
uncertainty into the crisis, making the permutations even less predictable—but there was uncertainty enough already. One ambiguity
concerned that concession in 'the law of the ten tribunes' (above,
pp. 283–4) allowing C. to stand for a second consulship in absence: as
Morstein-Marx emphasizes, this would be particularly valuable in
guaranteeing that there would be no repetition of the imbroglio of
60 BCE (13.1 nn.), costing C. the glory of a triumph. C. and his friends
would think it implicit that, if he were standing in absence, this would
be because his command would have been continued; Cicero too saw
it that way, *Att.* 7.7 (130).6 (cf. Gelzer 176 n.1, Raaflaub 131–2,
Morstein-Marx 171–2 and n. 62, Lintott, *Evidence*, 435, and below,
31.1 n.). But C.'s enemies could read the concession either as condi-
tional (if he is still in command, then he may stand in absence . . .) or
even as nothing to do with the command at all (he may absent himself

---

[14] Mommsen, *StR* ii. 248–9, assumed that the 'five years' would allow a magistrate
to take up a province on the fifth *anniversary* of taking up a consulship or praetorship
(i.e. after a four-year gap), so that a magistrate of 54 could take up a province in 49
rather than 48; but Dio's language (40.46.2 and 56.1, 'should not be allotted provinces
till five years had passed') suggests a full five-year *interval* between consulship and
proconsulship. (Dio 40.30.1, 'before the fifth year', might suggest the other interpretation, but that passage is anyway confused.) This would be analogous to the ten-year
gap demanded between two consulships, which certainly demanded a full ten-year
interval rather than a tenth anniversary. In Jan. 49 Domitius was indeed appointed to
Transalpine Gaul, five-year gap or not; but by then it is a war situation, and the other
appointments made at that time were equally in breach of the *lex Pompeia* (C. *BC*
1.6.5).

And senators could always discuss what they planned to decide once decision became formally possible. That could still leave it open for a partisan to claim that to initiate that sort of debate was itself a sort of 'proposal', and Hirt. *BG* 8.53.1 does claim precisely that ('Marcellus in the previous year had brought a proposal [*rettulerat*] to the senate prematurely in breach of the law of Pompey and Crassus'): the senate opposed Marcellus in a division (Hirt.'s word is *discessio*) on whatever proposal he made, so they, like Pompey, seem to have taken the same view that this was inappropriate. But it is not implausible that here at least interpretation of the 55 law could be contentious, and so this was a further important uncertainty. This does not mean that it was pointless in 55 to outlaw a formal proposal while inevitably allowing discussion: events themselves showed that such a provision made it much more difficult to supersede C.

(*b*) If the senate did take that view that Marcellus was in breach of the 55 law, they probably had some grounds. For Suet. 28.2 also makes it possible, perhaps even likely, that Marcellus went beyond mere 'discussion': 'M. Claudius Marcellus said first that he was going to make a proposal on the state, and then proposed to the senate that C. be superseded before time, given that the war was finished, it was peace, and the conquering army should be demobilized; and that C. should not be allowed to stand in absence, given that Pompey had not subsequently annulled the decree of the people', i.e. that which generally outlawed candidatures in absence (above, p. 284). Cic. *Att.* 8.3 (153).3 makes it clear that Marcellus 'tried to fix the Kalends of March as the terminal date for the Gallic provinces': that was 'before time', as it meant that a successor could arrive on the day—that is (on the view expressed here) it turned the date for a decision into a terminal date for the command, and in that case the decision would evidently have had to be taken some time before that specified date. Dio 40.59.1 is similar: 'among many other proposals Marcellus moved that a successor be sent to C. straight away, before the proper time'; App. 2.26.99 too seems to suggest the same. These authors may not be writing with constitutional precision (e.g. 'before time' could mean 'before C. could reasonably have expected' rather than 'before the legal date'), or may simply be wrong. Suet. at least seems to have thought that C. was due to stay in command till December 49 anyway (Hardy 152–3). Most likely, though, Marcellus' proposal really *was* illegal, and that was one reason why it was rejected.

We find that odd: consuls should not be making illegal proposals. But (i) Marcellus may have been implying a deeper point of legal principle, defending the position that the *lex Licinia Pompeia* was itself unconstitutional as it was the senate's right, not the people's, to determine foreign policy. Cic. *Prov. Cons.* 36 demonstrates that there were those in 56 who 'denied that this [in that case the *lex Vatinia*] was a law', even if their own proposals kept to its own terms. (ii) Senatorial debate was anyway a complex business, and frequently issues were debated when it would be clear that no decision could be taken, or at least none that would result in action. Very often a veto could be expected, and that was particularly so in these cases now the *lex Pompeia* had removed the ban on vetoing proposals to assign consular provinces (above, p. 289). That does not mean that debate was pointless. It was a way of testing or showing opinion; it was also a way to pursue an honour-based display of antagonism and power—I, as consul, *can* be rude and dismissive about C., I *can* force him to resort to the veto, I *can* air the prospect of superseding him whatever the law and his cronies may say. That in itself was humiliation; it was worth doing. Raising the political temperature was not a by-product of such gesture politics, it was the whole point.[17] It does not mean that Marcellus judged it all well; if the senatorial response was so negative and no veto was necessary, that may well have been a disappointment to him. But it was not a senseless exercise.

Marcellus, Lentulus, and their followers. The Greek phrase could just mean 'Marcellus and Lentulus' (cf. 31.2 n.), but probably it indicates deftly that there was a coherent group of intransigents who took a consistent line over the next few years. There is no need to assume that P. was confused, as Gelzer 170 n. 2 and Hardy 142 n. 1 thought. M. Claudius **Marcellus** was consul of 51 (*MRR* 240–1, *OCD*[4]), another indication that P. has moved forward a year: see above for his proposals to appoint a successor, and §7 n. for the

---

[17] Moderns have little intuitive understanding of such gesture politics: Hardy, for instance, thought it 'absolutely certain' that 'the constitutionalist party' would not propose anything illegal (153, cf. 165 and e.g. Stone 196, Stevens 171–2, Balsdon 175); yet the antics of Home Secretaries (especially Conservatives in the 1990s—'the constitutionalist party'), introducing politically loaded measures that they must have known would be contested and probably overthrown in the courts, may help to open British eyes. Writers from the Greek world understood such things better, especially Dio (e.g. 39.18, in that case on the courts; 39.34.3–4, of assemblies; 40.61.3, of the senate).

request from C. that he now opposed. L. Cornelius **Lentulus** Crus (10.6 n.) became consul in 49 (*MRR* 256, *OCD*⁴) and played a crucial role in the events of the first days of the year: 30.6, 31.2 nn. P.'s lack of sympathy for their hard line is clear: **They hated** (cf. p. 312) **Caesar anyway… some of their actions were quite unnecessary.** Contrast C.'s own requests, which appeared 'strikingly just' (30.1). P. is normally sympathetic to elite causes, but is more sympathetic still to a spirit of compromise and non-provocation, as *Advice on Public Life* makes clear.

A more positive view of the hardliners' strategy is possible: see below, pp. 311–12.

29.2. they took away the citizenship from the inhabitants of Novum Comum, a colony that Caesar had recently established in Gaul. In 89 the colonists of Comum (the modern Como) had been given 'Latin rights' (*OCD*⁴, s.v. *ius Latii*), and received a further group of settlers at C.'s hands in 59 (cf. 14.2 n., technically by a *lex Vatinia*), when it was refounded or at least renamed as Novum Comum. Perhaps 5,000 were settled in 59: so Strabo 5.1.6.¹⁸

P. clearly takes this to be a colony of Roman citizens, and many believe him (e.g. Holmes, *RR* ii. 317–20, Hardy 126–49, Brunt, *Manpower*, 199, Gruen 460–1, H. Mouritsen, *Italian Unification* (*BICS* Supp. 70; 1998), 107–8). On balance, though, it is better to follow App. 2.26.98, who says that the colony still had Latin rights: so e.g. Carsana, ad loc., G. Luraschi, *Atti del Convegno Celebrativo del Centenario della Riv. Arch. di Como* (1974), 363–400, and H. Wolff, *Chiron*, 9 (1979), 169–87. If so, it was probably (*pace* Mouritsen) already the case that those who had held a local magistracy would become Roman citizens: cf. E. Bispham, *From Asculum to Actium* (2007), 173–4 and n. 58. App. makes clear his view that only these ex-magistrates now had their citizenship removed, and that it was one of

---

¹⁸ Strabo 5.1.6 says that these 5,000 included 500 non-resident Greeks of distinction, and he gave 'these'—presumably the 500—'citizenship as well'. That passage is 'obscure' (A. N. Sherwin-White, *The Roman Citizenship*² (1973), 231–2), and it is not clear that the remaining 4,500 as well as the 500 received citizenship: Strabo's language suggests that they did not. Even if they did, Strabo may mean the citizenship of Novum Comum rather than of Rome. We cannot be sure that one of those 'citizens' was in point here, and it is certainly unlikely to be one of the 500 'Greeks', who as Strabo says were non-resident: Cic. *Fam.* 13.35 (306).1 seems to refer to one of those, who was clearly resident in Sicily. By then (46 or 45 BCE) this person had become a Roman citizen, but that might have been through the 49 enfranchisement.

them who fell foul of Marcellus in 51. It is this that P. captures, not very precisely, by **a councillor from Novum Comum,** which fails to bring out the importance of a (past) magistracy. For him the man's social standing highlights the indignity more than his precise legal claim to the citizenship (cf. 7.8 n.), rather as at 31.3 (n.) he stresses the insult at Rome to 'distinguished men' rather than the legal aspects of the tribunate; and, without interest in that legal claim, he would naturally but erroneously infer that the colonists had been settled as Roman citizens. Cic. *Att.* 5.11 (104).2 seems to confirm App.'s view that the magistracy was an issue, even if he also suggests that there was some doubt (or Marcellus' friends claimed some doubt) whether the man had really held office: Cic. says that the act was disgraceful 'even if the man may not have held a magistracy', and his subjunctive *gesserit* there leaves the issue open (see Shackleton Bailey's n.).

Such colonies were a long-established feature of Roman policy: see *OCD*[4], s.v. 'colonization, Roman'; the 89 settlement was the work of Pompey's own father (one reason, perhaps, why Cicero expected Pompey as well as C. to be offended by the incident, *Att.* 5.11 (104).2). Suet. 28.3 makes Marcellus propose 'taking away the citizenship from the colonists' on the grounds that C. had given it '*per ambitionem*' ('to further his own political ambitions', Graves, but there is also a suggestion of 'through sharp practice') 'and beyond what was prescribed': that is often taken as meaning that C. somehow exceeded the terms of the 59 bill, perhaps by settling too many or (as Wolff suggests) by organizing the local decurionate in such a way as to make it easy for a large number to become Roman citizens. Perhaps that is right; or perhaps Marcellus did not accept the validity of the 59 measure at all, given Bibulus' obstruction at the time (14.2 n.). True, the magistrates of Comum would probably have become Roman citizens even before 59, which makes Marcellus' flogging gesture seem incoherent. But 'New Comum' may have been regarded as different, and, if the man was one of C.'s new settlers, any magistracy he held could anyway have been seen as illegitimate. Nor, in the climate that Marcellus was helping to generate, was it the time for niceties, nor perhaps even for legality: cf. above, p. 293.

The point was particularly sensitive in 51, for shortly before this incident there was a rumour that C. had ordered the Transpadani to appoint magistrates as if they were Roman municipalities, i.e. as if all held the citizenship already. Cicero found this very worrying, *Att.* 5.2 (95); cf. Cael. *Fam.* 8.1 (77).2. It does look like a step along the

path towards giving the Transpadani full citizenship, as C. did in 49 (?
March, 37.2 n.). Cf. Williams 120–2.

his rods: i.e. the twelve fasces of office, normally only ceremonial,
each wielded by a lictor. The incident was apparently in June 51 (Cic.
Att. 5.11 (104).2). '...**to show you are not a Roman**'. Under a *lex
Porcia* Roman citizens could not be flogged without a right of appeal,
Cic. *Rep.* 2.53–4.

29.3. Gallic wealth: 20.3 n. **Curio** and **Paullus** are also linked by
App. 2.26–7 as C.'s prize purchases: they were already spoken of
together at the time, Cic. *Att.* 6.3 (117).4. C. Scribonius **Curio** was
son of the Curio of 8.3 n.: cf. *OCD*[4], no. 2, Gruen 470–97, Dettenhofer
34–63, 146–56. He became **tribune** on 10 December 51, so the
narrative has again jumped forward some months. He figures at
Ant. 2.4–5 as a youthful, hard-living, and free-spending crony of
Antony: *Caesar* is more concerned with his politics than his morals,
and **his many debts** are interesting only for the way they made Curio
susceptible to C.'s bribery. (According to App. 2.26.101 Curio cost C.
even more than Paullus; Val. Max. 9.1.6 speaks of 60,000,000 HS of
debt.) He had been an opponent of C. through the fifties, and strongly
opposed C.'s interests in late 51 (Cael. *Fam.* 8.9 (84).10, 8.10 (87).3);
in February 50 he suddenly changed sides (*Fam.* 8.6 (88).5), and
manœuvred skilfully for C. in the rest of the political exchanges
(30.1–2, 31.2, 59.3 nn.). W. K. Lacey, *Hist.* 10 (1961), 320–1, and
Gruen 473–4, 479–80 doubt whether he was straightforwardly bought
or bribed, but this may be less implausible with Curio than with
Paullus (see below). The agreement of P. and App. suggests that the
allegation goes back to Pollio; Cael. *Fam.* 8.4 (81).2 (1 August 51)
explains Curio's earlier hostility to C. in terms of his having so far
refused to spend money on him; and Dettenhofer 54–5 points out the
relevance of the imminent censorship now (see on Ap. Claudius, §5
n.), for Curio was a controversial figure and unless he could clear his
debts he might be expelled from the senate. Cf. Cael. *Fam.* 8.14 (97).4
for Appius' toughness on debt, and Dio 40.63.5 for the threat to
Curio. Dettenhofer also suggests that Curio was already on C.'s side
in 51, and the apparent fierce opposition then was a feint: that is
harder to believe, though it is true that both Caelius (*Fam.* 8.4 (81).2)
and Cicero (so he later claimed, *Fam.* 2.13(93).3) had their doubts
about him even then. He was killed in Africa in 49 (37.2 n.).

1,500 talents: i.e. 36,000,000 HS (1.7 n.): the detail matches the '1,000 talents' of 28.8. Both sides are dealing in vast sums. L. Aemilius **Paullus** (*OCD*[4], no. 3), consul in 50, had been a steady if not specially prominent optimate. C.'s funds may have been arriving for some time: in August 51 there were already doubts, it seems, as to how this might affect Paullus' political line (Cael. *Fam.* 8.4 (81).4 with Shackleton Bailey's n.). The link with C. was probably known when Paullus was elected, and some may have hoped that he would moderate his more extreme colleague C. Marcellus, the cousin of the consul of the previous year (§1 n.). But it does seem that he too, like Curio, came out for C. in early 50 in a way that had been unexpected (cf. Cael. *Fam.* 8.11 (91).1 with Shackleton Bailey's n.): Cicero found the news unpleasant, *Att.* 6.3 (117).4. Still, as with Appius Claudius at 21.5 (n.), P. probably overestimates the degree to which men of such nobility and pride could be turned into uncompromising supporters, however hard up Paullus may have been after his building extravaganza (below). True, the law of 52 (above, p. 287) might prevent him from recouping his outlays with a province immediately after his consulship, but he seems to have hoped for some exemption (Cic. *Att.* 6.1 (115).7, Cael. *Fam.* 8.10 (87).3, with Shackleton Bailey's nn.). App. 2.26.101 speaks of C. securing his neutrality ('so as neither to cooperate with him nor to oppose him'), and that emphasis—Pollio's?—is probably right. Paullus did not do much to check Marcellus: App. 2.27.103 simply has him 'staying silent' when Marcellus proposed appointing a successor. He was again effectively neutral in the Civil War.

This **basilica** is probably the same (*pace* E. M. Steinby in *LTUR* i.167–8) as the 'Basilica Paulli' that he had been building for some years (Cic. *Att.* 4.16 (89). 8, 54 BC), perhaps since an aedileship in 56. **it replaced the Fulvian basilica:** just to the north of the forum (*LTUR* i. 173–5, 183–6). This was a family matter, for the Basilica Fulvia was built in 179 in the consulship of Paullus' ancestor M. Aemilius Lepidus, and was further embellished by his father, the M. Aemilius Lepidus who was an agitatory consul in 78 (3.1 n.). Varro *LL* 6.4 (if the text is right) seems to refer to the old building as the *Basilica Aemilia et Fulvia*. It was eventually completed and dedicated by Paullus' son in 34, a year full of ostentatious building (*CAH* x[2]. 47). Its magnificence is clear: Pliny mentions its pillars of Phrygian marble (*NH* 36.102).

In 54 Cicero mentions that the new building has reused some of the old columns (*Att.* 4.16 (89).8), and also refers to a second building of Paullus, which is being built in magnificent style. This second building is a puzzle; it does not seem to be the separate Basilica Aemilia identified by Steinby immediately east of the temple of Castor (*LTUR* i. 168). Perhaps the 54 construction was simply a piece of temporary patching (hence the reused columns), and the second building replaced it on the same site (L. Richardson, in *Studies...P.H. von Blanckenhagen* (1979), 209–15). Or T. P. Wiseman's ingenious suggestion might be right, that Paullus planned this second building to the south of the forum, and it was eventually finished as the Basilica Iulia (see next paragraph); the transfer of funds from C. would in that case be a sort of purchase of the project (*Tria Lustra: Essays...John Pinsent* (1993), 181–2, 188).

Whether or not Wiseman is right, there is probably *some* link between Paullus' building and C.'s. In the late fifties C.'s own projects included the Forum Iulium (Suet. 26.2, *LTUR* ii. 299–306), just to the north of this new basilica, and the Basilica Iulia, directly opposite it (*LTUR* i. 177–9). Such building was a traditional way of celebrating foreign victories and using the wealth they generated—and of course marking the victor's claim for glory and further honours. C. may well have wished to be associated with Paullus' basilica as well, especially given the proximity. Certainly Cicero's letter of 54 is already treating Paullus' and C.'s own building projects in the same breath, and with the same tone: *Att.* 4.16 (89).8.

29.4. That finally brought Pompey to feel alarm: thus in *Caesar* mid-50 is when Pompey becomes alert, even if only transiently (cf. § 6); in *Pompey* we have a Pompey who has been alert for some time (28.2 n.), and mid-50 marks the point when he is lulled into overconfidence. That is because of the joyful reaction in Italy when he recovers from a serious illness, with crowds thronging to him and throwing flowers in delight and relief: 'this is said to have played as big a part as anything in bringing on the war' (*Pomp.* 57.1–4). The different interpretations each suit their *Life*: cf. *Plutarch and History*, 96–8. In *Pompey* this happy parade mirrors the earlier glory of the triumph in 61 (*Pomp.* 45); it also deepens the contrast between the true confidence and the false, and the true popularity and the false, of C. and Pompey. In *Caesar* Pompey's 'alarm' presages the panic that will shortly grip everyone (ch. 33), and continues the theme of C.

steadily duping everyone till it is too late (4.6–8, 13.6, 20.3, 21.9 nn.).
It leaves no room for the significance of Pompey's illness, which
Pollio too may well have stressed: cf. App. 2.28.107, and see 30.2 n.
on the pattern of flower imagery, 33.5 n. for the delay of an item from
that context.

**He now took action . . . to have a successor appointed to take over
Caesar's command.** In April 50 the consul C. Marcellus, backed by
Pompey, proposed to recall C., fixing 13 November 50 as the new
final date (Cael. *Fam.* 8.11 (91).3, etc.): this, he claimed, was 'equitable' to C.—language that suggests that it was presented by Pompey
as a compromise (so e.g. Hirschfeld 317, 320, cf. Girardet 701–2),
though it may simply have been an acknowledgement that 1 March
had come and gone. The proposal was vetoed by Curio (Cic. *Att.* 6.2
(116).6, etc.). It was unclear (and not at all straightforward, cf. above,
pp. 287–8) who would succeed C. if the proposal had gone through:
probably L. Domitius Ahenobarbus, legally eligible or not. (Under the
lex Pompeia he was probably ineligible till 1 January 48: above, p. 289.
Even if Mommsen's interpretation of the 'five years' is right (p. 289, n.
14), he would not have been eligible in November 50.) But this was
presumably not part of the proposal, and would have been the subject
of a second motion if the first had not been vetoed. Cf. §6 n. below on
Pompey's part in these manœuvrings. **he also sent to demand the
return of the soldiers he had lent Caesar for the Gallic Wars:** i.e.
those he had sent in 54/53, 25.2 n. In spring 50 (perhaps this too was
in April, Stevens 199 and n. 128) the senate called on both C. and
Pompey to give up one legion apiece for an anticipated war against
Parthia, and Pompey designated as his contribution the legion he had
lent C. (Hirt. *BG* 8.54); the idea of demanding it back had been in the
air since the previous summer, Cael. *Fam.* 8.4 (81).4. C. sent back this
legion (I) along with one of his own (XV): Brunt, *Manpower*, 467. The
Parthian threat was real enough, but the legions were kept in Italy and
were sent to winter in Capua (App. 2.30.115). Cf. 33.6 n. **Caesar duly
returned them—after giving each man 250 drachmas** (i.e. 1,000 HS,
1.7 n.): more than, perhaps more than double, a legionary's annual
pay (C. at some point doubled pay from 450 to 900 HS a year, but we
do not know when). Still, the sum could easily have been greater:
Pompey in 61 had rewarded his men with 6,000 HS apiece, and offers
of 2,000 HS and more became regular during the second triumvirate
(Brunt, *Manpower*, 412 and nn. 1–2).

29.5. The officers. At *Pomp.* 57.7 P. names 'Appius', and probably
thought this was the distinguished Appius Claudius of 21.5 (n.). That
may be right: for an earlier visit of this Appius to C. in Gaul, cf. Cic. *Q.
fr.* 2.14 (18).3. If so, that puts it in early summer 50, soon after Appius'
maiestas trial in the spring (Cic. *Fam.* 3.10 (73), 8.6 (88).1, etc.), for
Appius became censor in about July (Cic. *Fam.* 3.11 (74), etc.), and
was thereafter very active in Rome (*MRR* 247–8). Or the man may be
this Appius' nephew, the future consul of 38 (so Gelzer 186, Münzer,
R-E iii. 2853–4, no. 298), though if so P. probably did not realize it.
The non-naming here may be significant: see next note. **began a
shameful and disgraceful whispering campaign among the ordinary
people on Caesar's behalf.** Notice the stress on the 'ordinary people',
typical of *Caesar* but absent from the parallel *Pomp.* 57.7. Here there
is a clear implication that these officers were deliberately spreading
misinformation (cf. Pelling, 'Notes', 43–4): despite Pompey's new
alertness (§4), C. is still outwitting him on every front. In *Pompey*
'Appius' himself seems to be mistaken, as unwisely dismissive of C. as
the senatorial heavyweights will later be at Pharsalus (*Pomp.* 67, cf. 42
below), just as Pompey himself has just been misled by the joyous
reception in Italy (§4 n.). Pollio may have given both alternatives, for
App. 2.30.117 has the men acting 'either through ignorance or because they had been bribed': in each *Life* P. selects the interpretation
that suits the run of his narrative. Cf. *Plutarch and History*, 96. That
may explain why 'Appius' is not named here: it would sound less
plausible for so aristocratic a figure to be acting so subserviently for
C., especially if P. took it to be the uncle rather than the nephew; nor
in fact would it suit his politics, for he was by now firmly on the other
side. **on Caesar's behalf.** The Greek could just mean 'about Caesar',
leaving it more open (as at App. 2.30.117, above) whether the men
were wholly conscious of what they were doing. **in this festering state**
continues the illness imagery of 28.6 (n.). The phrase is a striking one,
and it may evoke Plato, *Gorg.* 518e, where 'the city swells and festers
beneath its flesh', with an illness that will soon destroy it: when that
happens, says Plato's Socrates, people will be swift to blame the
politicians of the day (cf. **envy** here), but will not see that the real
fault lay with those who pampered and 'banqueted' the people. Here
the man who 'banqueted' them is of course Caesar. P. also seems to
allude to the Plato passage at *Mar.* 35.1, as, more polemically, does
Ael. Arist. *Against Plato about the 'Four'* 36.125 J = 168 D.

monarchical ideas: again the recurrent theme of *Caesar* (Intr., p. 60), and again absent from the parallel *Pomp*. 57.7, which simply has 'that's how much they have come to hate C. and yearn for Pompey'.

29.6. giving the impression he had nothing to fear. The Greek leaves it ambiguous whether this is an impression that Pompey was deliberately and disingenuously generating (an analysis close to that given in *Pompey* of Pompey's earlier tactics, 28.2, 29.4 nn., and one that may be close to historical truth, Raaflaub 52–3), or whether Pompey was really misled; but **tickled Pompey's vanity** suggests the second. **with various speeches and proposals.** On the various anti-Caesarian proposals made during 50, cf. §4, 30.1, 30.4–6 nn. The lead was given by others, but Caelius thought that Pompey was behind it all (*Fam*. 8.14 (97).2). Perhaps that is too simple: Raaflaub 33–55 traces sensitively the predicament that Pompey faced, and has good reasons for thinking that he was not eager for a decisive break with C. (cf. above, p. 283; Seager 152–63 also has an insightful analysis). But the delicate path he trod involved several anti-Caesarian gestures. The compromise that he backed in April (§4 n.) led to a clash then with Curio; and Hirt. *BG* 8.52.5 says that 'Pompey's friends' were on one occasion responsible for preventing a senatorial vote in C.'s favour. Perhaps this too was in April: so Raaflaub, *Chiron*, 4 (1974), 302–6. **thinking Caesar . . . :** there is a gap here in the text, presumably a short one, and it is not even clear if 'Caesar' is the subject or the object of the phrase that would have captured Pompey's 'thoughts': anyway they would have been dismissive. The missing text will also have explained more about this **vote against Caesar**, presumably one of those calling for him to be superseded in Gaul.

29.7. that the senate was refusing to give Caesar any extra time in his command. So now the notion of an extension of command was in the air: contrast §1 n. App. 2.25.97 attaches his version of this story to the consulship of M. Marcellus in 51: if that is right, this centurion would not be one of the men sent back in §§4–5, but presumably had returned to vote, and to intimidate, in the elections (for such visits, cf. 21.6 n., *Pomp*. 51.5, *Crass*. 14.7, Cic. *Att*. 4.16 (89).6). Whichever year it was, C. need not have been seeking a full five-year extension like Pompey's own of 28.8 (n.): a shorter extension to bring him to 1 January 48 might have sufficed, or possibly even just to summer 49 to allow him to stand in absence. So App. 2.25.97, 'he schemed to keep his power until he should become consul, and asked the senate to allow him a little more time to retain his command in Gaul or a part of it'. (That further concession 'or a part of it' presumably hints at the offer of January 49 to retain only Cisalpine Gaul and Illyricum: 31.1 n.) **'They may not give it; this will,' he said, slapping the hilt of his sword.** According to App. 2.25.97, it was C. himself, not a centurion, who said this: P.'s version continues the emphasis on the devotion of C.'s men (15–17, 44.10–12 nn.), and gives the lie to the bland misinformation of §5. The same story was told of an officer of the young Octavian in 43 BCE (Dio 46.43.4), and, by a similar variation, of Octavian himself (Suet. *Aug.* 26.1); and also of Niger in 193 CE (Dio 75 (74). 6.2a). All of them may be true: male posturing has a limited range.

30.1. had the appearance: 31.1 n. **strikingly just:** cf. 29.1, 7 nn. Note how P. puts this: despite the stress on what appeared 'just' (the Greek word has a strong hint of legalism), he does not concentrate on the legal position: he knows that 'an extension of the command' was in the air (29.1, 7 nn.), but does not go into details, and the point is rather C.'s demand for equitable treatment with Pompey and the public response to his claims (note **appearance** here and cf. 31.1, 31.3 nn.). Nor does he stress the keynote of C.'s own propaganda, the protest that his *dignitas* was compromised by such opposition and that his achievements should have safeguarded him from such humiliation (16.1 n., esp. *BC* 1.7.7, 9.2, Cic. *Att.* 7.11 (134).1)—a more honour-based, less legalistic claim. That surfaces at 46.1 (n.), 'I, Gaius Caesar, victor in the greatest of wars . . . ': the word here for 'claim'— thinking something right or worthy—may hint at that too. But for the moment it is not developed. **His proposal was that he should lay down his arms and Pompey should do the same:** a proposal that Curio had been making strongly at least since late May 50, when C. Marcellus renewed his proposal (29.1 n.) to appoint an immediate successor to Caesar. Curio continued to veto; when M. Marcellus proposed applying pressure on Curio to withdraw the veto, the senate refused to back him (Cael. *Fam.* 8.13 (94).2, Cic. *Att.* 7.7 (130).5)—a sign of the moderate views that were to resurface at the end of the year (§5 n.). Curio repeated his proposal 'often' through 50 (Hirt. *BG* 8.52.4); C. himself confirmed his readiness to comply (cf. Cael. *Fam.* 8.14 (97).2, August), and repeated the offer again in early January 49 (C. *BC* 1.9.3, 5: §3 n. and 31.1 n., below). As Wiseman points out (*CAH* ix². 421), Curio does not seem to have specified *when* this should happen. There may even have been some gesturing on Pompey's part indicating some readiness to comply, as App. 2.28.107 and Vell. 2.48.5 suggest (cf. Woodman's n. on the Vell. passage). But ultimately the offer was unlikely to be accepted; even if the armies were demobilized, both sides knew that, as Suet. 29.2 observes, C. would be able to recall his veterans more swiftly and reliably than Pompey could summon his new recruits. Cf. R. Morstein-Marx, *Hist.* 56 (2007), 173 and n. 66.

and find what advantage they could from their fellow-citizens. The same phrase is used at *Pomp.* 56.3, but there it represents the propaganda of C.'s *enemies*, demanding that he give up his armies and 'find what advantage they could from their fellow-citizens': no mention of Pompey there. The phrase is an interesting one, used elsewhere to refer to the weak throwing themselves on the mercy of a conqueror (Arr. *Anab.* 3.21.5) or of a man of power (Xen. *Anab.* 7.1.31): it conveys the call for humility rather than assertiveness before these 'fellow-citizens'. It may well capture a phrase of contemporary debate, for 'kindnesses [*beneficia*] of the Roman people' is often used of elective magistracies, e.g. Cic. *2 Verr.* 4.25, 5.180, *Mur.* 2, 3, 86, 90, *Dom.* 110, *Sest.* 134, Sall. *BJ* 85.3, 26, and cf. Hellegouarc'h 169; C.'s enemies could well say that he should seek such a 'kindness' by standing for the consulship in person (cf. above, pp. 289–90). In the speeches he gives himself at *BC* 1.9.2 and 1.32.3, C. complains that his enemies have robbed him of the 'kindness [*beneficium*] which the Roman people had bestowed on him' already, i.e. the permission to stand in absence (cf. also Cic. *Att.* 9.11A (178A).2, Suet. 29.2); that could well be a riposte. If so, that suggests that the *Pompey* version, making 'find what advantage…' a point that is aimed at C. alone, is more accurate (Pompey had no such electoral canvass in prospect), and P. is again adapting here to develop the notion of a plea for equality (above, pp. 283–4). **tyranny…tyrant:** again (cf. 29.5 n.) the *Leitmotif* of this *Life*, but again such things were said at the time: cf. e.g. Cic. *Att.* 8.11 (161).2, 'both men want to be king'; *Att.* 9.4 (173) on all the 'tyrant' declamation themes to which Cicero's mind was straying; J. R. Dunkle, *TAPA* 98 (1967), 151–71. Curio himself apparently spoke of Pompey's *dominatio*, Hirt. *BG* 8.52.4: cf. Dettenhofer 53–4.

30.2. in the popular assembly. It is unclear exactly when. *Pomp.* 58.9 seems to suggest 1 December, after that day's senatorial debate:

both, he disarms both'. A month later Cato was taking a different line (31.2 n. and below, pp. 311–12).

30.6. Scipio forced the matter through. Scipio proposed on 1 January 49 that C. should dismiss his army by a specific date or be declared a public enemy: above, §4. This was vetoed by the tribunes Antony and Q. Cassius Longinus. There were further debates on 2, 5, 6, and 7 January, and on 7 January the so-called last decree (*senatus consultum ultimum*) was passed, encouraging 'the consuls, praetors, tribunes, and proconsuls in the vicinity of the city [i.e. Pompey] to take care that the state suffer no harm' (*C. BC* 1.5.3–4). **Lentulus the consul:** i.e. L. Cornelius **Lentulus** Crus (29.1 n.), who became consul on 1 January. His war cry—**arms were what were needed against this brigand, not votes**—conflates what in *Pompey* are two different outbursts, 'C. is a brigand and should be declared a public enemy unless he lays down his arms' (58.6) and 'I will not sit here and listen to words: I see ten legions already coming over the Alps, and I am going myself and will send the man to fight him for my country' (58.10). Yet in *Pompey* both remarks are attributed to Marcellus, the consul of 50, and at the time of the 370–22 vote (§5 n.) and the change of clothes (next n.) Lentulus is still consul designate, not 'consul' as here. Once again P. has probably shifted actions and remarks from one consul to another to smooth his narrative sequence: *Plutarch and History*, 107–8. **the senators put on mourning clothes to mark the civil discord:** as they had repeatedly in the last few years, in 63 (Dio 37.37.3), 58 (Dio 38.16.2), 56 (39.28.2–4, 30.4), 55 (39.39.2), 53 (40.46.1), and 52 (40.50.1). *Pomp.* 59.1 puts this in December 50, but in fact P. is probably right here to put it in early January 49: so Dio 41.3.1, and cf. Raaflaub, *Chiron*, 4 (1974), 307–9.

31.1. letters from Caesar: or 'a letter': the Greek plural *epistolai* can mean either several letters or, like the Latin *litterae*, just one. Particularly significant was one brought by Curio to the senate on 1 January: the tribunes Antony and Cassius (30.6 n.) had difficulty even in getting it read (*C. BC* 1.1.1; at *Ant.* 5.5 P. again refers to that letter with the plural *epistolai*). The sequence here of 30.5–31.1 might seem to suggest that the letter(s) came *after* Scipio's proposal and therefore after that 1 January debate; that implication is pressed by Raaflaub 67 and *Chiron*, 4 (1974), 316, though it causes difficulties in explaining how C. was able to react so quickly (Holmes, *RR* ii. 331–3). Raaflaub suggests that the concessions were offered not in a letter but by Curio in the next few days: on that view C. would have primed Curio on the further concessions he would be prepared to make. So also Meier 343–5. But it is better to assume that P. is again fusing the chronology of December and January (cf. 30.4–5 nn.), and the crucial letter offering concessions was in fact read at the same session as, and presumably before, Scipio made his uncompromising proposal. As an alternative, C. also repeated the offer to give up his army and command completely if Pompey—or this time more likely 'all other commanders'—did the same (30.1 n.): cf. C. *BC* 1.9.3, Suet. 29.2, App. 2.32.128, Dio 41.1.4; Raaflaub 61 and n. 241. He supported his claim with a catalogue of what he had achieved in Gaul. **gave the impression.** As at 30.1 ('appearance') P. is more interested in how things seemed at the time than in giving his own view of the rights and wrongs. P. stresses the continued moderation of C.'s proposals; so also, understandably, C. himself at *BC* 1.5.4 (he was waiting at Ravenna for a reply to 'his most modest demands'). Cicero thought the letter 'threatening and harsh' (*Fam.* 16.11 (143).2), though he did what he could to mediate. **on condition that he was granted Cisalpine Gaul and Illyricum:** cf. 29.7 n. App. 2.32.126 gives the impression that this concession was aired by C. in negotiations during December, but the chronology is very tight for such further comings and goings (Raaflaub, *Chiron*, 4 (1974), 312–15), and P. is probably right to imply that this offer was first made on (or if Raaflaub is right—see above—a few days after) 1 January. **until he stood for his second consulship.** This is probably also what is meant by Suet. 29.2 'until he should become consul', for 'become consul' is the regular phrase for 'be elected' (*OLD*, s.v. 'fio' 6b, Mommsen, *Rechtsfrage*, 54 n. 140); so also App. 2.25.97 and 32.126, 'until he should be elected consul'. We might have expected 'until he could take up the consulship' in January 48, but it does seem that C. had been forced back to an insistence on his permission to stand in absence, with its implication that he would retain his command until the elections (above, p. 289 and 29.7 n.) but not necessarily any further. Still, that might be enough: if immunity from prosecution was his concern (46.1 n.), it is possible though not certain that a consul designate could not be indicted for anything other than electoral malpractice (Sealey, *C&M* 18 (1957), 99). Anyway, if he could retain his province that long he would probably have little difficulty in continuing it for the rest of the year. The tribunes could continue to veto the appointment of a successor; and there was nothing irregular in retaining a command longer than the senate had decreed if there was no successor and the situation demanded it (cf. Cic. *Att.* 6.6 (121).3). **Cicero ... arrived** from his proconsulship in **Cilicia** on 4 January: 'I fell into the very flames of civil discord, or rather war' (*Fam.* 16.11 (143).2). C. had not forgotten him (cf. above, p. 283) during his governorship: when a thanksgiving was voted for a military victory of Cicero, C. had written to congratulate him—and to emphasize that Cato had voted against (Cic. *Att.* 7.1 (124).7, 7.2 (125).7, cf. *Fam.* 15.4–6 (110–12). Cicero's absence in Cilicia since mid-51 had made a difference, for had he been in Rome he would, with however much soul-searching, have been an important force for moderation. **Cicero ... was working for a reconciliation** by first proposing acceptance of C.'s proposals and suggesting that Pompey leave for Spain, then moving to the further compromise sketched in §2: Gelzer 191–2. Others too produced compromise proposals in the 1 January meeting (C. *BC* 1.2). A week or so earlier another idea had been that C. should retain *either* his army *or* his privilege to stand in absence: Cic. *Att.* 7.8 (131).4, 7.9 (132).2–3. Unsurprisingly, this was not acceptable to C. **Pompey responded by agreeing to the rest of Caesar's suggestion.** And that was the crucial part, for in that case C. would retain *imperium* until he became consul. **but insisting that he give up the soldiers.** App. 2.32.126 simplifies by saying that Pompey agreed to everything. P. is probably right, even though Pompey soon backed down on the soldiers too (§2): so Seager 162.

Some (esp. Ottmer 81–3) have doubted C.'s sincerity in these compromise proposals, suggesting he was already decided on war, knew that all proposals would be unacceptable, but hoped to split opinion in the senatorial camp by a display of moderation. But the proposals were taken seriously by Cicero, and it seems by Pompey too; the senatorial majority was not enthusiastic for war (30.1, 30.5 nn.); there was a real chance that the proposals might be accepted, and unless C. was 'sincere' he was playing with fire.

31.2. Cicero then urged Caesar's friends: in particular Curio, Cassius, and Antony. **together with just 6,000 troops:** i.e. one legion rather than the two C. had stipulated, §1. The hardliners called Cicero 'timid', and he does not deny it (*Fam.* 6.21 (246).1, a letter of January 45); but he also, reasonably, reflects that 'if Pompey had done what I had urged him to do, C. would indeed have been a distinguished private citizen, indeed the first man of the state, but would not have the power he has now' (*Fam.* 6.6 (234).5, Oct. 46). **Pompey was inclined to...allow this.** Thus Cato exclaimed that 'Pompey was being duped yet again', according to *Pomp.* 59.6; this concentration on the two protagonists fits both *Pompey* and *Caesar*, but *C.min.* 51.7 puts it rather differently, with less stress on Pompey ('deceiving and cheating the city'). **Lentulus, who was consul** (30.6 n.), **refused:** in the tense debates on 5 and 6 January. **he and his associates.** The Greek in fact has 'Lentulus and his associates, who were consuls, refused, and...'. The Greek phrase may again mean just 'Lentulus' (29.1, 30.5 nn.), and probably does mean that in 'who were consuls': his colleague (another C. Marcellus, a brother of cos. 51 and cousin of cos. 50) was admittedly no friend of C., but the focus is resting on Lentulus alone, who presided at the crucial sessions. (In fact this Marcellus may have been more moderate: cf. *BC* 1.6.4 and Raaflaub 203.) But the 'humiliation' is inflicted by the wider coherent group that P.'s language has already suggested at 29.1 (n.). **humiliated Antony and Curio and drove them out of the senate:** on 7 January. In this *Life* P. continues to stress Curio, in *Antony* Antony and Cassius (*Ant.* 5.9–10, cf. 30.6 n.), who as the two tribunes were constitutionally the important pair. The senate voted on that day to supersede C. in Gaul and to abrogate his right to stand for the consulship in absence; Antony and Cassius (30.6 n.) vetoed this, and the senate decreed that 'the consuls, praetors, tribunes and proconsuls near the city should take care lest the state suffer harm' (the so-called last decree). Antony and Cassius left the senate before the decree was passed (Dio 41.3.2–3, cf. App. 2.33.131, Raaflaub 74 n. 298), and fled to C. at once.

As is clear from the above nn., the tribunician veto was a critical weapon in the tactics adopted by Curio and Antony in the final months before the war; equally, the overriding of that veto on 7 January was central to C.'s argument in self-defence (cf. *BC* 1.5.1, 1.7.2–3, and Cicero's anticipation of this at *Att.* 7.9 (132).2 (27 December 50); also Dion. Hal. *Ant. Rom.* 8.87.7–8 with Raaflaub 108–9). P. does not bring this out, here or in his other versions: thus here he stresses the humiliation and threat to 'distinguished men', at *Ant.* 5.10 of the violation of their free speech. At 35.6 (n.) he similarly seems to overlook the importance of a veto. Elsewhere too he seems not to understand the veto, explaining it incorrectly at *Gracch.* 10.3 and *C.min.* 20.8 as if a tribune could veto only the act of a fellow-tribune. Cf. *Ant.* 5.8 n. and *Plutarch and History*, 219.

31.3. the best of his justifications: again (30.1, 31.1 nn.) P.'s preoccupation is with how it appeared. **his soldiers:** who needed little
stirring, as we have come to know: their loyalty has already been
stressed (15–17 nn., 29.7 n.). **display to them.** App. 2.33.133 confirms
that C. 'showed the tribunes in this condition' to the troops (he does
not say where[19]) and made a speech to inflame them. At *Ant.* 5.10 (n.)
P. transfers the indignant speech to Antony and Cassius themselves.
Cf. *Plutarch and History*, 93.

Where did this 'display' take place, at Ariminum after the crossing
or at Ravenna before it? At Ariminum, it seems, for C. *BC* 1.8.1 says
that the tribunes met C. there, as also seems to be implied by Cael.
Fam. 8.17 (156).1. According to his own account, C. had by then
already heard (presumably by courier) of the events of 7 January,
delivered a speech of self-justification and inspiration to the troops—
but without the tribunes—at Ravenna (*BC* 1.7), and launched the
invasion. Lucan 1.231–381 similarly puts the great assembly at Ariminum: so also Suet. 33, mentioning the tribunes, Dio 41.4.1, and
Oros. 6.15.3 (32.1 n.). Nothing excludes a double harangue, one at
Ravenna without the tribunes and one at Ariminum after they had
arrived: so Holmes, *RR* ii. 334–7 and Carter on C. *BC* 1.7.1. But that
would be too cumbersome for P., who implicitly here and explicitly at
Ant. 5.10–6.1 makes the tribunes' arrival trigger the invasion; they
therefore have to join C. before the crossing. Their journey decisively
moves the action from Rome to C.'s camp, and from now on C.'s
decisions and acts control the narrative. Notice, though, that here
P. does not make that sequence explicit: if it were too clear that there
was a public address before the crossing, the atmosphere of secrecy of
ch. 32 (cf. below, p. 313) would have been spoilt.

Urgent journeys to and from Ravenna seem to take three days
(App. 2.32.127; six days are needed for the return journey at C. *BC*
1.3.6), so the news may well have arrived on 10 January. The tribunes
were presumably also travelling at speed, so, if C. moved before their
arrival, it was probably on the evening of 10 January itself. **who had**

---

[19] He is usually taken as implying Ravenna, and that is how I took it in my note on
Ant. 6.1; but that misinterprets the sequence of 2.33.133–35.137. App. moves back in
time after the tribunes' arrival (notice the pluperfects of 2.34.134, now 'the war had
been begun on both sides...' and 136, C. 'had sent around to his troops'), and it is not
clear that the narrative of the Rubicon at 35 need be subsequent to the tribunes' arrival
at 33.133 (*pace* Carsana, ad loc.).

arrived in hired carriages and wearing slaves' clothing: so also *Ant.*
5.9–10; cf. 32.5 n. Though Seneca, *Clem.* 1.24.1, might suggest that
there was no distinction in clothing between slave and free (that was
also said of classical Athens, in disgruntled mood, by the 'Old Oli-
garch' (Ps.-Xen. *Ath. pol.*) 1.10), there is good reason to think that the
clothing of slaves was of recognizably poorer quality: K. Bradley,
Slavery and Society at Rome (1994), 96–9.

P. has cut away one or two important details here of the opposition,
not merely conflating two of C. Marcellus' outbursts and transferring
them to Lentulus (30.6 n.) but omitting another, when he responded
to the 1 December vote (30.5 n.) by telling the senate 'you have won—
to have C. as your master'. P. also omits the march of the senate, led
by Marcellus, to Pompey, the presentation to him of an emblematic
sword, and the call on him to save his country (*Pomp.* 59.1, App.
2.31.121), a moment that arguably marked a decisive stage in the
escalation (Raaflaub 33–55; it is discussed by H. Botermann, *Hermes*,
117 (1989), 62–85). Cato too played a part in stiffening Pompey's
resolve, *Pomp.* 59.6, *C.min.* 51.7 (cf. 31.2 n., C. *BC* 1.4.1, and, for
Cato's language, Vell. 2.49.3, 'one should die rather than accept terms
from a fellow-citizen'). Naturally those items focus more on Pompey
and his relations with the senatorial elite, and have less relevance for
Caesar: that may also be a reason why in *Pompey*, but not here,
P. clearly differentiates the role of the consuls of 50 and 49, Marcellus
and Lentulus (30.5–6 nn.). But the emphasis of *Caesar* also puts more
weight on Curio's and Antony's reception with the people of Rome
(30.2–3) and the army (31.3), factors that are more crucial to this *Life*,
and were coming to be more crucial in history, than the posturing in
the senate. The flight of Antony and Curio moves the action to C.'s
camp (31.3 n.); in *Pompey* the narrative focus remains in Rome, and
the subsequent events are controlled by the reception of news and
rumours of C.'s actions (60.1, 60.5, etc.).

It is easy to fault C.'s senatorial opponents for their intransigence,
and they must have known they were risking war. P. clearly found
them unsympathetic (29.1, 30.1 nn.). Yet, *given their standpoint*, they
had not done badly. If the traditional ways of the Republic were worth
defending, they had above all to be defended against the threat of the
returning general backed by an army. The threat presented by C. was
as great as any—yet it was not so great that it could not be opposed. If
C. could be faced down, that would be an important, probably a
decisive signal to any future general who tried to impose his will so

ruthlessly. By 50 his enemies had managed to manœuvre C. into a position where his tenure was legally questionable, not the main or the only issue but one that clearly mattered; where he had been deprived of some of his troops; where he had been forced into a treasonable attack on his own country; and, most important of all, where the state had Pompey, the one general of comparable stature, to lead the fight. The hardliners had even managed to keep Pompey on their side, despite all the temptations for him to side with C. When it came to the fighting, the chances were good, even if C. had an immediate advantage in the quality of his troops. In the sequel the Republicans really should have won, at Dyrrhachium and even at Pharsalus. Of course the risk was immense: and, given the hypocrisy, narrowness, and brutality of the Roman elite, it is not too cynical for a modern to question whether those traditional ways really justified a civil war to defend them. To judge from the senate vote of 1 December, others at the time thought the cost too great; as he travelled through Italy later in the month Cicero could find almost no one who preferred war to concession (*Att.* 7.6 (129).2, cf. 7.5 (128).4, 7.7 (130).5). Cicero's own feelings, despite a series of tirades against C. and a determination to vote with Pompey (*Att.* 7.3 (126).3–5, 7.6 (129).2, 7.7 (130).6–7, 7.9 (132).4), were privately not too different (7.5 (128).5). But, however negatively we judge the intransigents' cause, we should pay them credit for their tactics. It was they, not Pompey, who had manœuvred C. into a step more extreme than he surely wanted, though one he was ready to accept. And C. was no easy politician to outmanœuvre.

Not that their motives were necessarily as cool or thoughtful as the above analysis suggests. As Strasburger in particular stressed (*CUZ*), C. simply hated these people, and they hated him. They feared him too, after what he had done as consul in 59 (so 'certain people think...' (Cic. *Att.* 7.9 (132).3)). All the clearer they would be that he would not give in; and all the more eager, not merely willing, to make a great example of him.

32: THE RUBICON IS CROSSED   We are halfway through the *Life*. Cassius Dio expressively makes Curio's flight to C. (30.2 n.) the halfway point in his massive eighty-book history of Rome (40.66.5, cf. Millar 194); P. does something similar here, with this most dramatic of stories—very different in style from the taut political narrative and analysis of the previous few chapters—marking the decisive turning point. In those preceding chapters we have heard of C. only as his messages and offers have reached Rome. Now we see that he has been active too, summoning his forces from beyond the Alps (§1 n.). His insight that speed and daring are needed (§2) is what the earlier narrative had led us to expect of C., audacious and decisive as ever. The adroitness with which he maintains secrecy also fits the man we know, even if P. does leave it a little inconsequential: C. could hardly take Ariminum with just his 'lieutenants and captains', and, if he has already publicly harangued his troops (cf. 31.3 n.), it is unclear exactly who is supposed to be taken in by the mealtime deception, beautifully told though it is. He would do better to skip dinner and get on with it.

River-crossings are often momentous in Greek and Roman historiography, from Herodotus (stressed esp. by H. R. Immerwahr, *Form and Thought in Herodotus* (1966), see index, s.v. river motif) to Tacitus (R Poignault, *Lat.* 60 (2001), 414–32 at 427–32) and beyond: cf. D. Braund, 'River Frontiers in the Environmental Psychology of the Roman World', in D. L. Kennedy (ed.), *The Roman Army in the East* (*JRA* Supp 17; 1996), 43–7. The moment of doubt at the Rubicon comes as more of a surprise. For fuller discussion, see *Plutarch and History* (2002), 327–8, where I comment on how rare it is for P. to dramatize such internal agonizing; that contrasts with epic and tragedy, where internal debate is often a central mode of characterisation. This presentation is also comparatively unintegrated with the Caesar of the rest of the *Life*: not merely is such indecision out of character, even his concern with 'how great the story of it they would leave among later generations' (§7) is a theme that is undeveloped elsewhere. It could have been, given the interest in C.'s concern with glory; and in the paired *Life* Alexander was certainly presented as having an eye to future fame, *Alex.* 14.9. But in C.'s case that is left for the metatheatre of Shakespeare, *JC* iii.i.111–16. The technique here dramatizes and marks the importance of the moment, but it is less central to the characterization. Still, if even a man like Caesar feels hesitation, that makes that momentousness even clearer.

The agonizing here is also discussed by F. Frazier in I. Gallo and B. Scardigli (eds), *Teoria e prassi politica nelle opere di Plutarco* (1995), 147–71 at 152–4: comparing *Cic.* 19.5 and *Pyrrh.* 22.3–4, she comments that the stress in such passages falls less on the reasoning, more on the decisiveness once the mind is made up.

That momentousness is also marked by the 'unspeakable dream' of §9. I discuss this in *G&R* 44 (1997), 200–1, and suggest that P. leaves it unclear how it connects with the hesitation. Many dreams in P. are sent from outside, and come prophetically from the gods (e.g. *Rom.* 2.5, *Cic.* 44.3–4; on P.'s dreams in general, cf. Brenk 214–36 and *Lat.* 34 (1975), 336–49). This—so far—is a notably secular *Life*, but the godlessness may only be provisional (cf. Intr., p. 31), and, if C. fears that the gods may indeed be intervening, this may help to explain *why* he is so uncharacteristically hesitant. But there are also dreams that seem to be triggered internally, Marcellus so obsessed with fighting Hannibal hand to hand that he dreams about it nightly, or Brutus not being able to get dreams of killing C. himself out of his head (*Marc.* 28.4–5, *Brut.* 13.2). It may be that this dream too came *because* C. is uneasy, a reflection rather than a cause of his doubts. The reader cannot know. P. is here manipulating his material considerably: it seems that he has delayed this dream nearly twenty years from its historical context in 69–68 BCE (n.). But its contribution to the atmosphere is superb.

C. does not mention the Rubicon in *BC* 1. Those present 'included Asinius Pollio' (§7). The naming here almost serves as a source citation (for a similar technique, cf. 'Polybius' at *Phil.* 21.5 and 'Dellius' at *Ant.* 25), and P. surely draws the story from his history: the 'die' of §8 (n.) may itself be a pointer to that. Pollio—perhaps typically, cf. Morgan, 'Autopsy'—evidently stressed that he was there, an eyewitness. The closeness of the description to App. 2.35.137–41 would fit a derivation from Pollio, though in fact it is *so* close that App. may here be following P. directly: cf. Intr., p. 44. Other elements had attached themselves to the story, whether or not they came in Pollio, but P. finds them dispensable. One story was that, as C. hesitated on the bank, he was faced by a strange phantom who seized a trumpet and urged him on to the other bank (Suet. 32); or perhaps it was a different sort of spirit, the 'phantom of his terrified country', begging his army to relent (Lucan 1.185–94, probably adapting for his own chilling vision the more encouraging phantom that we later see in Suet. and adding a hint of Cic. *Cat.* 1.19–20). Either version would intrude the supernatural too grossly: P. prefers something subtler.

Suet. 30 takes this as his peg for discussing C.'s motivation for war: had he really planned it all his life (Intr., p. 60)? At *Ant.* 5–6 P. does something similar, there exploiting C.'s focus and decisiveness as a foil for Antony's aimless irresponsibility. Here we already know that C. has long decided to destroy Pompey (28.1 n.), and that is enough.

The various versions are discussed by L. Herrmann, *REA* 37 (1935), 435–7, E. Hohl, *Hermes*, 80 (1952) 246–9, R. A. Tucker, *Historia*, 37 (1988), 245–8, P. Bicknell and D. Nielsen in C. Deroux (ed.), *Studies in Latin Literature*, 9 (1998), 138–66 (interestingly suggesting at 152–6 that the Suet.'s phantom reflects a spectacle stage managed by C. himself in the manner of Pisistratus' Phye, Hdt. 1.60.4–5), E. Marinoni in P. G. Michelotto (ed.), λόγιος ἀνήρ: *Studi…M. Attilio Levi* (2002), 277–85, A. Rondholz, *Mnem.* 62 (2009), 432–50, and a paper of J. Beneker forthcoming in *Phoenix*. On Lucan's treatment, see esp. J. Masters, *Poetry and Civil War in Lucan's 'Bellum Civile'* (1992), 1–10, and now the comm. of P. Roche (2009); on Suet.'s, Steidle 46–8; T. P. Wiseman, *Roman History and Roman Drama* (1998), 60–3, who argues for the influence of drama; and Lambrecht 51–62, 79–80, who suggests that there are foreshadowings of later imperial practice, e.g. the parade of hesitation at the outset of reigns.

32.1. 300 cavalry and 5,000 infantry: so also *Pomp.* 60.2, App. 2.32.124, 34.136. The '5,000 infantry' = one legion, i.e. XIII (C. *BC* 1.7.8). But Oros. 6.15.3 speaks of C. addressing at Ariminum (31.3 n.) 'the five cohorts which were all that he then had, and with whom, as Livy puts it, he attacked the whole world': it is not clear whether Livy is there cited for the 'five cohorts' (i.e. half a legion) or just for the striking phraseology, and it is rash to put much weight on that (as Bicknell and Nielsen do, art. cit., 156–61, arguing that the other half of XIII was disaffected). **The rest of his forces had been left beyond the Alps, and he had sent men to bring them to him.** P. understates the degree to which C. had been preparing the ground in Cisalpine Gaul, even if his forces were not with him at Ravenna. In September 50 C. had been travelling around the area, and had been greeted with strong demonstrations of support (Hirt. *BG* 8.50–1). There were rumours too about troop movements, with talk that four legions would arrive at Placentia on 15 October (Cic. *Att.* 6.9 (123).5, 7.1 (124).1). The rumours were false, but there are still signs that C. was indeed concentrating troops: this was argued elaborately by Ottmer, esp. 15–39. Ottmer overstates the case (see my review in *Gnom.* 54 (1982), 212–13), but C. certainly raised twenty-two new cohorts in late 50 (C. *BC* 1.18.5), and it does seem that he had ten (*Pomp.* 58.10, cf. Suet. 29) or eleven (Cic. *Att.* 7.7.6) legions ready to invade: cf. Brunt, *Manpower*, 467–8. C. had summoned legions from **beyond the**

a second time where the Greek language matters (n.): together the two passages mark the beginning and end of the critical phase, the period where indeed the dice are still being thrown. The pattern is reinforced by 40.1, where Pompey is 'reluctant to let so much turn on the throw of a single battle': in the Greek the word for 'turn . . . on the throw of' is the same as for 'casting' the dice here. App. 2.69.287 similarly has Pompey 'playing dice with so many men's lives and his own reputation' at Pharsalus, suggesting that this patterning too goes back to Pollio. At *Brut.* 40.3 Cassius also uses similar language, again explicitly in Greek, before the battle of Philippi, one of several ways in which P. there intimates that the wheel has turned full circle.

'War was proverbially a gamble' (Nisbet and Hubbard on Horace, *Odes* 2.1.6, quoting among other passages Aesch. *Seven against Thebes* 414, 'Ares will decide the matter in his dice'; cf. also e.g. Plb. 1.87.8, Livy 31.35.1, 40.21.6, 42.50.2 and 59.10). At *Odes* 2.1.6 Horace acclaims Pollio as treating 'a work full of hazardous gambling', and the word for 'gambling' is *alea*, the same as for 'die' in Suet.'s version (below): the moment seems to have been a defining scene of Pollio's history. By a familiar trope (rather as pastoral poets 'become' shepherds themselves) Horace blurs the hazardous gambling that Pollio is describing, that of C., Pompey, and the rest, with the hazardous gamble for Pollio himself in treating such a theme. The phrase, not surprisingly, is picked up by later writers, particularly when intimating a link between their theme and (Pollionic?) civil war: most clearly at Petr. *Sat.* 122.173 (C. himself is there speaking), 'with Fortune to decide, let the dice fall'; also at Lucan 6.7 ~ 6.603, Manilius 1.916, and probably Livy 1.23.9.

The manuscripts of Suet. 32 have 'the die is cast' (*iacta alea est*), which is often emended to agree with P. by reading Erasmus' emendation *est<o>*, 'let the die be cast'. That is unnecessary: the shift from the proverbial imperative to the indicative is needed there because the phantom (above, p. 34) has already led the way, and C. is following. Acceptance that the decision has already been made for him is appropriate there, but not at all for P., where the agonizing must end with a decision by C. himself. We cannot tell whether the change to indicative was made by Suet. (so Hohl, art. cit., 249) or already by Pollio.

32.9. the night before he crossed, he dreamed a monstrous dream. P. has moved this from its original context in 69–8 BCE, when C. was quaestor in Spain (so Suet. 7.2, Dio 37.52.2), just as he moved the musings on Alexander from the same context to 11.5–6 (n.): cf. 5.6 n. The Alexander thoughts were repositioned at the point where C. began his path to world conquest; the dream is moved to the critical turning point along that path. The new setting makes it recall the similar dream of Hippias, another man who was trying to return to his country and become tyrant, on the eve of Marathon (Hdt. 6.107); and that was a dream that portended disaster for the dreamer. Nor is Oedipus far away, and all those unhappy associations for the tyrant himself and for his state.

P. makes the dream unambiguously **monstrous**: the sexual congress is **the unspeakable union**. Yet in themselves dreams of mother-intercourse were not so clear-cut. Artemidorus 1.79 even makes them a good sign for politicians and office-holders, because 'mother' signifies the native land and is figured as obedient and willing. Thus Suet. and Dio made their versions of the dream unambiguously propitious for the young C., intimating his future greatness, in that case (Suet. explains) because the mother stands for the whole earth. But Artemidorus does find such dreams particularly complex to interpret, and variations of sexual position carry vast differences of signification. Cf. J. J. Winkler, *The Constraints of Desire* (1990), 37–8, 42; G. W. Bowersock, *Fiction and History: Nero to Julian* (1994), 83–5. Had he chosen, P. might have used that complexity to create ambiguity as to whether this would turn out good or bad, generating an uncertainty that would mirror C.'s own (§§7–8); but he prefers to close down such ambiguity rather than encourage it. Any uncertainty centres rather on *how* the dream connects with C.'s own hesitation: above, p. 314.

33–5: The Conquest of Italy
The war has come; its 'gates' (35.1 n.) are open. All Italy is shaken, and the storm imagery of 28.5 (n.) sharpens to the 'torrent' of flights and migrations and the 'violent maelstrom' of 33.2—a very different sort of river from that last tranquil moment at the Rubicon. By 34.2–3 this torrent has left the city as a ship without a helmsman, drifting where it may: so much for the confidence at 28.6 that Pompey was the man to save Rome. Pompey's own alarm at 29.4, however transient (29.6 n.), set a pattern that is now repeated everywhere; and Pompey is as passive in dealing with it as he had been in facing the optimate extremists in 30–1.

The style changes again for this grand survey of tumultuous panic. A whole way of life is threatened, especially at Rome itself: 'no respect was paid to the laws of the city, just as none had been given to the boundary of Caesar's province' (33.1). That collapse of law may be overstated (there was little time for it, for C. was master of Italy in only sixty days, 35.3), but it inevitably recalls Thucydides on Corcyra, the great example of civic strife (3.82–3). Much of the language has a Thucydidean tinge too, especially at 33.3, both in content—the stress on 'contrary passions and violent impulses', and on the 'brash confidence' that brought further aggression and quarrels—and in style: like Thucydides, Plutarch here favours abstracts, especially a distinctive idiom using the neuter form of the participle or adjective. Thus the passage on 'jubilation', 'fear', and 'pain' is literally a clash of 'the rejoicing' element with 'that which had come to fear and was feeling pain': cf. e.g. 'the fearing' and 'the feeling confident' at Thuc. 1.36.1, 'the causing pain' at 2.61.2, or in the Corcyrean chapters 'the prudent', 'the cowardly', 'the intelligent' at 3.82.4. For similar affectations of Thucydidean style for political generalization, cf. 4.7 n. and *Cic.* 13.1 with *Plutarch and History*, 57; for general discussion, Pelling, 'Thucydidean Intertextuality'.

The Thucydidean model would lead us to expect not merely violent emotions but a vindictive ruthlessness issuing in indiscriminate bloodshed: that is the keynote of Thucydidean civic strife. All the more striking, then, that this does not happen. C. is as moderate now in victory (34.7–8) as he was in his negotiations of the previous weeks (30.1, 31.1 nn.). Still, once again that is exploited less for moralistic purposes than to stress the consequences, the beginning of a restored calm in the city (34.9, 35.4). Had P. wished to paint C. in the most favourable colours, he would not have given such emphasis to the scene with Metellus (35.6–11, cf. 35.5 n.), where his tone—'you are my slave, you and all the others I have captured who took sides against me'—is already that of the tyrant.

P. does not explain the campaign, concentrating instead on the single vignette of Domitius at Corfinium (34.6–9). Understandably, too, he does not dwell on Pompey's decision to evacuate Italy: contrast *Pompey* 63.1–2, where he debates its wisdom and quotes C.'s own criticism ('C. himself expressed amazement that, when Pompey was in possession of the city in such strength, was expecting his troops from Spain, and had control of the sea, he nonetheless left and abandoned Italy'). P.'s presentation there can be taken as an implicit defence of that controversial decision of Pompey (63–4, cf. *Plutarch and History*, 112 n. 35), whereas here it reads more as a natural continuation of the earlier panicky 'flights' from Rome (34.1– 4) and to Brundisium (35.2). C.'s rapidity too is here presented as natural for the man we have come to know; in *Pomp.* 62.2, but not here, P. explains that C. was eager to drive Pompey out of Italy before he could be reinforced by his troops from Spain (36.1 n.). Nor, in *Caesar*, is there any time now for talk, amid such panic on the one side and such decisive action on the other. In historical fact the transition from jaw to war was more blurred, as P. surely knew (*Pomp.* 63.3 mentions one initiative, and App. 2.36.143–5 has some senatorial wavering of resolve); there were further negotiations in mid-January, and C. was again moderate, even offering to give up both his province and his privilege of standing for the consulship in absence (C. *BC* 1.9–10, Cic. *Fam.* 16.12 (146).3, etc.; Gelzer 198–9, Shackleton Bailey *Cicero's Letters to Atticus*, iv. 441–7, Raaflaub 262– 72). C. made further approaches to Pompey after the fall of Corfinium (*BC* 1.24.5, 26.2–5), but was again rebuffed: cf. Raaflaub 273–6.

Some survey of the Italian terror probably stood in Pollio, but Appian has only 'there were flights and migrations from everywhere, as was to be expected amid such panic: people rushed around in disorder and tears, for they had no accurate reports and thought C. was advancing in strength with a massive army' (2.35.141). Terrible omens were announced (App. 2.36.143–5, cf. Dio 41.14), but P. is here moving too quickly for those: contrast 43.3–7, 47, 63, and e.g. *Ant.* 60.2–7 (nn.). Dio 41.7–8 expands on the agonized psychology of both those who left Italy and those who stayed, with his stress falling on the conflicting emotions that coexisted in the same mind: some of his language resembles P.'s: those who stayed 'were confronting different and contending passions...' (41.8.1, cf. §3 n.). In *Cic.* 37 P. had himself dwelt on Cicero's internal agonizings on which way to turn. Here the psychology is less tortured, and P.'s emphasis falls rather on the clash of different emotions felt (presumably) by differ- ent people ('jubilation... clashed with fear and pain'), then the se- quence of different feelings as the panic eased (34.9, 35.3).

33.1. gates of war: a familiar expression in Latin epic after Ennius *Ann.* 225–6 Sk. = 266–7 V. and one exploited by Virgil at *Aen.* 1.294–6 and 7.607–22, but it is much bolder in Greek than in Latin. It suggests the gates of Janus (*OCD*[4], s.v.), closed only when the

empire was at peace. P. knew of that custom (*Numa* 20.1–3 and *On
the Fortune of the Romans* 322a–c, using the same Greek phrase for
'gate of war'), and doubtless alludes to it here: yet now it is not a
matter of ritual nor confined to Rome, for the 'broad' gates open up
all land and sea to war's horrors. F. Fuhrmann, *Les Images de Plutarque* (1964) 209–10 n. 4, comments that the combination of 'sea' and
'gates' is 'peu logique'; but 'gates' (*pulai*) can be used of the Straits of
Gibraltar or the Bosporus (LSJ, s.v. II.3), or—seen differently, as a gate
that is closed rather than open—of the Isthmus of Corinth ('the gates
of the Sea' (Pi. *N.* 10.27: LSJ, s.v. II.2)). There may also be a suggestion
of *sluice*-gates, preparing for the 'torrent' of §2.

**33.2. Rome itself was filled by a torrent of flights and migrations
from the nearby towns:**   rather as Thucydides described Athens as
filled, tumultuously, at the beginning of the Peloponnesian War
(2.14–17), something that aggravated the disastrous plague and therefore hastened the collapse of law and custom (2.52): cf. *Per.* 34.5, and
that migration is also arguably a strong intertextual referent in *Theseus* (*Plutarch and History*, 180). This picture of a teeming city in 49 is
surely overstated: in mid-February Cicero is still *expecting* that Rome
might soon be full of honest men from the townships abandoned to
C., *Att.* 8.1 (151).3. **it was no easy matter for any leader to control the
city by persuasion or to restrain it by words:** as Thucydides' Pericles
used persuasion and words to 'restrain'—the same word as here—the
Athenian democracy 'in a manner worthy of free people' (2.65.8): cf.
Per. 18.2, 20.3–21.1, etc. The focus on leadership already prepares for
the lack of a helmsman at 34.3. *Pomp.* 61.3 gives a less developed
version of the same ideas, 'in so great a storm and tumult, the useful
element' (another Thucydidean neuter, cf. above, p. 320) 'in the city
was weak, while the undisciplined was strong and hard for leaders to
control'.

33.3. Contending passions . . . violent impulses   (lit. 'movements'):
all four words or roots (*antipalos, pathos, biaios, kin-*) are favourites
of Thucydides: in particular, war is a 'violent schoolmaster' in the
Corcyrean passage, 3.82.2, brutalizing human temper; 'passions' (the
word also means 'sufferings') are for Thucydides central to war,
especially the passion of unrelenting and murderous hatred; the
Peloponnesian War was a great 'movement', *kinēsis* (1.1.2), and in
the Corcyrean context 'virtually all Greece was later moved' by such
civic strife (3.82.1). The last three (*pathos, biaios, kin-*) are medical

terms as well, and so this takes further the medical imagery of 28.6 (n.); but it is no more likely that Pompey will be able to control this as 'doctor' (28.6) than as leader. **jubilation... fear... pain:** for the Thucydidean style, cf. above, p. 320. **in a great city:** perhaps a further echo, for in a key passage Thucydides makes the wranglings 'in a great city' lead to the Syracusan expedition (2.65.11). That is symmetrically echoed at 6.39.2, where the Syracusan demagogue Athenagoras talks of the difficulty of controlling oligarchic aspirations 'in a great city', this time Syracuse itself.

33.4. Pompey himself was bewildered, hounded on every side by conflicting criticisms: no Thucydidean Pericles, then. **Some accused him of being the one who had built Caesar's power:** not necessarily P.'s own view, at least in this *Life* (28.2 n.), but at 28.2 Pompey himself had looked at it in this way. **held responsible for.** The Greek word is *euthunai*, the 'holding to account' after office that was distinctive of Greek democracy. At *Pomp.* 61.1 Cato recommends appointing Pompey commander-in-chief, adding that 'those who do great harm must also cure it': that might be an echo of this same item, for by now *Caesar* has less room for Cato than *Pompey* does. **that Pompey had allowed Lentulus and his group to insult Caesar just when he was giving way and offering a reasonable solution:** close to P.'s own narrative emphasis, 30.1, 31.1–2, though in those passages it was not clear that Pompey had much choice in the matter. **Lentulus and his group.** The Greek could again (cf. 31.2 n.) mean just 'Lentulus'.

33.5. Favonius: 21.8 n. App. 2.37.146–7 makes Pompey give a spirited answer: 'You can have those armies, if only you follow me and do not think it so dreadful to leave Rome—and if need be Italy too. Power and liberty do not consist in the places and buildings which men own, but the men themselves have these in their possession, wherever they may be...'. But there is a hint of Thucydides' Nicias there too (Thuc. 7.77.7), as again at 2.50.205 and perhaps 2.58.240 ~ Thuc 7.50.4 (Pelling, 'Breaking the Bounds', 272 n. 34): not a good sign. **he had only to strike his foot on the earth to fill all Italy with armies.** *Pomp.* 57.9 had told this story earlier, in the context of Pompey's over-confidence in mid-50, a theme that P. passes over quickly in *Caesar*: cf. 29.4 n. Cic. *Att.* 7.16 (140).2 confirms that Pompey was still talking confidently in late January: he would have a strong army 'in a few days'. That may have been disingenuous (cf. 29.6 n.), and he soon changed his tune (§ 6 n. below).

Pomp. 60.6–7 also tells how 'Tullus' asked Pompey about forces, Pompey replied that those coming from C. (29.4–6) would suffice, and Tullus cried out 'you have deceived us, Pompey' and recommended sending an embassy to C. This 'Tullus' may be Cicero (i.e. Tullius), as App. 2.36.145 might suggest, but if so P. clearly did not realize it. On balance it is more likely to be L. Volcacius Tullus, cos. 66 (above, p. 288 n. 11: cf. Cic. *Att.* 8.9A (160).1): so F. X. Ryan, *Chiron*, 24 (1994), 75–82.

33.6. Even so, Pompey's force still outnumbered Caesar's. C. *BC* 1.6.1 makes Pompey assure the senate he has ten legions ready. Those include the two returned by C. (29.4 n.) and probably the seven in Spain (28.8 n.), though Ottmer 47–8 thinks that Pompey was excluding the Spanish legions and confident of raising seven or eight new ones in Italy. The dubious loyalty of the two who had served with C. was not difficult to guess: it was certainly soon clear to Cicero (*Att.* 7.13 (136).2, 23 January) and to Pompey himself (*Att.* 8.12 (162) A.2–3, C.4, D.1, 16–?18 February), and it is hard to think that this was a sudden revelation. (In the event, though, they stayed loyal to Pompey, and at Pharsalus were placed in a position of trust: C. *BC* 3.88, 94.3, with K. von Fritz, *TAPA* 73 (1942), 167–8, 174.) App. 2.34.134 tells of the senate instructing Pompey to raise 130,000 Italian soldiers, presumably 20 legions, and also as many men as possible from the neighbouring provinces. Recruiting was, however, understandably difficult and slow: Cic. *Att.* 7.21 (145).1. C. himself was soon joined by legions XII and VIII together with further reinforcements (C. *BC* 1.15.3, 18.5, 25.1): for those legions to arrive so promptly, C. must already have moved them into winter quarters south of the Alps (Ottmer 18–31, cf. 32.1 n.). By mid-February Pompey was in no doubt that in Italy he was seriously outnumbered and outmatched, as his letter in Cic. *Att.* 8.12c (162c).1 shows. **there was panic after panic.** C. *BC* 1.14 describes the terror when news of his early successes reached Rome, claiming that Lentulus broke into the inner treasury (35.6 n.) to seize money—something that P. might have stressed to balance the Metellus scene of 35.6–11, if he knew of it. But C. may well have coloured that episode misleadingly in *BC*: so L. de Libero, *Klio*, 80 (1998), 116–21. **The war was at the gates, they said, sweeping all before it:** 'C. was falsely reported to be on the brink of arriving, his cavalry to be here already' (C. *BC* 1.14.1). **He carried a vote to establish a state of emergency**: i.e. a declaration of *tumultus* (*OCD*[4], s.v., Lintott, *Violence*, 153–5): one point of this was to make it easier to raise levies through all Italy (Brunt, *Manpower*, 629–30). Dio 41.3.3 suggests that this was passed at one of the senate-meetings held outside the *pomerium* on perhaps 8 or 9 January; this may underlie C. *BC* 1.6.3, recording in that context a decision that 'a levy should be held in all Italy'. C.'s narrative concentrates on the inappropriateness of the 'last decree' (30.6 n.), 1.5.3, 7.5–6: he would understandably not complicate it by including the *tumultus* decree as well. So P. is simplifying, here and at *Pomp.* 61.6, by delaying the decree and presenting it as a sign of panic. **then left the city**: on the evening of 17 January. Despite P.'s implied approval in *Pomp.* 63 for Pompey's readiness to evacuate Italy (above, pp. 320–1), in a different train of thought he does criticize the decision to abandon the city (*Pomp.* 83 (3).6–8). It was very controversial: cf. *Pomp.* 63.1–2, quoting Cic. *Att.* 7.11 (134).3, and Cic. has other outbursts too, e.g. *Att.* 8.2 (152).2, 'no statesman or general anywhere has ever done anything so disgraceful...'. The great Napoleon too thought Pompey's strategy a bad mistake, *Précis* 125–6: cf. Ottmer 60–2. **forbidding anyone to remain whose allegiance lay with country and freedom rather than slavery.** *Pomp.* 61.7 personalizes the conflict more, 'Pompey proclaimed that he would regard anyone who remained as C.'s man'. That seems closer to the original, for C. *BC* 1.33.2 has Pompey saying that 'he would regard those who stayed in Rome in the same light as those who fought for C.'. (On this extreme and surely ill-judged tactic, cf. Raaflaub 230–2; Suet. *Nero* 2.3 says that Domitius (34.6 n.) was the only one to support it, though that leaves it inexplicable why it was adopted.) The formulation here coheres with the stress on tyranny: Intr., p. 21, and above, p. 320. But 34.4 (n.) soon establishes that personal loyalties are playing a part too.

34.1. The consuls fled, without even conducting the normal sacrifices before leaving. The text of C. *BC* 1.6.7 is corrupt, but may well have said something similar: cf. Carter, ad loc. The consuls left on 18 or 19 January, it seems (Carter on C. *BC* 1.14.1), and they and many of the senate gathered at Capua. This display of haste and horror may well have been deliberately overdone, to impress the public with the extremity of C.'s actions: Cic. *Att.* 7.11 (134).4

comments that the immediate reaction to this sight of a 'capital without magistrates and senate' was to swing opinion against him.

34.2. Even some of Caesar's most enthusiastic former supporters...: including his father-in-law Piso (14.8, 37.1 nn.): Cic. *Att.* 7.13 (136).1, *Fam.* 14.14 (145).2. **were so amazed:** 32.2 n.

34.3. The storm was sweeping down... like some ship left by its despairing helmsmen: 28.5, 33.2 nn. Once again (cf. 28.6 n.) the image was in people's minds at the time: Cic. *Att.* 7.3 (126).5, 'for me the only ship will be that with Pompey at the helm' (9 December 50), but by 7.13 (136).2 'we're committed—either by our own doing or our leader's—to leave harbour without a rudder and sail into the storm' (23 January).

34.4. Yet, for Pompey's sake, people even felt exile to be their home: elaborated at *Pomp.* 61.7: 'many criticized the generalship but no one hated the general; you would have found more leaving because they could not abandon Pompey than fleeing for freedom's sake.' Even Cicero, with vast reservations about Pompey's strategy and motives and lingering resentment about past treatment, felt something similar: 'a single man weighs with me: I ought to be his comrade in flight and his ally in regaining the state' (*Att.* 8.14 (164).2); cf. 9.1 (167).4, 9.5 (171).3, etc.; Gelzer, *Cicero* 247–8.

34.5. Labienus: 18.2 n. His defection was rumoured by 21 January (Cic. *Att.* 7.11 (134).1) and confirmed a day or so later (7.12 (135). 5, 13 (136).1). He originated from Picenum, the centre of Pompey's support, and Syme, *RP* i. 62–75, thought that a vital factor in his change of allegiance now. For alternative speculations, cf. W. B. Tyrrell, *Hist.* 21 (1972), 424–40 (a matter of principled support for the legitimate government); G. Wylie, *AHB* 3 (1989), 123–7 (personal resentment at C.'s lack of appreciation, exacerbated by the rise of Antony in C.'s favour). **who had... fought most valiantly in all the Gallic campaigns:** 18.2, 20.1, 20.8, 25.1, 25.2, 25.3–27, 26.6 nn. **Caesar sent all Labienus' possessions and equipment after him:** for such courtesy in war, cf. *Ant.* 63.3 (n.), Antony's treatment of Cn. Domitius Ahenobarbus before Actium (the Enobarbus of Shakespeare and the son of the Domitius of §6). D. Brutus did the same for a senator at Mutina in 43 BCE, Dio 46.38.3–4.

34.6. Then he moved on Domitius. C.'s first moves, esp. his capture of Arretium (C. *BC* 1.12), might have seemed aimed at Rome, whether or not this was in fact his strategy from the start (T. P. Hillman, *Hist.* 37 (1988), 248–52 doubts it). When it became clear that Pompey was moving eastwards, C. too changed direction. For a good brief analysis of the strategy, cf. Carter i–ii. 13–16; for a vigorous narrative, Holmes, *RR* iii.1–33; on C.'s own narrative technique in *BC*, Batstone and Damon 61–3. For L. **Domitius** Ahenobarbus, cos. 54, C.'s inveterate enemy and now designated to succeed him in Gaul, cf. 21.3–9, 23.7, 28.5, 29.1, and 29.5 nn.; *OCD*[4], s.v. (1). After his release here he fought again at Massilia and Pharsalus, where he was killed trying to escape. **Corfinium:** see Map 1. C. describes the seven-day Corfinium campaign (14/15–21 February) at *BC* 1.15–23: for good analyses of his narrative, see Batstone and Damon 12–18, 64–8, 139–41, 160–1. Domitius was trying to trap C. between himself and Pompey, who he hoped would advance from the south: that strategy was optimistic but not senseless. Pompey, however, pleaded with Domitius to withdraw (Cic. *Att.* 8.12 (162)a–c, C. *BC* 1.19.4), without perhaps being wholly candid about his own thinking about evacuation, but Pompey did not have the authority to insist. Cf. G. Veith, *Klio*, 13 (1913), 1–26; K. von Fritz, *TAPA* 73 (1942), 145–80, esp. 154–66; Shackleton Bailey, *Cicero's Letters to Atticus*, iv. 448–59; Seager 169–73; Gelzer 200–1. **thirty cohorts.** This might simply mean 'three legions' (12.1 n.), but in fact Domitius' force was a more ramshackle collection of smaller detachments (cf. Batstone and Damon 12–13): C. *BC* 1.15.6–7 suggests that Domitius had thirty-three cohorts, twenty of his own and thirteen brought by Lucilius Hirrus; Pompey thought he had thirty-one (Cic. *Att.* 8. 12a (162a).1). Cf. Carter on *BC* 1.15.7.

34.7. he heard that Caesar was treating prisoners with a remarkable generosity: in particular, Lentulus Spinther (cos. 57), who had pleaded with C. for mercy and was spared: that reassured many others in Corfinium (C. *BC* 1.22). **remarkable generosity.** Notice that P. avoids using any word for 'clemency' or 'mercy': cf. 48.4, 57.4 nn. and Intr., p. 20.

34.8. His doctor told him to take heart, for he had taken only a sleeping drug, and it was not lethal. Suet. *Nero* 2.3 tells it rather differently: Domitius was lacking in resolve, and after taking the poison changed his mind and deliberately vomited it up; the doctor had known his master well, and not given him a lethal draught. That inconstancy of Nero's ancestor is thematically useful for Suet.'s *Life*.

The story is also told by Sen. *Ben.* 3.24 and Plin. *NH* 7.186; like Suet., they do not have the news arriving of C.'s clemency and Domitius' regret at his premature decision, and that looks like P.'s elaboration.

Stith Thompson, *Motif-index of Folk Literature*, vi^2 (1958) 717, collects such tales of 'sleeping potion substituted for poison'. They are particularly frequent in love stories, for instance, in cases where a thwarted lover or husband tries to kill his unresponsive lady but she is spared by a friend who switches the drugs; cf. Xen. *Eph.* 3.5.9–8.2, where Anthia saves herself from an unwelcome new husband by drinking what she thinks to be poison but is in fact merely a sleeping draught. The motif sits oddly in a military narrative: 'a fairy-tale anecdote' (Batstone and Damon 17). **The delighted Domitius rose, went off to Caesar, and took him by the hand.** C. mentions the sparing of Domitius and his son, together with Lentulus, three other senators, and many more (*BC* 1.23): he adds that (amazingly) he allowed Domitius to keep a sum of 6,000,000 HS, something that the early reports apparently denied (Cic. *Att.* 8.14 (164).3). C. *BC* does not have the scene of the sleeping draught: that was not in C.'s style (though it may have been in Pollio's, Intr., p. 47). The story may also come from oral tradition: Intr., p. 54.

34.9. When this news reached Rome it raised people's spirits...: Cicero too comments on the way in which this clemency at Corfinium turned public opinion in C.'s favour: *Att.* 8.13 (163).2, 8.16(166), etc. Cf. Gelzer 201–2. **some who had fled turned back to the city:** Cic. *Att.* 9.1 (167).2 (6 March), 'I hear that Rome is now full of optimates...' (though 'optimates' may carry irony, cf. *Att.* 9.5 (171).3 and 9.9 (176).1): Gelzer 202 and n. 2.

35.1. Caesar enlisted Domitius' troops among his own army: C. *BC* 1.23.5, cf. Ottmer 43–4. **the levies of Pompey that he had overrun in the various cities:** including Auximum, Sulmo, Alba, and Tarracina (C. *BC* 1.13.4, 1.18.4, 1.24.3), then others during the march to Brundisium (*BC* 1.24.4). Other Pompeian troops had simply dispersed (*BC* 1.12.2, 15.3); some of these may also have now joined C.'s army. By the time he reached Brundisium, C. had six legions (*BC* 1.25.1). Cf. Ottmer 40–4.

35.2. Pompey withdrew before his advance. He may well have initially intended to challenge C. in north Italy, but the option of withdrawing to Greece was aired from an early stage: Cicero was talking of it in December, *Fam.* 2.16 (154).3. Many have thought that it was Pompey's firm plan from the outset: so, in otherwise partly divergent analyses, e.g. Holmes, *RR* iii. 12, von Fritz, *TAPA* 73 (1942), 145–80, Ottmer 55–62, and Raaflaub 52–3. I prefer to follow Seager 172–3 and Carter i–ii. 14–16 in believing that Pompey was keeping his options open for as long as possible, even if evacuation was always the most likely outcome; then C.'s early successes swiftly persuaded Pompey that this was the wiser course. (Dio too reconstructed Pompey's thinking in this way, 41.10.3.) By early February (Cic. *Att.* 7.20 (144).1) he had positioned himself at Luceria (see Map 1), a station that would still allow either option but already looked better suited for flight: that is the way Cicero saw it, *Att.* 8.1 (151).2, 8.3 (153).4, etc. By 13–15 February Pompey was thinking firmly of evacuation, as he made clear in his letter to the consuls (*Att.* 8.12A (162A).3) but perhaps less clear to Domitius (34.6 n.). **He fled to Brundisium.** Pompey left Luceria on 19 February and Canusium on the 21st (Cic. *Att.* 8.8 (158).2, 8.9A (160).1, 9.1 (167).1). **then sent the consuls with a force over to Dyrrhachium:** C. *BC* 1.25.2. They crossed on 4 March, it seems (cf. Cic. *Att.* 9.6 (172).3), with thirty cohorts (*Pomp.* 62.3) or perhaps 15,000 men (*Att.* 9.9 (176).2 with 9.6 (182).3). **he himself sailed after them a little later:** on 17 March (*Att.* 9.15A (184)). **as Caesar came up:** C. arrived before Brundisium on 9 March (*Att.* 9.13A (181A).1). **The details will be given more fully in my projected** *Life* **of Pompey.** And *Pomp.* 62 indeed gives extra details on the siege of Brundisium and Pompey's evacuation to Greece. Such cross-references are frequent in the *Lives*: I discuss them at *Plutarch and History*, 7–10. Often they excuse an abbreviated version, as here and at 45.9 (*Pompey* again), 59.4 (*Numa*), and 62.8 and 68.7 (*Brutus*): cf. 62 n. Usually P. refers to other *Lives* in the perfect tense, 'as has been written in ...', and he sometimes uses such perfects even in cases when the other *Life* has not yet been published. The future tense here is rarer, and in *Plutarch and History*, 34 n. 54, I wonder whether a longer interval was anticipated before the publication of *Pompey* than in the other cases. In any case, P. has clearly already considered the material and presentation of *Pompey* as well (Intr., p. 37), and it is understandable that he can already regard himself as engaged on that *Life*: at 45.9 below he refers to it in the present tense, 'we tell that story in his own *Life*'.

35.3. Caesar was eager to pursue at once, but did not have the ships: C. *BC* 1.29: 'although Caesar thought his best hope of finishing the business was to gather ships, cross the sea, and follow Pompey before he could strengthen his army with overseas reinforcements, he still feared the delay and the amount of time this would require, as Pompey had taken all the ships and therefore removed any chance of an immediate pursuit. The only remaining possibility was to wait for ships from more distant regions—Gaul, Picenum, and the Straits of Messina—and the time of year made that an extended and difficult prospect...'. The 'time of year' was mid-March by the calendar, but still late January by the season (32.1 n.). C. therefore decided to deal with the Spanish threat first (36.1 n.), leaving orders for the townships to send what ships they could to Brundisium in his absence (*BC* 1.29.3–30.1). **and so he returned to Rome:** in late March. In *Pomp.* 62.1–2 this return, together with the Metellus episode, is displaced for compositional reasons (*Plutarch and History*, 92–3) to before the siege of Brundisium.

35.4. he addressed them in moderate and popular tones. He convened the senate on 1 April (Cic. *Att.* 9.17 (186).1) and again on each of the next two days: at *BC* 1.32 C. summarizes this address, including a call on the senate to participate in the administration—and an indication that, if they did not, he would rule himself. He had earlier said something similar to Cicero in private, *Att.* 9.18 (187).3. P. provides his own version of that blend of the monarchic and the moderate (so does Dio 41.17.3, but more crudely): the word here for **popular** is *dēmotikos*, hinting at the style of the demagogue, and there is a contrast with the blunt tyrant-speak that follows (§§6–11, cf. above, p. 320), though that contrast is complicated by the familiar linkage of populism and tyranny (29.4 n.). **encouraging them to send envoys to Pompey to propose a reasonable settlement:** *BC* 1.32.8; cf. Raaflaub 230–1, 276–8.

35.5. But no one did. According to C. *BC* 1.33.1, the senate agreed to send envoys 'but no one could be found to do it'; Dio 41.16.4 suggests that envoys were nominated but refused. Cicero expected Ser. Sulpicius Rufus to be chosen, *Att.* 10.1A (191). **Perhaps they were nervous of Pompey, whom they had abandoned:** C.'s own explanation, *BC* 1.33.1–2. **perhaps they felt Caesar's fine words were insincere.** Cicero took this second view at the time, *Att.* 10.1 (190).3 and 1A

(191); later Dio read it the same way, with characteristic elaboration, 41.16. For such double explanations in P., cf. 8.3, 9.10 nn. Here, if anything, it is the explanation more to C.'s moral credit that the *preceding* narrative encourages: Pompey's proclamation of 33.6 would make anyone still in the city **nervous**, while the moderation of C.'s earlier proposals was stressed at 30.1 and 31.1. But in those passages (nn.) P. had stressed the way C.'s proposals 'appeared' or the 'impression' they left, just as at 29.4 and 31.3 he had talked of the 'justifications' he had exploited; the narrative was not concerned with his offers' sincerity, only with their impact. The *following* narrative, with the bluntness of §§6–11, may tilt the balance the other way, towards thinking that such **fine words** were indeed **insincere**, or at least that there was a more uncompromising side to C.'s demeanour too; and the difficulty in reading motives—both the senators' difficulty in reading C. and the reader's difficulty in reading the senators—itself tells a tale about the uneasy atmosphere generated by one-man rule.

   C. also, it seems, promised a grain distribution and a distribution of 300 HS per citizen (Dio 41.16.1, cf. Lucan 3.52–70), and it may also be now that the important enfranchisement of the Transpadani is to be dated (37.2 n.); but for the moment P. concentrates on the senate.

35.6. the tribune. L. Caecilius **Metellus** (*MRR* 259) was son of the consul of 68 and son-in-law of a 'Clodia' who was a sister of Clodius (10.2 n.) and of Ap. Claudius, cos. 54 (21.5n.); possibly even the famous Clodia of Cic. *Cael.* Metellus had earlier been with the consuls in Capua (Cic. *Att.* 9.6 (172).3). News of the present incident reached Cicero at Cumae by 14 April (*Att.* 10.4 (195).8): his visitor Curio also told him that C. had been 'so furious that he had wanted Metellus killed—which would have been the start of a great massacre'. So the atmosphere at Rome was clearly still very nervous. C. glosses over it in *BC* 1.33.3–4: 'L. Metellus, a tribune of the people, was put up by Caesar's enemies to delay this business [the proposal of negotiations] and hamper everything else he had decided to do. When Caesar realized this plan, as he had already wasted several days and was eager not to lose any more time, he left undone what he had intended to achieve, departed from the city, and went to Further Gaul.' C.'s implication there that he had 'left undone' (or 'unfinished') his plans leaves the misleading impression that Metellus' obstruction had succeeded, and passes over the crucial **money from the treasury**.

This episode is discussed by L. de Libero, *Klio*, 80 (1998), 111–33, and Woytek 46–57. Woytek thinks that P. has misplaced the confrontation and C. as a bearer of *imperium* remained properly outside the pomerium, but it is unlikely that such niceties were observed.

treasury. P. does not make it clear whether he means the *aerarium* as a whole or the 'more sacred treasury' in the temple of Saturn (*OCD*[4], s.v. *aerarium*, *LTUR* iv. 234–6), used for emergencies and fed by a 5 per cent tax on manumissions: de Libero, art. cit., 129–30 and Woytek 56–7 sensibly remark that he probably raided both, but it is the 'more sacred treasury' that figures more in contemporary accounts. According to C. *BC* 1.14.1 (33.6 n.), the consul Lentulus had already tried to take what he could in January, and in February there was a further unsuccessful instruction to the consuls to return to Rome and remove as much as possible (Cic. *Att.* 7.21 (142).2). In January Cicero had predicted that C. would not be slowed by a closed treasury (*Att.* 7.12 (135).2, cf. 7.15 (139).3). The amount he took is given by Plin. *NH* 33.56 as 15,000 ingots of gold, 30,000 of silver, and 30,000,000 HS. Pliny adds that the treasury was then richer than at any point in its history. Oros. 6.15.5 gives 4,135 pounds of gold and 900,000 (perhaps to be emended to 90,000) of silver. For an attempt to reconcile the data, cf. T. Frank, *AJP* 53 (1932), 360–4, who calculates that the total was equivalent to about 50,000,000 HS, enough to pay his legions for several months: that calculation may well be too low, and 75,000,000 might be nearer the mark. Cf. also Woytek 53–4, doubting Frank's attempt to reconcile Pliny and Orosius and placing more weight on Pliny. Some of the takings were juicier: there were also 1,500 pounds of *laserpicium*, i.e. Cyrenaic silphium (Plin. *NH* 19.40). **cited certain laws in his support:** perhaps those excluding the use of the gold deposited during the Gallic invasion of 387 BCE and declared 'sacred' (Livy 5.50.6, cf. Plin. *NH* 33.14); App. 2.41.164 and Lucan 3.159 indicate that this was the sum in question now, though it may just be that Metellus, and then C.'s other enemies in spreading the tale, made most fuss about this to stress the scandal of it all (de Libero, art. cit., 127–8). But Metellus doubtless also made much of the importance of his veto (P. may not have grasped this, 31.2 n.), and the 'laws' (or 'customs', *nomoi*) of tribunician sacrosanctity were also relevant: Lucan's 'Metellus' makes that clear, 3.123–6. In mid-April Caelius told Cicero that C. had left Rome 'furious at those vetoes' (*Att.*

10.9A (200A).1 = *Fam.* 8.16 (153).1), and the plural suggests that
Metellus vetoed actions in the senate as well (cf. *Att.* 10.4 (195).9 with
Shackleton Bailey's note). The precedent of Tiberius Gracchus effectively sealing the temple of Saturn (*Gracch.* 10.8–9) was an especially
close one, and it was most embarrassing for C. to be so brutal with
tribunes' rights so soon after going to war as their champion (31.3).
Cf. Raaflaub 177–9.

35.8. you are my slave: tyrant-speak, indeed: cf. above, p. 320.
Those suggestions were also caught by the American senator Henry
Clay in late 1833: in a fierce denunciation of President Jackson, Clay
likened the President's dismissal of Secretary of the Treasury William
J. Duane to C.'s seizure of the treasury as told by 'the venerable
biographer'. His point was precisely that Jackson was endangering
public liberty and setting up a tyranny.

35.9. The keys were nowhere to be seen.   According to Dio 41.17.2,
the consuls still held the keys (cf. §6 n.), but he is probably guessing.
They should, it seems, have been kept by the city quaestors: cf.
Gracch. 10.8, Plb. 23.14.5, *StR* ii. 132; de Libero, art. cit. (§5 n.), 112
n. 6 and 128 n. 96.

35.10. he threatened to kill him…: contrast Lucan 3.133–40, who
makes the furious Caesar *refuse* to kill Metellus, for he is unworthy of
so distinguished a death; there it is a 'Cotta' who dissuades Metellus,
with a rather tortuous argument about liberty's death. That is probably Lucan's own adaptation (so Hunink on 3.143), fitting into a
sequence of odious clemencies: cf. 2.511–25 (Domitius) and then
4.337–64 (Afranius, so degenerate as to plead for clemency himself).
Broughton was too trustful in including Cotta as a historical tribune
of the year (*MRR* 258). If there is any factual basis for this man, it may
be L. Aurelius Cotta, cos. 65 (above, p. 288, 60.2 n.: so J. L. Ferrary,
Mélanges… Heurgon (1976), i. 285–92, and cf. *MRR* iii. 30). But he
may well be pure fiction: perhaps even a foil for his near-anagram
Cato, with Lucan playing with different notions of freedom (cf. e.g.
2.234–325)? **'And, young man':** Greek *meirakion*, an especially suitable form of address for such dismissiveness: E. Dickey, *Greek Forms
of Address: From Herodotus to Lucian* (1996), 72–6.

35.11. into going away: presumably just 'from the treasury', but
predictably he at some point left Rome too and joined the Pompeians.
After Pharsalus he wished to return to Italy, but C. refused (Cic. *Att.*

11.7 (218).2). **ensured that everything else Caesar needed for the war was carried out readily and quickly.** But it also alienated opinion even among the *plebs*, if Curio read things aright (*Att.* 10.4 (195).8). Cicero believed him, *Att.* 10.8 (199).6.

36–8: Civil War: The Opening Moves

36: THE WAR IN SPAIN   Pompey's seven legions in Spain (28.8 n.) had already played a part in calculations. As P. explains at *Pomp.* 62.1 (above, pp. 320–1), C. was eager to conquer Italy before they could come to reinforce Pompey (cf. Cic. *Fam.* 16.12 (146).4 for the part those legions could play in a prolonged Italian campaign, and C.'s own criticism of Pompey for forsaking that advantage at *Pomp.* 63.2, above, p. 320). By *Att.* 9.15 (183).1 and 9.15A (184).1 and 9.18 (187).1 (25 and 28 March) it was clear that C. would move on Spain before Greece.

36.1. he launched an expedition into Spain.   C. left Rome around 6 or 7 April, initially for Gaul, where Massilia had refused to open its gates to him (C. *BC* 1.34–7): he invested the city before continuing to Spain, and after his departure the siege did not end till October or later (C. *BC.* 2.1–22). The Massilia fighting involved some spectacular siege works and sea encounters, which interested Lucan (3.298–762), but not here P., even though he has already referred allusively to 'the sea battle off Massilia' at 16.2 (n.). C. arrived at Ilerda (the modern Lérida/Lleida) on or around 23 June (Carter on C. *BC* 1.41.1). L. **Afranius** (*OCD*[4], no. 2), cos. 60, was like Pompey a native of Picenum: at *Advice on Public Life* 806a–b P. tells a story of his consular candidature that turns on his role as a loyal Pompeian acolyte. His career often took him to Spain. He fought there under Pompey in the seventies (*Sert.* 19); he may have been proconsul of Nearer Spain in ?71–67 (so *MRR* iii. 12–13, though the evidence is uncertain, *PRR* 515), and he celebrated a triumph; then after 55 he governed as Pompey's legate one or other Spanish province, probably again Nearer (*MRR* 220, etc.), with three legions (cf. 28.8 nn.). After this campaign he fought again at Pharsalus and at Thapsus, after which he was captured and executed (53.7 n.). M. Terentius **Varro** is the renowned antiquarian scholar; one earlier service for Pompey had been his composition of a memoir on senatorial procedure in 70. Like Afranius, he had also held a series of commands under Pompey, first in Spain in the seventies and then, after his praetorship, against the pirates in 67 (*MRR* 100, 149). He had probably been a Pompeian

legate in Spain for some time, possibly from 55 (*MRR* 253, 625). The
third legate was M. Petreius, a 'military man' (Sall. *Cat.* 59.6) who also
played prominent roles in the fighting against Catiline in 63 and in
the African campaign of 46 (52.9 n.), but Plutarch does not mention
him in any of the *Lives*. **Pompey's legates ... the forces there:** picking
up 28.8, 'he governed them [Spain and Africa] by sending out legates
and maintaining armies'.

**36.2. continued his pursuits and challenges and circumvallations
until he seized control of the enemy camps and forces.** A very
succinct summary of the complicated campaign that ended with C.'s
success at Ilerda (C. *BC* 1.37–87, 2.17–21): P. delays tactical detail for
the critical fighting in Greece, 37–46. P.'s phrasing hints at, but does
not elaborate, the tactical skill with which C.'s manœuvrings secured
victory over a formidable enemy force without a pitched battle.
The **ambushes** are probably an inexact version of the sequence of
C. *BC* 1.65–70, where both forces race to be the first to occupy high
ground flanking a narrow defile; for the difficulties caused by **lack of
food** and their subsequent relief, cf. C. *BC* 1.48–9, 52, 60. The tables
eventually turned, and it was shortage of food that forced Afranius
and Petreius to capitulate on 2 August 49. (On the campaign and C.'s
account, see Carter's comm.; Holmes, *RR* iii. 51–77, 388–408; Fuller
193–206; P. A. Stadter, *CJ* 88 (1992–3), 217–21; P. F. Cagniart, *AncW*
26 (1995), 29–44; Batstone and Damon 75–84. There is some reason
to think that the operations of *BC* 1.65–70 may have taken place
further east than they are usually put.[20]) P. does not develop
two other themes that apparently figured in his source (cf. App.
2.43.171–4, which may well derive from C. *BC*—so E. Potz, *GrB* 21
(1995), 85–94—but if so probably via Pollio): (*a*) the fraternization
between the two forces that won goodwill among the Pompeian
rank and file: it is abruptly and bloodily terminated by Petreius
(C. *BC* 1.74–6). P. makes something of a similar episode at *Ant.* 18,
but in *Caesar* the response of *enemy* soldiers is not an interest. P. also
omits (*b*) the ostentatious clemency that C. showed to both

[20] i.e., that Afranius may have been making for the defile of S. Juan, rather than the
somewhat notional defile of Ribarroja; that 'Octagesa' should be identified with Flix
rather than Ribarroja (Rice Holmes, Fuller, and many others) or Mequinenza (Cagniart); and that the conspicuous 'mountain' of C.'s narrative was one of the eastern
range including Granadella, possibly the height-system extending east of Carbonella,
rather than (as usually assumed) Monmaneu.

commanders and troops, an aspect that he stresses at *Pomp.* 65.3. In C.'s own account he demands only that the legions be demobilized (*BC* 1.85–6); App. has him release them, like their commanders, to rejoin Pompey; at *Pomp.* 65.3 P., like Dio 41.23.1–2, has him release the commanders and recruit the men himself. Here **the commanders took to flight** makes it sound as if the generals escaped rather than being released unharmed. A mention of the clemency might have continued the themes of 34.6–9, but 35.3–11 has by now moved the narrative emphasis to make C.'s behaviour more two-edged (cf. 35.5 n.).

So this chapter has moved very quickly and selectively: even the summarizing comment on Afranius' 'poor generalship' is left to be made in passing at 41.4. As on C.'s return to Rome at 37.1–2, the narrative briskness conveys the formidable and effective strategist. That, rather than any clemency or goodwill among the enemy troops, is the more relevant preparation for the decisive fighting.

37.1–2: CAESAR IN ROME, (?NOVEMBER–)DECEMBER 49 Varro's forces still remained (36.1), though support ebbed away after the capitulation of Afranius and Petreius (C. *BC* 2.17–21); C. accepted his surrender at Cordoba (?late September 49), then began the long march back to Italy. There were delays en route at Massilia and Placentia (below). His eleven days at Rome will have included at least some time before 9 December, Antony's last day in office, if Antony was the proposer of one of the bills and if C. was already present (§2 n.). P. simplifies by omitting the other developments of 49: the continuation of the siege of Massilia until C. accepted the surrender (36.1 n., C. *BC* 2.22); the command of Cato in Sicily (*C.min.* 53); C. Antonius' reverse in Illyricum (C. *BC* 3.4.2, 10.5, 67.5, and a full account may well have stood in a lost section of *BC* 2, as H. C. Avery suggested, *Hermes*, 121 (1993), 452–69); Curio's failure and death in Africa (C. *BC* 2.23–44), which was apparently described in some colour by the eyewitness Pollio (App. 2.45.185–46.187); and, most interestingly, the mutiny that C. faced at Placentia on his way back to Rome (Suet. 69, etc.). On this, see §§3–9 n.

The specific measures of C.'s dictatorship are described generously (§2 nn.), but §1 leaves no doubt that he was not in the mood for compromise, and it is again (cf. 36.2 n.) the speed that is emphasized as C. hastened onwards.

37.1. his father-in-law Piso: 14.8, 34.1 nn. He emerges several times as a peacemaker, and had offered to serve on a similar embassy himself in the crisis of early January (C. *BC* 1.3.6). P. Servilius **Isauricus,** the son of the Isauricus of 7.1 (n.), had supported Cato in the disturbances of 54 (28.4 n.), but had come over to C. since. 'A man of some competence' (Syme, *RR* 69), he went on after his consulship in 48 (§2) to govern Asia in 46–44. He later betrothed his daughter to the young Octavian and was again consul in 41, but P. never mentions him except for the two references here. He again (7.5 n.) introduces rather casually a figure who would not be very familiar to his readers.

37.2. Then the senate appointed Caesar dictator. He had in fact been named dictator while still en route back from Spain (C. *BC* 2.21.5), perhaps in October, but he took up the office only on his entry to the city: cf. Dio 42.21.3 on C.'s *second* dictatorship (?September/October 48, 51.1 n.), 'C. entered on his dictatorship immediately, despite being outside Italy', evidently an irregularity (*StR* ii. 152–4). 'The senate appointed' is loose (as is 'the nervous people appointed' at App. 2.48.196), for P. knew that dictators were nominated rather than appointed or elected: 'a dictator is not chosen by the people or the senate, but one of the consuls or praetors goes before the people and names the person of his choice as dictator' (*Marc.* 24.11–12). 'One of the consuls or praetors' glosses over the irregularity of nomination by a praetor, for this regularly fell to the consuls (Lintott, *Constitution*, 110); but the Pompeian consuls of the year (29.1, 30.5–6, 31.2 nn.) would hardly oblige and were anyway already in Greece. The constitutional problem was being discussed as early as March 49 (Cic. *Att.* 9.15 (183).2). It was met by the passing of a law, doubtless with senatorial backing (so P.'s language, like App.'s, is not altogether misleading; F. X. Ryan, *Hist.* 57 (1998), 253, is a little harsh), in consequence of which C. was nominated dictator by the praetor M. Aemilius Lepidus (63.7 n.): on Lepidus' role here, cf. K. Welch, *Hermes,* 123 (1995), 446–50.

He allowed some exiles to return: all except Milo (28.7 n.), say App. 2.48.198 and Dio 41.36.2; there were a few further exceptions, including C. Antonius (4.2 n.), according to Cic. *Phil.* 2.55–6, 98. This was done through a law proposed by M. Antony as tribune (*MRR* 258, Thommen 123, 126). C.'s intention to restore exiles had been anticipated at least since April: Cic. *Att.* 10.4 (195).8, 10.8 (199).2, 10.13

(205).1, 10.14 (206).3. Bruhns 64–70 notes that C. was slow to move on this (contrast the Transpadani legislation, probably in March: below), and suggests that he was treading carefully around a delicate topic: he also points out that the exiles that did return seem to have done little to help C. **restored their political rights to the children of those who had suffered under Sulla:** i.e. the children of the pro-scribed, possibly but not certainly under the same *lex Antonia*: it may be that C. simply announced that he would accept their candidature for office, on the assumption that the proscriptions were themselves illegal (A. Drummond, *Athen.* 87 (1999), 135 n. 50). At *Sulla* 31.8 P. expresses his indignation at Sulla's exclusion of the sons and grand-sons of the proscribed from political rights and the confiscation of their property ('the most unfair measure of all'). As P. himself brings out at *Cic.* 12.2 (so also Dio 41.18.2, 44.47.4, cf. Jehne 237–8), the most important aspect concerned their right to stand for office, for it is hard to think that any property could by now be restored. F. Hinard, *Les Proscriptions de la Rome républicaine* (1985), 92–100, 171–7 and *Sullana Varia* (2008), 107–20, considers whether any other restrictions might have still remained until they were now removed: possibly the right to initiate prosecutions. Dio 41.18.2 puts this measure under C.'s actions in March, before leaving for Spain (35.5 n.), and Hinard, *Les Proscriptions*, 217–19, differentiates two phases, first allowing candidatures in March and then retrospec-tively validating this by law in November: that is possible, but Dio may well be collecting items out of temporal sequence in 41.18, as is his wont. As C. *BC* 3.1.4–5 suggests, more immediately relevant and contentious was the restoration of some who had been condemned of electoral corruption under Pompey's law of 52 (*MRR* 234, cf. above, p. 277; *MRR* 257, 258), perhaps numbering as many as 40 (Bruhns 66); P. prefers to concentrate on the Sullan aspect, suggesting a continua-tion of C.'s 'Marianism' (5.2–5, 6.1–6, 18.1, 19.4 nn.). C.'s campaign about the proscriptions may in fact go back to his aedileship (6.6 nn.). **introduced some unburdening of interest to lighten the load on debtors.** The Greek for 'unburdening' is *seisachtheia*, a word that inevitably evokes Solon's acclaimed measure (cf. *Solon* 15–16); as P. himself notes in *Advice on Public Life* 807e, it is a positive word for the sort of 'cancellation of debts' that P. normally treats negatively as part of the demagogue stereotype (*Ant.* 9.1 with my n., *Popl.* 26(3).2, *Ag.-Cl.* 12.1, 38.5; Intr., p. 19). The fact that it granted remission only of *interest*, not of the whole debt, would make it more moderate in P.'s eyes: he is tempted by a similar interpretation of Solon's measure, *Solon* 15.3–4. 'Lighten the load' continues the image and the favourable tone. In fact the measures were more complicated, imposing a valuation of properties at their pre-war price if they had been used as security for loans, requiring creditors to accept such properties instead of cash, and imposing a limit on cash-holdings (C. *BC* 3.1.2 with Carter's n.; Dio 41.37–8; App. 2.48.198). Other measures may have dealt specifically with interest payments: Suet. 42 says that C. allowed interest already paid to be deducted from the valuation of the security, Dio 42.51.1 that he remitted interest due from the beginning of the war, but neither measure is securely dated (Dio seems to be speaking of 47): cf. M. W. Frederiksen, *JRS* 56 (1966), 133–5, with good remarks on the nature of the crisis; E. Rawson, *CAH* ix^2 (1994), 457–8, and C. Nicolet in the same volume, 641–2; Jehne 243–9; Woytek 68–9. **other similar measures, but not very many.** He also distributed corn, celebrated the Latin festival, designated some provincial governors (App. 2.48.197), and filled some vacant priesthoods (Dio 41.36.3). Dio also puts here the enfranchisement of the Transpadani, i.e. the inhabitants of Cisalpine Gaul, though it seems more likely that this had already been carried through in March by the praetor L. Roscius Fabatus (35.5 n.): so *MRR* 258, though cf. also *LPPR* 416, Jehne 154 n. 8. This was a measure of great political and administrative importance (cf. 5.6, 29.2 nn., Williams 120–6), but one that would have involved P. in a cumbersome and distracting explanation. **within eleven days:** so C. *BC* 3.2.1. That is, eleven days after his arrival in Rome, whether or not the dictatorship was counted as beginning then or on his nomination two months earlier (cf. on 'the senate appointed Caesar dictator' above). **declared himself and Servilius Isauricus consuls:** for 48, though it was irregular for the presiding magistrate himself to be a candidate (Frei-Stolba 40). The phrasing need not preclude a formal election by the *comitia centuriata*, whose results were then 'declared' by the presiding magistrate (cf. 58.2 n., and, for the language, cf. *Marc.* 5.1–3, *Ant.* 11.5, Frei-Stolba 47); but in the circumstances the election was doubtless indeed a formality. Lucan 5.392–6 waxes indignant. Normally it would be one or both of the consuls who would hold elections (Lintott, *Constitution*, 105), and here again (cf. on 'the senate appointed Caesar dictator', above) a constitutional difficulty was anticipated as early as March (Cic. *Att.* 9.9 (176).3). Dictators could hold elections in the consuls' absence, and this may well have been a prime reason why C.

took the office. The tone of *BC* 3.1 shows that C. was keen to make some parade of constitutionality.

37.3–9: THE MARCH TO BRUNDISIUM, DECEMBER 49–EARLY JANUARY 48   C. set sail from Brundisium on 4 January 48 (C. *BC* 3.6.1). His journey from Rome might take seven or eight days (§1 n.), and so the latest possible day for his leaving Rome would be 24 December (Carter on C. *BC* 3.2.1); but his eleven days in Rome will have included some time before 9 December (37.1–2 n.), and so we should assume that he spent some time at Brundisium before sailing. App. 2.54.221 confirms that C. arrived in Brundisium before the end of December.

There is no need to doubt that C.'s troops were disgruntled (§3 n.), but this episode seems to be an imaginative elaboration of P.'s own. It may be inspired by an item that he has just omitted but that apparently figured in Pollio (App. 2.47.191–5), the mutiny of the ninth legion that C. faced down at Placentia (? November): cf. also Suet. 69, Dio 41.26–36, and (with E. Fantham, *CPh* 80 (1985), 119–31) Lucan 5.237–373. Cf. S. G. Chrissanthos, *JRS* 91 (2001), 68. Its suppression required strong measures, the threat of dismissal and/or decimation, and the execution of twelve ringleaders. That does not suit P.'s picture of the 'remarkable enthusiasm and devotion' (16.1) of C.'s men; nor, admittedly, do these grumblings, but P.'s emphasis can now rest on the inspirational recovery of spirits, and no threats are needed.

37.3. he swept past the rest of his troops.   C. had ordered twelve legions and his cavalry to rendezvous at Brundisium (C. *BC* 3.2.2): that force will include some recent recruits (cf. 32.1, 33.6, 35.1 nn.; Carter on C. *BC*. 3.2.2, Brunt, *Manpower*, 467–8). Presumably four legions from Spain (C. *BC* 1.39.2, 2.21.4 with Carter's nn.) and one from Massilia (C. *BC* 2.22.6) were among those making their way to Brundisium. No wonder they were tired, fractious, and late: if they left Massilia in late October, they would need to cover some 900 miles in little more than two months to reach Brundisium before C. sailed. Normal speed might be 10–13 miles a day, with at least one rest day in five. Those who had fought in Spain would already have covered at least 400 miles before. C. *BC* 3.2.2 adds that they were suffering from disease in the oppressive south Italian autumn after the healthier climate of Spain and Gaul. No wonder, too, that C. swept past them: he would be travelling 40–50 miles a day, and might cover the journey from Rome in 7–8 days (Carter on *BC* 3.2.1; Horace's party took more like a fortnight, *Sat.* 1.6, but they were not in such haste). **with just 600 elite cavalry and five legions:** the MSS of C. *BC* 3.6.2 say 'seven legions', those of *BC* 3.2.2 that C. had sufficient ships to transport only '15,000 legionaries and 500 cavalry'. (That '15,000' is often corrected to e.g. '20,000' (so Carter) to give a more plausible equivalent for seven legions, even ones acknowledged to be under strength (*BC* 3.2.3).) App. 2.54.221–2 suggests that C. found 5 legions and 600 cavalry in Brundisium on his arrival and 2 more legions arrived in time to embark: that is probably the origin of the discrepancy between C.'s and P.'s figures for the legions, though the small anomaly on cavalry numbers remains (it may be the result of alternative roundings). P. omits another reason for the limited size of C.'s initial invasion force, the shortage of ships (C. *BC* 3.2.2).

the beginning of January, the equivalent of the Athenian month Posideon: 4 January by the calendar, but probably some sixty days earlier by the season (32.1, 59 nn.), so 'close to the winter solstice' (cf. 52.2 n.) is misleading. (So also *Pomp.* 65.4, *Fortune of the Romans* 319b, and App. 2.52.214, 54.221, but notice C.'s own mention of the oppressive *autumn* at *BC* 3.2.2, above.) Poseideon was the sixth month of the Athenian year, which theoretically began with the first new moon after the summer solstice, which, as it happens, fell twenty-six days after the solstice in 49. 'January' would seem a reasonable calendrical equivalent, but P. has failed to take into account the mismatch between Roman calendar and season: the Athenian calendar had many complexities—on these, see A. E. Samuel, *Greek and Roman Chronology* (1970), 57–64 and K. Clarke, *Making Time for the Past* (2008), 21–7—but it was kept closer in line with solar and lunar realities than the Roman. (D. Feeney, *Caesar's Calendar* (2008), 194–6, compares the two calendrical mentalities.) Such calculations of equivalences are still very precarious for reasons given by Samuel (64), but Pyanopsion or Maimakterion would be the most probable equivalent in 48. P. was interested in such calendrical matters, and wrote a treatise 'On days': some of its texture can be gauged from e.g. *Numa* 18–9, *Cam.* 19, *Roman Questions* 19 (267f–8d) and *Table Talk* 8.1 (717a–8b), and cf. 59 nn. He also sometimes explains Greek terms for his Roman audience: cf. Intr., p. 9. But he does not normally feel the need to gloss Roman month names: cf. e.g. *Cam.* 30.1, 33.7, *Marc.* 3.7, *Sulla* 27.13, *Lucull.* 27.9; at *Sulla* 14.10 he gives both Roman and Athenian dating, but that is because the capture of Athens is in point. Here the triple emphasis—winter solstice, January, Poseideon—ensures that the reckless bravery of such a midwinter crossing is felt, and that is fair: even with the late autumn date for his own crossing and even allowing that winter sailing was not irregular in wartime (K. Simonsen, *Mouseion*, 3 (2003), 259–68), he was committing the rest of his forces to cross in the worst sailing season (Plin. *NH* 2.125), through waters that were among the most treacherous in the Mediterranean in winter conditions (Simonsen 263), and against an enemy who would by then be alert (38.1 n.).

This decision of C. has been fiercely criticized, not least by the emperor Napoleon (*Précis*, 114–15). For an intelligent defence, see Ottmer 94–6. It was a risk, certainly, but—as the sequel showed, and as Antony was to find seventeen years later in the Actium campaign—it was no easy matter for any army or fleet based in Greece to prevent crossings from Italy, for the Greek coast offers many possible points of landing.

37.4. Crossing the Ionian Sea.   He disembarked on the morning of 5 January close to the Ceraunian range, 'at a place called Palaeste, without losing a single ship' (C. *BC* 3.6.3): see Map 7. Palaeste was a mere cove (cf. Carter on *BC* 3.6.3), and disembarkation must have been difficult: Pompeian forces had been stationed all along the coast (*BC* 3.5.1). C. then immediately sent the transports back to Italy, but thirty of them were intercepted and destroyed en route by Bibulus (14.2 n.), now in command of a large fleet based in Corcyra. **he took Oricum and Apollonia**: about 25 and about 60 miles respectively north of the landing ground. The operations are briefly recounted at C. *BC* 3.11–12: both towns according to C. came over willingly, forcing the hand of the Pompeian garrisons and commanders. Oricum may well have fallen on the day of C.'s arrival, 5 January. It would have taken a day or so more to reach Apollonia.

From Oricum C. sent L. Vibullius Rufus with peace proposals to Pompey (C. *BC* 3.10). P. recounts this at *Pomp.* 65.4–5, adding that 'Pompey regarded this as a trap' (not unreasonably, cf. Carter on *BC* 3.10.8); but here the item would have stood uneasily after C.'s rejection of a peace mission at 37.1, and P. understandably omits it.

37.5. these were men who were past their physical peak.   Unnecessarily patronizing (though Lucan liked the idea too, 'look at our white hair and our frail hands and our wasted shoulders...' (5.274–5), and it clearly goes back to a source: cf. also App. 2.66.274, of Pharsalus). These will have included some of 'the most long-standing veteran legions of singular virtue' (Hirt. *BG* 8.8.2), and even ten years of service does not turn a tough recruit into a decrepit old man. Hirtius was talking of several legions including IX, and it was the ninth whose mutiny at Placentia seems to underlie this account (§§3–9 n.).

37.6–7. 'Where is this man taking us now?...' P. is very sparing of his use of direct speech, and such passages typically point anecdotes or, if more extended, illustrate important themes: cf. my n. on *Ant.* 84.4–7. For such collective speakers, cf. *Popl.* 10.1–2 and esp. *Lucull.* 14.3, again pointing soldiers' grumbles but in a case that then shows a general at his worst rather than his best, and *Mar.* 16.7–10, articulating high morale rather than low; at *Galba* 22.6–8 unrest is articulated by an unnamed 'someone' among the group. The devotion of C.'s men, so stressed in the *Life* (ch. 16, and Intr., p. 21), may momentarily waver, but it is swiftly reclaimed even in C.'s absence by the qualities stressed in 17.1–3: 'That was what his men were like, full of spirit and enthusiasm, and Caesar himself cultivated those qualities and made them even more effective', partly by his 'prescription of long marches, strict personal regime, nights in the open air, and constant hard work'. Their dedication to their general will soon be seen to be vital once again: cf. esp. 38.7, 39.2–3, 44.10–12 nn.

37.9. They sat on the cliffs and gazed out towards the sea...carry them over to Caesar. Not unlike Odysseus, *Od.* 5.151–3; but Odysseus was desperate to go home and finish his wanderings, whereas C.'s men have now willingly given up their hopes of release. The tone is also almost erotic (so E. Fantham, *CPh* 80 (1985), 131, comparing Lucan 5.682–99), and recalls Ariadne who 'would sadly climb steep mountains to gaze out at the vast waves of the sea' (Catull. 64.126–7), desperate for her lover to return, or Hero looking out for Leander over stormy seas (Ov. *Her.* 19.21–2, 51; Musaeus, *Hero and Leander* 36): cf. also *Ant.* 51, Antony waiting restlessly for Cleopatra. As with lovers, too, moods shift quickly: like C. here (38.1), Ovid's Hero swiftly moves to reproaching Leander for missing his chance when the weather abated (*Her.* 19.24, 69–90); and by 38.7 C.'s men remonstrate with him for not trusting them enough, again rather like indignant lovers (Prop. 1.18.9–16, Ov. *Am.* 2.7, etc.).

38: CAESAR'S ATTEMPT TO SAIL BACK IN A SMALL BOAT The story is omitted by C. in *BC*, but it clearly became famous. If Weinstock 124 is right in relating to this a coin of 44 BCE (*RRC* 480.25, a *quinarius* of P. Sepullius Macer, the first representation of *Fortuna* with a rudder), it seems that some version of the story had become current before or soon after C.'s death, and was presumably encouraged by C. himself. (But that interpretation of the coin is uncertain: cf. the Addenda at Weinstock 415, and Greek *Tyche* was ruddered as early as Pindar fr. 40 M.) Whether true or false, it seems to have figured in Pollio (if so, notice again his taste for the sensational, Intr., p. 47), for it is told with similar detail by App. 2.56.234–57.237.[21] Dio 41.46 also has a version, but with fewer points of contact; Lucan elaborates at 5.497–702, briefly and well discussed by M. Leigh in *CJC* 246–7. The story also figures in P.'s *Fortune of the Romans* 319b–d, in more exuberant style: C. there bids the captain to 'unfurl his sails' to catch Fortune's wind (not just, as here, to press on): 'so confident was C. that Fortune was his fellow-voyager, fellow-traveller, fellow-soldier, fellow-commander—Fortune, whose task it was to impose calm on the waves, summer on winter, speed on the slowest, vigour on the most timid...'. In *Fortune of the Romans* P. uses this as evidence that it was Fortune that raised C. to greatness: rather inappositely, given that the voyage was a failure. Fortune is not a major theme of *Alexander-Caesar* (unlike, say, *Aemilius–Timoleon* or *Demetrius–Antony*: cf. S. Swain, *AJP* 110 (1989), 272–302), and the point here is one about human mentality, both C.'s own (his impatience and his self-confidence) and that of his men (§7 n.).

The story is discussed by Weinstock 112–27 (see §5 n.), C. Brutscher, *MH* 15 (1958), 75–83, and W.-H. Friedrich in

---

[21] App.'s account begins with C.'s encouraging his men to continue dining while he steals away in humble clothing, 2.57.235 (cf. § 2 here—of course, essential to this story, with its moment of revelation). Some echoes of the Rubicon seem clear, that earlier water-crossing driven by a trust in Fortune. Yet it was P., not App., who stressed the stealing away from dinner at the Rubicon (32.4 above: contrast App. 2.32.124); both P. (31.3) and App. (2.33.133) have the tribunes' humble disguises; P. does not here have the dining (though Val. Max. 9.8.2 does). Probably it was Pollio who introduced the echoing, and both P. and App. preserve fragments of it: cf. 30.2 and 66.10 and 12 nn. for similar cases (Intr., 47).

Thesaurismata: Festschrift für Ida Kapp (1954), 1–24, all of whom regard it as fictitious, and Veith, *Feldzug* 108–12 and F. Bömer, *Gymn.* 73 (1966), 63–85, who are prepared to believe it. Friedrich suggests that it has its origins in hostile propaganda (cf. App. 2.58.241, 'thus C. trusted in luck rather than rationality'), and argues that its development was influenced by the miraculous story of Alexander in Pamphylia which P. ridicules at *Alex.* 17.6–10: App. 2.149–150 indeed brings the two items together. If so, notice that P. avoids suggesting any parallel, and in particular there is no suggestion here that C. expected any such miraculous calm (like that of the gospel story, *Mark* 4.37–41 etc.) rather than simply survival. Cicero claimed more than that for Pompey, whose 'felicity' was such that 'even the winds and storms gave him good passage' (*de Imp. Cn. Pomp.* 48).

38.1. Caesar sat in Apollonia.   He was encamped on one bank of the River Apsus (= the modern Semeni): Pompey, who had been marching westwards along the Via Egnatia when he heard from Vibullius (37.4 n.) of C.'s landings, had hurried to defend Dyrrhachium, then marched south and taken a position on the other bank of the Apsus (C. *BC* 3.11–3). **Time went on, still the troops from Italy did not arrive.** It was always going to be more difficult for C.'s commanders in Italy, Antony and Calenus (39.9 n.), to force their crossing than it had been for C. himself to establish the bridgehead: the Pompeian admiral Bibulus, with sea domination, now knew exactly where the landing was to be expected, and his force duly patrolled the coast near Oricum and Apollonia. When Bibulus fell sick and died, tactics changed, and L. Scribonius Libo blockaded Brundisium instead. C. made the urgency clear to his subordinates, writing to them 'sternly': C. *BC* 3.25.3–4. His impatience is also stressed by App. 2.56.233–4 and esp. by Lucan 5.476–504, whereas at *Ant.* 7 P. puts more stress on the daring and seamanship shown by Antony when he did finally cross (39.1 n.).

38.3. The river Aous.   'Aous' is Dacier's emendation of the MSS's 'Anius' or 'Annius'. The Aous (= the modern Vijosë) flows into the sea just south of Apollonia. Equally palaeographically likely is 'Apsus', the river that was separating the two forces (§1 n.) and reaches the sea after a meandering course a little to the north. The mouth of the Aous fits the description of §4 better, but we cannot be sure how much of that is P.'s imagination, less gothic than Lucan's (5.597–677 with L. Pitcher, *CQ* 58 (2008), 243–9), but still quite capable of elaborating here. App. 2.56.234, 57.237 has only 'twelve stades' between C.'s camp and the point of the river where the boat was hired, and mentions the danger that the boat might be observed by the enemy. If right, both points suggest the Apsus, as Veith, *Feldzug*, 109, 111–12, observes; but App.'s geography is often impressionistic, and the danger may be his own elaboration. The text of Val. Max. 9.8.2 presents a similar problem: Shackleton Bailey and Briscoe read 'e flumine Ao<o>' (Gertz) for the manuscripts' *ac*, but 'A<ps>o' would also be possible. Veith, *Feldzug*, 111–12 points out that the Aoüs is better suited to seagoing vessels than the Apsus: still, he himself travelled the Apsus in a substantial motorboat (admittedly with 'very bad experiences' (111), but those are what C. suffered too). 'Aoüs' remains, but only marginally, the more likely.

38.5. Caesar's Fortune: cf. 57.1 n. Roman military heroes had often cultivated a link with *Fortuna*, (Good) Fortune: the view that Fortuna favours the brave took stronger root in Rome than it had in Greece, and became proverbial (Otto 144). C. himself often stresses the role of fortune in the *Commentarii*, and pointed out to Cicero (Cic. *Att.* 10.8B (199B).1) and, to judge from his own account, to his troops (*BC* 3.73.3, cf. esp. 3.26.4, 95.1) the indications that fortune—or Fortune, as one cannot firmly distinguish the two (A. Clark, *Divine Qualities* (2007), esp. 243)—was on his side. Others spoke similarly, including Cic. himself (*Marc.* 19). Elsewhere C. could talk of a setback as 'the only thing that was lacking to continue his fortune of old' (*BG* 4.26.5). Such language soon came naturally to imperial authors, as in several passages of Velleius, esp. 2.55 (with Woodman's nn. and Schmitzer 206–9): C. 'followed his fortune' to Africa, where he fought 'first with varying fortune, then with his own', and then 'his fortune accompanied him to Spain'. There is good reason to speak of a 'competition' between Pompey and Caesar, each claiming to be Fortune's favourite (Clark, *Divine Qualities*, 243–6).

 Whether C. himself actually talked so grandly and explicitly of 'Caesar's Fortune' is less clear: this story is the best evidence for it, for App. too has 'you are carrying Caesar and Caesar's Fortune'. Lucan simply makes C. say 'let Fortune be my sole companion' (5.510, cf. 593): that idea of Fortune as a protecting companion is an important one (A. D. Nock, *JRS* 37 (1947), 113, Woodman on Vell. 2.69.6), and is also felt here ('sails with us'). Dio 41.46.3 and Flor. 2.13.37 have just 'you are carrying Caesar'. The use of the third person reminds the

modern reader of C.'s use of it in his *Commentarii*, which might
have struck contemporaries too as distinctive (J. Marincola, *Authority
and Tradition in Ancient Historiography* (1997), 196–8; cf. Riggsby
150–5); but such self-naming, especially at times of extreme emotion,
is not unusual (e.g. *Pomp.* 74.5, *Ant.* 76.5, 84.5).

Weinstock 112–27 has a discussion that is on the whole cautious,
but rather surprisingly claims that the evidence for a planned cult of
Fortuna Caesaris is 'overwhelming' (112). He wonders (123) if the
notion of 'bearing the fortune of Caesar' originally attached to C.'s
own *successful* crossing (37.4 n.), and was then transferred by a hostile
critic to this failed re-crossing. If so, one would naturally think of
Pollio; but P. and App. were both used to imperial ideas of e.g. 'the
Fortune of Augustus', a slogan that appears on coins from Galba
onwards (J. Hellegouarc'h, *Hommages à M. Renard*, i (1966), 426–30,
Weinstock 127), and, even though the story does probably go back to
Pollio, we cannot be sure that this detail is his colouring rather than
theirs. We might also recall that C. would have spoken Greek, and
might have been thinking Greek too: so F. Bömer, *Gymn.* 73 (1966),
72, 84–5, arguing that C. was thinking in Greek terms of *Tyche* (the
word used by P. and App.) as a personal protecting deity, for which
the nearest Roman equivalent would be 'Genius' (rather than 'Fortuna') 'Caesaris'.

38.7. why was he taking these risks…?:   echoing those grumbles
of their colleagues in Italy, especially 'even a god cannot impose his
will on the winter season and the winds of the sea' (37.7), and the
word for 'taking risks' is then the same there as here. But this time the
complaints turn not on C.'s taking his men for granted but on his not
trusting them enough, and point confidence, not demoralization. The
lovers' tiff is over (37.9 n.), and these men sound like winners.

39: Dyrrhachium
The rhythm of initial near-catastrophe as a precursor to complete
victory is at least as old as the relationship of Thermopylae to Salamis
and Plataea (and familiar in modern warfare narrative and reality too:
one thinks of Dunkirk): cf. my n. on *Ant.* 48.

C. gives a long account of the Dyrrhachium campaign at *BC*
3.34–77, and it seems that Pollio too had a fair amount of detail.
P. drastically abbreviates, and gives little detail of the strategy of the
fighting at Dyrrhachium, which lasted several months and involved
some complicated contravallations (C. *BC* 3.43–9, 54, 58) and some

40.2. Pompey himself was cautious and reluctant to let so much turn on the throw of a single battle: echoing 32.8 (n.), 'let the die be cast': C. is the risk-taker, Pompey is not.

40.3. their age left them ill-suited to long marches...night watches: picking up the (overstated, cf. n.) description at 37.5. *Pomp.* 66.1 and App. 2.66.274 are similar, and so it seems to come from Pollio; App. makes it a perception of C.'s troops themselves as well as of Pompey. In C.'s own account Labienus is given a speech giving a different reason for Pompeian confidence: these are *not* the men who fought in Gaul, but largely new recruits (3.87). That is felt as overstated in *BC*—C. has just represented himself as reminding his men of their Gallic experiences (3.73.6, cf. 79.6; Batstone–Damon 108–9)—but he had indeed been recruiting heavily in 49: Brunt, *Manpower*, 475.

40.4. outlandish diet: 39.3 n. The report was accurate, 41.7–8 n.

41.1. Cato...when he saw the enemy dead lying on the field of battle: at Dyrrhachium, for Cato was not present at Pharsalus, having been left behind to guard Pompey's base (*Pomp.* 67.2–3, *C.min.* 55.1–3: see intr. n. to 41–2). *C.min.* 54.11 also mentions his tears, adding the moralizing gloss that suits the themes of that *Life* better than this: he 'lamented the destructive and ill-starred lust for power that had led to this'. **some thousand in number:** so C. *BC* 3.71.1. *Pomp.* 65.8 gets it wrong ('two thousand'), if the text there can be trusted.

41.2. 'Agamemnon' or 'king of kings'. Agamemnon is not in fact called 'king of kings' in the *Iliad*, though he is addressed by Nestor as the 'most kingly' one, *basileutatos*, at 9.69 and himself claims to be 'more kingly' than Achilles at 9.160 (echoed dismissively at 9.392 by Achilles himself); his normal epithet is 'lord of men'. Two aspects make the gibe especially pointed. First, as App. 2.67.278 explains, Pompey did indeed have kings effectively under his command, e.g. Deiotarus of Galatia and Ariobarzanes of Cappadocia (C. *BC* 3.4.3: cf. *Pomp.* 64.3, App. 2.71.295, Dio 41.55.2–3, 63.1). Secondly, the title 'king of kings' was not infrequent (cf. my n. on *Ant.* 54.7), but especially for *oriental* kings, e.g. Tigranes (*Lucull.* 14.6): the hint of eastern excess goes with other features of the representation of

Pompey's camp (*Pomp.* 72.5–6, echoing Herodotus' picture of the Persian camp after Plataea, 9.82: see 46.2 n.), and may well be a Caesarian riposte to attacks on C. himself for decadent or unroman behaviour (cf. A. Rossi, *CJ* 95 (2000), 239–56). **his one-man rule:** literally 'monarchy', *monarchia*, the same word as at 28.5–6. The recall of that passage suggests some ironies, though P. leaves the insights muted: then people had been content to accept a monarchy of Pompey as the least bad solution, but they did not like it now; and that dislike paved the way for the monarchy that was even more unwelcome, that of their enemy Caesar.

41.3. Favonius: 21.8, 33.5 nn. **Pompey's lust for rule:** *philarchia* in Greek, giving a jingle with *monarchia*. Pompey's *philarchia* is a recurrent motif in *Pompey* (30.8, 31.8, 53.7, cf. *Crass.* 14.5). But *Pomp.* 53.7 and *C.min.* 54.11 bring out what is again muted here, that this *philarchia* is a quality that C. and Pompey share: cf. 69.1 (n.). It is C.'s *philarchia*, even more than Pompey's, that will keep so many from returning to enjoy **the figs of Tusculum**—the best in Italy, claimed Varro (cit. Macr. *Sat.* 3.16.12).

41.4. Afranius, newly arrived from his poor generalship in Spain: 36 nn. **why they were not fighting against this merchant...:** on the face of it a surprising comment from one who was recommending return to Italy rather than immediate confrontation (intr. n., above), but Afranius might still have found the put-down irresistible. **to whom he had sold the provinces:** F. Fischer, *Klio*, 91 (2009), 439, notes that Afranius was (probably) proconsul of Cisalpine Gaul in 59 (cf. above, p. 288 and n. 12), and presumably expected to retain it for some time: the allocation to C. of Cisalpine Gaul for 58 would have been a big disappointment to him, and evidently happened with Pompey's connivance. In view of his steady Pompeian record (36.1 n.), Afranius had every reason to let that rankle still. **provinces:** plural, because Transalpine Gaul and Illyricum are relevant as well as the Cisalpina (14.10 n.).

41.6. Caesar's march was not an easy one. More details at *C. BC* 3.75–8. This will have been in the second half of July (Holmes, *RR* iii. 478–81). C. had to divert via Apollonia; Pompey, once he knew where C. was headed, had an easier direct route along the Via Egnatia. On the details, see Carter on *BC* 3.78.4. There was a real danger that Pompey would cut off Domitius Calvinus (39.9 n.) before C. could unite the armies, and *BC* 3.79 narrates how this was avoided in the nick of time. **everyone had heard of his recent defeat, and they were writing off his chances:** C. *BC* 3.79.4–5, 80.2–3.

41.7. Gomphi: some 35 km. south of Aeginium, where C. and Domitius' forces had joined (§6 n.), and some 65 km. west of Pharsalus. See Map 7. The town fell in a few hours. C. defends the plunder at *BC* 3.80–1: Gomphi, he claims, had broken faith after previously pledging its support; it was important to send a signal to other Thessalian towns, and nearby Metropolis was duly persuaded into meekness and was spared; the other cities of Thessaly followed suit, except for Larissa, where Scipio (39.10 n.) was based. Pollio seems to have added further details of the plunder at Gomphi: App. 2.64.268–9 agrees with P. on the drunkenness (the Germans were particularly boisterous), and tells of a scene where twenty of the city's notables were discovered dead in a doctor's surgery, peacefully lying where they had fallen after the doctor had served them poison. Plutarch was sensitive to the sufferings of Greece: cf. *Ant.* 62.1, 68.6–8, *Sulla* 43 (5).5. But here his focus rests firmly on the Roman troops: neither C. nor App. has P.'s item of their miraculous recovery.

41.8. wine   of various sorts, including unmixed, is often recommended by medical writers, not surprisingly in a culture when water was so often befouled. **the whole constitution of their bodies** also has a medical tinge. But **continued the march reeling about in drunken revelry** also recalls the gloriously drunken march of Alexander through Carmania at *Alex.* 67. That Dionysiac procession presaged Alexander's final days, where again drunkenness played a large part; this one is a preliminary for C.'s greatest success.

42–6: THE BATTLE OF PHARSALUS   The battle took place on 9 August 48 by the calendar, early June by the season. Much of this account is ultimately informed by C. *BC* 3.82–99 (nn.), but the continuing close parallels with App. suggest that their account derives from Pollio, whom P. quotes both here (46.2) and in *Pompey* (72.4, Intr., p. 43: App. quotes him too, 2.82.346. Both P. and App quote C.'s criticisms of Pompey's stand-and-receive tactics (44.8 n., *Pomp.* 69.7, App. 2.79.330). As at 22.2 (n.), that suggests that that citation too is taken over via Pollio. It is clear that Pollio at times followed C. fairly closely, but added some gripping material of his own, especially the

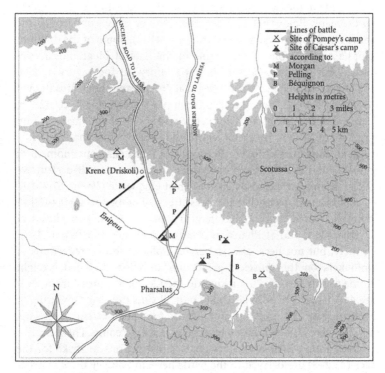

Map 8. Pharsalus

critical striking at the dandyish Pompeian horsemen's faces (42.3, 44.3, 45.2–5 nn., *Pomp.* 69.4–5, App. 2.76.318); he also included Caesar's words on the battlefield after victory was won, and some details of the scene in Pompey's camp (46.1–2 nn.). He seems too to have added or adjusted material in less dramatic ways—for instance, in some details of the dispositions and numbers (43.1–2, 44.3–4 nn.), and in gently improving C.'s words as he realizes that Pompey is willing to fight and in his dialogue with the centurion Crassinius/Crastinus (44.1, 44.9–12 n.). He also apparently corrected C.'s estimate of the numbers of Pompeian dead (46.3 n.). There were, it seems, some sombre reflections of participants on the sadness of it all (cf. App. 2.77), which P. elaborates at *Pomp.* 70. Dio 41.53–60 has a full account, but concentrates on reconstructing the psychology of the combatants: the details of the fighting (41.60) seem to be largely imaginary, though there is a hint of ultimate derivation from C. (60.3 ~ *BC* 3.84.3).

The account in *Pomp.* 67–73 is also detailed, and clearly not independent: the two versions are either drafted with the same source (presumably Pollio) before P.'s eyes on both occasions or based on the same notes (i.e. a *hypomnēma*, Intr., pp. 41–2). Some of the different emphases are explicable in terms of the 'law of biographical relevance'. For instance, *Caesar* but not *Pompey* has the augury of 43.4, the 'it was their choice' apophthegm at 46.1–2, and the Brutus item of 46.4; *Pompey* has more detail on Pompey's dream (68.2, cf. 42.1 n. here) and the luxurious banquet preparations found in his camp (72.5–6, cf. 46.2 n. here). Others fit the different role that the battle plays in each man's life. For Pompey this is the climactic moment of reversal, and P.'s comment on Pompey's calamitous, self-destructive failure to impose authority rises to great eloquence (*Pomp.* 67.7–10). It aids that emphasis that the pressure on Pompey to fight (41.1–5 here) is treated more elaborately in that *Life*, with two phases at Dyrrhachium and at Pharsalus clearly demarcated (66.2–5, 67.4–7). P. there, but not here, also elaborates Pollio's 'choric' reflections of onlookers on the senseless greed and ambition that had brought Rome to this (*Pomp.* 70, picking up the idea of a 'chorus' from 68.7: see 44.1 n. here). The avoidability of it all suits the tragic texturing of *Pompey*, but that mode of moralism is foreign to *Caesar* (Intr., pp. 19–21): here C.'s own tragic reversals are still to come. The narrative of the fighting itself is also varied. C.'s instructions to strike for the face (45.2–3) are delayed to the battle here; in *Pompey* these instructions are treated before the battle (69.4–5), where they contrast with Pompey's own advice to his infantry to hold still—mistaken advice, as P. emphasizes in both *Lives* (44.8 (n.), *Pomp.* 69.7), in each case quoting C.'s own insight. The effect in *Pompey* is to cast Pompey even more decisively as a loser even before battle begins (cf. 44.5 n.), and to do so by juxtaposing the differing insight of the two generals; in *Caesar* it is the juxtaposition of the two *armies* that is more stressed (44.12 n.), and that develops this *Life*'s emphasis on the importance of the devotion of C.'s men (ch. 16, Intr., p. 21).

In neither *Life* does P. mention C.'s famous instruction to 'spare fellow-citizens' in the slaughter (App. 2.80.336–8, Suet. 75.2, Lucan 7.318–9, 728–31, Flor. 2.13.50); at 46.4 he also makes less than we might expect of C.'s clemency to the surrendered Pompeians. Cf. Intr., p. 20.

On C.'s own account in *BC*, see esp. F.-H. Mutschler, *Erzählstil und Propaganda in Caesars Kommentarien* (1975), 214–25, and R. D. Brown, *CJ* 94 (1999), 342–57, both emphasizing C.'s contrast of leadership on the Pompeian side and on his own: C. may be harder on Pompey's lieutenants than on Pompey himself, but tellingly exposes Pompey's failure to match C.'s own harmony with his officers and men. Both features are also seen in P.'s account: the Crassinius scene is here especially telling (44.9–12 n.). Cf. also J. E. Lendon, *ClassAnt* 18 (1999), 273–329, who takes Pharsalus as his starting point for an insightful analysis of the factors C. recurrently highlights in his battle narratives. Lendon brings out that C.'s emphasis too falls on psychology (cf. 39, 44.8 nn.) and masculine courage (*uirtus*), in Pharsalus' case combined with a more traditionally 'Greek' emphasis on carefully orchestrated tactics. He also comments (321–2) that P. takes over that psychological emphasis and elaborates it, especially at 45.2–4 (see n.).

42.1. the district of Pharsalus: lit. 'Pharsalia', which is sometimes used to denote the battle as well as the district: along with 'Pharsalus', 'Palaepharsalus' or 'Palaeopharsalus' is also used by some authors— presumably an earlier settlement nearby. On the names, cf. R. T. Bruère, *CP* 46 (1951), 111–15, and J. Morgan, *AJA* 87 (1983), 27–8. The topography of the battle is much discussed. In an influential article, Y. Béquignon argued for a site south of the river Enipeus (*BCH* 84 (1960), 176–88), which is where App. seems to place it ('between the city of Pharsalus and the river Enipeus' (2.75.313)). I argued for a northern site in *Hist.* 22 (1973), 249–59, and so, in a position a few kilometres further west, did J. D. Morgan, *AJA* 87 (1983), 23–54. Carter iii. 203–4 follows Morgan and myself. See those papers for references to earlier treatments, and, for the various reconstructions, see Map 8. Morgan also produces strong arguments for identifying Palaepharsalus with the modern Driskoli (Krene) on the northern bank, and thinks this may be the origin of App.'s 'between Pharsalus [i.e. Palaepharsalus, whether or not App. realized it] and the Enipeus'. **a dream in which he had seen himself back in his theatre, applauded by the Romans:** on P.'s dreams, cf. 32 n. This one (unsurprisingly absent from C. *BC*) sounds encouraging, unlike those **unfavourable omens**, but *Pomp.* 68.2 adds that Pompey also dreamed he was 'adorning a temple of Aphrodite the Conqueror [i.e. Venus Victrix] with a mass of spoils': so also App. 2.68.284. It was C.'s descent from Venus that made the dream discouraging. (That dream is elaborated by Lucan, 7.7–28 ('Dreams', 204–5), but Lucan, stressing the dream's 'guise of joys', omits the Venus Victrix element: so does Flor. 2.13.45.) Some editors have emended the text here to clarify the train of thought, usually by marking a lacuna; Dacier and Langhorne simply inserted the *Pompey* passage verbatim into the text. But *Caesar* mostly suppresses mention of the gods (Intr., p. 31), and the Venus descent in particular: thus P. also here omits that C. sacrificed to Mars and Venus before the battle, App. 2.68.281, and that the Caesarians' watchword was 'Venus Victrix', App. 2.76.319: cf. Pelling, 'Notes', 44–5. The omission here does leave the logic of Pompey's hesitation unclear, but there is no need to emend. These negative omens contrast with C.'s more hopeful ones, 43.3–6 n.

42.2. Domitius and Spinther and Scipio: so C. *BC* 3.83.1: i.e. L. Domitius Ahenobarbus, cos. 54 (34.6 n.); P. Cornelius Lentulus Spinther, cos. 57 (34.7 n.); and Pompey's father-in-law Scipio, cos. 52 (30.4, 39.10 nn.). These were indeed the senior *pontifices* on the Pompeian side. The others of whom we know were Brutus and C. Fannius (L. R. Taylor, *AJP* 63 (1942), 385–412 at 406): Fannius, though a *pontifex* of perhaps fifteen years' standing (Taylor 398, *MRR* 186), was only of praetorian status, and Brutus did not reach the praetorship till 44. **to rent and put in early bids for houses that would be suitable for consuls and praetors.** They were no fools: the war had caused house prices to plummet (37.2 n., C. *BC* 3.1.2), but they could be expected to climb again once the victor was known. *BC* 3.82.3 makes it clear that the Pompeians also had their eye on the houses of Caesarian partisans: if those are meant here, the agents would be able to 'rent and put in ... bids' only after victory and the proscriptions that might be expected to follow (Carter, ad loc.).

42.3. The cavalry ... particularly impressive with their splendid arms and their well-fed horses and their handsome physical appearance. Pompey's superiority in cavalry would be expected to play a vital role in the fighting: those expectations had already played a role in determining both sides' strategy (C. *BC* 3.4.5, cf. 39.9 n.), and continued to do so now (44.3–6, cf. *BC* 84.3, 86.3–4). P. is just as interested in their 'splendid appearance', beginning the highly visual language of the battle description in which the same glittering word (*lampros*) for 'splendid' recurs, 44.3; cf. also 45.1, 4 (nn.). At 44.5 it is duly a 'splendid rout' that these cocky horsemen expect to inflict. But it is Crassinius' hopes of a 'splendid victory' that are better founded, 44.10, based as they are on toughness rather than show. The cavalry's pride in their appearance eventually plays a decisive part in their demise: 45.2–4. This picture of visually impressive and self-preening cavalrymen builds on classical stereotypes (Arist. *Clouds* 14–15, 119–20, *Knights* 554–5, 580, cf. Xen. *Hipparch.* 1.11–2, 3.1) as well as, doubtless, on reality; but C. *BC* makes nothing of it, and this will be an elaboration by Pollio or by P. himself. **7,000 of them to Caesar's 1,000**: so C. *BC* 3.84.4, and App. 2.70.289–90 agrees: see next n.

42.4. 45,000 men against 22,000: C. *BC* 3.88–9, adding that Pompey had a further 2,000 *euocati* (veterans recalled from retirement) and another 7 cohorts left to guard the camp. App. 2.70.289 agrees on C.'s 22,000, with Pompey having 'more than double'. App. makes a great deal of following 'the most credible Roman sources' on these numbers, and makes it clear that others hugely exaggerated. Flor. 2.13.44 shows such exaggeration: 'more than 300,000'. The numbers given by C. are much discussed: cf. esp. Holmes, *RR* iii. 472–6; Carter on *BC* 3.88.4, concluding that they are plausible.

43.1–2. Cornificius was close at hand with two legions. The manuscripts have 'Corfinius': cf. 51.3 n. 'Cornificius' is Xylander's correction, and makes P. refer to Q. Cornificius (*MRR* 276, E. Rawson, *CQ* 28 (1978), 188–201 = her *Roman Culture and Society* (1991), 272–88), who had been fighting in Illyricum (*B.Alex.* 42–7). Carter on C. *BC* 3.56.2 prefers to think this a reference to Calvisius Sabinus (see next n.), and implies a further force of new recruits: this seems less likely. In any case, this—like the reference to 'Megara and Athens' in what follows—has no counterpart in the

motions of men going to battle', then others report that the first ranks
are forming; C. exclaims that 'the day has at last come when he will be
fighting not hunger but men' (so also App. 2.73.303, but the direct
speech given by C. himself is different and less colourful, *BC* 3.85.4),
and he puts out the sign for battle; his men let out shouts of joy before
each takes up his position 'like a chorus'—the first of several tragic
touches (42–6 n. above).

44.2. Domitius Calvinus: 39.9–10, 41.6, 50.1 nn. **Antony took the
left wing and Caesar himself the right:** C. *BC* 3.89.4, making it
clear that P. Cornelius Sulla (*MRR* 281) had specific command
of the right, even if C. also initially took up his station there: it
was important that, as overall commander, 'Caesar could choose
to range where he wished' once the fighting started (Goldsworthy,
JCAR, 208). *Pomp.* 69 elegantly varies to present from the viewpoint
of Pompey, who 'stationed his father-in-law Scipio against
Calvinus in the centre...', etc. R. Ash in D. Levene and D. Nelis
(eds), *Clio and the Poets* (2002), 261, points out that, despite all
the detail of the dispositions, C. gives no attention to the subordinate
commanders in the battle description itself: the same is true of P.
and App.

**44.3. six cohorts should secretly move across to him from the
rear.** C. *BC* 3.89.4, 93.5, but the text of C. does not specify 'six'
(though Orsini restored it at 93.5). Frontinus 2.3.22 also has 'six
cohorts'. It seems that Pollio did give numbers in some form,
as App. 2.76.317 specifies '3,000' men, roughly equivalent in
theory (a fully manned cohort numbered 480 men) though probably
not by this stage of the campaign in practice. C.'s total of
80 cohorts in the battle-line numbered 22,000 men, *BC* 3.89.2;
proportionately, 6 cohorts might therefore number *c*.1,650 men.
On C.'s tactics here, see N. Rosenstein, *CJC* 94–6. **told them
what they should do when the enemy cavalry attacked.** We
have to wait till 45.2–5 to discover what the instructions were; C.'s
narrative does the same at *BC* 3.89.4, though his 'instructions'
there are less elaborate (45.2–4 n.). *Pomp.* 69.3–4 gives them now:
see 42–6 n.

44.4. Pompey commanded his own right wing...: so also *Pomp.*
69.1, and this fits 45.7, 'from the opposite wing': but C. *BC* 3.88.2, 89.3
puts Pompey on the left wing, opposite C. himself. It is conceivable
that Pollio here corrected C.'s own account: he certainly seems to
have added some detail not in C., for App. 2.76.316 adds that Pompey's right was commanded by 'Lentulus' (Lucan 7.218–20 gives him
the left and Domitius the right). This is probably L. Cornelius Lentulus Crus (29.1 n., *MRR* 276) rather than Lentulus Spinther (42.2 n.).
That is plausible, whether or not the supreme commander was
also stationed there (cf. C. and Sulla on *his* right, §2 n.). C. may
himself have got the Pompeian dispositions wrong, perhaps by mistake, more likely to highlight the idea of the two protagonists
facing up to one another. It would not be the only time that Pollio
corrected C. on a detail where we might have expected C. to know
the truth: 46.3 n., and Ll. Morgan, 'Autopsy', 58–9. But it may also
of course be P. who is mistaken, possibly misled by an ambiguity
in Pollio: App. too presents an oddity here (2.76.316, Pompey 'guarding the camp' along with Afranius). Alternatively, J. Morgan, *AJA* 87
(1983), 54, suggests that P.'s source may have put Pompey on
the right to distance him from responsibility for the ill-fated cavalry
attack.

**44.5. All the cavalry were stationed to throw their weight towards
the left.** C. *BC* 3.88.6.

**44.7. Pompey gave instructions that his legionaries should...stand
their ground firmly.** On the advice of one C. Triarius, C. *BC* 3.92.2.
Pompey had noticed, *Pomp.* 69.6 adds, that his line was wavering and
losing its formation through inexperience and nervousness. That
explanation is not found in C. (who explains the tactic differently
and not very plausibly, 3.92.2–3 with Carter's n.): it is another touch
that compounds the impression in *Pompey* of an army that will not
win (42–6 n.).

44.8. Caesar claims that this was another error: C. *BC* 3.92.4: 'This
seems to me a mistake by Pompey, for there is a certain stimulation of
the spirit and an innate eagerness which is inflamed by the enthusiasm for the fight'; cf. J. E. Lendon, *ClassAnt* 18 (1999), 273–329, esp.

279–90, bringing out how C.'s emphasis fits both his distinctive
interest in psychology (42–6 n.) and his portrayal of battle as a matter
of crashing impact rather than the Greek conception of sustained
'pushing'. The same passage of C. is quoted in *Pomp.* 69.7 and by
App. 2.79.330; that suggests that the citation stood in Pollio (Intr.,
p. 43). App. in fact quotes it from 'C. *in his letters*': for a similar oddity
in citation, cf. 22.2 n. ('journal'). Possibly C. *did* use the phrase in a
letter (cf. 46.2 n.) as well as the *Commentarii*, though if so it was
probably not in an official despatch to the senate; or possibly App.
was confused by some phrasing in the shared source. **the first clash of
arms…helps to inflame the men's spirit as it is fanned up by the
encounter.** I discuss the language at *Plutarch and History*, 79–80,
suggesting that the different imagery of *Pompey*—'the tightening
which comes from the charge…the surge of spirit and momentum',
and perhaps of *Apophthegmata* 206d, 'the tightening of the muscles
and the zing and spirit that men generate during a charge'—may be
closer to Pollio: App. 2.79.330 too talks of 'tightening'.

44.9–12: THE CENTURION CRASSINIUS   C. *BC* 3.91 gives his
name as 'Crastinus': so also Lucan 7.471. C.'s own account gives the
centurion two speeches, one encouraging his men and then this one
to C. himself (there 'I shall ensure, general, that today you are grateful
to me, whether I live or die'). Cf. C.'s similar portrayal of another
heroically loyal centurion, Petronius, at Gergovia, *BG* 7.50.
C. S. Kraus comments on that passage that '[c]enturions are Caesar's
favourite actors. They focus action, wield significant objects, are
granted rare direct speech, and generally serve as the stylized representatives of his legions, who through their leaders speak in (largely)
ultra-brave, ultra-Roman, ultra-loyal voices' (in Kraus, Marincola,
and Pelling (eds), *Ancient Historiography and its Contexts* (2010),
56). That is true of P.'s presentation as well.
   To judge from App. 2.82.347–8, P.'s dialogue form of the story
goes back to Pollio: it captures the harmony of general and fighting
soldier even more forcefully. Crassinius/Crastinus is reminiscent of
the wise centurion at *Ant.* 64 (see my n. on that passage), where once
again the significance is marked by direct speech. But in *Antony*
the centurion's advice is not taken, and we know Antony will lose.
Here the outcome is similarly predictable, with devotion like this to
drive C.'s men on.

44.10. he had fought many campaigns. C. *BC* 3.91.1 says that he was an *euocatus*, i.e. a re-enlisted veteran (42.4 n.), who the previous year had been *primipilaris* in the tenth legion. **called out to him by name.** C. also calls out to his centurions 'by name' in the Nervii battle at *BG* 2.25.2. The stereotypically inspiring general knows, and knows when to use, the names of at least his centurions and senior men: Livy 8.39.4 with Oakley's n., 10.14.12, Sall. *BC* 59.5, Tac. *Hist.* 1.23.1, Virg. *Aen.* 11.731. **a splendid victory:** 42.3 n.

44.11. 120 men: C. *BC* 3.91.4, adding that they were 'picked volunteers': so this charge was not spontaneous, and Crassinius/Crastinus' inspiring display may well have been a 'staged demonstration' (Brown, *CJ* 94 (1999), 350) preconcerted by C. himself.

44.12. He cut his way through ... a thrust of a sword through the mouth ... by the occipital bone: C. *BC* 3.99.2. The gruesome detail is in the manner of the *Iliad*, and it recalls the similar stories of ch. 16: here as there, the vigour and devotion of men like this are the hallmark of C.'s army, and presage his success. The delay of the detail on Pompey's effete cavalry (45.1–4) allows a telling juxtaposition: see 42–6 n.

45.1. in the centre. C. *BC* 3.91 makes it clear that Crassinius/Crastinus led his charge on C.'s right, but this detail may still be correct: Pompey's left was hanging back (§5 n.). *BC* 3.93.1 gives more details of the initial clash: C.'s men had double the expected distance to charge because of Pompey's stand-and-receive tactic, but they stopped halfway and caught their breath. **magnificent.** The word is again highly visual (42.3 n.); the speed with which such showiness collapses is striking.

45.2–4. Those had been Caesar's instructions ... protecting their faces: 44.3 n. The language of App. 2.76.318 and esp. of *Pomp.* 69.5 is similarly coloured, with some individual touches: e.g. *Pompey* describes the cavalry as 'experts at the pyrrhic dance'—i.e. an armed dance that *mimicked* warfare, and ironically seems to have celebrated the cohesion of a fighting force. The item clearly comes from Pollio, but it is a case where Pollio was elaborating C.'s account: *BC* 3.93.5–6 puts similar stress on this phase of the battle, but has nothing of the strike-at-the-face instructions. There the infantry reserve behind

the right (44.3 above) simply launches a vigorous attack on the
cavalry, and they turn tail. Despite C.'s silence in *BC*, the instruction
'strike at the face' became famous: Flor. 2.13.50, Front. *Strat.* 4.7.32.

Some have suspected reasons for the tactic of thrusting rather than
throwing that were not psychological. There is an obvious advantage
in reach of javelin over sword when striking up at a mounted cavalryman (F. Paschoud, *Hist.* 30 (1981), 184–5); and T. F. Carney acutely
points out that there was little advantage in casting a javelin against a
charging cavalryman, as, even if it stuck in the shield, it would not
slow him (unlike an infantryman, where a dangling javelin could
impede the run), but that it was important to thrust at exposed
flesh, for the soft iron of the Roman javelin would bend rather than
penetrate armour (*CR* 8 (1958), 11–13). Still, all that would be true of
any of the many battles where infantry faced cavalry. It would seem
that there was something unusual and noteworthy about this one,
either in the tactics or in the reasons for employing them, and the
psychological explanation may still be right: Pompey's cavalry were
not raw recruits, and they had seen much skirmishing action at
Dyrrhachium, but there was much less experience of pitched battles
on his side than on C.'s.

45.3. young and vain and proud of their good looks.   The word for
'vain' is *komaō*, literally 'wear the hair long': the literal meaning has
some force too, for long hair was part of the classical stereotype of the
conceited cavalryman (Dover on Arist. *Clouds* 14).

**45.4. they turned their heads away and covered them up, protecting
their faces:**   again very visual.

**45.5. the cohorts … went on to turn the flank of Pompey's
infantry:**   C. *BC* 3.93.8, and see Map 8. *Pomp.* 71.5 explains that
Pompey had delayed advancing his left wing in anticipation of the
cavalry encounter.

45.7. saw his cavalry routed: by seeing the dust raised by their
flight, *Pomp.* 72.1. **he had no memory that he was Pompey the
Great.** *Pomp.* 72.1 is closely similar. **he was more like a man whom
Heaven had robbed of his wits:** a rare hint of the supernatural in this
Life (cf. Intr., p. 31), but still he is only 'like' such a man, and Plutarch
does not commit himself to divine involvement. There are again close
similarities at *Pomp.* 72.1 ('most like someone who was out of his

mind and shaken out of his wits') and App. 2.81.340 ('being robbed of his senses by some god'). Both *Pompey* and App. also cite *Il.* 11.544–6, where Zeus instils fear into Ajax and 'he stood in amazement'. (Not in fact an especially apposite Homeric parallel for—presumably—Pollio to have taken, given that Ajax goes on to mount a stubborn and impressive retreat.) The account in C. *BC* 3.94.5–6 is much less coloured. **he moved away to his tent, sat down...:** like C. at Dyrrhachium, 39.9 (n.), but Pompey can now do no more than wait **for what was to come.**

45.9. we tell that story in his own *Life*: *Pomp.* 73–80. Cf. 35.2 n. The outlines are clearly taken as familiar, but **his death after entrusting himself to the Egyptians** ensures that even the less well-informed reader understands the sequel at 48.2–4. Pompey died on, probably, 28 September (48.2 n.).

46.1. 'It was their choice'. Literally, 'they willed it', as in the Latin version *hoc uoluerunt* (Suet. 30.4). **'I, Gaius Caesar, victor in the greatest of wars...':** in Suet. 'I, Gaius Caesar, with achievements that have been so great...' (*tantis rebus gestis*). In both versions the language reflects the claim most emphasized in C.'s own propaganda, the intolerable threat to his *dignitas* after he had achieved so much: 30.1 n. **'would actually have been condemned in the courts...'.** It is disputed how realistic any such fear was: not realistic according to Gruen 494–5, C. T. H. R. Ehrhardt, *Antichthon*, 29 (1995), 30–41, and R. Morstein-Marx, *Hist.* 56 (2007), 159–78; among those who disagree are Brunt, *JRS* 76 (1986), 17–18, K. M. Girardet, *Chiron*, 30 (2000), 686–9 and 707–8, and G. R. Stanton, *Hist.* 52 (2003), 67–94. But it was anyway in the air at the time: Cato had threatened as much (Suet. 30.3), and the tribune L. Antistius had tried to launch a prosecution in (?) 56 (21.3–9n., *MRR* iii. 17, E. Badian in J. A. S. Evans (ed.), *Polis and Imperium* (1974), 144–61)—even though in the late fifties Cicero and his correspondents did not rate the possibility even worth mentioning (Shackleton Bailey, *Cicero's Letters to Atticus*, i. 38–40, and *Cicero* (1971), 135). There is no need, then, to regard C.'s battlefield pronouncement as Pollio's fiction (Ehrhardt): whether or not C. really feared such a show trial, it made excellent propaganda for him to take his enemies at their word, and C. had doubtless rehearsed his remark carefully. He does not, however, include it in the account of *BC* 3, where the narrative register is different.

It remains striking that C. never mentions any threat of prosecution in the narrative of *BC* 1, for instance in his speeches to his soldiers at 1.7, to the senate at 1.22, or to Afranius at 1.85: probably 'he recognized that [this justification] would not stand up to public, nonpartisan scrutiny' (Morstein-Marx, art. cit., 164) once the passions of the moment had cooled. **'if I had given up my armies'**: in Suet.'s Latin 'if I had not sought help from my armies'. Both versions are possible—for the demand that C. 'give up his armies', cf. 29.4, 30.1, 30.4 nn.—but the Latin version carries an extra point, playing on the 'help' (*auxilium*) that a citizen might normally look for from the tribunes, when in this case their authority had been overridden (31.2 n.). Maybe that point was added in Pollio's translation of the original Greek (§2 n. below); maybe, as Hohl suggested (*Hermes*, 80 (1952), 248), Plutarch retranslated Pollio's Latin into Greek 'not wholly correctly'.

46.2. according to Asinius Pollio: Intr., p. 44. This is fr. 2 P. The eyewitness (Intr., p. 46) Pollio had other tales to tell of this moment too: *Pomp.* 72.4–5 (= fr. 2b P.) quotes his account of how the Caesarians 'gazed on their enemies' shallowness and folly, as every tent was garlanded with myrtle and equipped with flower-laden couches and tables full of goblets, and bowls of wine were there waiting: all the elaborate preparations had the air of men who were celebrating a festival and had already sacrificed, not of armed soldiers going to war'; cf. App. 2.69.285. This evokes the similar scenes in the Persian camp after the battle of Plataea (Hdt. 9.82: cf. 41.2 n. and A. Rossi, *CJ* 95 (2000), 239–56), and elaborates the original item of C. *BC* 3.96.1.

he uttered them in Greek at the time, then they were written down by Pollio himself in Latin: a puzzling passage, and the text translated here makes two alterations to the manuscript reading, which has 'he uttered them in Latin at the time, then they were written down by him [i.e., presumably, C.] in Greek'. The first, minor change is Schäfer's emendation of 'by him' (i.e. C.) to 'by himself' (i.e. Pollio). That is effectively only a matter of a rough or a smooth breathing, *hautou* or *autou*, and is really an interpretation rather than a correction of the manuscripts, for their reading may well be owed to a scribe who was himself interpreting in choosing what diacritical mark to add. The second, more substantial, is the reversal of 'in Latin' and 'in Greek'. Ziegler accepts the first alteration but not the second; E. Hohl, *Hermes*, 80 (1952), 246–9, accepts the second, and, though not accepting the first takes 'by him' to mean 'by himself'; Flacelière and Gärtner (in his 1994 addenda to Ziegler) accept both; Perrin and R. Häussler, *RhM* 109 (1966), 339–55, accept neither. Let us start with the manuscript reading.

(1) If it was 'written down by him [C.] in Greek' it would probably have been in a letter (cf. 44.8 n., the 'letter' quoted by App. 2.79.330, and 50.3 n., the 'I came, I saw, I conquered' letter: Intr., p. 48), and presumably one that became famous. (A less likely alternative would be the collection of *apophthegmata* mentioned at Suet. 56.7 and Cic. *Fam.* 9.16 (190). 4, but the Cicero passage suggests that these were not widely circulated.) That is possible, and would explain why Pollio and P. took the trouble to clarify which language was in fact used, as they would be correcting a version that was already well known. But we should have expected 'in a letter' to be specified, and the Greek is also awkward: we would expect 'and then he later wrote them down in Greek' rather than the shift to the passive.

(2) So on balance 'by himself', i.e. 'by Pollio', is more likely than 'by him'. (It is also possible, but less likely, that 'by him' should stand but be interpreted as 'by Pollio': so Hohl and G. Delvaux, *LEC* 56 (1988), 47.) Pollio wrote in Latin: Sen. *Suas.* 6.24 quotes his obituary notice of Cicero, and Val. Max. 8.13 ext. 4 describes him as 'not the least part of Latin stylistic achievement'. It is impossible to picture a Latin author putting the words in Greek, something that Roman historiography does not seem to admit, then adding that they were originally in Latin anyway. Hence R. Daebritz, *Philologus*, 70 (1911), 267–73, suggested that there also existed a Greek version of Pollio: so also P. Boyancé, *REL* 34 (1956), 121. Häussler, however, showed that this was unlikely (art. cit.), and the different technical terms App. and P. use for e.g. 'legion' and 'camp' suggest that they are independently using a Latin rather than Greek source (H.-P. Syndicus, *Lucans Gedicht zum Bürgerkrieg* (1958), 2 and 122–3 n. 12, and Scardigli, *Römerbiographien*, 132).

(3) So there is a strong case for following Madvig, Peter, Hohl, and Flacelière in reversing 'in Latin' and 'in Greek', and that is what I have preferred: this would make Pollio (or, less likely, C. if 'by him' were right) note, in Latin, that the original was in Greek.[23] (We need not assume that Pollio or C. clodhoppingly added 'and I have translated

[23] A. Strobach, *Plutarch und die Sprachen* (Palingenesia, 64 (1997), 153–4), thinks that it was P. rather than his manuscripts who was confused: his immediate source

into Latin', for that is of course implied: P. might, however, draw it out explicitly to explain why a Latin version had become well known.) C. may well have used Greek,[24] as he did at the Rubicon in the apophthegm with which this remark forms a ring (32.8 n., cf. also 66.8 n.); this also gives more point to P.'s noting the fact, as a Roman general speaking Greek is rather more remarkable than one speaking Latin, and the note also helps to mark that Rubicon ring.

At the Rubicon C. presumably spoke Greek because it was a Greek proverb, 32.8 n. Why he should have done the same now is another question. M. Dubuisson, *Annales*, 47 (1992), 193, suggests that Greek was felt appropriate for introspection ('la langue du retoir sur soi'), and—not very plausibly, cf. J. N. Adams, *Bilingualism and the Latin Language* (2003), 310—that it may have been the language he had learnt first as a child. Or perhaps, deep in Greece, there were simply some Greeks in his company; *Pomp.* 70.1 mentions 'some Greeks who were present but not participating in the battle', presumably men of some standing.

46.3. Most of the dead (Pollio goes on) were servants... not more than 6,000 soldiers were killed. The syntax makes it clear that this is also owed to Pollio (so also *Pomp.* 72.4): App. 2.82.346 also makes that explicit, citing Pollio for the '6,000' figure but making it clear that this refers only to Pompeian dead. C. *BC* 3.99 gives C.'s losses as 200 soldiers and 30 centurions, the Pompeians' as about 15,000. It looks as if Pollio was revising C.'s figures for Pompeian dead downwards, or at least insisting that the bulk of the dead were attendants rather than fighting men: the phrasing would sit well in a passage where he was discussing and rejecting higher estimates. The lower figure is more plausible: Brunt, *Manpower*, 696, Carter on C. *BC* 3.99.4. C.'s figures for his own dead may on the other hand be too low, whether or not Pollio pointed this out: cf. Carter on *BC* 3.99.1. Cf. Gerlinger 117–19.

---

noted that C. uttered the words in Greek but wrote them down in Latin, but P. garbled the story and reversed the languages. That seems much less likely.

[24] Suet. 30.4 quotes Pollio as giving C.'s words 'verbatim' (*ad uerbum*), and goes on to quote them in his Latin version: but that phrase can be used of a 'literal' or 'word-by-word' translation from the Greek (Cic. *de Fin.* 1.4, *Tusc. Disp.* 3.44, Quint. 7.4.7). It is not relevant (*pace* André 52 and Häussler) that Suet. is prepared to quote in Greek elsewhere, notably 'you too, my child' at 82.2 (cf. 66.12 n. below): if Pollio did not give the Greek, Suet. could not quote it from him.

46.4. He spared many of the more prominent figures as well: many, not all: C.'s old enemy L. Domitius Ahenobarbus (34.6 n., 42.2) was captured and killed, by C.'s cavalry according to *BC* 3.99.5, by Antony according to Cic. *Phil.* 2.71; Lucan 7.597–616 imaginatively has it happen in C.'s presence. According to Dio 41.62.1–2, C. executed those senators and *equites* whom he had already captured once and spared, except that his friends were allowed to nominate one man each to be spared; those now captured for the first time were released. Cf. 57.5 n. **Brutus, the man who went on to kill him:** cf. 62.3. Any attempt to keep suspense as to the end of C.'s story would be pointless: everyone knew how he died. P. prefers to lay a trail towards the downfall at the moment of triumph, just as his death scenes so often recall his subject's greatest moment (*Plutarch and History*, 375, and *Philosophia Togata*, ed. M. Griffin and J. Barnes (1989), 207–8). **when Brutus initially appeared to be lost:** more detail at *Brut.* 6.1: Brutus slipped out of a gate into a nearby swamp (that detail is relevant to the reconstruction of the topography, *Hist.* 22 (1973), 253, 256 n. 54, and J. Morgan, *AJA* 87 (1983), 46); then he escaped to Larissa, and wrote to C. from there.

47: Portents of Pharsalus

Like the Greek and Roman historians, P. is fond of using portents to mark important episodes and themes: cf. 43.3–6 and 63 (nn.), *Ant.* 60 with my note, and Brenk 30–8, 184–213. He often adopts a sceptical approach towards particular omens, acknowledging that some were the work of manipulative humans (*Numa* 8.4, *Them.* 10.1) and seeking rationalist explanations where possible (e.g. *Cor.* 38.1–3, *Lys.* 12); but he is equally clear that they should often be believed (cf. esp. 63 below, *Crass.* 38(5).3, *Cam.* 6.5–6, *Cor.* 38.5–7), and insists that rationalist explanations need not exclude the possibility of divine communication (*Per.* 6). Like his references to fate and fortune (Swain, *AJP* 110 (1989), 272–302), omens and portents tend to centre around themes of large historical consequence, in particular the rise of Athens and of Macedon and the fall of Persia, the spread of Roman power and the origins of the Roman Empire (Brenk 187–8). It is no coincidence, then, that they cluster in the second half of *Caesar*, just as P.'s readers would have been familiar with omens presaging the rise to power or the catastrophic end of individual emperors (on these, see A. Vigourt, *Les Présages impériaux* (2001)). There is a similar cluster towards the end of *Alexander* (57.4, 73–5; Intr., p. 29). The very spread of these particular omens—well to the east at Tralles in the Maeander valley, well to the west at Patavium—marks the wide significance of what was happening in Thessaly. Lucan 7.202–4 makes the point poetically explicit: if human augury had been adequate, 'Pharsalia was visible throughout the world'. The narrative vista will itself immediately broaden, to Egypt and Asia, then to further west in Africa and finally to Spain.

Naturally, accounts of omens normally precede the events they portend, as at *Ant.* 60 and here at 42.1 and 43.3–6. In this case the second omen (Patavium) occurred simultaneously with the battle rather than preceding it, and it would have been awkward to insert it before the narrative. It would also be awkward to discriminate pre-battle and simultaneous omens, and so P. leaves the timing of the first portent (Tralles) unclear: 'indicate the victory' could mean before or during or after the event. (C.'s own procedure is similar at *BC* 3.105.6, where he dates it 'around those days'.) Positioned here, the section also serves as a panel-divider: the first two-thirds of the *Life* have culminated in C.'s triumph; the last third remains, and will end in catastrophe.

The first omen is drawn ultimately, but presumably not directly, from C.'s own account: Pollio may again be the source, though this item does not figure in App. The second clearly originates with Livy, as does the portentous dream for which Livy is cited at 63.9 (n.), and is taken over from him by Lucan, Gellius, and Dio (§3 n.). See Intr., pp. 48–9: it is possible that, here as in other *Lives*, P. draws on Livy directly, and if so it was probably from memory; or alternatively he may owe the material to a slave or freedman helper.

The Patavium omen is discussed by K. Latte, *MH* 16 (1959), 140–2, who thinks it clearly a 'prophecy after the event'. He is doubtless right, but (*a*) he overstates his argument that the account makes no ritual sense (§6 n.), and (*b*) it was, one assumes, precisely because it seemed too good to be true that P. is so insistent that 'Livy firmly attests the truth of this'. (For similar source citations in support of omens, cf. 63.3 and 9 below, *Dion* 25.5–10, *Lucull.* 10.4, *Brut.* 48.2.) P. may have underestimated Livy's capacity for invention (so Latte), but he was not naively unaware that the story strained credibility.

47.1–2. There were many portents. P., as usual (Brenk 189–90), is selective. C.—rather unexpectedly (G. Reggi, *PdP* 57 (2002), 216–26, suspects interpolation), but this is the climax of his narrative—lists this and some further omens at *BC* 3.105, and those too are repeated by other authors, esp. Dio 41.61 and Val. Max. 1.6.12. P. probably thinks this the **most remarkable** as the one that most clearly indicates victory *for Caesar*: the others mark simply a great battle or the emergence of an unspecified victor, as in the case of a miraculous turning of an image of Victory at Elis. **at Tralles . . . in the Temple of Victory . . . a palm-tree sprang up:** ultimately from C. *BC* 3.105.6: the language is similar, though P. elaborates a little. Reggi, art. cit., 221, finds it odd that a statue of C. should already be standing in Tralles, given that Asia had closer links with Pompey, and suspects that the palm was only shown off and linked with Pharsalus some time later: perhaps, but it is conceivable that the statue of C.—and for all we know statues of others too, including Pompey—had been put there during the period of the two men's alliance; or perhaps earlier still, during C.'s activity in Asia during 74–73 (1.8–2.7 n.: thus A. E. Raubitschek, *JRS* 44 (1954), 65). In any case, the city doubtless made the most of anything they could as C. passed through or nearby on his way through Asia (48.1 n.), and at that time there may well have been some creative reformulation of their past, very likely including the omen: possibly even the statue itself may be as recent as that. The **palm** is a frequent signifier of victory: cf. Nisbet and Hubbard on Hor. *Odes* 1.1.5 and Oakley on Livy 10.47.3. At *Table Talk* 8.4 (723a–4f) P. discusses why that should be.

47.3. Gaius Cornelius . . . This omen is also mentioned by Lucan 7.192–214, Gell. 15.18, and Dio 41.61.3–5, all doubtless deriving from Livy. Gellius in particular is closely similar, adding (possibly from his imagination) that Cornelius accurately traced the course of the battle—'some retreating, some pressing on, the deaths, the flight, the soaring weapons, the beginning of the battle, the assault, the cries, the wounds . . .'. **happened to be sitting on that day studying the auguries:** §6 n.

47.4. according to Livy: fr. 43 W.–M. = 44 Jal; cf. Obsequens 65a. P. adds a Livian omen again at 63.9 (n.).

47.5. in a frenzy. The Greek word *enthousiasmos* suggests 'like a man possessed' rather than the modern 'enthusiasm': but, as Patavium in Cisalpine Gaul had received Roman citizenship on C.'s

initiative only a year before (37.2 n.), locals might indeed have been
excited by the prospect of C.'s victory.

47.6. the wreath from his head.   Gell. 15.18 notes that he was a
priest; the wreath presumably marked this out as he took the auspices,
but if so it was not in a way that duplicated Roman ritual: as Latte
notes (art. cit.), a Roman augur would view the auspices with hooded
head. Latte adds that auguries were typically taken to decide whether
a course of action did or did not enjoy divine favour, rather than to
discover what was happening or would happen elsewhere in the
world, and concludes that the story is ritually implausible. That is
premature: (*a*) Patavine ritual need not have been the same as
Roman: at the point where Cicero distinguishes Roman augury
from prophecy, he makes it clear that practice was different elsewhere
in Italy (*Div.* 2.70, cf. 1.105, 132); and (*b*) the point is presumably that
Cornelius was taking the auspices for some other reason, and was not
expecting to discover what he did. The scope of divination was anyway widening in the first century BCE (J. North in M. Beard and
J. North (eds), *Pagan Priests* (1990), 56–61), and some of the portents
recorded even for earlier times clearly do reveal hidden truths from
the present, such as the location of a lost object or the misbehaviour
of a Vestal virgin (North, 60–1: cf. e.g. Cic. *Div.* 1.16, Livy 2.42.9–11,
D.H. *Ant. Rom.* 9.40, Obsequens 37).

48.1: En Route to Egypt: Administrative Measures
P. gives the impression that not merely the grant of freedom to
Thessaly but also the similar grant to Cnidus and the revision of the
Asian tax system happened immediately after Pharsalus. Perhaps it
did, for C.'s move through Asia Minor was not as quick as all that
(48.2 n.); C. *BC* 3.106.1 confirms that he 'delayed for a few days' in
Asia, and he may well have stayed for some time at Cnidus (n.). There
may also be some historical basis for Lucan's account of his visiting
the site of Troy (9.961–99); if so, it may also have been now that he
granted freedom to Ilium (Strabo 13.1.27, cf. Carter on *BC* 3.106.1).
This will also be the context in which 'Caesar's law' set up a treaty
with the commune (*koinon*) of Lycia that was ratified in Rome two
years later (S. Mitchell in M. Pintadui (ed.), *Papyri Graecae Schøyen*
(*Papyrologica Florentina* 35; 2005), 161–258 at 232–7; Wiseman 198–
9). Not knowing quite what to expect in Egypt, he may well have
thought it worthwhile to play for the goodwill of regions that would

lie to his rear: in winter 31–30 Octavian similarly secured alliances in Asia Minor before the anticipated Alexandrian campaign. Equally, the tax revision in particular will have required some thought and taken some time, and it may be that P. has collected here material that was undated, or dated later, in his source.

48.1. Caesar gave the people of Thessaly their freedom to celebrate his victory: so also App. 2.88.368. Pliny *NH* 4.29, listing the towns of Thessaly, includes 'the plains of Pharsalus with their free state', suggesting that in Pliny's day Pharsalus alone enjoyed that status of *ciuitas libera*. Matters may have changed between C. and Pliny, but it *may* be that C.'s grant of the status of *ciuitas libera* was limited to Pharsalus alone and P. and App. are overstating (so e.g. Garzetti): in theory the rest of Thessaly had been declared free in 196 (Livy 33.32.5), though the status of Pharsalus itself was then left hanging (Livy 33.34.7 and 49.8 with Briscoe's nn.). Still, App. specifies that C.'s declaration was to acknowledge the support he had received in the war; 'all Thessaly except Larissa' had supported him (C. *BC* 3.81.2), so perhaps the declaration was as grand as P. and App. say. Perhaps the 'freedom' granted in 196 had by now been revoked or encroached upon; Rome could also insert specific, sometimes quite demanding qualifications in any declaration of freedom (A. N. Sherwin-White, *The Roman Citizenship*[2] (1973), 174–89, A. W. Lintott, *Imperium Romanum* (1993), 36–40), and those—in particular any direct or indirect taxation or obligation to give military support—may now have been adjusted or removed. Cf. on Cnidus, below. Alternatively, the gesture may have been little more than words; such declarations were on the way to becoming only 'an act of courtesy' (Sherwin-White 178). An honorary inscription from Demetrias in Thessaly seems to date from shortly after Pharsalus (A. E. Raubitschek, *JRS* 44 (1954), 66–7), doubtless marking the city's gratitude.

If any irony is felt in this grant of 'freedom' to celebrate the origin of Roman one-man rule, P. does not make anything of it.

then set off in pursuit of Pompey: on the third day after the battle (App. 2.88.368–9): i.e. 11 (counting inclusively) or 12 August. By then he had discovered Pompey's direction of flight, possibly from a conversation with Brutus (*Brut.* 6.1–4, which does not make it sound as if Brutus was reluctant to reveal whatever he knew). He crossed the Hellespont in a small boat, narrowly avoiding catastrophe when he ran into ten warships commanded by L. Cassius (Suet. 63:

App. 2.88.370–2 confuses this Cassius with the tyrannicide). The
journey through Asia took in Ephesus (C. *BC* 3.105.1–2), therefore
passing close to Tralles (47.1–2 n.), and then Rhodes (App. 2.89.373).
App. 2.116.486 also says that Artemidorus (65.1 n. and below) entertained C. in Cnidus, and that too was probably on this journey. C.
evidently had time to linger: §2 n.

   he liberated the Cnidians—that was a favour to Theopompus. An
inscription (W. Blümel, *Die Inschriften von Knidos*, 1 (1992), no. 71:
cf. C. P. Jones, *Proceedings of the American Philosophical Society*, 143
(1999), 596–7) records the death and funeral of a daughter or descendant of 'Theopompus, who obtained his country's freedom and
immunity from tribute' (*aneisphoria*). So in this case (cf. above on
Thessaly), exemption from direct taxation was indeed conferred
along with freedom: R. Bernhardt, *Hist.* 29 (1980), 192. Unsurprisingly, we know of delegations from and intercessions on behalf of
other cities too, Pergamum (*IGR* iv. 1677), Mytilene (*IG* xii.2.35; on
the date, R. K. Sherk, *GRBS* 4 (1963), 145–53), and more generally
'the Ionians, the Aeolians, and the other peoples of Asia Minor' (App.
2.89.373); cf. S. Mitchell, *Papyri Graecae Schøyen* (48.1 n.), 233–4.
Theopompus is mentioned by Strabo 14.2.15 as 'a friend of the divine
Caesar, one of the very powerful ones', and is presumably the same as
the Theopompus mentioned several times in Cicero's correspondence
(*Att.* 13.7 (314).1 with Shackleton Bailey's n., *Q.fr.* 2.11 (15).4, and
perhaps 1.2 (2).9). Artemidorus (65.1 n. and above) was his son.
Theopompus was honoured not merely at Cnidus, along with his
family (Blümel, *Inschriften*, nos 51, 56–8, 701), but also at Delphi,
Rhodes, and Cos (Blümel, p. 43): that suggests that he secured much
wider benefits from C.—or at least that those states hoped that he
might. By specifying him as a **collector of myths** P. is probably
suggesting that C.'s gift was in recognition of his cultural achievement. That is possible. Historians in the Greek world knew how to
write in ways that would flatter Rome and their powerful patrons
(K. Clarke, *Making Time for the Past* (2008), 354–63), and a Caesar-
friendly mythographer would doubtless have made much of the
Aeneas ancestry. If so, C.'s grant was matching the freedom Pompey
had earlier granted Mytilene in recognition of their pro-Pompeian
writer Theophanes (*Pomp.* 42.8). Still, we know nothing further of
this work (cf. *FGrH* no. 21), and Theopompus' services certainly went
beyond the literary: he was active in various negotiations on C.'s
behalf at least as early as 54 (Cic. *Q.fr.* 2.11 (15).4), and in 43 he

was an important enough figure in the Caesarian cause for Trebonius
to hound him to Alexandria, and for Antony to make capital from
it (Cic. *Phil.* 13.33).

**granted all the peoples of Asia remission of a third of their
tribute.** App. 5.4.19 makes his 'Antony' refer to this remission in a
speech to representatives of the Asian cities in 41 BCE, contrasting C.'s
generosity with the previous practices of the *publicani*: 'Caesar remitted a third of what you had been paying them and also stopped
their outrages, allowing you to collect the tribute direct from the
farmers.' Dio 42.6.3 also mentions that second measure, cutting out
the *publicani*. P. was well aware of the harm that *publicani* could do
(cf. *Lucull.* 7.6–7, 20, *Sert,* 24.5), and would have recognized the
importance of the second measure; but he does not interrupt the
narrative flow here to say so. Asia's normal tribute was probably
2,000–2,500 talents a year (*ESAR* iv. 563–4, estimating 2,400 talents =
14,400,000 denarii for 'a good year about 60 BCE when the yield was
greatest'), with more to be expected in times of war, including contributions from client kings and free cities (cf. App. 5.6.27). Asia
would have been squeezed hard by Pompey (C. *BC* 3.32 elaborates
the theme), just as it had been earlier by Sulla and would be later by
Brutus and Cassius and then Antony: cf. *Sulla* 25.4–5, *Brut.* 30–2,
Ant. 23.2 with my note. It is unclear whether C.'s remission now
applied to an estimate of their usual tribute, or to the amount
collected in the previous year by Pompey (cf. Gabba on App.
5.4.19): probably the latter, allowing C. to make an apparently more
generous gesture that would also make a propaganda point against his
enemy. The remission presumably applied only to the single year in
question.

This gesture did not prevent C. from extracting vast sums from
individuals who had helped Pompey, such as Pythodorus of Tralles
(property worth more than 2,000 talents, Strabo 14.1.42).

48.2–49.10: Caesar in Egypt
'A nasty little war' (E. Rawson, *CAH* ix² (1994), 434). Its first phase is
covered by C. *BC* 3.106–12; the later part is treated in the extant
Bellum Alexandrinum 1–33, possibly (K. Barwick, *Caesar und das
Corpus Caesarianum* (1938), 178–93) but not certainly by Hirtius: on
this cf. the differing views of A. Patzer, *WJA* 19 (1993), 121–6, and
L. Hall, *CQ* 46 (1996), 411–15. On the complicated Egyptian back-
ground, H. Heinen, *Rom und Ägypten*, is useful; it is reprinted in his

Kleopatra-Studien. M. Siani-Davies gives a very good sketch of the
tangled dealings of the late king Ptolemy XII with Rome during the
fifties in the Intr. to her Clarendon Ancient History Series edition of
Cic. *Rab. Post.* (2001), 1–38.

P. is very selective. It is unsurprising that he is economical on the
complicated political background and the details of the fighting (48.5
n.), but more striking that he gives us so little on Cleopatra (48.5, 49.3,
49.10 nn.). Of the two possibilities he raises at 48.5—'a shameful and
hazardous escapade, inspired by his passion for Cleopatra. Others
blame the king's courtiers'—P. gives some grounds for believing both:
C. was indeed 'captivated', 49.3, but more emphasis falls on the secret
plotting of, in particular, Pothinus. P. leaves unstated the obvious
(and fair) further question whether C. should not have disengaged
himself from the courtiers' imbroglio more promptly, given that his
Roman enemies were gathering their forces: and elsewhere (*Pel.* 2) he
is sharply critical of generals who expose themselves to physical
danger in the way that C. did here (49.7–8). Here he is content to
imply only that there is a case to answer.

Ironically, though, C. is reasonably adept at dealing with the deviousness (48.7–9) of these figures whose style belongs in a different
and unroman world. It is when the plots come from his own sort, and
in Rome, that he will be destroyed; and the eventual destructive 'passion' (*erōs*) will be, not for Cleopatra, but for a Roman throne (60.1).

48.2. He sailed into Alexandria just after Pompey's death.   Pompey
died on 28 September 48, the day before his birthday (Vell. 2.53.3
with Plin. *NH* 37.13); or, less likely, on the birthday itself (*Cam.* 19.1
and, by implication, Dio 42.5.5–6). *Table Talk* 8.1.717c notes both
versions; *Pomp.* 79.5 gets it wrong ('the day after'). I discuss P.'s
different versions in a paper to appear in a collection on the *Quaes-
tiones Conuiuales* edited by F. Klotz and A. Oikonomopoulou.

C. arrived on the first day or so of October. He will have come in as
much strength as possible, given that the Egyptian situation was
unpredictable, and there was also some possibility that Pompey
could head west to Cyrene and link with Cato (*Pomp.* 76.2, *C.min.*
56.1, Vell. 2.53.1). But in fact C. came with only two legions, totalling
3,200 men, and 800 cavalry (*C. BC* 3.106.1–2), a small fraction of
those who had fought at Pharsalus; and it may be that C. himself
arrived before his men in Egypt (App. 2.89.375–6) or at least at
Alexandria (Dio 42.7.2). The reasons were doubtless logistic, for the

legions needed to come from Thessaly and Achaea (C. *BC* 3.106.1). The land journey would be some 2,000 miles, impossible in so short a time (37.3 n.), so the troops must have been transported at least part of the way by ship. *BC* 3.106.1 mentions 'ten warships from Asia and a few from Asia', but some merchantmen would have been used as well. How many C. could raise, we do not know; and his command of the sea was not total (*Pomp.* 76.1–2, C. *BC* 3.101, cf. Lucan 8.272). All this understandably took some time (§1 n.).

What would C. have done had he found Pompey still alive? Executing him would have been most damaging to his parade of *clementia*. Perhaps some accommodation was not out of the question (so M. Jehne in G. Urso (ed.), *L'Ultimo Cesare* (2000), 153), just as five years later Antony and Octavian were allies against shared opponents only months after fighting one another bloodily at Mutina. Now too there were substantial senatorial enemies still to fight (52–4 n.), men about whom Pompey will not have felt much more warmly than C. Yet it would be no alliance of equals, and it was unlikely to be comfortable. Theodotus' reading of the situation was not a foolish one.

Pompey's death. The scene is vividly described at *Pomp.* 77–80, and P. does not duplicate it here. Cf. 45.9 n. **Theodotus** of Chios (so P.) or, less likely, Samos (so App. 2.84.354, but his account has other mistakes) is introduced without explanation: that is not unusual in P. (cf. 7.5, 8.3, 21.5, 32.3, 56.6 nn.), but here it may be because the story itself is assumed to be familiar. Theodotus is not mentioned in C.'s own laconic account of Pompey's death (*BC* 3.104), but at *Pomp.* 77.3–7 P. describes him as 'Theodotus the Chian, who had been hired as a teacher of rhetoric' to the 13-year-old king Ptolemy (so also *Brut.* 33.3), and says that he, Pothinus (48.5 n.), and Achillas (49.4 n.) were the most influential three figures at court. App. 2.84.253–4 is evidently based on similar material. Theodotus was eventually captured, tortured, and killed in 42 by Brutus (*Brut.* 33) or, less likely, Cassius (App. 2.90.377).

Theodotus' argument now was that it was too dangerous either to welcome Pompey or to refuse to receive him; the safest way to win C.'s favour was to admit him and then kill him. He added with a smile that 'a dead man does not bite' (*Pomp.* 77.6–7, *Brut.* 33.3–5). That last phrase sounds proverbial, like the later *mortui non mordent* ('dead men don't bite', said to have figured in advice given to Elizabeth I to execute Mary Queen of Scots) or 'a dead dog does not bite' (*canis mortuus non mordet*). As those formulations show, the punning wordplay makes it work better in Latin—but would Theodotus have been speaking Latin? Probably not, and more likely the pungency is due to a Latin source, very likely but not certainly Pollio.

he turned away: regarding him as *palamnaios*—someone polluted, with blood on his hands—as *Pomp.* 80.7 puts it in heightened language. C.'s own murderers will be similarly shunned by Caesarian loyalists after the Ides of March (*Ant.* 14.7 n.). **the man's signet ring**: with a seal of a lion carrying a sword, *Pomp.* 80.7. **and wept for him**: as Octavian would later weep for Antony, *Ant.* 78.2: see my n. on that passage for Hellenistic and Roman precedents for such displays of sensibility in a victor. The most famous case was that of Scipio Aemilianus weeping for Carthage (Plb. 38.21). The normal suggestion, especially with Scipio, is one of sensitivity to the human condition: the victor may one day be as vulnerable as the conquered. Cf. J. Hornblower, *Hieronymus of Cardia* (1981), 104–6. Such a perspective would not be out of place here, given that C.'s own treacherous assassination looms, but P. does not develop it. He leaves the impression that the tears are simply of distress for a former friend and relative, though §4 may also hint at disappointment at losing a chance to display clemency: cf. 54.2 n. Dio 42.8.2–3 and Lucan 9.1104–6 say that the hypocrisy of such a display was transparent. They are doubtless reconstructing onlookers' reactions, but may not be wrong.

C. also ordered the head's burial. The ashes were returned to Italy and buried by his wife Cornelia, *Pomp.* 80.10.

48.4. he wrote back to his friends at Rome: but doubtless for wider consumption. For C.'s paraded clemency (though P. avoids describing this as such), cf. 34.7, 57.4 nn. and Intr., p. 20.

48.5. the war in Egypt. Cleopatra and her brother were at war before C. arrived. Cleopatra had become queen at the age of 18 in 51, but was required by her father's will to share the throne with her brother Ptolemy XIII, then 10 years old, and in due course to marry him. In 49 they jointly sent a squadron to support Pompey (App. 2.71.296) on the request of his son Gnaeus (56.1 n.), but before the end of that year brother and sister were at odds, and some anomalies in the regnal years given by papyri in this year suggest uncertainties and disruptions concerning the throne (Sullivan 254–5). In December 49 Pompey and his 'senate' in Thessalonica apparently recognized Ptolemy alone as ruler (Lucan 5.58–64: Heinen, *Rom und Ägypten*, 57–60 = Heinen, *Kleopatra-Studien*, 60–2). Cleopatra was expelled, and by now she was gathering troops in Syria. Ptolemy's forces were

awaiting her invasion near Pelusium (see Map 3), and it was there
that Pompey had come to shore and been killed. On C.'s arrival
naturally both sides sought his aid: both brother and sister had
reasons to be nervous, given the help they had given Pompey. The
tales of Pothinus' arrogance (§§5–8) are doubtless 'exaggerated, for
Ptolemy's advisers had no interest in alienating the new master of the
Roman world. They look like propagandist self-justification for
Roman ears, receptive as they would be to tales of decadent and
arrogant eunuchs (cf. e.g. Hor. *Epod.* 9.13–14 with Watson's n.). C.
had better reasons for preferring Cleopatra, and those need not have
been limited to her sexual charms: C. was no bad judge of ability, and
the next eighteen years would show how valuable and loyal she could
be to her Roman allies.

   **some claim that it was unnecessary...Others blame the king's
courtiers.** See 48.2–49.10 n. **the eunuch Pothinus:** tutor of the young
king and 'the most important man at court' (Heinen, *Rom und
Ägypten*, 36 = Heinen, *Kleopatra-Studien*, 45): by now he had assumed the role of 'administrator of the royal finances' (*dioikētēs*, cf.
Dio 42.36.1, App. 2.84.354: Heinen, *Rom und Ägypten*, 37–40 =
Heinen, *Kleopatra-Studien*, 46–8), and C. could describe him as
exercising *procuratio regni* (*BC* 3.108.1)—practically a regency. **it
was he who had killed Pompey.** *Pomp.* 77.2–7 puts more weight on
the agency of Theodotus (cf. §2 n.), but makes it clear that it had been
Pothinus who convened the decisive council. **and had driven out
Cleopatra.** C. *BC* 3.103.2 says that Ptolemy had driven out Cleopatra
a few months earlier 'through the agency of his relatives and friends',
presumably Pothinus among others.

**48.6. this is why they say Caesar now began his practice of all-night
drinking parties:**   as did Alexander, especially towards the end of his
life: *Alex.* 67.3, 75.4. In earlier days that may have been through
Alexander's pleasure in conversation with his friends (*Alex.* 23,
though at *Table Talk* 1.6 623e P. takes a different view), but at the
end it was from a more macabre sort of fear of the supernatural, *Alex.*
75.1–2. C.'s nervousness is in contrast wholly secular, and does not
seem ungrounded (though see also 49.4 n.): cf. Intr., p. 29.

**48.7–8. claiming that Caesar had taken all the gold and silver to
settle a debt.... now he demanded the ten million immediately
for the support of his army.**   It certainly seems that C.'s demands

for money were a principal reason for his lingering in Egypt, and for the popular disturbances he faced: Dio 42.34.2 says that the extraction of treasure from temples caused particular distress, and Oros. 6.15.29 that it was the king's advisers who raided the temples to make the point that the royal treasury was exhausted.

48.8. Caesar was in fact owed 17,500,000 drachmas . . . the father of the present king. Ptolemy XII had in 59 BCE allegedly paid C. and Pompey 6,000 talents = 36 million drachmas/denarii to have C. as consul obtain the recognition of his throne (Suet. 54.2). A further 10,000 talents = 60 million dr./den. were needed in 55 to secure Ptolemy's restoration by A. Gabinius, or so it was said (Cic. *Rab. Post.* 21, 30–1): that was initially raised from Roman speculators, and Rabirius Postumus was then the man charged with collecting in Egypt the sum that was owed. On these complicated events, see D. Braund, *Rome and the Friendly King* (1984), 59–60; Sullivan 234–51; M. Siani-Davies, *Hist.* 46 (1997), 306–40 at 333–40 and her edition of *Pro Rabirio Postumo* (2001), 1–38. So debts of nearly a hundred million dr./den. had in fact been incurred, though not all to C. personally. Some, though probably not much, may have been repaid by the late king; some may have been remitted to Ptolemy's children on his death (cf. next n.). Some had also been raised since C.'s arrival now, amid predictable turbulence. Siani-Davies, *Hist.* 46 (1997), 336–7 and in her *Rab.* edn 71–2, 207–8, suggests that the 17,500,000 drachmas refers to 'Caesar's share of the unpaid loan raised by Rabirius Postumus, possibly consolidated with the financiers' other debts after his failure to gather the necessary money'—i.e., that C. was one of the speculators involved in Rabirius' enterprise, perhaps underwriting investments made by others; similarly also Woytek 160. That is very possible. Most (e.g. Braund 69 n. 36, Sullivan 244) have assumed that the debt dated from 59. If the debts had simply accumulated, it may well have been unclear which remained unsettled; and no one, anyway, was in a position to quibble. **He had previously granted the old king's children remission of everything beyond ten million drachmas:** when? Possibly in 51 on the king's death, though it is hard to see why C., far away in Gaul, would then have remitted a personal debt; possibly in 49, as a way of countering Pompey's bid for the co-monarchs' support (so Heinen, *Rom und Ägypten*, 80 = Heinen, *Kleopatra-Studien*, 77); or possibly now, shortly after his arrival but before relations with the court worsened.

48.9. and attend to his great affairs: biting sarcasm, if historical: no wonder C. preferred to support Cleopatra. Dealing with **Egyptian advisers** like this would carry little appeal—and little prospect of raising the money he needed. **to come from the country:** from the east, where the king's army was mobilized against her (§5 n.).

49.1. Apollodorus of Sicily: not otherwise known. The name is frequent in Sicily (*LGPN* iiiA. 50) as elsewhere.

49.2. she got into one of those sacks that are used for bedclothes: the origin of the legend of Cleopatra and the 'carpet'. These 'sacks' were 'something like a sailor's kitbag which could have been tied up and slung over one's shoulder' (J. Whitehorne, *XXII congresso internazionale di papirologia* ii (2001), 1287–93). They could be filled with other things in case of need, a talent of silver (Aeschin. *de Falsa Leg.* 99), or the 'literary contributions'—i.e. the books—that Athenaeus' diners bring to the banquet (Athen. 4b); App. 4.40.167 tells of an exciting escape during the proscriptions when a wife hid her husband in one. North's translation has 'mattress or flockbed' (i.e. bedding stuffed with flock), whence Shakespeare's 'mattress' (*A&C* ii. vi. 70). Langhorne's 1770 translation introduced a 'carpet', in the now obsolete sense of 'a thick fabric, commonly of wool, used to cover tables, beds, etc.' (*OED*, s.v. 1a), and the word enters Shakespearian criticism before the end of the eighteenth century (S. and E. Harding, *Shakespeare Illustrated by an Assemblage of Portraits and Views* (1793]), i, s.v. 'Cleopatra'). As the sense of 'carpet' changed, so did the popular picturing of the scene: a carpet, in the modern sense, features in art at least as early as Jean Léone Gérôme's *Cleopatra before Caesar* (1866); then Shaw's *Caesar and Cleopatra* (1898) lavishes attention on it ('It is a Persian carpet—a beauty!'). So, rather differently, does *Carry on Cleo* (1965): C. (Kenneth Williams) to the bearer: 'Where's Cleopatra? In the carpet? Oh, all right. Beat it.'

The trick is alluded to at Petr. 102, when Eumolpus suggests a similar escape plan, in that case putting his friends into two leather sacks and hiding them amid the boat's baggage. Encolpius is scathing, 'even if the trick worked once': what happens if one sneezes or snores?

brought it in through the doors to Caesar. Deliveries of bedding would not normally be made to the great man in person. If Cleopatra did indeed emerge before his eyes (and P. does not quite say so), it will be because he was already in on the plan.

49.3. the trick showed such style, and he was also overcome by all the charm and grace with which she behaved towards him. And that, together with 48.5, is all we get on Cleopatra's charms in this *Life*: cf. §10 n. and Intr., p. 23. P. waxes more eloquent on her looks and her captivating accomplishments at *Ant.* 27.3–5: see my nn. on that passage. Dio 42.4–6 has a similar but less elaborate introduction in the present context. **He reconciled her with her brother, and arranged that the two would rule jointly.** Perhaps mid–late January 47 (= late October or November 48 by the season). More detail of the settlement is given at C. *BC* 3.107–8. C. claimed the right as representative of the Roman people and as consul and dictator to hear the cases of brother and sister: their father's will of 51 BCE had specified that they should be joint heirs (48.5 n.), and had 'called the Roman people to witness', a phrase that should be interpreted as asking the Roman people to guarantee the succession rather than act as the siblings' 'guardians' (as Dio 42.35.4–6 has it, followed by Braund, *Rome and the Friendly King* (1984), 137 and Sullivan 244–5): cf. Heinen, *Rom und Ägypten*, 9–23, esp. 14–15 = Heinen, *Kleopatra-Studien*, 26–36, esp. 29–30. By this point, so C. claims, Pothinus in the city had already been in contact with Achillas in the camp near Pelusium (48.5 n.), and Achillas' army was approaching Alexandria: see §4 nn.

C. also granted Cyprus to the younger siblings Ptolemy (later Ptolemy XIV) and Arsinoe.

49.4. a plot was being hatched ... Achillas the general and Pothinus the eunuch. P. evidently does not realize that Achillas was still with the army (48.5 n.). He seems to be thinking of a 'plot' of the sort C. was guarding against at 48.6, a matter of a sudden furtive assault in the bedchamber, and the same impression is given by Lucan 10.395–9; but the item probably originally concerned the secret messages from Pothinus to Achillas that C. mentions at *BC* 3.108.2–3 and 112.12, urging him to bring up the army and attack the palace. Cf. Heinen, *Rom und Ägypten*, 95–6 = Heinen, *Kleopatra-Studien*, 88–9. **Achillas the general.** C. *BC* 3.104.2 introduces him as the *praefectus regius*, which naturally suggests 'commander of the king's army'; 3.108.2, though, suggests that he was formally appointed to that role only after C.'s arrival and the concentration of the

Egyptian forces. Cf. Heinen, *Rom und Ägypten*, 41–2 = Heinen, *Kleopatra-Studien*, 48–9. C. also calls him 'a man of remarkable nerve' (Carter's trans.).

Achillas' forces now moved on Alexandria (? early February 47 = November 48 by the season).

49.5. to surround the banqueting hall. There is a wordplay in the Greek that would sound even more forced in English: C. 'surrounded' the hall with guards, Achillas 'surrounded' (i.e. 'enveloped') C. with a difficult war. **then had Pothinus killed.** This did not happen until some time after the fighting started (C. *BC* 3.112.12). **Achillas escaped to the army camp:** wrong: he was already there (§4 n.). He was eventually killed within his own camp, the victim of a plot of the eunuch Ganymedes and the princess Arsinoe (§3 n.): *B.Alex.* 4. **with so few men of his own:** cf. 48.2 n., C. *BC* 3.109.2. More men were coming from Asia (C. *BC* 3.107.1, cf. *B.Alex.* 1.1, 26), but they naturally took some time to arrive: the first ones to do so also found difficulty in landing (*B.Alex.* 9.3–4).

49.6. the conduits were dammed by the enemy: *B.Alex.* 5–9. **nearly cut off from his fleet:** C. *BC.* 3.111. 2–6: if the enemy had captured them, they would have been able to blockade the harbour. Once C. had fought off the attack, he burnt all the ships in the harbour, as he was unable to protect them adequately with his forces. This presumably was the **fire** that went on to destroy docks, storehouses, and—so P. says—**the great library.** This was the most famous and largest of the world: see P. M. Fraser, *Ptolemaic Alexandria* (1972), i. 320–35; R. MacLeod (ed.), *The Library of Alexandria* (2nd edn, 2004). Fraser i. 324–5 thinks that this formed part of the Mouseion, and MacLeod 3–4 agrees that the two were closely adjacent: if so, the library lay 'fairly near the shore' (Fraser i. 15), and would be highly vulnerable to such a fire, though it is also possible that the real damage was done to warehouses storing its books. The library's stocks are most reliably given as 400,000 'mixed' and 90,000 'unmixed and simple' volumes (Tzetzes, *CGF*, pp. 19, 31): i.e. respectively rolls with several works and rolls with only one. An eleventh- or twelfth-century copyist of this *Life* was moved to add a cry of pain to his margin: 'alas for the library!'

The damage done by the fire is controversial, but there are good reasons for thinking that it was very substantial, and it could plausibly be claimed as destroying most or all of its stock: see Fraser i. 334–5, ii. 493–4, and (more sceptical) Holmes, *RR* iii. 487–9, and R. Barnes in MacLeod, 70–2. The evidence is confusing. Gell. 7.17.3 confirms that 700,000 volumes (apparently: a less well-attested variant has 70,000) had been gathered by the Ptolemies, and 'all these' were burnt. The text of Sen. *de Tranq.* 9.5 gives the loss as 40,000 volumes, and in context seems clearly to mean the library rather than a warehouse: he quotes Livy, who also probably lies behind Oros. 6.15.31–2, speaking of the destruction of 400,000 volumes 'stored in a nearby building' (but the Latin for 40,000 and 400,000 is so similar—*quadraginta* or *quadringenta milia*—that one or other of those passages is likely to be corrupt: 400,000 seems the more likely reading, though it may well be an exaggeration). Dio 42.38.2 simply mentions the destruction of 'very many and excellent books'. Amm. Marc. 22.16.13–4 has 700,000 volumes destroyed, but confuses the great library with a second, 'daughter' library in the Serapeum.

Strabo, describing the Mouseion a generation later (17.1.8), does not say anything of the library, only of the 'learned men' that gathered there. That silence may be explained variously, especially if it formed part of the Mouseion (Fraser). Was the presence of books taken for granted as less important than the people and the culture (as we may talk of an Institute for Advanced Study and *assume* the presence of a research library)? Or was the damage so great that for the moment the library was non-existent? True, by Strabo's time Antony had allegedly transferred 200,000 volumes from the Pergamene Library (*Ant.* 58.9), presumably to compensate for the loss; but P. himself casts doubt on those allegations (*Ant.* 59.1).

49.7–8. there was a battle around the island of Pharos: which C. had occupied (C. *BC* 3.112.1–4), as its possession gave control of the harbour entry. In fact there were several battles, described at *B.Alex.* 15–22; cf. Dio 42.40.3–5. **he only just managed to escape by swimming . . . According to the story . . .** *B.Alex.* 21.1–3 mentions the escape by swimming and the sinking of the boat, but is very restrained. The tale was probably told by Pollio, as a brief version appears in App. 2.90.377. App. and Dio add that the Alexandrians captured his general's cloak and displayed it as a trophy; Suet. 64 has C. save the cloak by dragging it with his teeth.

49.9. the king left to join the enemy: perhaps mid-February 47 (Heinen, *Rom und Ägypten*, 128 = Heinen, *Kleopatra-Studien*, 112). According to *B.Alex.* 23–4, the army leaders pretended that they wished to consult with the king on the terms of a possible surrender; C. was not taken in, but let him go anyway. Doubts may reasonably be felt about that version, and Heinen, *Rom und Ägypten*, 120–6 = Heinen, *Kleopatra-Studien*, 106–10, thinks that C. was playing for time while waiting for the reinforcements (next n.). **Caesar marched on their forces and defeated them in battle.** He attacked once those reinforcements from Syria and Cilicia arrived, *B.Alex.* 26. On the manœuvres, the battle, and the capture of the king's camp, *B.Alex.* 27–31. The date of the battle was 27 March 47 by the pre-Julian calendar, early–mid January by the season. **Many were killed, and the king disappeared.** He drowned in the Nile: *B.Alex.* 31.6 represents it as an accident.

49.10. Caesar left Cleopatra in control of Egypt. Three legions were also left to support her. Cleopatra would be co-ruler with an even younger brother-husband, the 11- or 12-year-old Ptolemy XIV. He too did not prosper: he died in a further outbreak of violence shortly after C.'s death in 44, allegedly poisoned by Cleopatra, who then elevated the 3-year-old Caesarion to share her rule. **a little later she bore him a son ... Caesarion:** born 23 June 47 = 6 September by the pre-Julian calendar (H. Heinen, *Hist.* 18 (1969), 182–3 = Heinen, *Kleopatra-Studien*, 156). The boy was to be a factor in the exchanges between Cleopatra/Antony and Octavian: cf. *Ant.* 54.6 with my n., 184, 250–1, 261, 295, 298, 312. Egyptian inscriptions call him 'Ptolemy Kaisar' or 'Kaisaros': it appears that C. authorized that use of 'Caesar', and it was current in Rome by the time of C.'s death (Cic. *Att.* 14.20 (374).2, cf. Heinen, art. cit., 196–7 = Heinen, *Kleopatra-Studien*, 169). Understandably, the parentage was disputed, in particular by supporters of Octavian, for whom a biological son of C. was very inconvenient: cf. esp. Suet. 52. He was killed on Octavian's orders in 30 (*Ant.* 81.5–82.1).

P. omits another item that figured in the historical tradition (App. 2.90.379, cf. Suet. 52.1), C.'s Nile cruise with Cleopatra—a pleasure cruise, so it was claimed, though there was precious little time to dawdle before C. left (next n.): on this see T. W. Hillard, *CQ* 52

(2002), 549–54. Once again (cf. §2 n.) P. makes less of Cleopatra than he might. Cf. Intr., p. 23, and 48.2–49.10 n.

Caesar himself set out for Syria. It seems likely that he left only a few weeks after the battle: here the elaborate calculations of L. E. Lord, *JRS* 28 (1938), 19–40, still seem largely cogent, despite the reservations (partly well founded) of Heinen, *Rom und Ägypten*,148–58 = Heinen, *Kleopatra-Studien*, 126–33. So also A. Aly in *Roma e l'Egitto nell' antichità classica: Atti del I Congresso Internazionale Italo-Egiziano* (1992), 48–9. The stay in Egypt was thus probably a little more than six months, though App. 2.90.378 says 'nine'.

50: The War against Pharnaces, Summer 47

Like our other sources, P. dwells on the swiftness of the decisive fighting. However fair, that emphasis obscures that the campaign with its extensive marches took much longer, and seriously delayed C.'s return to Rome, where, as he already knew in the spring, grave problems awaited (*B.Alex.* 65.1, cf. 51.2 n.). It also allowed more time for the defeated Pompeians to regroup (52.1 n., cf. Cic. *Fam.* 15.15 (174).2). Had he returned direct from Alexandria, he might have been in Rome by July; as it was, he could not return till October (51.1 n.). Positive as well as negative spin could be put on this: cf. *B.Alex.* 65.1, 'although he could see that all these factors demanded his presence, he nevertheless thought the priority was to leave the provinces and regions he had visited ordered in such a way that they should be freed from domestic discord, that they should receive laws and justice, and should lay aside fear of foreign wars'. But P. prefers to leave the impression that only Alexandria raised the slightest question of propriety (48.5 with 48.2–49.10 n.); the brevity of the description of the Pharnaces war reflects 'the sharpness and speed' of the outcome, and contrasts with the more dangerous and laborious Roman conflicts to come.

The campaign and its background are described at *B.Alex.* 34–41, 67–78.

50.1. he travelled on through Asia: via Syria, where he heard news of Domitius' defeat and of the disruption in Rome (51.2 n.), and then via Cilicia: *B.Alex.* 65–6. On his route and the time it would take, see L. E. Lord, *JRS* 28 (1938), 19–40. As in his previous journey through Asia in 48 (49.1 n.), he took the opportunity to settle various administrative affairs en route (*B.Alex.* 65.4, Gelzer 258–9). In particular, he arbitrated on wrangles among the ruling class of Judaea, establishing

Hyrcanus II as high priest and Antipater as *epitropos* ('procurator'), and regulating taxes: Jos. *BJ* 1.194–200, *AJ* 14.137–44, 190–210; on the difficulties presented by Josephus' documents, see E. Schürer, G. Vermes, and F. Millar, *The History of the Jewish People in the Age of Jesus Christ*, i (1973), 272–5. **Domitius:** Cn. Domitius Calvinus (39.9–10, 41.6, 44.2 nn.), the consul of 53, 'to whom C. had entrusted administration of Asia and the neighbouring provinces' (*B.Alex.* 34.1: cf. *MRR* 277). **Pharnaces:** king of Bosporus since the death in 63 of his father **Mithridates**, the great adversary of Sulla, Lucullus, and Pompey. On Pharnaces, see Sullivan 155–8: it was said that his revolt against his father had pushed Mithridates to suicide (*Pomp.* 41.7). He had now been ravaging Lesser Armenia and Cappadocia (*B.Alex.* 34.1–2), evidently taking advantage of the civil war and the absence of kings Deiotarus and Ariobarzanes (41.2 n.) at the fighting; Deiotarus had called on Domitius to intervene. Pharnaces won an emphatic victory over the combined forces of Domitius, Deiotarus, and Ariobarzanes at Nicopolis in Lesser Armenia in late 48: *B.Alex.* 34–40. **and had fled from Pontus with a few followers:** 'into Asia' (*B.Alex.* 40.4–5).

Pharnaces…was already master of Bithynia and Cappadocia, with aspirations to take over the land called Lesser Armenia. *B. Alex.* 34–5 gives the impression that Pharnaces had already overrun much of Lesser Armenia before the battle; also some parts of Cappadocia, though he had since withdrawn from these. It was now Pontus, the former realm of his father Mithridates, that he occupied, with (according to *B.Alex.* 41) accompanying atrocities: App. 2.91.381 and Dio 42.46.3 say that the town of Amisus suffered particular cruelty. Strabo 12.3.14 agrees, adding that C. granted the city freedom (cf. 48.1 n.), presumably as a mark of respect or compensation. **the kings and tetrarchs.** 'Tetrarch' was indeed the correct word for some of the local rulers (*B.Alex.* 67.1, 68.1, 78.3, etc.), but the coupling of the words was anyway a Roman cliché to summon up oriental power and splendour: e.g. Sall. *Cat.* 20.7, Cic. *Dom.* 60, Hor. *Sat.* 1.3.12, Tac. *Ann.* 15.25.3, and see my n. on *Ant.* 56.7.

50.2. with three legions. C. had brought from Alexandria the remains of the sixth legion, now depleted to fewer than 1,000 men; in Pontus he was reinforced with one 'legion' that Deiotarus had armed and trained in the Roman fashion and two that had fought with Domitius (*B.Alex.* 68.2–69.1). P. or his source may not be counting the Galatian legion, which had anyway suffered severe losses at Nicopolis (*B.Alex.* 40.4). **A great battle ensued at the city of Zela:** *B.Alex.* 72–6. Its date was 2 August 47 (= late May by the season). **Caesar drove Pharnaces out of Pontus and destroyed his entire army.** *B.Alex.* 76 stresses the large number killed or captured. Pharnaces 'fled with a few horsemen' (*B.Alex.* 76.4), and later suffered a further defeat at the hands of Asander, his rebellious governor in Bosporus, and died of his wounds (App. *Mith.* 120.595, cf. Dio 42.46–7). C. transferred Bosporus to Mithridates of Pergamum, who had been instrumental in bringing the Syrian and Cilician reinforcements to Egypt (49.9 n.)—but it was specified that he would need to defeat Asander first in order to claim it (cf. Dio 42.48.4). He did not; Mithridates was killed, and Asander continued to rule until his death in 17 BCE. Cf. Sullivan 158–60; H. Heinen, in R. Günther and S. Rebenic (eds), *E fontibus haurire* (1994), 63–79.

50.3. the sharpness and speed of the battle: within five days of his arrival and within four hours of coming within sight of the enemy, according to Suet. 35.2: nothing in the narrative of *B.Alex.* makes one doubt it. **Matius:** Cichorius' plausible emendation (*Römische Studien* (1922), 245–50) of the manuscripts' 'Amatius' or 'Amantius', here as at 51.3 (n.). C. Matius had accompanied C. in Gaul, and during the civil war was active on his behalf in Rome and Italy (a 'Caesarian business man' (Syme, *RR* 71)). He was a friend of Cicero as well as C., and played an important part in easing the relations of the two men both during the fifties and then, particularly, in 49–47 (Cic. *Fam.* 11.27 (348)). 'A man of moderation and good sense' (*Att.* 9.11 (178).2), he is notable for writing in 44 a letter that Holmes, *RR* iii. 349, called 'the noblest that has come from antiquity', defending his loyalty to C. in response to a hypocritical Cicero: *Fam.* 11.28 (349). **'I came, I saw, I conquered':** the canonical English rendering (at least as old as Philemon Holland's 1606 Suetonius) of *ueni uidi uici*. According to Suet. 37.2, this was the inscription on a placard carried at the triumph (55.2 n.); App. 2.91.384 agrees with P. that it was used in a letter 'to Rome'. Both versions may well be right: P.'s naming of the recipient suggests good information for the 'letter' version, but once C. had coined the slogan he was unlikely to waste it. It is also echoed, presumably as an allusion that readers will recognize, in the phrasing adopted for the battle by Flor. 2.13.63 and by Dio 42.48.1 and 44.46.1. Florus adds a less striking boast of C., 'we beat them before we even

saw them'; Suet. 35.2 a less gracious one, that Pompey was a lucky man
to win so much glory from such feeble enemies. **In Latin... the
compression of the phrase is very powerful.** For P.'s explanation of
Latin to a Greek audience, cf. Intr., p. 9. At *Dem.* 2.4 he says he has
not had time to develop a deep appreciation of Latin style (Intr., p. 43),
but, like any modern student, he can understand the brilliance of *ueni
uidi uici.*

51: Caesar Returns to Rome

See Intr., pp. 21–2, for the importance of this chapter in the *Life*'s
structure. The various forces that built C.'s greatness—troops, people,
friends—are all beginning to contribute to his downfall: C. can see
what is happening, but is trapped by 'political considerations'—
trapped, in fact, both by the present needs and by his own past. P.
deserves credit here for perceptiveness as well as literary craft. It is no
surprise that observers could see that C.'s freedom of action was
constrained by the depth of the crisis: Cic. *Fam.* 9.17 (195).3 (?
September 46), 'we're slaves to him, he to the times'; 4.13 (225).2.
But Cicero also emphasized, and feared the extent of, C.'s obligations
to his friends: *Fam.* 9.17 (195).2, 12.18 (205).2, 4.9 (231).3. Cf.
Strasburger, *CUZ* 63; Jehne 238–41; Batstone and Damon 168–9.

So perceptions mattered, as the taste of C.'s power was beginning to
sour, and C. himself was sensing it. P.'s focalization technique now
becomes most skilful as he explores those perceptions, and once
again, as is usual in this *Life* (Intr., p. 20), he affords material for
moral judgement without enforcing it on the reader too stridently. In
§3 it matters that 'tongues' started 'wagging against C.', and the views
of those critics help to texture the language: 'Dolabella's madness' and
'Matius' avarice' are the sort of terms that they would have used. At
the same time P. does not distance himself from the language, and
some of it is factual enough: Antony *was* drunken, as *Ant.* 9.5–9
makes clear. The phrase 'political considerations' is again blurred in
its focalization (n.): in part that may reflect 'the needs' of the state
(and P., monarchist as he was (Intr., pp. 11–12), would not have
disagreed); but it is C.'s 'political line', and the premisses that under-
pin it, that are defining what is necessary.

Some of this material overlaps with *Ant.* 9–10.1 and 21.2–5 (nn.),
and *Antony* too emphasizes that the excesses in C.'s absence aroused
popular disapproval; that *Life* has also already adopted the analysis

developed here, that it was the conduct of C.'s friends rather than his own that damaged his reputation (*Ant.* 6.7). If the *Lives* were prepared as part of a single project (Intr., p. 36), that is no surprise, as P.'s reading about each individual contributes to his presentation of the other. 'Asinius', i.e. Asinius Pollio, is named in *Ant.* 9.2 among those who opposed Dolabella's agitation, and he doubtless described these events in his history. But *Ant.* also draws heavily on Cicero's *Second Philippic*, and the item on Antony's drunkenness and his treatment of Pompey's house (§3 n.) is influenced by that. The 'rebuilding' of that house is, however, not mentioned either by Cicero or in *Antony*: perhaps that is P.'s own imaginative elaboration, inspired by his picture of Pompey as 'a man admired as much for his moderation and his regular and ordinary lifestyle as for his three triumphs' (*Ant.* 21.2)—so he would, of course, have lived too modestly for Antony's tastes; or perhaps that is drawn from Pollio, who may also be the source for 'Matius' avarice'.

51.1. Caesar then crossed to Italy: to Tarentum, where he arrived in late September 47. Cicero hurried to meet him, and the two made their peace (*Cicero* 39.4). **and travelled to Rome:** arriving in early October (Gelzer 261). He took a devious route from Tarentum, going via Brundisium: he may well have been nervous of travelling via Campania, where the mutiny remained unresolved (§2 n.). **It was just at the end of the year for which he had been elected dictator for the second time.** C. had been nominated dictator when the news of Pharsalus reached Rome, probably September 48 (Dio 42.18–20 seems to place this after the news of Pompey's death reached Rome, which might suggest late November: so M. Jehne in G. Urso (ed.), *L'Ultimo Cesare* (2000), 166–7 n. 100. But it is characteristic of Dio to group such honours 'out of time', and no weight can be put on this sequence.) Broughton, *MRR* 272 and 284–5 n. 1 and A. E. Raubitschek, *JRS* 44 (1954), 70–1, assume that the dictatorship began only when C. himself was notified of this in Alexandria, presumably in November 48. That is probably right, though the constitutional position will not have been clear: this appointment was anyway irregular, as C. was outside Italy (37.1 n.). Antony was his *magister equitum*, and was active in that role by December (*Ant.* 8.4 with my n.); K. Welch, *Antichthon*, 24 (1990), 55–7, notes the novelty of a *mag. eq.* who was basically filling an urban administrative role. We should also note the extreme constitutional irregularity of this year 47, which has no consuls till September, when Q. Fufius Calenus and P. Vatinius were elected after C.'s return (*MRR* 286): cf. Frei-Stolba 46. **though this office had never before been an annual one.** Dio 42.20.3 says that C. in 48 'received the privilege of being named consul for the next five years and as dictator not for a six-month period but for a full year'. (Misleading, for C. was not consul in 47, as Dio knew: 43.1.1.) Dictatorships had previously been for specific purposes, with either no time limit or one of six months (Lintott, *Constitution*, 110). **He was now declared consul for the following year:** but not dictator: C. did not reassume a dictatorship until April or perhaps even July 46 (*MRR* 294–5, iii. 107–8: Raubitschek, art. cit., 71). His reasons were 'probably propagandistic: the Pompeians made a great deal of their legitimacy, and he could oppose them more effectively as holder of the regular supreme office...' (Jehne 39 n. 4). Q. Fufius Calenus and P. Vatinius were also elected consuls for the last few months of 47 (*MRR* 286): C.'s own consular colleague for 46 was to be Lepidus (*Ant.* 10.2, *MRR* 293–4). In principle C.'s election as consul might seem a potential constitutional embarrassment, as only one year had elapsed since his consulship of 48 instead of the legally demanded ten (cf. 28.7 n.), and in 50–49 P. had based much of his self-justification on his claim to a second consulship at the proper time: thus M. T. Boatwright, *CJ* 84 (1988), 31–40. But C. had then protested at his being allowed *less* than his legal entitlement; the principle that the ten-year gap could be waived at times of crisis had already been established by Pompey's sole consulship of 52, only three years after his 55 consulship, and there had also been talk of electing C. at that time after only a six-year gap (28.7, 29.1 nn.). If anything underlies the garbling of Dio 42.20.3 (see above, on 'though this office...'), it may be that in 48 C. was allowed the privilege of *standing for* the consulship for any of the next five years without any restrictions on such iteration (Jehne 41).

51.2. He was met by popular disapproval. *B.Alex.* 65.1 says that C. was informed about the disruption in the city while in Syria (50.1 n). Cic. *Att.* 11.10 (221).2 (19 January 47) refers in passing to 'the desperate situation in the city', which continued throughout the year. It is discussed by K. Welch, *G&R* 42 (1995), 182–201, stressing the role of Antony's wife Fulvia, and by M. Jehne in G. Urso (ed.), *L'Ultimo Cesare* (2000), 151–73. **his soldiers had mutinied:** in Campania. It was a most serious outbreak (S. G. Chrissanthos, *JRS* 91

(2001), 63–75), probably involving all nine of the legions quartered there: and these were valuable veteran legions, expected to be crucial once fighting resumed. They had not received the rewards that C. had several times promised them (see below, on the 'thousand drachmas'), and had probably not even been paid for some time. Trouble began as early as June 47, fanned by several military tribunes and other officers (*B.Af.* 54); Campanian cities were plundered; Antony was unable to deal with it (*Ant.* 10.1, Dio 42.30). On C.'s return in October he first sent C. Sallustius Crispus (the historian Sallust) with a further promise of bonuses; that failed, and Sallustius was lucky to escape with his life. The soldiers marched on Rome, killing on the way **the two former praetors, Cosconius and Galba.** The first is probably C. Cosconius, praetor in 54 (*MRR* 221 and iii. 77, *PRR* 538). The second is more difficult to identify: possibly the P. Sulpicius Galba who was praetor in 66 or before (*MRR* 132), as suggested by Shackleton Bailey on Cic. *Att.* 1.1 (10).1 and by Garzetti; but there are other possibilities. See *MRR* iii. 201. In Rome the troops met C. himself in the Campus Martius.

Caesar had ventured no harsher punishment than to call the men 'citizens': i.e. 'Quirites'. P.'s emphasis is notably different from that of most sources, who prefer to emphasize the authority by which C.'s use of the single word quelled the rebels: so App. 2.93–4, Dio 42.53–5, Suet. 70, Tac. *Ann.* 1.42.3. P.'s historical sensibility here deserves credit, for contemporary observers were indeed likely to sense the mildness rather than the firmness of C.'s response. The Italian public were doubtless no friends of the soldiers, even if many came from a similar background, and Cic. *Phil.* 2.62 suggests that trouble started with billeting in the Italian cities during winter 48–47. Chrissanthos, art. cit., has good reason to emphasize the lavishness with which C. now bought his troops off, and only five of the nine legions in fact fought for C. in Africa. Nor was C. yet strong enough to punish the ringleaders: he did that a few months later in Africa (*B.Af.* 54, Dio 42.55.2, cf. 43.13.1). **a thousand drachmas:** presumably realizing the bonuses promised at Brundisium (37.3–9 n.) and before Pharsalus: App. 2.47.191, 92.386. **parcelling out ... in land grants.** P. correctly implies that many of them were discharged (so 'citizens' indeed). App. 2.94.395 gives the impression that the grants were rather promises for the future, but the land commissioners were at work within a few months. Dio 42.55.1 says that those immediately settled were 'the turbulent ones, and not all of them but those with some

experience of farming'. See Chrissanthos, art. cit., 74, and, on C.'s
settlements, Keppie 49–58.

51.3. Dolabella: P. Cornelius Dolabella, tribune in 47 (*MRR* 287)
and Cicero's son-in-law: 'ambitious beyond character or capacity,
Dolabella may be described as pseudo-dynamic' (Syme, *Hist.* 29
(1980), 431–5 = *RP* iii. 1244–8, speculating rather extravagantly that
he may have been C.'s own biological son). On his character and
career, cf. esp. Dettenhofer 119–22, 165–83 ('he was openly aspiring
to the succession to Clodius' (172)), 310–14. **madness:** language in
the style of the late Republic: 14.6 n. Here P. allusively refers to the
events of *Ant.* 9.1–4, Dolabella's advocation of rent reform and 'a
cancellation of debts' and the subsequent violence, with troops of
Antony and Dolabella fighting in the forum and leaving many dead
(*MRR* 287, Bruhns 126–37, P. Simelon, *LEC* 53 (1985), 387–405). P.
says nothing of C.'s own attempts to relieve the financial crisis, which
included a limit on rents (Suet. 38.2): on these measures, cf. 37.2 n.,
M. W. Frederiksen, *JRS* 56 (1966), 133–5, Bruhns 125–6, Jehne 249–
50, 292–4, and Woytek 169–71. **Matius' avarice.** 'Matius' is again (cf.
50.3 n.) Cichorius' emendation for the manuscripts' 'Amatius' or
'Amantius': a figure as prominent as Dolabella and Antony is needed,
and Matius fills that bill. In his letter to Cicero of 44 (*Fam.* 11.28
(349).2, 50.3 n.) Matius claims 'I did not fall victim to the temptations
of honour or of wealth, while others who had less influence with
Caesar abused those rewards without restraint': but (*a*) we need not
believe him, (*b*) the emphasis may suggest a self-defence against
criticisms ('false rumours' (*Fam.* 11.28 (349).8)), (*c*) his restraint
may have been only relative, and most importantly (*d*) these criticisms
are partly focalized through the eyes of the victims (cf. 51 n.), and
Matius may well have been gathering money ruthlessly for C.'s re-
quirements rather than his own, especially the need to pay the troops
(§2 n.). Those suffering at his hands were not likely to care about the
distinction. In that same letter Matius claims that he actually lost
money by one of C.'s laws. Frederiksen, *JRS* 56 (1966), 138, suggests
that this was a law of 46 that allowed and regulated the transfer of
property to settle debts, and that Matius was a creditor who had
hitherto done well through demanding cash. If so, that too could
well be felt as 'avarice' by those he was dunning. **Antony's drunken
excesses:** again alluding to material handled more expansively in
Antony (9.5–9), drawing heavily on Cicero's *Second Philippic*: see my

comm. on the *Antony* passage. **his ransacking and rebuilding of
Pompey's private house:** treated more fully at *Ant.* 21.2–3, and
drawn ultimately from Cic. *Phil.* 2.64–9, though the 'rebuilding' element does not come from Cicero (see above, 51 n.). The manuscripts
have 'Corfinius' ransacking and rebuilding': Koraës deleted 'Corfinius'
to make the reference continue to be to Antony. That seems correct:
Antony 'was the only person' (Cic. *Phil.* 2.64) to bid for Pompey's
house and was still in possession of it ten years later (*Ant.* 32.4). The
manuscripts also insert 'Corfinius' in error at 43.1 (n.). One might
otherwise have thought again of Q. Cornificius (43.1 n.), as did
Cichorius (*Röm. Studien* 246) and E. Rawson, *CQ* 28 (1978), 192 =
her *Roman Culture and Society* (1991), 277, but Cornificius was in
Illyricum, not Rome (*MRR* 288), and it does not sound as if the ill-will
was simply incurred by the man's agents.

51.4. Political considerations.   The Greek has 'the *hypothesis* ["pre-
miss", something from which conclusions may be inferred] of the
politeia [either "the state" or "his political line"]': so P. leaves it nicely
ambiguous whether it is 'the needs of the state' (cf. e.g. *Arist.* 25.2) or
'the principles on which C. was basing his own political programme'
(cf. e.g. *Ag.-Cl.* 2.7, *Arat.* 43.2) that are forcing C.'s hand. So once
again the focalization is blurred, and P. leaves it open whether he
himself endorses C.'s programme and the helpers it required. Cf.
Pelling, 'Focalisation', 513–14.

52–4: The War in Africa
C.'s position was precarious. 'It looks as if he had largely wasted his
success at Pharsalus, and that in September 47 he was no better off
than he was before Pharsalus' (M. Jehne in G. Urso (ed.), *L'Ultimo
Cesare* (2000), 152). His enemies had gathered a considerable force in
Africa, even if they no longer had a general of Pompey's stature to
command them; many of C.'s own troops were reluctant to fight (51.2
n.); and, as P. has just brought out, Italy itself was a disaffected base.
There is indeed a good case for regarding Thapsus rather than
Pharsalus as the decisive battle of the war. P. himself does not go so
far, and Pharsalus remains the high point of the *Life*'s story of success:
but the Thapsus campaign repeats much of the rhythm of Dyrrhachium and Pharsalus, with a bold winter crossing (52.2 ~ 37.2 nn.)
quelling the doubts of his own men (52.2 ~ 37.4–8), a return to
the main force (52.3 ~ 38), hardships caused by a shortage of food

(52.6 ~ 39.2–3), a series of perilous encounters culminating in one of particular danger (52.7–9 ~ 39.4–8), an intervention of C. himself to try to stem a rout (52.9 n. ~ 39.6), an enemy general emboldened to try a decisive battle (53.1 ~ 40.1, 41.5), and a failed race against time to catch the enemy figurehead before his death (54.2 ~ 48.2).

Thapsus was decisive emblematically as well, for it led to the death of that figurehead, Cato. P. gives Cato's suicide a lavish treatment in *C.min.* 58–72 (cf. M. B. Trapp, in A. Pérez Jiménez, J. Garcia López, and R. M. Aguilar (eds), *Plutarco, Platón y Aristoteles* (1999), 487–99, A. V. Zadorojnyi, *CQ* 57 (2007), 216–30); here he has only the curt 'when news came that Cato had killed himself' (54.2). No more was necessary for an audience that would clearly know the story, but there is certainly no musing on the death of the Republican cause. Here the moral problematic lies in C.'s own behaviour towards Cato—would he really have spared him? Can he be excused for the *Anticato*? P.'s judgement is cool: the possibility of a political aim for the *Anticato* is raised, but only as one that 'people infer' (54.4), not one that P. himself endorses: and even on that view the 'ambition' is not a matter of calm calculation, but of irritation (54.6 n.). Cato, P. suggests, brought out the emotional worst in C., just as the battlefields of Pharsalus and Thapsus showed him at his best. Any calculation seems rather to come in the blandness of 54.2, 'Cato, I grudge you your death, just as you grudged me the chance of saving your life'. Even more clearly than with Pompey (48.2 n.), there is a strong savour there of hypocrisy.

The war is narrated in *B.Af.*, the work, it seems, of a trained soldier and eyewitness, though not a man in C.'s confidence: on its Latin— unciceronian rather than unrefined—see J. N. Adams in T. Reinhardt, M. Lapidge, and J. N. Adams (eds), *Aspects of the Language of Latin Prose* (2005), 73–96. P.'s account is largely, perhaps wholly, independent of *B.Af.*, dwelling on only a few episodes and making no attempt to describe the complicated series of engagements. The mention of Pollio at 52.8 is, and was probably meant as, an indication that his account comes from that source (Intr., p. 46), which, to judge from App., was itself selective. For modern accounts, cf. Holmes, *RR* iii. 236–75, 516–36; Gelzer 264–71.

The incident of Granius Petro (16.8–9) may fit somewhere into his campaign: see n., ad loc.

52.1. the followers of Cato and Scipio had taken refuge in Africa. *C.min.* 56–7 relates how Cato met up with Sextus Pompey in Africa in late 48, and heard from him of his father's death. Cato was urged to assume leadership: he heard though that Metellus Scipio (30.4, 39.10 nn.) had been well received by Juba and that P. Attius Varus, the Pompeian governor of Africa (*MRR* 260, 275, iii. 29), was with them with an army. Cato joined them after an epic march, and deferred to the consular Scipio as the senior commander. Relations among the Republican commanders had been stormy even before Cato's arrival (*C.min.* 57.1, Dio 42.57.1), and continued so: Scipio was anxious for action, Cato advocated a waiting game (*C.min.* 58.7, cf. below, 53.1 n.), and was accused of cowardice for his pains. **King Juba** of Numidia (*OCD*[4] (no. 1)) was a long-standing enemy of C.: there was talk of an insult he had received, presumably in Rome when on an embassy (C. grabbed his beard, Suet. 71). In 49 he had defeated Curio decisively (37.1–2 n.). *C.min.* tells tales of his arrogance (57.1–5. cf. *B.Af.* 57.4–6) and of his desire, unopposed by Scipio but thwarted by Cato, to massacre the people of Utica (58.1–2). Doubtless his Caesarian enemies, Pollio among them, have blackened his portrayal. **they had by now gathered a considerable force.** *B.Af.* 1 gives the reported strength as 'four legions and a large number of light-armed troops provided by the king, and ten legions, 120 elephants, and several fleets of Scipio himself'; there were also some 18,000 horsemen. Cf. Brunt, *Manpower*, 473–4. C.'s initial force comprised five legions of new recruits, one legion of veterans, seven further cohorts, and some 2,000 cavalry; reinforcements eventually strengthened it with four further veteran legions and an extra 4,000 men (Holmes, *RR* iii. 534–6), but it remained weak in horse.

52.2. around the time of the winter solstice: echoing 37.3, but again (cf. n. on that passage) misled by the vagaries of the calendar: C. crossed to Sicily on 17 December and to Africa on 25 December 47 (*B.Af.* 1.1, 2.4), but this would be only early–mid October by the season. The solstice itself was not till the pre-Julian beginning of March. Dio 42.56.1, 'although winter had set in', is better; Cic. *de Div.* 2.52 has C. ignoring a diviner (cf. 63.5 n.) warning him not to cross *ante brumam*, which could be either 'before winter' or 'before the solstice' (cf. *OLD*). Cf. E. Rawson, *JRS* 68 (1978), 142–3 = *Roman Culture and Society* (1991), 307–8. **pitched his tent on the seashore**

itself: at Lilybaeum in west Sicily, *B.Af.* 1.1–2. **with 3,000 infantry and a small force of cavalry:** *B.Af.* 3.1 ('3,000 infantry and 150 cavalry').

52.3. He managed to land these: near Hadrumetum (*B.Af.* 3.1). **unobserved:** contrast *B.Af.* 3.1: C. could see enemy forces on the shore. P. does not tell a famous anecdote here that he probably knew: as he came ashore, C. stumbled and fell, but quickwittedly kissed the soil and said 'I have you, Africa!' (Suet. 59, Dio 42.58.3). **immediately put to sea again:** *B.Af.* 10–11. This was not quite 'immediate', in fact: *B.Af.* 3–10 details several engagements, and C. had by now moved first to Lepcis, then to Ruspina.

52.4. an ancient oracle, which said that it was the prerogative of the Scipios always to win mastery in Africa. At *C.min.* 57.7 it is simply that 'Scipio's name gave the ordinary soldiers confidence that they would win, with a Scipio in command in Africa'; Dio 42.57.1 has this as 'a strange, irrational belief', but does not mention an oracle. Suet. 59 refers to 'prophecies'. The allusion is not merely to the exploits of Scipio Africanus, the victor of Hannibal, but also to Scipio Aemilianus and his part in the destruction of Carthage in 146 (57.8 n.). Cf. Intr., p. 31, on the *Life*'s, and C.'s, generally sceptical attitude to anything supernatural.

52.5. Scipio Salvito. His name is uncertain: this is Ziegler's correction of the manuscripts' 'Sallutio'. At 42.58.1 Dio's manuscripts have 'Salutio'. Some MSS of Suet. 59 have 'Salvito', some 'Salutio', adding that the name was given him because of 'his disgraceful lifestyle'. Pliny seems to call him 'Salvitto' (thus most of the manuscripts at *NH* 7.54, 35.8), and says that he was nicknamed after a pantomime actor of that name.

Caesar was indeed forced to engage the enemy frequently. P. does not go into details on the various operations at Ruspina, Lepcis, Uzitta, and Aggar recounted in *B.Af.* 9–78.

52.6. short of food: *B.Af.* 20.4–21.1, 24.2, 47.4. **give the horses a diet of seaweed:** *B.Af.* 24.4, though **adding a little of the local grass to disguise the flavour** may be P.'s own addition.

52.7 they were being entertained by an African, who was a gifted dancer and flute-player. This episode is otherwise unknown.

Garzetti thinks it may relate to the surprise Republican attack late in the day at Uzitta (*B.Af.* 52): that may well be right.

52.8. Asinius Pollio: Intr., p. 46, and 52–4 n.: this is doubtless drawn from his history.

52.9. another battle, too, when the enemy were getting the better of the engagement. This seems to be the battle described, with varying details, at *B.Af.* 18–19 and by App. 2.95.399–400 and Dio 43.2.1–2, shortly after C.'s arrival, and therefore probably before the incident of §§7–8. The enemy attack was led by Petreius (36.1 n), who was seriously wounded, and Labienus (18.2, 34.5 nn.). **Caesar, so they say, grabbed the standard-bearer . . . 'the enemy are over there!':** a more successful equivalent of the episode at Dyrrhachium, 39.6. The story is also told by Val. Max. 3.2.19, making it clear that the standard-bearer belonged to the *legio Martia*. Such scenes are a stereotypical mark of the good general: cf. e.g. Livy 6.8.1–2 with the nn. of Oakley and Kraus, 3.70.10, Tac. *Hist.* 3.17.1, Frontin. 2.8.1–4, 4.5.3. But it doubtless sometimes happened, and may well have happened now.

53.1 These successes encouraged Scipio to risk a decisive battle: the battle of Thapsus (6 April 46), described at *B.Af.* 79–86.

P.'s language suggests some rashness on Scipio's part in taking such a risk, and *C.min.* 58.7 describes the disagreements between Cato, who wished to avoid battle (as he had also recommended before Pharsalus, *C.min.*53.5), and the more bellicose Scipio. App. 2.97.405 similarly suggests that Scipio was criticized for not adopting a strategy of attrition, though also (not altogether coherently) for not following up his earlier victory (52.9 n.). But (*a*) Scipio's earlier strategy had largely, though not entirely, been one of attrition, with some partly successful attempts to cut C. off from water (playing C. at his own game of Ilerda, 36.2 n.): *B.Af.* 51.5, 69.5, 76.2, 79.1; (*b*) with numerical superiority even after C.'s reinforcements had arrived (52.1 n.), there was much to be said for battle: C.'s men had good reason still to be nervous both of Scipio's elephants and of his cavalry, and the chances of Republican success were good.

He left Afranius and Juba in separate camps nearby: one of several details not in *B.Af.*; it may have been inferred from a narrative of the rout, where each camp fell in turn (§3, cf. *B.Af.* 85—but *B.Af.*

does not name Afranius). P. does not bring out that Scipio was drawn to Thapsus by C.'s manœuvring (*B.Af.* 79). For Afranius cf. 36.1 n. **a lake:** for the topography, cf. *B.Af.* 80: a narrow neck of land ran between this salt lake, which was a prominent feature of the landscape (Strabo 17.3.12), and the sea. Both sides tried to fortify it.

53.2. He surrounded... in a frontal charge. There was also a sea-borne attack synchronized with the land assault, *B.Af.* 80.5. But it was all rather less ordered than P.'s account would suggest: C.'s troops joined battle before the order was given (*B.Af.* 82.3–4), one of several signs of unaccustomed indiscipline in this (largely newly recruited) Caesarian force. Cf. §7 n.

53.3. Juba... fled. He 'hid on a mountain with a few companions' (*C.min.* 60.5).

53.4. In a small part of a single day. But Dio 43.6.4 brings out that there were preliminary manœuvrings and skirmishes for several days before the battle; App. 2.97.403 that the fighting itself was very fierce and lasted till evening. **had taken three camps and killed 50,000 of his enemy, losing fewer than 50 of his own men:** *B.Af.* 86.1 has '10,000' enemy dead and '50' Caesarian. ('10,000' is tacitly emended to '50,000' in the Oxford text of *B.Af.*, which misled Brunt, *Manpower*, 474.) For once, the large figure of enemy dead may be no exaggeration: Brunt points out that the Pompeian soldiers who escaped to Spain were re-formed into only one legion (*B.Hisp.* 7.4) from an original fourteen, though admittedly not all the survivors will have been keen to fight on.

53.5–6. Others say that Caesar was not on the field himself... passed the battle there undisturbed: a familiar type of story, as enemies tried to diminish a general's achievement: cf. 18.2 n., *Ant.* 22.3 and my note. This particular charge is not known from elsewhere, and is inconsistent with the narrative of *B.Af.* (83.1); conceivably it originated as an excuse for the excesses of C.'s troops in victory (§7 n.), as Gelzer 268 n. 3 suggested. In P.'s narrative it gives some preparation for 60.6–8 (n.), reminding the reader of C.'s **usual illness,** i.e. epilepsy (17.2 n.): here we see rational self-control as C. the general handles a genuine attack of the illness, but then at 60.6–8 the excuse is false, and marks how C. the politician is losing his grip.

53.7. A good many men of consular and praetorian rank survived the battle. Scipio himself initially escaped and 'anchored by a cliff not far from Utica, where he, like Juba, waited on events' (*C.min.* 60.5). **some took their own lives.** Juba and Petreius killed one another in a suicide pact; Scipio's fleet was attacked, and he stabbed himself and leapt overboard to avoid capture; Cato killed himself, memorably and messily, at Utica. **Caesar put many to death himself.** There is uncertainty here (cf. M. Jehne, *Chiron*, 17 (1987), 322–4), and some sources again prefer an emphasis along the lines that 'C. showed the same clemency to his defeated enemies as in the past' (Vell. 2.55.2). At *C.min.* 73.1 P. acknowledges that C. spared Cato's son. C. also pardoned the people of Utica, except for those of the Council of 300 whom he could find (or so App. says, 2.100.416). Suet. 75 says that only three of C.'s enemies were executed except on the battlefield (and all of these it seems were after Thapsus), Afranius (36.1 n.), Faustus Sulla (14.7 n.), and the younger L. Caesar, and that even these were killed against C.'s own wishes. Earlier P. Ligarius had also been executed (*B.Af.* 64.1). *B.Af.* 85.7–8 makes it clear that there was a general massacre after the battle and C. was unable to stop it—more indiscipline (§2 n.)—and in such circumstances uncertainty is understandable on responsibility for deaths. Thus *B.Af.* 89.4 is explicit that C. pardoned his distant relative L. Caesar, and this squares with Suet., but Dio 43.12.2 puts the responsibility for L. Caesar's death squarely on C. himself; similarly, *B.Af.* 95 gives the impression that Afranius and Faustus were killed by soldiers ('after a disagreement arose in the camp'), but this was on C.'s orders according to Dio 43.12.2, Flor. 2.13.90, and Oros. 6.16.5 (this, then, was probably the Livian version); cf. Gelzer 269–70 and n. 1. Florus and Orosius (hence again probably Livy) also claim that C. executed Pompey's daughter (Faustus' wife, 14.7 n.) and grandchildren, but *B.Af.* 95.3 says that he saved them, and App. 2.100.416 adds that he sent them to Cn. Pompey in Spain. That seems right: Pompeia herself certainly survived, to be touted as a possible wife for Cicero (*Att.* 12.11 (249)) and then to marry L. Cornelius Cinna (cf. Dio 55.14.1, Sen. *Clem.* 1.9.2): Miltner, *R-E* 21 (1952), 2263–4.

P.'s siding with the less positive sources, together with his focus only on 'men of consular and praetorian rank'—he does not even mention Juba—prepare for the scepticism in the next chapter about whether he would have spared Cato. If we remember 48.4—'this was the greatest and most delicious reward of victory, the chance to save one man after another who had fought against him'—we will be even more inclined to sense hypocrisy in those bland words of C.

C. also annexed territory from Juba's kingdom as the new province of *Africa Nova*, and left it under C. Sallustius Crispus (Sallust) as proconsul: *MRR* 298.

54.1. Cato was one man he had ambitions of taking alive, and he hurried to Utica: *C.min.* 71–2. **ambitions:** the word is echoed at §4, 'political ambition'—in the Greek, *philotimia*. That becomes a loaded word at 58.4 (n.) ~ 62.8: for the moment this is the bad side of C.'s 'ambition' or 'eagerness for glory', and 58.4 will show the good.

54.2. Cato had killed himself. 12 April 46. **'Cato, I grudge you your death, just as you grudged me the chance of saving your life':** so also *C.min.* 72.2, Val. Max. 5.1.10, and in less sharp formulations App. 2.99.414 and Dio 43.12.1.

54.3. the work he wrote later against the dead Cato: the *Anticato*: §§5–6 nn., Intr., p. 48. **would he really have spared him alive, when he poured out so much anger on the man when he was a senseless corpse?** Yes, perhaps he would: the humiliation of Cato in owing his life to a fellow-Roman's mercy (cf. Cic. *Phil.* 2.5) would have been as welcome as the parade of clemency itself (57.4 n.). The rhetorical question and the metaphor ('poured out') mark the intensity of P.'s engagement. At *C.min.* 72.3 P.'s words have some edge: 'What in fact Caesar would have done is unclear: but people prefer the more favourable interpretation concerning Caesar.' There as here (§4 n.), P. distances himself from that view: the word order in *C.min.* suggests 'it being Caesar, people give him the benefit of the doubt'—possibly because C. was so merciful a person, but more likely because of his power and the consequent necessity to guard one's tongue.

54.4. he was generous towards Cicero: *Cic.* 39.4–6. **and Brutus:** 46.4, 62.2 nn. **leads people to infer:** 'people', but not necessarily P. himself: 54.3 n.

54.5. Cicero had written a eulogy of Cato ('Cato' was in fact its title). He was at work on it soon after Cato's death (*Att.* 12.4 (240).2, ? May 46), and it was being copied in (?) July (*Fam.* 16.22

(185).1). K. Kumaniecki, *Forschungen zur röm. Literatur: Fschr....*
Karl Büchner (1970), 168–88, largely followed by Tschiedel, *Caesars*
'Anticato' (§6 n.), 8, thought that Cicero's work was not published
before November 46, because the replies began to emerge only in
early 45: that inference is insecure. C. was following a conciliatory
policy through summer 46 (55 n.), and may have thought it unwise to
stir up anger if the work had been published at that point; equally,
Cicero was eager to express support for C. in the autumn (the *pro*
Marcello, 55 n.), and publishing the *Cato* makes less sense then than a
few months earlier. It was only after Munda that C. might feel it
timely to try—unsuccessfully, as it turned out—to counter the mar-
tyrology that Cato's name was beginning to attract. Cf. 56.9 n.

'Eulogy' (*enkōmion*) is also the word P. uses at *Cic.* 39.5: Cicero
himself calls it a work of 'praise' (*Att.* 12.4 (240).2, 12.40 (281).1), and
Gell. 13.20.3 too calls it a 'praise of Cato' (*Laus Catonis*); cf. Tac. *Ann.*
4.34.4, 'praising Cato to the skies', quoted more fully in §6 n. below.
But C. P. Jones, *RhM* 113 (1970), 188–96, argued that this was overall
'less than entirely favourable to its subject', and that *C.min.* 50.2 may
come from that work: 'Cicero takes him to task for failing to meet the
demands of a crisis which called for a leader of Cato's calibre, and
making no effort to win over the people with a show of generous
bonhomie but giving up and resigning the struggle for the future...'
(this refers to Cato's style of candidature and mild acceptance of
defeat when he stood for the consulship of 51). It is true that Cicero's
feelings about Cato were mixed: even in *de Officiis* (44 BCE) the
strongly expressed admiration for Cato (1.112 and esp. 3.66) is
tempered by an explicit statement that the two men often disagreed
(3.88). A scholiast on Juvenal (6.338) calls the work a 'dialogue', and
Jones 194–6 suggests that this may be right, thus allowing discordant
views to be heard. That would certainly suit Cato as a man about
whom people loved to disagree, just as Satyrus' dialogue *Lives* suited
the likes of Euripides. But, even if so, the descriptions of this as a work
of praise still carry weight, and it is likely to have been highly
complimentary overall.

Yet perhaps *C.min.* 50.2 does not come from that work at all. As
Jones 192 observes, it has much in common with the criticism that
'Cato speaks as if he were in Plato's *Republic*, not in Romulus' cesspool' (*Att.* 2.1 (21).8), which P. quotes in *Phoc.* 3.2: Cicero was there
writing in 60 BCE, much earlier than Cato's failed candidature, but in

Phoc. too P. relates it to that consular rebuff. Jones wonders if the cesspool remark too was repeated in the *Cato* (if it was, it might even have been recast as a compliment); but it is more likely that P. is misremembering the 60 letter both in *C.min.* and in *Phoc.* (Intr., pp. 17–18, 52, and n. 136).

composed by the most accomplished of orators: echoing 3.3–4 (n.).

54.6. That irritated Caesar ... So he ... published them under the title 'Anticato'. P. simplifies a complicated sequence of laudation and counter-laudation. Cicero's work came first, and the first reply to that came from Hirtius (early 45? Cicero had it at least by May, *Att.* 12.40 (281).1); C.'s then followed, written 'around the time of the battle of Munda' (Suet. 56.5: March 45, 56.2 n.) and in circulation by August (*Att.* 13.50 (348).1). By then Brutus had also written his *Cato* (*Att.* 12.21 (260).1, March 45); Fabius (or Fadius) Gallus added a further *Cato* before August of that year, *Fam.* 7.24 (260).2), and at some time Cato's companion Munatius Rufus composed a work from which P. drew, perhaps indirectly, a good deal of material in *C.min.* (Intr., p. 51). Cf. Gelzer 302–4, H. J. Tschiedel, *Caesars 'Anticato'* (1981), 6–12, and, on Munatius, J. Geiger, *Athen.* 57 (1979), 48–72.

It is clear, though, that C. framed his work as a reply to Cicero in particular: that is implied by 3.4 above, C.'s plea 'not to compare his style with Cicero's', and it is what Cicero himself anticipated in May 45 ('I can see what to expect from Caesar's denunciation in reply to my work of praise' (*Att.* 12.40 (281).1)). So also *Cic.* 39.5, adding that C. 'praised Cicero's rhetoric and his life as similar to Pericles and Theramenes'—a remark with some edge, as the implication was surely that Cicero's rhetoric was Periclean and Olympian but his life was more like that of the trimmer Theramenes. So Tschiedel, *Caesars 'Anticato'* 79–83. Cf. 3.4 n. for another *Anticato* remark that was more barbed against Cicero than P. perhaps realized.

he collected many charges against Cato and published them under the title 'Anticato': the *Anticato* in two books, sometimes therefore called *Anticatones*, written in Spain in early 45 (56.1 n.). H. J. Tschiedel, *Caesars 'Anticato'* (1981), gives a very exhaustive treatment of what we know of the work. It was probably in speech form: cf. Tac. *Ann.* 4.34.4, quoted below. *C.min.* quotes several passages, sometimes explicitly and sometimes under a thin disguise of 'someone says', with P. often expressing indignation: it included attacks on the way Cato treated his friends (*C.min.* 36.5) and his wife

(52.6–8), with a hint of an affair with his own sister or niece Servilia
(54.2: Tschiedel 111–13 doubts the sexual suggestions, I think
wrongly); on his over-fondness for wine (44.1–2, cf. Plin. *Ep.*
3.12.2–3); on his lack of dignity (57.4); and C. was evidently the
'someone' who claimed that 'Cato sifted and filtered his brother's
ashes looking for melted gold among the remains of the fire. The man
who said that did not have any consequences or cross-examination to
fear, and this amounted to exploiting that confidence with the pen,
not just the sword' (*C.min.* 11.7–8: on the 'pen'/'sword' conceit, see
J. Geiger, *CQ* 52 (2002), 632–4). Fair comment, perhaps: but C. also
deserves credit for encouraging an atmosphere where Cato's admirers
felt free to write, and the vitriolic elements of his own work were
firmly in the imaginatively scurrilous tradition of Roman invective.
The exchange was surely meant to signal a return to rhetorical
normality, not tyranny: 'M. Cicero wrote a book praising Cato to
the skies—and what did C. as dictator do except write a speech in
reply, as if he was putting his case to a jury?' (Cremutius Cordus in
Tac. *Ann.* 4.34.4). There was a certain pointedness in encouraging
such freedom of speech when Cato's worshippers were celebrating
him as liberty's martyr.

Both works have many admirers, for Caesar's and for Cato's sake:
a more measured and balanced verdict than in *C.min.*: see previous
note. But even here P. makes it clear that C.'s response was more
emotional than was usual in so calculating a performer ('Caesar was
clearly very annoyed...he poured out so much anger...That irritated Caesar').

P. makes no claim to have seen either Cicero's *Cato* or C.'s *Anticato*
himself, and probably knew of C.'s attacks via Munatius Rufus
(above, on 'That irritated Caesar...'), who will have included material in reply to them. P. may well have known Munatius only at
second hand, as it was Munatius whom Thrasea Paetus 'followed as
his main authority' in his own laudatory biography of Cato (*C.min.*
37.1). That may help to explain the hostile tones in which he treats the
Anticato. Cf. Intr., pp. 48, 51.

55: Caesar in Rome, 46 BCE
P. concentrates on C.'s cultivation of the people and of his soldiers,
two of the three elements that had figured so strongly in ch. 51 (n.).
Other sources give more attention to his dealings with the senate, and
senatorial supporters and opponents (thus at §1 P. has a speech to the

people, Dio to the senate); in P. these are delayed till ch. 57, where they can be gathered together with similar material relating to the period after Munda. That in its turn will lead naturally into the continuing and increasing alienation of the senate (59.6–61), which forms the essential background for the conspiracy (62). The structure is neat, but it gives an unbalanced picture of C.'s priorities between his return to Rome in late July and his departure in early November: he spent some effort on building bridges with his previous senatorial opponents, 'on every matter and in every way consulting the leading senators and sometimes the senate itself' (Dio 43.27.1). In particular, he made a show of referring to the senate the question of his bitter enemy M. Marcellus (29.1 n.) and signalling that he would not oppose his recall from exile. Cicero's letters from the period, despite all their gloom, also show an increasing strain of muted optimism (naturally modulated according to the circumstances of his addressee: *Fam.* 9.16 (190), 12.17 (204).1, 13.68 (211).2, 6.10.5 (222.2), 6.13 (227).2, and esp. 6.6 (234).8–11), together with a reluctance to blame C. himself for what had gone wrong (51 n.); C.'s friends were certainly making a point of cultivating Cicero himself (*Fam.* 9.7 (178).1, 9.16 (190).2, 9.15 (196).4). Cicero's *pro Marcello* of September 46, with its strong programme of revival and reinvigoration (§§23–4), is best seen not as a presumptuous protreptic to controversial policies, still less as a coded clarion call to the disaffected (R. R. Dyer, *JRS* 80 (1990), 17–30), but as a gesture of confidence that this is the advice that C. will welcome and a signal of Cicero's own backing for his policies.

Another conciliatory gesture at this time was the holding of an open form of 'trial' of Q. Ligarius in October 46, leading to his recall from exile. P. tells a story of the trial at *Cic.* 39.6–7, but gives it no space in the fast-moving narrative here.

On C.'s conciliatory line in these months, cf. Gelzer 279–82, 292, Bruhns 119–23, 173; on Cicero's response, Gelzer, *Cicero* 276–81; on *pro Marcello*, Dobesch, *AS* i. 155–203, esp. 177–80, 200–1; M. Winterbottom, in J. F. Miller, C. Damon, and K. S. Myers (eds), *Vertis in Usum: Studies in Honor of Edward Courtney* (2002), 24–38; H. Botermann, *Klio*, 74 (1992), 183–6; and, briefly, Pelling in M. Wyke (ed.), *Julius Caesar in Western Culture* (2006), 17–18.

55.1. Caesar now returned from Africa to Rome. He sailed from Utica to Sardinia on 13 June, left Sardinia on 27 June, and arrived at Rome on 25 July. **First he gave a grand speech about his victory to**

the people. As it happens, no other source mentions this, but C. surely did make such a speech to the people, and this suits P.'s thematic emphasis (above). Dio 43.15–18 describes a conciliatory speech to the senate, promising to be leader rather than tyrant: a reassuring speech of some sort is plausible (above, 55 n.), whether Dio's content rests on source material (thus, tentatively, J. Rich in A. Cameron (ed.), *History as Text* (1989), 96 n. 55) or on Dio's own reconstruction (F. Millar, *A Study of Cassius Dio* (1964), 81, finding its detail anachronistic). **he had conquered land.** Gaul and Africa (53.7 n.) provided new territory for Rome, while the success in Pontus could be claimed to reassert Roman control. **large enough (he claimed) to produce ... a yearly income of 200,000 Attic bushels of grain and 3 million cups of olive oil:** 1 bushel = 6 Roman *modii*. 'Cup' translates the Greek *litra* (= the Latin *libra*), which can be a measure either of weight or of liquid quantity (cf. LSJ): presumably here the latter, with one 'cup' being about a quarter of a modern litre. The phrasing gives the impression of a yearly tribute in kind, though it is possible that this reflects C.'s framing of the tribute in terms of equivalents that his public would find attractive (thus Dobesch, *AS* i. 149 n. 19); it may have come from Africa in particular, for the '300 million *librae* of olive oil' is the figure given by *B.Af.* 97.3 for the annual payment imposed on 'Leptis'—perhaps Leptis Minor, between Hadrumetum and Thapsus (so P. W. Townend. *CPh* 36 (1940), 274–83), perhaps the better-known Lepcis Magna (so R. M. Haywood, *CPh* 37 (1941), 246–56, and A. Bouvet in the Budé *B.Af.*), but in either case it will refer to a region much larger than the city itself. It was Gaul that generated most new tribute, but this would not have been in kind: Suet. 25.1 gives an annual figure of 40 million sesterces, which Woytek 16–17 finds surprisingly small. P.'s figures here are of the same order of magnitude as those given by Suet. 38.1 (cf. Dio 43.21.3) for a one-off distribution made now to the Roman people, 10 *modii* of grain and 10 *librae* of oil apiece. If the 150,000 figure of 55.5 is right for the number of recipients, then 1,500,000 *modii* or 250,000 bushels and 1,500,000 *librae* will have been distributed: that may have been presented either as the first instalment of tribute or at least (thus Dobesch) as a foretaste of the lasting benefits the conquest would bring.

55.2. Then he celebrated his triumphs, from Egypt, from Pontus, and from Africa: all in September 46, with intervals of a few days:

Gelzer 284–5. In fact there were four triumphs, the first being from Gaul, and Suet. 37 says that this was the most excellent of them all; it also featured a famous accident when the axle of his chariot broke. It was followed by the execution of Vercingetorix. P. has already pointed forward to this Gallic triumph at 27.10 (n.), and Ziegler and Flacelière add 'from Gaul' here before 'from Egypt': that is perhaps right, but P. may just be using the triad of names to round off and reprise the themes of the last few chapters. **the last masqueraded as a victory over King Juba rather than Scipio.** Thus C. avoided placards carrying the names of his defeated Roman enemies; as later in Octavian's declaration of war against Cleopatra (*Ant.* 60.1 with my n.), this will also have intimated that Juba's Roman allies were traitors to Rome (Gelzer 285). Pictorial representations nevertheless included the deaths of Scipio, Petreius, and Cato, and these caused offence (App.): cf. 56.7 n.

Further details of the displays are given by Suet. 37, Flor. 2.13.88, Dio 43.19, 21–2, and App. 2.101.418–20: cf. Weinstock 60–79; M. Beard, *The Roman Triumph* (2007), esp. 102–4, 145, 154, 234–6. The senate had voted C. the privilege of using white horses rather than the usual black (Dio 43.14.3), a remarkable honour that carried a strong association with Jupiter (Weinstock 68–75, Beard 234–6); but it is not clear that C. availed himself of that privilege, though modern scholars normally assume that he did. Dio often makes no distinctions between honours accepted and honours simply offered (57.2 n.), and at *Cam.* 7.1 P. says that Camillus' triumph featured white horses 'and no one else has ever done this, before or since'. (Admittedly that may anyway be mistaken: white horses seem to have featured in the expectations for imperial triumphs, Beard 235.) The use of elephants in one or more of the triumphs is better attested (Suet. 37.2, Dio 43.22.1, cf. A. Bell, *Spectacular Power in the Greek and Roman City* (2004), 41, 164–6), and C. may have thought that sufficient, not least because it would revive memories of a famous hitch in the young Pompey's African triumph when his elephants were too big to get through a gate (*Pomp.* 14.6, cf. Beard 17, 236, 317–18).

55.3. Juba, the small son of the king. See *OCD*[4] (no. 2); *FGrH*, no. 275. We do not know how old he was: P.'s language suggests an infant ('at most two years of age' (D. W. Roller, *The World of Juba II and Kleopatra Selene* (2003), 59)). He was brought up in Italy, was given Roman citizenship, and in 25 BCE was installed by Augustus as king of

Mauretania; before 20–19 he then married Cleopatra Selene, the daughter of Antony and Cleopatra, who had herself walked as a child in Octavian's triumph over her parents in 29. At *Ant.* 87.2 P. calls him 'the most civilized of kings' and at *Sert.* 9.10 'the most historically accomplished among kings', alluding to the writings that justified his being **counted among the most learned of Greek authors**: these included writings on Libyan, Arabian, and Assyrian as well as Roman history and antiquities and works on painting and theatre. P. knew his works by the time he wrote *Caesar*: he had already used his researches on Roman antiquities in, particularly, *Romulus* (14.7, 15.4, 17.5), *Numa* (7.11, 13.9), and *Roman Questions* (264d, 269b–c, 278e, 282e, 285d), where he is treated with more respect than any other source (Roller 170, cf. 173); and at some point P. also drew from him some engaging details on elephant behaviour in *On the Cleverness of Animals* (972b, 977d–e). It is uncertain how far his Roman history extended. P quotes him at *Sulla* 16.15 for an event in 86 BCE concerning Chaeronea, but that may not come from the history: wherever it came from, P. will have picked up eagerly this titbit about his native town. There anyway seems no hint that he covered the fighting of his father against Rome or the history of his mother-in-law (those would be most uncomfortable themes), and he is unlikely to be a significant source for this *Life* (though cf. 59 n.). Cf. D. Braund, *CQ* 34 (1984), 175–8; D. W. Roller, *The World of Juba II and Kleopatra Selene* (2003), and *Scholarly Kings: The Writings of Juba II of Mauretania, Archelaos of Kappadokia, Herod the Great, and the Emperor Claudius* (2004).

55.4. he gave great rewards to the soldiers: 'besides the 2000 sesterces that he had paid out at the beginning of the conflict, he gave 24,000 sesterces apiece to soldiers of his veteran legions by way of booty; he also gave them lands, but not in unified settlements, to avoid dispossessing those who owned them' (Suet. 38.1). Dio 43.21.3 and App. 2.102.421 give a figure of 5,000 dr./den. = 20,000 sesterces rather than Suet.'s 24,000: the discrepancy is odd, as we should not expect the Greek authors to round down, but here as elsewhere in 37–9 Suet. may be running together two separate rounds of distribution, one now and one after Munda in 45. (Woytek 184 prefers simply to reject Suet.'s figures.) App. adds that centurions received twice as much as ordinary soldiers, and military tribunes and cavalry captains four times as much. P. omits an episode that would not fit the picture: some soldiers objected at the money being squandered on the people, and C. dragged one man off personally to be executed; two more were then ceremonially slaughtered (Dio 43.24.3–4).

On the land settlements, cf. 57.8 n., Gelzer 283–4 n. 1, and Keppie 49–58, esp. 50–2. It is hard to discriminate settlements of 46 from those of other times during 47–44 (51.2 n.).

cultivated the people with banquets and spectacles: recalling the techniques of his early career, 4.4–7, 5.8–9 nn. This now becomes a *leitmotif* of the closing chapters: cf. 57.8 (n.). But the damage to his popularity has already been done (51 n.). On these banquets and spectacles and their political value, see R. C. Beacham, *Spectacle Entertainments of Early Imperial Rome* (1999), esp. 74–81; A. Bell, *Spectacular Power in the Greek and Roman City* (2004), esp. ch. 2.
banquets: Vell. 2.56.1 speaks of 'the celebration of banqueting through many days', probably referring to individual dinners after each triumph rather than a continuous single occasion; Pliny *NH* 9.171 speaks of a 'loan' (whatever that may mean—it would be hard to repay) of 6,000 lampreys by C. Hirrius for C.'s 'triumphal banquets', i.e. now and after Munda (56.7); at 14.97 he then has details of the wine served now—the first occasion when four separate wines were served, Falernian, Chian, Lesbian, and Mamertine—and after Munda. **spectacles:** many more details at Suet. 39, though it is not clear which ones belong now and which ones after Munda, and at Dio 43.22–4. **22,000 separate triple-couches:** 'which, according to the usual understanding that a *triclinium* comprises three couches with three diners each, means a grand total of 198,000 diners' (M. Beard, *The Roman Triumph* (2007), 259). That is more than the 150,000 corn-recipients of §5, but (*a*) we do not know how rigorously the feasting was limited to adult males; (*b*) P.'s sequence may well be correct, with the banqueting preceding the census; and, most important, (*c*) J. H. D'Arms suggests that the 198,000 included not merely the *plebs frumentaria* but also 'all others of superior wealth and station, from legionaries to other sub-equestrians to senators' (*JRA* 13 (2000), 192–200 at 197, clarifying a suggestion he had made in M. Cima and E. La Rocca (eds), *Horti Romani* (1998), 33–43 at 41–2). In that case the numbers might fit well enough. **gladiatorial shows and mock naval battles:** so also Vell. 2.56.1, adding that there was a mock land battle involving infantry, cavalry, and—spectacularly and predictably—elephants. Cf. also Suet. 39.3–4, App. 2.102.423, and Dio 43.23.3–4, with further details also of the naval battle, which was the

first entertainment of this sort at Rome: the principate was to see
many more. It involved 'Tyrian and Egyptian biremes, triremes, and
quadriremes' (Suet.), and was fought in the Campus Martius. App.
mentions 4,000 oarsmen and 2,000 marines. **his daughter Julia, who
had died years earlier:** 23.5–7 (n.). This too should be seen as part of
the conciliatory line towards former enemies, for Julia's name would
recall not just her father C. but her husband Pompey. Cf. Cic. *Fam.*
6.6 (234).10 (? October 46): C. 'never speaks of Pompey except in
terms of the greatest respect'.

P. omits one further part of the usual suite of demagogic techniques, grain and cash distributions: on the grain distributions, cf. §1 n.;
Suet. 38.1, App. 2.102.422, and Dio 43.21.3 all mention a cash distribution to the people of 400 sesterces = 1 Attic *mina* apiece.

55.5. 150,000…before it had been 320,000: so also Suet. 41.3;
Livy *per.* 115; App. 2.102.425 says that the previous number was
halved. Suet. makes it clear that the numbers refer to a revision
(*recensus*) of the register for free corn rather than a full census, as
the Greek authors' language would suggest: so, rightly, T. P. Wiseman, *JRS* 59 (1969), 62–3. So great a depletion is not credible in terms
of war casualties alone, for Rome itself had escaped most of the
miseries of the war, and not many of the urban poor would have
been among both sides' new recruits. Dio 43.25.2 agrees that there
had been great loss of life, but at 43.21.4 he also says that C. inves-
tigated eligibility for corn distribution and struck off half of the
names: that is probably exaggerated, but additional rigour is confirmed by Suet. 41.3 and explains most of the diminution in the
number. Previous distributions and measures had been heavily politicized, not least those of Cato in 62 (8.6–7 n.) and Clodius' in 58
(*MRR* 196), and there may have been good short-term reasons for not
scrutinizing claims too closely. Cf. Brunt, *Manpower*, 106 and esp.
381; E. Rawson, *CAH* ix^2 (1994), 456 and n. 196; Jehne 91–4, 304–8;
Woytek 186–9. There may also have been some change in the method
of registration and/or distribution: so C. Virlouvet, *Tessera frumentaria* (1995), 166–71.

56: The Campaign of Munda, 46–45 BCE

The narrative is brisk, omitting the various preliminaries—the speed
of C.'s march, the preliminary manœuvres (§1 nn.), the sieges that
followed (§6 n.). There is some emphasis on the danger ('perils that

were nearly the end of him... never before to survive'), fitting the pattern whereby intense danger precedes sudden and complete deliverance (39 n., *Ant.* 48 with my n.). Still, this is not elaborated with narrative detail (contrast e.g. Flor. 2.13.73–87), and at §§1 and 2 (nn.) P. neglects chances to repeat the rhythm of Pharsalus and Thapsus (52–4 n.). Instead, various closural techniques reinforce the way that 'this was Caesar's final war' (§7 n.). A generalizing remark is a typical terminal feature (B. Herrnstein Smith, *Poetic Closure* (1968), 182–6), and here the generalizing apophthegm of §4 (n.) also echoes and develops that of 39.8, the Pompeians' lack of a 'winner' to press home their advantage at Dyrrhachium: especially in P., ends often reprise critical or glorious moments of a career in this way (Intr., p. 32). The calendrical coincidence of §5 marks full circle (cf. Shakespeare, *JC* v. iii. 23–5, in the different context of Brutus' birthday, 'Time is come round, | and where I did begin, there shall I end': cf. Herrnstein Smith, 129–30); and it is a particularly frequent closural characteristic to end with a death, §6 (*Plutarch and History*, 365–6; Herrnstein Smith 175–82). This concentration of features partly reflects the way that '[c]losural signals begin to accumulate toward the end of any work' (D. Fowler, in D. H. Roberts, F. M. Dunn, and D. Fowler (eds), *Classical Closure* (1997), 21), but there is also a particular irony that the apparently closural apophthegm—'I have often fought to win, never before to survive'—presages the real threat to his survival, which will come in Rome, in a milieu where the great general is less at home.

The campaign is described in the *Bellum Hispaniense*, the work of an eyewitness fighting on C.'s side. His accumulation of detail of many exchanges produces a confusing narrative, which is made more difficult by many textual problems; yet that confusion may be truer to the realities of conflict than the smoothly selective campaign narratives of writers, including C. himself, working more closely within the historiographic tradition. His closeness to the events also produces an unusually clear impression both of the atrocities of war (Pelling in *OCD*[4]) and of the fierce loyalty and admiration the writer feels for C. himself (R. Cluett, in F. Cairns and E. Fantham (eds), *Caesar against Liberty* (Papers of the Langford Latin Seminar 11; 2003), 118–31). For modern accounts of the campaign and C.'s subsequent settlement, cf. Holmes, *RR* iii. 293–312, 541–52; Gelzer 292–9.

56.1. he was declared consul for the fourth time, then set out to Spain. P.'s sequence seems to be wrong: C. was not declared consul for 45 until the end of 46, with M. Lepidus convening the assembly in his absence (Dio 43.33.1). The error is shared by Eutr. 6.24.1. The irregularity of the delay is notable, as the elections could have been held in C.'s presence during the summer (Bruhns 145, cf. Frei-Stolba 51–2); perhaps other concerns were too pressing (Bruhns), perhaps he thought it less invidious for this to be delayed to his absence. He was to be sole consul on the model of Pompey in 52 (28.7 n.), and continued as dictator, with the dictatorship now to be for ten years (*MRR* 304–5, iii. 107–8; cf. 51.1, 57.1 nn.). **set out for Spain:** in the second intercalary month (59 n.) = early November by the season. Making remarkable speed, he arrived at Obulco (the modern Porcuna) twenty-seven days later: App. 2.103.429, Strabo 3.4.9. **the sons of Pompey:** i.e. Gnaeus and Sextus. See *OCD*[4]; M. Hadas, *Sextus Pompey* (1930), 44–55; B. J. Lowe, in A. Powell and K. Welch (eds), *Sextus Pompeius* (2002), esp. 65–77. In 49 Gnaeus had secured an Egyptian fleet from Cleopatra and Ptolemy (48.5 n.), and operated in the Adriatic to harry C.'s transports; during the African War he had first occupied the Balearics, then crossed to Spain. Sextus had accompanied his father to Egypt, then after his father's death joined Scipio's army; after Thapsus he had joined his brother in Spain. **They were still young.** Gnaeus was aged about 33; the date of Sextus' birth is disputed (see J. Rougé, *REL* 46 (1968), 180–93, Woodman on Vell. 2.73.1), but it is hard to reject the tradition that at the time of Pharsalus he was with his mother in Mytilene (*Pomp.* 74.1 etc.). If so, he was probably no more than 18 then, perhaps 21 now.

a force of astonishing size. *B.Hisp.* 7.4 appears (though the text may be deficient) to say that there were thirteen legionary eagles, but the only reliable legions were two that had defected from the Caesarian proconsul C. Trebonius (cf. *MRR* 289, 299), including at least one locally levied in Spain; a further one recruited from the Spanish colonies; and one constituted from the fugitives from Africa (53.4 n.). The light-armed troops and cavalry were far inferior to C.'s. Cf. Brunt, *Manpower*, 230–1. App. 2.103.406–7 also mentions 'a great number of slaves' who had been training hard for over three years: that looks like Caesarian propaganda, but *B.Hisp.* (12.1, 20.5, 34.2) and Dio (43.39.2) also mention slaves on the Pompeian side. On

the composition of the Pompeian forces, cf. B. J. Lowe, in A. Powell
and K. Welch (eds), *Sextus Pompeius* (2002), 72–7. **daring.** App.
2.103.427 mentions disagreement between Gnaeus and his more
experienced generals: they urged delay on the basis of their experiences in Greece (40.2 n.) and Africa (53.1 n.), Gnaeus insisted on
fighting C. immediately on his arrival, and if this figured in Pollio it
may be what underlies this stress on 'daring'. If so, here as at §2 (n.) P.
does not take the chance to echo the rhythm of the earlier two
campaigns, with their similar debates. In fact, though, there were
some considerable preliminary manœuvres around Ulia, Cordoba,
Ategua, and Ucubi (*B.Hisp.* 3–27): it was some time before Gnaeus
thought it wise to risk a decisive battle (*B.Hisp.* 26.5, Dio 43.35.2).
their claim to leadership: interesting language: it could mean 'their
claim to lead these Republican armies' (cf. e.g. *Aem.* 10.6, *Crass.* 7.1,
Flam. 7.3, *Them.* 11.2), but *hēgemonia*, 'leadership', is also regularly
used for the 'rule' of a *princeps* (*Galba* 4.5, 5.3, 6.3; *Otho* 9.4, 15.5,
18.6, etc.). Whether or not the sons of Pompey were fighting to
establish their own control over the Roman world (we may recall
the suspicions that their father was over-fond of 'monarchy', 41.2 n.),
this is increasingly the texture that can be assumed for these civil
wars.

56.2. The great battle took place near the city of Munda, some 90
km. south-west of Cordoba and 10 km. west of the ancient Urso (=
Osuna): *B.Hisp.* 28–31. The most plausible site is that identified by
Kromayer and Veith, *Antike Schlachtfelder*, iv. 562, 573, the Cerro del
Pradillo. The date was 17 March 45 (§5 n.). **he himself dashed amid
the weapons and the ranks.** According to App. 2.104.431–3 and
152.638, he took off his helmet to inspire his men through his
visibility; then seized a shield, sprang to lead the attack against the
enemy, and was the target for 200 missiles; then first his officers and
then his men rushed to protect him. The story was well known (cf.
Vell. 2.55.3, Frontin. *Strat.* 2.8.13, Polyaenus 8.23.16, and Flor.
2.13.81–3), and P. probably knew its detail, especially as App. may
well have drawn it from Pollio. If so, such charismatic personal
leadership again (cf. §1 n. on 'daring') offered the chance to echo
Pharsalus and Thapsus (39.6, 42.9 with 52–4 n.); but here too P.
leaves it undeveloped. Florus 2.13.83, Suet. 36, and Oros. 6.16.7 add
that the danger was such that C. contemplated suicide.

56.3. It was a hard fight and it required much strenuous effort. The bloodiness of the battle is also stressed by Dio 43.37, with some probably imaginative elaboration, and by Flor. 2.13.85 and Oros. 6.16.9. **killing over 30,000 of the Pompeians but losing 1,000 high-quality men of his own.** *B.Hisp.* 31.9–11 gives Pompeian losses as 'about 30,000 or a little more' infantry and 'about 3,000 cavalry', and C.'s as 'about 1,000, partly infantry and partly cavalry' (though R. G. Böhm, *Vigiliae Hibericae* (1988), 244–5, there emends to '3,000', partly on the grounds that P.'s 'high-quality men' should refer only to elite troops).

56.4. 'I have often fought to win…never before to survive': not in *B.Hisp.*, but so also App. 2.104.433. **fought to win:** for instance, at Dyrrhachium, 39.8, 'Today the enemy might have won—all they needed was a winner'. 'Victory' language was also especially prominent in the Pharsalus narrative (42.2, 44.10, and five times in 47.1–48.4). The exposure to physical danger in earlier civil campaigns (38, 39.6–7, 49.7–8, 52.8–9), as already in Gaul (20.8), makes **never before to survive** seem an overstatement; that does not mean that C. did not say it. For his taste for post-battle epigram, cf. 46.1–2 as well as the 39.8 instance.

56.5. on the feast of the Dionysia: i.e. the *Liberalia* (*B.Hisp.* 31.8), 17 March—but the Greek Dionysus carries more connotations of violence and uncontrolled frenzy than the Roman Bacchus (= *Liber*), and that is not inappropriate to the growing note of unease at this stage of the *Life*. **Pompey had left for the war:** i.e. when he left Italy (17 March 49, 35.2 n.) rather than Rome (17 January 49, 33.6 n.). The reform of the calendar in 46 (59 n.) is not taken into account, so in fact rather more than **four years had passed.** Oros. 6.17.8 makes a similar comment; it may come from Livy, but the coincidence would doubtless have been marked by many.

56.6. The younger of Pompey's sons escaped: Sextus, who had been at Cordoba during the battle (*B.Hisp.* 32.4). He took refuge in Catalunya (M. Hadas, *Sextus Pompey* (1930), 52–3). **a few days later Didius brought in the head of the elder:** more detail at *B.Hisp.* 32, 36–9 and App. 2.105.434–9. Other notable deaths included that of Labienus (18.2 n.). **Didius.** For the unheralded and unexplained individual, cf. 7.5 n. This is C. Didius, who had earlier won a naval victory over the Pompeian Attius Varus: *MRR* 300, 311. He died shortly afterwards in battle with the Lusitanians (*B.Hisp.* 40). **brought in the head of the elder.** Gnaeus reached the sea at Carteia, but was wounded when disembarking, then captured and killed. His head was brought to C. at Hispalis on 12 April, and put on display there.

P. says nothing of the siege of Munda and the capture of Cordoba and Hispalis after the battle (*B.Hisp.* 32–6, 42), nor of the fighting in which Didius lost his life (*B.Hisp.* 40). C. in fact spent several months in Spain after his victory reorganizing the administration, and did not arrive back in Rome until October 45 (Vell. 2.56.3). P. knew some further details of that return journey, and at *Ant.* 11.1–2 describes C.'s journey through north Italy with Antony at his side and the young Octavian and D. Brutus (64.1 n.) following behind; 'all the notable men of Rome' came out from the city to greet him, and Antony himself travelled as far as Narbo (*Ant.* 11.1, 13.2). Here P. prefers to move swiftly back to give a sharp contrast between C.'s success on the battlefield and the ham-fisted use he made of it in the city.

56.7. This was Caesar's final war. The *Life* begins to echo the patterns of the end of *Romulus*: here cf. *Rom.* 26.1, 'This was Romulus' last war'—and there too it is immediately followed by an alienation of the Roman people. See Intr., p. 34. **The triumph that he celebrated for it.** In early October, *MRR* 305. More details at Vell. 2.56.2 (apparatus of polished silver) and Suet. 37 (two separate public banquets, the second four days after the first): cf. also 55.4 n. A fragment of the *Fasti Cuprenses* has been plausibly associated with this triumph; if this is right, a reference to the 'Tiber' suggests that the 'gardens across the Tiber', later to figure in C.'s will as a gift to the Roman people (68.1 n.), were opened on this occasion to hold his banquet(s). So G. V. Gentili, *Epigraphica*, 10 (1948), 136–8 = *AE* 1950, 93b and esp. J. H. D'Arms, in M. Cima and E. La Rocca (eds), *Horti Romani* (1998), 33–43, bringing out how C. was following but also outdoing the practice of Pompey and Lucullus in 'admitting large members of the *plebs urbana* into . . . private *horti* in order to promote . . . political aims': cf. *Pomp.* 44.4 (Pompey in 62 BCE). C.'s triumph was followed later in the year by those of his generals, Q. Fabius Maximus (by then also suffect consul, 58.2 n.) on 13 October and Q. Pedius on 13 December: *MRR* 304–5, 309, Jehne 62–4. According to Dio 43.42.1–2 this gave rise to ridicule. **was the most**

distressing thing of all to the Romans. For such 'characterization by reaction', see Intr., p. 25; but here it is more than a way for P. to convey his own disapproval, even though that disapproval—understandable in the author of *On Inoffensive Self-Praise*—is strongly felt. It becomes an important part of the political analysis as well.

56.8. Caesar had destroyed the sons: in fact, only the one son, as Sextus escaped (§6 n.)—but that may not have been known at Rome. **and the entire family:** probably just in the sense of destroying his future lineage by killing the 'sons', but there may also be a hint of the (false) allegation that he had killed Pompey's daughter and grandchildren after Thapsus, 53.7 n. **the man who had been the greatest of the Romans, and who had fallen on misfortune:** cf. 57.1 n., and for the respect felt for Pompey *Ant.* 21.2, 'a man who was admired no less for his sobriety and his modest, orderly, and democratic way of life than for the fact of his having earned three triumphs'. For similar outrage at the humiliation or slaughter of fellow-citizens, cf. *Gracch.* 38.8–9 (121 BCE), *Pomp.* 10.4–6 (82 BCE).

56.9. especially as before this Caesar…shun that sort of glory. And P. also implicitly suggests a contrast with the African triumph that 'masqueraded as a victory over King Juba rather than Scipio', 55.2 (n.). P. correctly notes the change of tone, but is more concerned to trace its political consequences, carrying further that popular alienation that he had begun to trace at 51 (nn.), than to offer any explanation. P.'s delay and suppression of senatorial material in 55 (n.) has obscured the way that the change was more far-reaching, for in 45 C. seems to have been less conciliatory of senatorial opinion than in 46: this may explain the delay in publication of the *Anticato* (54.5 n.). With victory firmly won, it was time to define his own position in a new order (60.1, 61.4 nn.), where his enemies needed to accept their role as vanquished. C. is the master now, and the older civilities were out of date. The 'preening' on his victory, and more especially the humbling of his enemies, represented conscious policy, however ill-judged this might later appear.

For this change in C.'s governmental tone, cf. Bruhns 173–6.

57–61: Caesar as Dictator
P.'s treatment both of the honours (57.2 n.) and of C.'s own measures is extremely selective. Had P. been interested in the ways that C.'s

measures anticipated or contrasted with those of Augustus or the emperors of his own day, other matters would have commanded space: the expansion of the senate or of the number of magistracies, the grants of citizenship, the reforms of taxation, the tribunicial sacrosanctity, the oaths taken by magistrates to respect his decisions and by all citizens to protect his person, the renaming of the month which would now be July. (On all this, see briefly *MRR* 305–6 and 317–18, Syme, *RR* 52–3 and on the new senators 78–96, more fully Gelzer 283–91, E. Rawson, *CAH* ix^2 (1994), 438–67, and in great depth Jehne.) But P. concentrates on a few themes that illustrate most sharply the continuities with C.'s earlier behaviour, his attempts to retain popularity and support, and his uneasy relationship with his senatorial critics.

'This was acknowledged tyranny' (57.1 n.) echoes the end of Plato *Republic* 8, 'This would be acknowledged tyranny...' (569b), of the classic process whereby a demagogue seizes tyrannical power. In some ways that fits C.'s career, with all those earlier demagogic methods (Intr., p. 21, cf. Duff 303); but by now the picture has become complicated, and we also notice the ways that C. does *not* fit the Platonic stereotype. Plato's demagogue does not shrink from bloodshed (566e, 57.1 n.) and ruthlessly eliminates anyone who is a threat (567b–c); C. in contrast practises clemency (57.4 n.), even giving honours to old adversaries (57.5), and fails to move against Brutus and Cassius despite his suspicions (62.9–10). Plato's tyrant protects himself with a bodyguard (566b, 567d–e); C. ostentatiously refuses one (57.7). Plato's tyrant behaves well in his first days in power, 'smiling and greeting everyone he meets... and pretending to be benign and mild to everyone' (*Rpb.* 8.566d–e). But that is indeed a pretence, and does not last: C.'s 'mildness' (57.4)—the same word as in Plato—goes much deeper, and he knows, as P. himself knows, that popular goodwill is a better way to protect one's power (57.1 n.).

Many of these actions are clearly commendable, but P. is not particularly interested in drawing up a moral balance sheet: contrast Suet. 76.1, after listing the positive features of the dictatorship, 'nevertheless his other deeds and words outweigh these, so that the verdict is that he abused his power and that his killing was justified' (Intr., p. 18). Nor is this to be seen as providing a template for the guidance or evaluation of later emperors, which is one way of interpreting Suet. (Intr., p. 5; Pelling in *CJC* 259–65). His accent rather falls on the way that it is too late: try though C. may to break the pattern of tyrannical oppression and popular hostility, his own die is already cast, and the old demagogic techniques (57.8 n.) no longer work. That is partly because the forces that built his power have now turned against him (51 n., Intr., p. 22). In particular, his friends, so vital to his success, are now leading him astray (60.8). It is also partly because his enemies show such intransigence and political deviousness (57.2). Early in the *Life* he had deftly manipulated his supporters, and they had 'sought new offices and new honours to repay him' (5.9), a phrase that had prepared for these later themes (at the expense of anachronism, n.); now the tables are turned, and his opponents are the ones looking for the new honours and playing the subtle, manipulative, popular game. Even C.'s earlier preference for politics over rhetoric (3.2–4) now becomes a two-edged sword as the rhetorical master Cicero scores several damaging points (58.3, 59.6, though note also 57.2 n. and 57.6). But some causes for his downfall are also to be seen in his own behaviour. He crossed the Rubicon after senators had contemptuously insulted his supporters (29) and humiliated his tribunes (31.2–3); now it is he who insults the senate (60.4–8) and humiliates tribunes (61.1, 61.8–10), and the people are as offended now (60.5, 61.9–10) as once they were strident in his support. That love affair with the people and his soldiers (Intr., p. 21) gives way to new lusts, first his 'passion for new glory' (58.4) and then, more destructively, his 'passion to be king' (60.1 n.), and he no longer treats his public with the skills of old (60.5, 61.10). In chs 60–1 it is the people's responses that are stressed (they are outraged even when it is the senate or magistrates who are insulted or attacked, 60.5, 61.10), and it is duly 'the ordinary people' who turn to Brutus (62.1) for action, whereas in *Brutus* it seems to be 'the first and most powerful of the citizens' (10.6), and this was probably the emphasis Plutarch found in his main source (cf. App. 2.113.472). The introduction of the conspirators and their motives is thus delayed to a point (62 (n.)) where C.'s fall has come to seem inevitable. Its explanation is in terms of him, not them.

Many items in these chapters come out of their chronological order: for instance, the dictatorship for life, mentioned first (57.1), was in fact one of the latest honours; the calendar reform (59) then dates from two years earlier; the sequence of events involving the Lupercalia, the crowning of statues, and C.'s treatment of the tribunes (61) is given differently in P.'s different accounts (nn.). Possibly P. found at least some of the material more chronologically organized in his sources; more likely, as with C.'s first consulship in 59 (14 n.), most of the items were already out of sequence in those accounts, with only a few indications that (say) the Lupercalia and the treatment of the tribunes came close to the end, and P., like our other sources, rearranged everything to suit his own purposes. See also 60.4 n.

57.1. the man's fortune: cf. 38.5 n. But 'fortune' is in the Greek the same word as for Pompey's 'misfortune' just before at 56.8 (cf. 45.9): C.'s own fortune is in increasing danger of replicating that of his adversary. **bridle:** Greek *chalinos*, a familiar image of tyranny, used for instance of Zeus' autocratic imposition of his will in [Aesch.] *Prom.* 672 and 1009–10, and by Sophocles' unattractive figures Aegisthus (*El.* 1472 with Finglass's n.) and Creon (*Ant.* 477–8) when they parade their power. It is not a pretty picture: 'Greek bridles and bits included spikes that bloodied the horse's mouth if it resisted' (Griffith on Soph. *Ant.* 477–8). At *C.min.* 59.9 Cato uses similar language in urging the council of Utica that things are not hopeless, as Rome has 'not yet accepted C.'s bridle'; but, at least by now and for the moment, he was wrong, and Romans have indeed **accepted** it. Their reasons develop the thinking of 28.6 (n.), where 'sensible people' were coming to acknowledge 'that the state could be cured only by a monarchy, and the right thing to do was to take the remedy from the gentlest of the doctors who were offering it'. At that point the malaise was one of urban turbulence, and they meant Pompey; but turbulence has now escalated to war, and a new 'gentle doctor'— 'gentle' renders the same Greek word as C.'s 'mildness' here at §4—is at hand.

Still, 'bridling' is no way to establish 'rule over willing subjects' (58.1): 'they use bridles and collars to control violent horses and disobedient dogs, but for one human to make another gentle and submissive nothing works so well as confidence in one's goodwill and a reputation for good behaviour and fairness' (*Advice on Public Life* 821b). The paradox is that C. knows this and does his best: 'gentle' ('mildness') and 'goodwill' become watchwords for him too (§§2, 4, 8 nn.).

Thinking that monarchy could afford a respite from civil war and national calamities: a classic justification for the principate, one with resonance for P. and his audience that goes beyond C.'s own career: 'in my sixth and seventh consulships, after bringing civil wars to an end, by universal consent I acquired absolute power...' (Augustus, *Res Gestae* 34.1, going on to claim that he 'transferred the government of the state to the authority of the senate and people of Rome'); Augustus 'imposed the laws whereby we might enjoy peace and the principate' (*pax et princeps*, Tac. *Ann.* 3.28.2). An awareness of the blessings was still strong: 'consider the greatest goods that the cities can possess, peace, freedom, prosperity, a healthy population, and concord: as far as peace is concerned, the people have no need for politicians at present, for all Greek and all foreign war has been banished; as for liberty, they have as much of it as our masters allow, and to have more might be no great boon...' (*Advice on Public Life* 824b–c). Cf. Intr., p. 11.

they proclaimed him dictator for life: in or shortly before February 44: *MRR* 317–18, iii. 107–8; Jehne 32 and n. 63. P. picks this out as particularly monarchic: cf. *Fab.* 3.7, 'everyone agreed that the circumstances required sole rule (*monarchia*) of a man who could not be held to account—a dictatorship, as they call it'; *Cam.* 18.6; *On the Fortune of the Romans* 318c, '*monarchiai* and dictatorships'. For C.'s other titles and honours, cf. §2 n.

This was acknowledged tyranny: Plato, *Republic* 8.569b, 'This would be acknowledged tyranny...': the phrase is also echoed at *Tim.* 1.6 and by Cic. *Att.* 2.17 (37).1 (of Pompey), Dion. Hal. *AR* 4.41.3 (of Tarquinius Superbus), and App. 1.101.473 (of Sulla). See above, 57–61 n. Plato has there been tracking the process whereby the cycle of constitutions terminates with the change from democracy to tyranny, with the demagogue emerging as tyrant (565c–6d): on this model, see 28.5 n., and cf. Intr., pp. 63–4. For Plato it was the consequence of 'excessive' or 'extreme' liberty, 564a, and arises from internal disorder: that has ultimately been the case here and C., the archetypal demagogue, fits the Platonic picture (28.5 n.), but C.'s military skills and the need for a civil war have complicated and delayed the way in which it has come about (57–61 n.). Plato's demagogue too 'does not shy from internecine bloodshed' (566e), but operates by ruthless elimination of his internal enemies rather than on the battlefield. **unaccountability:** i.e. the freedom from any need to render account of one's action: a defining feature of tyranny (Hdt. 3.80.3, Arist. *Pol.* 4.1295a20, cf. e.g. Arist. *Wasps* 587, Plato *Laws* 9.875b, Dion. Hal. *AR* 8.81.4), but it can be used of monarchy more generally (Plb. 27.10.2, Dio of Prusa 3.43, 56.5, Diod. 1.70.1): it is applied to earlier dictatorships as well as C.'s, *Fab.* 3.7 (quoted

above), Dion. Hal. *AR* 5.70.2, 6.2.3, etc. In fact, the 'accountability' of
a dictator was a matter of constitutional uncertainty (Lintott, *Constitution*, 111–12), but it does at least seem that any charge could be
laid only after the dictator had demitted office (Livy 9.26.21, and the
lex repetundarum of 111 BCE §§8–9: Lintott, *Judicial Reform and Land
Reform in the Roman Republic* (1992), 90, 114). Thus C.'s 'unaccountability' arguably depended more closely than P.'s language suggests
on the **permanence** of this 'dictatorship for life'.

P.'s emphasis on the historical significance of this is justified.
Republicans could no longer hope that C. might one day abdicate,
Sulla-like; this was 'the final slamming of the door on Republican
hopes' (Rawson, *CAH* ix² (1994), 463, cf. Jehne 38). Nepos, writing
under the triumvirate, reflects such thinking at *Miltiades* 8.3, when he
explains the Greek general's loss of popular support: 'everyone
is called and thought to be a tyrant who holds permanent power in
a state that has enjoyed liberty' (cf. A. C. Dionisotti, *JRS* 78 (1988),
47–8).

57.2. The first honours were proposed: disentangling the sequence of honours is not easy. P. has no interest in giving details:
Suet. 76.1 lists the 'excessive honours' as 'continuous consulship [in
fact for ten years], permanent dictatorship, prefecture of morals, and
also the *praenomen* of Imperator, the *cognomen* of Father of his
Country, a statue among the kings, a dais in the orchestra. He also
allowed things to be decreed that were too great for the pinnacle of
human achievement, a golden throne in the senate and before the
tribunal, a wagon and carrying-frame for a procession in the circus,
temples, altars, images next to the gods, a divine couch, a priest,
luperci, a month named after him; and every manner of honour he
both accepted and granted according to his whim.' (On 'Father of his
Country', see Intr., p. 4.) Even fuller lists are given by App. 2.106.440–
3 and esp., with some distinction of sequence, Dio 43.14.3–7 (46 BCE),
43.42.2–46.1 (45 BCE) and 44.3–47.3 (apparently 44 BCE). Dio's distinction of those three phases suggests that **the first honours** here
may represent a retrospect of those voted in 46, on his return from
Africa (55.1)—not that Dio's listing suggests that those were particularly restrained or particularly **appropriate to a human being**. They
indeed included the decree that his chariot should be placed on a
plinth facing the statue of Jupiter, and a statue of himself should be
placed bestriding a globe with a dedication indicating that he was a

demigod (43.14.6). True, Dio may characteristically not have fully
distinguished honours accepted from those declined (H. A. Andersen,
Cassius Dio und die Begründung des Principates (1938), 10–14, 16–17,
26, cf. Jehne 101–4), despite his claim in this context to do exactly that
(43.14.7); but P.'s point here concerns the decrees as much as their
acceptance. The alternative would be to assume that P. is simply
concerned with honours voted in late 45 and 44. All these honours
are much discussed: cf. Weinstock, esp. 270–86; Jehne, esp. 191–220.
Many do suggest present or future divinity (67.8 n., Weinstock 281–6,
Jehne 217–20) rather than anything 'appropriate to a human being',
but P. leaves that theme relatively undeveloped: contrast e.g. *Ant.*
24.4, 55.9, 75.4–5, and, for the importance of the contrast with
Alexander, see Intr., pp. 30–2.

   Cic. 40.4–5 also notes **Cicero**'s role in proposing honours, but no
other source mentions this, and P. may be elaborating his presence: cf.
57–61 n. above and Intr., p. 25. In what follows the rhythm of Cicero's
comments mirrors that of these 'honours' in general: his first comment seems wholly laudatory (§6 n.), but further jests carry more edge
(58.3, 59.6), and reflect, perhaps partly orchestrate, the mounting
resentment. *Cicero* itself does not develop the theme so dynamically:
only the first, positive remark (~ 57.6 here) is there mentioned, and it
simply points Cicero's 'ambition always to make some novel remark
about C. and his actions'.

   they rendered the man offensive and loathsome. P. limits the
significance to this human-level response: there is no suggestion, for
instance, that C.'s pre-eminence might itself evoke divine envy. **to the
most mild-mannered of observers.** 'Mild-mannered' is the same
word as for C.'s 'mildness' in §4: C.'s quality is not being repaid in
kind.

**57.3. They say that those who hated Caesar were no less active here
than his flatterers:** so also Nic. Dam. 67, 'some were playing for C.'s
favour, others were insidiously welcoming the excessive measures and
making sure everyone knew about them to generate envy together
with suspicion...'. But Nic. Dam. represents C. as taken in by the
flattery, 'given that he was a simple man at heart and unfamiliar with
political technique because of the time he had spent campaigning
overseas'. (The point is probably to contrast with Augustus, the
subject of Nic. Dam.'s *Life*: see M. Toher in M. Wyke (ed.), *Julius
Caesar in Western Culture* (2006), 29–44.) Dio 44.3 and 44.7.3

similarly has C. 'stirred up and puffed up' by the honours to make mistakes, and he presents the senators, some with insidious motives, as both inventing the honours and then blaming C. for accepting them. In P. there is no such misreading: C. is aware of the dangers (62.6–63.1 nn.) of conspiracy and objects to excessive honours (60.4), though the negative response to his demurring also suggests the delicacy of his predicament (60.5). Thus Dio 44.3.3: 'he did not dare to reject everything, as that would give the impression of contempt, and yet it would not be safe to accept them ...'. Cf. also §7 n.

57.4. For Caesar himself behaved in a way that was unimpeachable, now that the civil wars were over.   Cf. esp. *Brut.* 55(2).2 and *Ant.* 6.7, cited at 28.6 n., and Intr., p. 20. **unimpeachable.** The word has a forensic ring. It need not imply that he was flawless, as 60–1 go on to demonstrate: but C.'s mistakes were of diplomacy and tact rather than the more violent transgressions that were usually associated with tyranny and that the Platonic colouring might suggest, elimination of rivals (*Rpb.* 8.567b–c), use of a bodyguard (567d), violation of women (Hdt. 3.80.5, etc), and so on. **in gratitude for his mildness.** Contrast the emphasis on fearfulness at App. 2.106.443, which may reflect App.'s experience of imperial realities: 'they dedicated many temples to C. as a god and one jointly to him and to Clemency, representing them as clasping hands: that is how fearful they were of him as a master, and prayed that he would be merciful to them.' 'Mildness' and 'clemency' are both good qualities, but as that passage shows they can carry an edge: they mark the conduct of the powerful towards the powerless, and are in fact the words that P. used of C.'s behaviour to the defeated Gauls at 15.4 (n.). So the language here reinforces the 'acknowledgement' of tyranny of 57.1: it may also echo 28.6, the readiness to accept monarchy from the 'gentlest' doctor, where 'gentle' is the same Greek word as 'mild' here (57–61 n.). On the delicate issues involved in a parade of 'clemency' see esp. M. T. Griffin in F. Cairns and E. Fantham (eds), *Caesar against Liberty* (2003), 159–82, and previous literature cited there. C. avoids the word *clementia* in *BC*; it was Cicero who trumpeted the word in his orations of 46–45 and elsewhere (Weinstock 236–7, Griffin 163, A. Clark, *Divine Qualities* (2007), 247–9), though this senatorial decree suggests that C. did not resist it. **decreed a temple to Clemency:** some time in 45, though it is not clear that it was ever built. It may have been rather to 'Caesar and clemency' (App., cited above) or even 'Jupiter Julius and

Clemency' (Dio 44.6.4); coins of 44 BCE also depict the (planned) temple, with the legend 'Caesar's Clemency' (*clementia*) on the obverse (*RRC* 480/21). Cf. Weinstock 233–43, 308–10.

I translate 'Clemency' to avoid historical confusion, but the Greek word is in fact *epieikeia*, which is more generally 'Reasonableness': cf. 34.7 n. Like *clementia* it is especially appropriate to the mighty who are generous to those within their power (especially in treating them with equity rather than with strict application of the law: O. Murray, *JRS* 55 (1965), 177); it is already used of Rome's mercy to the conquered in Polybius, Posidonius (Weinstock 235), Dionysius of Halicarnassus, and Diodorus. It is, however, more unambiguously positive than *clementia*, especially given the associations *clementia* had come to have with the autocratic principate (on which see esp. Griffin, art cit.; cf. M. Schettino in P. Stadter and L. van der Stockt (eds), *Sage and Emperor* (2002), 205); and one might debate whether it was right to be clement in a particular case, but hardly whether it was right to be reasonable (Pelling in R. H. Sternberg (ed.), *Pity and Power in Ancient Athens* (2005), 278). Earlier too P. describes C.'s generosity to captive enemies in terms that are clearly positive: 34.7, 48.4 nn.

Again there is a contrast and a comparison here with Plato's demagogue-tyrant, who becomes an object of hatred to the 'reasonable' among the citizens (*Rpb.* 8.568a, cf. 9.577c–d, Arist. *Pol.* 5.1314a19–23): but in Plato's case it is because of, in C.'s case largely despite, his behaviour in power.

57.5. He pardoned many of those who had fought against him. On C.'s generosity to defeated Pompeians, see 55 n. (Marcellus and Ligarius) and esp. M. Jehne, *Chiron*, 17 (1987), 313–41: an essential criterion for mercy was whether a man had already benefited from C.'s clemency after a previous capture (cf. 46.4 n.). Those who returned to arms had failed to respect the obligations incurred through such a kindness (*beneficium*). Suet. 75.4 also mentions a decree 'during his final period in power' in which he 'permitted even those whom he had not yet pardoned to return to Italy and assume magistrates and commands': similarly App. 2.107.448, though noting that he excepted those who were in exile 'on irremediable charges'. **even gave offices and honours to some.** That reflects one of Aristotle's ways by which a tyrant can cement his position through goodwill (§8 n.), 'giving honour to those who have good qualities in such a way as to convince them that they would not have received more at the hands of free citizens', *Pol.* 5.1315ᵃ4–6. Here the phrase picks up C.'s own rule and honours of §§1–2, as C. tries to deflect the unpopularity by giving similar recognition to others. **such as Brutus and Cassius.** Cf. Bruhns 120: others were Varro (36.1, 37.1–2 nn.), given a special commission in 45 to organize public libraries (58.4–10 n., *MRR* 314); P. Sestius, who served with Domitius Calvinus (50.1 n.) in Asia Minor (*MRR* 278, iii. 197); C. Messius, who held a command in Africa (*MRR* 301); C. Ateius Capito, agrarian commissioner in 45 or 44 (*MRR* 332); and probably A. Terentius Varro Murena, aedile in or before 44 (*MRR* 322, iii. 204). Apart from Varro with his libraries—clearly a special case—those others did not hold especially prominent positions, and Brutus and Cassius were evidently the most notable. **Both men became praetors.** In 44 BCE: 62.4–5 (n.).

57.6. Nor did Caesar allow the statues of Pompey to remain lying on the ground: not just Pompey's, but Sulla's too (Suet. 75.4, Polyaenus 8.23.31): they had been 'thrown down by the people' (Suet.), presumably after Pharsalus and presumably with an eye to C.'s Marian connections (1.2, 5.2, 6, 19.4 nn.). Dio 43.49.4 mentions the restoration of a particular statue of Pompey in the forum, and dates it to 44. **Cicero remarked that by raising up Pompey's statues he had firmly fixed his own:** also noted at *Cic.* 40.5 (§2 n.) and at *How to benefit from one's enemies* 91a, yet here there is a particular irony: a statue of Pompey will play an emblematic role as C. falls, 66.1 n. On the importance of statues in this pair, cf. Intr., p. 30.

57.7. His friends: probably a reference to Hirtius and Pansa, who 'always told C. that he had won his power through arms and should hold on to it through arms' (Vell. 2.57.1). **urged him to use a bodyguard:** as tyrants stereotypically did: Plato *Rpb.* 8.566b, 567d–e (57–61 n., above), and e.g. *Pyrrh.* 8.2, *Dion* 19.8, *Advice on Public Life* 801d, Hdt. 1.59.5, 98.2, 5.92η.3, Xen. *Hiero* 5.3–4, Arist. *Pol.* 5.1315ᵇ27–9, Dion. Hal. *AR* 4.41.3. A 'monarchy without bodyguards', as here, thus becomes a paradox: *Arist.* 7.1. **he would not allow it.** He even dismissed an earlier bodyguard, consisting of Spaniards (Suet. 86), doubtless to parade the fact that he was no tyrant. Cf. K. Kraft, *Der goldene Kranz Caesars und der Kampf um die Entlarvung des 'Tyrannen'* (1952/3), 47; Dobesch, *AS* i. 427–32; Jehne 256–7, 453–4. **Better to meet death once ... than always to be**

anticipating it. Just as at 63.7, he expresses a preference for dying 'unexpectedly'.

'Cowards die many times before their deaths; | the valiant never taste of death but once' (Shakespeare, *JC* ii. ii. 32–3). But Shakespeare's C. gives more fatalistic reasons than P.'s: 'death, a necessary end, | will come when it will come'. Some preservation of his public face may also there be sensed beneath the bravado: 'Danger knows full well | that Caesar is more dangerous than he' (ii. ii. 44–5). See Intr., pp. 68–9. This Caesar is more enigmatic than Shakespeare's (Intr., p. 29): but P.'s point in context is C.'s exemplary behaviour and preference for an authority based on goodwill, and so here too his remark may be a well-judged public gesture rather than (or as well as) a reflection of his true mentality.

C.'s reasons for dismissing his bodyguard were clearly a matter for debate. Suet. 86 reports that 'some think' he was over-confident because of an oath sworn by the senate to protect him (cf. Suet. 84.2), others—apparently, though the text is defective—that he preferred to face danger once rather than always to fear it. The first explanation is similar to those favoured by Dio 44.7.4 and Nic. Dam. 80, both speaking of 'decrees' rather than an oath: it fits their interpretation that C. was beguiled by the flatteries (§3 n.). The second is in line with the words P. gives to C. here, with Vell. 2.57.1, 'he preferred to die than to fear', and with the less forceful version at App. 2.109.455, 'nothing is worse than a continuous guarding: it is a sign of perpetual fear'. Cf. also *Dion* 56.3, where Dion similarly hears rumours of conspiracies and says that he will die willingly 'if the alternative is to live in perpetual guard against not just his enemies but also his friends': and Dion, like C., does indeed soon meet his death.

The dismissal is clearly essential to explaining why C. was so open to attack: contrast Antony, who surrounded the senate with armed men later in 44 (a contrast greatly exploited by Cicero in the *Second Philippic*, 112, 116–17). It is C.'s good points, not his bad, that leave him so vulnerable at the end: 64–5 n.

57.8. He regarded people's goodwill as at once the fairest and the firmest protection . . . : so also Nic. Dam. 80, with Toher's n. This, effectively, was one of Aristotle's ways for a tyrant to protect his power, by (as he puts it) making the tyranny more like a kingship: *Pol.* 5.1314^{a}29–15b10, cf. 60.1 n. Such claims had become part of the recipe for good kingship and of the repertoire for flattering tyrants: Isoc. *Nic.* 21, *Hel.* 37 (both cited by Toher); O. Murray, *JRS* 55 (1965), 168; cf. also *Arat.* 25.7. **he put this on as a magic charm.** 'Put this on' is literally 'put it around him', presumably around his neck as an amulet: cf. *Per.* 38.2 with Stadter's n. The phrasing may link with the gesture at 60.6 and the killing at 66.6–7: see nn. and Intr., p. 70. **he cultivated the people with banquets and doles and the military with colonies:** the same old techniques: cf. 4.5, 5.9, 55.4. It is hard to separate the evidence for these entertainments, distributions, and settlements from those earlier in 47–45: cf. 51.2, 55.4 nn. Jehne 286–331 analyses in detail C.'s treatment of the urban *plebs* and their reaction to him. **Carthage and Corinth** were famously linked in their destruction in 146 BCE (*MRR* i. 465–7): for its ideological point, see N. Purcell in D. Innes, H. Hine, and C. Pelling (eds), *Ethics and Rhetoric: Classical Essays for Donald Russell* (1995), 133–48, with good remarks on the suggestive symmetry of east and west in both the destruction and the refoundation (138–41). For these refoundations some time between 46 and 44, see *MRR* 294, Brunt, *Manpower*, 593, 598; C. Bearzot (Corinth) and G. Zecchini (Carthage) in G. Urso (ed.), *L'Ultimo Cesare* (2000), 35–53 and 353–62 respectively (Zecchini 137–45 has another version of the second); on Carthage, also C. van Nerom, in *Hommages à M. Renard*, ii (1962), 767–76, B. D. Shaw, *Hist.* 30 (1981), 424–71 at 438–40, A. Cristofori, *Antiquités africaines*, 25 (1989), 83–93; on Corinth, 58.6 n. Carthage in particular represents a continuation of C.'s 'popular' policies, reviving a famous initiative of C. Gracchus despite the sacral controversy that it caused at the time (*Gracch.* 32). The refoundation may have been in 46, i.e. precisely a century after the sacks (Purcell 139), but Diod. 37.27.1 has 'about a hundred years' and App. *Lib.* 136.648 has '102 years', i.e. in 44. The centenary gesture remains important, even if the century was only approximate: D. Feeney, *Caesar's Calendar* (2007), 145. We know of many other colonies too, in Gaul, Spain, Epirus, Asia, and Bithynia-Pontus, as well as Italy (Keppie 49–58) and elsewhere in Greece and Africa (Shaw, art. cit., 436–8): cf. *OCD*[4], s.v. 'colonization, Roman'; Gelzer 290, 297, and 311–12; E. T. Salmon, *Roman Colonization under the Republic* (1970), 132–7; E. Rawson, *CAH* ix[2] (1994), 445–8; Brunt, *Manpower*, 255–9, 319–24, 589–601; Jehne 139–52, 343–7, with extensive bibliography. According to Suet. 42.1, C. settled 80,000 people overseas. But P. dwells on the two names that appropriately conjure ideas of greatness, transience, and calamity, themes that by now have resonance for C.'s own fate.

A tale was told of C. encamped near Carthage during the Africa campaign of 46, and having a dream of a whole army weeping, at which he immediately wrote a memorandum authorizing the colony (App. *Lib.* 136.645–6). The story may well have been put about by C. himself or his supporters ('simplistic propaganda' (Shaw, art. cit., 440)): it was a modern counterpart of the famous tears of Scipio Aemilianus as Carthage fell (Plb. 38.21–2), and like those tears radiated the humane sensibility of the victorious general who was sensitive to the transience of empire.

58.1. As for the men of power…positions of authority and honours: awkwardly separated from the 'offices and honours' given to 'some', including Brutus and Cassius, at 57.5: it is effectively the same item. But the repetition gives a transition to the Caninius Rebilus item of §§2–3, and that allows P. to end this initial collection of dictatorial material with a gibe that fits into the mounting refrain of senatorial unrest. **he promised some of them consulships and praetorships.** C. had the right to nominate half of the magistrates (except the consuls) while the people elected the rest, Suet. 41.2; but in effect his control over all elections was complete, Dio 43.51.3. Cf. Frei-Stolba 58–76; Jehne 110–30. Hirtius and Pansa were formally designated consuls for 43, and D. Brutus and L. Munatius Plancus for 42; it appears that Brutus at least was to be consul in 41 and possibly Cassius too (62.4 n.), though it is not clear whether they were formally designated. Cf. Syme, *RR* 95, Frei-Stolba 59–60; Dettenhofer 233–4 doubts the plan for 41 on the grounds that the two most prominent ex-Pompeians would be a surprising and provocative combination, but that may have been precisely the point that C. intended to convey. Those designations were to cover the period when C. was expecting to be absent in Parthia (58.5 n., Dio 43.51.2), normally but insecurely assumed on the basis of Dio to be three years: see Toher on Nic. Dam. 41. On praetorships, cf. 62.5 n.: this passage prepares for that. **courting:** more erotic vocabulary (Intr., p. 21, 57–61 n.), as C. seeks to turn into marriage his love affair with those who are now his **subjects**; but that affair is already cooling, and C. will shortly show a real 'passion' for a clearer sort of **rule** (60.1). The same image of 'courting monarchy' is used of Pompey at *C.min.* 45.7, quoted at 28.5 n. **rule over willing subjects:** by now a cliché: cf. 57.8 n. Ael. Arist. (*Panath.*

p. 158 J) and Dio of Prusa (34.50) claim it for at least the first stages of the classical Athenian empire, Dionysius of Halicarnassus makes it a (sometimes abused) catchword of early Roman politics (*AR* 6.64.3, 6.85.1, 11.11.2), Cassius Dio has it as an aim of Augustus (53.2.6), Philo describes in these terms the authority of Moses (*Life of Moses* 1.163). But Arist. *Pol.* 3.1285ª26, 1285ᵇ3, 1295ª16, etc., regards this as a feature of kingship as opposed to tyranny: similarly Xen. *Mem.* 4.6.12, Plb. 6.4.2, [Plato] *Theages* 126a7–8, and Strabo (5.3.2) of King Numa. Thus not merely the 'courting' but also the 'willing subjects' prepare for that 'passion to be king' (60.1).

58.2. Maximus: Q. Fabius Maximus, suffect consul in the last months of 45 (*MRR* 304–5): cf. 56.7 n. for his triumph in October. **he declared.** As at 37.2 (n.), this does not exclude some sort of electoral procedure, even though this would be only a formality (§1 n., cf. *Ant.* 11.5 with my n.): C. conducted the election as dictator and 'declared' the result. Cf. Frei-Stolba 54–6, 75. **C. Caninius Rebilus:** succeeded Fabius Maximus when he died on 31 December (*MRR* 305). Caninius had fought for C. in Gaul in 52–49, in Africa in 46 as proconsul, and in Spain. Jehne 375–6 observes that the brief suffect consulship of Fabius Maximus had aroused public derision (Suet. 80.2); the even briefer appointment of Caninius may have been a pointed gesture of C.'s disdain for such criticisms. But Weinstock 276 argues that C. was in fact being constitutionally scrupulous in ensuring that the consul was replaced, and similar brief end-of-year tenures are attested for other years (admittedly later ones, 44, 43, and 30 BCE) without public outcry: any indignation, he thinks, was misplaced. Still, indignation there was: 'these things make sorry hearing, and they were sorrier to see than to hear' (Cic. *Fam.* 7.30 (265).1–2)— though Cicero doubtless played up the farcicality to make his good lines seem even better (§3 n.). See also Bruhns 155 n. 65.

58.3. 'let's hurry,' said Cicero, 'or his consulship will be over': not the only nor the best witticism of Cicero on the subject: better was 'Caninius was so conscientious a consul that he never slept a wink in office' (*Fam.* 7.30 (265).1, *SHA* 24.8.2, Macr. 2.3.6), and there were others too (Macr. 7.3.10, cf. A. Corbeill, *Controlling Laughter* (1996), 204). But P. selects the story that best captures the courtier's plight.

58.4–10: CAESAR'S LAST PLANS   The theme recalls *Alex.* 68.1, where Alexander too towards the end of his life planned a grand circular journey, in his case to the south around Africa: cf. Intr., p. 28. Other versions made Alexander plan a loop to the north rather than south, taking in the Black Sea, Scythia, and Lake Maeotis (Arr. 7.1.3). He too, like C. (§5 n.), was 'contending only with himself' (Arr. 7.1.4). Other, more elaborate versions of Alexander's last plans existed, based on 'memoranda' said to have been left at his death (Diod. 18.4.1–6). They are much discussed: cf. A. B. Bosworth, *From Arrian to Alexander* (1988), 185–211, with further bibliography; Hamilton on *Alex.* 68.1.

Suet. 44 similarly stresses the magnificent plans that were interrupted by C.'s death, but he especially emphasizes building projects in the city (a temple of Mars and a theatre on the Tarpeian mount) and in Italy (a road from the Adriatic across the Apennines to link with the Tiber valley), a plan to codify civil law, and the commission to Varro (57.5 n.) to organize Greek and Latin public libraries on the biggest scale possible. Those are largely themes that provide more of a template for the activity of later emperors, but have less interest for P.: cf. §7 n. for his avoidance of contemporary resonance.

Normally such material would provoke scepticism, as the modern debate about Alexander's last plans shows: 'a fabricated concatenation of unrealized intentions may be logical, artistic and persuasive, but it is not history' (Syme, *RR* 271, of the alleged intentions of Antony and Cleopatra; cf. *RR* 53 and 55 and esp. *The Provincial at Rome* (1999), 174–92, of C.). But some at least of C.'s plans were certainly in the air at the time: the diverting of the Tiber, the draining of the Pomptine marshes, and especially the Parthian campaign (nn.), together with some extravagant urban building plans (Cic. *Att.* 13.20 (328).1, 33a (330).1, 35 (334).1). Cf. Gelzer 314, 322. Other alleged plans are less plausible, such as the campaigns in the north and west of §§6–7—probably the result of P.'s own recasting, §6 n.—and the idea of transplanting the capital to Alexandria or Troy (Suet. 79.3, Nic. Dam. 68 with Toher's n.). Similar things were to be said twelve years later about Antony (Dio 50.4.1).

58.4. eagerness for glory: in the Greek, *philotimia*, a quality we have seen before as C.'s career developed. It has been used of 'ambitious' measures and rivalries and displays (5.9, 6.1, 6.3, 7.2, 11.3) as well as the spirit that inspired them (3.2, 17.2, 54.1, 54.4). As at 5.9

(n.), there is some play here between the *philotimia*, lit. 'love of honour', and the *timai*, 'honours', that his supporters sought at 5.9 and that are now showered upon him: but such shallow senatorial 'honours' are not now enough to satisfy C.'s drive. What had once typified C. was his capacity to inspire and match a similar quality in his men (17.1 (n.) ~ 17.2). Now too C.'s own *philotimia* will be mirrored by the same quality in others, but to his catastrophe rather than his triumph: for 'eagerness for glory', again the same word, is what is triggered in Brutus at 62.8. **the spark that inflamed his thoughts for the future.** The word for 'spark' (*hupekkauma*) is especially associated with ambition: cf. *Pomp.* 30.8, *Should an old man engage in politics?* 787a, and esp. *Ages.* 5.5, where the Spartan lawgiver 'seems to have injected an eagerness for glory [*philotimon*] and a contentiousness [*philonikon*, cf. §5 n.] into the state as a spark to inflame virtue…'. **a passion for new glory:** more erotic language (Intr., p. 21; 57–61 n.): this passion is an *erōs*, a 'lust', which will be matched by his 'passion to be king' (60.1). Similar language is used of Pompey at *Pomp.* 38.4, where again (*pace* Heftner, ad loc.) a hint of Alexander is felt (§7 n.), and of Sulla at *Sulla* 13.1. On the 'glory', cf. 69.1 n.

58.5 envy of himself. 'Envy' is frequently inspired in others when a person's 'enthusiasm for glory', *philotimia*, is strong, e.g. at *Them.* 21–2: cf. F. Frazier, *RPh* 62 (1988), 121–2. It is so frequent a response that it can be a matter of comment if an act of *philotimia* does *not* evoke envy, as with Poplicola's triumph (*Popl.* 9.9–10). Now C.'s bizarre self-envy—*zēlos*, suggesting 'emulous rivalry'—palely mimics the much more destructive envy felt by his enemies, for which the stronger word *phthonos* is used, 64.5, 69.1. **he was eager to contend with his past achievements and outdo them with those to come.** He had earlier 'washed away' the ambitious achievements (*philotimiai*) of his predecessors, 5.9: now there is only himself to beat. The idea is not original: Cic. *Marc.* 12 uses it of C., though in that case it is his peacetime generosity that has outdone, first, all other victors in civil wars and, now, himself and his own victory. Arr. *Anab.* 7.1.4 applies the conceit to Alexander (§§4–10 n., above); Livy 6.6.9 makes Camillus use it of himself. By P.'s time it had become a commonplace of panegyric (Plin. *Pan.* 13.5) and of flattering letters (Cic. *Fam.* 9.14 (326).6, 11.15 (422).2, *Q.fr.* 1.1 (1).3, Plin. *Ep.* 8.24.8): P. uses it admiringly of the young Coriolanus (*Cor.* 4.2), though that *Life* may also suggest that the later excesses spring from a version of the same competitive drive. As Oakley notes on Livy 6.6.9, the idea is particularly suitable to panegyric of monarchs; it may therefore go with that 'passion to be king' that becomes so important here (60.1)—but in C.'s case the conventional formulation is no more than the truth.

eager to contend with. The word for this eagerness is *philonikia*, 'contentiousness', which would probably suggest to a Greek ear both 'love of victory (*nikē*)' and 'love of quarrels' (*neikē*): cf. *Plutarch and History*, 345 and 347 n. 24. It is particularly often paired with *philotimia* as that quality's more aggressive and disquieting counterpart, as in *Ages.* 5.5, quoted in §4 n., and particularly in *Phil.–Flam.*, where 'the one man's [Flamininus'] mistakes came through *philotimia*, the other's [Philopoemen's] through *philonikia*': cf. *Plutarch and History*, 243–7. Here the word does not negate the impressiveness of C.'s irrepressible drive, but it does suggest an element of excess and unease.

58.6. an expedition against the Parthians. This could be represented as unfinished business as long as Crassus' disaster in 53 (28.1 n.) remained unavenged, but it had a dimension that related to the civil wars: the Pompeians had looked to Parthia for help (Dio 41.55.3–4), and the Parthian king Orodes had not been unsympathetic. Pompey had thought of fleeing there after Pharsalus (*Pomp.* 76.6). In late 45 the Parthian prince Pacorus came to reinforce the Pompeian Q. Caecilius Bassus, continuing the struggle against C. in Syria, and Pacorus defeated C.'s legate C. Antistius Vetus at Apamea: *MRR* 308, Gelzer 304–5, D. Timpe, *MH* 19 (1962), 114–15. C.'s Parthian plan had been known at least from May 45 (Cic. *Att.* 13.27 (298).1, 31 (302).3), well before Pacorus' attack. He was planning to leave for the campaign on 18 March.

On the planned war, see Toher on Nic. Dam. 41; J. Malitz, *Hist.* 33 (1984), 21–59. Suet. (44.3 and *Aug.* 8.2) and Vell. 2.59.4 say that the Dacian campaign (§6 n.) was to come first, and App. 3.25.93 that Antony said the same in 44 when arguing for a Dacian war;[25] P. may have altered the order (*a*) to play down the Dacians (§7 n.) and (*b*) to

---

[25] But App. 2.110.459 should not be quoted in support of Suet., despite White's Loeb translation 'The Getae … were to be attacked first'. Rather 'He was launching a pre-emptive strike against the Getae …'. Carter's Penguin gets it right.

develop the idea of the Alexander-like grand 'circle' (§7) that C.
envisaged. This adaptation has, however, serious implications for
the plausibility of these plans. P.'s sequence and idea of a circle
bring in not merely Dacia but also Scythia and Germany, which
scholars (e.g. G. B. Townend, *Lat.* 42 (1983), 601; Syme, *Provincial
at Rome*, 176) have found the least plausible targets for conquest; both
are absent from Suet.'s version of the plans at 44.2. Without those,
C.'s plans could be described in similar terms to Pompey's at *Pomp.*
38.4–5: 'a certain passion and emulation came over Pompey to recover Syria, drive through Arabia to the Red Sea [probably here
meaning the Indian Ocean, including both the modern Red Sea and
the Persian Gulf: cf. my n. on *Ant.* 69.4], and reach in triumph the
Ocean that surrounds the human world…': this further conquest
might have allowed Pompey to 'complete *the circuit of his campaigning* by linking it to the Red Sea'. The reference there is to Pompey's
previous triumphal campaigns in Africa, Spain, and Asia; C.'s own
previous successes in Spain, Gaul, and Africa would allow a similar
claim to a worldwide 'circuit' if a further Parthian conquest brought
him to the eastern Ocean, not at all a wild idea given that even the
Caspian Sea could be envisaged as an inlet of Ocean (Malitz, art. cit.,
53–4; P. A. Brunt, *Roman Imperial Themes* (1990), 107–8 = *JRS* 53
(1963), 175). Such an aspiration to outdo Pompey's 'circuit' is not
implausible, and need not imply, as P.'s language does, a commitment
to further campaigns in the north and west. But G. Dobesch, *Die
Kelten in Österreich nach den ältesten Berichten der Antike* (1980),
352–4, esp. 353–4 n. 21, defends the north-western aspect of the plan
as well.

There is some debate on C.'s aims. Did he intend permanent
conquest of the Parthian empire, as P.'s language at 60.1 (n.) might
suggest and as Suet. 44.1 arguably implies with his phrase 'protect and
expand the empire' (G. B. Townend, *Lat.* 42 (1983), 601–6)? Or
simply to make a show of force and inflict some exemplary defeats
(W. C. McDermott, *AncSoc* 13/14 (1982–3), 223–31)? To drive the
Parthians back to beyond a new boundary of the Euphrates (Ph.-St.
Freber, *Der hellenistische Osten und das Illyricum unter Caesar*
(1993), 172)? Or to use the legions, or some of them, merely as a
sabre-rattling threat with the hope of recovering Crassus' lost eagles
through diplomacy, as Augustus regained them twenty-four years
later (Syme, *Provincial at Rome*, 188–9)? Most likely, C. left matters
vague, at least in public: any or all of these could have been

represented as a brilliant success, just as both Gaul and Britain (23.2 n.) had been paraded as different sorts of success in the previous decade, and C. was shrewd enough not to specify war aims that he could later be criticized for not achieving. Cf. 60.2 n.

According to App. 2.110.460, C. 'sent in advance' across the Adriatic 16 legions (probably the same number as Antony deployed 8 years later, Brunt, *Manpower*, 503–4, and substantially more than C. had used in Gaul) and 10,000 cavalry: the cavalry would be especially important against Parthians. The transport of troops eastward had been in train for some time (Cic. *Fam.* 12.19 (206).2, December 46), and by 44 most, perhaps all, of these legions were already east of the Adriatic: cf. Malitz, art. cit., 43–4 (for a Dacian campaign, 3 legions in Illyria; for Parthia, 6 in Macedonia or Greece, 3 or 4 in Egypt, 2 coming to Syria from Pontus, and 3 from Bithynia);[26] Brunt, *Manpower*, 480 (6 in Macedon, 6 in Syria, 4 in Egypt); Syme, *Provincial at Rome*, 185–6 (6 in Macedonia, 3 in Egypt, 3 in ?Bithynia, 3 in ? Cilicia—but Syme thinks that 10 at most of these were to go to Parthia). Some supplies, however, were still in Italy awaiting transport (App. 3.11.39).

Hyrcania: on the south-east coast of the Caspian, in the north of the modern Iran. **Scythia:** a vague word for peoples to the north and north-west of the Black Sea, but one that had considerable resonance still for Romans: cf. Nisbet–Rudd on Hor. *Odes* 3.24.

58.7. Germany's neighbours: i.e. the Dacians, or (as they are more often called by Greek authors) the Getae: their king at the time was Burebista (Strabo 7.3.6), and they had already been making incursions into Pontus, presumably hoping to capitalize on the uncertainties following C.'s campaign of 47 (50.2 n.), and into Thrace (Suet. 44.3). The Dacian campaign was probably to come before the Parthian (§6 n.), and Syme, *Provincial at Rome*, 174–92, and Ph.-St. Freber, *Der hellenistische Osten und das Illyricum unter Caesar* (1993), 157–76, argue that Dacia rather than Parthia was C.'s more important target: if so, the purpose was presumably 'not the annexation of Dacia itself but the repulse of the Dacians over the Danube and the breaking of their power' (Syme, *Provincial at Rome*, 180–1), as a

---

[26] J. Malitz, *Hist.* 35 (1984), 44, thinks that at least one legion had not yet crossed, the one Lepidus had near Rome on the Ides (App. 2.118.496); but there is no indication (as he admits) or likelihood that this had been destined for Parthia rather than as an intimidating presence for urban peacekeeping.

prelude to the conquest of Illyricum and the establishment of a new frontier at the Danube. Possibly so: but in that case C. was playing a dangerous game in making so much of Parthia in his propaganda at Rome, running the risk that he could again be presented, as in the Alexandrian War (48.2–49.10 n.), as allowing a distraction—this time Dacia—to compromise a higher priority. The phrasing of Suet. 44.3, 'to restrain [*coercere*] the Dacians, who had poured into Pontus and Thrace, and then to invade Parthia...', gives the impression of a punitive and exemplary Dacian campaign as a preliminary to Parthia.

At the time when P. wrote *Caesar* Trajan's Dacian campaign was a current theme: P.'s avoidance of the name is striking. Cf. Intr., p. 3, and, for the possibility that P. has misrepresented C.'s planned sequence, above, §6 n.

that would have Ocean alone as its boundary: 12.1, 23.2 nn. Similarly Nic. Dam. 95 (with Toher's n.), and *Pomp.* 38.4–5 of Pompey in 63 BCE. The language again recalls Alexander (cf. Weippert 174–5, Intr., p. 28), though it need not follow that C. himself was concerned with Alexander imitation (so, rightly, P. Green, *AJAH* 3 (1978), 15).

58.8. to dig a canal through the Isthmus of Corinth: so also Suet. 44.3, Dio 44.5.1; the work was later taken up by the emperors Gaius and Nero (Plin. *NH* 4.10). The canal was finally built in 1893. Possibly P.'s implication ('During this expedition') is right, and this would serve the military purpose for the war—evidently, to help naval movements from the Adriatic to the Aegean; but the advantage was marginal, and it is better to connect this with the recolonization of Corinth (57.8 n.). †**Anienus.** The '†' marks that the name is corrupt: it is not known as a name in either Latin or Greek. Reiske suggested 'Anicius', Garzetti 'Aninius' or 'Annius'; the Greek name 'Aniketos' would be as good or better palaeographically (and the wordplay of an 'Unconquerable' would fit the chapter well). In any case, P. has again (cf. 7.5 n.) introduced an unexplained person whom his readers would find unfamiliar. **Circeum:** a promontory (San Felice Circeo) some 20 km. west of **Tarracina** (Terracina/Anxur). At first sight this sits oddly with the plan to develop Ostia (§10), but the plan was presumably to divert part of the Tiber stream rather than, as P.'s language suggests, all of it. Cic. *Att.* 13.33a (330).1 (July 45) mentions a (presumably separate) plan of diverting the Tiber within the city itself to flow west rather than east of the present Vatican.

form in the MSS of *Numa* 18 and at Cinc. fr. 10 Funaioli: Festus
111.15 L. has *Mercedonios*. This was an unofficial name, it seems, for
it does not appear in official lists (A. K. Michels, *The Calendar of the
Roman Republic* (1967), 18; Samuel, *Greek and Roman Chronologies*
161 n. 1); Ziegler pointed to the obscure MERK in two columns of the
fasti Maffeiani (*CIL* i² p. 225), but those relate to July and September,
not February, and indicate a market (*mercatus*): thus Degrassi in *Insc.
It.* xiii.2 78 and 80. J. Rüpke, *Kalendar und Öffentlichkeit* (1995), 321–
2 suggests that 'Mercedonius' was a nickname based on *merces*, 'fee',
and was a joke at the expense of those who used the intercalary
months to manipulate their interest payments.

59.4. as I explained in his *Life*:   *Numa* 18, where P. explains that
Romulus' year had been one of 360 days but his months had had no
real system at all; Numa introduced a year of 365 days and a sequence
of months that regularly totalled 354, and reconciled the two by
inserting a 22-day intercalary 'Mercedinus' (§3 n.) 'after' or 'on to'
(*epi* + dative) February in alternate years. This is slightly inaccurate:
the intercalary month was inserted when February would otherwise
still have had 5 days (or possibly 4—below) to run, and those 5 days
were added to the end of the intercalary month to make it up to
27 days. Censorinus 20.6 and Macr. 1.13.12 also say that alternately
22 and 23 days were intercalated, to give extra months of 27 and 28
days; or possibly the intercalary month was always 27 days, but when
an extra day was needed the month was inserted after 24 rather than
23 February (A. K. Michels, *The Calendar of the Roman Republic*
(1967), 160–3, followed by Samuel, *Greek and Roman Chronologies*,
160–1). On *Numa* 18, see also J. D. Cloud, *LCM* 4.4 (1979), 65–71,
though P. is a good deal less confused than Cloud's treatment suggests.

the best philosophers and mathematicians of the day: 59.5.
particularly Sosigenes of Alexandria (*R-E* 3A (1927), 1153–7), who
published three treatises on the subject, progressively correcting
himself (Pliny *NH* 18.211–12): one hopes that all three pre-dated
the reform. Appian (2.154.648), himself a native of Alexandria, Dio
(43.26.2), and Macrobius (1.14.3) also stress the use of Egyptian
models. Not that the Egyptian calendar itself was at this stage particularly in kilter with the natural year: Blackburn and Holford-Strevens, *Oxford Companion to the Year*, 707–10. **his solution:** this
famously included the lengthening of the months to create a lunar

year of 365 days and the insertion of a leap day every fourth year to correct almost totally for the true length of the solar year (just over eleven minutes short of 365 and a quarter days). The slight remaining misalignment adds up to one day every 128 years, and was eventually corrected in the Gregorian calendar by omitting the leap day on three out of four 'century' years. The Julian calendar was replaced by the Gregorian in 1582 in many European countries, in 1752 in Britain, in 1918 in Russia, and in 1923–4 in Greece, but is still used for fixing some feasts in Russia, Serbia, and elsewhere.

With the exception of the 28-day February, Numa's months had either 31 days (March, May, Quinctilis (renamed July in 44 BCE), October) or 29; C. left non-leap-year February and the 31-day months alone, but lengthened the 29-day ones to either 30 (April, June, September, November) or 31 (January, Sextilis, December). One minor social consequence affected rents and interest payments, both of which were levied on a monthly basis: cf. on 'Mercedonius', §3 n. above. Unless there was some compensatory increase in rates (and we do not hear of any), the effect of C.'s longer months was to reduce the amounts payable by approximately 3 per cent. Cf. 37.2 n. for an earlier, more far-reaching 'lightening of the load' on debtors and renters.

combined them in an individual way to produce a more accurate correction. The 365¼-day solar year had been known to Babylonian astronomers, and had been familiar in Greece since at least the fifth and possibly the sixth century (Samuel, *Greek and Roman Chronologies*, 40, 155). Ptolemy Euergetes had proposed a four-yearly intercalary day in Egypt in 238, but that failed through resistance of the priests (Blackburn and Holford-Strevens, *Oxford Companion to the Year*, 709). This was not the only means available, however: more obvious and probably less controversial would have been to rationalize intercalation and apply it in a more rigorous and regulated way, as Cicero had recommended in *de Leg.* 2.29. Cicero's comments incidentally demonstrate that this was a topic of contemporary debate: C.'s reforms did not come out of the blue. Thus, rightly, Malitz, art. cit., 109–12.

The months presented the bigger problem. There was no pretence that months would begin or end in a way that accurately mirrored any particular phase of the moon, any more than their Republican predecessors had done. There remained the problem of retaining traditional festivals on dates that would in a sense be new, though described in the same words ('fifteen days before the Kalends of...'); and finding a start date for the newly defined year—not a question with an obvious answer, for 1 January might, for instance, have been synchronized more precisely with the winter solstice (cf. *Roman Questions* 268d, with Feeney, *Caesar's Calendar*, 204)—which would best fit those festivals, geared as many were to the agricultural year or in some cases to the rising or setting of constellations. It seems that a work 'On the stars' was published by C. or under his name, including an astronomical calendar for the year: it is cited as a source by Pliny the Elder (index of authors to *NH* 18, cf. 18.214). On its possible inaccuracies, cf. §6 n.; Le Bonniec and Le Boeuffle's Budé edn of Pliny *NH* 18, 262–3; Malitz, art. cit., 121–4.

Beyond subtlety, what was needed was the willingness to see a point in achieving harmony between civil and celestial years and to adopt a radical measure to do so, the decisiveness in giving priority to alignment with the solar rather than the lunar phenomena, and particularly the combination of sacral and secular power that allowed C., as pontifex maximus and dictator, to impose a unilateral solution.

The Romans still use his system. But it fell into confusion very soon after his own day through including leap days every three years instead of every four, perhaps through misunderstanding of some phrase such as *quarto quoque anno* ('every fourth year'), and C.'s original system had to be 'restored' by Augustus: Suet. *Aug.* 31.2, Macr. 1.14.13–15. Cf. Blackburn and Holford-Strevens, *Oxford Companion to the Year*, 671; L. Polverini in G. Urso (ed.), *L'Ultimo Cesare* (2000), 248–58 at 249–52. Malitz, art. cit., 116 n. 64, suspects that the misunderstanding was wilful 'sabotage' by C.'s enemies, but that is not plausible; neither Lepidus, C.'s successor as pontifex maximus, nor the other men of power in the thirties had any interest in damaging C.'s posthumous image.

59.6. tomorrow the constellation Lyra would rise: 'tomorrow' would presumably be 5 January, on C.'s system the day of the rising of the Lyre (Ov. *Fast.* 1.315–6, Pliny *NH* 18.234, Columella *RR* 11.2.97). It is generally assumed that this was 5 January 45, when the new calendar would only just have come into effect, rather than 44. If so, C. was safely (or so Cicero might hope) far away from the orator's crack, campaigning in Spain (56.1n.). **as if this too was an imposition that mortals had to accept:** not, on the face of it, the point of the joke, which was that C. was imposing a new order on the firmament, not just on mortals. This is probably not a matter of P. missing the point (Feeney, *Caesar's Calendar*, 295 n. 133)—it was hardly abstruse—but of his bending his emphasis to focus again on the gathering human resentment at such cosmic bossiness. But there may be more to it, for even under the new calendar there was apparently a mismatch between the constellation's notional rising on 5 January and its actual rising in November or even earlier (Bömer on Ov. *Fast.* 1.315; Le Bonniec and Le Boeuffle's Budé edn of Plin. *NH* 18, 262–3). A. Le Boeuffle, *REL* 42 (1964), 329–30, suspected an underlying confusion between two different constellations called 'the Lyre'. Thus P. may have conveyed something of the point after all, if Cicero was implying that mortals had to go along with the pretence that C. had brought everything into cosmic order: so A. W. J. Holleman, *Hist.* 27 (1978), 496–8, and Malitz, art. cit., 125–6. Cicero, the translator of Aratus' *Phaenomena*, was astronomically informed enough to notice that something was amiss.

60–1: CAESAR'S 'PASSION TO BE KING' P. again uses erotic language: this is *erōs*, love or lust, for the position of king (*basileia*): cf. Intr., p. 21. C. already enjoyed 'a monarch's unaccountability', and 'a monarch's permanence' (57.1), so this was a matter of titles and emblems, as P. goes on to make clear. The title, however, was important. The distinction between kingship and 'tyranny' was a traditional one, with kingship implying legitimacy and, in particular, consent: Xen. *Mem.* 4.6.12, Arist. *Pol.* 1285^{a}24–9, 1313^{a}5, 1314^{a}36–7, Plb. 5.11.6, 6.4.2, 6.6–7, with O. Murray, *JRS* 55 (1965), 161–82, esp. 165–6; cf. 57.8 n. So far C. has been setting about it in the best possible way in P.'s narrative, regarding 'people's goodwill' as his 'magic charm' (57.8) and 'courting rule over willing subjects' in a way that seeks a quasi-marital legitimisation of this 'passion' (58.1 n.); but chs 60–1 now trace the ways in which he loses his popular touch.

It is disputed how far C.'s ambitions were really for 'kingship': cf. esp. E. Rawson, *JRS* 65 (1975), 148–59 = *Roman Culture and Society*, 169–88, for discussion of the ambivalent mix of fascination and disdain that could figure in Roman reactions to kings. Rawson herself is surely right to say, there and at *CAH* ix^2 (1994), 463–5, that the evidence for C.'s aspirations to divinity (67.8 n.) is stronger than that for ambitions for royalty, and doubtless 'a passion to be king' puts it all too crudely; but it remains plausible that C. was seeking new ways to define his position, that those might not all be conciliatory to the old elite (56.9 n.), and that some of the strands that C. wove into his new presentation borrowed elements from Hellenistic and from old Roman kingship (61.4 n.).

60.1. his passion to be king: similar language at Nic. Dam. 69, where C. objects to the tribunes' (61.8) attempt to paint him as 'in love [*erōs*, as here] with an illegal dominion [*dynasteia*]'; also at *Ant.* 6.3, where Plutarch draws the comparison with 'Alexander before and Cyrus long ago'. At the expense of some consistency—**the first grievance** ignores the popular disapproval at 56.7–9—the emphasis now shifts back towards **the ordinary people** from **those who had long nursed their resentments.** The second group presumably refers to the senatorial opponents who are already familiar (57.2–3, 58.3, 59.6) and whom we have already seen manipulatively looking for **pretexts,** 57.3 (the same word as here). Cf. 57–61 n.

60.2. those who were trying to procure this honour for Caesar: an extension of the pattern whereby his friends are now the problem (Intr., pp. 21–2; 51 and 57–61 nn., and §8 below). But §1 has left no doubt that they were doing as C. wished. It is not clear that P. is right about this. K. Kraft, *Der goldene Kranz Caesar und der Kampf um die Entlarvung des 'Tyrannen'* (1952/3), 56–8, suggests that this proposal, or at least the rumour, came from those who were trying to embarrass C. (cf. 57.3 n.), and that one reason C. felt he should attend the senate on 15 March (64.3 n.) was his irritated determination to repudiate the idea. **in the Sibylline books.** The 'official' Sibylline oracles (*OCD*[4], s.v. 'Sibyl', Ogilvie on Livy 5.13.5) could in theory be consulted only on the senate's command (Cic. *Div.* 2.112), though this had been over-ridden in 56 BCE to publicize the controversial oracle concerning the restoration of Ptolemy (Dio 39.15–16, cf. 21.3–9 n.); rumours of what they might contain might anyway be exploited politically (e.g. *Cic.*17.5 ~ Cic. *Cat.* 3.9, Sall. *BC* 47.2), and even official revelation by the *quindecimuiri* (see below) did not end suspicions of falsification, as that controversy over Ptolemy in the mid-fifties makes clear (Cic. *Fam.* 1.4 (14).2. etc.: cf. Siani-Davies on Cic. *Rab. Post.* 2.10).

   that Parthia would only fall [lit. 'could be taken' or 'captured'] **if the Romans marched on them with a king.** The language of Dio 44.15.3 is closely similar; Suet. 79.3 has 'the Parthians could not be defeated [*uinci*] except by a king', App. 2.110.460 'that the Parthians would never submit to the Romans unless a king campaigned against them'. Of these, P.'s and Dio's language most clearly suggests a plan for full conquest, not just for an exemplary campaign (cf. G. B. Townend, *Lat.* 42 (1983), 605; Ph.-St. Freber, *Der Hellenistische Osten* (58.6 n.), 173). In fact it is unlikely that C. himself, or any oracle that his supporters might conveniently find, would be so clear-cut (cf. 58.6 n.), and—assuming that the proposal *does* reflect C.'s own wishes (but see above on 'those who were trying to procure the honour for Caesar')—Suet.'s formulation of 'defeat' is the most likely. That would not *exclude* the possibility of full-scale conquest, especially as the implication might be that Parthia, so used to royalty, would submit only to switching one king for another, just as Persia had with Alexander. Cf. Weinstock 340–1.

It was said, 'truly or falsely' (Dio), that L. Aurelius Cotta, a *quindecimuir* (one of the body of priests who were official guardians of the Sibylline oracles), was going on to propose the title of king on these grounds 'at the next senate', i.e. presumably that of 15 March itself (Suet. 79.3, Dio 44.15.3–4, though notice also *Brut.* 10.3, 'the Kalends of March'): cf. 64.3 (n.) below. (Cotta, cos. 65, was related to C. on his mother's side: 1.4 n. and p. 288.) Cic. *de Div.* 2.110 doubtless puts the content of the alleged oracle tendentiously, but confirms the expectation that it would be raised in the senate: he refers to the 'recent false rumour' that a Sibylline priest 'was going to say in the senate that the man who was our king in reality should also have the title of king: our survival depended on it!'

60.3. Caesar was returning to the city from Alba: i.e. from the celebration of the *feriae Latinae* on the Alban Mount, 26 January 44: Weinstock 320–31. This may well have been the same occasion as that of the decoration of the statues with diadems (61.8 n.), whether or not P. realized it. If he did, the separation of the two items allows the emphasis here to rest on the title or name of king, at 61.8 on C.'s strong reaction and the consequent popular disaffection: the hailing of the tribunes as 'Brutuses' also helps the transition to the conspirators (61.9 n.). **they:** either 'those supporters', the same people as were damagingly meddling at §2, or a vague 'people on the way'. **'Caesar', not 'King':** so Suet. 79.2, App. 2.108.450. The play is on the Roman word *rex* ('king'), and C.'s descent from Ancus Marcius and the Marcii Reges (Suet. 6.1). **Everyone fell silent.** P. again (cf. 14.12,

67.7 nn.) knows how to exploit the dramatic silence: there is nothing similar in Suet. or App. **annoyed ... looking sullen and displeased.** Given C.'s 'passion to be king', the text implies that it was the negative reaction rather than the royalist gesture that caused C.'s dismay.

60.4 above the rostra.   We would naturally say 'on the rostra', but the reference is to the beaks of captured ships that decorated the front of the orators' platform at the western end of the Roman Forum: cf. 61.4 (n.). (It, and they, were moved a few metres by C. as part of his building of a new senate house.) Yet this incident took place 'in front of the temple of Venus Genetrix' (Suet. 78.1, Livy *per.* 116, cf. Dio 44.8.1), which places it in the Forum Iulium rather than the Roman Forum. P.'s mistake may go back to (a possibly unclear remark in) his source, as App. 2.107.445 has 'in front of the rostra' (as he does for the Lupercalia, 2.109.456: cf. 61.4 n.). As Dio makes clear, the senate had voted the honours in C.'s absence (we do not know where: not all meetings took place in the *curia Pompeii*, 66.1), and now came out to address C. formally; according to Nic. Dam. 78, C. was engaged in letting contracts for his building work at the time. The incident is discussed at length by Dobesch, *AS* i. 275–361, detecting Pollio as the source of Dio's detailed and balanced account of these final months. The date was before C.'s assumption of the title 'dictator for life' (57.1 n.), if Dio 44.8.4 can be trusted. But perhaps he cannot; there are so many uncertainties in sequence about these incidents that it is likely that they were remembered as free-floating individual stories, and each narrator imposed his own order: so, rightly, Toher on Nic. Dam. 69–79, against Dobesch, and cf. next n. and 57–61 n. On Dio's tendency to prefer thematic to chronological arrangement, see also Lintott, *ANRW* ii. 34.3 2503–8. **the consuls ... approached:** so also App. 2.107.445, but Nic. Dam. 78 has 'the consul': if Nic. Dam. is right, then that points to a date in 44, when 'the consul' will be Antony (*MRR* 315–16); the other consul would have been C. himself. If P. and App. are right and it was 'consuls', this will be late 45, when C. was not consul (*MRR* 304–5, 58.2 n.): thus Weinstock 275, Dobesch *AS* i. 407–26 (esp. 416–17), Toher on Nic. Dam. 78. **the whole senate following behind.** Some 400 had attended the senate at the crucial vote of 1 December 50 (30.5 n.). Many had died in the war, but C.'s new senators again numbered some 400. Dio 43.47.3 puts the total now at 900; Syme, *RP* i. 98, thinks 800 more likely. A good number of these would be abroad, and not all at home would be present; but this would still have been a massively impressive parade. According to Nic. Dam. 78, ordinary people were also following in vast numbers behind the senate. **Instead of standing up to receive them...** It may be that C., as dictator and superior magistrate, was formally in the right to remain seated (so Weinstock 275–6), but this clearly caused offence. Such deference became an important part of protocol in the early principate, with emperors doubtless learning from C.'s lesson: Augustus made a point of saluting the senate when they were seated and he was arriving or leaving (Suet. *Aug.* 53.3), Tiberius of getting to his feet before the consuls (*Tib.* 31.2), and Claudius of rising before magistrates presiding at the games (*Claud.* 12.2).

60.5. That distressed the people as much as the senate. For the emphasis, cf. 57–61 n.; for the light cast on the difficulty of C.'s position, 57.3 n.

60.6. he drew his toga away from his throat. The gesture looks back to the people's goodwill that he put on like an amulet around his neck (58.8 n.), but now the goodwill is being lost; and forward to the killing at 66.6–7, when **his friends** indeed strike. App. does not have this but does have a very similar gesture of Bibulus in 59 BCE, 2.11.39: Pollio may well have had both gestures, with the later recalling the earlier, and if so the whole system may go back to him. For similar cases, cf. 30.2, 66.10, 66.12 nn.

At *Ant.* 12.6 P. attaches this episode to the Lupercalia. That is probably a displacement in *Antony*, where P. does not use the 'not rising to the senate' item but may well have been reluctant to lose this part of it; or perhaps this was another free-floating story of these final months (cf. §4 n.), which P. could anchor as he chose. Shakespeare also attaches it to the Lupercalia (*JC* I. ii. 260–4), possibly following *Ant.*: Intr., pp. 67–8.

60.6–7. Later he blamed it on his disease... faintness and loss of consciousness: i.e. his epilepsy, 17.2 n.: Suet. 45.1 says that attacks of epilepsy were especially frequent during C.'s later years, App. 2.110.459 that they tended to come especially when he was 'inactive' (i.e. not on campaign): both may be generalizing from this single case. In P., note the contrast with the genuine onset of the disease at Thapsus, 53.5–6 n. According to Dio 44.8.3, this explanation was put about by his friends. Other excuses were clearly offered too, itself an indication of the embarrassment the incident caused. Nic. Dam. 79 says that C. was deep in conversation, and did not notice the arrival of the train 'as they were coming up at an angle' (hardly plausible, and anyway, as Toher notes, he does not say that C. rose when he *did* notice them); Dio 44.8.3 also reports the explanation that C. was suffering from diarrhoea and 'there was a danger of a sudden flux'—very likely a scatological parody of the epilepsy excuse, as Dobesch, *AS* i. 284–5 suggests.

This false excuse seems to have been the inspiration for Shakespeare's remarkable emphasis on C.'s frailty in *JC*: Intr., p. 71.

60.8. people say: similarly Suet. 78.1, 'some people think that' Balbus encouraged C. to remain seated. **one of his friends, or rather his flatterers:** continuing the analysis of 51 and 60.2–3 nn.: 'flatterers' also echoes 57.3, and the emphasis on the disastrous effect that a flatterer may have is a favourite Plutarchan theme, treated at length in *How to Tell a Flatterer from a Friend* and traced emphatically in the narrative of *Lives* such as *Demetrius, Antony*, and *Alcibiades*. The rare and striking use of direct speech (37.6–7 n.) marks the importance of the theme. **Cornelius Balbus:** from Gades, immensely rich, by now C.'s 'chief agent in public affairs' (*OCD*[4], cf. Syme, *RR* 72); he was to be consul in 40. K. Welch, *Antichthon*, 24 (1990), 60–9, speculates that he may have been appointed *praefectus urbi* in 45. **'Remember you are Caesar':** hinting at the resonance the name was coming to have, and continued to have in P.'s own time. He was indeed '"Caesar", not "King"' (§3), but that might now be the greater name, and almost a title already.

Another friend, C. Trebatius, urged C. to stand and received a withering look for his pains (Suet. 78.1). If P. knew this item, he would naturally suppress it: he is interested in the *damaging* friends.

61.1–7: THE LUPERCALIA   The date was 15 February 44. Here and at *Ant.* 12 P. draws much of his detail from Cic. *Phil.* 2.84–7, but App. 2.109.456–8 suggests that he will also have found an account in Pollio. Dio 44.11 is similar, Nic. Dam. 71–5 rather different.

The significance of the incident was discussed in antiquity: Nic. Dam. 73–4 and Dio 44.11.3 and 46.17–19 record various guesses, and different interpretations are also in play at App. 2.110.459 (Pelling, 'Focalisation', 521–2). Conceivably Antony was acting independently, though if so it would surely have been a gesture that he expected C. to find welcome. More likely, though, C. had arranged it himself, and P. makes it clearer here than in *Antony* that this is his own view: the applause was 'prearranged' (§5), and it was an 'attempt' (§7) that 'failed'. In *Antony* he is more concerned to follow the cue given by Cic. in *Phil.* 2, and blame Antony for his irresponsibility rather than C. for his misjudgement. If C. did set it all up, it remains unclear whether he hoped that popular applause would allow him to keep the diadem, which is the interpretation most in line with P.'s emphases; or intended to give a public indication of his refusal to take the title of king, as Kraft and others have thought and as is probably most likely; or was testing the water to see how far he could reasonably go. Of the many discussions especially useful are Weinstock 331–40; K. Kraft, *Der goldene Kranz Caesars und der Kampf um die Entlarvung des 'Tyrannen'* (1952/3), esp. 39–58; K.-W. Welwei, *Hist.* 16 (1967), 44–69; and now J. A. North, *JRS* 98 (2008), 144–60, countering Weinstock's suggestion of a Hellenistic coronation ritual. Cf. also my n. on *Ant.* 12.

An evil omen, a heartless bull or a headless liver, may have marked a bad start to a bad day for C. on 15 February: see 63.4 n.

In *JC* Act I, scene ii Shakespeare exploits the Lupercalia (which he fuses with the triumph over Pompey's sons) to emphasize the contrast of C.'s position and aspirations ('he was very loath to lay his fingers off it', 239–40) with his human feebleness: we hear of a fever and of his deafness (119–21, 212), and C. eventually collapses in an epileptic fit (244–51). That may be suggested by the excuse of epilepsy raised at 60.6–7: see n. there, and on the frailty further Intr., p. 71.

61.1. his insults to the tribunes. It was the festival of the Lupercalia. P. thus immediately ties these two incidents together, wrongly: cf. §8 n. **Lupercalia:** 15 February 44. The festival is much discussed: see esp. T. P. Wiseman, *Remus* (1995), 75–88, and *JRS* 85 (1995), 1–22, and recently J. A. North, *JRS* 98 (2008), 144–60, all with further bibliography; also North and N. McLynn, *JRS* 98 (2008), 178–9, on the essential continuity of the festival between C.'s time and P.'s. P. in fact knew a fair amount about it, and gives more detail at *Rom.* 21.4–10, *Roman Questions* 280b–c and 290d, and (more briefly) *Ant.* 12.2. **ancient pastoral festival.** Its origins were obscure and disputed (cf. Ogilvie on Livy 1.5.1–2, Bömer on Ov. *Fasti* 2.267), but were associated in various ways with Romulus, as at *Rom.* 21:

cf. P. Marchetti, *LEC* 70 (2002), 77–92. C. was becoming linked with Romulus in other ways—for instance, in having his own statue placed in the temple of Quirinus (Weinstock 174–99, esp. 186–8); this will have seemed an appropriate setting for the offer of kingship, as Dio 46.19.6 makes his 'Calenus' observe, or at least to convey and clarify C.'s relationship to the early kings. North, art. cit., similarly emphasizes that the display would have suggested an affinity with Romulus, in particular his and Remus' role as city-founders. For P.'s own suggestions of a Roman cycle that begins with Romulus and ends with C., see Intr., pp. 34–5. **with some similarities to the Arcadian Lycaea.** P. here abbreviates and simplifies an issue on which he held firm views, for at *Rom.* 21.4–5 he expresses doubts about the usual view that the Lupercalia derived from the Lycaea and the cult of Lycaean Pan: for this, cf. Livy 1.5.2, Ov. *Fasti* 2.267–452 with Bömer on 271, and Virg. *Aen.* 8.343–4. The perception of similarity rested partly on the name, with *lup-* and *luk-* both being taken to refer to wolves, though the Arcadian cult in fact takes its name from Mt Lycaeon; both festivals may also have been genuinely associated with Pan, as Wiseman in particular has argued for the Lupercalia, *JRS* 85 (1995), 1–22.

61.2. nobles.   Here, as e.g. at *Sulla* 1.1, the word = 'patricians', though P. also often uses it in a less specific sense: cf. 9.2 n., *Plutarch and History*, 232–3 n. 88. **through the city:** in particular, up and down the Sacra Via in the forum. On the route, cf. Wiseman, *Remus* (1995), 81–2, and North, *JRS* 108 (2008), 148 (with bibliography in n. 27).

61.3. they think...to conceive if they are barren: so also *Rom.* 21.7, Ov. *Fasti* 2.425–8, etc (with North, art. cit., 149–53). Shakespeare makes his Caesar tell Calpurnia to 'stand...directly in Antonius' way' and make sure she is touched in order to shake off her 'sterile curse' (*JC* I. ii. 1–9), an early indication in the play of the importance of succession: cf. Intr., p. 73 and Julia Griffin in *CJC* 385.

61.4. above the rostra.   The same phrase as at 60.4 (n.), and the echo may be sensed: it is as if C. has failed to learn his lesson from only a few weeks earlier. This is close to where the run would finish: cf. North, art. cit., 156–8. Several Latin sources (Suet. 79.2, Vell. 2.56.4, Florus 2.13.91) speak of C. as seated *pro rostris*, which is sometimes translated as e.g. 'before the *rostra*' (thus Edwards in the *World's Classics* Suet.): so also App. 2.109.456. That would make Antony's gesture easier, but the Latin phrase probably means 'in a forward or prominent position on, on the edge of' (*OLD*, s.v. *pro* 1b), and Cic. *Phil.* 2.85 is explicit that Antony had to 'climb up' to offer the diadem. Cf. Wiseman 172–3: Antony 'had probably come up by the steps at the back' of the new Caesarian *rostra*, whose platform was some 3.7 metres high. **on a golden throne:** an honour granted in early 44, and possibly depicted on coins of 43 (*RRC*, no. 491). It caused offence (Suet. 76.1). Cf. 66.6 with 66.4 n.; Weinstock 272–3. **wearing rich triumphal dress.** In my n. on *Ant.* 12.2 I attempted to distinguish the elements in C.'s dress that were genuinely 'triumphal' (such as perhaps the golden crown visible on coin portraits) from those more redolent of the Alban kings ('the dress the kings once wore' (Dio 44.6.1 and 11.1, Weinstock 107–9, 271)), such as a purple toga (rather than the more richly embroidered triumphal equivalent)—not, of course, that anyone had accurate knowledge by now of what the kings had *really* worn. But M. Beard, *The Roman Triumph* (2007), 276, is doubtless right to insist that this sort of distinction could not have been drawn by contemporary observers. She and I agree that various traditions—triumphal, ancient kings, Hellenistic monarchy, divinity—all contributed as C. sought to present, and his audience to grasp, the character of his rule.

An important conclusion remains: 'The Roman people were not antiquarians or theorists: they may not have known quite what to make of C.'s insignia, but in their eyes the diadem could still be offered and refused as signifying a *regnum* which he did not yet possess' (my n. on *Ant.* 12.2).

61.5. Antony was one of those running the sacred race, for he was consul. In fact he was running the race not as consul but as captain of one of the three colleges of *Luperci*, the *Iulii*, now added to the ancient *Fabiani* and *Quinctiales* as an honour to C. (Weinstock 332–3). This emphasis on Antony as consul may derive from Cic. *Phil.* 2.85, stressing that C. was 'your colleague' to emphasize Antony's humiliating subservience.

Here and in *Ant.*, P. mentions only Antony, following Cic. *Phil.* 2.85 (esp. 'you alone, you scoundrel, were found...'); other sources do the same, with the exception of Nic. Dam. 71–2, who says that

'Licinius', Cassius Longinus, and P. Casca were the first to offer the diadem: Licinius laid it at C.'s feet, Cassius with Casca lifted it on to his knees, and only then did Antony come up and place it on C.'s head. It is unlikely to be coincidence that Cassius and a Casca figured among the conspirators, and it may also be that 'Licinius' conceals the name of another conspirator, L. Cinna (68.6 n.), and 'P. Casca' should in fact be 'C. Casca' (66.7 n.): so Toher, ad loc. and in F. Cairns and E. Fantham (eds), *Caesar against Liberty* (2003), 141–2. Possibly, then, that whole version was a fabrication either to blacken the tyrannicides as 'hypocrites and cowards' (so E. Hohl, *Klio*, 34 (1941–2), 92–117 at 108) or to represent them as continuing the manipulative game of overdoing the honours (57.3); but it may also be that, as Toher argues, Nic. Dam. has accurate material after all, and that the future conspirators were indeed playing this manipulative game. Dio 44.9 gives a similar interpretation of the crowning of the *statues*, §8 n., and that certainly seems to be Nic.'s own interpretation here: the nuance of his Greek suggests that Cassius in particular was only *pretending* goodwill. **a diadem with a laurel crown wound around it.** Thus also Nic. Dam. 71; the laurel may have been to conceal the diadem before it was offered, or perhaps C. was being invited to put on both laurel and diadem together. The diadem was a simple cloth strip, usually white, worn as a headband: it was a familiar symbol of Hellenistic kingship. From Cicero on (*Phil.* 2.86, 3.12, 13.17), most sources speak in terms of Antony placing the diadem on C.'s head, as does P. himself at *Ant.* 12.3. But C. was already wearing a *golden* crown (Cic. *Phil.* 2.85, Dio 44.11.2), presumably the crown visible on his coin portraits (on which see Crawford, *RRC* i. 488 n. 1). Perhaps Antony tried to remove that crown, though given C.'s show of reluctance that would imply an unseemly tussle; perhaps the diadem would be wound round C.'s forehead below the crown, as in Hellenistic coronations a diadem was added to the Macedonian and/or Persian headwear that was already in place (Weinstock 339, Ramsey on Cic. *Phil.* 2.85); or perhaps P. is right here and the diadem was simply offered.

A similar theme had figured prominently in Roman partisan exchanges eighty-nine years earlier, when opponents claimed that a gesture of Tiberius Gracchus implied that he aspired after the diadem (*Gracch.* 19.3, cf. 14.3): that may be recalled here (Intr., p. 35).

61.6 the people cried loudly in approval ... again everyone cheered. The sources mostly agree with Cic. *Phil.* 2.85 that the popular reaction approved C.'s rejection more than Antony's offer; the exception is Nic. Dam. 72, who has the nearest in the crowd encouraging C. to accept the diadem and those in the distance applauding him when he rejected it (though Nic. may be implying that those within C.'s sight thought it prudent to strike an enthusiastic note). But Toher thinks that Nic. Dam. may be right about the popular enthusiasm for C. to become king (n. on Nic. Dam. 71–5). **Caesar rejected it:** throwing it into the crowd, says Nic. Dam. 72, though it clearly remained available to be sent elsewhere later in his narrative (§7 n.). Nic. Dam. may be elaborating Cic. *Phil.* 2.85–6, who speaks of C.'s 'throwing away' the diadem: but that could just mean 'removing' it (so Ramsey, ad loc.) or 'throwing it down' at his feet.

61.7. the crown: i.e. , the laurel crown in which the diadem was concealed; despite *Ant.* 12.7 (below), one would assume that the diadem was sent too, whether or not the two were still wound together. **to be taken and dedicated on the Capitol:** to Jupiter Optimus Maximus (Nic. Dam. 73, Suet. 79.2) as 'the only king of the Romans' (Dio 44.11.3). Contrast *Ant.* 12.7, where the diadem is placed on one of C.'s statues: that may reflect the alternative version of Nic. Dam. 75, where Antony tells some bystanders to place the diadem on a nearby statue. This all looks like confusion with the separate story of §8, and in *Ant.* P. uses that version as a transition to a brief mention of the tribunes' instructions to take down the diadem and C.'s removal of the tribunes: that, presumably, is why he uses that version there but not here, where he wishes to allow the tribunes fuller and separate treatment.

Antony ordered an inscription to be made in the *fasti* as an additional note on 15 February: 'M. Antony, consul, on the instructions of the people offered kingship to C. Caesar, dictator for life. Caesar refused' (Cic. *Phil.* 2.87).

61.8. His statues were also seen decorated with royal diadems: or perhaps a single statue decorated with a combination of laurel crown and diadem (cf. §5 n.), as Suet. 79.1 and App. 2.108.449 suggest ('a laurel bound with a white fillet'). *Ant.* 12.7, Dio 44.9.2, and Nic. Dam. 69 similarly have only a single statue, according to Nic. and Dio 'on the rostra': the rostra, symbolic as they were of frank and open public speech, become a charged setting in these weeks, 60.4, 61.4 nn. Plutarch makes statues a suggestive theme as well: Intr., p. 30. Despite

P.'s ordering here, this was in fact earlier than the Lupercalia, as Nic. Dam. 71 makes explicit. Suet. says that it was on C.'s return from the 'Latin sacrifice', i.e. the festival on the Alban Mount on 26 January, 60.3 n.; Dio 44.10.1 says it was earlier than that. For the reasons for P.'s ordering, 57–61, 60.3 nn.: we should not draw any conclusion about the order in his source, as Dobesch does, *AS* i. 217. **Two tribunes, Flavius and Marullus:** L. Caesetius Flavius and C. Epidius Marullus, *MRR* 323–4. It is a telling irony that C.'s insulting treatment of *tribunes* should play so critical a part in his fall, given the capital he had made of the humiliation of his own tribunes, 31.2–3: Intr., p. 33. **the first to hail Caesar as king:** 60.3 n.: this may confirm the association of the statue-crowning with the events of 26 January, though it is also possible that the connection of Flavius and Marullus with both incidents led to their conflation. **and hauled them off to prison:** so also App. 2.108.449, though he has just a single man imprisoned, and it is for crowning the statue; 108.451 (possibly but not certainly a doublet, as Dobesch, *AS* i. 338 thought) then has the tribunes *summon* the man who began the shouting. Suet. 79.1 and Dio 44.10.1 also have just a single culprit, for Suet. the man responsible for crowning the statue, for Dio the first man to shout.

61.9. called the men true Brutuses. The 'true Brutuses' aspect is not mentioned by our other sources for these events, and at *Ant.* 12.7 P. just has 'the people escorted them with enthusiastic applause': it is presumably P.'s own additional touch, as he begins here to contrive his transition to the conspirators. **Brutus was the one who overthrew the regal dynasty:** traditionally, in 509 BCE, following which Brutus became one of the Republic's first two consuls: see *OCD*[4], s.v. Iunius Brutus, Lucius, and T. P. Wiseman, *Unwritten Rome* (2008), 293–305. His statue stood on the Capitol, suggestively placed among those of the kings (*Brut.*1.1, Dio 43.45.4, etc.). For P.'s version of the immediate aftermath of the regime change and L. Iunius Brutus' part in it, see *Popl.* 1–9. The famous story that Brutus executed his sons for plotting against the new Republic (*Popl.* 3–6) allowed doubts whether the conspirator Brutus was a true descendant; P. discusses the issue at *Brut.* 1.6–8, quoting the view of Posidonius that there was a further infant son who survived, and this interpretation seems reflected at *Popl.* 3.5, where L. Brutus has 'several' children and only 'the two who were adult' are implicated. Another problem, as P. himself notes at *Brut.* 1.6, was that the Iunii

Bruti were a plebeian *gens*, and one would expect the first consul to have been a patrician.

61.10. Caesar was furious.   It appears that he objected, and then the tribunes issued some edict in defence of their freedom of speech. C.'s more decisive action was stimulated by that edict. But the details of this sequence are disputed, and the edict (mentioned only by Dio 44.10.2) has been doubted, though probably unnecessarily: cf. Dobesch, *AS* i. 101–43 (plausibly arguing at 111–14 that C.'s speech against the tribunes was one of those that were published, Suet. 55.3), H. Kloft, *Hist.* 29 (1980), 315–34, Toher on Nic. Dam. 69, and Woodman on Vell. 2.68.4. **Marullus and his colleague:** the idiomatic phrase (7.5, 29.1, 30.5, 31.2, 68.7 nn.) that means literally 'the associates (or 'followers') of Marullus' and can sometimes mean just 'Marullus'; here it clearly means 'Marullus and Flavius'. App 2.108.451–2 uses the same phrase, and perhaps Marullus was felt to be the dominant partner. **dismissed . . . from office:** whence Shakespeare's elegantly ominous 'are put to silence' (*JC* i. ii. 283). The dismissal was apparently on the proposal of their co-tribune C. Helvius Cinna (Dio 44.10.3, 46.49.2: cf. 68.3 n., *MRR* 324), and they were then expelled from the senate: C. here acted as censor according to Vell. 2.68.5. There were precedents both for such censorial action (M. Duronius in 97, *MRR* 6–7) and for the involvement of fellow-tribunes in sponsoring such proposals (most obviously with Ti. Gracchus in 133, *Gracch.*15: Thommen, 34, 92–6). This gesture of tribunicial solidarity in censure was clearly felt to be important: a year later P. Servilius Casca was similarly expelled from the senate on the proposal of his fellow-tribune P. Titius (*MRR* 340, iii.194–5). Now Marullus and Flavius went into, perhaps notionally voluntary, exile. The stated reasons may well have included the charge, as Liv. *per.* 116 and Val. Max. 5.7.2 have it, 'that they were stirring up unpopularity against C. as being one who had aspirations to kingship': that could be taken as, and perhaps was, an insinuation that their treatment of the culprits was so heavy-handed as to suggest that there was a genuine regal issue at stake when in fact there was not. That is consistent with the emphasis of App. 2.108.452 and Nic. Dam. 69. But, if that was C.'s (or Helvius Cinna's) argument, it failed to take into account how readily the punishment could be taken as an indication that C. indeed wanted kingship and resented any gesture of opposition. Cf. Suet. 79.1: 'either because he was annoyed that the suggestion of kingship had not gone down well or because, as he said himself, he had been deprived of the glory of refusing it.' According to Vell. 2.68.4, C. also emphasized that he had not used his dictatorial powers to impose a harsher punishment, and 'bore witness that he greatly regretted having to make the choice between acting out of character or allowing his dignity to be damaged': that echoes C.'s *clementia* (34.7, 48.4, 57.4 nn.) and his distinctive concern for his *dignitas* (16.1, 30.1 nn.), but there was a genuine broader point that the dignity of the dictatorship called for defence. **in his invective against them.** According to Nic. Dam. 69, this was in a senate-meeting summoned in the temple of Concord (an expressive setting), and C. also accused them of planting the statue diadem themselves as part of a conspiracy to kill him (i.e., presumably, to endanger his life by creating such an impression of unacceptable tyranny: Dobesch, *AS* i. 121–2). Thus Nic. Dam. 'has C. see a false conspiracy even as he fails to perceive the real conspiracy that is forming against him' (Toher). **insulting to the people as well.** P. reverts to his favoured theme: 57–61 n., Intr., p. 21–2, 59–60. Presumably the point is that C.'s ridiculing of the tribunes constituted also a ridicule of those who had applauded them and, assuming that the reference to the legendary Brutus is felt (see next n.), had viewed them in such an idealized way: cf. Dobesch, *AS* i. 108 and n. 23, 133–5.

As at 35.6 (n.), it was embarrassing for C. to be so cavalier with tribunes' rights after making so much of them in going to war (31.3); and, as at 35.8 (n.), his treatment of them, however masked in constitutionalism, could easily be seen as 'tyrannical'—i.e. at verifying the charges by precisely the way at which he took offence at them.

There was a further brush with a tribune that P. omits: Pontius Aquila, alone of the tribunes, refused to rise in C.'s honour as he passed by, and C.—so Suet. 78.2 says—angrily cried out 'so, Aquila! Act the tribune, and claim back the state from me!' The next few days (Suet. goes on) he added to every promise he made, 'provided, that is, that Pontius Aquila permits'. Pontius was tribune in 45 rather than 44 (*MRR* 308), so this belongs before the Flavius and Marullus incidents: as his tribunate terminated on 9 December, it may have been the first of the final sequence of C.'s misjudgements.

'Brutuses' and 'Cumaeans'. The inhabitants of Aeolic Cyme had a reputation for simple-mindedness (Strabo 13.3.6); Philogelos 154–82 duly collects 'there was a Cumaean...' jokes, some of them quite good (e.g. the first: a bystander at a funeral asked who was being buried, and the Cumaean mourner said 'the man lying there'). 'Brutuses' too will reflect the Latin *bruti* = 'stupid', but there is evidently a hint of the expeller of the Tarquins as well, particularly as legend had it that he had concealed his disaffection by himself pretending stupidity (Livy 1.56.8 etc.). C.'s point may therefore have been 'you're not *that* sort of Brutus: you're just the Cumaean, stupid sort'.

Still, there is presumably (*pace* Garzetti) a double meaning in 'Cumaean' as well. For Romans the important Cumae was the one in Campania: that was the home of the Sibyl, the Sibyl was in the news (60.2 n.) and may well have been mentioned by the tribunes themselves; and Epidius may even have been a native of the area, where the name is not infrequent (Kloft, art. cit., 329 n. 62). In that case 'Marullus and Flavius become "stupid regicides" who have arrived from Cumae spreading unbelievable prophecies' (A. Corbeill, *Controlling Laughter* (1996), 201). That allows a further 'Cumaean' twist, for retrospectively C. would be sensed as speaking with more mantic insight than he realized with this talk of 'Brutuses'; and people may also have recalled that the first Brutus too had drawn strength from knowledge of an oracle, in his case one from Delphi (Livy 1.56.4–12).

62: The Conspiracy

P.'s fullest account of the conspiracy is given in *Brutus* (8–13), there telling it from the conspirators' viewpoint and giving a much fuller account of their motives: the cross-reference to *Brutus* at §8 thus excuses and explains the brevity on such matters here, just as a similar cross-reference to *Caesar* at *Brut.* 9.9 explains the brevity there on the activities of C.'s flatterers and the offence they caused. This is in line with the 'law of biographical relevance' (Intr., p. 22), and thus *Brutus* but not *Caesar* also discusses why the conspirators selected the senate for their attack (14.2–3) and their discussion whether Antony should be killed too (18.5–6, cf. *Ant.* 13.3–4). The narrative of the morning of the Ides will then be divided along similar lines at 64–5 (n.) and *Brut.* 14–16. C. Stoltz might therefore have cited these cases when he showed that P.'s cross-references could not simply be deleted as interpolations (*Zur relativen Chronologie der Parallelbiographien Plutarchs* (1929), 20–2, 43–8): in these cases as in the others analysed by Stoltz, the narrative would have been constructed differently had P. been unable to economize by making reference to other *Lives* in the series. Cf. 35.2 n.

As we have seen (57–61 n.), in *Caesar* P. has delayed any concentration on the conspirators to the point where C.'s own actions are already precipitating his downfall, and the narrative continues here to concentrate on C.'s own treatment and view of Brutus and Cassius. One consequence is to deflect attention away from the classic question of the moral rectitude of their act (Intr., p. 20): Brutus' 'ingratitude' (§6) becomes relevant only in the sense that C. cannot believe in it, and hence is over-trusting. So once again the focus rests on C.'s own contribution to his fall.

The close similarities with Appian's narrative continue (nn.), but there are also an increased number of non-Appianic items such as the 'Brutus will wait for this flesh' and the 'thin and pale' stories of §§ 6, 9–10. These may well come from the reading that Plutarch had undertaken 'for' *Brutus*: cf. Intr., pp. 37, 51–2.

62.1. the ordinary people: see 57–61 n. **turned to Marcus Brutus.** So Brutus is immediately more emphasized than Cassius: that is largely because of the artfully managed transition from 61.8, but it also reflects the way that the tradition came to concentrate more on Brutus where moral rights and wrongs were in point, though just as much on Cassius when it came to the campaigning issues of 43–42 BCE: cf. E. Rawson in I. S. Moxon, J. D. Smart, and A. J. Woodman (eds), *Past Perspectives* (1986), 101–19 = *Roman Culture and Society* (1991), 488–507. Brutus has already been briefly mentioned at 46.4 (n.) and, with Cassius, at 57.5. **He was thought to descend from that ancient Brutus.** P. does not here commit himself to the truth of this 'descent': that may reflect the difficulties aired at *Brut.* 1.6–8 (61.9 n. above), but anyway the relevant point for 44 BCE is what was popularly 'thought'. **on his mother's he belonged to the Servilii.** his mother Servilia was the daughter of Q. Servilius Caepio, a significant player in the political wranglings of the 90s (*OCD*[4], s.v. 'Servilius', no. 2), and of his wife Livia; Livia's second husband was Cato's father M. Porcius Cato. Most strikingly, P. does not mention Servilia's notorious affair with C. himself, a theme that is emphasized at *Brut.* 5.2–4 and *C.min.* 24.1–3 and mentioned in the present context by App. 2.112.468–9. As at 8.2 (n.), this *Life* again shies away from personalia, even in this case where we might expect this to have affected Brutus' and C.'s relationship. Cf. Intr., p. 23. **another distinguished family:** and also, as P. makes clear at *Brut.* 1.5 but not here, one with its own tradition of anti-tyrannical bloodshed, for Servilius Ahala was remembered as the killer of the would-be tyrant Sp. Maelius in 439 BCE. **the nephew ... of Cato,** who was Servilia's half-brother (above). **and son-in-law:** so also *Brut.*

2.1 and Dio 44.13.1, though in fact Cato was already dead when his daughter Porcia married Brutus in 45 BCE. Porcia is allowed a memorable role at *Brut.* 13 and in Shakespeare, but in this *Life* P. retains his strong focus on C. himself.

62.2. He had received honours and favours at Caesar's hands: 57.5 n. Besides the praetorship and anticipated consulship (§4), these included the governorship of Cisalpine Gaul in 46–45 (*Brut.* 6.10–12, *MRR* 301, 311). **these had blunted his own zeal to overthrow the monarchy.** *Brutus* leaves a different picture, portraying Brutus as 'listening to his friends who were constantly warning him that he must not allow himself to be charmed or softened up by Caesar, but make a point of refusing a tyrant's generosity and favours' (7.7). In *Caesar* P. is less concerned with Brutus' moral stature; the effect is also to put more weight on the effect of the pamphlets and of public opinion in bringing so sudden a turnaround.

62.3. he had been rescued at Pharsalus: 46.4 (n.), *Brut.* 6.1; cf. 48.1 n. for his revealing conversation with C. after his 'rescue'. **he had even been allowed to extend this rescue to many of his friends:** so also *Brut.* 56(3).4, where this becomes a crucial point in discussing the morality of Brutus' turn against his benefactor: Intr., p. 20.

62.4. the most distinguished of the praetorships: i.e. the urban praetorship, as *Brut.* 7.1 and App. 2.112.466 explicitly say: the *praetor urbanus* heard cases of dispute between citizens, the *praetor peregrinus* (4.2 n.) those where a non-citizen was involved. The elections for the praetorships of 44 were apparently held in December 45. Caesar had in fact raised the number of praetorships from eight to first ten, then (for 45) fourteen, then (for 44) sixteen. **He was also going to be consul in three years' time:** i.e. in 41 BCE: 58.1 n. **Cassius had been his rival:** for the praetorship, P. says at *Brut.* 7.1, and App. 2.112.466–7 agrees; but P.'s language here gives the impression that it was for the consulship of 41 (58.1 n.), and that is also the version of Vell. 2.56.3, C. 'had not managed to win over the one [Brutus] by promising him the consulship but had offended the other [Cassius] by putting him off'. Cic. *Phil.* 8.27, however, implies that Brutus and Cassius were to be consuls together, presumably in 41: possibly Ciceronian wishful thinking, but it does not sound like that. Possibly Vell. and Cicero are both right, if the promise to Brutus was given before that to Cassius.

As at 5.1 (n.), the word for 'rivalry' is quite strong, and suggests some wrangling between the pair: *Brut.* 7 gives more detail, including the suggestion that C. might have provoked the disharmony himself. W. Huß, *WJb* 3 (1977), 115–25, stresses the relations between the two, arguing that before the Ides they had little in common.

62.5. Cassius' claim was the fairer.   As *Brut.* 7.3 makes clear, Cassius' claim would have rested in particular on his military record: he several times emerges as a voice of caution during Crassus' Parthian campaign of 54–53 BCE (*Crass.* 18, 20, 22, 23, 27), and eventually managed an enterprising getaway (*Crass.* 29). He had then organized the defence of Syria, crushed a revolt in Judaea, and in 51 defeated Parthian invaders near Antioch (*MRR* 229, 237, 242). **he himself would not pass over Brutus:** slightly differently at *Brut.* 7.4, 'the first prize must be given to Brutus', corresponding to that *Life*'s interpretation that the rivalry was over the most prestigious praetorship ('the first prize') rather than the consulship (§4 n.).

62.6. and accused Brutus—the conspiracy had already begun.   Like §§9–10, this prepares for 63.1 (n.) and the question whether the assassination was anticipated. In fact the notion was in the air as early as September 46, for Cicero acknowledges and exploits the danger in *pro Marcello* (21–3). Suet. 75.5 also speaks of multiple 'conspiracies', to which C. simply responded with edicts indicating that he was aware of them. **'Brutus will wait for this flesh':** so also *Brut.* 8.3, in the less punchy version 'What? Do you not imagine Brutus would wait for this poor piece of flesh?' **The implication was . . . ingratitude or dishonour.** For this emphasis on C.'s misreading, cf. 62 n. above. As *Brut.* 8.3–4 brings out, the more interesting implication would seem to be that C. envisaged Brutus as a possible and willing successor, at least to a position of 'first man in Rome' (8.4) if not to one of tyranny or monarchy.

62.7. covering with writings his tribunal and the chair where he sat for official business as praetor: so also *Brut.* 9.7. Most translators from Amyot and North onwards have assumed that this means 'papers' ('billets et écritaux', Amyot, whence North's 'sundry papers'; Perrin is more non-committal). In fact we should think of graffiti, here as on the statues: that is particularly clear at *Brut.* 10.6, where Cassius goads Brutus by saying 'do you think it is weavers and

shopkeepers that are *writing on* your tribunal', and the 'writings' of
Gracch. 8.10 (below) are clearly graffiti. App. 2.112.469 conveys the
same impression, lumping together all the slogans as things 'secretly
written on the statues of the ancient Brutus and on the place of
justice'. Shakespeare follows North in talking of 'this paper' (*JC* I.
iii. 142–6, etc.): he makes it all a machiavellian plot of Cassius. Roman
graffiti were extremely important as a mode of communicating popular dissent, especially in extreme situations such as those of the
Gracchan agitation or of 44 BCE: on this see a forthcoming article
by Robert Morstein-Marx, who agrees that it is graffiti rather than
papers that are here in point. He suggests that these graffiti represented a furtive nocturnal retort to the night-time decoration of the
statues (61.8 n.): 'the symbolic war being fought out in the chilly
nights of January, 44 was a complex one, with moves and counter-
moves ranging from the Forum and the Capitol and back again.'
'Brutus! You are asleep!' or possibly 'are you asleep?' Only a question
mark distinguishes the two formulations in Greek: we cannot be sure
that the original graffito artist was careful to add punctuation, and it
may never have been clear which was meant. The same goes for **'You
are no Brutus'**, or alternatively 'Are you not Brutus?' (though the
version in *Brut.*, 'you really are no Brutus', is more difficult to take as
a question). The statue of the legendary Brutus (61.9 n.) was also
daubed with graffiti along the lines 'we wish you were alive now!'
(*Brut.* 9.6, etc.). That is particularly emblematically charged if Morstein-Marx (above) is right to infer from *Brut.* 1.8, the observed
likeness between Brutus and the statue of his ancestor, that 'the statue
was itself a kind of touchstone of Brutan identity by the late Republic'.
If so, this had been true for some time before 44: in the *Brut.* passage
Plutarch is citing Posidonius, who died in 51 BCE. Suet. 80.3 also
mentions a graffito on a statue of C. himself, 'Brutus threw out the
kings, and so was made first consul; this man threw out the consuls,
and was at the end made king'.

Several graffiti at Pompeii similarly have 'you are asleep!' (*dormis*),
e.g. *CIL* iv. 1190, 'wool-scrubber, you are asleep!', or 7464, 'Sutoria
Primigenia and her family say, Ceius Secundus for duumvir! Astylus,
you are asleep!' Cf. also the clarion call that Sallust's Cato gives to his
indolent colleagues, 'wake up some time and put your hands to the
state!' (*Cat.* 52.5).

Tiberius Gracchus was similarly roused to action when 'the people themselves...inscribed writings (*grammata*) on porticoes, monuments, and the walls of houses, calling upon him to recover the public land for the poor' (*Gracch.* 8.10): cf. Intr., p. 35.

62.8. his eagerness for glory: in Greek *philotimon*, a key word and concept: see 58.4 n., Intr., p. 69. **Cassius...began to press him harder than before:** more details at *Brut.* 8–10 and, evidently from the same source, App. 2.113.470–2. **as we have explained in the *Brutus*:** *Brut.* 8.6–7, instancing a case when C. appropriated some lions in Megara that Cassius had procured for a show (though, as Garzetti suggested, that may be a confusion with his brother L. Cassius Longinus, who we know was in the area, 43.1–2 n.: cf. App.'s confusion at App. 2.88.370–2, 48.1 n.). D. F. Epstein, *Lat.* 46 (1987), 566–70, and R. Storch, *AHB* 9 (1995), 45–52, argue that such personal grievances were more important in the conspiracy than the ideological emphasis of the tradition allows. We cannot know; perhaps the conspirators did not fully know themselves; but any follower of contemporary politics knows that, when the knives come out for a struggling leader, career disappointments and smarting pride do play a big part. P., more clearly in *Brutus* than here, allows space for personal resentment, Republican (or at least anti-tyrannical) idealism, and the charisma of Brutus all to play a part. For the cross-reference, cf. 62 n. above; for the implications for P.'s method of work, Intr., p. 37.

62.9. was in fact suspicious of Cassius: again (§6 n.) preparing for 63.1. **'I do not like him: he is too pale.'** Cf. §10 n.

62.10. that Antony and Dolabella were plotting. P. gives more detail of the squabbles of Antony and Dolabella (51.3 n.) at *Ant.* 9.1–4 and 11.3–6. Dolabella there is described at 9.1 as 'a young man with a young man's revolutionary ambitions' (see my n. ad loc.), but that seems to refer to his plans for e.g. debt reform rather than to any danger that C. personally might have to **fear**. The version of C.'s remark at *Brut.* 8.2 does not have 'fear', but 'it is not these fat, long-haired fellows *who bother me*, but the pale and thin ones'. If that is the original version, the point was probably that C. would prefer irritating squabblers to dangerous conspirators. But *Ant.* 11.6 also has 'fear', and so does *Sayings of Kings and Generals* 206e.

In all three of P.'s versions, **fat** suggests intellectual slowness as well as gastronomic self-indulgence, and **long-haired** the effete affectations of the young elite; **thin and pale** in contrast points to the untanned and unexercised body shape of the intellectuals who have spent far too long indoors or in the shade. Cf. my n. on *Ant.* 11.6, where P. quotes the same remark of C., and Dover's on Ar. *Clouds* 103. **meaning Cassius and Brutus.** So the train of thought has brought the narrative round to suggesting that C. *did* suspect Brutus after all, despite the emphasis of §6.

'Let me have men about me that are fat, | sleek-headed men, and such as sleep-a-nights. | Yond Cassius has a lean and hungry look; | He thinks too much: such men are dangerous' (Shakespeare, *JC* I. ii. 191–4). 'Such as sleep-a-nights' is a new Shakespearian touch, appropriate for a world in which the insomniac Brutus (Act II, scene i, etc.) will prove such a threat. But notice that Shakespeare limits C.'s fears to Cassius (Intr., p. 74). That is perhaps influenced by P.'s own limitation of the first 'he is too pale' to Cassius at §9, but it also prepares for the distinction of characters of Cassius and Brutus that will be important later in the play: that is inspired by P.'s own characterization in *Brutus*, but the distinction is not important here in *Caesar*. Shakespeare's 'he thinks too much', reflecting the same suspicion of the intellectual as in the Greek, is then developed accordingly in his further remark on Cassius, 'he reads much, | he is a great observer, and he looks | quite through the deeds of men' (I. ii. 200–2): that presages the shrewdness of Cassius which contrasts with Brutus' political naïveté, most strikingly at III. i. 231–43, where he sees the dangers of letting Antony speak. Shakespeare indeed has Cassius as an even shrewder figure here, for he makes him the author of the graffiti campaign of §8. Morstein-Marx (§8 n.) wonders whether that might even be right.

63: Omens; the Night before the Ides

63.1 introduces the notion of 'fate', and the supernatural dimension, hitherto rather played down in the *Life* (Intr., p. 31), is then developed in the list of omens and other uncanny occurrences: this fits P.'s general habit of limiting talk of fate and destiny to matters of great significance, on the level of the birth of Rome or the revolution from Republic to Principate (47 n., S. Swain, *AJP* 110 (1989), 272–302), and also of using such language and such catalogues of omens to prepare for and separate off narrative climaxes (my nn. on

Ant. 56.6 and 60.2–7), in this *Life* first C.'s triumph (43.3–6, 47 nn.)
and now his disaster. And the earlier turning point of this *Life* was the
Rubicon, introduced by C.'s own mother-dream, 32.9; his end is
introduced by a wife-dream here, §§8–10. In each case they might
have warned him to desist; in each case he hesitates; in each case he
still goes on, first to glory and now to death.

P.'s language at 63.1 could in itself mean '[C.'s] fate *was* more
unavoidable than it was unexpected', and 62.6–10 has shown that
rumours of conspiracy were in the air: that does suggest that the death
was not 'unexpected', and the omens of this chapter evidently themselves encouraged expectations ('for ... to show what was to come'
(63.1)). But whose expectations? Were those suspicions and denun-
ciations of 62.6–10 enough to make C. himself expect, or half-expect,
assassination? His own outburst at §7 could be taken in different
ways. Is his preference for 'the unexpected' death to be taken simply
as an indication that he did not expect what was coming? Or that
sudden death was weighing on his mind? Or is his 'crying out'—the
word marks unusual behaviour—itself to be taken as a sort of omen
(as with an uncanny utterance of Brutus in a different context, *Brut.*
24.6)? At least by the end of the chapter, some unease if not 'expectation' of C. is certainly seen, just as there was a muted sense of 'fear' at
the end of ch. 62 (n.). Cf. Intr., p. 29, on P.'s enigmatic characterization here and the contrast with Alexander's explicitly bizarre psychology as he neared his end.

On these and earlier prodigies, cf. esp. Weinstock 342–6;
E. Rawson, *JRS* 68 (1978), 142–6 = *Roman Culture and Society*
(1991), 307–12.

**63.1. Yet fate, it would seem, is not so much unexpected as
unavoidable.**   The formulation is not original: Cic. *Div.* 1.119, discussing the omens of mid-February (§4 n.), makes 'Quintus' say that
'the immortal gods sent him these portents so that[27] he would see his
coming death, not that he would try to avoid it'—but that makes it
explicitly a matter of C.'s own expectations, whereas P. is more
enigmatic, 63 n. Other parallels to the thought are collected by
Pease and by Wardle in their nn. on Cic. *Div.* 1.119: notice in
particular Tac. *Hist.* 1.18.1 on Galba's insistence on ignoring ill
omens and going forth on 10 January 69 CE, a sequence that has

---

[27] Or, less likely, 'with the result that', as Wardle argues ad loc.

several features in common with this: 'he despised such things as matters of chance—or perhaps what is fated cannot be avoided, however much it may be signalled in advance'.

63.2. the blazing lights in the sky.   Both the blazing lights and the strange night-time sounds figure in Ovid's list of evil omens at *Met.* 15.783–93. **the strange sounds... at night.** It was the arms of Mars, according to Dio 44.17.2, that were deposited in the residence of the pontifex maximus (§9 n.) and now started noisily moving around. **or the birds that swooped down into the forum by day:** a difficult passage. 'By day' translates my emendation *hēmerinous* for the *erēmous* of the manuscripts: *erēmous* would mean 'isolated', possibly pointing to the omen recorded by Suet. 81.3 (below) but unintelligible in the absence of further detail (*Ant.* 60.7 shows what would be needed). Ziegler's *anēmerous*, accepted by Flacelière, would mean 'wild', but that seems pointless: most swooping birds are wild. 'By day' would give a contrast with the strange night-time flashes and noises: bad omens beset Rome through all twenty-four hours. (Amyot indeed expanded his translation to 'des oiseaux solitaires [i.e. *erēmous*], qui, *en plein jour*, se vinrent poser sur la grande place...', whence North's 'solitary birds to be seen at noondays...': Shakespeare could do nothing with the 'solitary' but could with the 'noonday', 'and yesterday the bird of night did sit, | even at noonday, upon the market-place, | hooting and shrieking' (*JC* i. iii. 26–8.) Presumably the point is not simply of a swooping flock coming into land, though that would be striking enough in a crowded forum, but rather particular sorts of birds that signalled bad luck (whence Herwerden's *dusphēmous*, 'of ill omen', but that is too distant from the manuscript reading): for instance, owls (Obsequens 26, 30, 32, and several other cases), a bad omen when they come by day (Plin. *NH* 10.36: cf. Shakespeare's neat twist, above), or the mysterious 'firebird' (Obsequens 40, 51, Plin. *NH* 10.36), or 'another, unknown bird' of equally ill omen (Obsequens 27a).

This may, however, be a distant variant on the omen recorded by Suet. 81.3 for the day before the Ides: a 'kingly bird' (i.e. a wren) carrying a laurel branch flew into the 'Pompeian *curia*' (66.1 n.) and was chased and torn apart by other birds gathering from a nearby grove.

63.3. the philosopher Strabo narrates: Strabo of Amiseia (*OCD*[4]): as well as the extant *Geography*, he wrote an influential history in forty-seven books. The present item presumably figured in his history, as the word for 'narrates' (*historei*) suggests, and Jacoby prints it as *FGrH* 91 F 19: P. quotes the history also at *Lucull.* 28.8 (F 9), and the further quotation at *Sulla* 26.4 is also presumably from that work (F 8). Cf. Intr., p. 48–9. Why, then, Strabo 'the philosopher'? Strabo himself tells us that he studied philosophy (16.2.24) with the Peripatetic Xenarchus (14.5.4), his geographical work shows Stoic tendencies and philosophical interests (D. Dueck, *Strabo of Amasia* (2000), 62–9), and he begins it by presenting it as a 'philosophical project' (1.1.1, cf. 1.1.22–3). Yet we know of no more conventionally philosophical work, and this description is still striking. It is not, however, isolated: Suda similarly has 'Strabo: a man of Ameiseia and a philosopher' and Stephanus of Byzantium has 'the Stoic philosopher'; and *Lucull.* 28.8 is closely similar, 'Strabo, another philosopher [i.e. as well as Antiochus, whom he has just quoted], says in his *Historical Notes* that . . . '. Presumably P.'s point in both passages is to add authority: 'philosophers' are assumed to be more critical and less credulous than others. Cf. 'Posidonius the philosopher' at *Brut.* 1.7, recounting the item on Brutus' descent (61.9, 62.7 nn.) that almost certainly figured in his *History* rather than his philosophical works, and similarly 'Nicolaus the philosopher' at *Brut.* 53.5.

63.4. Caesar himself found that the heart was missing from an animal he was sacrificing: also mentioned by Cic. *Div.* 1.119 (followed by Val. Max. 1.6.13 and Plin. *NH* 11.186) and 2.36–7: it was a 'prime bull'. Cf. Wardle's comm. on 1.119. Cicero adds that Spurinna (§5 n.) warned of a danger 'that counsel and life might fail, as both come from the heart', and the next day there was an animal with no 'head' to the liver; he also dates the first omen to 'the first day when C. sat on the golden throne and came out in purple dress', i.e. at or before the Lupercalia on 15 February (cf. 61.4 nn.). If it is right to connect this with Spurinna's warning that he should 'beware the next thirty days' (§5 n.), that again points to mid-February: counting inclusively, the first day of the thirty should be either 14 or 15 February, depending on whether 44 was a leap year, and it probably was not (A. E. Samuel, *Greek and Roman Chronology* (1972), 156–8). If, then, it was 14 February, then the second, 'headless liver' omen would fall on the day of the Lupercalia, not inappositely given the emblematic importance later that day of C.'s own head and its crown or diadem. The issue is discussed by A. Alföldi, *Caesar in 44 v. Chr.*

(1985), 163–4, Zecchini 72–3, Wardle on Cic. *Div.* 1.119, and (best)
J. T. Ramsey, *CQ* 50 (2000), 445–6.

63.5. a certain soothsayer: Spurinna, possibly a Vestricius Spurinna of illustrious Etruscan ancestry: cf. E. Rawson, *JRS* 68 (1978),
143–6 = *Roman Culture and Society* (1991), 308–12. He had a
prominent role as *haruspex* under C.'s dictatorship, and may have
been the 'leading diviner' who advised C. not to cross to Africa before
winter in 46 (Cic. *Div.* 2.52, cf. 52.2 n.); he may also have been the
haruspex, or one of them, that C. adlected to the senate in 46–45 (Cic.
Fam. 6.18 (218).1). He was notorious enough for Cicero to use his
name in a rather laboured augury-jest at *Fam.* 9.24 (362).2 (but it
misses the joke to infer that he was 'a friend of Cicero', as Weinstock
346 n. 1 has it: Zecchini 74–5 also takes it too literally). It is perilous to
draw from Spurinna any inferences about (elite Etruscan? haruspi-
cal?) opposition to Caesar (thus in particular Zecchini 69–76, and,
more cautiously phrased, G. D. Farney, *Ethnic Identity and Aristocratic Competition in Republican Rome* (2007), 161–2). It is true that
most surviving omen- and auspices-stories of C.'s final years are those
of warnings, often those that he ignores or disingenuously manipu-
lates: cf. 52.2–4 nn., Suet. 59, App. 2.116.488, and notice also the
ambivalence of 43.3–4 (n.). But it is in the nature of historical
memory to dwell on, and doubtless to improve, such material only
when the prophecies or warnings turn out to be justified. And, if the
story is true, Spurinna—who will have believed in his auspices even if
C. did not, and had perhaps himself had got wind of a conspiracy—
may for all we know have genuinely been trying to help: so L. Aigner
Foresti in G. Urso (ed.), *L'Ultimo Cesare* (2000), 19–21.

**to beware of a great danger on the day of March that the Romans
call the Ides.** P. simplifies. Spurinna warned C. 'to beware the next
thirty days as fateful: the last of these was the Ides of March' (Val.
Max. 8.11.2, cf. 'not later than the Ides of March' (Suet. 81.2)). That
points to a warning delivered on 14 or 15 February, §4 n. The basis for
Spurinna's prophecy—*not* astrological—is discussed by J. T. Ramsey,
CQ 50 (2000), 440–54: he also (452) brings out the frequency with
which 'thirty days' figure in such warnings. P.'s limitation to the
single day may owe something to the 'one day' that in tragedy can
be the term of a divinity's anger (Soph. *Ajax* 756–7, and when Medea
asks for only one day's grace at Eur. *Med.* 340 we sense that she too

has superhuman power), or that is enough to bring down even the greatest of powers (Soph. *OT* 436, Aesch. *Pers.* 431–2). **that the Romans call.** P. does not usually make such a meal of explaining Roman calendrical terms (37.3 n., cf. e.g. *Brut.* 10.3 'the Kalends of March'), and this of all dates was hardly unfamiliar to his audience. So, here as at *Brut.* 14.3, the heavy circumlocution is presumably to emphasize the moment.

63.6. as he left for the senate: thus jumping ahead to the context of 64.6. Like Shakespeare (*JC* I. ii. 18–23, III. i. 1–2), P. could have separated the initial prophecy and the final exchange, but combining them here allows a different, more secular group of warnings to dominate when the narrative reaches that stage (64.6–65.4). Val. Max. 8.11.2 puts the exchange with Spurinna at the house of Cn. Domitius Calvinus, Master of the Horse designate for 43, and says that it was 'early'; App. 2.149.619 says 'around dawn', without giving a location. But, if there is anything in P.'s account of the troubled night, that does not suggest that C. left the house early. Suet. 81.4 also puts the encounter later, as C. was about to enter the senate. If Val. Max.'s location is right, it may be that C. took a mild detour on his way to the senate. Calvinus' house, on the south slope of the Velia, was not far from C.'s own: see J. T. Ramsey, *In Pursuit of Wissenschaft: Festschrift... Calder* (2008), 353, though Ramsey believes in an early morning meeting and thinks it was connected with sacrifices for the festival of Anna Perenna that day. Cf. 66 n. **'The Ides of March have come...'** The story is even more beautifully told in the Greek, where the nuancing particles *men dē* could readily imply that a second, contrasting clause was to be anticipated (J. D. Denniston, *The Greek Particles* (2nd edn, 1954), 258–9): C. presumably would have gone on 'but nothing bad has happened'; the soothsayer corrects to 'but they have not gone'. The Latin of Suet. 81.4 is less dramatic, that of Val. Max. 8.11.2 more heavy-footed: 'do you realize the Ides of March have come?' 'Do you realize they have not yet gone?'

63.7. Marcus Lepidus had been entertaining him to dinner. M. Aemilius Lepidus is the future triumvir (*OCD*[4], no. 3). K. Welch, *Hermes*, 123 (1995), 443–54, gives a cool assessment of his abilities and politics under C.: 'it was not only his reliability but his lack of independence and imagination which led to his success during the dictatorship and his humiliating failure after it' (443). Similarly,

L. Hayne, *Acta Classica* 14 (1971), 109–17, 'a natural second-in-command rather than a leader' (111). **'Unexpectedly':** 57.7 n.

The dinner and the remark are also mentioned by Suet. 87. App. 2.115.479 says that it was C. himself who proposed the subject for discussion (Syme, *RP* vi. 127, here goes astray), and that D. Brutus was one of the other guests. In the draft biography of Caesar that Sir Ronald Syme left unfinished at his death in 1989, he memorably reconstituted most of the rest of the guest list: Antony, Dolabella, Hirtius, Pansa, Balbus, and one other (the manuscript is not clear: probably C. Trebonius, as Mark Toher has conjectured from the rest of Syme's argument). If so, it was a *very* businesslike dinner. Syme thought that it was to discuss the wranglings of Antony and Dolabella (51.3, 62.10 nn.).

If there is anything in the story at all, the topic of death—whoever proposed it—had some edge: there was enough talk of assassination in the air (62.6–10, 63.1 nn.) to make sure of that.

adding his personal notes to letters: not quite 'signing', as most translators, but adding personal greetings at the bottom of a document written by a secretary: see F. Millar, *The Emperor in the Roman World* (1977), 221–2; J. Reynolds, *Aphrodisias and Rome* (1982), 47–8. **as usual:** not an endearing habit. C. would also attend to his correspondence at public games, and people took offence (Suet. *Aug.* 45.1).

63.8. his wife: Calpurnia, 14.8 n. Note that C. and his wife are still sharing a bed, which is not necessarily what we would expect: the bedroom scene mixes the domestic and the macabre. **suddenly all the doors and windows of the room flew open.** Suet. 81.3 and Dio 44.17.2 both mention 'doors' flying open. Obsequens 67 also has similar detail in his excerpt of Livy's omens (though he has Calpurnia rather than C. wakened by the **moonlight**), and that suggests that these details of their disturbed night also figured in Livy's alternative version of the dream (§9 n.). A similar omen is recorded for Nero (Dio 63.26.5).

63.9. She was dreaming that she was holding Caesar's murdered body in her arms and weeping for him: so also Val. Max. 1.7.2. This was the classic gesture of (esp. female) mourning, usually with the head in the woman's lap: cf. Hom. *Il.* 18.71–2 with Edwards's n., 23.136, 24.724, and in P. the similarly morbid dream of Alcibiades as his own death approaches, *Alc.* 39.2. Shakespeare's transformation of Calpurnia's dream (*JC* II. ii. 71–90) starts from this version, but develops in most interesting, partly Christianizing fashion: see Pelling, 'Roman Tragedy', 280–1.

a different one:... a gable ... Calpurnia dreamed that this had broken off and she was weeping in frenzy for it. Suet. 81.3 combines this alternative version of the dream with that of §9: Calpurnia dreamed that the gable had collapsed and her husband was being stabbed in her arms. Dio 44.17.1 gives it rather differently: the house had collapsed, the wounded C. had fled to her arms, and then C. himself was raised to the clouds and to grasp the hand of Zeus. Suet. 81.3 also mentions C.'s dream of being raised to Heaven and to Jupiter. Presumably that element post-dates C.'s consecration in 42 BCE (67.8 n., Weinstock 346), and it may even be influenced by Virg. *Ecl.* 5 and/or Ov. *Met.* 15.803–52.

Notice the different suggestions: Suet. and Dio suggest apotheosis, whereas P.'s collapsing 'gable' directs attention to the *puncturing* of divine pretensions (below). If P. knew of the other version, it is not surprising that he suppressed it: so clear-cut a suggestion of C.'s divinity does not yet suit his narrative (Intr., p. 31).

according to Livy's account. So, as at 47.4–6, Livy is adduced for an omen. Here as there, it is possible that P. (or an assistant) has gone to Livy to supplement the account in Pollio, as App. has no suggestion of the 'gable' version. Cf. Intr., p. 49. It is anyway striking that as at 47.4 and 63.3 source citations accompany omens. P. presumably assumed that his readers might otherwise be sceptical, at least of omens as startling as these.

voted by the senate as a mark of honour and distinction. That vote is mentioned by Cic. *Phil.* 2.110 and Flor. 2.13.91, and the gable itself by Suet. 81.3. This 'gable' or pediment added to the house the impression of a temple. C. lived in the *domus publica* on the Sacred Way (9.7 n.), and as the official residence of the pontifex maximus this already carried some religious connotations; but the gable marked something more. Cf. Weinstock 280–1.

63.11. he knew that Calpurnia had never before succumbed to such womanly superstition. So, even here, C.'s 'misgivings and unease' are not directly caused by the supernatural elements themselves, but are affected by his response to the humans around him. It is her superstition, not his, that is foregrounded. Contrast Shakespeare, where it is C. himself who 'is superstitious grown of late' (*JC* II. i. 195): cf. Intr., p. 70.

63.12. The soothsayers duly sacrificed... the omens were unfavourable. *Brut.* 15.1 and Dio 44.17.3 also have unfavourable sacrifices before C. left home, Nic. Dam. 86, Suet. 81.4 and App. 2.116.488–9 and 153.641 put them as C. is about to enter the senate (where it was regular to sacrifice): it may be that both are right, and the sacrifices were repeated.

64–5: The Morning of the Ides
Once again (62 n.) *Caesar* controls the narrative from C.'s viewpoint, and it moves with him from his house to the senate; *Brut.* 14–15 does the opposite, focusing on the behaviour of Brutus and Cassius, particularly during the nervous hours before C.'s arrival, while C.'s own reasons for delay are there mentioned only briefly (15.1). Similarly, *Caesar* dwells on the moments when C. might genuinely have been told of the conspiracy, first by the servant of 64.6 and then by Artemidorus; *Brutus* on those when the conspirators *think* news may have leaked out, with their misreadings of the behaviour of Casca (15.2) and then Popillius Laenas (15.4, 16.4–5). So again the two accounts interlock with minimal repetition.

Why, for P., does C. agree to go? 63.11–12 has brought out his unease. Decimus touches two raw spots, the thought of kingship (which may well be P.'s elaboration, 64.3 n.) and the political damage that would be caused by such disdain for the senate; enemies and friends (64.4–5 n.), those two groups whose complex combination of responses has done so much to create the crisis (Intr., p. 22), are critical factors once more. But there is also a sense that C. himself finds himself almost bullied by Decimus, in this moment when, as before at the Rubicon (32 n.), he is so uncharacteristically hesitant. He eventually submits to being led by the hand, and Decimus' motives are very different from those of the Euripidean Theseus who may there be evoked (64.6 n.). The tense domestic scene swiftly gives way to the jostle of the crowd, at his door (64.6) and in the street (65.3–4); and notice how *accessible* C. is, accepting petition after petition, with no bodyguard (57.7 (n.)) to keep back the throng or the jostling senators of 66.5–6. This is not the stereotyped Greek tyrant, strongly guarded, keeping a remote distance (most memorably with Deioces, Hdt. 1.96–101: cf. Xenophon's Cyrus, *Cyrop.* 7.5.37–58, or his picture

of the fourth-century Persian king, *Ages.* 9.2; also Thuc. 1.130.2). It is
again (57.7 n.) C.'s good qualities, not his bad, that bring him down.

64.1. Decimus Brutus Albinus.   P. names him elaborately to distinguish him from Marcus. On that name, cf. D. R. Shackleton Bailey,
Two Studies in Roman Nomenclature (2nd edn, 1991), 76: he will have
been adopted by a Postumius Albinus, probably the consul of 99 or
his son. He had fought for C. with distinction in Gaul (22.1–5 n.) and
in the Massilia campaign (36.1 n.), then governed Transalpine Gaul
in 47–6 (*MRR* 291, 301, iii. 112–13), where he suppressed a revolt of
the Bellovaci. By 45 he was back at Rome, probably as praetor (*MRR*
307, iii. 113), and toured Italy in C.'s train (56.6 n.). He was consul
designate for 42 (58.1 n.). His career is discussed by R. Syme, *Hist.* 29
(1980), 426–30 = *RP* iii. 1240–4 and by Dettenhofer 72–8, 183–91,
256–62, 287–93. At *Brut.* 12.5 P. is cool about his qualities, surprisingly so in view of the way he keeps his nerve now: 'This man was not
particularly vigorous or brave, but he was important to the conspirators because of the numbers of gladiators whom he was keeping at
Rome in preparation for a public show, and he also commanded
Caesar's confidence.' For these gladiators, cf. Nic. Dam. 98–9 with
67.7 n. below.

    he was included in his will among the second class of heirs. So
also Suet. 83.2, etc.: such an heir would inherit only if the first
class renounced their shares of the inheritance. Decimus was also to
be one of the guardians of any son that C. should have. Syme, art. cit.,
428, was impressed by this and by Decimus' swift rise under C.'s
patronage, and as with Dolabella (51.3 n.) speculated that Decimus
might have been C.'s biological son: but Suet. makes it clear that
'several of the assassins' were named as potential guardians. App.
2.143.597, 146.611 wrongly states that Decimus was also adopted
in C.'s will.

64.2. treating them like playthings: the same phrase as at *Gracch.*
17.6, §4 n. below. The Greek concept is *truphē*, hard to capture in
English. It refers to the extravagant, pampered life that can lead a
person of power to treat the rest of the world with arrogant casual-
ness.

**64.3. to vote for him to become king of the overseas provinces and
to wear a diadem wherever he travelled outside Italy:**   reflecting the
expectation that L. Cotta would raise the kingship question (Suet.

79.4, cf. 60.2 n.). This 'outside Italy' suggestion—App. 2.110.461 phrases it as 'some people saying' that C. ought to be 'king of the nations that were subject to Rome'—could be represented as a compromise, enough to satisfy the demands of the Sibylline oracle concerning Parthia (60.2). Whether this was really the topic for the day is another question (and also, if it was, whether the point was to accept the offer or to scotch the idea, as K. Kraft thought, 60.2 n.). Even if there were rumours that the kingship question would be raised, it is not clear that they were accurate (60.2 n.), and P. may only have inferred this part of D. Brutus' argument from the rumours that he knew were circulating—App.'s 'some people were saying'—and from P.'s own view of C.'s 'passion to be king'. Nic. Dam. 84, otherwise similar on Decimus' role (see next note), does not have this: notice his 'which *has* honoured you'. The arguments that Dio 44.18.2 gives Decimus are also different, and simpler: the senate was 'exceedingly eager to see him'. That fits Dio's C., who is taken in and 'puffed up' by the senate's flatteries: 57.3 n.

64.4. reconvene on some day when Calpurnia's dreams had improved.   Nic. Dam. 84 is fuller and more blunt: 'What, Caesar? Are you, a man of your years, going to pay attention to a woman's dreams and to idle rumours, and insult the senate by not attending— the senate which has honoured you and which you have yourself summoned? If you will take my advice, you will not do that, but throw away all thought of such dream-traffic and go: it has been sitting there waiting for you since early in the morning.' Cf. Toher, ad loc., and on 'early in the morning' see 66 n.

64.4–5. what would be said by those who were jealous of him? And who would listen to his friends if they denied that this was tyranny and slavery?   On the enemies and their envy, see 57.3 and 58.5 nn.; on the friends, 51, 60.2–3, 60.8 nn.

Gracch. 17.6 is similar, as Blossius of Cumae argues that Tiberius Gracchus should not be put off by a bad omen from going into public: 'that would be a disgrace—but his enemies would treat it as no laughing matter, but would denounce him before the people as one who was already playing the tyrant and treating others like playthings' (§2 n.). The echo between the *Lives* may be suggestive: Intr., p. 35. But Blossius means well; D. Brutus does not.

64.5. make the announcement of a postponement in person. *Brut.*
16.1 makes it clear that it was indeed C.'s intention to postpone the
sitting when he arrived, making the excuse that he was unwell: Suet.
81 and Nic. Dam. 83 add that he really was ill. App. 2.115.481 also
confirms C.'s intention to postpone. If the senate was indeed to be
postponed, it could only be for a day or so if it was to meet before C.'s
departure on 18 March (58.6 n.).

64.6. he took Caesar by the hand: so also Nic. Dam. 87. The
gesture is a powerful one, as the great man becomes the dependent
follower: it recalls Theseus' taking Heracles by the hand and leading
him off in friendship to a new life (Eur. *Her.* 1398–1404). For all its
theatricality, this gesture is dropped by Shakespeare, for his C. insists
on his independence and grandeur to the end: 'I will not come today'
(ii. ii. 62, 64) and 'The cause is in my will: I will not come' (71) give
way to 'I will go' (ii. ii. 107). In P.'s narrative the gesture is mirrored at
68.3 (n.). **and began to lead him out:** 'at about the fifth hour', Suet.
81.4. **a slave ... forced his way into the house ... had great matters to
reveal to him:** similarly App. 2.116.485, without the detail that the
slave 'belonged to someone else' (that may be P.'s own inference,
explaining how he would have had access to others' conversations)
but drawing the conclusion that the slave was not fully informed,
for he anticipated that C. would return. The contact between
App. and P. on this and on Artemidorus (65 nn.) makes it likely
that this motif—'how close C. came to being saved!'—was highlighted
by Pollio.

65.1. Artemidorus: son of Theopompus (48.1 nn.). Like his father,
he was a big man at Cnidus (Strabo 14.2.15): his countrymen voted
him divine honours, a tomb in the gymnasium, five-year gymnastic
festivals to be known as the Artemidoreia, and a statue to share the
temple of Artemis (W. Blümel, *Inschriften von Knidos* 1 (1992), no.
59; L. Robert, *Ant. Class.* 35 (1966), 420–1). He is named also by App.
2.116.486 (see §4 n.), but not by other sources who know of this
document that C. was handed but could not read: Nic. Dam. 66, Vell.
2.57.2, Suet. 81.4, Dio 44.18.3, Flor. 2.13.94. **a Greek sophist, and for
that reason close to some of Brutus' followers.** Only P. gives this
explanation of how Artemidorus could know so much. It may be his
own inference based on the intellectualism of Brutus' circle.

65.2. 'Read this... your own person.' On the direct speech, cf. 37.6–7n.

65.3. he could not read it, though he tried time after time: very different, then, from Shakespeare's Caesar, who makes a show of refusing to read: 'What touches us ourself shall be last served' (*JC* III. i. 8).

65.4. Some claim that it was some other person... That is the version of App. 2.116.486, who has Artemidorus run into the senate to find C. already dead, after the document has been given to C. 'by another person'; that is oddly emphatic, and App. seems to be rebutting the Artemidorus version that P. puts first. Possibly Pollio mentioned both alternatives.

66: Assassination
C. had left home at 'the fifth hour', i.e. between 10 and 11 a.m. (64.6 n.). Depending on the jostle and on his route (cf. 63.6 n.), it might take him anything between ten minutes and three-quarters of an hour to reach the senate house of Pompey (§1 n.). Any failed sacrifices (63.12 n.) will also have taken time; so C. fell some time between 11 a.m. and noon. The senate had been assembled 'since early that morning' (Nic. Dam., cited at 64.4 n.), but not 'since dawn', as is often stated, for otherwise Cassius would not have arranged a *toga virilis* ceremony for his son (*Brut.* 14.4): so, rightly, Toher on Nic. Dam. 84 and J. T. Ramsey, *In Pursuit of Wissenschaft: Festschrift...* *Calder* (2008), 351–63 (who also allows time for an early meeting of C. and Calvinus, 63.6 n.). The conspirators numbered more than sixty in number according to Suet. 80.4 and the Livian tradition (Eutr. 6.25, Oros. 6.17.2), more than eighty according to Nic. Dam. 59. That need not conflict with the number of 'twenty-three wounds' and P.'s detail that 'each person' there needed to land a blow (§11), as not all the conspirators need have been senators: there had been earlier debate on other possible locations and occasions, and non-senators might certainly have had a role to play had, say, the alternative been adopted of an attack during the (consular?) elections or as he walked along the Sacred Way (Suet. 80.4, Nic. Dam. 81).
    A good deal of P.'s narrative, here and in *Brutus*, continues to show contact with App. 2.117.490–3, and there is another indication too (the wild beast image of §10, n.) that both authors are drawing on

Pollio here. Still, other sources may continue to contribute (Intr.,
p. 51–2), and the closeness of some but not all to Nic. Dam. suggests
either that P. also looked at Nic. and exploited him very selectively or,
more likely, that much of the detail is historically accurate, despite the
confusion that we would expect to attend so swift and tumultuous an
event. That confusion is itself well caught (esp. §§10, 14); and P.'s
rapid and vivid style creates a powerful visual picture that adapted
very readily for Shakespeare's theatre. Notice particularly the physio-
logical detail of the blows, reminding one of the anatomical precision
with which wounds are described in the *Iliad*, and that tinge is then
picked up in the brief simile of §10 (n.). The names help too, as P.'s
readiness to introduce unexplained characters (7.5 n.) allows him to
bring Tillius Cimber and Casca on to the stage, adding more colour
than a simple 'one of the conspirators' and 'another' would allow:
contrast Dio 44.19.3–4. The shift of gaze from intense participants to
startled and terrified observers (§9, 67.1) is again a distinctive Plutarchan touch: cf. for instance the end of *Pompey* (70, 78–80), and my
Ant. comm., index, s.v. 'characterisation by reaction'.

   For details of the day, see N. Horsfall, *Greece and Rome*, 21 (1974),
191–9, though he is corrected on one important detail (above) by
Toher and Ramsey. For a perceptive and highly readable modern
account of the assassination, see G. Woolf, *Et tu, Brute?* (2007), who
goes on to cover the resonance of the murder in the early principate
and to debate some differences between ancient and modern political
assassinations. For the details of the killing, see Wiseman 211–15.
Appian's account is discussed by V. Pagán, *Conspiracy Narratives in
Roman History* (2005), 109–22; Suet.'s by H. Gugel, *Gymn.* 77 (1970),
5–22; Nic. Dam's by Dobesch, *AS* i. 205–3 and in Toher's comm.;
I discuss P.'s in 'Caesar's Fall', and Shakespeare's adaptation of P. in
Intr., Section 5 (above), and more fully in 'Roman Tragedy'.

66.1. the place where the senate had gathered on that day: the
'senate house of Pompey' (*curia Pompeii*): see below. **it had a statue
of Pompey standing there.** And it had been C. himself who had
raised up Pompey's statues, 57.6 (n.). 'Just so in tragedy do the statues
of the gods preside' (J. Mossman in M. A. Flower and M. Toher (eds),
Georgica (*BICS* Supp. 58; 1991), 98–119 at 117)—for instance, the
statues of Artemis and Aphrodite in *Hippolytus*: this skilful thematic
use of statues is typical of P.'s artistry, as Mossman's paper brings out.
as one of the additional decorations to his theatre: on the theatre, see

Pompey 40.9, 42.9, and esp. 52.5, its opening and the attendant celebrations in 55 BCE. At *Brut.* 14 'Pompey's portico' is also specified as the place where the assassins waited and where Brutus calmly transacted business as praetor. This great rectangular portico lay to the east of the theatre, and the 'senate house of Pompey' opened on to that, facing the theatre. The complex was in the Campus Martius, about half a mile to the west of the forum: see Map 6, *LTUR* i. 334–5, iv. 148–50, and v. 35–8, R. Étienne, *Hommage à la mémoire de J. Carcopino* (1977), 71–9, and Woolf, *Et tu Brute?* 1–3. **made it plain.** P. here strongly implies that that there really was a cosmic dimension, and that is also the emphasis of Nic. Dam. 83. Suet. 80.4 prefers to suggest that the choice of Pompey's senate house was a factor in the conspirators' planning: see §12 n., where P. too refocuses on the human aspects. **some heavenly power:** in Greek, *daimōn*, preparing for the importance of C.'s 'great guardian spirit'—*daimōn* again—in the final chapter (69.2 n.). See Intr., p. 66–7. The technique is similar in *Brutus*, where *daimōn* at 14.3 prepares for a development, more complex than here, of 'daimonic' themes later in the *Life*: I discuss these in 'Augustus' Autobiography', 52–7. Nic. Dam. 86 refers to an *alastōr*, an avenging spirit, that the seers felt they could see in the failed sacrifices (63.12 n.).

66.2. even though Cassius was sympathetic to Epicurean doctrine. The point is partly that an Epicurean would think that death finishes everything, and hence the mortal Pompey would no longer have any concern for what was happening; and partly that any gods that existed would anyway not concern themselves with human preoccupations.

66.4. Antony... and so Brutus Albinus kept him outside the senate: wrong: it was C. Trebonius (Cic. *Phil.* 2.34, App. 2.117.490 and 3.26.101, Dio 44.19.1), as P. knows at *Brut.* 17.2. This is probably just a mistake here, though just possibly P. is eliminating a complicating individual (he never mentions Trebonius in this *Life*, but in *Brutus* he recurs at 19.5). At *Ant.* 13.4 P. speaks vaguely of 'some of the conspirators' who were detached to delay Antony. In my n. ad loc. I suggest that this was fudging on P.'s part once he had noticed the discrepancy between his other two versions.

No mention here of the conspirators' debate whether to kill Antony too, relevant in different ways to *Brutus* (18.4–5) and *Antony* (13.3–4). In my n. on the *Antony* passage I discuss P.'s differing narrative emphases.

66.5. the senate rose as a mark of respect.   The language echoes 60.4, where C. does not 'rise', and 60.8, where Balbus encourages C. to expect such 'respect'. As with the 'chair' and the 'neck' (§6 nn.), the denouement recalls the chain of events that provoked it. **Tillius Cimber:** L. Tillius Cimber, another who had been well treated by Caesar (Cic. *Phil.* 2.27) and was influential with him (Cic. *Fam.* 6.12 (226).2). He had probably been praetor in 45 (*MRR* 307), and was appointed governor of Bithynia (*MRR* 330), probably by C. himself before his death (App. 3.2.4) rather than after the murder (*Brut.* 19.5). His **brother** may be the 'Tillius' mentioned at Hor. *Sat.* 1.6.24–5 who lost and then regained the status of senator (*MRR* iii.205), but M. Toher, *CQ* 55 (2005), 183–9, suggests that Horace may be referring to Tillius himself rather than his brother.

66.6. the chair: presumably the golden throne mentioned at 61.4 (n.): on its significance, cf. §5 n. above, though it is admittedly more stressed in other accounts, esp. Dio 44.17.3 and Flor 2.13.95. **They responded by pleading with ever greater force.** *Brut.* 17.3–4 says that they grasped his hands—thus making it more difficult for him to fight back, as Nic. Dam. 88 makes clear—and kissed his breasts and head. C. was trying to stand up when **Tillius grabbed C.'s toga with both hands.** Apart from exposing his neck and giving the signal to the others, this would also drag him back down into his seat. Nic. Dam. 88 has Cimber drag the toga down in such a way as to restrain C.'s hands, but if this was the intention it did not succeed: C. fought back well (§7 n.). Cimber also cried out 'what are you waiting for, my friends?' (App. 2.117.491). **ripped it down from the neck:** on the symbolic importance that C.'s 'neck' and throat have come to acquire, see 57.8, 60.6 nn.

66.7. Casca struck first.   He was standing behind C., *Brut.* 17.4 and App. 2.117.492: cf. 'spin round' here. We should think of an upward slope of kneeling petitioners, C. struggling to rise, and the standing Casca at his back. The kneeling becomes a most expressive gesture in Shakespeare too (Intr., p. 70), and Shakespeare too clearly staged

Casca as standing 'behind' (v. i. 43). P. Servilius Casca Longus later became tribune in 43, then fought for Brutus and Cassius in the East in 42 (*MRR* 340, 366). He fought at Philippi (*Brut.* 45.8–9), and he and his brother (§8 n.) apparently killed themselves after the battle. **by the side of the neck:** the left, according to Nic. Dam. 89. If Casca was standing behind C., perhaps he was left-handed. The blow slipped past the neck and hit the chest, App. 2.117.492. At *Brut.* 17.4 P. specifies the 'shoulder' (twice) rather than the 'neck': in *Caesar* the neck matters more (§6 n.). Wiseman 212 suggests that Casca was aiming for the heart, but the throat is just as effective a way of killing. **grasp the dagger, and hold it firm.** C. also stabbed Casca back through the arm with his writing stylus (Suet. 82.2).

66.8. in Greek: presumably to evoke Hellenic traditions of tyrannicide, but the moment also forms a trio with C.'s own Greek utterances of 32.8 and 46.2: those marked C.'s highest success, this his catastrophe. Casca's **brother** was Gaius, and he eventually shared Publius' fate after Philippi (§7 n.). It is uncertain whether he was one of the plotters, or was simply called on as an onlooker. Dio 44.52 has a (dubious) story of Gaius issuing a proclamation that he was not involved as he feared he might share the fate of Cinna (68.3–7 (n.)), but Nic. Dam. 89 has him joining in the murder and striking a crucial blow.

66.10. each brandishing a naked blade. The Greek *xiphos* can be used of either 'sword' or 'dagger', but as the blades had been concealed under togas (*Brut.* 16.4) we should think of daggers (so Moles, *Brutus*), as explicitly at §7. The phrase is echoed at 67.3, when the conspirators brandish their 'naked blades' in triumph rather than in violence, and 69.14, when the phrasing is echoed as Brutus dies; Cassius' dagger also becomes important at 69.3. **like some wild beast.** The brief simile carries on the Iliadic character that the anatomical detail of the blows has already generated: cf. *Il.* 11.544–55 and esp. 12.41–8 for extended similes where wild beasts thrash around, and 3.449, *Od.* 14.21 for the brevity of an unelaborated 'like some wild beast'. Here App. 2.117.493 and 147.612 has the same image. At 'Breaking the Bounds' 264 I suggest that this, like the description of the bestiality of C.'s troops at 39.3, may go back to a more extended system in Pollio, as App. describes C.'s men repeatedly as 'wild beasts' (2.61.252, 71.297, 75.312, 151.632), Cato's death throes too showed him 'like a wild beast' (2.99.412, 101.420), and Cinna is also hunted down 'like a wild beast' (2.147.613). Cf. on 'flower-throwing', 30.2 n., and for further similar possibilities see p. 344 n. 21, 28.6 n., 60.6 n., and below, §12 n.; Intr., p. 47 and n. 113.

66.11. each person there needed to begin the sacrifice. For the sacrificial imagery, cf. *Brut.* 10.1; it is reflected also in 'needed', as if each of the conspirators was bonded by this ritual act. Nic. Dam. 90 gives a meaner impression, perhaps influenced by Hom., *Il.* 22.371, of every conspirator getting in his blow at the lifeless corpse 'so that he too would seem to have played a part in the act'. Shakespeare too makes much of the notion of sacrifice ('Let us be sacrificers, but not butchers, Caius...' (*JC* ii. i. 165); interestingly, the translations that provided Shakespeare with his material (the French Amyot, translated into English by North) had toned down P.'s sacrificial ideas, only for Shakespeare to restore them. Cf. Intr., p. 65–6.

Brutus too struck a single blow to the groin. App. 2.117.493 says 'to the thigh', Nic. Dam. 89 has Decimus Brutus strike C. 'right through below the flanks' (possibly but not necessarily a confusion with Marcus: cf. Toher, ad loc.). The 'groin' version is likely to link, unpleasantly, with the notion of C. as Brutus' biological father: see next n.

66.12. Some say that... when he saw Brutus with drawn blade he pulled his toga over his head and gave in before the attack. This is the version given, without the 'some say' qualification, at *Brut.* 17.6. 'Pulled his toga over his head' recalls the similar gesture as Pompey fell, *Pomp.* 79.5. It is hard, though not perhaps impossible, to find this expressive across different *Lives*, but anyway it may well go back to a patterning that was already there in Pollio (cf. §10 n.). Possibly the echo of Socrates' death may also be felt (Plato *Phaedo* 118a, cf. H. Gugel, *Gymn.* 77 (1970), 17); if so, the point is presumably to contrast the serenity of the philosophical end with the messy violence of the politicians'.

It was also now that, so some people told, C. said to Brutus in Greek 'You too, my child?' That is recorded by Suet. 82.2 and Dio 44.19.5, though both authors prefer the version that C. said nothing. For discussion, see esp. J. N. Adams, *Bilingualism and the Latin Language* (2003), 310. The 'my child' need not be interpreted literally

(so, rightly, M. Dubuisson, *Lat.* 39 (1980), 881–4), but some may well
have taken it so, especially as the vocative *teknon* is much more
regularly used than the alternative *pai* by real fathers or those in
loco parentis (E. Dickey, *Greek Forms of Address: From Herodotus to
Lucian* (1996), 65–72; but Dickey also observes that *teknon* is the
more suitable word for addressing non-kin adults, 68–9). This may
therefore be the origin of the version that Brutus was C.'s own
biological son (*Brut.* 5.2, App. 2.112.467–8, etc.). More interestingly,
'you too' is a frequent phrase on curse inscriptions, turning a curse
back on the person who made it: 'And the same to you' (J. Russell in
B. Marshall (ed.), *Vindex Humanitatis: Essays in Honor of John
Huntly Bishop* (1980), 123–8). P. may have known the item, but
probably did not (so Moles, *Brutus*). He might have suppressed it
here (any possible hint of parentage would not fit, 62.1 n.), but he
would surely have used it in *Brutus*, which both includes the possible
parentage (5.2) and hints at that notion of a recurrent pattern, with
Brutus falling to similar forces to those that destroyed C.—'and the
same to you!' That second theme is then much more developed in
Shakespeare (Intr., Section 5), though his *et tu Brute* (iii. i. 77) does
not have the same 'and the same to you' resonance, even if it derives
ultimately from Suet. (If it does, the derivation is probably not direct:
Shakespeare seems to have drawn the Latin from previous English
dramatic versions of the death. See Pelling, 'Roman Tragedy', 266–7.)

   P. Arnaud, *Lat.* 57 (1998), 61–71, prefers to think that the story
represents death as interrupting C. in mid-line, and it would have
gone on 'and you too, my child, will one day taste this power of mine'.
That is what Augustus (Suet. *Galba* 4.1) or Tiberius (Dio 57.19.4) is
reported to have said to Galba, taken by Arnaud to be echoing the
story of C.'s end. The insinuation will have been that Brutus was
himself driven by power hunger rather than idealism, and he thinks
that the story was made up soon after the events as anti-tyrannicide
propaganda. A. J. Woodman, *CQ* 56 (2006), 183–4, follows Arnaud in
emphasizing also the implied prediction of the *dangers* of power: that
takes us in the same direction as the curse interpretation.

   He fell: taking care to fall decorously, Suet. 82.2, Val. Max. 4.5.6—a
version evidently influenced by Euripides' Polyxena, *Hecuba* 569,
a famous line echoed also by Ovid (*Met.* 13.479–80, *Fasti* 2.833–4)
and Pliny (*Ep.* 4.11.9). **perhaps by chance, perhaps dragged there by
the assassins:** §1 implied that Pompey's emblematic presence might
indeed reflect something cosmically ordained; here the second

suggestion—'perhaps dragged there by the assassins'—refocuses on the possibility that it was more a matter of the conspirators' thinking, making the most of Pompey's name and cause. That is the emphasis also of Suet. 80.4 (§1 n.).

66.13. gave the impression: again (§12 n.) more non-committal than at §1.

66.14. twenty-three: so also most of our other sources, but Nic. Dam. 90 says thirty-five. Only one wound was in itself fatal, according to the doctor Antistius (Suet. 82.3). 'There must have been a lot of blood' (Wiseman 215). **many of the assailants were wounded by one another:** Brutus himself received a stab in the hand, perhaps from Cassius (*Brut.* 17.7, App. 2.122.512, Nic. Dam. 89).

67–8: Aftermath

The events in the hours and days after the killing are complicated and controversial. P.'s most extended version is in *Brut.* 18–23; shorter and simplified versions come at *Cic.* 42, *Ant.* 14, and here. App. has an extended version that shows sufficient contact with P. to suggest that both derive much of their material from Pollio, though both authors probably draw from other sources as well (*Plutarch and History*, 14–15). Nic. Dam. 91–106 has some material that coincides with the App./P. tradition and a good deal that differs, some of it probably accurate (cf. Toher's comm.). The narrative in Dio 44.20–53 is principally concerned to provide a framework for the extensive speeches he gives to Cicero and Antony.

P.'s various accounts largely follow 'the law of biographical relevance' (Intr., p. 22), which explains why the *Brutus* account is fullest; *Antony* in particular dwells on the diplomatic achievement of Antony himself (67.9 n.), an aspect that this *Life* ignores, just as it omits Cicero's role in pleading for amnesty (67.8 n., *Cic.* 42.3). That 'law' naturally operates rather differently here in *Caesar*, as it is Brutus and Cassius and then the senate who dominate the action; yet in a way it still applies, as it is the impact of the dead C. that is most emphasized. Thus the panicky response of senators and bystanders receives as much emphasis here as in *Brutus*, building here on the paralysed horror of 66.9 and contrasting with the 'radiant' assassins (67.1, 3) and those who wish to join the bandwagon (67.4–6); but attention soon switches to the recrudescence of popular support for C., and that theme frames (67.7, 68) the attempt of 'the senate' to calm the situation (67.8)—no named individuals here, unlike in the other *Lives*, and this itself recalls the senate/people polarity that has been recurrent in the *Life* (Intr., p. 59). The effect is to underline how delusory that impression of 'stability' and of a satisfactory 'compromise' (67.9) may be: 'compromise' is literally 'blending' (n.), a mixing together of the various elements and interests, yet the forces embodied in the people are too great for such a mix to work. The violent end of Cinna (68.3–6) rams the point home.

'The people' therefore matter most: it looks as if Pollio had a similar emphasis, and included at this point an unsympathetic analysis of the composition of the urban 'people'. This is hinted at *Brut.* 18.12 ('the people, despite being of mixed composition and ready to make trouble') and 21.3 ('amid crowds that lent themselves to unpredictable and swift impulses'), and developed more at App. 2.120.503–7. App. mentions the growth of the urban populace through immigration, the extensive manumission of slaves, the influx to Rome from other parts of Italy of those attracted by the corn doles, and the crowded presence of discharged soldiers waiting to leave for their new settlements. He also seems to have acknowledged the continuing presence of 'the uncorrupted part of the populace' (App. 2.121.510, 125.523, 126.527), who remained loyal to C.'s memory. Despite the importance of 'the people' in this *Life*, P. never gives an analysis in this depth. He is interested in tracing the effects of popular forces, not in the particular factors that generated them. This need not be explained in terms of a deficiency in analytic curiosity, nor even of the demands of the biographical genre: the aspects that App. emphasizes are those that are specific to one city and one set of historical circumstances, whereas P.'s interests are in the universal and the timeless. See Intr., pp. 61, 76.

The revival of popular enthusiasm after death again recalls the rhythm of the *Gracchi*: see Intr., p. 35.

P. also ignores several military factors, the gladiators of D. Brutus (67.7 n.) and the legion that M. Lepidus had on the Insula Tiberina (67.2 n.). Nic. Dam. 94, App. 2.119.501, Dio 44.51.4, and Flor. 2.17.2 all also emphasize that the conspirators were nervous of C.'s own veterans 'who were present in the city in considerable numbers' (App.), and more swiftly gathered from nearby colonies (Nic. Dam. 49, 103); almost immediately, their land grants were explicitly confirmed, but Antony could certainly use the fury of 'soldiers and *plebs*' to sabre-rattle in negotiations with D. Brutus (Cic. *Fam.* 11.1 (325).1).

On these soldiers, see H. Botermann, *Die Soldaten und die römische Politik in der Zeit von Caesars Tod bis zur Begründung des Zweiten Triumvirats* (1968), 1–14, 197–200. The *Life* has not neglected the importance of soldiers before: cf. esp. 51.2, 57.8; but here P. simplifies by concentrating on the urban *plebs*.

For modern narratives, see Woolf, *Et tu Brute?* (66 n.), 10–20, and E. Rawson, *CAH* ix² (1994), 468–71. For particularly perceptive analyses, see Dettenhofer 262–80, Morstein-Marx 150–8, and Wiseman, 215–34; Wiseman argues that the popular reaction to the killing was unequivocally negative, while Morstein-Marx stresses the difficulty of reading public opinion even at the time and the deft attempts on both sides to manipulate it. Cf. also Z. Yavetz, *Plebs and Princeps* (1969), 58–82, arguing that Antony systematically underestimated the importance of the *plebs*, and U. Gotter, *Der Diktator ist tot!* (*Hist*. Einz. 110; 1996), esp. 21–7.

**67.1. Brutus came forward before the senators to say something...
The senators would not let him:** so also *Brut*. 18.1, App. 2.119.499.
Some shut up their houses ... some were rushing to the place to see what had happened, others were rushing back once they had seen the sight: elaborating the similar but briefer description at *Brut*. 18.1; Nic. Dam. 91–2 and Dio 44.20 give vivid accounts; App. 2.119.499 is less coloured. We can readily believe that non-senators too came crowding into the senate house in the confusion: App. 2.116.486 says that Artemidorus (65.1 n.) ran in and found C. already dying.

67.2. Antony and Lepidus ... stole away into other houses. P. describes this a little more fully at *Brut*. 18.6 and *Ant*. 14.1, both concentrating on Antony (but Lepidus here was important at 63.7) and having him don slave's clothing: that may be implied here by the furtive 'stole away', and the item would have offered P. a chance to echo 31.3, but the narrative is now concentrating on the tyrannicides.
other houses: a minor problem, though the passage has not troubled editors or translators. The Greek *heteras oikias*, 'other houses', should mean 'other than the one(s) mentioned or implied already'. That is not easy, but it might just mean 'other than the ones nearby that the panic-stricken householders had closed' (§1), which would otherwise have been the first refuge. Translators from Amyot on, including Perrin, Warner, and Chambry, take the phrase as meaning 'other people's houses', but (*a*) that is impossible Greek (it would be different if 'their own houses' had just been mentioned), and (*b*) it is

inaccurate for both Antony and Lepidus: Antony went to his own house (Cic. *Phil.* 2.88) and barricaded himself inside, while Lepidus left, not for a 'house', but to join a legion of soldiers that he had on the nearby Insula Tiberina (App. 2.118.496, cf. Map 6). Even my interpretation makes the text misleading as regards Lepidus, but it is hard to find any interpretation or emendation that captures the historical reality. One further possibility is <*sph*>*eteras oikias*, 'their own houses', an emendation of Ewen Bowie reported in Moles, *Brutus*; still, that too is wrong for Lepidus.

Lepidus made sure that his military force was visible during the next few days, not least by occupying the forum on the night of 15–16 March: Nic. Dam. 103, App. 2.126.525–7. His actions on 15–17 March are analysed by L. Hayne, *Acta Classica* 14 (1971), 109–17: he acted 'skilfully and consistently'.

67.3. brandished their naked blades: 66.10, 69.14 nn. So also Nic. Dam. 91, 94. **to the Capitol:** 'a symbolical act, antiquarian and even Hellenic', Syme, *RR* 99, the equivalent of occupying an Acropolis (Moles, *Brutus*); and there may have been a practical purpose too, as the threat from the veterans in the city was a real one. **their faces were radiant with pride and confidence:** a highly visual detail not given in *Brutus*; App. 2.119.499 is also very visual, with the further detail that one of them was carrying a cap of freedom on spear-point. 'Radiant' is a favourite word of P. for such delight at a moment of triumph, and is especially used of inspiring leadership: P. uses it again of Brutus at *Brut.* 16.4 and 52.4, and cf. e.g. *Crass.* 16.5, *Otho* 15.4, *Table Talk* 620d–e, and the interesting role reversal at *Ant.* 43.2, where it is Antony's troops that inspire their general (see my n.). **called the ordinary people to freedom:** reflecting their self-portrayal as 'Liberators' from a tyranny, 57.1 n.: but 67.7 and esp. 68 show that they did not succeed in gaining popular recognition for this image (Z. Yavetz, *Plebs and Princeps* (1969), 64, cf. Wiseman 215–34). The respect afforded Brutus at §7 will be wholly personal. **welcomed the men of quality among those they met:** not just a casual reflection of ancient snobberies: P. is preparing for the tyrannicides' failure to appeal sufficiently to the ordinary people.

67.4–6. There were some … what they wished they had done: again, not in *Brutus*. **Gaius Octavius:** probably C. Octavius Balbus, who was proscribed and killed in 43 (App. 4.21.84–6, Val. Max. 5.7.3):

MRR iii. 151, T. P. Wiseman, *CQ* 14 (1964), 124. **Lentulus Spinther:** son of the consul of 57 (34.7, 42.8 nn.). A letter of his to Cicero (*Fam.* 12.14 (405).6) rather disingenuously claims credit 'for sharing with Brutus and Cassius in that deed and that danger'. He was active in the fighting of 44–42 (*MRR* 325, 344, 364, iii. 70) and seems to have been executed after Philippi.

Lentulus but not Octavius is also named by App. 2.119.500, along with 'Favonius, Aquinus, Dolabella, Murcus, and Patiscus': i.e., M. Favonius (21.8 n.), M. Aquinus, who was to fight under Cassius in 43–42 (*MRR* iii. 25), the Caesarian P. Cornelius Dolabella (51.3 n.) with his insignia as *consul suffectus*, whose antics on the day included a suggestion that the day should be consecrated as the birthday of the republic (App. 2.122.511) but who was certainly playing a more complicated game than glory-hunting, L. Staius Murcus, who was shortly to take up the proconsulship of Syria (*MRR* 330, iii. 200), and 'Patiscus', who was to fight as legate in 43 (*MRR* 348). See also next n.

67.5. they were put to death by Antony and the younger Caesar: i.e. (as we normally call him) Octavian: for their deaths, see previous n. Of the others mentioned by App. (last n.), Favonius at least was also executed after Philippi (Suet. *Aug.* 13, Dio 47.49.4), so P. might have mentioned him here. **they did not even win the glory for which they died:** similar reflections at App. 2.119.500 and Dio 44.21.4.

67.7. Next day Brutus and his followers came down from the Capitol, and Brutus made a speech: or possibly just 'they made speeches': 'Brutus and his followers' is the idiomatic phrase (7.5, 61.10 nn.) that can mean either 'Brutus' or his whole group. 'Came down' probably means the group, but the speechmaking may be Brutus' alone: notice the **respect for Brutus** in the response. There were indeed other speeches, as the fuller narrative of *Brutus*, App. 2.122.513, and Dio 44.21.1 all make clear, but that *Brutus* narrative (below) also makes it clear that the response to others was not so respectful.

In any case, P. clearly simplifies here (and 'next day' is an error), even though not all the details of the sequence can be reliably reconstructed. P.'s fullest version is in *Brut.* 18. That in *Antony* revises in several respects: see my n. on *Ant.* 14.1–4. According to *Brutus*, when the panic died down 'the senators and many of the ordinary people' went up to the Capitol, and Brutus made a speech there that was well judged and attractive to the people. The good response to this encouraged Brutus to come down to the forum, and there he was heard with respect and in silence, but the people's true feelings emerged in a much more violent response when, according to *Brutus*, L. Cornelius Cinna (68.6 n.) followed with a denunciation of the dead C. At this they returned to the Capitol. In *Brutus* all this would seem to be on 15 March rather than the 'next day'. App. 2.121.509–123.515 has a different sequence of speeches: first Cinna spoke, followed by Dolabella (§§4–6, 51.3 nn.); then Cassius and Brutus came down alone (whereas *Brutus* has them 'escorted by many distinguished men') and spoke; then, still apprehensive, they returned to the Capitol. App. later has a popular attack on Cinna on the morning of the 17th, 2.126.526–7. These two versions are discussed by J. L. Moles, *RhM* 130 (1987), 124–8, who has good reason for thinking P.'s version of Cinna's speech superior to App.'s, though App. may be right in having a further, separate attack on Cinna on the 17th. Nic. Dam. is simpler: he has an initial calming speech of Brutus to the people immediately after the killing (92) and before the move to the Capitol—this contrasts with the impression left by P. of a swift progression to the Capitol; then, later on the 15th, a descent and a further, tentative speech of Brutus, followed by return to the Capitol (99–101). It also appears that Brutus made a further speech on the Capitol on the 16th, though the dating is not quite certain: Cic. *Att.* 15.1a (378).2, App. 2.137.570–142.592, cf. Wiseman 227. **their utter silence... respect for Brutus.** P. thus omits the response to Cinna, above. App. 2.142.592 makes the popular response to Brutus more unequivocally favourable (and once again he prefers noisiness to a dramatic silence, 60.3 nn.), but he too brings out how swiftly the mood changed after the will was read (143.597) and especially after Antony spoke (146.611).

P. also passes over some other important elements, first that the tyrannicides had already sent some money to win goodwill (App. 2.120.503, cf. 121.511), and secondly the role played by the gladiators of D. Brutus (64.1 n., *Brut.* 12.5): these rushed alarmingly to the senate house (App. 2.118.495), then later served as bodyguards as Cassius and Brutus moved to and from the Capitol. Nic. Dam.'s account gives them particular prominence (81, 92, 94, 98). P. further omits the tense negotiations with Antony and Lepidus on the evening of 15 and throughout 16 March; also the conciliatory dinners, with Antony and Lepidus entertaining Cassius and Brutus respectively (*Brut.* 19.3 and *Ant.* 14.2), and the child hostages, with the sons of Lepidus and Antony deposited with the tyrannicides (*Ant.* 14.2, etc.). In this *Life* the emphasis falls on 'the senate' (§7) as a whole, not on individuals: 67–8 n.

67.8. The senate tried to bring about some sort of amnesty and general reconciliation. Though P. does not make it clear, this is another day later, on 17 March, and the senate met this time in the Temple of Tellus—surely itself a calming gesture, to avoid the passions roused by the site of the killing, though App. 2.126.525 says that Antony chose it simply because it was near his house. On this senate-meeting, cf. also *Ant.* 14.3 and esp. *Brut.* 19, P.'s fullest account. *Brutus* distinguishes two senate-meetings on, presumably, 17 and 18 March, though P.'s own account there leaves the impression of the 16th and 17th: it is possible that he is right to distinguish two sessions, but more likely that there was only a single meeting on the 17th (see *Plutarch and History*, 37 n. 90, and my n. on *Ant.* 14.3). It was anyway on the 17th that 'Antony, Plancus, and Cicero' spoke in favour of an amnesty (*Brut.* 19.1, whereas *Cic.* 42.3 mentions only Cicero). **amnesty:** recalls the famous decision in Athens in 403 to wipe the slate clean after the Thirty Tyrants ('on the model of the Athenians' (*Cic.* 42.3)), and that accurately reflects the language of the time: cf. Cic. *Phil.* 1.1, 'I revived that ancient example set by the Athenians: yes, I took over that Greek word…' (presumably *amnēstia*, the word used here: thus Ramsey, ad loc.).

so they voted that Caesar should be honoured as a god. It is hard to know what this refers to, as our other detailed narratives of these events do not mention any such decree. Still, probably something was indeed voted at this stage: that is probably the reference of *de uir. ill.* 85.1, 'Antony…crowned C. with a diadem at the Lupercalia, and decreed him divine honours once he was dead', and Suet. 88 refers to the games of 44 as the first in C.'s honour 'after his deification' (69.4 n.). Many such divine honours had of course already been voted during C.'s lifetime, and some continued to be given during the following few years: cf. 57.2 n., Weinstock, esp. 281–317, 386–91, M. Beard, *CAH* ix^2 (1994), 749–55; cf. also 60–1, 63.9 nn. **that there should be no alteration in even the smallest particular of anything he had planned.** As App. 2.128.535–129.541 brings out, there were good pragmatic reasons for C.'s *acta* to be ratified, as so many vested interests were involved, including the veterans' land allocations and the legitimacy of tenure of all current magistrates. But it understandably led to much dispute over the following months, especially as **planned**—not just 'enacted'—accurately captures what was agreed. The difficulties are touched on at *Ant.* 15.2–5: see my nn. there.

67.9. provinces and appropriate honours were given to Brutus and his friends. At *Brut.* 19 P. puts the honours at the first, the provinces at the second of his two sessions (§8 n.). **provinces:** yes. For the details, see my n. on *Ant.* 14.3; the account in *Brutus* is confused. **honours:** no: this was apparently the proposal of Ti. Claudius Nero (Suet. *Tib.* 4.1), but became a flashpoint (App. 2.127.530–3), and it was apparently not even put to the vote. **So everyone thought that the situation had stabilized, and the best possible compromise had been reached.** Antony, as the surviving consul, took a lot of the credit for this, as Cicero allows (*Phil.* 1.2, 1.31, and esp. 2.90). Hence, more colourfully than here, *Ant.* 14.3, 'Antony left the senate as the most brilliant man alive: it was felt that he had delivered Rome from civil war...'. **compromise:** literally a 'mixture' reached by a blending of different elements, which may echo Thuc. 8.97.2, praising the 'Constitution of the 5000' of 411 BCE (see Hornblower, ad loc., on the language); that period was in people's minds at the time and would be in P.'s mind too, with 'amnesty' recalling events of 403 (§8 n.). There may be an echo here too of the 'mixed constitution' that Polybius thought so distinctive of Rome (6.3–10) and that Tacitus treated with such scepticism (*Ann.* 4.33.1). But here the 'blending' is not a matter of a continuing constitution or (as Hornblower finds in Thuc.) a behavioural pattern, but of a highly politicized response to an immediate crisis. It is not surprising that any 'stability' proved only momentary.

68.1. Caesar's will was opened: on the insistence of his father-in-law L. Piso (14.8 n.). P. here omits the controversy over whether the will should be read: Antony demanded that it should, Cassius strongly opposed, but Brutus—naively, as P. and others rightly thought—was willing to agree (*Brut.* 20.1–2). **a sizable sum to every single Roman citizen:** 75 dr./den. apiece (*Brut.* 20.3), i.e. 300 sesterces (Suet. 83.2). C.'s gardens 'across the Tiber' were also left for public use. Shakespeare integrates the will-reading with Antony's brilliantly devious 'Friends, Romans, Countrymen...' funeral speech, though in fact the will was probably read on 18 or 19 March and the speech given and the body burnt on the following day. Shakespeare builds on the brief mentions of the speech at *Brut.* 20.4–5 and *Ant.* 14.6–8, where see my n., though he may also have known of App. 2.144.600–146.609. **saw the body as it was borne through the forum... brought benches and railings and tables from the forum...:** i.e. from other parts of the forum and the surrounding buildings—tribunals, courts, workshops. *Brut.* 20.5 is similar, adding 'as had happened before in the case of Clodius the demagogue' in 52 BCE, a precedent that was doubtless in people's minds now (Wiseman 232): the rioting then had been so serious that the senate house was set on fire (Cic. *Mil.* 91–2), an episode that App. 2.147.613 mistakenly transfers to the present context. But one house was indeed burnt: Cic. *Phil.* 2.91. **and set it alight:** the word for this at *Brut.* 20.6 and *Ant.* 14.8 (cf. my n.) is *kathagizein*, with a suggestion of solemn religious ritual, especially as in *Brutus* P. notes that the spot was 'surrounded by many temples, sanctuaries, and holy places'. That religious dimension is not developed here.

More detail is given at App. 2.147.612–148.616, Dio 44.50, and Suet. 84–5; cf. Weinstock 350–5. A pyre had been prepared in the Campus Martius, but the mob first bore C.'s body to the Capitol; there they were turned back by priests, so they rapidly built the pyre in the forum. Actors and musicians threw on their costumes, legionaries their decorations, mothers their children's clothes. Then the violence started.

68.2. lit blazing torches and ran to the houses of the assassins... they were all well barricaded away.   *Brut.* 20.7 is very close.

68.3. Cinna: C. Helvius Cinna, 'Cinna the poet': cf. esp. T. P. Wiseman, *Cinna the Poet and other Essays* (1974), 44–58, and on P.'s treatment A. Zadorojnyi (as 'Zadorojniy') in C. Schrader, V. Ramón, and J. Vela (eds), *Plutarco y la historia* (1999), 497–506 at 500–2. In fact only *Brut.* 20.8 describes him as a poet, whence Shakespeare's scene in *JC*—'Tear him for his bad verses, tear him for his bad verses!' (III. ii. 30). Our other sources prefer to stress that he was currently tribune, and therefore implicitly sacrosanct: that magnifies the outrage. He had in fact been active in C.'s support, 61.10 n. For his poetry, see E. Courtney, *The Fragmentary Latin Poets* (1993), 212–24. His mini-epic *Zmyrna* is acclaimed by Catullus 95, and Virgil mentions him as a benchmark of quality, *Ecl.* 9.35. His death is obliquely referred to by Ovid, *Ibis* 539–40 (J. D. Morgan, *CQ* 40 (1990), 558–9). The scholar Parthenius of Nicaea, important for Roman poetry, was brought to Rome after capture in the Mithridatic Wars by 'Cinna': that is perhaps this man if he held the tribunate at an unusually but not impossibly late age (Wiseman), more likely 'the *father* of the poet (or a close relation)' (J. L. Lightfoot, *Parthenius of Nicaea* (1999), 11–13). **Caesar led him along by the hand:** 64.6 n. *Brut.* 20.8 has him led by the hand 'to a vast and murky place'.

68.6. there was a man of the same name among the conspirators: L. Cornelius Cinna, son of the Cinna who 'had once been monarch' and brother of Caesar's first wife Cornelia (1.1 nn.): he was probably not a conspirator in fact, though he spoke in the tyrannicides' support after the killing (67.7 n.). He was praetor, but had ostentatiously discarded his insignia 'as the gift of a tyrant' (App. 2.121.509, *MRR* 320); he quickly resumed them, App. 2.126.526.

68.7. a few days later they left the city. Exactly when they left is unclear. *Ant.* 15.1. *Brut.* 21.1, and App. 2.148.615 all give the impression that their departure was almost immediate; *Brutus* and Nic. Dam. 50 add that they went to Antium. In fact Brutus and Cassius were still in Rome *c.*11 April (Cic. *Att.* 14.5 (359).2, 14.6 (360).1), Ramsey on Cic. *Phil.* 2.31), but Toher on Nic. Dam. 50 may be right in suggesting that they left Rome for a few days after the funeral, then returned. Their departure in mid-April may well be connected with Octavian's arrival on the scene: so Toher, *CQ* 54 (2004), 180–1. Brutus was then reported seen at Lanuvium in mid-April (Cic. *Att.* 14.7 (361).1). **In the *Brutus*:** *Brut.* 21–53. **before they met their ends:** carefully phrased, leaving the 'ends' themselves for the next chapter.

69.1: Summing up
For such death notices, often noting age and (where appropriate) length of reign, cf. e.g. *Rom.* 29.12 (with Intr., p. 34), *Ages.* 40.3, *Artax.* 30.9, and especially the remarkable shared notice of Antony and Cleopatra at *Ant.* 86.8, with my n. This is one of several cases where the notice is resumptive, returning to the death once the narrative has moved on some way past it: cf. *C.min.* 73.1 and again *Rom.* 29.12; the paired *Life* of Alexander was here probably similar, though its ending has been lost (Pelling, *CQ* 23 (1973), 343–4).

The summary reprises, but also repoints, themes familiar from the *Life*, particularly its closing chapters. For the 'dominion and power', cf. esp. 3.3 and 57.1 (nn.); but P. here avoids the question of whether it should be called 'tyranny' or 'kingship', despite the way that this has become a flashpoint (57.1, 60.1, 61, 67.3 nn.). For the 'envy' cf. 58.5, 64.4–5 nn. 'Fame' (or 'glory' or 'reputation', *doxa*) has often been C.'s spur, strikingly in his last plans of 58.4–10 (the word is used at 58.4) but also at 16.1, 22.6, and 28.3. But this is the wrong sort of 'fame' and 'reputation', one that destroys the mortal man rather than staking his claim for immortal memory. Nor, as sometimes elsewhere in P. (e.g. in *Alcibiades*, cf. my *Literary Texts and the Greek Historian* (2000), 54–7), is there any suggestion that the destructive reputation has come to be at odds with a man's real actions. Here the power, and the unpopularity it caused, are real enough.

The most striking new perspective is the way that P.'s tone raises the question whether it was all worthwhile; whether that choice of C. since his early years was really the right one, to give 'his attention to becoming first in power and in armed strength' (3.3); whether the other possible lives he might have led would have produced more contentment, or at least whether different choices might be wiser for any of P.'s readers pondering C. as a model. A big question, indeed: cf. Intr., pp. 23–4, 76.

69.1. after living fifty-six years.   C. was in fact 55: 'in his fifty-sixth year', say Suet. 88 and App. 2.149.620, which implies, doubtless rightly, a birth date of July 100. But P. may be counting inclusively. **outliving Pompey by a little more than four years.** In fact a little less, though the exact length is complicated by the calendar reform of 46. **He had sought dominion and power all his days:** Intr., p. 21. **the only fruit it bore him:** §5 n.

69.2–14: Vengeance

Many of P.'s *Lives* take the narrative on past the death of the principal, especially when that death is avenged: I discuss such 'completions of the death' at *Plutarch and History*, 365–7. Other features too are characteristic: for the last word to be one of death, but of someone else's death (*Plutarch and History*, 382 n. 5); for features of the closure to mirror critical moments of the *Life*'s narrative, often elsewhere the man's greatest triumph, here the moment of the slaying for which the assassins pay the price (§§3, 14 nn.: *Plutarch and History*, 374–5,

Pelling, 'Roman Tragedy', 275–6). A further perspective is given by
the emphasis on the supernatural, when C. himself and the *Life*'s
earlier narrative have tended to play this down: despite the occasional
omens to suggest divine interest (43.3–6. 47, 63), there has certainly
been no suggestion so far of a 'great guardian spirit' to guide C.'s
successes. Cf. Intr., pp. 30–2, and, for the suggestion that this arresting closure may also help to explain the absence of a synkritic
epilogue, pp. 32–3.

P. treats the Philippi campaign in more detail at *Brut.* 24–53, and
here he takes the outline for granted: notice the way P. mentions 'the
defeat at Philippi' as familiar at §3, and then proceeds without needing to explain that the items of §§6–14 refer to events of the same
campaign. The 'spirit' or *daimōn* is important in *Brutus* too, and great
weight is placed on its double appearance (*Brut.* 36–7, 48). In that *Life*
there are also hints of some divine protection for Octavian, and in
'Augustus' Autobiography' I suggest that that contrast is important in
keeping that *Life*'s moral balance: Brutus is both sympathetic, for his
ideals and for the cosmic hopelessness of his struggle, and wrong, for
history is on the Caesarians' side. Questions of sympathy are less
important here, and so is any notion of future history: this 'great
spirit' is animated by backward-looking vengeance, not by any concern to shape the future empire.

69.2. His great guardian spirit: in Greek, *daimōn*: cf. esp. *C.min.*
54.9, where it is 'C.'s *daimōn*' that robs his enemies of total victory at
Dyrrhachium (39.8 n.). *Daimones* play an important and not always
consistent role in P.'s theological and cosmic universe. As here, they
are sometimes connected closely with particular individuals and
guide their lives, especially at *Socrates' Sign* 591d–4a: thus at *Mar.*
46.1 the dying Plato praised 'his own *daimōn* and fortune' for making
him human, a Greek, and a contemporary of Socrates, while at *Ant.*
33.3 Antony's *daimōn* stands in awe of Octavian's. Sometimes, as
again in *Socrates' Sign* (593d–e), *daimones* appear to begin as human
souls; sometimes they represent human intellect; and/or they can be
envisaged as an intermediate being between gods and mortals, helping to interpret and mediate between both; and sometimes a *daimōn*
seems to capture a larger concept of 'The Divinity', or, as we might
say, 'Heaven' (e.g. at *Brut.* 55(2).2), cited at Intr., p. 20). For a good
brief treatment, cf. D. A. Russell, *Plutarch* (1972), 75–8; for more
extensive discussion, Y. Vernière, *Symboles et mythes dans la pensée*

de Plutarque (1977), 249–62, and F. E. Brenk, *In Mist Apparelled* (1977), esp. 49–64, 84–112, and 130–2, and *CJ* 69 (1973), 1–11. Brenk also discusses the Brutus case in *Actes du VIIIe Congrès de l'Association Guillaume Budé, Paris 5–10 Avril 1968* (1969), 588–94, and in *Relighting the Souls* (1998), 118–27.

What relation does this 'great *daimōn* of C.' have to the phantom that appears to Brutus, which in that case is Brutus' own 'evil' *daimōn* (§11)? Surely there should be some, as D. Babut, *Plutarque et le stoicisme* (1999), 433, insists; Brenk's view that '[t]he term [*daimōn*] seems to be tossed about here with an almost reckless abandon' (*CJ* 69 (1973), 10) seems unlikely in so carefully wrought a conclusion. Shakespeare apparently took them as identical, with the same manifestation being both 'Caesar's ghost' (stage direction in Act IV, scene iii, and Brutus himself at v. v. 16) and Brutus' own 'evil spirit' (as the ghost announces himself at IV. iii. 279). In this he went beyond North's translation, which followed Amyot in giving a much blander rendering: see Intr., pp. 66–7. Possibly P. too implies such a fusion, and that spirit that guided C. can indeed be 'evil' for Brutus; if so, it turns on its head what a protective *daimōn* might be expected to do, not here nurturing but rather marking destruction, but such a negative inflection is possible enough. Something similar seems to underlie *Alex.* 50.2, where Cleitus' own *daimōn* works together with Alexander's drunken rage to destroy Cleitus; and cf. the different but related idea at *Peace of Mind* 474b, where each of us has at birth not just a positive but also a negative *daimōn*. Whether or not P. himself goes quite as far as Shakespeare, in other *Lives* he certainly plays with the notion that two people's fates can become one, most notably in the intertwining of the lives of Antony and Cleopatra; in some ways *Brutus* too intermeshes the lives of Brutus and Cassius. Here in *Caesar* we have the even eerier notion that Brutus' and Caesar's *daimones* are either identical, or at least inextricably and catastrophically linked.

Whatever the case in *Caesar*, there is no suggestion in *Brutus* of identity with any 'spirit' of Caesar (so, rightly, Moles, *Brutus*); it is simply Brutus' 'evil *daimōn*'. In the proem to *Dion–Brutus* P. plays with what he calls a 'most outlandish' view, that 'evil and mischievous daimonic things' might be envious and hostile towards good men, making their virtuous path more difficult to avoid their gaining 'a better fate after death' than the *daimones* themselves (*Dion* 2.5–6). That rather unPlutarchan view is not straightforwardly developed in the pair itself, but at least prepares for the suggestion of hostility. The notion that a *daimōn* might resemble an avenging force also fits the parallel vision in *Dion* 55, where a 'great woman, in dress and appearance just like a tragic Erinys', appears to Dion after he has murdered his rival Heracleides.

until not one remained. The universal vengeance is also stressed by Suet. 89, 'hardly any of the assassins lived on for more than three years or died a natural death'. Suet. also mentions some who died 'by shipwreck'; we know of none, but this may underlie **over every land and sea** here. The vengeance theme is also tracked by Appian: Trebonius the first to die, 3.26.101; D. Brutus, 3.98.408–9; Brutus and Cassius, 4.135.568. **in thought or in execution.** The phrase may hint that non-senators were involved (66 n.), as all the senators had a share in the execution (66.11), or may point to the death of Cicero, a non-involved sympathizer and supporter (*Cic.* 42.1–2, *Brut.* 12.2, etc.).

69.3. after his defeat at Philippi: in the first battle, §12 n. below. *Brut.* 43.4–9 gives a fine description of his suicide, including the detail that he drew his cloak over his head (just as C. had done on the Ides, 66.12 ~ *Brut.* 17.6), but P. does not there mention that he used the same dagger. *Brut.* 45.2 does, however, report that Cassius' blade was brought to Antony on the following day. Suet. ends his *Life* with the note that 'some' destroyed themselves with the same dagger as they had used on the Ides (89).

69.4. the great comet: 'Caesar's star' of Virg. *Ecl.* 9.47–9, where it is supposed to promote joyful fertility in the land; but here the results are anything but fruitful, §5. Cf. Weinstock 370–84; Intr., p. 31. This 'star' was believed to be the spirit of C. ascending to a welcoming Heaven (Suet. 88, Plin. *NH* 2.93, Dio 45.7.1, etc.), but it is notable that P. does not bring out this implication. In themselves, comets could more readily be seen as bad rather than good omens (Weinstock 371), and the quick transition here to the 'dimming of the sun' does not suggest much joyfulness. Cf. Virg. *G.* 4.488, when 'grim comets' are the culmination of the bad celestial signs marking C.'s death (§5 n.), and contrast the acclamation normally given to the 'star' in Augustan poetry, e.g. at Ov. *Met.* 15.848–50 and Prop. 4.6.59; it also appears on Caesarian coinage, for the first time in 38 BCE (Crawford, *RRC*, nos 534–5 with p. 744). Plin. *NH* 2.93–4 says that Augustus privately took it as indicating his own future divinity: cf. Nisbet–Hubbard on Hor. *Odes* 1.12.47. **for seven nights:** 'for seven days in a row, rising around the eleventh hour' (Suet. 88); but Serv. on *Aen.* 8.681 says 'a period of three days'. It appeared in the constellation of the Bear, Obsequens 68. **after Caesar's death:** at the time of 'the first games which his heir Augustus gave in his honour after his consecration' (Suet. 88), i.e. the 'games for C.'s Victory' or 'for Venus the mother': both names were used. On these games, see Weinstock 88–91. They were first held in 46: those of 20–30 July 44 would be the first after 'his consecration' (cf. 67.8 n.), and on Octavian's initiative they were combined on this occasion with funeral games for C. (Weinstock 89, 368).

69.5. For that entire year the sun rose pale . . . the lack of radiance to penetrate it: cf. esp. Virg. *G.* 1.466–8, the first of the ways in which the sun marked the death of C.: 'it shrouded its bright head with dark shades of rust, and the godless generations stood in fear of endless night.' An eclipse (admittedly later, in November 44) may lie behind this, as perhaps behind *de uir. ill.* 78.10, 'when his body was exposed before the *rostra* the sun is said to have shrouded its head'; but Obsequens 68 also says that, following an initial omen of three suns in the sky (cf. Wardle on Cic. *Div.* 1.97), 'the light of the sun was sickly for several months': see Weinstock 382–3. There are parallels too with the omens listed by Ov. *Met.* 15.782–98 in clear imitation of Virgil, esp. 785–6, 'the sun too showed a grim appearance, providing a wan light to the worried earth'; but those are explicitly omens that *preceded* the Ides. **The fruits of the earth:** i.e. the crops. The word in Greek is the noun form of the verb rendered in §1 as 'the only fruit it bore': unsatisfactory fruit for the land, then, through his death, just as the fruits of his power were unsatisfactory for C. himself.

69.6–11: THE FIRST APPARITION   The tale is told at *Brut.* 36–7 with several close verbal echoes, and with even more dramatic and atmospheric detail ('the hour was late, and the whole camp was wrapped in silence . . . When the phantom had vanished, Brutus called his servants, but they assured him that they had neither heard a voice nor seen any apparition'). P. there appends a discussion with Cassius on the interpretation of such phantoms, one in which Cassius is generally supposed to be giving an Epicurean view: in fact it is not at all Epicurean (D. A. Russell, *Plutarch* (1972), 77; F. E. Brenk,

Relighting the Souls (1998), 118–27).[28] Whatever the strength of his rationalist arguments, Cassius is presumably felt as misguided in explaining the apparition away as *wholly* non-supernatural. App. 4.134.565 mentions the phantom's appearances briefly but with similar detail; Flor. 2.17.8 has the first appearance alone, and therefore omits 'you will see me at Philippi', retaining only 'your evil genius'.

A very similar story was told of another of the assassins, Cassius of Parma, just before Actium (Val. Max. 1.7.7). Possibly the story was falsely transferred from one person to the other, in which case it may well have been from the less prominent Cassius of Parma to the famous Brutus: Brenk, *In Mist Apparelled*, 186, 206, suggests that P. might have transferred it himself. Still, P.'s closeness to App. suggests that the story was already told of Brutus in Pollio. In that case it is more likely that the Cassius of Parma version was meant to echo the Brutus story: the 'evil spirit' was ranging still, hunting down one of the last surviving assassins just as it had earlier hunted Brutus. A different story is also told of the other Cassius, the co-leader, confronted by a terrifying, larger-than-life apparition of C. on the battlefield of Philippi (Val. Max. 1.8.8).

69.7. Brutus was about to transport the army from Abydus to the other continent: probably August 42. Meanwhile the Caesarian forces had crossed to Macedonia, and were marching eastwards. For a narrative, and some attempt to analyse the strategy, cf. *CAH* x^2 (1996), 5–8.

69.8. needed less sleep than any other general in history: More on his habits at *Brut.* 36.3–4: he would sleep in the evening after supper, then spend the rest of the night dealing with urgent business or reading. The apparition appeared 'in the third watch', i.e. (it seems) shortly before dawn.

69.12. Brutus faced Antony and the young Caesar in battle at Philippi.   By now Cassius has disappeared from the narrative. He and Brutus arrived in the region of Philippi in September 42. **In the**

---

[28] One suggestion made in passing by Brenk (122) deserves further attention, the proposal to read *humeteros* rather than *hēmeteros* at *Brut.* 37.2: this would make the Epicurean Cassius give Brutus a version of 'your', i.e. an Academic and/or Aristotelian, rather than 'our' doctrine. As Brenk might have added, *humeteros* is in fact the manuscript reading; *hēmeteros* is Xylander's emendation.

first battle: early October 42. **he defeated and forced back the detachment stationed opposite himself.** Brutus commanded the right wing, *Brut.* 40.10–12. The account in *Brut.* 41–3 suggests a less ordered engagement. Brutus' main force indeed **defeated and forced back the detachment stationed opposite,** and cut to pieces three legions in hand-to-hand fighting, 42.1. Some troops under his command did reach and **destroy Caesar's camp,** but largely because they lost contact with one another in the charge, and some 'overlapped Octavian's left wing and were carried past it' (41.5). This undisciplined pursuit opened a gap between this right wing and the centre, and that is where the Caesarians successfully counterattacked (42.2). The Republicans' left was routed, their camp too was captured (42.3–8), and Cassius, prematurely assuming that all was lost, killed himself (43).

69.13: THE SECOND APPARITION   This apparition is also mentioned at *Brut.* 48.1: it was the night before the battle. P. there adds several other omens, which he explicitly draws from Volumnius (Intr., p. 52), though he also notes that Volumnius makes no mention of the apparition. **When he was about to fight the second battle.** The date of the battle was 23 October 42: this was the night before. **plunged into danger in the battle.** The language here suggests rashness, but *Brut.* 49–50 rather stresses Brutus' caution in the battle's initial stages. His left wing was, however, crushed, and he found himself encircled.

69.14. he took refuge on a rocky prominence: 'a place where the ground was hollow and had a great rock in front of it' (*Brut.* 51.1; then 51–2 go on to give further details of the death, including some inspiring last words which would be wholly out of place here). **his naked blade:** less explicitly than with Cassius (§3), this too echoes the assassination and the triumphant moment that followed (66.10, 67.3, 69.3 nn.) **with a friend, so they say, adding weight to the blow.** This conflates what *Brut.* 52.7–8 gives as two versions, the first that Brutus pushed the blade into himself with both hands and fell on it, the second that his friend Strato reluctantly held the blade, eyes averted, and Brutus ran on to it. **death:** an appropriate last word for a *Life*, but here as elsewhere (above, 69 n.) P. makes it an avenging death, one that marks the final, and in a way vindicating, completion of the central figure's story.

Notice the ways P. does *not* choose to end: not with the young Caesar, despite his brief mention at §12; not with any hint of the charismatic effect of C.'s name in the next fifteen years (contrast *Brut.* 57(4).4, 'Caesar's fame guided his friends to success even after his death, and his name raised its holder from a defenceless child to become the first man at Rome...'), nor of the continuing bloodshed of civil war; no mention of those future emperors who would be Caesars (contrast *Ant.* 87), or who—as with Trajan—would echo C.'s achievements as well as his name; but simply with the elegant and restrained suggestion that C.'s own story is complete.

Index of Names

Romans are listed under the name by which they are most familiar: hence 'Cicero' and 'Cato' for M. Tullius Cicero and M. Porcius Cato, but 'Cassius' for C. Cassius Longinus. References to Appian, Dio, Suetonius etc are listed only when their material is discussed in the notes, not for occasions where they simply figure in a list of supporting passages.

Parthenius of Nicaea 493
Parthia 3, 9, 71, 98, 119–20, 258, 262,
  275, 288 n. 13, 289, 299, 432–9, 446–7,
  462, 475
Pasion 209
Patavium 111, 374–6
Patiscus 488
Paullus Aemilius Lepidus (cos. 34) 297
Paullus, L. Aemilius (cos. 182 etc) 195
Paullus, L. Aemilius (cos. 50) 99, 289,
  296–8, 305
Pedius, Q. (cos. 43) 419
Pelopidas 13, 33
Pelusium 383, 386
Pergamum 78, 378, 388
Pericles 35, 322–3, 407
Persephone 177
Persia 355, 370, 373, 447, 454
Persian Gulf 437
Petra 350
Petreius, M. 282, 335–6, 402, 404, 411
Petronius 385
Petronius, M. (centurion) 366
Pharmacusa 77, 139
Pharnaces 114, 390–3
Pharos 113, 388
Pharsalus 27, 31–2, 37–8, 46, 53,
  108–11, 114, 122, 245, 300, 312,
  317–18, 324, 327, 333–4, 343, 353–76,
  380, 394, 396, 398–9, 402, 415–18,
  429, 436, 461
Philip II of Macedon 132, 156
Philippi 1, 38, 52, 68, 70, 127–8, 248,
  316, 318, 481, 488, 495–501
Philo 142, 433
Philogelos 458–9
Philonicus, Licinius 195
Philopoemen 436
Philotas 29
Phrygia 83, 176–7
Phye 315
Picenum 326, 330, 334
Pictones 265
Pindar 344
Pisistratus 202, 315
Piso Caesoninus, L. Calpurnius (cos. 58)
  87, 104, 193, 198, 305, 326, 337, 491
Piso, C. Calpurnius (cos. 67) 81, 161–2,
  169
Piso, C. Calpurnius (historian) 50 n. 125
Piso, M. Pupius (cos. 61) 285 n. 11
Placentia 315, 336, 340, 343

Plancus, L. Munatius (cos. 42) 432, 490
Plataea 347, 355, 370
Plato (comic poet) 55
Plato (philosopher) 18, 52, 55, 63–4,
  157, 197, 278, 280, 300, 406, 421, 424,
  427–8, 482, 495
Plautus 26 n. 55
Pliny the elder (C. Plinius Secundus) 19,
  50, 131 and n. 2, 203, 208, 297, 332,
  377, 401, 413, 443, 497
Pliny the younger (C. Plinius Caecilius
  Secundus) 4, 483
Plotius 150
Plowden, Edmund 75 n. 179
Pollio, C. Asinius 40, 43–9, 53, 101, 111,
  115, 145, 186, 190–5, 203–6, 210–11,
  219–23, 234, 243–4, 250, 253–6, 258,
  260, 263, 267, 270–82, 296–300, 304,
  314, 317–18, 321, 328, 335–6, 340, 344
  and n. 21, 347–58, 360–74, 382, 388,
  394, 399–402, 417, 448–50, 472,
  476–7, 481–2, 484–5, 499
Polyaenus 138–9, 222
Polybius 16, 46, 63, 191, 314, 428, 491
Polyxena 483
Pompeia (daughter of Pompey) 198,
  283, 404, 420
Pompeia (wife of Caesar) 57, 80, 83–4,
  152–3, 175–80
Pompeii 463
Pompeius Strabo, Cn. (cos. 89) 295
Pompeius, Cn. (son of Pompey) 117,
  382, 404, 416–19
Pompeius, Q. 152
Pompeius, Sex. (son of Pompey) 117,
  400, 416–20
Pompey (Cn. Pompeius Magnus) 12,
  19–20, 26–8, 30–1, 37–8, 49–50, 53,
  59–60, 68, 80, 85–8, 92–118, 122,
  124–7, 134, 138, 144, 148–50, 153,
  174, 181–204, 209, 212, 225, 234–6,
  241–9, 256–9, 262–3, 273–384, 391–8,
  398–9, 411, 414–20, 423, 428–9, 432,
  435–7, 477–9, 482–4
Pomptine Marshes 119, 434, 440
Pontus 3, 114, 117, 119, 391–2, 410, 431,
  438–9
Popilia 151
Popillius Laenas 473
Popillius, C. 79, 149
Poplicola, P. Valerius 435
Porcia 68 n. 170, 69–70, 76, 461

General Index

ambition *see philotimia*
amnesty 490
apophthegmata 24–5, 144–5, 158, 180, 426
  suitable for biography 15, 24–5
  of Caesar 24–5, 144–5, 226, 351, 369–72, 415, 418, 429–30, 464–5, 482–3
  of others 25, 144, 156, 158, 192, 426, 433, 481
assistants for research 38, 49, 374, 472
augury 111–12, 123, 232, 374–6, 469–70
  see also omens

banquets 113, 358, 387
  public, as demagogic technique 80, 117–18, 147–8, 300, 413–14, 419, 431
barbarian characteristics 208–11, 227, 229–31, 233–4
beards 178
biography 13–25, 32–3, 59, 160, 186, 205, 207 *see also* 'law of biographical relevance'
  biographies as sources 49–52
bodyguards 64, 421, 427, 429–30, 489
bribery
  as feature of Roman politics 98, 148, 159, 174, 186, 249, 277, 288
  as used by Caesar 154, 296–7
  Plutarch's treatment 59, 154, 159, 186, 249, 274–7

calendar 54, 119–20, 341–2, 400, 418, 421–2, 440–5, 470
casualty figures, *see* numbers
cavalrymen, preening 360–1, 367–8
census 117, 414
centurions 197, 213, 231, 240, 260, 301–2, 366–7
characterization by reaction 25, 156–7, 247–8, 278, 419, 478
Christianity 73, 472
chronology, relative, of *Lives* 34, 36–7

citizenship 99, 294–6, 339, 375–6
  see also Index of Names, s.v. Transpadani
clemency 20, 64, 118, 208–9, 238–9, 327–8, 335–6, 358, 382, 404–5, 421, 427–8, 458
closure 32–3, 35, 415, 493–5, 501
colonization 86, 118, 196, 295–6, 339, 375–6, 431–2
comparison 25–35, 61, 207, 495 *see also* Index of Names, s.v. Alexander
contemporary relevance, 2–13, 75–6, 152, 421, 423–4, 501
corn-distributions 83, 171–2, 339, 414
corruption *see* bribery
creative reconstruction 57
'cross-fertilization' 37, 49–53, 460
cross-references 37, 329, 459, 464
crowns 121, 177, 214, 276–7, 422, 453–6, 468
curses 483

daimōn, daimones 31, 66–7, 351, 379, 495–501
debt
  feature of Roman politics 63, 99, 181–2, 274, 296, 383–4, 397
  Caesar's debts 19, 80, 153–4, 181–2, 185, 383–4, 397
  Caesar's measures to deal with debt 61, 63, 85, 104, 185, 338–9, 443
  Plutarch's treatment of 19, 61, 296, 338–9
delay, narrative 59
demos and demagogues
  Plutarch's emphasis on Roman people 21–2, 59–60, 136, 143, 145, 160–1, 170, 174–5, 196, 204–5, 241, 244–5, 249, 300, 311, 393, 408, 419–22, 458, 484–7, 492
  demagogic techniques 61, 147–9, 153, 157, 160, 175–6, 196, 199, 231, 236, 277–8, 330, 421–2, 424, 428, 431